DECONSTRUCTING DEVELOPMENT DISCOURSE IN PERU

A Meta-Ethnography of the Modernity Project at Vicos

REVISED EDITION

William W. Stein

University Press of America,® Inc.
Lanham · Boulder · New York · Toronto · Oxford

Copyright © 2003 by
University Press of America,® Inc.
4501 Forbes Boulevard
Suite 200
Lanham, Maryland 20706
UPA Acquisitions Department (301) 459-3366

PO Box 317
Oxford
OX2 9RU, UK

ISBN 0-7618-2650-5 (clothbound : alk. ppr.)
ISBN 0-7618-2651-3 (paperback : alk. ppr.)

Contents

Preface

"[D]econstruction cannot be applied." Why? You know the program;
it cannot be applied because deconstruction is not a doctrine; it's not
a method, nor is it a set of rules or tools; it cannot be separated from
performatives, from signatures, from a given language. So, if you
want to "do deconstruction"– "you know, the kind of thing Derrida
does"–then you have to perform something new, in your own
language, in your own singular situation, with your own signature, to
invent the impossible and to break with the application, in the
technical, neutral sense of the word. So, on the one hand, there is no
"applied deconstruction." But on the other hand, there is nothing
else, since deconstruction doesn't consist in a set of theorems, axioms,
tools, rules, techniques, methods. If deconstruction, then, is nothing
by itself, the only thing it can do is apply, to be applied, to something
else, not only in more than one language, but also with something
else. There is no deconstruction, deconstruction has no specific
object, it can only refer to, apply to .... It can only apply. (Jacques
Derrida 1996a:217-218.)

It seems absurd, then, to begin by saying that I intend to apply
deconstruction to applied anthropology in this work. Deconstruction
applies itself. To anthropology and, likewise, applied anthropology–but
their universes are huge and quite beyond my capabilities to apply them,
apply to them, apply for them, apply with them, or apply within them.
Derrida (1995:28) says that deconstruction is destined "to erring and
voyage, which is to say, to a destination and destinerrance." I apply my
word-processing instrument more simply to the task of writing a book

about an internationally famous applied anthropology project that was carried out a half century ago by professional scholars, working in universities in Peru and North America, in a small community in Peru. That makes me an applicator of something. Whether or not what that "something" is, is deconstruction is undecidable for, as Derrida writes, it's impossible and yet there's nothing else. But I insist on my "right to deconstruction," which Derrida (2001a:26) defines as

> an unconditional right to ask critical questions not only to the history of the concept of man [sic], but to the history even of the notion of critique, to the form and the authority of the question, to the interrogative form of thought. For this implies the right to do it performatively, that is, by producing events, for example by writing, and by giving rise to singular *oeuvres* (which up until now has been the purview of neither the classical nor the modern Humanities). With the event of thought constituted by such *oeuvres*, it would be a matter of making something happen to this concept of truth or of humanity, without necessarily betraying it, that is, to the concept that forms the charter and the profession of faith of all universities

Derrida's work in philosophy is not irrelevant to anthropology but, rather, reaches out to it. Christopher Norris (1987:156) writes:

> Derrida has devoted the bulk of his writings to a patient working-through (albeit on his own very different terms) of precisely those problems that have occupied philosophers in the "mainstream" tradition, from Kant to Husserl and Frege. And this because those problems are indubitably *there*, installed within philosophy and reaching beyond it into every department of modern institutionalized knowledge.

Here I quote from Derrida's (2002a:9) recent deconstruction of the university, only substituting for "philosophy" and "philosophical" the words "anthropology" and "anthropological," and I don't think this does damage to Derrida's purpose:

> What has been called "deconstruction" is also the *exposure* of this institutional identity of the discipline of anthropology: What is irreducible about it must be exposed as such, that is to say, shown, watched over, laid claim to, but in that which opens it and ex-propriates it, as what is proper in its properness distances itself from itself in order to relate to itself–first of all, in the least of its questions about itself. Anthropology, anthropological identity, is also the name of an experience that, in identification in general, begins by ex-posing

itself: in other words, expatriating itself. Taking place where it does not take place, where the place is neither natural, nor originary, nor given.

It's also useful to note, at the outset and *with* Derrida (103) that: "[T]here is no *one* deconstruction. There are only singular movements, more or less idiomatic styles, strategies, effects of deconstruction that are heterogeneous from one place to another, from one (historical, national, cultural, linguistic, even 'individual') situation to another. This heterogeneity is irreducible and taking account of it is essential to every deconstruction." Furthermore, in response to criticism that deconstruction doesn't deconstruct itself, we should understand that when deconstruction is applied it is a *permanent* application quite unlike "permanent revolution" in which something revolves and ultimately keeps showing the same face again and again. Gayatri Spivak (1976:lxxvii-lxxviii), in her "Translator's Preface" to Derrida's *Of Grammatology*, expresses this neatly:

> Derrida acknowledges that the desire of deconstruction may itself become a desire to reappropriate the text actively through mastery, to show the text what it "does not know". And as she deconstructs, all protestations to the contrary, the critic necessarily assumes that she at least, and for the time being, means what she says. Even the declaration of her vulnerability must come, after all, in the controlling language of demonstration and reference. In other words, the critic provisionally forgets that her own text is necessarily self-deconstructed, always already a palimpsest.
> The desire of deconstruction has also the opposite allure. Deconstruction seems to offer a way out of the closure of knowledge. By inaugurating the open-ended indefiniteness of textuality—by thus "placing in the abyss" (*mettre en abîme*, as the French expression would literally have it—it shows us the lure of the abyss as freedom. The fall into the abyss of deconstruction inspires us with as much pleasure as fear. We are intoxicated with the prospect of never hitting bottom.
> Thus a further deconstruction deconstructs deconstruction, both as the search for a foundation (the critic behaving as if she means what she says in her text), and as the pleasure of the bottomless. The tool for this, as indeed for any deconstruction, is our desire, itself a deconstruction and grammatological structure that forever differs from (we only desire what is not ourselves) and defers (desire is never fulfilled) the text of our selves. Deconstruction can therefore never be a positive science. For we are in a bind, in a "double (read abyssal) bind" . . . We *must* do a thing *and* its opposite, and indeed we desire to do both, and so on indefinitely. Deconstruction is a perpetually self-deconstructing movement that is inhabited by difference. No text is ever *fully* deconstructing or

Deconstructing Development Discourse in Peru

deconstructed.

I am grateful to Derrida for his help with my work, and I hope he will be grateful to me for extending his work into a subject where one would not expect to find it, but as he himself points out: "[Deconstruction] is the most thankless thing in the world, a kind of ethics of ingratitude . . . , a practice of implacable ingratitude, without thanks, *sans merci*. Deconstruction is merciless. On the other hand, as a thinking of the gift, of a gift beyond the debt and a justice beyond the law, deconstruction should, on the contrary, be devoted to grace and gratitude, thus to a gratitude without thanks, without exchange or, if you prefer, according to an exchange that carries beyond exchange" (Derrida 1995:15-16). That's all impossible, and it's impossible to write a book about it. But, while it's impossible to write a book, there's nothing else here but the text of a book. A text which deconstructs its self as it goes along. This is not the first impossible book I've written. I still don't understand completely why I engage in such a thankless task. This text is unruly, rude, unmanageable, like a misbehaving child. It mocks me, the one who should be the author of everything in it (doesn't it bear my signature?), by telling me it's nothing but a collage of other authors.

Why does anyone write a book? Roland Barthes (1972a:279) says: "One writes in order to be loved, one is read without being able to be loved, it is doubtless this distance which constitutes the writer." Peter Weiss (1976-81, 2:33, quoted in Bürger 1992:140) remarks with regard to plastic art: "It had never been so clear to me before how in art values can be created which overcome the experience of exclusion and loss, how the attempt can be made to alleviate melancholy through the power of shaping vision." While some of my critics might balk at the thought of calling this text "art," Weiss's words seem familiar to me because they apply to writing as I experience it. Thus, a passage in Jean-François Lyotard's (1997:232) *Postmodern Fables* can be extended:

> Differences between the fine arts proceed from differences between these matters, that is, from the various ways, all contingent, the body has of being threatened by nullity, of being anesthetized: deaf, color-blind, bedridden, etc. Aesthetics is phobic, it *arises* from anesthesia, belonging to it, recovering from it. You sing *for* not hearing, you paint *for* not seeing, you dance *for* being paralyzed.

And you write *for* not acting out your desire. So I echo Nicolas Abraham's (in Abraham and Torok 1994:214) assertion that "everything in my book is good for me and everybody else should recognize that the same thing applies to all of us." There is no end to application. Here, now, is a story about an event that took place when I was in Lima in 1996 for the *presentación* of my book on the Hospital Víctor Larco Herrera (*Un hospital psiquiátrico peruano*. Lima: Mosca Azul Editores, 1996). A day or two after the ceremony, the Director of the Hospital invited me to give a *charla*, a talk, to his staff in a Hospital lecture hall. I think around sixty or seventy people attended and listened politely as I discussed, in my halting Spanish, my current impressions of the Hospital as compared with what I remembered of 1959, the date of my research. I then tried to respond to questions from the audience, and I believe I was performing as expected when a young bearded man–my guess was that he was a resident–suddenly asked me why it took me over thirty years to write the book and why I chose to study a psychiatric hospital in the first place. How revealing was I to be with people I did not know personally? What was I expected to expose, and how much of it? I responded simply that it had taken me thirty years to overcome a writing block, that anthropologists studied the exotic, and that I had believed a psychiatric hospital was an exotic place. Fortunately for me, we had come to the end of the time allotted for the *charla* and everyone had to return to work. But that response remained with me, teased me, played with me. It was only partly true. I suffered no block when it came to writing about people, places, and events in the Callejón de Huaylas; and, despite the fact that my works had not always received the kindest of receptions, I had not ceased to write. However, thirty years earlier I ceased to try writing about the Hospital because I did not know what to say about my research experience or how to say it. I placed all my notes into a cardboard carton which I stored on top of a bookcase. Whenever I moved I carried this carton with me. For me the carton was enchanted: I could not open it, yet I could not part with it. Thus, I can understand "from the inside" how a researcher can experience ambivalence regarding what he/she has researched. It was not until I found a mode of writing that was deliberately and consciously, or preconsciously,[1] *both* autobiographical and ethnographic–one which incorporated my fears and desires, yet one which discussed the Hospital–that I was able to take the carton down, look through the contents and organize them, and complete the book. And that took place at a much later time, in the early 90s, a period of great stress and change in my life. I did both the library research on madness, psychiatric hospitals, and psychiatry, *and* the writing as conscious "occupational therapy" designed to keep myself out of trouble–which it only partially did. One of my projects was the reading of Sigmund Freud's nearly two dozen volumes of psychological works, because I did not feel I could properly understand the field of psychiatry without some grasp of

Freud's work which had had such great impact. I do not pretend that I understand all of what Freud is trying to tell us, or that I am a "convert" to Freudian psychology as some might have it, but what I did learn changed my perspective which has not been the same since.

In my research I was indeed searching for the exotic, far from the other in me. The *pabellón* in which I did most of the work very soon lost its "exotic" flavor and became a very ordinary place with what seemed to me like ordinary people in it. As for my desire to look at the forbidden, a voyeuristic impulse to gaze behind locked gates, I soon lost it in what I was gathering of the "imponderabilia" of daily life in the Hospital. It got lost but it did not disappear. Rather, it formed part of the spectral aura around my box of data that haunted me. What had impelled me, in the first place, to study psychiatric staff and patients was my ambivalence toward madness, my own included, and a preconscious need to situate myself close to psychotherapy. And, during my youth, a close relative was "locked away" in a psychiatric institution, a traumatic experience which still haunted me. At the time of my research, medical anthropology was in a formative state, and I also believed that I could enhance my career with it as a specialty. Besides, the Hospital was there and it welcomed my presence as a social anthropologist. All of this said, it is quite apparent to me that I have only started to respond to the young "resident"'s questions. Why someone engages in research and writing is overdetermined. I should have told the young "resident": "I will spend an hour a day explaining my answers to you for six months, if you will match it by spending an hour a day explaining to me why you asked those questions!" Alas! he and I never had the opportunity to pursue farther the questions and the answers.

One also writes about something because it *is there*. Roland Barthes (1972a:xiii) remarks that "one writes perhaps less to materialize an idea than to exhaust a task which bears within itself its own satisfaction." But later he adds:

> To ask oneself why one writes is already an advance over the blissful unconsciousness of "inspiration," but it is a dispiriting advance–there is no answer. Apart from demand and apart from success, empirical alibis much more than real motives, the literary act is without cause and without goal precisely because it is devoid of sanction: it proposes itself to the world without any *praxis* establishing or justifying it: it is an absolutely intransitive act, it modifies nothing, nothing *reassures* it. ... So then? Well, that is its paradox; this act exhausts itself in its technique, it exists only in the condition of a manner. (134-135.)

Writing is also work, and I think immediately of the Vicosino who told his interviewer that when he was not working he was crying (see Chapter 3). Probably that is reason enough to keep writing. Like Foucault (1997:114), I believe that "I have to be convinced that their inability to situate me has something to do with me." Trouble, of course. Trouble, a mode of existence. Judith Butler's (1990:vii) words in the "Preface" to her book on *Gender Trouble* also apply to me:

> To make trouble was, within the reigning discourse of my childhood, something one should never do precisely because that would get one *in* trouble. The rebellion and its reprimand seemed to be caught up in the same terms, a phenomenon that gave rise to my first critical insight into the subtle ruse of power: The prevailing law threatened one with trouble, even put one in trouble, all to keep out of trouble. Hence, I concluded that trouble is inevitable and the task, how best to make it, what best way to be in it.

So, Old Friend Trouble, here I am! I spent the first half of my adult life running from trouble, and never quite managing to keep ahead of it. I had a general writing block–as if the act of scribbling with a pencil or pen, or pounding the keys of a typewriter, were producing, constructing, or erecting some unacceptable horror that I desperately feared–but always contrived to "pass" courses by writing acceptable nonsense. I wrote my dissertation in 1955 while I was undergoing psychotherapy for depression, and finished my first book in 1960 again in psychiatric care and under the influence of anti-depressants and energizers. Two things helped me begin to begin to be together, one an event and the other a movement. First, the Stonewall Rebellion—it was more than a series of "riots"—demonstrated that harassment of homosexuals was *political* and unjustly deserved, and that Queer people could *proudly* resist repression.[2] Second, I'm indebted to feminism of the early 70s for suggesting to me that one could indeed make friends with one's body and that one was not personally responsible for the compulsions of patriarchy and hetertosexism. I had a moment of epiphany in late 1970 in, of all places, a Queer bookstore. I finally discovered Michelet's "cure" for a writing block in the early 1970s by turning around to confront my own homophobia.[3] The "cure" is described by Georges Bataille (1973:56):

> [Michelet] was obviously dominated, and even bewildered, by anxiety as he wrote [*La Sorcière*]. In a passage from his diary (I have been unable to read it since it is still inaccessible, but a third party has provided me with adequate information), he said that as he worked he would suddenly find that he lacked inspiration. He then would leave

his house and go to a public convenience where the stink was stultifying. He would breathe in deeply and then, having "got as close as possible to the object of his disgust", return to work.

I began to write easily only then. Circumstances, as I defined them, "forced" me to continue to pass as heterosexual, except for a small circle of gay friends and lovers, and I had to continue to visit the latrine a few more times. Now I'm out forever! Confession? No way! An assertion of who I am with pride and dignity. There's no need to hide. No mistake. Susan Stewart (1980:49) says: "If we agree about what a mistake is, we can begin to agree about what is not a mistake." I can't do anything about mistakes I've made in the past–sure, all of them undecidable–but it's not a mistake to claim agency now. Besides, this might just make it easier for someone else to come out. And then. as Naomi Zack (1993:51-52) advises:

> Don't forget who you are, because if you do, you will say and do things in your forgetfulness which will harm others who are what you are; identify yourself so that you will not be ignored or harmed under the guise of a false neutrality.

I used Marxism as a closet door; that is, I hid behind it. (And isn't someone, these days, who believes in a "proletarian dictatorship" to come at least a little "queer" intellectually?) I'm sure that many of my former and present colleagues believe I'm a "Marxist." (One of them even flatulently introduced me to a new colleague as "our departmental Marxist".) I'm not happy with that, but it's the way things were.

How did I come to write *this* book? First, I wanted to bring together some published materials on the Modernity Project at Vicos and make them more available to Peruvian readers. A first edition was published in Lima as *Vicisitudes del discurso del desarrollo en el Perú: Una etnografía sobre la modernidad del Proyecto Vicos* (Lima: SUR, Casa de Estudios del Socialismo, 2000). I wanted, also, to combine these with some unpublished materials whose nature held up writing until this late date–not a writing "block" *per se*, but a courtesy toward persons who no longer exist. I wanted to reexamine "development", on both the personal level and what has been taking place in Vicos and in Perú, in the light of the library work I have done over the last decade. I wished also to assess the changes that had taken place in me. I promised myself that I would contest images of the "modernity project at Vicos," as well as images of Vicos, that have been constructed over the past half century with counter-hegemonic images of ambiguity and undecidability and, thus, to turn "doxic truths" into topics that can be debated. The object here is to make the ethnography of this development project into something negotiable, in accord with contemporary conceptions of meta-ethnography,[4] and to reclaim for myself some of the agency I would have lost had I not challenged the very concept of agency. It seems to me, also, that I wanted to get on speaking terms with some ghosts of mine so that they might cease to haunt me and, indeed, become part of me. So, very much like Catherine Liu (2000:50), I want to point out that the "Oedipal aspects of my engagement" with Allan R. Holmberg "are obvious." Allan was the chair of my graduate committee at Cornell University and thus in a relationship with me that was "by turns . . . inspiring and infuriating." But where it is that one of leaves off and the other begins, I'm undecided. This book deals with ghosts, too. Avery Gordon (1997:22) says:

> To be haunted and to write from that location, to take on the condition of what you study, is not a methodology or a consciousness you can simply adopt or adapt as a set of rules or as an identity; it produces its own insights and blindnesses. Following the ghosts is about making a contact that changes you and refashions the social relations in which you are located. It is about putting life back in where only a vague memory or a bare trace was visible to those who bothered to look. It is sometimes about writing ghost stories, stories that not only repair representational mistakes, but also strive to understand the conditions under which a memory was produced in the first place, toward a countermemory, for the future.

This edition is designed to make explicit the "deconstructive turn" that was implicit in the original edition. It is also reparative.[5] In reconstructing a counter-myth to "development", with concepts of the fetish, the phallus, patriarchy, and the commodity, as I do later in the book, my aim is to combine the somewhat autobiographical mode with the critical ethnography of a North American research and development project in relation to the Vicos workers, as well as to observe deconstruction in process. My approach to the data is post-structuralist, and I thoroughly enjoy working with Derrida, not to omit Bourdieu and Foucault, although this does not mean the abandonment of structure. It may even be postmodern. In his exploration of postmodern art, Mark Taylor (1993:173-174) points out that postmodern artists attempt "to resist . . . commodification" with "[o]bjects constructed to disappear and works built in inaccessible spaces." A book the page proofs of which I have prepared myself with a limited run of a few hundred copies, many of which I give away: what could be less of a commodity, short-lived, and unheralded? Taylor continues:

> While many modern artists attempt to break out of the grid of knowledge to establish an immediate experience that is self-authenticating and universally valid, postmodernists realize that consciousness is inevitably mediated by structures of awareness that are historically relative and culturally conditioned. In different terms, knowledge is always already encoded. What we take to be an object of direct perception is actually a fabrication of the knowing subject's constructive imagination. Every representation, therefore, is a re-presentation of an antecedent representation. Awareness is never original but is forever secondary to an origin that *cannot* be present. Instead of attempting to deny the belatedness of awareness in artworks that claim to be original, postmodern artists admit the inescapability of the network of images and language that constitutes not only cognition but the very structures of subjectivity. To explore the human condition in the age of postmodernism is to examine not only the mediation of knowledge but the mediation of reality.

My intentions have changed so much over the last three decades–and especially over the last crucial one for the world and for me–that I decided to rewrite around the same data, erasing much of what I had written before. I am reminded here of what Spivak (1990:36-37) says about change-mindedness: "When someone stands up in the audience and presents some problem with what I have said, then great. I will learn too, in that situation. At the same time, if someone says that they read in an interview I gave in 1986, something that was different to what I said in, say, 1976, I would simply say 'Too bad!'–and that is that!"

Acknowledgments

For this book I have made use of field data collected in Vicos by the staffs of both the Vicos Project and the Methodology Project. There is no need for me to fear acknowledgment of all this book's contributors for, as Clifford Geertz (1995:62) says, "to acknowledge that one has put something together rather than found it glistening on a beach is to undermine its claim to true being and actuality. But a chair is culturally (historically, socially . . .) constructed, a product of acting persons informed by notions not wholly their own, yet you can sit in it . . . ." Without the good work of Buenaventura Armas Montoro, William C. Blanchard, Paul L. Doughty, Juan Elías Flores, Carlos Gómez, *Sarah Levy, Héctor Martínez Arellano, Abner Montalvo Vidal, Norman Pava, Eduardo Soler Bustamante, Froilán Soto Flores, and Mario C. Vázquez, I could not have composed this book. They are its authors too. But I should not leave out all the Vicosinos who served as informants and observational objects for these field workers: they are too numerous to mention individually, but they are also its co-authors, indeed the senior ones. All of these persons, and others whom I have cited and who have provided guidance, are this book's context. And I must not leave out the other or others in me, who certainly had an influence, if not a hand, in the writing. As Derrida (1982b) maintains, "There is nothing outside context."

The field materials, which may be consulted in the Archives of the Vicos Project, consists of raw notes which I have taken the liberty of editing for clarity and style. Neither the field workers nor the Vicosinos are responsible for my interventions or my conclusions. I am most grateful to Mrs. Laura Holmberg for encouraging my first visits to the Project's Archives when it was stored in the Department of Anthropology, Cornell University, and to that Department for assisting me in getting started in 1970 and 1971. Also to the staff of the Department of Manuscripts and University Archives, Olin Library, Cornell University, for granting me access to these records several times in the mid-1970s, providing me with copying facilities, and giving me direction. The Archives are now located in the Rare and Manuscript Collections, Carl A. Kroch Library, Cornell University, and I thank the latter for permitting my recent visit in November, 1997.

Vicos was one of the field stations organized by the anthropologists of what was then the Department of Sociology and Anthropology of Cornell University in the early 1950s, with the assistance of funds from the Carnegie Corporation. In 1953 the Vicos Project played host to the Cornell Cross-Cultural Methodology Project, organized by the sociologists of the same Department and funded by the Rockefeller Foundation.

As I've indicated, Allan Holmberg was my mentor and friend during my graduate work at Cornell University. He was human, and so both negative and positive statements can be made about him. He was absent during my final year at Cornell, and I wrote my doctoral thesis with Morris E. Opler. Allan came back just in time to chair my defense. I remember both men as kind and gentle. I visited Vicos many times in 1952, and I am grateful to Allan and Laura Holmberg for their hospitality on those occasions. I was not a member of the Project, however, for I was funded in 1951 and 1952 by the Social Science Research Council and the Wenner-Gren Foundation for Anthropological Research, and spent most of my time working in Hualcán, a rural community in the Province of Carhuaz, north of Vicos. I have been excluded from work on the Project and from the Project's works, but this is more the consequence of my own self-exclusion than anyone else's intentions. My research in Hualcán, an intense experience, inevitably contributes to my image of life in the Callejón de Huaylas, and may carry over into many of my observations of Vicos. In 1962 I was a guest of the Project for three months in Vicos, as Field Instructor in the Summer Field School at Vicos, in a program carried out jointly by Columbia, Cornell, Harvard, and Illinois Universities, and funded by the Carnegie Corporation. I still hope some day to publish the biographical and oral history data I collected then. I spent another two months in Vicos in 1971, continuing my work on oral history, funded by the Research Foundation of State University of New York, and I made a brief visit to Vicos in 1977 while I was in the Callejón de Huaylas searching for data on the Atusparia Uprising of 1885, also funded by the Research Foundation of State University of New York.

I want to thank Paul L. Doughty for sending me a copy of Cheryl Chadbourn's (1962) summer essay on disease and curing in Vicos. It is also on file in the Kroch Library archives, along with Price's (1961) work on trial marriage, Lancaster's (1965) essay on the Huaraz hospital, and other works by the students of successive years of the Summer Field School.

In 1968, Rose K. Goldsen of Cornell's Department of Sociology (the sociologists and anthropologists had split apart by then) presented me with the files of the Methodology Project. I thank her for this gesture of support at a time when my identity as a Peruvianist appeared to be in suspension.

I thank Cliff and Zelda Barnett in a note in Chapter 2, but I want to reiterate my gratitude to them for their hospitality and willingness to share their memories of Vicos with me in Palo Alto, California, in November, 1997.

I also want to acknowledge a debt to Teófilo Altamirano, Blanca Figueroa, Nelson Manrique, and Gonzalo Portocarrero, whose comments at the presentation of the Spanish version of this book in Lima on December 8, 2000, have assisted me to rethink parts of it for this revision. I thank Blanca for allowing me to reproduce her contribution here.

I retired from the teaching faculty of State University of New York at Buffalo in 1994, and soon moved to Lubbock, Texas, where I have received much hospitality, interest, support, and kindness from Texas Tech University, without which the preparation of the manuscript for this book would have been much more difficult. Somehow, a dys-placement seems to have been displaced by a re-placement, but the many errors of commission and omission I have made in writing, as well as in the judgment of distinguishing these, are mine alone.

Susan Stein has read portions of the manuscript of this book and made many insightful suggestions for improving its style. So did Daniel Stein. If I have not written up to their standards, the fault is all mine and none of theirs. An earlier version of this book was originally published in Spanish by the Casa SUR in Lima, in 2000. I want to thank my fellow *socios* of that organization for their patience with me and for making me one of them. My work with Maruja Martínez, who translated the manuscript into Spanish, was close, despite the thousands of miles which separated us and her questions, interventions, and corrections seem to have been a creative encounter for both of us. John Leavey (1999:149) provides an impressive metaphor: "One tongue in the mouth of the other, a French kiss: such is translation." Maruja's influence extends to this new version. I remember her lovingly for being there and for her steady support via e-mail. That she is there no longer leaves a hole in the world which can never be filled.

Finally, I want to thank the following for permission to reprint published materials:

William P. Mangin, for his "Thoughts on twenty-four years' work in Peru: The Vicos Project and me." In *Long-Term Field Research in Social Anthropology*, George M. Foster, et al., eds. New York: Academic Press, 1979.

Routledge, Taylor & Francis, Garland Publishing for: Homi K. Bhabha, *The Location of Culture*. London and New York: Routledge, 1994.

Sage Publications for: Henry F. Dobyns, Paul L. Doughty, and Harold D. Lasswell, eds., *Peasants, Power, and Applied Social Change, Vicos As a Model*, Beverly Hills, California: Sage Publications, pp. 14, 15, 18-19, 19-20, 34, 43, 92, 142-44, 172, copyright (c) 1971 by Sage Publications. Reprinted by Permission of Sage Publications, Inc.

The University of Chicago Press for: Nicolas Abraham and Maria Torok, *The Shell and the Kernel, Renewals of Psychoanalysis*. Edited, translated, and with an Introduction by Nicholas T. Rand. Chicago and London: The University of Chicago Press, 1994.

Lubbock, Texas, February 27, 2003

William W. Stein

Notes

1. According to Laplanche and Pontalis (1973:326), "[T]he preconscious system is governed by the secondary process. . . . [T]he term . . . is used above all, adjectivally, to describe what escapes immediate consciousness without being

unconscious in the strict sense of the word."

2. See Martin Duberman's (1994) excellent collage of the event in which Gay Liberation began.

3. Don Kulick (n.d.:3-4) says, regarding this term: "'Homophobia' is a problematic word. It was first popularized in the early-mid 1970s to refer to an irrational fear of homosexuality. In this, the word is directly linked to the diagnosis of 'acute homosexual panic', which is a psychiatric condition that was first proposed in 1920. It is interesting . . . that in its original formulation, 'homosexual panic' did not refer to a fear of homosexuals. Instead, it referred to cases where men who had been in intensively same sex environments became aware of homosexual desires that they felt unable to control, and unable to act on. The original formulation of the disorder was based on diagnosis of a small number of soldiers and sailors in a U.S. government mental hospital after WWI. These men were not violent—they were on the contrary passive. The disorder was characterized by periods of introspective brooding, self-punishment, suicidal assaults, withdrawal, and helplessness." I'm most grateful to the author for permission to quote this unpublished material.

4. I am grateful to Thomas Eriksen (1997:109-111) for the model that inspires these thoughts. In a section of an essay on Norwegian historical metaphors entitled "Contesting the past," he writes: "The 'tradition' on which nationalism and national identity feeds has been deconstructed in this way, and the great tradition of nationhood is increasingly being fragmented into several lesser histories which point out the ambiguities involved in interpreting the past, and which reveal nationalist versions of history as compounds of fact, myth, and interpretations which are open to discussion. With the increased influence of these counter-hegemonic interpretations of the past, it has become more difficult for the nationalists to expropriate the childhood recollections of the citizens: formerly doxic truths have been moved to the realm of opinion. And, it must be added, when it is shown in this way that the biography of a nation is negotiable, it becomes evident that so, too, is the biography of the individual citizen."

5. Melanie Klein (1975:83) writes of human development: "Love, desires (both aggressive and libidinal) and anxieties are transferred from the first and unique object, the mother, to other objects; and new interests develop which become substitutes for the relation to the primary object. . . . When depressive anxiety arises . . . the ego feels driven to project, deflect and distribute desires and emotions, as well as guilt and the urge to make reparation, on to new objects and interests. These processes . . . are a mainspring for sublimations throughout life." And then: "The contrast between persecutory and idealized, between good and bad objects–being an expression of life and death instincts [i.e., psychic drives] and forming the basis of phantasy life–is to be found in every layer of the self. Among

the hated and threatening objects, which the early ego tries to ward off, are also those which are felt to have been injured or killed and which thereby turn into dangerous persecutors. With the strengthening of the ego . . . the injured object is no longer predominantly felt as a persecutor but as a loved object towards whom a feeling of guilt and the urge to make reparation are experienced." (241-242.)

A Note on Quechua

I am taking some liberties with Quechua orthography which I hope will not offend linguists. The i/e and u/o sound shifts which are heard before and after q, but which are not phonemic, are retained (harmlessly, I think), as in *qepa muruy*, "late planting." The first word, meaning "behind, back of," (e.g., *qepaykicho*, [qipe:kicho:], "behind you") should be spelled /qipa/ by all purists. In the second word, *muruy*, "planting," pronounced [muri:], might be phonemically rendered as /muruy/ in the Callejón de Huaylas, the -*uy* ending corresponds with other Quechua varieties, as does my writing of the -*ay* ending, as in *pishtay*, "to slaughter, cut a throat," pronounced [pishte:], the root of the well-known *pishtaco*, "cutthroat." To render it phonemically "/pishte:/" would bring the shunned e into linguistic existence in a different way.

Ancash Quechua is different from other varieties, and the language spoken in the northern provinces of the Callejón, including Carhuaz where Vicos is located, drop the initial h of *ara*, "maize," *ampi*, "remedy/antiremedy," *aka*, "cuy," etc., heard in the southern provinces. Similarly, the northern *shuti*, "name," appears as *huti* in the extreme south of Ancash, as does the northern *qotza*, "lake," appear as *qocha*, and *patza*, earth, as *pasa*. "Earth" is *pacha* in other varieties of Quechua, so that the well-known *Pachamama*, "Earthmother," makes little sense in Ancash (see Chapter 4, Note 31). Other famous Quechua utterances, like *Tawantinsuyu*, the Incas' name for their "Land of the Four Divisions," likewise mean nothing in Ancash where the word for "four" is *chusku*!

Bruce Mannheim (1991) discusses the many varieties of Quechua, although his focus is on the more homogeneous Southern Quechua dialects. Ancash Quechua is neither "purer" nor more "corrupt" than the others, despite the misunderstandings of local peoples throughout the Andes. Marisol de la Cadena (1996:313) writes: "The Academy of Quechua language [of Cusco] was crucial in fashioning Cusco's special role within the national identity. This institution fosters the old and still current belief that the Cusco region has produced the 'purest' and most cultivated Quechua in the Andean area. Since its XVIth century inception, this belief has been an important pillar of Cusqueño identity as hegemonic among other Andean sites." Evidence for the widespread acceptance of this illusion is to be found in von Gleich and Wölck's (1994:36) Ayacucho survey in which 62 per cent of a sampling of communities in Ayacucho responded that the "best Quechua" was spoken in Cusco.   Nancy Hornberger (1995:197) adds that the Academy takes "Cusco Quechua to be the mother language of all the Quechua varieties, . . . the standard against which to measure all Quechuas," as opposed to Peruvian linguists who, "on the basis of historical inguistic analysis, archaeological evidence, and Andean social history, establish the earliest origins of Quechua in the central part of Peru."

Chapter 1

The Modernity Project at Vicos.[1]

> Justice is not the same as rights; it exceeds and founds the rights of man
> [sic]; nor is it distributive justice. It is not even, in the traditional sense
> of the word, *respect* for the other as a human subject. It is the experience
> of the other as other, the fact that I let the other be other, which
> presupposes a gift without restitution, without reappropriation and
> without jurisdiction. . . . [It is] giving not only what one has but what one
> doesn't have. This excess overflows the present, property, restitution, and
> no doubt law, morality, and politics, even though it should draw them in
> [*aspirer*] or inspire [*inspirer*] them. (Jacques Derrida 2002b:105.)

It is hard to "let things be" and not to touch them, feel them, stroke them,
handle them, possess them, know them. Can we "let the other be other"?
And in the presence of absence, can we let it be not?

The activity of the modernizers in the Peruvian community of Vicos is
the subject of this book. I write its deconstruction which, as Paul de Man
(1979:249) points out, "always has for its target to reveal the existence of
hidden articulations and fragmentations within assumedly monadic
totalities." I show how the Vicos Project was more than itself, how it
contained alterities that it did not recognize, how its "nature" engendered
other "natures" that it did not anticipate, and how it presented and represented absence. De Man continues: "[N]ature turns out to be a self-
deconstructive term. It engenders endless other 'natures' in an eternally

repeated pattern of regression. Nature deconstructs nature." Thus I make no claim that "I deconstruct" anything here, for the subject deconstructs itself. Meanwhile, the "I" that also appears here is busy deconstructing its self.

The Vicos Project is a well known but poorly understood applied anthropological study that took place between 1952 and 1966 in Vicos, a rural community located in Peru's Callejón de Huaylas, an intermontane basin in the north central part of the country. This research was undertaken by a group of scholars, both Peruvian and North American, who identified themselves as applied anthropologists. In his overview of the field, John Bennett (1996:S23) traces the development of "applied anthropology" to an emerging "mixture of New Deal humanitarian liberalism and progressive industrial management ideology" in the United States and "a humanitarian advisory function for colonial administration in Africa" in Britain.[2] The term refers "mainly to the employment of anthropologists by organizations involved in inducing change or enhancing human welfare." The modernity project at Vicos tried to be all of that, and more.

Deborah Poole (1992:210) situates Andean Studies in the "academic field of Latin American Studies" which was "created at the end of World War II" as one branch of "area studies," a Cold War device for the United States to accumulate "knowledge about those parts of the world in which it had definite political and economic interests."

> The character of Andean Studies in the United States has been formed and defined by its multiple forms of affiliation or association with the widest intellectual and political planning of area studies. During the decades of the 1950s and 1960s the dominant theoretical paradigm of the social sciences in the United States was modernization theory. As a product of this influence, Latin American Studies incorporated the principle that the "traditional" cultures of Latin America constituted separate social orders that were fundamentally different from "modern" state formations and national societies. This theory maintained that unless rural indigenous peoples "overcame" past traditions and were assimilated, Latin American countries could not modernize completely or become integrated democratic nations.

In their study of "development" both the North American researchers and their Peruvian counterparts identified themselves as modernizers–hence the "modernity project" in the sub-title of this book–whose aim was to "rationalize" their subjects, the Vicosinos, people of Vicos. They spoke of "economically underdeveloped" areas, but it will be quite apparent in the documents I am going to present that they considered the people in these areas to be "underdeveloped" as well. They piously hoped to eliminate poverty but, unconsciously, they merely desired its modernization, "not only to create consumers but to transform society by turning the poor into objects of knowledge and management" (Escobar 1995:22-23). However, by failing to recognize the nature of their desire these developers defeated their own stated rational purposes. So this book is also about misrecognition of desire, like that of the nineteenth century colonial project of confounding a "natural" state with an "unnatural" one. Robert Young (1995:98) suggests residues of racism, self-aggrandizement, and erotic fantasy in his portrayal of "colonial desire":

> Colonialism . . . was not only a machine of war and administration, it was also a desiring machine. This desiring machine, with its unlimited appetite for territorial expansion, for "endless growth and self-reproduction," for making connections and disjunctions, continuously forced disparate territories, histories and people to be thrust together like foreign bodies in the night. In that sense it was itself the instrument that produced its own darkest fantasy–the unlimited and ungovernable fertility of "unnatural" unions.

Thus, although they were not conscious of it, these modernizers were also immersed in what Homi Bhabha (1994:70-71) calls "colonial discourse":

> It is an apparatus that turns on the recognition and disavowal of racial/cultural/historical differences. Its predominant strategic function is the creation of a space for a "subject peoples" through the production of knowledges in terms of which surveillance is exercised and a complex form of pleasure/unpleasure is incited. It seeks authorization for its strategies by the production of knowledges of colonizer and colonized which are stereotypical but antithetically evaluated. The objective of colonial discourse is to construe the colonized as a population of degenerate types on the basis of racial origin, in order to justify conquest and to establish systems of administration and instruction. . . . Therefore, . . . colonial discourse produces the colonized as a social reality which is at once an "other" and yet entirely knowable and visible. It resembles a form of narrative whereby the productivity and circulation of subjects and signs are bound in a reformed and recognizable totality. It employs a system of representation, a regime of truth, that is structurally similar to realism.

Bhabha's statement is inspired by Edward Said's discussion of "Orientalism," which Said (1978:3) defines as "the corporate institution for dealing with the Orient–dealing with it by making statements about it, authorizing views of it, describing it, by teaching it, settling it, ruling over it." However, Said adds, it "is–and does not simply represent–a considerable dimension of modern political-intellectual culture, and as such has less to do with the Orient than it does with 'our' world" (12). "Colonial discourse" or "Orientalism" may be less satisfying to purists who do not wish to be limited to only a part of the Third World and might propose a "neocolonial" or "post-colonial" discourse. This does not change the nature of the intellectual and political "apparatus." Arturo Escobar (1995:9) proposes the term: "development discourse . . . governed by the same principles, . . . [which] has created an extremely efficient apparatus for producing knowledge about, and the exercise of power over, the Third World."

David Ludden (1992:247-248) identifies "development discourse" as based on an organic analogy: "Economic development appears to be a process of quantitative growth and structural change that, like growth and differentiation among cells, occurs in the object world, independent of the numbers that measure it and the conditions that affect it." Thus: "'Underdeveloped' and 'developing' imply immaturity and unrealized potential; development discourse is replete with the assumption that the realization of potential lies in mature capitalism." And he adds: "Imperialist politicians project power from the heights of capitalist maturity and routinely speak as adults talking about children, in the rhetoric of national superiority, responsibility, philanthropy, and self-defense . . . . In this way, the language of history and politics defines the world by development, its absence, and its spread from the West." Colin Leys (1996:5) traces the origin of "development theory" to its emergence "in the 1950s to deal" with the problem of "how the economies of the colonies of Britain, France, Portugal and other European powers, colonies comprising some 28% of the world's population, might be transformed and made more productive as decolonization approached, in the context of the still 'semi-colonial' condition of the former colonies of Latin America (accounting for a further 7%)." The self-proclaimed "developed" part of the world had practical interests in "development," and it figured as well in the Cold War of the times. Leys (6) notes, however, that "'development studies' tended to be conducted, at least until the mid-1960s, as if they had no significant historical or philosophical roots or presuppositions; and while 'development theorists' were usually glad to affirm their strong normative reasons for being concerned with development, they rarely acknowledged the extent to which their thinking reflected their own political commitments."

Pierre Bourdieu (1991:153) characterizes such discourse as "ideological": "The institutionalized circle of collective misrecognition, which is the basis of belief in the value of an ideological discourse, is established only when the structure of the field of production and circulation of this discourse is such that the *negation* it effects (by saying what it says only in a form which suggests that it is not saying it) is brought together with interpreters who are able, as it were, to *misrecognize again* the negated message; in other words, the circle is established only when what is denied by the form is 're-misrecognized', that is, known and recognized in the form, and only in the form, in which it is realized by denying itself. . . . Ideological production is all the more successful when it is able to *put in the wrong* anyone who attempts to *reduce* it to its objective truth. The ability to accuse the science of ideology of being ideological is a specific characteristic of the dominant ideology: uttering the hidden truth of a discourse is scandalous because it says something which was 'the last thing to be said.'"

We are discussing metadiscourse, a discourse on discourse, or discourse defined discursively. I employ the term "discourse" here in Michel Foucault's (1972:38) sense: "Whenever one can describe, between a number of statements, such a system of dispersion, whenever, between objects, types of statements, concepts, or thematic choices, one can define a regularity (an order, correlations, positions and functionings, transformations), we will say, for the sake of convenience, that we are dealing with a *discursive formation.*" I also endeavor to follow Foucault's (27-28) model in treating a "discursive totality" in order to "rediscover beyond the statements themselves the intention of the speaking subject, his [or her] conscious activity, what he meant, or, again, the unconscious activity that took place, despite himself, in what he said or in the almost imperceptible fracture of his actual words; in any case, we must reconstitute another discourse, rediscover the silent murmuring, the inexhaustible speech that animates from within the voice that one hears, re-establish the tiny, invisible text that runs between and sometimes collides with them. The analysis of thought is always *allegorical* in relation to the discourse that it employs. Its question is unfailingly: what was being said in what was said?" Thus, "in one way or another, things said say more than themselves" (110).

This is not all. It will also be useful for us to view discourse as taking place in a field of symbolic power:

The structure of linguistic production relation depends on the symbolic power relation between the two speakers, i.e., on the size of their respective capitals of authority (which is not reducible to specifically linguistic capital). Thus, competence is also the capacity to command a listener. Language is not only an instrument of communication or even of knowledge, but also an instrument of power. A person speaks not only to be understood but also to be believed, obeyed, respected, distinguished. Hence the full definition of competence as the right to speech, i.e., to the legitimate language, the authorized language which is also the language of authority. Competence implies the power to impose reception. (Bourdieu 1977a:648.)

[A] field may be defined as a network, or a configuration, of objective relations between positions. These positions are objectively defined, in their existence and in the determination they impose upon their occupants, agents or institutions, by their present and potential situation (*situs*) in the structure of the distribution of species of power (or capital) whose possession commands access to the specific profits that are at stake in the field, as well as by their objective relation to other positions (domination, subordination, homology, etc.) (Bourdieu *in* Bourdieu and Wacquant 1992:97.)

[I]f we want . . . to determine the structure of what is said in the place where we are, it's not sufficient to make an analysis of the discourse; we have to grasp the discourse as the product of a whole process of work on the group (invitation and non-invitation, etc.). In short, one needs an analysis of the social conditions of the constitution of the group in which the discourse is produced, because that is where one finds the true principle of what could and what could not be said there. More profoundly, one of the most effective ways a group has of reducing people to silence is by excluding them from the positions from which one *can* speak with people who will only say what the field authorizes and calls for. (Bourdieu 1993:92.)

To change the world, one has to change the ways of world-making, that is, the vision of the world and the practical operations by which groups are produced and reproduced. Symbolic power, whose form par excellence is the power to make groups . . . , rests on two conditions. First, as any form of performative discourse, symbolic power has to be based on the possession of symbolic capital. The power to impose upon other minds a vision, old or new, of social divisions depends on the social authority acquired in previous struggles. . . . Second, symbolic efficacy depends on the degree to which the vision proposed is founded in reality. . . . Symbolic power is the power to make things with words. It is only if it is true, that is, adequate to things, that description makes things. In this sense, *symbolic power is a power or consecration or revelation*, the power to consecrate or to reveal things that are already there. (Bourdieu 1989:23).

Symbolic power is exerted only with the collaboration of those who undergo it because they help to *construct* it as such. But nothing would be more dangerous than to stop short at this observation (as idealist constructivism, in its ethnomethodological or other forms, does). This submission is in no way a "voluntary servitude" and this complicity is not granted by a conscious, deliberate act; it is itself the effect of a power, which is durably inscribed in the bodies of the dominated, in the forms of schemes of perception and dispositions (to respect, admire, love, etc.), in other words, beliefs which make one *sensitive* to certain public manifestations, such as public representations of power. (Bourdieu 2000a:171).

There is one more thing to note regarding discursive formations, and that is that they are impermanent. In his discourse on "the chain of discourses," Roland Barthes (1986:317-318) writes:

It is because language is not dialectical (permitting the third term only as a formula, a rhetorical assertion, a pious hope) that discourse (discursivity), in its historical development, moves by fits and starts. Each new discourse can emerge only as the *paradox* which reverses (and often opposes) the surrounding or preceding *doxa*; it can be generated only as difference, distinction, standing out *against* what sticks to it. . . . Hence, we must always try to find which *doxa* an author is opposing (it may be an extremely minority *doxa*, governing a limited group). Teaching can also be evaluated in terms of paradox, provided it is based on the conviction: that a system which calls for corrections, translations, openings, and denials is more useful than an unformulated absence of system; we may then avoid the immobility of prattle and join the historical chain of discourses, the progress (*progressus*) of discursivity.

Vicos and the Vicos Project

Vicos, at the time of the Project's research, was a community of about 2,200 people belonging to over 250 farming households. These rural laborers paid labor rent to a landlord in return for family plots. The community is located at altitudes of 9,000 feet and higher in an upland basin of the Marcará River, a tributary of the Santa River which flows northwest for some 125 miles between two ranges of the Andes forming the Callejón de Huaylas. The Marcará River flows down about 25 miles from glacial sources in the Cordillera Blanca, a range of mountains with many peaks of 20,000 feet and over, and connects with the Santa at the town of Marcará, the District capital six kilometers below Vicos and over a thousand feet lower than the Vicos bottom lands. According to Humberto Ghersi's (1959 I:142) census of 1952, the town had a population of 958 persons almost all of whom were farmers and farm laborers, which would give it a much smaller population of culturally "urban" people. The political District of Marcará is located in the Province of Carhuaz, the capital of which is the town by the same name, twelve kilometers to the northwest. Carhuaz, with over 3,000 inhabitants, was larger but, again, the "urban" elite, known as "mestizos," was small. When our little group of graduate students in anthropology from Cornell University[3] arrived in the Callejón de Huaylas in 1951 we did not encounter slavery *per se* but we did observe a social arrangement which equally offended our modern sensibilities: labor rent, which we identified as a "feudal" arrangement. The payment of three days' work a week in return for a few miserable plots of land for subsistence farming was a *visible* form of exploitation we North Americans easily recognized. Agnes Heller (1990:152) observes: "Slavery is an anomaly in modernity, whereas the unequal distribution of wealth is not." She continues:

> If some (not all) people are freely born, their freedom is determined by the very existence of those born unfreely. What they can do and others cannot is what "being born freely" means. If every human being is freely born, the concrete content of having been freely born disappears. Freedom becomes an abstraction, an empty possibility. . . . Modernity is about the concretization of "freedom." There is no longer a 'social pyramid.' The modern world is flat because it is symmetrical.

Immanuel Wallerstein (1991:120-121) comments: "The so-called 'subsistence farmer' quite frequently turns out on closer inspection in fact to be transferring surplus-value to someone by some means." He defines "eight varieties of proletarians, only one of which meets the classic model: the worker who transfers all the value he [sic] has created to the 'owner' and receives in return money (i.e., wages). In other boxes of the matrix, we can place such familiar types as petty producer (or 'middle peasant'), tenant farmer, sharecropper, peon, slave." However, there is another "dimension" to consider:

> There is the question of the degree to which performing the role in a particular fashion is accepted by the worker under the pressures of the market (which we cynically call "free" labor) or because of the exigencies of some political machinery (which we more frankly call "forced" or "coerced" labor). A further issue is the length of the contract–by the day, the week, the year or for life). A third issue is whether the producer's relationship to a given owner could be transferred to another owner without the producer's assent. . . .
> The difference between a peon and a slave was in the "theory" to be sure, but in two respects in the practice. First, a landlord could "sell" a

slave but not usually a peon. Second, if an outsider gave money to a peon, he was legally able to terminate his "contract". This was not true for a slave. . . .

Since wages are a relatively costly mode of labor . . . it is easy to understand why wage labor has *never* been the exclusive, and until relatively recently not even the principal, form of labor in the capitalist world economy.

While we had observed gross inequalities in the distribution of wealth at home in North America, as well as elsewhere in Peru, we did not recognize them as exploitation that we had anything to do with but, rather, misrecognized them as "poverty." (A few years later the concept of "culture of poverty" became quite popular in both social studies and politics, to the point where politicians could declare "war" on it and give many scholars the distinction of being front-line troops.) That is, we accepted inequalities and injustices as eternal verities. I believe that the asymmetries and irrationalities of the hacienda system, with its farmer-laborers in lifetime "contracts," grated on our nerves, more because they were something other, something beyond our perception, than because they were oppressive and exploitative. The world seemed no longer "flat" or "symmetrical," because we were on the other side of something we did not recognize, an otherness in ourselves. We viewed the abolition of the hacienda as a progressive step toward modernity. We believed in "area studies" and "community studies," and thereby failed to see how what we were studying was as intimate as it was. Our ethnography produced local subjects, according to our desire to isolate what we were studying, but it ignored *local* production of locality. Arjun Appadurai (1996:181-182) comments on this limitation and points to a new possibility:

> If a large part of the ethnographic record can be reread and rewritten as a record of the multifarious modes for the production of locality, it follows that ethnography has been unwittingly complicit in this activity. This is a point about knowledge and representation rather than about guilt or violence. The ethnographic project is in a peculiar way isomorphic with the very knowledge it seeks to discover and document, as both the ethnographic project and the social projects it seeks to describe have the production of locality as their governing telos. . . .
>
> The value of reconceiving ethnography (and rereading earlier ethnography) from this perspective is threefold: (1) it shifts the history of ethnography from a history of neighborhoods to a history of the techniques for the production of locality; (2) it opens up a new way to think about the complex coproduction of indigenous categories by organic intellectuals, administrators, linguists, missionaries, and ethnologists, which undergirds large portions of the monographic history of

anthropology; (3) it enables the ethnography of the modern, and of the production of locality under modern conditions, to be part of a more general contribution to the ethnographic record *tout court.*

We had traveled to Peru to engage in ethnographic and ethnological projects, a justification for crossing the border between our society and that of the Other, but our "treasonous impulse to intercourse with foreigners" is interpreted by Alphonso Lingis (1998:185) in different terms: "[W]e travel also, in every case, to flee our faces–to be anonymous, unrecognized, to dissolve the crust of our identity. We travel to break the enchainment of acts in time, to be in the instant. We travel to lose sight of the traffic patterns and the map of the future, our eye on a horizon as vaporous and nebulous as the sky. We travel under the gray clouds and invisible winds of the skies, pure realm of chance. We give ourselves over to chance encounters, chance infatuations, chance passions. . . . We travel to divest ourselves, to expose ourselves, denude ourselves."

It is this divestiture, exposing, and denuding that I explore in this book. Less like confession, though, and more like deconstruction. That is, to write the truth about the Vicos Project, truth not in any essentialist sense but as truth that constructs me as I construct it. Foucault (1980:131) observes:

> The important thing here, I believe, is that truth isn't outside power, or lacking in power: contrary to a myth whose history and functions would repay further study, truth isn't the reward of free spirits, the child of protracted solitude, nor the privilege of those who have succeeded in liberating themselves. Truth is a thing of this world: it is produced only by virtue of multiple forms of constraint. And it induces regular effects of power. Each society has its régime of truth, its "general politics" of truth: that is, the types of discourse which it accepts and makes function as true; the mechanisms and instances which enable one to distinguish true and false statements, the means by which each is sanctioned; the techniques and procedures accorded value in the acquisition of truth; the status of those who are charged with saying what counts as true.

We anthropologists of the early 50s did not really understand "the modern" because we thought we were it. De Man (1983:144) reminds us: "It is perhaps somewhat disconcerting to learn that our usage of the word goes back to the late fifth century of our era and that there is nothing modern about the concept of modernity." We came to modernize but we did not see that our modernity project could not be completed because of the privilege of our own modernity. The fact that only some Vicosinos,[4] Vicos people, were enabled to take advantage of the improved productive capabilities of the community, the educational opportunities offered, and the new freedoms, while most of the others continued in poverty, was in our eyes a function of this new, more rational world. A modernity project is, thus, an enlightenment project, a rationality project. Habermas (1987:1-2) traces the concept of "modernity" to Max Weber who "described as 'rational' the process of disenchantment which led in Europe to a disintegration of religious world views that issued in a secular culture":

> With the modern empirical sciences, autonomous arts, and theories of morality and law grounded on principles, cultural spheres of value took shape which made possible learning processes in accord with the respective inner logics of theoretical, aesthetic, and moral-practical problems.
>
> What Weber depicted was not only the secularization of Western *culture*, but also and especially the development of modern *societies* from the viewpoint of rationalization. The new structures of society were marked by the differentiation of the two functionally intermeshing systems that had taken shape around the organizational cores of the capitalist enterprise and the bureaucratic state apparatus. Weber understood this process as the institutionalization of purposive-rational economic and administrative action. To the degree that everyday life was affected by this cultural and societal rationalization, traditional forms of life–which in the early modern period were differentiated primarily according to one's trade– were dissolved. . . .
>
> "Modernization" was introduced as a technical term only in the 1950s. It is the mark of a theoretical approach that takes up Weber's problem but elaborates it with the tools of social-scientific functionalism. The concept of modernization refers to a bundle of processes that are cumulative and mutually reinforcing: to the formation of capital and the mobilization of resources; to the development of the forces of production and the increase in the productivity of labor; to the establishment of centralized political power and the formation of national identities; to the proliferation of rights of political participation, of urban forms of life, and of formal schooling; to the secularization of values and norms; and so on.

Secularization? De Man (1979:245) remarks wryly: "If . . . we are tempted to convert ourselves to 'theism,' we stand convicted of foolishness in the court of the intellect. But if we decide that belief, in the most extensive use of the term (which must include all possible forms of idolatry and ideology) can once and forever be overcome by the enlightened mind, then this twilight of the idols will be all the more foolish in not recognizing itself as the first victim of its occurrence."

Appadurai (1996:6) points out in his critique of the critique of modernity that the modern world has not grown "into an iron cage," nor has the human imagination been "stunted by the forces of commoditization, industrial capitalism, and the generalized regimentation and secularization of the world," nor has there been a "shrinking religiosity (and greater scientism), less play (and increasingly regimented leisure), and inhibited spontaneity at every level." A radical rejection of modernity, as Nancy Fraser (1989:35-36) indicates "is at best modern and at worst antimodern," for it rejects "the very commitments to truth, rationality, and freedom that alone make critique possible." But rationality and irrationality are not poles of a binary opposition which must be resolved through some third term. Shoshana Felman (1985:36) brings them together in her work on *Writing and Madness*:

> What characterizes madness is . . . not simply blindness, but a blindness *blind to itself*, to the point of necessarily entailing an *illusion of reason*. But if this is the case, how can we know where reason stops and madness begins, since both involve the pursuit of some form of reason? If madness as such is defined as an act of *faith* in reason, no reasonable conviction can indeed be exempt from the suspicion of madness. Reason and madness are thereby inextricably linked; madness is essentially a phenomenon of thought, of thought which claims to denounce, in another's thought, the Other of thought: that which thought is not.

Thus, rationality which fails to see its own irrationality is not rational. In place of binary opposition–and this goes for the functional and dysfunctional sides of any practice–, Derrida (1982:41-42) asks us to "proceed using a double gesture, according to a unity that is both systematic and in and of itself divided,"

> On the one hand, we must traverse a phase of *overturning*. To do justice to this necessity is to recognize that in a classical philosophical opposition we are not dealing with the peaceful coexistence of a *vis-a-vis*, but rather with a violent hierarchy. One of the two terms governs the other . . ., or has the upper hand. To deconstruct the opposition, first of all, is to overturn the hierarchy at a given moment. To overlook this phase of overturning is to forget the conflictual and subordinating structure of opposition. Therefore one might proceed too quickly to a *neutralization* that *in practice* would leave the previous field untouched, leaving one no hold on the previous opposition, thereby preventing any means of *intervening* in the field effectively. We know what always have been the *practical* (particularly *political*) effects of *immediately* jumping beyond oppositions, and of protests in the simple form of *neither* this *nor* that. When I say that this phase is necessary, the word *phase* is perhaps not the most rigorous one. It is not a question of a chronological phase, a given moment, or a page that one day simply will be turned, in order to go on to

other things. The necessity of this phase is structural; it is the necessity of an interminable analysis: the hierarchy of dual oppositions always reestablishes itself.

It is the same with our Andean ethnographic project which sought to place us inside our subjects' skins while maintaining our apartness. We see the beginnings of this early in the sixteenth century. With a remarkable sensitivity to the conditions of ethnographic practice Todorov (1984:247-248) makes this observation of the conquest of Mexico:

> Since the period of the conquest, for almost three hundred and fifty years, Western Europe has tried to assimilate the other, to do away with an exterior alterity, and has in great part succeeded. . . . This extraordinary success is chiefly due to one specific feature of Western civilization which for a long time was regarded as a feature of [people themselves], its development and prosperity among Europeans thereby becoming proof of their natural superiority: it is, paradoxically, Europeans' capacity to understand the other. Cortés affords us a splendid example of this, and he was conscious of the degree to which the art of adaptation and of improvisation governed his behavior. Schematically this behavior is organized into two phases. The first is that of interest in the other, at the cost of a certain empathy or temporary identification. Cortés slips into the other's skin [a play on the Aztec practice of dancing in the flayed skins of human sacrifices], but in a metaphoric and no longer a literal fashion: the difference is considerable. Thereby he ensures himself an understanding of the other's language and a knowledge of the other's political organization, whence his interest in the Aztecs' internal dissension, and he even masters the emission of messages in an appropriate code: hence he manages to pass himself off as Quetzalcoatl returned to earth. But in so doing he has never abandoned his feeling of superiority; it is even his very capacity to understand the other that confirms him in that feeling. Then comes the second phase, during which he is not content to reassert his own identity (which he has never really abandoned), but proceeds to assimilate the Indians to his own world.

This was our unconscious model at mid-century. To paraphrase Pierre Bourdieu (1977b:167), it went without saying because it came without saying. We could not question it because we were not aware of it. We could call it a part of our *habitus*, a term Bourdieu (72) defines as "systems of durable, transposable *dispositions*, structured structures predisposed to function as structuring structures, that is, as principles of the generation and structuring of practices and representations which can be objectively 'regulated' and 'regular' without in any way being the product of obedience to rules, objectively adapted to their goals without presupposing a conscious aiming at ends or an express mastery of the operations necessary to attain them and, being all this, collectively orchestrated without being the product of the orchestrating action of a conductor." Bourdieu (2000a:143-144) adds:

> In so far as it is the product of the incorporation of a *nomos*, of the principle of vision and division constitutive of a social order or a field, habitus generates practices immediately adjusted to that order, which are therefore perceived, by their author and also by others, as 'right', straight, adroit, adequate, without being in any way the product of obedience to an order in the sense of an imperative, to a norm or to legal rules. This practical, non-thetic intentionality, which has nothing in common with a *cogitatio* (or a noesis) consciously oriented towards a *cogitatum* (a noema), is rooted in a posture, a way of bearing the body (a *hexis*), a durable way of being of the durably modified body which is engendered and perpetuated, while constantly changing (within limits), in a twofold relationship, structured and structuring, to the environment. Habitus constructs the world by a certain way of orienting itself towards it, of bringing to bear on it an attention which, like that of a jumper preparing to jump, is an active, constructive bodily tension towards the imminent forthcoming (*allodoxia*, the mistake we sometimes make when, waiting for someone, we seem to see that person in everyone who comes along, gives an accurate idea of this tension).

Thus "[g]uided by one's sympathies and antipathies, affections and aversions, tastes and distastes, one makes for oneself an environment in which one feels 'at home' and in which one can achieve the desire to be which one identifies with happiness" (150).

As you will see, such *habitus* guided the Peru-Cornell Project at Vicos or, as it is known in the English-language literature, the Cornell-Peru Project. I will call it simply the Vicos Project. And to simplify matters at the beginning I will try to account for my relationship to it. Although I was an occasional guest researcher in Vicos, and I worked twelve months in 1954-55 in Ithaca, New York, as a research assistant on field materials that were collected in Vicos in 1953 by a "guest project" (see Chapter 2), I was never a member of the Vicos Project. I was certainly closely related to it while I was doing field work in Hualcán, a rural community about fifteen kilometers to the north of Vicos. With a growing family and an academic position to fill, it was not possible for me to travel to Peru as often as you might think a Peruvianist should. In view of my absence during the initial years, critical ones for Vicos, I was unable to observe at first hand the Project's activities between 1952 and 1962. I carried on field research in Vicos from June to September of 1962, and from

September to October of 1971, and perhaps that qualifies me to write this book.[5] However, while no work of mine on Vicos has been or will be the critical evaluation of the Project that needs to be done, it is very likely that such a "final" evaluation will never be made. Therefore, this book will have to serve.

The Vicos Project came into being at the end of 1951, with funds from the Carnegie Corporation of New York,[6] through an agreement between the Indigenous Institute, a Peruvian governmental agency, and Cornell University–although ethnographic work began in Vicos in 1949 with Mario C. Vázquez who later became what Enrique Mayer (1991:475) calls "the architect of the Peruvian agrarian reform."[7] At that time Vicos belonged to the Public Benefit Society of Huaraz, the largest city in the region and capital of the Department of Ancash, 40 kilometers southeast of Marcará. Holmberg (1952:1-2) writes of the uncertainty with which the Project was initiated and the fortuitous set of events which made it possible:

> When funds were received for carrying out the project, it was not certain that the hacienda under study could be obtained for experimental purposes since it was leased by a commercial firm whose contract still had five years to run. Accordingly, on first arriving in Peru in August 1951, it was necessary to see what arrangements could be made to take over the existing contract. Having been invited as a delegate to the Primer Congreso Internacional de Peruanistas [First International Congress of Peruvianists] and the Conferencia de Ciencias Antropológicas [Conference of Anthropological Sciences] which were held in Lima from August 16 to August 26, I utilized my participation in these congresses to explain the aims of our projected program in Peru. Through these congresses, I was fortunate in establishing most friendly rapport with Dr. Carlos Monge who as President of the Instituto Indigenista Peruano [Peruvian Indigenist Institute] immediately took a very active interest in sponsoring our project in Peru. Through him contact was made with the Minister of Labor and Indigenous Affairs, General Armando Artola, who also immediately became a very strong supporter of our program. With General Artola, Dr. Julio Pereyra (Chief of Indigenous Affairs of the Ministry of Labor and Indigenous Affairs), and Dr. Monge, a working agreement of collaboration between Cornell and the Instituto Indigenista Peruano . . . was drawn up and was immediately approved by the President of Peru [Manuel Odría]. On the basis of this a Supreme Decree was issued by the Government which gave the projected program official sanction and which authorized the collaboration of agencies of the Peruvian Government.

Holmberg (1971a:34) describes the legal and social connection of Vicos to the Benefit Society (in Spanish, the Sociedad de Beneficencia Pública de Huaraz):

> Vicos was a public hacienda, a type not uncommon in Peru. The title of Vicos was held by the Sociedad de Beneficencia Pública de Huaraz which rented the hacienda out to the highest bidder at public auction for periods ranging from 5 to 10 years. Vicos was one of 56 such properties owned by the Sociedad de Beneficencia Pública de Huaraz which used its income from rent to maintain the largest, though woefully inadequate, hospital in the Andean area of the department of Ancash. The rent paid for Vicos amounted to approximately $500 a year. The Beneficencia board, appointed by the Minister of Health and Social Service [head of the national agency in Lima] and in theory responsible to the ministry, was in fact autonomous to a large degree. Members of the Beneficencia board were of the regional upper class residing in the departmental capital of Huaraz and were often themselves *patrones* of similar estates.

The renter of Vicos would take over the Hacienda as *patrón*, that is, supreme authority on the estate as well as its operator and take whatever surplus over the rental fee he could. "Supreme authority" should be understood here as a relative, rather than absolute, term since close surveillance of the population of over 2,000 Vicosinos, Vicos people, would have been inconvenient and costly, if it were indeed possible on a large property such as Vicos. However, to say that Vicos workers and their families possessed some capacity for negotiation, as will be seen later in this book, does not mean to imply that the hacienda system was not exploitative and oppressive. To paraphrase Ann Zulawski's (1995:104) conclusion to her study of labor and its exploitation in colonial Upper Peru, which is now Bolivia:

> There are limits to the amount of control one can "give" Andean people in shaping their world without denying their exploitation and espousing a kind of relativism that scarcely distinguishes between dominated peoples and dominators. While Andean peoples certainly have been subjects, not merely objects, of history, the surplus extracted from them *has* facilitated development elsewhere, and it is absurd to suggest that this process has been effected without enormous suffering and emotional and cultural loss on the part of Andean peoples.

The *patrón* of Vicos was in the position which Gonzalo Portocarrero (1993:33) calls "total domination": "This concentration of power allows the dominator to turn the dominated into an instrument of his/her will; into a labor apparatus to exploit and an object for the satisfaction of aggressive and sexual impulses. Typically this relation creates on one side despotic personalities who exercise their rule arbitrarily, without limits, and on the other perpetually fearful and unquestioning servile personalities. Past renters of Vicos conformed to this pattern, and I vividly recall a dignified old man, in 1971, bursting into tears of impotent rage as he reported a physical attack by a *patrón* when he was a young Hacienda worker.

The highest bidder of the periodic auction of Vicos would take possession of the Hacienda and take what profit he could get from an estate described by Holmberg (1971a:34):

> Vicos consists of approximately 18,000 acres of land of which about 10,000 acres are now under cultivation. It is rocky and hilly rising from an elevation of 9,000 feet to over 14,000 feet. Most of the Indians, of whom there are 2,250 . . ., live in dispersed homesteads on the lower parts of the hacienda and they occupy roughly 85% of the arable lands. For the privilege of living on these lands, the Indians worked 3 days a week for the hacienda without pay except for 20 Peruvian centavos a day as gratification given for the purchase of coca. . . . Previously, the hacienda had been rented to the highest bidder . . . and each renter had always tried to take as much off the land as possible. Consequently, when we took over in January there was not a building on the hacienda in enough repair to occupy, there were no storage facilities for products, the lands were badly eroded, and the Indians had not even been paid their gratification for over a year.

Holmberg's use of the term "Indians" was more acceptable in the early 1950s than it is now, but even then, as I learned in Hualcán,[8] it was not heard kindly by rural people in reference to them. "Indian" is an epithet in the Callejón de Huaylas, the large intermontane basin in which Vicos and Hualcán are located. Olivia Harris (1995:376) says of the Andes as a whole: "Indians do not think of themselves primarily as 'Indians' but use the term ironically with reference to how they are classified by outsiders. They express their identity more in affiliation to local or regional groups." The word "*campesino,*" peasant,[9] is easily substituted but, as Marisol de la Cadena (1998:43) points out, it provides a term that implies "Indian," *indio* in Spanish, without actually saying it. "Indian," thus, is under erasure. We can see this as an example of undererasure, since *under* erasure there is still ("always already") a trace which is felt, heard, seen, and known of what is *under* it. Nevertheless, Cecilia Méndez (1992:41) writes:

> "Indian" is no longer a referent for understanding Peruvian reality. It is

useless to say that I am not referring to phenotypes. Culturally speaking, the word has been associated with a peasant culture; today it no longer refers to the majority. In this sense, strictly, it would appear that we have become a "republic without Indians." Although the paths which have brought us–or are bringing us–to this are very far from the liberal dreams of Bolívar, and in the antipodes of the Civilistas' [a nineteenth century modernizing political party] projects to whiten the country. Nevertheless, the cost has been high. Nobody could foresee the levels of violence in which the greatest disturbance which has ever shaken Peru would develop [i.e., the Shining Path movement and the government's equally violent response]. Indian Peru is disappearing together with oligarchical Peru, as was to be expected, given that the latter is defined as a function of the former. There are those who lament, and publish nostalgic Incaist or Indianist essays, as a reaction to what they conceive as the country's 'loss of identity.' But if there is any "loss of identity," this has more to do with their self-definition as intellectuals than with the country. These are discourses which rise up once more to mark ethnic and cultural differences–in an unconscious or a deliberate manner–at the precise moment when these differences are becoming less and less distinguishable."

Mirko Lauer (1991:6) comments ironically: "With the condition that in the 80s modernity has ceased being something which is offered, chosen, accepted, or rejected: the inner distance which maintained the difference has exploded, and now there are no real differences between Andean and non-Andean in Peru. A larger problem brings us together and defines us. All 21 million Peruvians will be Indians in the twenty-first century, whether our bourgeoisie likes it or not."

The historical conjuncture in Peru in the early 1950s was different. What de la Cadena (2000:87) describes for Cusco in the 1920s is quite applicable to Ancash a generation later: "Defining who the Indians were from the dominant viewpoint was neither a political nor an academic debate in the 1920s. Regional racial/cultural identity politics allowed an economically privileged cluster of individuals (male or female, literate or illiterate, but usually rural) to self-identify alternatively as mestizos or Indians, depending on the specific circumstances of their interactions. Yet the dominant intellectual and political definition of Indianness overrode this dynamic and rigidly defined Indians as illiterate agriculturalists who lived communally in highland *ayllus* [communities] . . . . This simplification required therefore that literate Indians become non-Indian, that is, mestizos."

"Indian"—*indio* in Spanish—is, nevertheless, a word. *It exists in language if nowhere else.* As such it can be interrogated as to its meaning. (See Stein 2001a.)

In 1951 the 2,000 people of Vicos were called "*colonos*", "serfs." The Project adopted the latter term uncritically and viewed the Hacienda as a "feudal manor." This is what Johannes Fabian (1983:50) calls the construction by anthropology of its object "by employing various devices of temporal distancing, negating the coeval existence of the object and subject of its discourse."[10] Townspeople in the Callejón de Huaylas, the main valley above which Vicos is located, referred to the Vicosinos and other rural people living in communities in the heights as "*indios*," Indians, as I have indicated, an insulting term in Peruvian Spanish, really an epithet. Vicosinos referred to themselves as "Vicosinos," or "*hacienda nuna*," hacienda people. Some simply identified themselves as "*obreros*," workers. I prefer the latter term, workers, because I think it is appropriate at the turn of a new century to de-exoticize the Other, to view Vicosinos not as "serfs," "peasants," or "Indians," but as people.

If I lean in the opposite direction and end up by exoticizing the Project it will be corrective of the positivism and antiseptic objectivity of social "science" which makes its objects into otherness.[11] Paul Rabinow (1986:241) shows why this is a healthy turn: "We need to anthropologize the West: show how exotic its constitution of reality has been; emphasize those domains most taken for granted as universal (this includes epistemology and economics); make them seem as historically peculiar as possible; show how their claims to truth are linked to social practices and have hence become effective forces in the social world." We treat the Vicos Project as an ethnographic object, with the understanding that ethnography is exaggeration. James Boon (1982:26) observes:

> Experience across cultures, like communication across languages, is neither unique nor universal. Its advantage lies rather in the sense of exaggeration it ensures. Every culture appears, vis-à-vis every other, exaggerated (just like every language), hence the exhilaration of the imperfectible effort we call translation. I propose, then, that ethnographic writing about other cultures consists, like cultures themselves, is an exaggeration of differences. We start with the exaggerations (the languages, the cultures), and only certain kinds of theories–each itself an unwitting exaggeration–and attempt to compromise the mutual exaggerations into cozy universals. . . . This discourse of cultures confesses its own exaggeration and seeks to control and assess it by becoming interpretive, at times even literary, while remaining both systematic and dialectical.

But more than an exaggeration, as Bourdieu (2000a:54) says of ethnographers who intrude their own theoretical views in their questions which lead the Others "to adopt a theoretical viewpoint on their own practice": "[I]t is no doubt the powerful, fascinating experiences of being a stranger that makes [them] forget, in the literary self-indulgence of exoticism, that [they are] no less [strangers] to [their] own practice than to the strange practices [they] observe."

In Vicos, in 1951, the current renter was faced with a failing linen business and was willing to assign the estate to another party on a sublease, while Professor Allan R. Holmberg was ready to enter as the representative of Cornell University. According to Barbara Lynch (1982:20) this sublease "was contingent upon the maintenance of traditional hacienda labor relationships [and] hacienda lands had to remain intact and work obligations fulfilled." (See also Vázquez 1955:9.) Thus, the directors of the Beneficencia, influential members of the regional elite, protected themselves from any challenge to what they conceived as "established" practices. In this way, Cornell, but more concretely Holmberg, became the ruler of Vicos. This was a more traditional role than Holmberg, really, wished to play; but he had no choice in the matter, and so the Vicos workers continued to pay labor rent to the Hacienda for their individual holdings for another five years, until the sublease expired.

Holmberg (1952:4) tells how the Project operated within these limits:

> In as much as our plans were aimed at working as much as possible with the Indians themselves, we dispensed with all outside employees except one, the administrator of the Hacienda [Enrique Luna, a mestizo, i.e., a person fluent in both Spanish and Quechua and so an intermediary, from the town of Marcará] who had considerable experience in back of him, is from the area, well-liked, and influential in the local situation. . . . [I]t was found advisable also to dispense immediately with all free services to the Hacienda and its employees. In place of these free services, volunteer paid Indian employees were hired for strategic jobs. At the suggestion of Indian leaders no basic change was made in the methods of work, but it was made clear to them that in consultation with the people all profits from their work would be invested to their interest on the Hacienda–in such works as better housing, schools, recreation, medical facilities, and improved agricultural practices.

It appeared that the Project had control of a number of major variables, to the extent that it could introduce innovations, since it held power in Vicos. Adams and Cumberland (1960:188) comment: "To actually 'rent' a population in which experimental introductions could be carried on would come excitingly close to the long-sought laboratory of human society of which sociologists and anthropologists have often dreamed." What was problematic, however, was that in reality few, if any, variables were controlled. An examination of the texts written by Project personnel were controlled. An examination of the texts written by Project personnel reveals that they saw themselves as initiators of change. This is an unfortunate anthropological habit: Mary Des Chene (1997:68) calls attention to "a feature of anthropological discourse . . .: that the ethnographer has arrived just prior to momentous changes and things will never be the same again." Contemporary anthropology is moving beyond such a naive view, but in the early 1950s this ethnographic *habitus* left Vicos "without history" (cf. Wolf 1982) in the eyes of the ethnographers.

In fact, Vicos had never been sealed off from an "outside world" but has always been one part of the flow of events in Peru. Vicosinos had participated in a local labor protest in the mid-1920s, which successfully cause the reduction of an Hacienda obligation of four days' work per week to three. Clifford Barnett (1960) ably documents the Vicos labor movement in a dissertation that was never published and remains unknown in anthropological literature. I continue to believe that this work was deliberately suppressed because it chronicled an assertion by Vicosinos of their civil rights and a "contamination" of Vicos by Peruvian anarcho-syndicalism which was incompatible with the construction of a purer "serfdom" by the Project. The populist Aprista Party's regional membership was active in Vicos in the 1930s and beyond. An account of the operations of the *Alianza Popular Revolucionaria Americana*, or APRA, in Chachapoyas, a town in northern Peru is provided by David Nugent (1997) who describes the "new persecuted political party" as "deeply committed to transforming regional society so that equality and justice would obtain, so that the individual would be freed from relations of servitude with the more powerful" (232). The history of the 1930s in the Callejón de Huaylas parallels Nugent's case. Joan Snyder (1960:434) sets forth the aims of the Peasant League of Ancash, organized by the Apristas in those times, as: "reduction of illiteracy, restraint of abuses by authorities and landlords, education of Indians, organization of workers, elimination of coca and alcoholism." She mentions that this organization "gained adherents among Vicosinos" (436). This dissertation also did not find its way to publication.

Archival research reveals that Vicos had been the scene of labor unrest in the nineteenth century too (Stein 1991a). The Callejón de Huaylas had been invaded by Chilean expeditionary forces in 1839 and 1883. A massive insurgency, known as the Atusparia Uprising from the name of its farmer-artisan leader, Pedro Pablo Atusparia, took place there in 1885. I have called this a "popular movement" because it was composed of most sectors of the society. The rebels succeeded in driving government troops out in February, but the region was recaptured in a bloody military campaign in May with the help of grapeshot (Stein 1988).[12] Some

Vicosinos participated in the revolt.

Vicos was inserted into regional and sub-regional social structures. Most Vicosinos remained immersed in the sub-regional patronage network,[13] in close relations with townspeople[14] in Marcará and Carhuaz, the provincial capital twelve kilometers away, or attached as "retainers"[15] to other Vicosinos. Perhaps the Project's belief that it had "excluded other would-be wielders of power" by asserting its own "power domain" (Holmberg and Dobyns 1969:409) under which Vicosinos could take shelter, led its staff to fail to see what Bourdieu (1977b:191) refers to as the "euphemized" and "symbolic violence" in social relations: "when domination can only be exercised in its *elementary form*, i.e. directly between one person and another, it cannot take place overtly and must be disguised under the veil of enchanted relationships, the official model of which is presented by relations between kinsmen; in order to be socially recognized it must get itself misrecognized.." Patronage, in the form of fictive kinship, fits this conception of euphemized violence.

Harold Lasswell's (1971:172) view of the pre-Project Vicosino as an "isolated peasant . . . more an object than an initiator of history" is inadequate. To the extent that this conception of the peasantry influenced the Project it was both a failure of vision and the dys-construction of a seeable Vicos. It was a limited binary view of Vicos as an "inside" world surrounded by an "outside" world, and represents the conventional understanding of Vicos history as beginning with the Project. Marcus and Fischer (1986:78) provide an alternative understanding: "Most local cultures worldwide are products of a history of appropriations, resistances, and accommodations. The task . . . is thus to revise conventions of ethnographic description away from a measuring of change against some self-contained, homogeneous, and largely ahistoric framing of the cultural unit toward a view of cultural situations as *always* in flux, in a perpetual historically sensitive state of resistance and accommodation to broader processes of influence that are as much inside as outside the local context."[16]   James Clifford (1988:25) asks: "If ethnography produces cultural interpretations through intense research experiences, how is unruly experience transformed into an authoritative written account? How, precisely, is a garrulous, overdetermined cross-cultural encounter shot through with power relations and personal cross-purposes circumscribed as an adequate version of a more or less discrete 'other world' composed by an individual author?" The Vicos Project did not provide answers.

All of this is not intended to suggest that the abolition of labor rent, the provision of more food, an education so that people could read the Republic's Constitution and know their rights, the acquisition of skills and trades, and living better in general, were not good. Paul Doughty

(1987a:437) states: To remain acquiescent in the face of manifest human need and deprivation and not use one's professional skills to address the situation was anathema to . . . the spirit of the Project." P. H. Gulliver (1985:50-52), an Africanist, identifies himself as "an ameliorist" in the colonial system of the 1950s, which was at the time "the going system . . . and it appeared preferable to work within it and do what one could . . . to do something that could help the colonized, make their voices heard more clearly and articulately and even, perhaps, assist in hastening the process towards decolonization." He adds: "I believe that I was able to help people in need and suffering some injustice. I did not believe that I could destroy the system which, in large part, had created those needs and injustices."

Yet there was something "wild,"[17] something uncontrolled and unconscious, in the Project's interventions, something that was unable to prevent it from using its power against Vicosinos, and protecting its clients from using their new powers against themselves. In a servile social order, Michel Foucault (1980:125) points out, power functions "through signs and levies," signs of respect and deference toward patrons and rituals, and levies of tribute and pillage. In the case of Vicos, people furnished labor power as rent and celebrated festivals to the saints. With development, Foucault continues, power has "to be able to gain access to the bodies of individuals, to their acts, attitudes and modes of everyday behavior." A new discipline of the market replaces an old discipline of the hacienda system. But trading one discipline for another may not respond to a client's need. You will confront in the chapters which follow several demonstrations of the Project's failures in this regard.

But what was this fascination with an oppressive hacienda, a left-over from colonial times? Hema Chari (2001:279) suggests what has been enthusiastically misrecognized until now: "[T]he gaze of the imperial voyeur is directed elsewhere, not necessarily or always on the female, but glancing askance on the colonized men. . . . Colonial power sustained its domination and status by appropriating a contradictory but systematic process of avowal and disavowal of sexual desire between men in the colonies. Further, the ambivalence of colonialist masculine erotics, which is simultaneously a promise and a threat, powerfully substantiates my claims that discursive practices of deferred and displaced homoeroticism underwrite colonial rule, and in fact continue to dominate the politics of postcoloniality." The Project, male and homosocial[18] with few exceptions (for a notable exception see Chapter 2), was designed to study male patrons exploiting male workers–the sexual imagery of penetration and passivity is clear[19]–and "cure" the perversity of both, removing the former and empowering the latter.

Another set of uncontrolled variables had to do with what Jorge Osterling (1983:356) calls the "feuds" among Peruvian scholars, rivalries which were known but which were never openly spoken about. Such tensions mounted into animosities and reached into Peruvian politics. Regretibly, this meant the incorporation of some scholars into the Project and the exclusion of some highly competent persons. Murra and López-Baralt (1996:27) touch on this in a footnote to one of José María Arguedas's letters:

> There was a program of applied anthropology in the Hacienda Vicos by the Instituto Indigenista Peruano and Cornell University in the Department of Ancash during the 1950s. Allan Holmberg participated for Cornell and William Mangin, in the absence of the former, directed the project. Mangin continued his research, studying Vicosinos in the marginal settelemts of Lima. The Peruvian anthropologist, Mario C. Vázquez, also participated. There was opposition to the project in the University of San Marcos, led by José Matos Mar, because it was considered by some intellectuals as imperialist and connected with APRA. (Mario C. Vázquez belonged to that party.)

Despite its lack of control, the Project's interventions had positive effects. When the sublease expired in 1957, the Project had introduced improvements in agricultural production, a complete primary school, and a clinic, among a number of strategic changes. The Peruvian Government then intervened to expropriate the estate so that negotiations could take place for the sale of Vicos to its inhabitants, a transaction which was finally completed in 1962. William Mangin (1979:76) relates how, after the Beneficencia had been threatening to reclaim the Hacienda Vicos, expropriation was accomplished through a series of fortuitous[20] events which recall the earlier uncertainties of the negotiations to assume the sublease in 1951:

> In late summer 1961, Senator Edward Kennedy visited Peru with a small group of American advisers. He wanted nothing to do with the [United States] embassy, but its officials . . . wanted him to go to Vicos. A Cornell anthropologist, Paul Doughty, met the senator's plane when it arrived at the Huaylas airport and, by chance, found that one of Kennedy's advisors was an ex-Cornell Professor whom he knew. Kennedy rode with Doughty through the valley, where not surprisingly many thought he was the president of the United States. Upon arrival in Vicos, Senator Kennedy heard a very emotional speech by an accomplished Vicosino orator describing past abuses . . . and was much moved. When he returned to Lima he had an audience with President Prado of Peru and later told embassy officials that Prado had never heard of Vicos. Kennedy

reportedly asked the president how Peru could ask for a several million dollar land reform loan when his government had been unable over a 10-year period to expropriate this small property. Prado said he could indeed do it, and he called the two ministries involved (Public Health and Labor and Indian Affairs) and so ordered. But even with this chance intervention of the brother of the President of the United States, it took Carlos Monge another year of maneuvering . . . to get the "final" decree of expropriation. Incredibly, until that time only one hacienda in Peru had ever been expropriated, a small place taken by the national police for a horse farm; and the owner had successfully sued and gotten it back! The Prime Minister of Peru had told a [North] American Embassy official that Vicos would never be expropriated and just to forget about it. Monge got out of a sickbed when he heard that the military were about to depose President Prado. . . . He knew that with a new government the Prado decision would be meaningless. Miraculously the papers were signed the day before the coup.

When the hacienda system was abolished, Vicos organized itself as a production cooperative. The former Hacienda lands were retained as commons, worked by the community for its own benefit. Holmberg (1958:13) stated his method: "[W]e used our power to share power to a point where we no longer hold power, which is just as matters should be." The Project remained in Vicos to observe, but it no longer was an hacienda. Barbara Lynch (1982:21-23) observes:

> The goals of the Peru-Cornell Project were framed in an atmosphere of optimism and faith in the power of democratic institutions and technological innovation and diffusion to overcome poverty and oppression. Holmberg and many of his fellow workers believed in progress–that the betterment of one group of individuals could take place without the impoverishment of other groups and that conflict need not be zero-sum. . . . Holmberg also expressed a strong faith at the outset in the eventual modernization of the Sierra [the Andean highlands] and its integration on an equal basis with the coast. He saw integration and self-determination for Vicosinos as compatible goals. . . . Participation in the national society would bring with it expanded employment opportunities, access to goods from outside the region, mobility, an expanded world view, and a role in shaping the future of the nation. Vicos's low standard of living and inward turned world view was assumed to be a function of isolation; improvement would come with integration.

"Integration" was a key concept in the 1950s when many white social scientists and politicians held it as a pious goal. Inspiration came from the "Chicago school of sociology" under Robert E. Park, whose "thinking shaped the dominant theoretical and methodological assumptions about race relations for the greater part of this century." Park's "race relations cycle" consisted of four steps: "Contact, conflict, accommodation, and assimilation," which appeared to work with immigrant "ethnic"[21] groups in North America and was expected to work with racial minorities. However: "These assumptions are as much political and ideological as they are theoretical. They neglect both the institutional and ideological nature of race in America, and the systematic presence of racial dynamics in such social spheres as education, art, social policy, law, religion, and science. Instead they focus attention on racial dynamics as the irrational products of individual pathologies" (Omi and Winant 1994:10). The aim of developers, then, in Peru as in North America was to rationalize and, as it were, "de-pathologize" such aberrations. This runs counter to the spirit of anthropology, at least as it has influenced researchers in its ethnographic subfield. Marcus and Fischer (1986:24) point out that "the main motif that ethnography as a science developed was that of salvaging cultural diversity, threatened with global Westernization, especially during the age of colonialism." Thus, if the Vicosinos were assimilated they would no longer be Vicosinos but Peruvians. The Vicos Project was working against itself, to the extent it desired both rationality and difference:

> Expert advice and expert-designed objects which allow their possessors to act in a way authorized by expert knowledge cater also for another crucial need of the individual: that of *rationality*. Characterized as it has been from its inception by a radical intolerance of any form of life different from itself, modern society can conceive of such difference only as ignorance, superstition or retardation. A form of life may be admitted into the realm of the tolerable and offered a citizenship status in the land of modernity only if first naturalized, trimmed of all oddity and in the end subjugated: only in a form, that, is, in which it can be fully translated into the language of rational choice, which is modernity's own. (Bauman 1991:224.)

Mangin (1979:67) comments on Holmberg's purposes:

> He wanted the anticipated results of the Vicos project diffused throughout Peru and the world, for he felt he was developing a model that would aid greatly in solving universal problems of poverty, exploitation, and racism. Basically, the project represented for him the opportunity to demonstrate the capacity of the "common man" to assume the responsibility for his own life and well-being, given the opportunity to do so. His . . . thinking conformed closely to that of other social reformers of the time, especially those concerned with community development. But he differed from

them in a very important way: the key to the problem, as he saw it, lay in the combination of applied research and political action.

Other commentaries on the Project vary from extraordinary praise to sharp criticism. George Foster (1969:33-34), a defender, says: "[T]he results are impressive. Applied social science revolutionized the way of life of an indigenous group, and in so doing learned a great deal about the processes of accelerating development and modernization. . . . Vicos is justly famous, and the Cornell Peru-Vicos Project will rank as a milestone in the development of applied social science." In contrast, the most negative criticism I have read is made by Glynn Cochrane (1971:18): "The kinds of results which were obtained were no more spectacular than those achieved by nonanthropologists in community development projects over the world. . . . Vicos shows an absence of any real appreciation of what development work is all about. At Vicos the anthropoologist apparently made all the major decisions." Bennett (1996:31) mentions the Vicos study as an example of one of "a few disasters or at least awkward projects in which the applied anthropologists had difficulties with the indigenous population." Dobyns and Doughty (1971b:19-20), heirs of Holmberg's work, which was never completed for he died prematurely, describe him as "a truly revolutionary anthropologist," and the Project as "a revolutionary anthropological program"–although they qualify the Vicos "revolution" as "peaceful social reformation." Holmberg (1960:81-82), with characteristic modesty, wrote:

> Changing this state of affairs without a large investment of resources or without a revolution, would seem at first glance to be an almost insoluble problem. To be sure, it was and still is no easy task. Yet it is not as hopeless as it might seem. In the case of Vicos, at any rate, it has been possible, on the basis of careful studies carried out in advance of initiating any action, to design a modest program of technical assistance and education which has gained fairly wide acceptance and has helped to awaken most members of the community to new opportunities for improving their lot through their own efforts.

Of all Holmberg's short articles, in my opinion, the one which conveys the standard to which he aspired, his ego-ideal, is "Participant intervention in the field" (1955). It is a brief, lucid, brilliant, and, for a professional scholar, rather unusual discussion of progress at Vicos to date and outline of the research model. He states his concern with the study of two processes: first, "changing the initial (and expected) image" of the Project "from that of hostile *patrones* to friendly consultants and observers"; and, second, "developing independent problem-solving and decision-making organizations among the indigenous population which could gradually assume the control and direction of community affairs in a rational and humane manner" (24). Near the end of this essay, Holmberg, who had been exposed to the psychobiological ambience in the Institute of Human Relations during his studies in Yale University,[22] introduces the analogy of "the psychoanalyst in the therapeutic situation." On the basis of this metaphor he proceeds to relate a narrative which touches matters of human existence, expressed with a rare beauty and sensitivity. Here is a dramatic "policy statement." But it is a discourse, as Renato Rosaldo (1986:96) puts it, "that denies the domination that makes its knowledge possible," like an ego-ideal on stage and a superego in the wings. Holmberg (1955:26) views himself in a role analogous to a psychoanalyst in a therapeutic situation

> What does the analyst do? He [sic] starts with a patient who desires but is unable to function to his [sic] fullest capacity in the world in which he interacts. The fact that he cannot do so may be the fault of the society in which he lives, but if the patient is to make a satisfactory and desirable adjustment to life, he must change his behavior in various ways. The analyst cannot change this behavior for him; the patient must do it for himself. Ideally, what happens is this: Through a process of self-enlightenment, with occasional strategic intervention by the analyst, the patient cures himself so that he can face up to his anxieties and shoulder his responsibilities to the best of his native abilities. When he reaches this point, the analyst is out of a job.
>
> It seems to me that the role of the participant interventionist in the process of community development is much the same. His job is to assist the community to develop itself, and to study this process while it is taking place. He cannot "cure" the community as a surgeon cures a patient; the community must perform the operation on itself. At first, to be sure, as our experience in Vicos indicates, the investigator may have to intervene frequently and boldly, but as problem-solving and decision-making skills are developed, the investigator intervenes less and less until he works himself out of the role of intervener and into the role of consultant and observes. At Vicos, I must admit, we are not yet in the final state of devolution, but the process is well underway.

"Working oneself out of a job" can be read in more than one way, whatever the author's intention. I read a desire to be not, a desire for absence, as well as a process of letting go. I also read a yearning for healing in the text as a whole.

Holmberg's text can be called a "policy narrative" because it corresponds to Emery Roe's (1994:34-35) definition of "stories (scenarios and arguments) which underwrite and stabilize the assumptions for policymaking in situations that persist with many unknowns, a high degree of interdependence, and little, if any agreement." He adds:

[R]ural development is a genuinely uncertain activity, and one of the principal ways in which practitioners, bureaucrats, and policymakers articulate and make sense of this uncertainty is to tell scenarios and arguments that simplify or complexity that reality. . . . Indeed, the pressure to generate policy narratives about development–where, again, policy is broadly defined–is directly related to the ambiguity decision makers experience over that development. Other things being equal, the more uncertain things seem everywhere at the microlevel, the greater the perceived scale of uncertainty at the macrolevel and the greater the perceived need for explanatory narratives that can be operationalized into standard approaches with widespread application. . . . Thus, the failure of field blueprints based on policy narratives often serves only to reinforce, not reduce, the appeal to some sort of narrative that explains and addresses the persisting, even increasing, uncertainty.

Roe's statement not only has much applicability to policy decisions in the contemporary world but to theory and method in the human sciences, including psychoanalysis. It has great relevance to the Project's activities and decisions in Vicos, all of which were carried out in local and regional contexts ruled by uncertainty, ambiguity, and ambivalence.

We may question Holmberg's failure to consider the weight of external structure on the community, as well as the porosity of the boundaries between Vicos and its "outside," much as we understand Sigmund Freud's limits which are clearly expressed in his classic offer to his patients in 1895 of the choice between the "hysterical misery" of neurosis and "the common unhappiness" of the life of the Viennese bourgeois society.[23] However, what seems highly significant to me is Holmberg's stubborn faith in an evolutionary and psychological, rather than an economic and political, discourse of development. Colin Leys (1996:65) points to a change from "the original optimistic assumption of orthodox development theory, that the process of development involved drawing the populations of the Third World out of their traditional isolation [sic] into a modern social system that would be participative, pluralistic and democratic," to one which "turned from a concern with the processes of 'modernization' (the processes of transformation into advanced, capitalist and hence pluralist and democratic societies) to a concern with the maintenance of social control." Holmberg's insistence on "working himself out of a job" was doubtlessly unattractive to many later developmentalists. But I read nothing resembling a "code of pacification" or a "prose of counter-insurgency" (Guha 1988a:59) in *this* text byHolmberg. His goal was the empowerment of Vicosinos, if not of himself.

The sudden illness which put an end to Holmberg's life[24] interfered with the accomplishment of many of the Project's goals. The Project operated, too, with a chronic insufficiency of funding. Himes (1981:178), after searching financial records of the Carnegie Corporation, reports that of a larger grant made to Cornell University, a total of "$126,336 was spent on field operations in Peru during the period 1949-60." This was not the total funding for the Project, since other grants were made "principally for research and graduate student training." Paul Doughty (1982:10) adds: "On the Peruvian end, funding came from its regular ministerial budgets, principally Labor and Indian Affairs, Education, and Agriculture. The general financing of the Project came from the Vicos community itself which, after redeveloping the agricultural base, was able to fund construction of several buildings and other aspects of Project activity." Adams and Cumberland (1960:192) comment:

> One derivative of the underfinancing was that Holmberg could not take as active a role in the development of the Project as was needed to achieve coordination. His duties on the departmental staff at Cornell made it impossible for him to get to Peru except during the summer time. As a result, he was able to oversee almost none of the field research . . . nor was he able to keep up satisfactory communication with the field. . . . The excessive load . . . made coordination from a distance almost impossible. This, in turn, tended to lead to the development of misunderstandings between the personnel in Vicos and Ithaca.

Holmberg (1958:12) himself said very candidly,

> had I known then what I now know, I am not so sure that I would be willing to repeat the experience, even though it has been one of the most rewarding ones of my whole Professional career. My doubts lie not so much with the fruitfulness or legitimacy of the research and development, as contrasted with the strictly research, approach to the study of the social process but more with the wear and tear that it might cause to the inadequately financed or inadequately staffed anthropologist or other behavioral scientist who is brash enough to attempt to apply it, especially in a foreign area.

Holmberg spent much time, which might have been put to more effective use, preparing grant proposals, and I think he tended to view as a personal failure his inability to attract greater funding. However, on the basis of nearly five decades of association with professional scholarship, the more I think about it the less I see anything "wrong" with Allan Holmberg in that regard. As William Mangin (1979:67) notes, Holmberg "came from a Minnesota farm environment and, like others born and raised under similar conditions, he felt that midwestern American farm and small town life was a desirable model for many other societies." As a populist and humanist, his utopian vision was one of prosperous operators of small farm and other enterprises, not the accumulation and concentration of capital. His aim was human freedom and dignity. He encouraged self-help, self-development, and self-determination. His program in no way offered aid and comfort to monopolizers of power and wealth. Instead of the extended reproduction of wealth and power, he urged, as I have noted earlier, "working one's way out of a job." There was nothing in his model of fomenting small production that was of any use to agribusiness, transnational capital, or superpower. In short, he was moving counter to trends in development discourse. He even cited Marx in reporting that Vicos data tended to confirm the hypothesis "that the alienation of people from control over the means of production retards social and economic development" (Holmberg (1959:9). Certainly, small grants might have been obtained for such work, as was actually the case, but big money is granted by big funding agencies for big projects.

Holmberg (1971:58-59) reports on the sale of Vicos to the Vicosinos, that during the years between 1957 and 1962 negotiations were carried on by the Project with the Beneficencia. The latter demanded at one time the excessively high price of the equivalent of slightly over $260,000, in contrast with "a ministerial estimate" of $26,000. The property was finally handed over to the people of Vicos at the price of $74,626, surely much more than it was worth, with one-fourth of that amount payable immediately, one-fourth in three years, and half on an interest-free government loan for twenty years.

Fortunately, the Vicosinos had accumulated savings from the extraordinarily good potato production of the late 1950s; with a 600% increase in that cash crop, they had a bank account of $10,000, according to Holmberg (1959:9). Mangin (1979:80) says that Vicos prosperity continued into the 1960s: "At this time potatoes brought a high price and the Vicosinos were harvesting crops and marketing them easily. They had converted the ex-hacienda fields to communal ones and to one variety of large, tasteless, high priced potato. . . . [They] have made regular payments on the mortgage and, for a few years in the late 1960s they were quite prosperous." Doughty (1987:144) reports that Vicos paid the final installment of 100,000 soles in 1968, just a year before the sweeping land reform decree-law of 1969. Doughty (1986:113-114) comments: "Anxious to place their own ideological stamp on progress, government representatives decreed a reorganization of Vicos to make it conform to the new national peasant community regulations. . . . Manipulated by government interests and its leadership, misled by corrupt ministerial employees . . . , the community dropped into a relatively disorganized state in the mid 1970s. Adding to its problems, a regional potato blight sharply lowered Vicos income." However, by 1983 Vicos had rebounded . . . and was proceeding with its plans, which include finishing the new high school building, extending the 5-year-old residential electrical system, fixing its roads, and initiating ambitious plans for formalizing its new urban area."

Holmberg had a high tolerance for weaknesses in others, perhaps unfortunately too high. He accepted grandiosity and pomposity, and endured meanness and stupidity. His permissiveness was a self-constructed trap which led him to encourage some with lesser talent and ignore others with greater. I think he perpetually maintained the optimistic expectation that people would grow into social human beings. However, he was unable to prevent the assumption of the *patrón*'s role on the part of Mario Vázquez, not altogether due to the latter's thirst for power but because the Vicosinos wanted it (Lynch 1982:71, 95). By 1971 this former member of the Project held an important office in Lima, as I have indicated, but I recall that Vicosinos took no important action without receiving confirmation from him. Perhaps Holmberg's errors in choosing personnel to manage the Project in his absence is simply one more illustration of Freud's (1965a:129) point that "belief in the 'goodness' of human nature is one of those evil illusions by which mankind expect their lives to be beautified and made easier while in reality they only cause damage."

Holmberg also allowed the intrusion of what Mangin (1979:70) aptly calls "some inappropriate and rather silly categories designed by Harold Lasswell, an American [i.e., North American] political scientist," into the Project's work. These categories are listed by Dobyns, Doughty, and Lasswell (1971b:15) as the: "Values-institution groups of power, wealth, skill, enlightenment, affection, respect, rectitude, and well-being." They are used, Mangin (1979:70) says, "to demonstrate the complex interplay of institutions in terms of the attributes of human relationships as they develop and change in the context of power." Because they did not fit into this scheme, Holmberg might have been swayed to suppress Mario Vázquez's (1955) thesis on technological change in Vicos and to ignore Clifford Barnett's (1960) dissertation on Vicos protest movements which, of all reports produced by the Project, probably has the most long-term value for Andean studies.

Paul Doughty (1971:92) notes that in 1952 Vicosinos were identifiable in the towns of the Callejón de Huaylas by their distinctive style of clothing. Mestizos, who defined themselves as *gente decente* ("decent people"), believed that "Indians" were generically inferior, "brutes," "ignorant, slow, drunken, humble or simple." Marisol de la Cadena's (1996:42-43) description of "decency" in Cusco earlier in this century as "a moral definition of race" corresponds closely to that in the Province of Carhuaz:

[T]he practice of denying one's Indianness was not an exclusive prerogative of the elite. On the contrary, such denial was common among the lower echelons of Cusqueño society, and was a source of tension with Cusqueños of higher social statos, who perceived them as Indians. Since "white" occupied the apex of the Cusqueño racial hierarchy, with "Indian" at the bottom, the Cusqueño population made efforts to whiten themselves. . . . Decencia [decency] was an important component of the social taxonomy in Peru in general. Broadly defined ,"decency" was the local interpretation of colonial honor, reformulated in a republican era in which caste-like distinctions were to have been superseded. Specifically, in Cusco it helped local intellectuals to broaden the genetic concept of "race," moving from the phenotype criterion to a certain kind of refined morality, education, and culture, capable of being biologically inherited. While inspired by liberalism, some of the legal, administrative barriers separating "higher" and "lower" groups had fallen, "decency" allowed the local brown skinned elites to partially challenge and diverge from European definitions, inasmuch as it emphasized cultural criteria in the definition of "race" while at the same time enabling liberal intellectuals to imagine a region where distinctions arose from premises of equality.

According to Doughty (1971:92), in 1952 there were 23 Vicosinos who could speak Spanish. Everyone was illiterate. They "did not participate in public affairs, held no official public offices, and none would have been entitled to vote." The situation has now changed in Peru. In 1986, Doughty (1987b:147) reports, 1800 Vicos voters, both men and women, formed the largest block in the municipal elections of the Province of Carhuaz. Three Vicosinos were candidates for posts on the provincial council and one was elected mayor of Marcará.

Doughty (1982:17) calls attention to the losses of mestizo towns when they were bypassed by Vicosinos:

There was a tendency on the part of Project staff and students, as well as Vicosinos, to gloat over the impacts of the changes on the . . . "upper class". . . . Such things as the Vicosinos refusing to be bullied into working for a pittance any more, preferring to sell their goods in markets where they could get better prices, challenging a merchant's addition, and demanding to be registered to vote were applauded in Project circles. . . . Nevertheless, there is no doubt that a more profound, long-term strategy would have been to pay considerable attention in design terms to this issue for the reason that once the Project folded its tents, the community would have to fend for itself and it would be better to do this with strong regional allies and sympathizers. In my view, this was a major failing of the Project although understandable in light of the many program complications.

In any assessment of the Project, it should be remembered that Holmberg was operating as a professional anthropologist of his time. If he overlooked some significant external variables, it was not an error that his colleagues were not making. Moreover, I also remember Allan Holmberg as a teacher who urged his students to feel free to make mistakes, as long as we learned something in the process. Incompetence, in fiction, can be "purposeful and accomplished," as Susan Stewart (1980:206-208) tells us, in a "domain of reversibility where mistakes 'do not count.'" She continues: "The other face of this device is the mistake-on-purpose, the planned mistake that does count, that, indeed, counts as skill in the fictive domain. In nonsense, the mistake repeated is not evidence of an inability to 'learn from one's mistakes,' but rather a play gesture, a gesture that effects a reversible world where mistakes are their proper nots, a gesture that promises mastery and threatens infinity." And then: "Nonsense gives information on the level of learning about learning, presenting a critique of learning manifested on the level of the 'mistake-on-purpose.' Convention proceeds not merely according to an organization of social life, but according too the shape of mistakes in such an organization. Nonsense gives us information about paradox, reflexivity, and the processes of interpretation by which it (nonsense) is manufactured." But this was written in the next generation.

Barbara Lynch (1982:24-26) notes:

> Despite the continued emphasis on integration of Vicos into the national society . . . Holmberg clung tenaciously to the belief that improvements of a permanent nature could be made at the community level without far-reaching changes in the national and regional social structures. . . .
> Holmberg and other Project staff members held assumptions about the introduction of innovations common to the diffusionist perspective. He believed that changes could be initiated in a small area or among a small population, and that when the efficacy of these changes was demonstrated, they would be adopted by other individuals and communities. The diffusionist perspective fostered a preoccupation with the identification of potential innovations to these key individuals. . . .
> In summary, most of the assumptions underlying the Peru-Cornell Project were widely shared by social scientists and policy makers in the postwar era. Poverty was seen as a product of isolation from, rather than

integration into western society. It was believed that knowledge and technological diffusion could eliminate poverty and that the elimination of poverty was a necessary and sufficient condition for the realization of basic human dignity.

The Project has not been discussed as much by Peruvians. A brief descriptive account is to be found in Osterling and Martínez (1983:345-346). A more extended presentation and critique is provided by Martínez and Samaniego (1978:157-171), who view it "as a great disappointment in several aspects." They note that the theoretical goals, with few exceptions, were not developed;   measuring instruments were not improved; interdisciplinary research did not take place;   and most of the Project's scholarly production is out of Peruvians' reach.

With regard to this last point, it is unfortunate that while the Vicos Project hosted several North American anthropologists, both professionals and students, during its life from 1952-1966 and a number of Cornell dissertations were based on data gathered there, most Peruvian professionals tended to be excluded from access to the Project's resources. The Project employed some Peruvian students as data-gatherers who filled stacks of file cabinets with information on Vicos but published very little on what they had contributed. Himes (1972:130-132) comments on this under-utilization:

> The information obtained from Peruvians who worked in Vicos as students suggests that for the most part they were left with a favorable impression of their Vicos experience as an early training opportunity. . . . Nearly all of those interviewed, however, expressed serious concern about the weakness of the theoretical or conceptual framework underlying their empirical work in Vicos. This misgiving came both from those who were generally positive about the Project . . . and from others who were very critical. . . . [Humberto] Ghersi, in a statement consistent with one made by [Mario] Vázquez as well, suggested that the administrative responsibilities of the anthropologists absorbed much more time in Vicos than had been anticipated and that this factor accounted for some of the neglect of the theoretical significance of the empirical findings of Vicos. [Rodrigo] Montoya asserted that the U. S. anthropologists were applying theoretical concepts which were wholly inadequate to analyze social reality in Peru. Unfortunately, he said, none of the Peruvians including himself was sufficiently well prepared at the time of their work in Vicos to question the imported theories and to develop others which would more adequately explain the phenomena they were observing. The Peruvians were employed principally as "*dateros*"–gatherers of raw data.
> Although this point was made only by [Héctor] Martínez . . ., I was left with the impression that the Vicos experience was much less adequate as a

training opportunity for Peruvians in those cases where it was not followed by more formal academic study in anthropology at the graduate level. Although part of Cornell's agreement with the *Instituto Indigenista Peruano* had been that fellowships would be negotiated by the Project for Peruvian participants, apparently only two Peruvians obtained graduate degrees abroad as a result.

While my indignation and anger on contemplating this mistreatment of defenseless and trusting people is autobiographical and highly personal,[25] it relates as well to the Peruvians who worked hard gathering data which they were neither enabled nor encouraged to publish. This could be easily explained if the North Americans who staffed these research endeavors had preempted the Peruvians' work and gone on to publish the books and articles the data-gathering deserved.   In fact the North Americans published rather little for all the effort that had taken place. This carries events far beyond exploitation to absurdity. If Allan Holmberg was short-funded, overloaded with administrative and teaching responsibilities, and supervised the work of many students,[26] this is no excuse for his epigones, the other North Americans who had participated in the Project and who closed it down after his death.[27]

The most detailed critical appraisal of the Project that I know of is the one made by Carlos Aramburú (1978:12-18) who observes that in the Project's conception of culture, people's value-orientation is emphasized. In this focus on values what is missing is "a historical explanation of the development of these values and the function and relation which they have to other social institutions." This is not simply the theoretical orientation of the Project but of "a whole school of thought in social anthropology." He suggests that the theoretical confusion is heightened by the use of the terms "mestizo" (Spanish-speaking, urban-oriented person) and "Indian" (Quechua-speaking peasant) "which denote racial characteristics but which nevertheless allude basically to class situations." Thus,

> the principle of inequality characteristic of the cultural orientation of Indian society would not be the result of a political and economic dynamic, which generates inequality and which requires for its reproduction that this inequality be maintained, as for example in the case of the highland hacienda, but, rather, would be a peculiar form of cultural orientation.   Similarly, confusion exists in stating the internalized, unconscious character of culture, and affirming that mestizos utilize this principle of inequality to reaffirm their privileged position. If mestizos participate in national culture, in which the dominant cultural orientation is equality, why do they reaffirm traditional values of inequality in their relations with Indians? Obviously, the problem appears insoluble to the

extent that analysis is not focused on the opposed class interests of mestizos and Indians, the first as proprietors of the means of production, and the second as peasants without land who are subject to relations of exploitation.

Aramburú (16-17) concludes:

> In our opinion, changes in relations of production and property were because the *"new patrones"* had an interest different from that of earlier landlords in bringing about a transfer of property and control of the hacienda, the central elements which explain causality existed between economic and social changes and the ones that took place on an ideological level . . . . Insofar as the isolated experience of Vicos did not create the conditions affecting the capitalist character of the economy, and did not weaken the dominant classes' interests on the regional level, its weakness and isolation impeded all demonstration effect and greater extension in promoting conditions for the liberation of the peasant population.

Aramburú's appraisal is a good example of the Project's impact on social studies in Peru. But for the purposes of this book I carry the analysis beyond socio-economic class to the discourse of race which offers another approach to the complex relations of people who are "more or less" mestizos and others who are "more or less" something else, what Mary Weismantel (2001:xxxviii) calls a "vicious binary." This will, in the end, assist our interpretation of the fate of the Vicos Project. Deborah Poole (1994:6) observes:

> In Peru . . . one of the most important cultural frameworks shaping both personal identity and public understandings of ethnicity and culture is the decidedly non-local discourse of race. While the biological category of race has been long since overturned by, among other things, the theories of socially constructed identity advocated by ethnicity theory, the concept and reality of race as a social and discursive category continues to mold individuals' perceptions of self, other and society. Racial terminology permeates nearly every aspect of daily life and social intercourse in Peru . . ., while ideologies of racial inferiority and superiority inform dimensions of social practice ranging from the most mundane negotiations of power in small Andean villages to the brutal counterinsurgency doctrines of the Peruvian armed forces. Indeed, given the acknowledged presence of racial and racist discourses in Peru, what is most striking is the absence of any serious discussion in the Andeanist literature of how race affects Peruvians' understandings of such things as culture, power, ethnicity, and resistance itself.

Mary Weismantel (1997:11) points out how anthropologists are "blinded by our awareness of the biological falsity of race." Weismantel and Eisenman (1998:121) state: "As long as any mention of race was understood to be an appeal to biological essentialism and thus itself an expression of racism, scholars felt compelled to ignore or minimize the importance of racial politics in the communities where they worked, even in the face of compelling evidence to the contrary. In their haste to disassociate themselves from the racist past of the social sciences, anthropologists forgot the Durkheimian mandate to treat social facts as real." Race is not merely a matter of anthropometry, but it is what people feel, see, think, say, and write. Poole (1997:216) concludes her work on Andean visual anthropology with these words: "In the end, I suggest that the mysterious, even subterranean ways in which racial discourse moves through history are more difficult–if not impossible–to grasp if we focus only on 'race.' The very slipperiness or 'race' is the strongest indication of its power, its hold on our own social and political imaginations, and its presence in the shaping of modernity. It is also an indication that 'race' may never be understood in its own terms." What North Americans, being themselves permeated with what may well be the grossest racism on earth, may easily fail to understand is that Peruvian racism is Peruvian, not North American. A good example of Poole's (190) characterization of one variety of it as "a constantly shifting and historical current of identity . . . an attitude and a pose, rather than an ineluctable or inherited fact of nature."

I think that one of the many uneasinesses which overcame some of us in the Callejón de Huaylas in 1951 was our uncanny[28] perception of something familiar in the otherness that surrounded us. That is, we were inclined to see the reflection of our own racism–which as budding anthropologists we would have strongly denied–in the social order we confronted. And we were inclined to deny it in that otherness, as well, by searching for one or another kind of class analysis. There is something of what Freud called "primary process"[29] in this. Young (1995:94) observes that "race theory possesses its own oneiric logic that allows it to survive despite its contradictions, to reverse itself at every refutation, to adapt and transform itself at every denial." Peter Gose (1994:165-166) points to anthropologists' "rush to demonstrate the non-racial referents of racial discourse": "One need only to listen to Andean people discuss their society for a short while to discover that they believe it to be composed of 'Indians,' '*Mestizos,* and to a lesser extent, 'Whites.' Each 'race' is thought to be defined by a substance, 'blood,' which is common to all its members, creates a solidarity among them and specifies their conduct. . . .

Anthropologists have had little choice but to conclude that these 'racial' terms provide imaginary vehicles for the apprehension of power relations in society. What they have not really explored are the implications of representing power relations in this totemistic manner." As Rattansi (1994:56-57) writes: "The only way to make sense of these complex and ever-changing reconfigurations of what one might call color, culture, and political discourse is to decenter and de-essentialize concepts of 'race,' ethnicity and nation. . . . There are, moreover, shifts of discourse and policy depending upon targeted populations–'Black,' 'Asian,' 'Oriental,' 'Celtic,' and so on. In other words there are racisms, not a singular racism." And so we now need to shift from the singular to the plural, recognizing that not all discourses of race are the same.[30]

To bring the discussion back to Vicos and its region, I quote a passage in which Himes (1981:192-193) reports on an interview he had with Enrique Luna, the ex-*mayordomo*, or overseer, of the Hacienda Vicos:

> "The Project really accomplished a lot in Vicos." Thanks largely to the Project, Luna said, people can now see that the *vicosinos* are able and hard working. "Before 1952 I myself considered them as savages." Some of Luna's pre-Project attitudes began to reemerge, however, toward the end of our lengthy conversation. Three *vicosinos* across the street from his shop in Marcará caught his eye; they were about 25 years old and dressed traditionally in homespun cloth. "Look at those *vicosinos*," he said, "dressed exactly as they dressed in Vicos 20 years ago." But the Indians, Luna went on, are fine people (*un gran elemento*) when properly trained. "The Indian is like a mule when domesticated. One has to know how to manage him and one has to show him affection . . . ."

Enrique Luna's words recall to me many of my own conversations with mestizos who tended to essentialize farmers and rural workers as "Indians," that is, to speak about them as if they were an invariant and undifferentiated category of people. It is just too easy to conceive of the population of the Callejón de Huaylas as being divided into two kinds of people, and I think this binary construction that was presented to us a half century ago misled us by assisting our receptive minds to confirm, rather than to question, this image of a bifurcated social order.

Andrew Vayda (1994:320) suggests that in anthropology "pattern and order have been exaggerated or unduly emphasized and . . . variations and variability need to be studied more." Thus, he continues, there has developed an "anti-essentialist view." Pnina Werbner (1997:228-229) defines essentialism: "To essentialize is to impute a fundamental, basic, absolutely necessary constitutive quality to a person, social category, ethnic group, religious community, or nation. It is to posit falsely a timeless continuity, a discreteness or boundedness in space, and an organic unity. It is to imply an internal sameness and external difference or otherness." However, she adds: "Attempts to avoid essentializing the social collectivities we study lead . . . to a series of conundrums. If to name is to re-present, to imply a continuity and discreteness in time and place, then it follows that all collective namings or labellings are essentialist, and that all discursive constructions of social collectivities–whether of community, class, nation, race or gender–are essentializing." We are well advised not to carry anti-essentialism to the point where we essentialize it! (I will return to this in Chapter 6.)

The mestizo view is summarized by Mario Vázquez (1967:32) who offers a listing of peasant characteristics, as mestizos see them: "Lazy, lying, dirty and lice-ridden, venal, thieving, stinking, cheating, ignorant, drunken, coca-addicted, ravenous, savage, stupid, clumsy, noisy, lascivious, shameless, or brazen."[31] I did not believe any of that racist discourse, nor do I now, but my own essentialisms surprise me: I first set foot in the Callejón de Huaylas with the conviction that I was going to study "Indians" who represented an earlier, and happier, "stage" of human development than my own. I recall my acute disappointment when I found myself among poor people. Delmos Jones (1997:193) tells of a similar experience in his first field research in Arizona: "I saw the Papago more as poor people than as 'Indians'. . . . What I saw were people who lived [like] the rural Black and White people of my childhood in . . . Alabama." Truly, as Naomi Schor (1994:43) points out, "essentialism is not one."

If, as Derrida (2002c:156) suggests, a "deconstruction implies a process of de-metaphorization," we can express strong doubts that the Vicos Project's psychoanalytic metaphor might "cure" racism when justice was required, not "therapy." To the extent that Sigmund Freud's (1965a:100) maxim, "Where id was, there ego shall be," was a part of the very complex motivation of this development effort to bring relative "primitives," people dominated by unconscious drives, into the light of rationality, a hidden discourse of race appears. Yet community development work is not psychoanalysis. There was no "free association"[32] and the analysis that did take place–i.e., the Lasswellian "values-institution groups" I have already outlined–was "wild."[33] (This did not affect the Vicosinos as much as it contributed to misunderstandings in North American anthropology.) Assuming the psychotherapeutic model as directing the Project's work, we may well wonder at the intrusion of the interventionists' needs. Frieda Fromm-Reichmann (1959:101) states: "[T]he psychiatrist's attitude toward the patient should not be dictated by his [sic] feelings of frustration and/or hostility which patients' communications may elicit in him. . . . What has *not* been mentioned most crucial constructive adjuvant in spotting and coping with the patient's problems that brought about the anxiety." But anxieties in Project personnel were not used in support of Vicos. And, finally, there can be no "therapy" if the psychoanalyst, psychiatrist, psychologist, counselor, psychiatric nurse or social worker, or other clinician is absent most of the time.

Lyotard (1993:6) says, "If the Ego should come to take the place where the Id is, it would immediately cease to be Ego." The Project's object was in no way the extinction of the Vicosinos. But if Vicosinos were turned into Peruvians, in the complete sense of the word, wouldn't they cease to be Vicosinos? Thus, as Nikos Papastergiadis (1998:7) sees ethnographic nostalgia in the process of "moving on with modernity," Vicosinos are leaving, have left, home:

> The concept of home is not safe in modernity. One of the clear objectives of modernism is to move out of the old home but the precise shape and location of the new home of modernity is never specified. The old home needs to be left behind because from the modernist's perspective it is locked into the frozen time of the past: bound to unchangeable customs; restricted to pure members; ruled by strict authoritarian father figures; stifled by superstitious beliefs. In short the old home represents closed traditions. To stay there is to atrophy. In contrast, modernity promises a sense of the present which is open, encourages mobility over stability, promotes difference as the stimulus for novelty, suggests that decision making should be participatory, and recognizes that reason bows to no God. The spirit of modernity is defined by the dynamism for change; the significance of place is always secondary in this revolution against the rooted practices of being and belonging.

Papastergiadis (8) suggests the threat in moving away from home: "a looming fear of living in a state of permanent homelessness." Here is an aporia that may have blocked the reports which the Project's work really deserved. It is an irresolvable ambivalence, a mutual incompatibility between the Vicos modernity project and the ethnographic project.

James Clifford (1988:17) points to an oscillation in ethnography "between two metanarratives: one of homogenization, the other of emergence; one of loss, the other of invention. In most specific conjunctures both narratives are relevant, each undermining the other's claim to tell 'the whole story,' each denying to the other a privileged, Hegelian vision." Clifford (218, 231) proceeds to a view of ethnography– by way of "gathering" or "collecting" (one might even say "foraging") which "involves the accumulation of possessions, the idea that identity is a kind of wealth (of objects, knowledge, memories, experience) . . . a strategy for the deployment of a possessive self, culture, and authenticity"—as a form of culture collecting (not, of course, the *only* way to see it) highlights the ways that diverse experiences and facts are selected, gathered, detached from their original temporal occasions, and given enduring value in a new arrangement. Collecting–at least in the West, where time is generally thought to be linear and irreversible–implies a rescue of phenomena from inevitable historical decay or loss. The collection contains what "deserves" to be kept, remembered, and treasured. Artifacts and customs are saved out of time. Anthropological culture collectors have typically gathered what seems "traditional"–what by definition is opposed to modernity. From a complex historical reality (which includes current ethnographic encounters) they select what gives form, structure, and continuity to a world. What is hybrid or "historical" in an emergent sense has been less commonly collected and presented as a system of authenticity.

I am impressed with the resemblance of this conception of ethnography and its object to Foucault's (1994:40) characterization of "nature" in sixteenth-century natural historians' eyes as "an unbroken tissue of words and signs, of accounts and characters, of discourse and forms"--

> When one is faced with the task of writing an animal's *history*, it is useless and impossible to choose between the profession of naturalist and that of compiler: one has to collect together into one and the same form of knowledge all that has been *seen* and *heard*, all that has been *recounted*, either by nature or by men, by the language of the world, by tradition, or by poets. To know an animal or a plant, or any terrestrial thing whatever, is to gather together the whole dense layer of signs with which it or they may have been covered; it is to rediscover also all the constellations of forms from which they derive their value as heraldic signs.

De Man (1979:16) points out: "The deconstruction of metaphor and of all rhetorical patterns . . . that use resemblance as a way to disguise differences . . . puts into question a whole series of concepts that underlie the value judgments of our critical discourse: the metaphors of primacy, of genetic history, and, most notably, of the autonomous power to will of the self." If development brings with it hybridization, blurred identities, deconstruction of self, loss of "form, structure, and continuity," if the "dense layer of signs" with which people have been "covered" is broken up, and if difference emerges from the process–then, what to write? How to write it? Which meta-discourse to choose? And so the master monograph on Vicos, a document which would have served "as a vehicle for career enhancement and, on a larger scale discipline formation" (Manganaro 1990:30), never appeared. Himes (1981:189) reports:

According to interview data and information in the Carnegie records, Holmberg always intended to publish a complete account on Vicos in a thorough and detailed anthropological report. The Carnegie files indicate that materials totaling 600-700 pages and requiring only "polishing up of the manuscript, editing and shortening" were ready in mid-1969. A number of sources have suggested that Holmberg's greater skills as a social science and development practitioner than as a scholarly writer and intellectual, account for the fact that the book never appeared. Several concluded that part of the price of combining action with research in the manner chosen by the Vicos project was the opportunity forgone to achieve systematic reporting and publication of the results in a more definitive form than was usually accomplished.

And writing resists itself. In 1969 Holmberg had been gone for three years. Why did his heirs not finish the volume Himes describes? If I may venture a hypothesis, it was because they were speechless. We are not to assume that people *have* something to say, or write, as Derrida (1997:218) suggests:

> [A]bove all else, doomed as it may be to hyperbole, the logic of agreement or hyperbolic consent presupposes a little too quickly that the person addressing the other wishes to be heard, read, or understood, wishes first of all to address some*one*–and that this desire, this will, this drive, are *simple*, simply identical to their supposed essence. If we believe and are saying that this is in no respect true, it is not to make a case for the demoniac by allowing it to appear, by staging it or leaving the stakes of the question in its favor. But we cannot, and we *must* not, exclude the fact that when someone is speaking, in private or in public, when someone teaches, publishes, preaches, orders, promises, prophesies, informs or communicates, some force in him or her is also striving not to be understood, approved, accepted in consensus–not immediately, not fully, and therefore not in the immediacy and plenitude of tomorrow, etc. For this hypothesis there is no need–this may appear extravagant to some people–to revert to a diabolical figure of the death instinct or a drive to destruction.

In other words, while wanting to understand is acceptable, we should not wish or need to understand everything since this is not possible. If writing is overdetermined, so is not-writing.[34] And so, while we may engage in overinterpretation of what is spoken or written, there is no interpretation of silence or a blank page by itself. The Vicos Project's low productivity is partially explained by Allan Holmberg's academic overload, the lack of funding with which to buy release from it, and his acute final illness as constituting both a physical and mental brake on his activity. I wish here only to indicate that it is also possible that he resisted himself. As an ethnographer *and* a developer he confronted the aporia of the Vicos Project, a desire to engage in two contradictory discourses, an essential ethnography and participant intervention, a binary opposition privileging development which he could not deconstruct.

But desire itself is unending. Baudrillard (1981:205) amplifies this: "Objects, and the needs that they imply, exist precisely in order to resolve the anguish of not knowing what one wants," where: "Desire . . . is signified throughout an entire chain of signifiers. And when it happens to be a desire for something experienced as lost, when it is a lack, an absence on which the objects that signify it have come to be inscribed, does it make any sense to treat such objects literally, as if they were merely what they are? And what can the notion of need possibly refer to in these circumstances?" (69, note 6). Thus, desire is also *un*-ending in the sense of end as impossible. This is why the conclusion of the Vicos Project and conclusions regarding it are undecidable.

Notes

1. This chapter is in part based on an article, "Reflexiones críticas sobre el proyecto Perú-Cornell," *Revista del Museo Nacional* (Lima) 48:287-316, 1986/1987, later published in English as "To let those we study come first: critical reflections on the Peru-Cornell Project," in *Fieldwork in Cultural Anthropology*, Mario D. Zamora and Bjørn B. Erring, eds. New Delhi: Reliance Publishing House, 1991. It is retitled and rewritten for this book.

2. John Van Willigen (1996:S44) corrects Bennett: "The emergence of conceptualized applied anthropology is much earlier. . . . The first published use of the term 'applied anthropology' apparently was in a 1906 [article] that described the training program in the Department of Anthropology at Cambridge University. . . . A similar pattern appears in the United States, where the initial program of the Bureau of American Ethnology was focused on what was called 'applied ethnology' as early as 1879. . . . Following [World War II] the amount of applied anthropology in Britain was greatly reduced, along with the size of the empire. In the United States what emerged was an anthropology of the cold war in which the use of anthropology in the design and evaluation of international aid programs increased dramatically."

3. This group consisted of Richard W. Patch, Joan Snyder, my wife Rhoda, our baby Daniel, and myself. We were soon joined by William and Vera Mangin. I recall our prolonged wait in the hotel in Chancos (the lowest part of Vicos) for

Allan Holmberg our Cornell mentor, who was busy in Lima arranging the transfer of the Vicos estate, whom we hoped would tell us what to do. Meanwhile, we visited in Vicos, Recuayhuanca, the community across the Marcará River, and the towns of Marcará and Carhuaz, as well as the city of Huaraz.

4. In Spanish, the term *Vicosinos*, a generic term for both men and women, is gendered masculine. In order to avoid cluttering up the text with repetitions of "Vicosinos (-as)" I hope we can agree that the English word is ungendered, much as "Angelenos" refers ungenderedly to the people of Los Angeles, male and female, where "Angelenas" would have no meaning to Anglos other than the plural for women named "Angelina."

5. All this does not mean that have not reported on Vicos. I reported on labor relations, a personal document, and medical problems in Vicos in Stein (1991).

6. The essays of Allan R. Holmberg, principal investigator of the Vicos Project, which are cited in the text, have been translated into Spanish and published in book form (Holmberg 1966) in Lima. The major work in English on the Project continues to be Dobyns, Doughty, and Lasswell (1971). The basic ethnography of Vicos, in Spanish, is Vázquez (1952). See also Holmberg 1967, Dobyns (1974), Babb (1980), Köhler (1981), and Himes (1981). Doughty (1987a and 2002) chronicles the major events in Vicos

7. Paige (1975:168) identifies Vázquez as "director of the Bureau of Peasant Affairs under the revolutionary military regime."

8. But not well enough to keep it out of my early work (Stein 1961)!

9. Michael Kearney (1996:1) begins his critique of the "peasant" concept by suggesting that "the category *peasant*, whatever validity it may once have held, has been outdistanced by contemporary history. Within anthropology and within peasant studies generally, '*the* peasant' was constructed from residual images of preindustrial European and colonial rural society. Informed by romantic sensibilities and modern nationalist imaginations, these images are anachronisms, but nevertheless they remain robust anachronisms even at the end of the twentieth century. As such, they are appropriate targets for a housecleaning that clears space for alternative theoretical views." Kearney points out that just as the term "primitive" began to be shunned at mid-century, "anthropology in no small measure reconstituted itself by making the peasant the primary form of the Other . . . . It is no exaggeration to say that the discipline as a fieldwork-based form of natural history was saved from obsolescence by the simultaneous discovery and invention of the peasant" (39).

10. Fabian (1983:30) says: "Physical time is seldom used in its naked, chronological form. More often than not, chronologies shade into *Mundane* or

the former where their "attitude [is] one of deference and politeness [and] they . . . try to coax the individual . . . to concede assistance which [is] seen as an extension of personal charity."

14. Linda Seligmann (1995:11) says: "Although to some extent useful analytical tools, the terms *urban* and *rural* are misnomers. It is the constant movement between these two spheres, neither of which is homogeneous in terms of ethnicity or class, that really captures the well-trained eye and ear."

15. I have borrowed the term "retainers" from John Murra (1966:36) because it seems less contaminated with "models from European social and economic history" than "client," "serf's serf," or "slave."

16. As evidence that Vicosinos are "change-minded," see my (Stein 1991b) essay in which a Vicosino, in 1953, tells of the many changes he has experienced throughout the more that two decades of his existence.

17. I am using the term "wild" in Hayden White's (1978:179) sense: "[I]n modern times, the notion of 'wild man' has become almost exclusively a psychological category rather than an anthropological one, as it was in the seventeenth and eighteenth centuries." I will explore some of the psychoanalytic implications of it later in this chapter.

18. Eve Sedgwick (1985:1-2) defines "homosocial" as "a word [which] describes social bonds between persons of the same sex; it is a neologism, obviously meant to be distinguished from 'homosexual.' In fact, is it applied to such activities as 'male bonding,' which may, as in our society, be characterized by intense homophobia, fear and hatred of homosexuality. To draw the 'homosocial' back into the orbit of 'desire,' of the potentially erotic, then, is to hypothesize the potential unbrokenness of a continuum between homosocial and homosexual–a continuum whose visibility , for men, in our society, is radically disrupted."

19. The Project appears in this aspect to have fit in with Andean conceptions of phallic vampires and female victims. See Mary Weismantel's (2001) magnificent work on these themes.

20. Paul Doughty (1987b:444) describes the "fortuitous event . . . which broke the stalemate" between the Beneficencia as consisting of Edward Kennedy's visit: "Kennedy was convinced to request, upon his return to Lima that [President] Prado permit the sale of Vicos to its serfs as an act of 'good faith,' since Prime Minister Beltrán was at that time attempting to negotiate United States financial support for 'studying' agrarian reform." Doughty continues, in a footnote (ibid.: note 11): "He effort made by the writer and other [Project] personnel, summer anthropology students, and the Vicos community to win Kennedy's understanding and support followed other lobbying efforts which had become part of the project strategy.

Kennedy, like other invited dignitaries, was given a tour of the community, held a head-to-head meeting with the Vicos council for more than an hour, and was treated to a 'pachamanca' (a highland barbecue). When Kennedy interviewed Prado the following day, his first point was to push for the sale of Vicos, according to both U.S. Chargé d'affaires Douglas Henderson and John Plank, a Harvard political scientist who accompanied him (personal communications):"

21. I cannot use this term without at least putting it into quotes. See my work , *Lo post-étnico y la persistencia de la diferencia* (Stein 2001).

22. Donna Haraway (1989:68) writes that this was an endeavor "to coordinate research on personality, development, social groups, culture, psychology and medicine, law and religion under the rubric of social harmony and personal adjustment."

23. Freud (1955a:305) wrote: "When I have promised my patients help or improvement by means of a cathartic treatment I have often been faced by this objection: 'Why, you tell me yourself that my illness is probably connected with my circumstances and the events of my life. You cannot alter these in any way. How do you propose to help me, then?' And I have been able to make this reply: 'No doubt fate would find it easier than I do to relieve you of your illness. But you will be able to convince yourself that much will be gained if we succeed in transforming your hysterical misery into common unhappiness. With a mental life that has been restored to health you will be better armed against that unhappiness.'"

24. Mrs. Laura Holmberg (personal communication, March 18, 1998) reports that her husband "had been and continued to be in good health until he had a burst appendix in 1963 in Lima. What I believe may have been the cause of the subsequent acute leukemia of which he died was that he was left under an x-ray machine in the British American Hospital in Lima and burned. I cannot, of course, prove that is what happened but he was never as robust after that. However, he continued to work, was Chair of the Department and went to Vicos every summer. He was diagnosed in 1965 with acute leukemia and he died a year later."

25. Although such exploitation is common in scholarly settings, I am thinking here mainly of the exploitation of small children by adults, and the possibilities of reducing adults to the status of children. In our exchange relating to the translation of the Spanish edition of this book, Maruja Martínez adds: "I remember that my mother and grandmothers dressed their domestic servants in children's clothing, even when they were 20 or 30 years old."

26. "At one time, he was a member of 43 graduate committees and he served the last five years of his life as Chair of the Department and continued to teach." (Mrs. Laura Holmberg, personal communication, March 18, 1998.)

27. Reporting on the Project is far from zero. Paul Doughty (1987a:458) observes: "The difficulty of producing the systematic publication of findings in all aspects of the program was a deficiency noted by many persons. Although there were well over two hundred articles, reports, monographs, and books published about Vicos and the [Project], more findings might have been published by more of the participants. The use of this material is also limited in part because of its dispersal among numerous journals, books, and 'fugitive reports.'"

While I am uncertain as to the meaning of "fugitive reports," I have in my personal library a number of mimeographed documents on Vicos that I am reasonably certain did not have wide circulation. Very little of this production would have been available to North American, much less Peruvian scholars and students. This excuses nobody but may shed some light on the problem.

28. I use this word in Sigmund Freud's sense as he applied it to the task of deconstructing the meaning of the German words *heimlich*, pertaining to the home or the familiar, and *unheimlich*, opposed to the familiar, the strange, or that which causes fear (Freud 1955b). He says that the uncanny is related to themes of the double, "the repetition of the same features or character-traits or vicissitudes, of the same crimes, or even the same names," but what makes the double uncanny is that it stems "from the fact of the 'double' being a creation dating back to a very early mental state, long since surmounted," which "has become a thing of terror, . . . the gods turned into demons." What inspires fear is that "every affect belonging to an emotional impulse, whatever its kind, is transformed, if it is repressed, into anxiety, [so that] among instances of frightening things there must be one class in which the frightening element can be shown to be something repressed which *recurrs*.

29. Laplanche and Pontalis (1973:339) offer this discussion of "primary process": "The study of symptom formation and the analysis of dreams led Freud to recognize a type of mental functioning that was very different from the thought-processes which had been the object of traditional psychological observation. This method of functioning, which had its own mechanisms and which was regulated by specific laws, was particularly well illustrated by dreaming. . . . The mechanisms which are in operation here, according to Freud, are displacement, on the one hand, whereby an often apparently insignificant idea comes to be invested with all the psychical value, depth of meaning and intensity originally attributed to another one; and, on the other hand, condensation, a process which enables all the meanings in several chains of association to converge on a single idea standing at their point of intersection." Freud (1965:639) himself said of this process: "It is unable to do anything but wish." It is no great leap over "mechanisms" and "laws" to view it as *desire*.

30. Because racism takes on a "plurality of forms. . . not simply between societies but within them also," Paul Gilroy (1990:265) points out, "there is no racism in general and consequently there can be no general theory of race relations or race and politics."

31. Peasants have their own essentializings of mestizos. Vázquez continues, in the same text, with this other listing of what peasants see in *their* others: "Lazy, lying and promise-breaking, immoral, venal, plundering, evil-smelling (men), swindling, know-it-alls, card-players or cardsharps, cigarette-smokers, rapists (men), cut-throats or *pishtacos*, crazy, weak, womanizers (men)." I wonder (as far as I know, nobody has ever researched this question) if they are able to see in mestizos what Mangin (1955:182) writes of as "the fear of being Indians."?

32. Holmberg encouraged participation by the Vicosinos and desired as much feedback from them as possible. He tells of the staff meetings, seminars, meetings with *mayorales* (Vicosino sub-overseers), and gatherings of the Hacienda labor force: "On Wednesdays, taking advantage of an ancient custom, that of [the] *mando* when the hacendado [operator of the Hacienda] told the Indians what they were to do the following week, we hold a meeting with all of the Indians who work for the Hacienda and discuss with them the agreements arrived at with the *mayorales* the previous day. Modifications can thus be made to best suit the group as a whole. . . . This meeting also serves as a means of reporting back to the people the results of our studies and the progress of our program. In this connection it is of interest to note that at the first of such meetings hardly a voice was raised, while now after five months of reunions most everyone wants to talk at once. Sometimes as many as three or four hundred Indians or heads of families participate in these meetings. . . . We do not yet have the response from these meetings that we would like to have but feel that we have made fair progress in approaching the problem of greater group participation in our program." (Holmberg 1952:6-7.) This is not "free association," however much the psychoanalytic model may have been present in the design.

33. Laplanche and Pontalis (1973:480) define "wild" psychoanalysis as "the procedure of amateur or inexperienced 'analysts' who attempt to interpret symptoms, dreams, utterances, actions, etc., on the basis of psychoanalytic notions which they have as often as not misunderstood. In a more technical sense, an interpretation is deemed 'wild' if a specific analytic situation is misapprehended in its current dynamics and its particularity–and especially if the repressed content is simply imparted to the patient with no heed paid to the resistances and to the transference." I suppose there may be "wild" revolutions, too, in which leaderships call up mobilizations with unanticipated consequences, as in the failed Peruvian "revolution" of 1968-1980, with emphasis on the "first phase" to 1975. Susan Stokes (1995:12) says of the military government's project that it "failed brilliantly." And one might add that the light of this failure still illuminates Peru.

34. John Murra (2000:101), one of the most seminal of the Andeanists of the past century, reports that when Sol Tax, a member of Murra's doctoral committee at the University of Chicago, asked him how it was that he, Murra, had taken so long to write his dissertation: "I asked him, 'Do you really want to know?' He said yes, so I explained to him psychoanalytically how it was with people who were afraid of

their own creativity." We can not be certain that Murra, who had undergone a Jungian analysis, was aware of the *psychoanalytic* symbolism of his statement. There is, likewise, no clue in his discussion of "Andean verticality," the concept for which he is justly acclaimed. Nevertheless, I wonder if a writing block, overdetermined as it is, might not *also* contain a fear of falling?

Chapter 2, Part I:

Sarah Levy's Profession/Sarah Levy's Confession[1]

One must underscore that constative utterances and discourses of pure knowledge, in the university or elsewhere, do not belong, as such, to the order of the profession in the strict sense. They belong perhaps to the craft, career, the *métier* ("competence, knowledge, know-how), but not to the profession understood in a rigorous sense. The discourse of profession is always, in one way or another, a free profession of faith; in its pledge of responsibility, it exceeds pure techno-scientific knowledge. To profess is to pledge oneself while declaring oneself, while *giving oneself out to be*, while promising this or that. . . . [T]o profess philosophy [is] not simply to be a philosopher, to practice or teach philosophy in some pertinent fashion, but to pledge oneself, with a public promise, to devote oneself publicly, to give oneself over to philosophy, to bear witness, or even to fight for it. And what matters here is this promise, this pledge of responsibility, which is reducible to neither theory nor practice. To profess consists always in a performative speech act, even if the knowledge, the object, the content of what one professes, of what one teaches or practices, remains on the order of the theoretical or the constative. *Because the act of professing is a performative speech act and because the event that it is or produces depends only on this linguistic promise, well, its proximity to the fable, to fabulation, and to fiction, to the "as if," will always be formidable.* (Jacques Derrida 2002c:214-215;

the last emphasis is mine.)

Professing anthropology–or sociology, as in the case we examine here–is a responsibility and a promise, neither of which is always easy to take or keep. Professing can and does slide easily into fiction which lies beyond truth and falsity. I examine such a slippage here, mainly through the eyes of someone who deposited a bundle of documents in the Archives of the Peru-Cornell Project (the "Vicos Project") many years ago, some of the presence and interventions of North Americans in Peru at mid-century. These documents consist of letters which Dr. Sarah Levy, a sociologist, wrote home from Vicos, plus some related letters written after her return to Ithaca, New York, by herself and others.[2] They were intended to constitute a set of "field notes" of Levy's experiences in Peru and Vicos. As ethnographic texts they are not a good recording of the Andean world in which she resided. However, as self-ethnography they are a rich source of information about the adventures of modernizers and rationalizers in the Third World. But perhaps ethnography should be precisely ethnography of the self as much, if not more, than surveillance of peoples who are powerless to redirect the Other's gaze. But these documents are much more than this. They also constitute a narrative of the vicissitudes of subaltern gender at mid century. I am employing the term "subaltern" here and elsewhere in this work as it was developed by a group of South Asian scholars to "name . . . the general attribute of subordination . . . whether this is expressed in terms of class, caste, age, gender and office or in any other way" (Guha 1988b:35).

Sarah Levy's story, then, is one of a *woman* sociologist in a men's project. It is a confession with many excuses, but "without alibi," since an "alibi always tells the story of lying" (Derrida 2002b:xxvi), and Levy does not lie even though she does not always narrate truth. Bill Readings (1989:236) tells this "apocryphal story" about Paul de Man: "[W]hen asked what his 'blind spot' was, after his statement that every discourse had an enabling 'blind spot', he replied that he had none." De Man (1984:81) himself said: "Autobiography veils a defacement of the mind of which it is itself the cause."

In reading Sarah Levy's story of the experience of a lone woman contending with a group of bonded males I would like to be guided by Derrida's (1978a:53) extension of Nietzsche's thoughts on "woman":

> [T]he credulous and dogmatic philosopher who *believes* in truth just as he believes in woman, this philosopher has understood nothing. He has understood nothing of truth, nor anything of woman. Because, indeed, if woman *is* truth, *she* at least knows that there is no truth, that truth has no

place here and that no one has a place for truth. And she is woman precisely because she herself does not believe in truth itself, because she does not believe in what she is, in what she is believed to be, in what she thus is not.

Julia Kristeva (1981:166, cited *in* de Laurentis 1984:95) observes: "Believing oneself 'a woman' is almost as absurd and obscurantist as believing oneself 'a man'." This is to be read in the Levy documents which reveal a drama of people who believe they see "woman" and "man" in themselves and each other. In the case of Derrida's text we may ask: exactly *which* woman is Derrida writing about? And *where* is she? I provide some answers in *my* text as I write the deconstruction of Sarah Levy's. You are not obliged to accept my answers. You are free to read the documents and come to your own conclusions. Meanwhile, we both will do well in eschewing credulity and dogmatism by affirming both our disbelief and our belief: we may believe our disbelief and disbelieve our belief. But I inform you here at the outset that this chapter is impossible, impossible to write and impossible to read, first, as Shoshana Felman (1985:21) notes, because "texts exceed the knowledge of their speaking (writing) subjects," and then later, when she asks: "How can we understand the Subject without transforming him (or her) into an object? Can the Subject comprehend itself? Is the Subject *thinkable*, as such? To put the question differently: is the *Other* thinkable? Is it possible to think the Other, not as an object, but as a subject, a subject who would not, however, amount to the same?" (42). "How can we read the unreadable?", Felman (187) asks,

> This question, however, is far from simple: grounded in contradiction, it in fact subverts its own terms: to actually *read* the unreadable, to impose a *meaning* on it, is precisely *not* to read the unreadable *as unreadable*, but to *reduce* it to the readable, to interpret it as if it were of the same order as the readable. But perhaps the unreadable and the readable *cannot* be located on the same level, perhaps they are *not* of the same order: if they could indeed correspond to the unconscious and to the conscious levels, then their functionings would be radically different, and their modes of being utterly heterogeneous to each other. It is entirely possible that the unreadable as such could by no means, in no way, be made *equivalent* to the readable, through a simple effort at better reading, through a simple *conscious* endeavor. The readable and the unreadable are by no means simply *comparable*, but neither are they simply *opposed*, since above all they are not *symmetrical*, they are *not* mirror-images of each other. Our task would perhaps then become not so much to read the unreadable *as a variant of the readable*, but, to the very contrary, to *rethink the readable*

itself, and hence, to attempt to read it *as a variant of the unreadable.* The paradoxical necessity of "reading the unreadable" could thus be accomplished only through a radical modification of the meaning of "reading" itself.

How are we, then, to read Sarah Levy's unreadable narrative, and here, following Teresa de Laurentis (1984:81), we should not read "narrative" in its "narrow sense of story (*fabula* and characters) or logical structure (actions and actant), but in the broader sense of discourse conveying the temporal movement and positionalities of desire." De Laurentis later continues:

> The work of narrative . . . is a mapping of differences, and specifically, first and foremost, of sexual differences into each text; and hence, by a sort of accumulation, into the universe of meaning, function, and history, represented by the literary-artistic tradition and all the texts of culture. But we have learned from semiotics that the productivity of the text, its play of structure and excess, engages the reader, viewer, or listener as subject in (and for) its process. Much as social formations and representations appeal to and position the individual as subject in the process to which we give the name ideology, the movement of narrative discourse shifts and places the reader, viewer, or listener in certain portions of the plot space. . . . [W]e reach a provisional conclusion: in its "making sense" of the world, narrative endlessly reconstructs it as a two-character drama in which the human person creates and recreates *himself* out of an abstract or purely symbolic other–the womb, the earth, the grave, the woman.

Thus, as Levy constantly creates and recreates herself in her narrative, I create and recreate myself in my writing about it, and you create and recreate yourself in your reading of it.

Levy's narrative contains unpleasures for everyone. It was never intended to be a pleasuring one for, as June Jordan (1981:180) tells us in writing about her kind of subalternity as an African American woman:

> If you make and keep my life horrible then, when I can tell the truth, it will be a horrible truth; it will not sound good or look good or, God willing, feel good to you, either. There is nothing good about the evils of a life forced into useless and impotent drift and privation. There is very little that is attractive or soothing about being strangled to death, whether it is the literal death of the body or the actual death of the soul that lying, that the humiliation and the evil of self-denial, guarantees.
>
> Extremity demands, and justifies, extreme response. Violation invites, and teaches, violence. Less than that, less than a scream or a fist, less than

the absolute cessation of normal events in the lock of abnormal duress is a lie and, worse than that, it is blasphemous ridicule of the self.

We will do well, in the event that we read "bad" in Sarah Levy's story, to suspend judgment and any disappointment we may feel.

The name *Sarah Levy, is a pseudonym, as are others in this essay, and I indicate this anonymity by using asterisks when some names are first mentioned. Thus I find myself located between two seemingly opposed promises, one a promise to reveal how great research efforts had such scant results, the other a promise to conceal identities in order to protect the privacy of several of the people involved, for the right to privacy extends to those who are no longer with us. Revelation and concealment, in a sense, constitute the context of this chapter. Each is a metaphor for the other. They so surround and penetrate each other that they no longer are two separate promises but a single promise which promises to make itself known, to reveal a truth.[3] This is overdetermined because I protect my own privacy too while relating to you matters which I think you ought to know about in order to evaluate these events, decisions and actions, which took place a half century ago. Here I play with what Tyler and Marcus (1990:125-126) envision as "*con*-text ('against text')" and "con-*text* ('with text')," so as not to be "conned by the artifice of the text," and with viewing as clearly as possible our influence on Sarah Levy, displacing her influence on us. Levy and I thus engage in what Erving Goffman (1986:180) calls a "containment competition," in which there are "two sides each trying to con the other, knowing that the other is trying to con it, but each trying to outcon the other."

Here is the context. A year and a half after the Vicos Project began it played host to another set of investigators in the Vicos phase of the Cornell Cross-Cultural Methodology Project (the Methodology Project). The Department of Sociology and Anthropology at Cornell University had received a grant to fund research which would compare several types of structured and non-structured methods of obtaining cross-cultural data. According to the "Final Report" of this project (Cornell Methodology Project 1956:2-3) of the latter:

> The Cornell Cross-Cultural Methodology Project was begun in February 1953, under a three-year grant of $64,900 from the Rockefeller Foundation. Its objectives were to develop and test diverse techniques of collecting and analyzing social science data from economically underdeveloped areas.
> From February to May 1953 the Project staff, in consultation with a committee of sociologists and anthropologists working in different culture

areas, developed a design for original research on the problem of acceptance of social and technological changes in three major areas, Peru, Thailand, and India, where the Department maintains field stations. . . .

From June to October 1953, field work was carried out in the first field station, Hacienda Vicos, Ancash, Peru. This field station is directed by Dr. Allan Holmberg . . . who collaborated with the Methodology Project's field directors . . . . The data gathered in Peru have been processed and analyzed, and are now being prepared for publication. . . . The Peruvian experience served as a pilot study, on the basis of which the subsequent research design for the equivalent study of social change in Thailand and India was drawn up.

The Methodology Project's "Progress Report" (Cornell Methodology Project 1955:1) provides a brief account of the preparation for the study in early 1953 along with the Peruvian phase of the study which took place later that year:

> During this period the staff, in consultation with anthropological and sociological research works and with area experts, specified the relevant areas of methodological research to be considered within the scope of the Cross-Cultural Methodology Project. A major accomplishment of this period was the definition of substantive areas for research which would be equally applicable to the diverse cultural areas and within which varied methods of data-collection and analysis could be applied. . . .
>
> [T]he staff conducted field studies at the Cornell University Field Station in Vicos Peru, focusing upon the effectiveness of varied methods of studying the substantive problem of Westernization accompanying the introduction of certain modern innovations in indigenous behavior and institutional forms. The field experiences encountered in executing this design resulted in revisions and rephrasing of the methodological tests, and accompanying redesign of field work techniques.

These two paragraphs are followed by tightly written sections describing a third analytic phase with the Vicos materials from November 1953 to October 1954 consisting of "analysis of the data-gathering process," "analysis of the analytic procedures," "statistical analysis of the quantitative material," "inductive content analysis of the qualitative materials," and "deductive content analysis of the qualitative materials." They need not be reproduced here but it may be noted that they display discursive mastery, optimism, and satisfaction with staff competence.

It will be difficult for turn-of-the-century readers to understand the context of these mid-century reports. That con-text is long gone. Himes (1972:56) says, for example, that "Vicos offers a sort of 'Free World' or 'democratic' answer to socialism, communism, or pan-Indian peasant movements." Now, in the year 2000, the Cold War is over, McCarthyism is as dead as the Edsel,[4] "underdeveloped" economies have not "taken off," the Eisenhower years are long past, the "Free World" is not as free as we then thought, and "Indians" do not legally exist in Peru. We read these texts today in a different context. Despite the intentions of their authors, their meaning, which at first seemed so permanent, turns out to be fluid, ephemeral, and fleeting, but also unlimited and unlimitable (Derrida 1988a). The authors believed that they were writing to a funding agency and doubtlessly desired to present themselves seductively; but they also intended to include colleagues among their readers and surely wished to avoid the exposure of incompetence and to conceal any shame or guilt they felt about "jobs" not completed; and they were writing, as well, for student consumption for they desired to maintain their authority over those who would replace them.

Here is the way in which the guest project came to Vicos: Although the principal investigator of Vicos Project, Professor Allan R. Holmberg, was an anthropologist and its field staff were also anthropologists, the Methodology Project was firmly in the hands of the senior sociologists at Cornell who assigned responsibilities to *their* junior colleagues who, in turn, employed North American and Peruvian anthropology students as research assistants (I served as one of these and worked under the direction of Professor Rose K. Goldsen in Ithaca from 1954 to 1955). When the senior sociologist, *Dr. Arthur Silver, who was one of the principal investigators, felt certain that the funding for the Methodology Project would be forthcoming, he, with his senior colleagues, set about finding a professional scholar who would take responsibility to direct the field research as guest of Cornell University's several field stations. They fixed on *Frank Nolan, a younger sociologist who had established his reputation, with the help of two highly competent English-speaking field assistants, by writing a book on a nation-state which had been recently freed from colonialism. They believed that his cross-cultural experience suited their need, and they also believed that he was competent in both structured, particularly social surveys, and non-structured methods. Nolan, who had been teaching and writing at a "second tier" state university in the midwest, had received good reviews of his book and seemed ready to be tried out in one of North America's elite universities, Cornell. The Department of Sociology and Anthropology decided that he would first visit the Peruvian site and furnished him with a graduate assistant, *Peter Quiller, a recent Cornell graduate who had remained at the university as a first-year graduate student. Quiller was an anthropologist who had accompanied Professor Holmberg to Peru two years earlier, knew Vicos, and was able to communicate in Spanish. Nobody understood that while this young man was an exceptionally intelligent individual, a true prodigy, he suffered from alcoholism, an affliction which is difficult to "cure" and even more difficult for light drinkers to understand. It turned out that Nolan was a heavy drinker, possibly a borderline alcoholic, so the two made a dysfunctional team. Nolan arrived in Ithaca, with his family, and took up his teaching duties while he prepared for the work in Vicos.

Nolan and Quiller arrived in Peru early in June, 1953. In Lima, Quiller found three anthropology students in the University of San Marcos, whom Nolan readily accepted as field assistants. The two proceeded to Vicos, followed by their field staff. Nolan designed his "rationality" project and gave instruction to the Peruvian students, between and during their drinking bouts. Nolan did not know Spanish but had to rely on Quiller to translate for him. The two, together with their three assistants, and with considerable help from the staff of the Vicos Project managed to carry on for a while, but they accomplished very little. Meanwhile, the senior faculty members at Cornell University had observed Nolan's work during his first year there and were beginning to discuss his possible "unsuitability," i.e., his possible incompetence. They realized that he was unprepared to conduct a social survey in Vicos and they searched for means to save the Methodology Project. They decided to act with caution.

Dr. Sarah Levy, an adjunct faculty member who held a temporary position as "research associate" in the department, funded by grant money, who had been involved in the planning of the research, and happened to know Spanish because she had done research in Latin American countries and was living with a Latin American companion, was selected to go to Vicos as co-director of the project. However, apparently neither she nor Nolan were advised of the reasons for this decision. Levy was suddenly ordered to go to Vicos as a second field director to work on the Methodology Project. She was glad to accept the assignment because she was interested in social science methods, viewed the work as an opportunity for career enhancement, and felt it might improve her chances to move into a tenure-track position at Cornell–although it meant suspending the research she was already carrying on. With no preparation other than her control of the language, she arrived in Lima on June 27, 1953, and drove to Vicos with Professor *George Rogers, a Cornell anthropologist, on July 9, after the Methodology team had arrived and set itself up in Vicos. This ambiguous situation with two directors of one Methodology Project continued for nearly a half a year.

All the major participants in the drama that developed no longer exist and it is possible to tell the story of the guest project mainly through

Levy's letters, intended to be "field notes," which she wrote home to her companion, Rosa Sánchez, in Ithaca and which were later deposited in a packet in the Vicos Project's archives. I am going to treat these letters as texts, the language of which is subject to overinterpretation: that is, this language carries multiple meanings, as in the language of dream-texts, poetry, drama, and the novel. I see no reason why the "field notes" of a social scientist cannot be put to the same kind of analytic treatment. However, as Stephen Tyler (1986:135) points out, a text cannot

> dictate its interpretation, for it cannot control the powers of its readers. They respond to a text out of various states of ignorance, irreceptivity, disbelief, and hypersensitivity to form. They are immune in the first extreme to any nuance of form, reading through it, not by means of it, unconscious of it except perhaps in confusion or annoyance. In the second extreme a paranoid conviction of authorial deceit feeds a search for hidden meanings–and the finding of them; or, in one with heightened sensibility to the necessary structures of thought and language, the search is less for things hidden by the author than for things hidden from the author by the structure of language and thought. Of these latter two, the one thinks the author a charlatan, the other a dupe, but to both the text is a coded secret hiding a necessary inner meaning irresponsive to those obscuring or concealing appearances of outer contingencies that implicate a community of belief. Because the text can eliminate neither ambiguity nor the subjectivity of its authors and readers, it is bound to be misread, so much so that we might conclude . . . that the meaning of the text is the sum of its misreadings.

In Levy's texts a theme which I call a "work ethic" occupies (and preoccupies) major space. She is constantly concerned about "work" and "working": whether or not people are "working," and whether or not "work is getting done." The English word "work" is *charged*–my word and one that is also loaded with metaphor–with a wide range of meaning, as, for example, in the simple physical notion of "work" as the expenditure of energy in contrast with the idea of "work" as "drudgery," or the conception of one's "working," as opposed to "playing," enjoying pleasure, which one might rather be doing. When one is "out of work," one has lost one's identity as a "worker": indeed, "[n]on-work is . . . only the repressive desublimation[5] of labor power" (Baudrillard 1975:40).[6] Then there is "pointless work, work for work's sake," created in order to control people (Foucault 1980:42).[7] We also speak of "working" in the case of the transformation of a liquid mixture of grain or fruit with sugar and yeast into a potable beverage. An author's, or a composer's "works," like other "works" of plastic art, are creations which he or she has conceived and formed. An electrical or electronic appliance is "working" when it is functioning, and "not working" when it is in disrepair. To "work out a problem" is to solve or resolve it. The human body is "working" when it is ingesting food and liquids, processing them into energy and wastes, and eliminating the latter in the form of various body emissions. When this alimentary apparatus is "not working," one is constipated, one is not producing on demand, and one may feel psychic anguish because one is not performing to expectations. Whose expectations? One's own, of course, but as well the expectations of caretakers early in life which one has introjected. Joseph Gusfield (1996:70) notes that for someone who finds leisure spiritually problematic "'play' is an abomination." He contrasts the "workaholic" with the alcoholic:

> In the perpetual struggle of the individual toward self-expressiveness and social integration, the conflict between work and play, day and night, gains intensity. Release is both a boon and a danger. The alcoholic is the obverse of the workaholic. (Note how the word has been adapted to both poles.) The alcoholic becomes one of the symbols of a fear of falling; of a threat in the personal drama of success and failure that is the key story of American careers. The workaholic is the opposite. Here the danger lies in the inability to let go; to enjoy release from role. That one is pathology and the other only troubling is the difference between cultural subordination and dominance.
>
> Drinking in America remains a point of political, legal, and social conflict. While it retains meanings of cultural remission, the society is able to institute social controls that generally bound and limit the "time-out" character of play.... That others find "playing" with social controls threatening to their own self-control and to the social organization is testimony to the fear that the "wild man" in us is uncontainable. Once let loose he may not show up for church on Sunday or for work on Monday.

Even the "industrial leisure" of modern society can be transformed into work, as Arjun Appadurai (1996:80) shows: "the harried vacation packed with so many activities, scenes, and choices, whose purpose is to create a hypertime of leisure, that the vacation becomes a form of work, of frenetic leisure–leisure ever conscious of its forthcoming rendezvous with work time." And: "Consumption has now become a serious form of work, however, if by *work* we mean the disciplined (skilled and semiskilled) production of the means of consumer subsistence. The heart of this work is the social discipline of the imagination, the discipline of learning to link fantasy and nostalgia to the desire for new bundles of commodities. This is not to reduce work to a pale metaphor, mirroring its strong anchorage in production. It is to suggest that learning how to navigate the open-ended temporal flows of consumer credit and purchase, in a landscape where nostalgia has become divorced from memory, involves new forms of labor: the labor of reading ever-shifting fashion messages, the labor of debt servicing, the labor of learning how best to manage newly complex domestic finances, and the labor of acquiring knowledge in the complexities of money management" (82-83). Work becomes a fetish, a ghostly object (see Chapters 3 and 4), when it takes the form of a tourist attraction, as described by Dale MacCannell (1976:6):

Wherever industrial society is transformed into modern society, *work* is simultaneously transformed into an object of touristic curiosity. In every corner of the modern world, *labor* and *production* are being presented to sightseers in guided tours of factories and in museums of science and industry. In the developing world, some important attractions are being detached from their original social and religious meanings, now appearing as monumental representations pf "abstract, undifferentiated human labor," as Karl Marx used to say. The Egyptian pyramids exemplify this. Sightseeing at such attractions preserves still important values embodied in work-in-general, even as specific work processes and the working class itself are transcended by history.

It is only by making a fetish of the work of others, by transforming it into an "amusement" ("do-it-yourself"), a spectacle (Grand Coulee [a well known North American dam]), or an attraction (the guided tours of Ford Motor Company), that modern workers on vacation, can apprehend work as a part of a meaningful totality.

Thus, one can direct one's gaze at others working without working oneself and one can do what Donald Horne (1984:110, 115) calls "industrial archaeology" by visiting technological museums in which "[r]everence is encouraged towards machines for their own sake–as if all machines are necessarily good, and their results progressive: human progress can seem to depend on machine begetting machine, without human agency." This is paralleled in the cases we are examining here by the overvaluation of mountains of field notes, which are not put to use, by social scientists who do little or no field work themselves, preferring to gaze at the work of others. Pierre Bourdieu (2000a:202) writes: "The experience of labor lies between two extremes, forced labor, which is determined only by external constraint, and scholastic labor, the limiting case which is the quasi-ludic activity of the artist or writer. The further someone moves from the former, the less they work directly for money and the more the 'interest' of work, the inherent gratification of the fact of performing the work increases–as does the interests linked to the symbolic profits associated with the name of the occupation or the occupational status and the quality of the working relations which often go hand in hand with the intrinsic interest of the labor." The "symbolic profits" extracted from the work of others, then, makes one a "symbolic capitalist."

This said, let us now examine the series of documents by Sarah Levy, some written in a peculiar but readable Spanish. Her Spanish here is translated into English, as well as I can do it, only slightly edited, and set in italics to distinguish it from her English. The first letter is dated July 14, 1953:

Dear Rosita, It makes me happy this morning to receive a letter from you. Listen, girl, I'm feeling better than I felt up to now. I sleeps a lot, I eats a lot, I goes around a lot on foot and by horse, but I'm not working very much. This Nolan is a pendejo![8] Heavens, I've never seen the like. It's very hard for me not to blow my top, but I must be patient. I tell you that I never have suspected that the field of anthropology and sociology was so full of pendejos and "phonies." Look, this pendejo has been here for more than a month. He hasn't gone more than maybe 5 kilometers from the center of the Hacienda. He hasn't tried to converse with anyone who speaks Spanish or Quechua. He only speaks English (so I don't think that he's to blame) but he hasn't made any attempt to learn a word. As I said, he's been here more than a month and he hasn't taken any notes (and that is almost a rule for fieldworkers). Well, I don't want to continue with this subject because the thought pains me to the heart that this project's report will end up, certainly, on top of my desk because there isn't any doubt that this pendejo is a pendejo.

Well, today I went around with Enrique [Enrique Luna, the Marcará mestizo who served as overseer of the Hacienda Vicos during the first years of the Project] *who is the boss of all the peons of the Hacienda. More or less, we went visiting a lot of fields because Allan* [Holmberg] *has brought from a hacienda around Vicos a new seed potato which is much better than the seed that the Vicosinos were using for 400 years. Then Enrique had to make sure that the peons were seeding well; that is, putting the plants more or less 18 inches separately. They have to level off and to use DDT and other insecticides that the Hacienda gives. These are experiments that Allan and his project is directing to see if some people do these practices and what happens. Who are those who imitate the new practices? Why? Also, who are those who don't accept the practices, and why?*

Well, look. I'm going through the heights of the Andes, crossing creeks and rivers and steep slopes and abysses on horseback. And I wasn't at all afraid. I think that I'll never have "the shakes" again. Remember one day a few years ago when we went to rent horses in Central Park, and I was afraid when mounted because it seemed to me so high? Today I enjoyed myself a lot, and also I had the courage to whip the horse and go at a gallop! If you were here, Rosita, look, there's a school which Allan has had built with workers from the Hacienda where the boys and some girls go (there aren't more than six girls because the Indians don't like to educate women). They come in rags, and so dirty. You couldn't imagine. They're very little. A boy of fourteen doesn't seem more than ten. And they don't speak Spanish, but the woman teacher is teaching in Spanish, teaching the young people Peru's national anthem (and remember that the Vicosinos don't know that they are living in a country that's called Peru, or who is President, or that the country has a President). But the little ones are very lovely and I like them a lot. They seem very friendly to me. They're always laughing and playing. You ought to see them. The school cooks a lunch for the pupils at noon, but they have to wash their hands before eating, and then they have to wash their plates after eating. They don't know anything about cleaning up and so they get wet and leave streaks of soap, but they don't forget to fix their hair! And when Allan and I visited the school the pupils tried to clean themselves even better to "show off."

The image of Sarah Levy riding horseback over the Andean heights has its libidinal implications but it is also an image of an imperialist "modernizer"riding Peru with the aim of "rationalizing" those backward schoolchildren who, dressed "in rags, and so dirty," do not even know what country they are living in. However, as I have noted, racism and colonialism are also libidinal. We should not judge her harshly for the latent, i.e., unconscious, content of her letter, but it is noteworthy that she was as ignorant of who those schoolchildren were and how they were formed historically in Peru as they were of the foreign language in which their teacher was attempting to instruct them. With regard to the "dirty" children, it would seem that the power of modernity had not yet filtered into their small bodies, so that they might fulfill the condition of "health and physical well-being of populations" which "comes to figure as a political objective which the 'police' of the social body must ensure along with those of economic regulation and the needs of order," in order to display "the imperative of health: at once the duty of each and the objective of all" (Foucault 1980:170-171). As a feminist, however, Levy did notice that "the Indians don't like to educate women."

Her complete rejection of Frank Nolan as a "*pendejo*" has also to be an assertion of her own adherence to a work ethic, and perhaps a reaction formation opposed to the pleasures in which Nolan was indulging; and while Levy admits that "I'm not working very much," she presents evidence of great activity. And, after all, she has only recently arrived in Peru and has been in Vicos all of five days, so she deserves forgiveness for accomplishing little. It should be noted that her attitude toward Nolan has formed on the basis of her situation: an adjunct research appointee, a woman, and a Jew, competing for a permanent faculty appointment with a tenure-track, male gentile. Levy finds it "very difficult for me not to blow my top, but I must have patience," which amounts to an admission that she feels she must exert self-control in order to hold her rage in. What may have precipitated that rage? Although we cannot say for certain, we know that Levy was suddenly called away from home and on-going research in Ithaca, to take up the work in Vicos–doubtlessly by a hope for continuing employment, scholarly success, as well as duty and fear of her superiors. These are sufficient grounds for anger, without searching for earlier reactions to parental orders, although something of the repetition phenomenon seems likely. Levy, at any rate, is searching for the "courage" she found on horseback in Central Park. She asserts, "I don't think I'll ever have 'the shakes' again.'" At the same time, she says, "I am sick at heart" when she thinks of the work that Nolan is incapable of performing and that she will have to do. Perhaps her heart hurts, too, upon the occasion of directing her gaze at Nolan, not-working, the *"pendejo* [who] is a *pendejo,"* such a terrible sight, so unspeakable that *words fail her* and she can only repeat the same word, *"pendejo."* Since this is a recurring knot in Levy's narratives, the "unspeakable" is worth emphasizing. Nicolas Abraham and Maria Torok (1994:128-129) suggest:

> Because our mouth is unable to say certain words and unable to formulate certain sentences, we fantasize, for reasons yet to be determined, that we are actually taking into our mouth the unnamable, the object itself. As the empty mouth calls out in vain to be filled with introjective speech, it reverts to being the food-craving mouth it was prior to the acquisition of speech. Failing to feed itself on words to be exchanged with others, the mouth absorbs in fantasy all or part of a person–the genuine depository of what is now nameless. The crucial move away from introjection (clearly rendered impossible) to incorporation is made when *words* fail to fill the subject's void and hence an imaginary thing is inserted into the mouth in their place. The desperate ploy of filling the mouth with illusory nourishment has the equally illusory effect of eradicating the idea of a void to be filled with words. We may conclude that, in the face of both the urgency and the impossibility of performing one type of mouth-work– speaking to someone about what we have lost–another type of mouth-work is utilized, one that is imaginary and equipped to deny the very existence of the entire problem.[9]

Bourdieu (1993:51-52) says:

> One of the important properties of a field lies in the fact that it implicitly

defines "unthinkable" things, things that are not even discussed. There's orthodoxy and heterodoxy, but there is also doxa, everything that goes without saying, and in particular the systems of classification determining what is judged interesting or uninteresting, the things that no one thinks worthy of being mentioned, because there is no *demand*. . . . It's important to wonder about these things that no one says, when one wants to do the social history of social science, if one wants to do something more than distribute praise and blame. It's not a question of setting oneself up as a judge, but of understanding why these people could not understand certain things, could not raise certain problems, of determining what are the social conditions of error–necessary error, inasmuch as it is the product of historical conditions, determinations. In the "goes-without-saying" of a particular period, there is the *de jure* unthinkable (the politically unthinkable, for example, what is unnameable, taboo, the problems that cannot be dealt with–and also the *de facto* unthinkable, the things that the intellectual tools of the day do not make it possible to think.

Levy's statement that "I'm feeling better than I felt up to now" also merits some comment. It suggests that during her first days in Vicos she had not felt well. This, in all likelihood would have been due to the hypoxia, known as *sorroche*, from which many newcomers to high altitude suffer. On the basis of observations of myself and others adapting to life at high altitudes, I believe it is highly relevant here to point out that, in addition to the physiological changes that come with exposure to a new and very different physical environment, well documented by Baker and Little (1976), and considering the sensory and cognitive overload created by exposure to a new and very different social environment, significant character changes in persons also occur. The latter response has been called "culture shock."[10] Roy Wagner (1981:6-7) identifies this disorder:

In [culture shock] the local "culture" first manifests itself to the anthropologist through his [sic] own *inadequacy*; against the backdrop of his new surroundings it is he who has become "visible." The situation has some parallels within our own society: the freshman first entering college, the new army recruit, and anyone else who is compelled to live in "new" or alien surroundings, all have had some taste of this kind of "shock." Typically the sufferer is depressed and anxious, he may withdraw into himself, or grasp at any chance to communicate with others. To a degree that we seldom realize, we depend upon the participation of others in our lives, and upon our own participation in the lives of others. Our success and effectiveness as persons is based upon this participation, and upon an ability to maintain a controlling competence in communicating with others. Culture shock is a loss of the self through the loss of these supports.

Persons newly arrived in the Andes may exhibit hypomania, mild to moderate depression, and mild to moderate paranoia. Some individuals carry on with their work, and after a few weeks or months appear unimpaired. Others are unable to perform as effectively as they can at sea level. And a few are unable to perform at all and, after trying for a while, leave the heights to seek alternative research or administrative possibilities. Hypoxia and culture shock are mutually reinforcing: rapid movement causes breathlessness and panic, and one searches for something that is "wrong" in one's surroundings. The Andes can, thus, turn one seemingly into a "completely different person."

Hypoxia could make Levy's "look, I'm going through the heights of the Andes, crossing creeks and rivers and steep slopes and abysses on horseback and I wasn't at all afraid," something of a cover for, if not a hypomanic defense against, other adaptation difficulties. Levy tended to stay close to the Vicos Project quarters, unless she was accompanied by someone like Enrique Luna, and she avoided gross culture shock by less frequent interaction with Vicosinos. As it turned out, she was unable to avoid interpersonal friction with Peruvians. You have already had the opportunity to read about her intolerance for Nolan, and you will read more about her problems with others.

In her next letter–this one in English–, dated July 23, 1953, Levy "musters the strength to write." She does not berate Nolan as harshly for his failure to perform, except for references to him and Quiller "drunk as hoot owls" and the two of them "drinking themselves blind," but complains that she "felt like the wrath of God all day." It is worthy of note that instead of asserting, "the water is contaminated," she says that she *does not trust* it. Might this be an indication of some sense of the physical environment as potentially unstable and threatening?

> The last letter I received from you said that you hadn't heard from me since I arrived in Vicos. However, I have written several times so I hope you have received *cartas* [letters] from me by now.
> There is much to describe. The last few days have been very hectic, and after a forlorn dinner at which only Cliff [Clifford R. Barnett], Mario [Mario C. Vázquez], I, and the kitchen staff were present, I am mustering the strength to write. The rest of the borachos [*borrachos*, drunks] were in bed, drunk as hoot owls.
> It all began on Monday. That was the day we dedicated the new grade school at Vicos. Two *ministros* [officials from government ministries] came. One of them was *padrino* [godfather] and I was *madrina* [godmother]. I got all dressed up in a clean suit, stockings, heels, the

works, including makeup which I never wear here. The two ministers arrived at 20 minutes before 9, 20 minutes earlier than they were expected, which is unheard of, as you know, in Latin America where all events are two hours later than scheduled. They came in about a half a dozen cars with about 30 people in their party. They had left another 30 behind in Chancos [3 kilometers below Vicos on the way to Marcará], all suffering from sirroche [i.e., *sorroche*] because they were unaccustomed to the altitude. The *maestra* [woman schoolteacher] and the *maestro* [man schoolteacher] had the school kids lined up since about 8 o'clock, as ragged a bunch of sufferers as you would ever want to see. Poor kids, they were on their feet–and bare feet at that–for more than an hour waiting for everything to be over. Mario made a speech, the *ministro* made a speech, the director of public schools for this district made a speech, and a few more people made speeches. The priest read prayers and made a speech. Then the school kids sang the *Himno Nacional* [National Anthem], but *más o menos* [more or less] if you know what I mean. As a matter of fact, in his speech the *ministro* said that he was very gratified to see that whereas a year ago these Indian children had not even a vague idea of the national anthem, this year they knew it and sang it "*casi bien*" [almost well]. The *maestro* was horrified at this slight. In fact, the next day he asked me if I would come to the school and play the tune with my recorder while he attempted to instruct the kids better. I said I would be glad to. The kids were really pretty good. I think there must be lots of school kids their age back home who don't know all of the Star Spangled Banner, no?

Anyway, the occasion was an excuse for a fiesta at Vicos. Nobody worked all day. We imported a caterer from a nearby town and after the ceremony at ten o'clock in the morning, *fíjate* [look]!, he served champagne cocktails, martinis, and manhattans, with hors d'oeuvres. All the dignitaries drank numerous *saludes* [toasts; "*¡Salud!*" means "to your health!"], and ate numerous hors d'oeuvres. We drove with a few of the visitors to Caraz, about 40 miles away, to see their town, and there they had another party, also with numerous *saludes*. Only this time it was beer. Again everyone made a flowery speech at the slightest provocation. I stuck close to the priest because I thought I'd have a better chance to lay off the liquor. But he drank more than anyone. The way they do it here is that someone thinks of a toast to something or other, stands up and makes a speech, everyone hollers "*salud*," and then you have to drain your glass empty and turn it upside down, whether it is beer, or wine, or a cocktail, or whatever. There never is any whisky which is the only drink I can comfortably drain at one swallow. I finally caught on that you can fake it by just touching your lips to the glass and grinning, but until I discovered this I had drunk champagne, martinis, beer, and pisco, and had a pretty bad *dolor del estómago* [stomach ache].

By the time we got back to Vicos for lunch, the Indians were pretty drunk and whooping it up. They marched around to the back door with drums and homemade bamboo flutes and called us out to dance. We danced the *huayno*. It's easy. You just sort of march about and bob up and down without any reference to anyone else, just being careful not to trip over the stones, because the terrain of the plaza is by no means like a dance floor. We took motion pictures of the dancing, including ourselves behaving like idiots. I didn't want to dance at first, but one of the old *mayorales* [Vicosino leaders of work parties] grabbed my hands and was insistent that I dance with him, so I started marching around rather sedately until I caught the spirit of the thing. Then I was as active as anybody.

This turned out to be a bit too strenuous for me [i.e., the effects of hypoxia], however, so I grabbed my recorder and joined the flute section. The men were quite interested in my instrument, although it's no match for theirs. They play about twice as loud and shrill as a fife. One of the old guys showed me how to manage the *caña* [perhaps a reference to the Andean cane flute, never referred to as a "*caña*!], and then I joined in with that. We moved away from the *casa de hacienda* [guest quarters and community center] and settled down in front of the church. There we had more dancing and more music, me still with the flute section playing Bach. Somebody broke out a bottle of pisco and somebody else found a shot glass, the greasiest, dirtiest glass I've ever seen. They passed the glass around for everyone to take a swig. When it came to me, I refused, but the cook who was with me said I ought to drink with them. I gritted my teeth and got it down, but I also saw the spirochetes and intestinal worms dancing around the glass. I only hoped that the alcohol would kill them before they settled comfortably in my stomach.

The fiesta lasted all night for the bitter-enders. I stuck with the flute section until supper time, but then withdrew because I was so beat.

I forgot to mention one thing about the ceremony. It seems that an essential piece of equipment for such dedications is a pair of satin ribbons, one red, one white, representing the colors of Peru. Nobody can even imagine what would happen if anything were ever dedicated without these ribbons. Of course it turned out when the great day approached that we had forgotten to buy some. It got pretty desperate until Enrique, the administrator of the hacienda, commandeered one of the cars which brought the dignitaries, sped into the nearest town, Marcará, and sped back again with the ribbons Everything went all right after that.

Well, that seemed like a lot of fiesta to me. It distresses me that I can't get anyone to do any real work, they're so busy drinking and dancing. But yesterday was the birthday of Alirio [reference to Aliro Almandoz], the handyman of the Hacienda and a pretty nice guy. What happened was that Mario and Enrique and [*Patricio] Gutiérrez, one of our project men, came back around 9 o'clock with Chinese firecrackers. I hadn't been feeling too well all day, so after dinner I had taken two aspirins and put on my pajamas, and was sitting in front of the fireplace with the idea of going to bed when the boys came back with the firecrackers. At ten I put on a skirt and rolled up the legs of my pajamas, and we all went to Alirio's house where the boys started to light the firecrackers. In a minute it looked, sounded, and smelled like a battlefield. Alirio and his wife were in bed, but they got dressed and came out. Before you knew it, the *maestra* and a friend of hers, the *maestro*, *Roberto's [Roberto Mendoza, a Peruvian field worker for the Vicos Project] last year's girl with the baby she had by him, and a few other unidentified people had all turned up at Alirio's and were drinking more *saludes*. Somebody broke out a guitar and the music and dancing started again. The *sala* [livingroom] in Alirio's home is a fair sized room, made out of mud and whitewashed. There are about three rickety chairs, a pile of potatoes in one corner, a cat in a basket with new kittens in another. Some sitting places are against the wall, made out of mud or rock and covered with a poncho. There are shelves high up on the wall with cooking utensils and junk on them (very meager and very poor). No light or heat, so we sent back to the hacienda for coleman lanterns and a kerosene stove. This time the liquor was either sweet vermouth or something called "*wasi-wasi*" [*huashco*, alcohol mixed with water?] which in my opinion is raw alcohol, so I was stuck with the sweet vermouth. Clearly, I couldn't drain a glass of that stuff, so I clutched one glass all night and at every *salud* I just touched my lips to it. This wasn't as easy as it sounds, either, because there were only about three glasses, and they had to do for everyone, so for me to keep a glass to myself all night was quite a feat.

At midnight we brought the whole party back to the casa hacienda for bacon and eggs, and then began singing, dancing, and speech making. George [Rogers, the Cornell anthropologist who was in charge of the Vicos Project at the time, and with whom Levy came to Vicos] made a speech of thanks to Alirio for his good work during the year. Again I was *madrina*, this time of a 500 sol note as a gift to Alirio from all of us. After George's speech, Mario made one. Then the *maestro*, then the *maestra*, then everyone else bobbed up and down to get in his oration, including the *saludes*. The gringos got together in one corner and sang barbershop harmony which the *maestra* said, in all sincerity, enchanted her. Then the Latinos started to sing. The *maestro* went back to his room and broke out a notebook in which he had copied Indian songs he had picked up here and there, so I brought out the recorder and played while the rest sang. They were very lovely, plaintive work songs which I plan to copy before I leave. Then someone turned on the radio and caught a corny dance orchestra from Lima playing tunes popular in the thirties, so Cliff and I showed them some steps of that vintage, which again "enchanted" everyone. Then Latin music and *huaynos*. Then Alirio asked one of the women to rhumba with him (he's damned good at it) and they danced. The singing and dancing went on till about two, when a few less hardy souls conked out, and then the remainder of the party adjourned again to Alirio's house, this time with guitar music and singing.

I must say I had a helluva good time until about 4:30 a.m. when I decided to go to bed. The bitter-enders stayed up all night without one bit of sleep and were at work again this morning until lunch. (I forgot to say that at 4 a.m. we had a full chicken dinner.) At lunch Alirio invited all of us again to his house. The table was set in the patio. With chickens running around, large cow turds lying in the yard, and Indians wandering through every now and then, God knows why. Again the *saludes*. A very good lunch which I could hardly eat, except it was too good to resist, consisting of chicken soup with *trigo* [wheat] in it, and *cuy*–that's guineapig–fried, seasoned mainly with *aji* [hot pepper] and served with further seasoned potatoes. By this time my stomach was rebelling, as you can imagine, but I managed to put away the food although I refused to drink either the sweet vermouth or the *wasi-wasi* or the raw pisco. I stuck to beer. But I have had diarrhea all day and couldn't do a bit of work, although I haven't been as bad off as Cliff who's been running to the john every half hour. George and I got away shortly after lunch, but Pete [Quiller] and Frank [Nolan] stayed on drinking themselves blind. At one point I looked out the window and saw Pete climb on a horse without a saddle, but I didn't pay much attention, thinking he was going somewhere. Later the cook told me that he was goading it till it threw him. He climbed back on and it threw him again. Everyone was out cold all day, and even now George just got up (it's nine at night). Frank and Pete are still in bed. God knows how Alirio, Enrique, and Alirio's wife are, to say nothing of the maestro and Gutiérrez. When I saw those two last they were snoring away in the *sala* covered with a joint poncho.

I must say that the fiesta last night was a helluva lot of fun, but I'm not sure it was worth the loss of a day's work, and I certainly couldn't carry it through today the way the rest of the boys did, nor would I want to. I think it served a purpose in a way, since I now have some pretty good friends among the mestizos and also among the Indians. The mestizos say I am a *chola* [urbanized "peasant" woman], which means just like a Peruvian. The Indians say I am very Vicosina, which means like a Vicos Indian. But I felt like the wrath of God all day and only now do I feel somewhat recovered.

I forgot to mention that yesterday morning I had been out riding the rounds with Enrique, about four hours on a pretty tough trail and under a sun so hot and beating on top of my head, and eating the dust his horse kicked up–I ride behind him, obviously--, and unable to take a drink because I don't trust the water, and without a bit of shade anywhere. I thought I would drop, and the only thing that kept me upright was the thought of the Indians who had to work threshing wheat on the top of the mountain while all I had to do was sit on a horse and let him carry me.

Today is the 23rd, only five days before the 28th when everything stops cold and people celebrate Peru's independence day. There will be bullfights in Carhuaz, which I want to attend immediately after I finish being *madrina* of the volleyball net at the primary school in Marcará. It will be impossible to get any work done at all for at least two days, the 28th and the 29th, so the next few days we'll have to get on the ball. I expect Frank and Pete to be hung over tomorrow again, so that leaves it up to me. I wouldn't mind, if only they'd lay off the field crew and let them keep sober enough to do a day's work. Well, let's see what happens. Forgive me for writing so long a letter, but I have made a carbon and it is as much a record for me as it is a letter to you. I hear that New York is suffering a heat wave and, Rosita, I'm glad you're out of the city and close to the lake. I take it that you're not working too hard, and I hope it doesn't get on your nerves. How is the [research] report? More specifically, where is it? I miss you all, and my animal family too. My little partridge died the day after he was given to me. Enrique's dog follows me around, the rangiest goddamned filthiest animal I have ever had nuzzle his wet nose into my hand, with a broken leg that never healed properly so he limps, who recently got over some kind of sickness which meant he couldn't eat so every rib sticks out, and with a tumor on his neck. He is such a pitiful animal that I can't find the heart to kick him away or throw him out. All he wants is to be loved, and he is the most unlovable animal I have ever seen. Poor beast.

Write to me. Everybody got about a half dozen letters today except me. I got none. Makes me feel like an outcast. Bless you all, Sarah.

In this letter Levy's complaints become more generalized.. She has stomach problems: "my stomach was rebelling," "I have had diarrhea all day." And this despite her attempts to avoid drinking. Her work ethic nags at her: she says, "it seemed like a lot of fiesta to me" because its consequence was distress that "I can't get anyone to do any real work"; and while "the fiesta last night was a helluva lot of fun . . . I'm not sure it was worth the loss of a day's work." She feels she should be working, not indulging in pleasure, to the point where she resists and even resents pleasure, "fun."

The sun is hot. She must eat the dust Enrique Luna's horse kicks up: as a woman, "I ride behind him, obviously." And, of course, Frank and Pete will be hung over which means "that leaves it up to me." What stands out in Levy's text is the positioning of her characterization of Enrique Luna's dog, "the rangiest [possibly this is a slip of the pen for "mangiest"] goddamned filthiest animal," "the most unlovable animal I have ever seen," but so "pitiful" that "I can't find the heart to kick him away or throw him out," when "all he wants is to be loved," and her own failure to receive mail, when "everybody got about a half dozen letters except me," which makes her feel like an "outcast," possibly as unloved and unlovable as the dog. I will also note that while Levy usually refers to almost everybody connected with the work at Vicos by their first names–Enrique, George, Mario, Frank, Pete–the Methodology Project's data gatherers are often referred to as "the boys" or by their last names. Why are they not "men," and why cannot Gutiérrez be called "Patricio"? Levy clarifies her attitude later in the correspondence. But, meanwhile, there is her letter–in Spanish–of July 30, 1953 to examine:

Yesterday we went to the bullfight in Huaraz. The day began badly with a "mixup" in transportation. Mario went first to get two girls–sisters whose names are Susa, the younger one, and Rosario, the one who is in love with Pete but he doesn't like her. We, the two Blanchards [William C., or Bill, and Max, the Vicos Project's Field Director and wife who had arrived in Vicos on July 24, recently appointed for a two-year period], *Frank, Pete, and I, were in the Jeep. We went to Marcará, hoping that Mario would be there waiting for us. We had to pick up Enrique and his wife, and with the two cars we hoped that there would be enough places. But what happened was that Mario went in his car with the two girls, and that Enrique had invited his sister, Doña Juana, and Gutiérrez. So there were ten of us in one Jeep when Mario had no more than three in his car. Clearly it could not be like that, and so the Blanchards and Nolan stayed in Marcará, and seven went on to the bullfight in the Jeep. This car jumps like a burro, and the roads are bad, and I almost died till we arrived* ["*arivamos*"] *in Huaraz, 40 miles* [actually 40 kilometers] *from Marcará. As Enrique said, if I had not had cusionings I would have been dead.*

When we arrived [this time "*llegamos*"] *in Huaraz, we looked for our "box." This box was nothing more than some sticks, in two floors, one above and the other below. We went into the box above. When I looked at this box, I had the thought that it didn't appear very secure and that there was no way to estimate the weight that happened next. And look what happened. The bullfight began and after more or less five minutes– phhttt!–the box broke and everybody above including me fell down. Everybody below were squashed and pounded. The women screamed, the children cried, and I was afraid of panic in the crowd. Enrique "took over" and controlled the situation, giving orders, getting people out, etc. Nobody was hurt, fortunately, but there sure was a lot of damage. I had a place on top of one of the corral's posts, with my legs hanging inside the corral. So the first bull was killed directly under my legs. That made me dizzy. It was nasty, a savagery. These "matadors" were butchers! They had to cut this bull's throat because the sword didn't kill it.*

They continued with this nastiness until the last bull came in. I liked one of the matadors, a young man about 20 years old. He made some passes at this bull and was hit by the bull's horns. People yelled and whistled. Then this matador took off his jacket and came in again in his shirt. He was hot and he began to fight with the bull, walking and stepping like a storm. When he had to pick the bull with bandilleros [i.e., *banderillas*], *he broke the bandilleros on his knee and scraped the points against the side of the corral, until the bandilleros were half their original size. Then with his hands tied together* ["*amarradas con una ligatura*"], *and with these short bandilleros, he thrust the bandilleros into the bull's back. It was very exciting. And then he thrust his sword up to his fist–he was the only one who did this. The others only pricked the bull with their swords and they had to cut the bull's throat to kill it. This young man had a lot of courage and great spirit but, poor man, he was hurt very badly. I still haven't seen a newspaper to see how he is. But I* wish I had his telephone number.

In any case it's difficult for me to understand the mentality of people who like this form of "esport." It seems to me like butchery. There's a lot of blood and cruelty. Maybe, if I'd been able to see a more professional bullfight, I'd value it more, but this bullfight was terrible in my estimation. Nevertheless, the people enjoyed it a lot, the women screamed and applauded the same as the men.

Listen, Rosita, we have to return here some day together, because I know without a doubt that you would enjoy it quite well. It's not yet too late to make plans.

Well, I'm happy that Gorgon [her dog] *is better now and that Ming* [another dog] *is feeling better. Thanks for taking care of them for me. I have a bird as a* "pet" *now. An Indian brought a little partridge no more than two days old, and here it is now inside a basket, with its nest of Kleenex that I have made. But it doesn't want to eat anything. I forced its mouth open and put in water with an eyedroppper. The Indians say that it's going to escape or die, because partridges can't be domesticated. I hope not. I haven't yet given a name to the bird but if it lives I'll call it "Rosita."*

Thanks for taking care of my bills. I don't know what you should do about the matter of Margaret and her car. I've sent a check in my last letter to you. So cash it for about $100 and use that money to pay her and any person to whom I owe money. And if you need money, use it. Here one can't spend anything! If I lived here two or three more months I could be rich!

Have patience with Art and Bert [*Arthur Silver and *Bertram Post, two of the senior sociologists at Cornell]. *According to what I've seen here, they aren't the only ones who are pendejos and it's no business of yours if they don't know what to do with the work* [the research Levy had to leave in order to go to Vicos?] *Do what you can and don't be bothered and don't worry about their work. This is their own business and not yours. No?*

Write me, because I'm happy to hear from you and about my family. I'm pleased that the dears from the house at the side of the street are visiting you because I like them a lot, and I was always happy to see them, and I always got out something for the children to eat, like a piece of candy or a "cookie," *or chocolate cigarettes, or whatever I had in the house. They're very friendly, aren't they? Even though the mother is impossible.*

Well, "chao" as Peruvians say, or better "chaocito." That's a little chao. It means "so long." *Kisses, S.*

> *P.S. Look at me giving instructions to students from the University of*
> *San Marcos who are working for our project in Spanish! I don't know*
> *how to speak, as you say, but I try, and I don't know how, but I can*
> *communicate with them. Poor boys, it could be that their heads ache*
> *trying to understand me.*

In her postscript Levy recognizes her problems with Spanish, which do not seem insuperable to me. Why would she be concerned that she is a "headache" to others? To the young male field workers of the Methodology Project? Is she sensing their misogyny? The big event in her letter, however, consists of her trip to Huaraz in an overcrowded jeep to witness the bullfights. She has mixed feelings about them. In one way they are "a nastiness," "*un* savagery," and "it is hard for me to understand the mentality" of those who like them. Her gaze takes in "a lot of blood and cruelty." At the same time, in the case of the matador she liked, her feeling that "it was very exciting" slips through, and she says in English, "I wish I had his telephone number." She employs the epithet "*pendejos*" to mask her fear of the superiors at Cornell, the ones who ripped her from her home and her ongoing work to send her to Vicos to be the lone woman researcher and where her status is not clearly defined, where she finds it difficult to perform according to her work ethic, and where she must deal with drunks, diarrhea, and unlovable dogs who need love. I am intrigued by the positioning of "butchers" who "slit the throat" [would this involve her self-image as a woman with a slit, as opposed to the phallic knife-wielding "butchers"] close to Arthur Silver and Bertram Post, who will decide her professional future at Cornell. She admires, to the point of wishing for his telephone number, the brave young matador who was "hurt" by the bull he successfully put down. This was the "exciting" part of what otherwise was "a nastiness."

We can feel certain that Levy's attitudes toward her fellow North Americans appeared and were perceived, whether or not she tried to hide them. Relations between her and this group of male misogynists had to be stamped by a male assertion of her proper place as a "dissatisfied" woman who should "know better." It may be that the all-male staff had achieved or was achieving what Kate Millett (2000:49-50) refers to as the "phallic state" of "men's house culture," before Levy "intruded" herself, in which "[t]he tone and ethos . . . is sadistic, power-oriented, and latently homosexual, frequently narcissistic in its energy and motives." In her next letter–in English–, written on August 1, 1953, in which she recounts how "the lid blew off," she tells us something about gender relations in North America and her own womanly rage:

Well, the lid blew off tonight. I don't know what happened, whether George was drunk or just sadistic, but he lit into me for no reason that I can discern. He said: "I told you that it would be like this but you didn't believe me." "Like what?" "That you wouldn't like it here, that things would go the way they are." "What things? How are they going?" "That you wouldn't be able to design your study."

I just can't understand why on earth George would say that. In the first place, I have always said, and honestly, that I love it in Vicos, that I have never had such comfortable field conditions, etc., etc. In the second place, for the past two weeks I have been most pleased about the way the study is going, and feel that Frank and I have ironed out our difficulties, even if we don't agree. That is, even if we disagree we are both talking about the same thing for the first time since the study began. As far as I can see, George's statement was based on absolutely no fact at all but just on what he supposes is the case, or what he wishes were the case, or God knows what.

Another thing he said to me is "you're plastered." I hadn't even had a single drink! I had made martinis for everyone, but had given mine up. George made the second round, and I had drunk exactly one martini! I certainly wasn't lit in the slightest degree!

I blew my top and left the table, finishing my dinner in the kitchen. I even shed a few tears of outrage.

I don't know what to do. My impulse is to leave here and move to Chancos [where a hotel had been built near the Chancos hot springs and was in operation at the time]. If I could have a horse, I could make it back and forth to Vicos. What disturbs me is what the hell people would think. I mean the boys. Coshta and Agustín [Vicosinos who helped project staff around the house] were in on the whole blow-up, and I suppose tomorrow it will be all around Vicos, anyway, so it wouldn't make much difference if I actually got out.

A second difficulty in moving to Chancos is that the lines of authority between me and Frank and Pete are so ambiguous. If I am not actually on the spot here, I haven't even the slightest idea of how things would be handled. I could finesse myself out of the so-called field work and concentrate on drawing up the questionnaire–but how the hell am I going to have access to the boys' field notes and impressions if I don't have access to the boys?

I am absolutely baffled. I don't know what to do or how to handle this situation, or why it occurred, or what on earth it was that makes George think I don't like Vicos or I'm not pleased with the way the study is going. Of course he has succeeded now in taking all the savor and gusto out of the place for me. I feel like a goddam fool since I never even had the slightest suspicion that I wasn't welcome here, or that he felt I disliked it–or whatever the hell is on his mind which I, for one, can't even begin to fathom!

I guess my best bet is to inspect Chancos tomorrow and see if I can rent

> a horse and get an alarm clock. I suppose that Mario could pick me up
> every morning, for that matter, just as he picks up the boys, and return me
> at night the way he does them. Why not? Just public relations and lines
> of authority. How the hell do I decide this dilemma?
> I shall write the survey and then beat it.

Here Levy is able to focus anger ("I blew my top . . . I even shed a few
tears of outrage") on George Rogers, whom she accuses of "being drunk
or just sadistic." In his criticism of Levy, and especially in his prediction
of her failure, Rogers was asserting the patriarchal "Law of the Father,"
the well known Lacanian "*'Non' du père*" in the "*Nom du père*," (the
father's "no" in the father's name), under which Judith Butler (1993:153)
states:

> Enduring and viable identity is thus purchased through subjection to and
> subjectivation by the patronym. But because this patronymic line can
> only be secured through the ritual exchange of women, there is required
> for women a certain shifting of patronymic alliance and, hence, a change
> of name. For women, then, propriety is achieved through having a
> changeable name, through the exchange of names, which means that the
> name is never permanent, and that the identity secured through the name
> is always dependent on the social exigencies of paternity and marriage.
> Expropriation is thus the condition of identity for women.

Levy seems not to have been fully conscious of the implications of
Rogers's scolding, but in her relentless pursuit of "symbolic capital,"
critical insistence on the production of work, hard-lined promotion of
structured sociological method, and refusal to exchange her patronymic,
"sociologist," she was disobeying his "Law." Rogers, in turn and
undoubtedly unconsciously, by depreciating her was exercising not
insignificant symbolic violence. Bourdieu (2000b:50) notes: "By
understanding 'symbolic' as opposed to real and effective, we suppose
symbolic violence to be a purely 'spiritual' violence and actually without
real effects. This ingenuous distinction, typical of a primary materialism,
is what the materialist theory of the economy of symbolic goods . . . tends
to destroy, allowing the objectivity of the subjective experience of
domination to occupy its theoretical space." Symbolic violence has real
effects: "Symbolic force is a form of power which is exercised directly
upon bodies and as though by magic, at the margin of any physical
coercion; but this magic only operates by basing itself on certain
dispositions, as if they were keys to the deepest parts of bodies. If it is
capable of acting like a *trigger*, that is, with an extremely low expenditure
of energy, it is because it is limited to freeing dispositions which the labors

of inculcation and assimilation have carried out in those males or females who, thanks to that fact, give it nurture. In other words, symbolic intertwining finds conditions for its realization, and its economic (in the wide sense of the word) counterpart, in the immense labor that has gone on before which is necessary for the operation of a lasting transformation of bodies and the production of permanent dispositions which it frees and awakens; an action of transformation all the more powerful to the extent that it is exercised, essentially, in an invisible and insidious manner, through insensible familiarization with a physical world that is symbolically structured and through precocious and prolonged experience in interactions penetrated by structures of domination" (54-55). In this way we can establish a context in which to view both Rogers's and Levy's extreme reaction to an extreme and permanent provocation.

Millett (2000:32-33) places Levy's insurgency in the context of masculine-feminine "sexual politics": "The arbitrary character of patriarchal ascriptions of temperament and role has little effect upon their power over us. . . . Politically, the fact that each group exhibits a circumscribed but complementary personality and range of activity is of secondary importance to the fact that each represents a status or power division. In the matter of conformity patriarchy is a governing ideology without peer; it is probable that no other system has ever exercised such a complete control over its subjects." The letter is best interpreted in the light of Adrienne Rich's (1986:40) strong statement of male feelings:

> The ancient, continuing envy, awe, and dread of the male for the female capacity to create life has repeatedly taken the form of hatred for every other female aspect of creativity. Not only have women been told to stick to motherhood, but we have been told that our intellectual or aesthetic creations were inappropriate, inconsequential, or scandalous, an attempt to become "like men," or to escape from the "real" tasks of adult womanhood: marriage and childbearing. To "think like a man" has been both praise and prison for women trying to escape the body-trap. No wonder that many intellectual and creative women have insisted that they were human beings first and women only incidentally . . . .

Levy's high standards are already apparent, as are her harsh judgments of anthropology and anthropologists–not without foundation. We do not know what Levy may have said or done to indicate to Rogers her very negative appraisal of his work and we also know little of Rogers's own pain. My reading of her narrative suggests that Sarah Levy also represented Roger's threatening superego to him, possibly a repetition of a generalized fear of women's judgments (and punishments) of him. The scene that she describes–really a "primal scene" for her, with all its implications of the abuse of women by men, and perhaps a repetition of patriarchal humiliations she had experienced many times earlier in her life–reveals a homosocial bonding on the part of the principal male actors in this drama, with its misrecognized homosexual-homophobic images, if not an outright oedipal compact not to attack each other but to attack Levy instead! This was not simply Rogers's problem. Not one of these principal researchers had been satisfying his own self-expectations in regard to research and scholarship in general, and they all knew this about each other. Thus, George Rogers may well have been listening to an other's language, and hearing a critical feeling he had about himself and his homosocial cohorts, which all had nothing to do with Levy, as well as allowing two martinis to liberate some general feelings of misogyny to focus on her. He and the other principals like almost all other men in the early 1950s were insensitive to the patriarchal atmosphere that pervaded North America, including North American academia. "At the core of patriarchy," Rich (1979:78-79) states, "is the individual family unit with its division of roles, its values of private ownership, monogamous marriage, emotional possessiveness, the 'illegitimacy' of a child born outside legal marriage, the unpaid domestic services of the wife, obedience to authority, judgment, and punishment for disobedience. . . . The sacredness of the family in the patriarchy–sacred in the sense that it is heresy to question its ultimate value–relieves the titular head of it from any real necessity to justify his behavior." Allan Johnson (1997:84-85) describes such patriarchal "family values" in terms of a culture:

> Patriarchal culture includes ideas about the nature of things, including men, women, and humanity, with manhood and masculinity most closely associated with being human and womanhood and femininity relegated to the marginal position of "other." It's about how social life is and how it's supposed to be; about what's expected of people and about how they feel.
> It's about standards of feminine beauty and masculine toughness, images of feminine vulnerability and masculine protectiveness, of older men coupled with young women, of elderly women alone. It's about defining women and men as opposites, about the "naturalness" of male aggression, competition, and subordination. . . . Above all, patriarchal culture is about the core value of control and domination in almost every area of human existence. From the expression of emotion to economics to the natural environment, gaining and exercising control is a continuing goal of great importance. Because of this, the concept of power takes on a narrow definition of "power over"–the ability to control others, events, resources, or oneself in spite of resistance–rather than alternatives such as the ability to cooperate with others, to give freely of oneself, or to feel and

act in harmony with nature.

Trinh Minh-ha (1998:39-40) provides a much more biting commentary on the patriarchal image of "woman":

> Woman can never be defined. Bat, dog, chick, mutton, tart. Queen, madam, lady of pleasure, MISTRESS. *Belle-de-nuit*, woman of the streets, fruitwoman, fallen woman. Cow, vixen, bitch. Call girl, joy girl, working girl. Lady and whore are both bred to please. The old Woman image-repertoire says She is a Womb, a mere baby's pouch, or "nothing but sexuality." She is a passive substance, a parasite, an enigma whose mystery proves to be a snare and a delusion. She wallows in night, disorder, and immanence and is at the same time the "disturbing factor (between men) and the key to the beyond. The further the repertoire unfolds its images, the more entangled it gets in its attempts at capturing Her. "Truth, Beauty, Poetry–she is All: once more all under the form of the Other. All except herself", Simone De Beauvoir wrote. Yet, even with or because of Her capacity to embody All, Woman is the lesser man, and among male athletes, to be called a woman is still resented as the worst of insults.

Instead of being "All," and even while she is stirring cocktails for the men, Levy is a highly competent critic and rival. If the scene were being played now, at the turn of a new century, Rogers might have gained a greater sensitivity to the advances feminism has made and Levy might have acquired an assurance of her right to exist as her own woman in Vicos as well as an ability to defend herself better. Instead, unable to exit from the dominant patriarchal discourse, she appears to undergo a decompensation, a loss of defenses and consequent depression. She is like a rape victim, except that she has been violated symbolically and not physically. When she says, "I don't know . . . what on earth it was that makes George think I don't like Vicos," she is, in effect saying, "What have I done?" Nikos Papastergiadis (1998:155-156) illustrates these psychic processes eloquently in his discussion of how a raped woman always stands accused of provoking aggression:

> The effect of patriarchal ideology is thus projected as the cause of rape. Self-recrimination is accounted for in these terms: she provokes sexual aggressivity because the husky desire of being taken is already within her, and he [the rapist] both obliges by giving "it" to her and then punishes her for taking "it" from him. A cycle of vengeance and retribution. She wanted "it" and therefore deserved being violated. After the rape there is the further "self" punishment that comes from a sense of worthlessness, a feeling which follows the experience of appropriation, which is how the

rape began. The raping continues as it rebounds inside the memory of the act and against the consequences of the act itself. A murderous cycle of victimage and self-destruction begins with the expression, "I must have deserved it."

As you will see in the documents still to be examined, Sarah Levy's character is strong enough not to remain depressed. Later she experiences a re-compensation in which she acts out the role of patriarch (or matriarch–or could it be phallic mother?) the only one left to her by Rogers and the other dominant males of the two projects. As Rich (1979:80) says: "Within the patriarchal family, the maternal element has also been variously misread, distorted, and corrupted. We all know the ways in which maternal care and concern can turn into authoritarian control. It is a truism to say that the channeling of female energy into domesticity can produce overprotectiveness, overscrupulosity, possessiveness disguised as sacrifice, and much repressed and displaced anger." I can come to no other conclusion from my reading of these texts. However, the Sarah Levy I knew as a graduate student and research assistant at Cornell University before and after her trip to Vicos was kind, thoughtful, and generous with students, had a wry sense of humor, and was creative in the classroom. The only possible connection she could have had to tyranny would have been in the role of anti-tyrant.

The text of Levy's letter is marked by depression. Levy feels abandoned by Rogers, from whom she has expected caretaking, which perhaps "represents the insuperable trauma inflicted by the discovery–doubtless a precocious one and for that very reason impossible to work out–of the existence of a *not-I*" (Kristeva 1989:241). And, as I have suggested already, would it also represent for her a repetition of a "primary scene" of perceived paternal violence? From this point on, Rogers represents Otherness to her. She wishes to escape. She says, "My impulse is to leave here"; she plans to complete her work "and then beat it." But, she adds, "what disturbs me is what the hell people would think." Who are these "people?" Would they represent more than the staff people in Vicos, including probably the senior sociologists at Cornell, who are to decide on granting her a tenure-track position, and perhaps residues of parental figures in her own superego? Her statement, "I have been most pleased about the way the study is going, and feel that Frank and I have ironed out our difficulties, even if we don't agree," is a contradiction of what Levy has said about Nolan and what she is going to say in future letters; it represents a defensive position, which Levy badly needs at this point, more than the reality of the relations between the two. As for Nolan, we do not know whether or not he understands that he is finished at Cornell or whether he still hopes to remain there, but we can guess at his confusion upon Levy's arrival in Vicos, when he found himself demoted to "co-field director," with a woman (he seems to have been more comfortable in a patriarchal division of labor) and, probably, with a Jewish one at that. And we can also guess about Nolan's own hostility which finds a receptive target in Levy, so that the two are very likely engaging in a kind of negative reciprocity. Levy points to the ambiguity of "the lines of authority," and this in itself is corrosive to on-going research.

The expressed "impulse" to run away from Vicos contrasts starkly with Levy's statement, "I have always said, and honestly, that I love it in Vicos, that I have never had such comfortable field conditions." It is true that the *casa hacienda*, the two-storey building which was both Project and Hacienda headquarters, provided comforts unexpected in an Andean rural community. One of the first things Allan Holmberg did, after he took over the Hacienda Vicos in early 1952 was to employ the Hacienda labor force in rebuilding that central structure into residence and Project office, with living space for project personnel and guests upstairs, including a livingroom with a fireplace, bedrooms, kitchen and pantry, and even a toilet, and additional rooms downstairs.[11] Levy could not have found better physical surroundings elsewhere in the Callejón de Huaylas, except perhaps in the tourist hotel in Monterrey near Huaraz. But the point here is not the comforts offered by the *casa hacienda*. It has to do with Levy's desire to escape from her rage and fear.

In the next letter, that of August 5, 1953, evidence of depression continues:

> That very night Pete came up to explain what had happened. George was drunk. Pete says his problem is that he is worried about the project, that is, his own, that he is not really working but spends his time repairing equipment and his conscience bothers him, that he reproaches himself for not doing a real job, and when he is drunk he projects his own insecurity to others. I don't know. All I know is that I feel very unwelcome. George seems to me a completely different person. The day after this blow-up we had a picnic up in the hills–a *pachamanca*–and I had a miserable time. George had no recollection the next day of what had happened (he had stayed up very late drinking and picking on Cliff after I left the room) and behaved very cordially to me; but I simply couldn't look him in the eye. I felt as if he were a stranger to me. Pete said I had better forget about the whole thing, and I don't dare leave here to stay in the hotel because I'm afraid of the gossip that would spread around Vicos and I don't dare take the chance. But I am very uncomfortable here. Frank is a stupid man and is hell to work with. Pete who is nominally our assistant views Frank as his boss and does what Frank tells him (which is

nothing). The field workers are very confused–they get it from all ends and don't know what's going on. If it were up to Frank, we'd have very highbrow discussions all day and all night but no data. As a matter of fact, I have seen no field notes for over a week! The boys could be out drinking themselves silly every day for all I know.

I wish I could get out of here and chuck the whole study in Frank's lap, but I hate to do it because I really think he would end up with absolutely no data. Or, I wish he would get the hell out and leave me to handle it alone. The situation is very difficult as it is and I get more discouraged every day.

To be without a car is also very irritating. You know how I hate to be dependent on others, and without a Peruvian license (which I stupidly neglected to get in Lima) I don't dare use the project car which everyone else uses. Several times during the past 10 days Pete or Frank have gone off on trips to nearby towns and have not asked me along–which means I am stuck here, unable to move! I could, of course, request one or both of them to take me to Carhuaz or Huaraz, but I just won't! That means my only alternative is to hire a car, which I can do, but it's a big deal and requires planning in advance and a given destination, whereas I would just prefer to bum around a bit, aimlessly, just to look around without any real destination or purpose. I have another alternative, of course, and that is to make trips on the trucks that drive through the Callejón on their various routes. But I hate to do it alone since I don't know the country or the roads. But I think I shall do it sooner or later, if only to get a breathing spell away from these disagreeable people.

I can't convey to you how foolish I think Frank is in terms of research. This week, for example, he spent at least 3 hours lecturing our field workers in English (Pete translating in bad Spanish) on theories of integration, assessment of community, psychological adjustment, homogeneity and heterogeneity, anomie, etc. These boys, mind you, are between 24 and 28 years old. They are undergraduate students at a 10th rate university where their course of study is about 20 years behind the times and concentrates most strongly on Peruvian archaeology. It is as if I got a job as a laboratory assistant in Oak Ridge [site of early research in nuclear fission] which required me to measure the temperature of certain vessels; and instead of showing me how to use the thermometer my boss instead lectured me (in Greek) on the theory of nuclear fission and thermodynamics!!

Well I wouldn't mind his assininity so much if personal relations here weren't so strained that it's impossible to work. George left the day after our argument–for Lima, to attend to some affairs with the government. I am glad he's gone because, as I told you, he is a totally different person here than the guy I liked so much–just like a stranger whom I just met a week ago for the first time!!!

If it weren't for these jerks I'd love it here. I like the people, the staff, the country, the work–everything, in fact, except the goddam gringos who are impossible!!! In short, they have spoiled the trip, the country, and the

study for me and I am no longer happy here, anxious to get away from
here and from them.
I miss hearing from you. Much love, S.
PS. Enclosed picture shows me as *madrina* of the volleyball net on the
28 de julio [July 28, Peruvian Independence Day] in Marcará.

Here is more of depression and the repetition of old feelings: "I feel
very unwelcome," "I am very uncomfortable here," "I am stuck here,
unable to move," "it's impossible to work," and "I wish I could get out of
here," though getting out means that there would be nothing (Levy says
that getting out would mean that Frank, and the Methodology Project,
"would end up with absolutely no data"). Does this represent a suicidal
seduction? Levy "had a miserable time" at the picnic-*pachamanca* unable
to look Rogers in the eye. In Levy's eyes, George Rogers seems like a
stranger, "a totally different person here than the guy I liked so much," one
who is "not really working." Levy's loss of mobility "is irritating," but she
feels that she does not "dare leave here" (in contrast with her desire to run
away, expressed in the earlier letter). Frank Nolan is "stupid," "foolish,"
"hell to work with," and Pete Quiller "does nothing." Consequently, "the
field workers are very confused" and she has "seen no field notes for a
week." Levy "hates to be dependent on others" but "just won't" ask for
help. Nothing and nobody is working: it is like Levy is frozen to the spot.

Quiller is hardly the one to be assessing an alcohol problem; indeed, he
could be projecting aspects of his own character into Rogers. I recall
George Rogers as a very permissive person who did not like to intrude his
personal solutions into problems in working with others, sometimes to the
point of not offering warnings of impending danger. He had designed
research which involved massive "participant intervention" in Vicos life,
but I am not certain that he foresaw the moral dilemmas that he was to
experience upon setting the research in motion. So he hesitated, remained
uncertain, and sometimes avoided making decisions, though I remember
him once, near the end of his life, advising me, "Bill, don't worry about
your decision, just make it!" I also recall him telling the story of how he
had to fire one of his field directors for "acting like an *hacendado*,"
because the man made too many decisions, too easily. Rogers's
relationship with Levy, then, is not simple. Rogers may also have been
reflecting back to Levy the criticism Levy was unconsciously conveying to
him, a turn in their relationship against which Levy would have brought all
her defenses–although, as I have pointed out, people tended not to contest
the doxa of patriarchy in those times. We also have "hypoxia" to consider
as a part of these interpersonal frictions.

Levy's hostility takes the form of belittling attacks on the University of

San Marcos for being "10th rate" and "20 years behind the times," and providing inadequate training for "the boys," who turn out to be men in their middle and late twenties. In contrast, Nolan indulges in "highbrow discussions" with them through Quiller.

Levy dreams of being able to "bum around a bit, aimlessly, just to look around without any real destination or purpose," but is blocked because she does not "know the country or the roads." This may be a disguised critique of her own training to "work." Does it mean that she is less consciously pondering the origins of all these bad social relations in herself? But bad they are: "If it weren't for these jerks, I'd love it here." She likes everything "except the goddam gringos who are impossible."

In her next letter, Wednesday August 12, 1953, Levy only mutes her glee at the impending departure of Nolan and Rogers by her irritation at their relations with her:

Dear Rosita, My last letter was a sad one, no? Well this one is a mixed happy and sad one. Happy is that Frank and George are leaving Saturday for Lima, and Wednesday for the States. Don't ask me to tell you how Frank made his decision to leave. Nothing, but nothing has been done that warrants his leaving. The field work is not half-finished, the survey isn't even written. He is just fucking off and leaving me holding the bag. (I wish I had thought of it first.) I consider my job here to have been [research] design and nothing more. He was field man and was supposed to direct the field work. His notion of "directing field work," however, turns out to be to lecture these poor, uneducated, bewildered, non-English-speaking students in English, in terms that even graduate students at Cornell can scarcely be expected to understand, and these highbrow lectures, in turn, were translated into Spanish by poor Pete Quiller, whose Spanish, God knows, is limited enough! He has never gone over their notes with them, or suggested that Pete do so, for the purpose of training them, or criticizing their work, or approving it–apparently it never occurred to him they were supposed to do so–or made any effort to find out whether they were doing what they were supposed to do, or whether they understood the field task, or anything of the sort. As a result, I have leaped into what I considered to be a vacuum, and look at me! Left holding the bag on design and also on field work! I wish I didn't have such a pricking conscience, and could just tell him to go fuck himself and let the study conk out. The way it looks, I won't be able to leave here until the middle of October, if everything is to get done so that the whole summer will not have been a total loss. We have to finish the field tasks on qualitative investigation, also write the survey and train survey interviewers, get the survey moving and finished–and that will take until October 9th, the way I figure the calendar. I would like to take at least one side trip in Peru to see what the hell the country is like, which means, counting only 5 days or so, that I wouldn't be able to get back until the

15th!

I don't know what your schedule is, when you want to leave for New York or whether you plan to stay on a while in Ithaca and sell the apartment. The only thing I can ask you to do for me is this: If you have to leave before I get back, please put the animals in a good kennel. I am enclosing another blank check (you never told me whether you got the first one I sent) in case you need money for anything. I think my bank account is in pretty good shape–I haven't drawn one cent since I've been here. That certainly cheers me up. Every time I get down, I think how much money I shall have saved this summer by having all my living expenses paid here, and having to meet only minimum obligations in Ithaca. So don't hesitate to draw on my account for anything, whether household or personally for yourself, or whatever.

As I told you, I love Peru and especially the sierra. I really don't mind having to stay on, except that all my other work in Ithaca is waiting for me and I am worried about how it will get done, and also I don't like being saddled with the complete responsibility. If this were my only commitment I would be happy to stay a little longer, but as it is it louses up my own work on [a topic in medical sociology], on values, on core training [training in sociological methods that was going on at the time at Cornell], and on a lot of other stuff. Indeed, I like Peru so much that I had a brilliant idea. There is an industrial plant [the linen factory at Pati] about 7 miles from here lying idle since the end of the war, when the linen manufacturing operation which was being conducted there went bankrupt.

George and Pete and I have discussed the possibility of getting foundation funds for the purpose of putting that plant back in operation and studying the economic and social aspects of such industrialization, much in the same way that George is studying the effects of an agricultural operation in Vicos. I was quite excited about it, not only because it's an interesting study in sociology and economics but also because I was figuring out how you and I could come here for a year to set things up and then arrange to make trips a few months out of each ensuing year, more or less the way George does in Vicos. I had even written a letter to you, telling you about it in detail, when that blow-up with George occurred. Moreover, Frank moved himself in on the study–and since I don't want to work with either of them, if I can help it, in more than a casual way, I soured completely on the idea and just turned it over to Pete, who is still interested. I told Pete I would help him draft a study proposal and try to help him peddle it [to granting agencies], but I certainly wouldn't want to work closely on it with those other two guys. So I tore up the letter I had written to you about it.

It's hard to explain about George, because he's so exaggerated from the way I knew him in Ithaca that it's almost like a caricature. He's all right when he's sober, but as soon as he smells a drink he's impossible. He gets argumentative and mean, and talks about things that are so unrelated to the topic of discussion that you begin to feel as disconnected as, for example, when you walk in, in the middle of a movie. You talk to him about research and pretty soon you find yourself in the middle of a discussion about the day's food bills. Or how hard it was to install the pump. Or what it was like among the [people Rogers had studied at the beginning of his career]. Until I caught on to this about George I tried to keep him to the topic under discussion, or else somehow to relate what he said to what we were talking about and respond in kind. I know enough now just to skip it. But it is maddening and requires a great deal of self-control. Cliff has already moved out of the hacienda and is living in an Indian household. This is the same thing that, I have learned, has happened with all his field staff.

Frank is another dish of tea. As far as I can discover, he has never done an honest day's work in his life, but has always picked up some kind of assistant (whom he called an "interpreter"), letting that poor chap do all the work, and then analyzing his data. He *still* doesn't have the slightest notion of what this methodology study is all about, hasn't made a single suggestion or put a single field task into operation in a way which the point of the study demands. Moreover, his personal attitude and behavior are insulting–both to me and, I think, to the Peruvians. He is insulting to me because he never consults with me about anything related to the study, but just goes ahead with his highbrow lectures as if I didn't exist. He is insulting, in my opinion, to the staff, because he makes no effort to communicate with them or to get to know them. He sends them out into the field and makes no effort to look at their work or evaluate it or say it's good or bad, or appreciated, or essential to the study. It's as if, after his fancy lectures, he just pushed them off into another planet and let it go at that. He countermands my instructions, does not acknowledge any status or authority which I might have (imagine what that does in the eyes of the field workers!) and, more important, stays sober too rarely. Since he has decided to take off Saturday, he has been doing a job of work–for all of this last week! But it's the first work he's done. I am so mad at his incompetence, his sabotage, his insulting behavior, and now, finally, his irresponsibility in just taking off, that I daydream about just leaving the study first and letting him handle it himself, as he has, in effect, done to me. This is the craziest goddam setup I have ever been in!

I am pleased, however, that they are going because it means that I have at least a couple of months to get some work done. I wouldn't give you two cents for what has been accomplished up to now by anyone, including me. I have had to spend so much time fighting with myself for self-control and trying to get some semblance of field work going on that I consider all the time everyone has spent here practically wasted.

As you can tell, my morale is almost completely shot. For example, I have two jobs to do right now, write a progress report and a structured field task; and instead of doing it, I am sitting here and writing to you. I just don't have a real interest in the work. Things have been so disheartening, and every time I think of that jerk taking off and leaving everything unsettled I alternately seethe with anger and breathe a sigh of relief that we can get something done for a change, without nonsense and sabotage.

Another thing this experience has brought home to me again (it's not the first time) is my old feeling that with all the phonies in this goddam field, maybe I'd better get the hell out of it. I can count on my fingers the people in this field that I think have the understanding to appreciate what a job of work is and what, on the other hand, is a bunch of crap. What the hell am I knocking myself out for, if there's nobody around to know the difference between me and a Frank Nolan? Beats me.

Well, this is a self-centered letter, isn't it? I miss hearing from you and wish you'd write. I got a note from Mrs. Johnson [her landlord in Ithaca] about the gas heat. She says if she installs gas heat the rent goes up to $60. I figure that during the winter I pay between $25 and $30 for heat, which means that 8 months a year I pay $65 to $70, and 4 months $40–$720 rent per year including heat. If I pay $60 for 12 months, that means $720 per year without heat. The question is, is the improvement in efficiency and looks worth the extra money? She wants me to write her to say whether I'm willing to pay the increased cost. What do you think?

How are the animals? I miss them very, very much. The dog [Enrique Luna's] I described to you died yesterday. He ate strychnine and had convulsions for a whole day and a night. It was pitiful. I can't get used to the casual and matter of fact way in which people around here accept death. This goes for bullfighting, for funerals of people, and for the equanimity with which everyone continued with their daily routine while the dog was dying, just as if they didn't notice it. I kept insisting that someone put him out of his misery, and finally two peons took him off and drowned him, or he'd have been in his death agony another night. Now there is absolutely no affection in this house, and I feel lonely and lost and unloved. I wish you were here with Gorgon and the two girls so I'd feel like a human being instead of a machine.

Write to me and tell me how you are and how the animals are, and whom you see and what you do and how the work is and how my friends are and what your plans are and anything else you can think of. Love, S.

P.S. As you can guess, I'm smoking myself into a stupor all day and all night. I tried to lay off cigarettes, but I am so tense all the time in this *manicomio* [insane asylum] that I decided it was either cigarettes or dope–so I chose cigarettes.

As Levy says at the beginning of this letter, it is a mixture of happiness and sadness. We do not know for certain what caused Nolan to bring his work in Vicos to an end: it could have been a recall from the senior sociologists at Cornell; it could have been his desire to be with the woman with whom he had had an extramarital affair; it could have been his inability to get adequate work done at high altitude; it could have been his sexist refusal to tolerate joint labors with Levy; or it could have been a combination of all of these, plus factors of which we are completely ignorant. Levy is happy to see both Nolan and Rogers leave Vicos, although she feels left "holding the bag" by the departure of the former because this increases her work load and delays her own return to her home and work in Ithaca. "The bag" contains what? Is it nothingness, the unspeakable? Or is it a "*cojudo estudio*," "stupid study," as she sometimes likes to call it.

Perhaps Levy's seniors at Cornell could have provided her with a clearer direction to begin with, but they were undoubtedly uncertain themselves and possibly they still hoped that Nolan would perform according to their expectations. There is nothing in Levy's correspondence, at this point, to indicate that she had even a minimal understanding of the deep trouble Nolan was in. But she understands quite well Nolan's basic confusion and misreading of the expectations which brought him to Vicos and of the tasks confronting him. Instead of focusing on the analysis of the results of the several non-structured and structured tasks of observation and interviewing which his field workers were to be engaged, he gives them "highbrow" (the use of which term undoubtedly reflects the Levy's training in a different graduate department) lectures, takes no interest in his crew, drinks too much, and, what is worse, is "insulting" when he "countermands my instructions" and "does not acknowledge any status or authority which I might have." "*Might* have"? Does this mean that Levy is also unsure? Is she unconsciously employing the patriarchal code, reciting a patriarchal narrative? But certainly Levy's vulgarity in describing Nolan's behavior as "just fucking off" is an indication of strong and certain feelings about the uselessness of Nolan's feeble efforts, as well as a displacement of fear that she herself is not working.

Levy tells Rosita about the "brilliant idea" she had of researching the effects of industrialization in the Callejón de Huaylas, and how "excited" she was about it until the "blow-up." That Nolan "moved himself in on the study" could not have helped. In consequence, Levy says, "I soured completely on the idea." She adds, "It's hard to explain about George, because he is so exaggerated from the way I knew him in Ithaca that it's almost like a caricature." She then goes on to describe Rogers's rapid changes of subject in conversation as "maddening." Just as I recall George Rogers as permissive and non-intrusive, I remember well his use of metaphor to convey his opinions. Literal-minded people, like Levy, not to mention countless naive graduate students, were likely not to get his point and to leave him in frustration. (There's a double meaning in this: *whose* frustration, is open to conjecture.)

A thought that "cheers her up" is "how much money she shall have saved" by doing the work at Vicos. She seems generous with Rosita, offering her access to his bank account, but later calculates heating costs in detail. She claims to "love Peru and especially the sierra," but later states, "I can't get used to the casual and matter of fact way in which people around here accept death." The case of the dying dog bothers her and she intervenes to have the dog killed. She thus attempts to say the unsayable, but she also wishes to "get the hell out of" her profession, and then says, "my morale is completely shot" and, finally, "there is absolutely no affection in this house, and I feel lonely and lost and unloved." For Levy, Vicos is a "*manicomio*." All these themes carry over into the next letter, of Thursday, August 13, 1953:

Dear Rosita, I just got your letter with the news about Gorgon and yourself. I am glad I mailed you another blank check yesterday, in case you need money. I hope you will take care of yourself properly and not go through that [word blacked out] business again. I wish I were with you. I would holler and scream, but I would take care of you and at least know you are well, instead of being worried and uneasy as I am now. Please cable me that you are all right. I am worried.

About Gorgon, I am also worried. I didn't know he was so old. The vet at the Cornell clinic told me he was at most 6 years old. I am sorry as hell that you are saddled with his illness. Somehow I shall make it up to you, I don't know how right now. If anything should happen to him in my absence, I should feel just utterly rotten and callous. On the other hand, if he is going to be sick and miserable, I should want him destroyed. I do not want him to suffer. I wish I were home right now taking care of my family, as I should be. Write me all the details about your own ordeal, and for Christ's sake don't be so secretive. What do you mean "troubles with the apartment?" When your letter came today I let out a moan as I read it, and George, who will be in Ithaca next week, asked if there was anything he could do to help. I only told him that Gorgon was sick, but I am more worried about you. I wish there were some way I could telephone. The connection from Marcará is impossible. Cliff called his wife last week in New York (she is about to have a baby and he wanted to know how she is) and he came back just fuming because he had such a poor connection. So I have decided not to telephone, since he said he couldn't hear a word.

I am so fed up with this study, and now the news from you makes me want to get the hell out of here. How can I do it with Frank taking off the way he is? I wish you could have been present at a so-called meeting we had this morning. Every time a subject came up for discussion, there were just blank stares. It was so funny and so idiotic, I just burst out laughing for a long time, and nobody understood what I was laughing at. I have been trying to get our field men to get their notes typed now, for four solid weeks, and so far not one word has been put to paper. This time the reason given was that the paper they have is not the right size! Therefore,

Pete told them to wait until we can order the right size paper from Lima! This is what happens all the time. A subject is brought up (usually by me), and I try to get discussion. Instead I get these blank stares, or idiotic reasons. I stick it out for a while, staring back, or saying outright, "What is your opinion?" and then–you know me–I make a decision. At that point all hell breaks loose. I am absolutely fed up, and I mean fed up. And now your letter is the last straw. I feel as if I were in prison, just waiting to be released. I think I shall try a bit of fucking off myself. I was looking forward to Frank's leaving here so I could whip the survey into shape. As it stands now it's a bunch of highbrow stuff addressed to these poor Indians as if each of them had completed a Ph.D. in sociology. However, I think I'll just put it through as it is, cleaning up only one or two sections so we won't look like complete idiots when it's published (if ever). I don't know whether I'll have the courage to be that irresponsible, but I certainly think I have ample justification for being so.

George, since he has decided to leave, has been as sweet as pie. He only backslid once–at dinner last night he had a couple of cocktails and got mean, but everyone ignored him and it passed over. Although I understand that after midnight he started it again, goading Pete this time until 2 a.m. But he's obviously trying to be nice to me. I guess that now, since he is leaving so soon, he wants to smooth over any ruffled personal feelings.

Please cable me that you are all right. I shall be worried until I hear from you. If you need money, use the check I sent. You know what my balance is (I don't). In addition I have about $100 in travelers' checks, plus project money, so I can manage. Don't be stingy with yourself. [Here seven lines, apparently having to do with Rosa Sánchez's health problem, are blacked out.]

Rosita, take care of yourself and cable me. Love, S.

Levy expresses concern for her companion's health and that of one of her dogs. She says, "I wish I were home right now." She uses as a metaphor for her much more generalized sense of isolation, which she has expressed again and again, the problems with telephone service. She repeats how "fed up with this study" she is, and relates the story of the staff meeting she attended that morning: "Nobody understood what I was laughing at" probably means *nobody understands me*. "Not one word has been put to paper," and this because Pete has decided that the project's paper is not the right size! Levy expresses her desire in her assertion, "I think I shall try a bit of fucking off myself." Does "fucking off" mean that she is seduced by pleasure? Hardly, with her tendency to defer, reject, and repress pleasure. Perhaps it represents only a seduction by not-work, *not-being*. We have seen this before, in her wish to "bum around, aimlessly." She soon rejects this: "I don't know whether I'll have the courage to be that irresponsible." We may well ask why irresponsibility would require courage? She had hoped to "whip"–a singularly punitive term–"the survey into shape," and was contemplating "just putting it through as it is . . so we won't look like complete idiots when it's published," but will not settle for this in the terms dictated by her work ethic. Her feelings of immobility and suspension are expressed in her statement, "I feel as if I were in prison, just waiting to be released." These themes continue in Levy's next letter, Thursday, August 20, 1953, together with some new ones which enter upon the departure of Nolan and Rogers:

Dear Rosita, "Another day, another dollar"–here I sit in Vicos trying to retrieve this *cojudo estudio* and calling myself all kinds of names for getting Frank's coals out of the fire. The disenchantment is setting in. I am becoming a real Latin, ordering the servants around, hollering at them, making demands on the field workers, letting them know who's boss, etc. This was not possible when Frank was here, because he fucked me up every time I turned around with his cojudoism. But now that he has gone I am trying to take hold. *A ver* [We'll see].

[Now in Spanish,] *I'm thinking of you–if you're well, what happened with the matter in New York, how much it cost, where the money came from, if you visited my friend as I wrote you, and where you are now. Today I received a letter written by Marge Johnson. She told me everything about her new car and the painting course in which she enrolled by mail, but she didn't mention anything about you. I still don't know how you are, or Gorgon either. I'd like to know all the news about my family.*

I'm well enough, but I just have a lot of work and little motivation. It's impossible to tell you how this study is fucked up. *I doubt if I can fix it, or if it is already too late.*

Today was a great day for Vicos. The electric light plant finally arrived, which the electrician installed and tonight it was functioning for the first time. The house looks very mich like Times Square. *Only we are missing a* Nedick's [a New York fast food chain] *stand. It's very fine, with one exception–the plant needs a gallon of gasoline to work for just an hour. And for every gallon of gasoline–which is cheap enough here in Peru–it needs a pint of oil, which costs 48 soles* [over three dollars at the time]! *We need a pile of money to make the light work.*

The Indians are pleased with the light, because they say that when they get drunk they won't break their heads. You ought to see them when they're drunk. They can't walk, and they fall down on the ground or in the acecia [*acequia*, irrigation channel] *where they sleep all night! They drink chicha* [home brew], *which is very much like beer, but it's made from corn–and washcu, which is just pure alcohol* [actually, it is cane alcohol mixed with water]. *The day before yesterday I drank this chicha and washcu, and I almost fell off my horse!*

Write to me how you are and what happened in New York. I worry a lot. Affectionately, S.

The expression, "Another day, another dollar" is a North American military expression, popular during early World War II, when common soldiers received the pay of thirty dollars per month. Levy suggests, in this way, that she feels she is in a kind of disciplinary limbo in which one day is the same as another, and she exists from day to day. "Here I sit in Vicos," she says, "trying to retrieve this *cojudo estudio*," and she adds that she is "calling herself all kinds of names for pulling Frank's coals out of the fire." Thus, she is not only experiencing "outrage" at Nolan but some "inrage," as well, which is indicated by the unnamed epithets she is directing toward herself. Why does she not direct some of those epithets toward the senior sociologists who put her in the situation, in the first place? Switching to Spanish, she worries about Rosita's health, says she is well enough, but then complains, "but I have a lot of work and little motivation." The research is so "fucked up" that "I doubt if I can fix it or if it is already too late."

At the same time, now that Nolan is gone and despite the "disenchantment" she feels, she is taking charge of things by commanding the servants and the field workers, "letting them know who's boss," like what she believes is a "real Latin," which looks like ethnocentrism at best but carries with it undertones of racism. She is also pleased by the installation of electric lighting in Vicos-- as if "the electrification of Peru" were going to bring with it "great white [in more than one sense] ways" and fast food stands, and thereby utopia–but cannot refrain from another ethnocentric comment on the contradiction between the relative costs of gasoline and oil.

The next letter is dated, August 31, 1953:

Dear Rosita, If you knew what was going on here you would be amused and disgusted at the same time. I guess by now you have an idea of the *ambiente* [atmosphere] of this cojudo place. I was left here high and dry, never having been introduced to anyone formally, my position here never having been specified, my authority never having been acknowledged–a bad setup at best, no?, and especially for a Latin culture where authority is so important. In addition, Frank and George when they were here, and Pete too, did nothing but drink all day and all night, so that night after night we had these drunken brawls. Our so-called field men moved in, and instead of an *ambiente* conducive to work, and an example set by Frank, George, and Pete, the acknowledged bosses, they found these crazy gringos just lapping up liquor, challenging everyone to drinking bouts, and all the rest of it. Well, you can't blame the poor boys. Here they are, set up as if at the Waldorf Astoria, good food, lots of service, lots of liquor, and no work. *Fíjate cómo fuera* [Look how it was]!

Bueno [Well], about 12 days ago I blew my top and said things had to change around here, or else, and parceled out *tareas* [tasks], etc., but instead of taking over the reins myself I still left a great deal to Pete, counting on him to go over the field tasks, to see to it that the agenda I make up every day was carried out, and, in short, to help me. Getting him to do something is like wrestling with a keg of molasses without the keg, because he'd go off on another drinking bout, *sacando* [taking out] the boys with him–and next morning nothing accomplished.

Well, today I blew my top again, after a drinking bout all day Sunday, lasting well into the night. Actually, I had to come downstairs, bang the table with my fist, and shout, "*Señores, este no sirvirá. Tienen que dejar. Nadie puede trabajar!*" [Gentlemen, this is no good. You have to stop. Nobody can work!] That served not to stop the brawling, but only to tone down mildly the terrific noise and singing, and I myself turned off the radio. This morning I was down to breakfast at 7, summoned each man as if he were shit, held a meeting which lasted all morning, went over their *tareas* sentence by sentence, deposed Pete from his position of apparent authority (they all think he is more boss than I because he was here first, and because Frank and George let it go at that). I told them exactly what I wanted done, hour by hour during the day. I told them that the brawling had to stop. I asked them to bring me their tasks, which I knew damned well hadn't been done because they'd been drinking instead of working, and when these tasks were not forthcoming I scolded each as if he were a ten-year-old. I checked up on everybody every hour to see if he were actually doing what he had been told to do. And, after dinner, when they were all about to go off to their nonsense again, I pulled each man back to the table and gave him more work to do. Unfortunately, we had hired a new interpreter to work with one of our men and today was his first day here. Poor fellow, he came in completely unprepared for this authoritarian figure who was unfriendly and amagro [*amargo*, bitter]. By now our staff represents all stages of *malogrado* [out of order]. Gutiérrez was the one who moved in first, and he was exposed to absolutely the worst brawling and idiotically permissive behavior and no-work *ambiente*. *Castillo moved in about 10 days later, after I had already blown my top once and the brawling and idiocy was on the decline. *Pepe [José Benavides], whom Quiller always refers to by his nickname, a new man, came only about three days ago. He was present only at the brawl I just described, and the morning after when I changed my personality and redefined this *cojudo* situation. And our new interpreter, as I said, doesn't know what the hell is going on here.

I have allies here in the person of the Blanchards who understand the whole fucked up situation and how I was left holding the bag here, not only because all the work is on *my* desk but also because the situation was so *malogrado* by the crazy behavior of the men allegedly in charge. And Cliff Barnett also understands what went on and is, in a way, an ally. But they are of no use, since Cliff is here for a year and the Blanchards for two. When I think of Frank and George, already in Cornell, and God knows what they are saying. And Pete, who is returning in 12 days or so, an ally of both George [Quiller was George Rogers's student] and Frank, because he always played along with them while I fought like hell, is also *caliente conmigo* [burned up at me] because I am finally getting him off his ass. I simply don't know how I can handle the situation when I return. George doesn't have the slightest idea that Frank is completely a phony. Pete, I think, knows it, but considers Frank his best friend and, moreover, is counting on Frank to help him get to India and Thailand as his assistant. Obviously, he cannot, under these circumstances, be counted on to evaluate this situation objectively. I cannot honestly say that any one of the three has done two solid days' work all the time they've been here, a period of one and a half months for Frank [an error: if Nolan had been in Vicos one and a half months on August 31, he would have arrived on July 15, after Levy!] to almost three months for Pete. Not only have they done no work themselves, but they have spoiled everyone else. Our field men are not worth a penny. Just to add a little local color to the fraternity-house atmosphere here, last night, during the brawl I described, Mario sneaked out to go to a party in Huaraz. Pete wanted to take the jeep (which is on loan to our project for essential errands) and drive, drunk as he was, with all the field men to Huaraz. Bill sneaked the car away so Pete couldn't drive. Thus the boys were mad at Mario, who had gone away in his own car, leaving them with no means of transportation. Therefore, they dismantled his bed and dragged it way the hell out to the *molino* [mill]. When Mario got home he had to sleep on the floor in his sleeping bag. So he got mad and threw Pete's eyeglasses into the *basura* [garbage]. And so on and on and on. I am so mad I could chew nails.

Changing my role and deposing Pete so he has no authority is all very well for improving morale, but it means that I have all the work to do with practically no help from him. As a result, I am sitting here typing this letter to you at midnight, having just finished my day's work: meeting all morning with the field men, going over pretests and field tasks during the afternoon, and finishing writing the questionnaire (which goes into the field this week) tonight. Carramba [*¡caramba!*, my goodness!], I wish you were here with me so we could get this situation back in line and *arreglar* [fix] it.

Incidentally, I wish you were here so you could laugh at my Spanish. Imagine me holding meetings in Spanish, scolding people in Spanish, criticizing their work in Spanish, hollering at the cook in Spanish, and writing the questionnaire in Spanish! I have improved a great deal, and now can follow almost all of a discussion when I am talking with just one person, although I miss a lot when everyone is talking at once. But I am not afraid and, as you say, I just talk and to hell with whether it's right or wrong. Somehow, people understand me.

Well, it's tough going with one hand tied behind my back, so to speak, but by God I'll get this fucking job done and that will be that. After all,

the most important thing is to accomplish what we set out to do, and I
have to remember that and not let my gripes interfere with getting the
pendejo job done. No? Anyway, that's what I keep telling myself.
Much love and *cariño* [affection] and *besos* [kisses] to you and my
adored family, S.
　　P.S. Are you going to be staying in Ithaca? *A ver* [let's see]. S.

Levy is optimistic about the improvement in her Spanish. She can find
the resolve: "By God, I'll get this fucking job done and that will be that."
She "blew her top," intervening to reduce the "drunken brawling," "crazy
gringos lapping up liquor," "deposing Pete so he has no authority,"
summoning each field worker "as if he were shit," and scolding each "as if
he were a ten-year-old." At the same time, getting Pete "to do something
is like wrestling with a keg of molasses without the keg." However,
Quiller had been an alcoholic for years, then, and had no desire to cease
his intake of his favorite toxic substance, but, rather, could not function
without it. Moreover, he carried others with him into what Levy sees as
"drunken brawls." If Quiller were unable to control his alcohol intake,
how could Levy hope to do it, no matter how many times she let her anger
show or how hard she tried to control the project that was now "hers?" It
is not surprising that Levy feels "left here high and dry." The men of the
Methodology Project indulge in "drinking bouts"; they give themselves
over to a pleasure which she can not, will not feel.

She senses that she has allies in the persons of the Blanchards and
Barnett but, she says, "all the work is on *my* desk because the situation was
so out of order by the crazy behavior of the men allegedly in charge." She
is concerned because Nolan and Rogers are back in Ithaca, "and God
knows what they are saying"; and she is also concerned because she
believes that "George doesn't have the slightest idea that Frank is
completely a phony." This is odd because Levy has all the information
she needs to feel comfortable about Rogers's estimation of her
competence, and to feel secure in her field directorship. She probably
knows something about the situation, and that before the summer's field
work began Nolan was viewed as problematic by his senior colleagues at
Cornell, as well as that her very presence in Peru was required by Nolan's
personal and professional problems. She has, in this correspondence made
very harsh but accurate evaluations of Nolan's understanding of his job
and skill in performing it. However, her personal insecurity, uncertainty,
and hesitation have her in this repetitive cycle of casting obscene blame
and playing victim. In her eyes, nobody has been getting any work done
because "they have spoiled everything." And now that "they" have gone,
the drinking bouts and petty quarreling (surely "their fault") go on and

Levy is "so mad she could chew nails." Levy will not give up her defenses, and her desire to hate herself takes shape as a hatred of where she is and what she is doing: "this *cojudo* place," "this fucking job," "this *cojudo* situation," "this fucked up situation." There is no pleasure here. Levy's major accomplishment is the transfer of her field workers to Vicos from the private homes in which they were residing in Marcará. There is no insecurity, uncertainty, or hesitation in this. She has them installed at project headquarters, in a kind of Foucauldian "panopticism" in which "[i]nspection funcions ceaselessly" and "[t]he gaze is alert everywhere" (Foucault 1977a:195).[12] The aim is "not so much to punish wrongdoers as to prevent even the possibility of wrongdoing, by immersing people in a field of total visibility where the opinion, observation and discourse of others would restrain them from harmful acts" (Foucault 1980:153). She can now engage in a twenty-four hour surveillance of their activities, to make sure they are working and not "fucking off" in the many ways possible when they are out of her sight. They are not to seek pleasure but to work. Metaphorically, this kind of surveillance is a control over their sexuality (cf.150). Foucault (1977a:143) defines the kind of space Levy has created:

> Disciplinary space tends to be divided into as many sections as there are bodies or elements to be distributed. One must eliminate the effects of imprecise distributions, the uncontrolled disappearance of individuals, their diffuse circulation, their unusable and dangerous coagulation; it was a tactic of anti-desertion, anti-vagabondage, anti-concentration. Its aim was to establish presences and absences, to know where and how to locate individuals, to set up useful communications, to interrupt others, to be able at each moment to supervise the conduct of each individual, to assess it, to judge it, to calculate its qualities or merits. It was a procedure, therefore, aimed at knowing, mastering and using.

With this said, let us read the next document, written on September 3, 1953:

> Dear Rosita, Another letter for the record. Please keep it. I'll need all this information when I get back.
> As you might have gathered, all hell has broken loose here. I think I told you that three of our field men had moved into the house. In addition, there is Enrique, *el administrador* [the administrator], Mario, Allan Holmberg's Peruvian anthropologist, Alirio [Aliro], the handyman, and his family. In addition, we have assorted other field men, 5 in all, who come and go every day.
> You must by now know the kind of atmosphere I inherited here.

Nobody has done a lick of work ever. Fiestas every night for one reason or another. Since Frank left, I have taken over the reins, have been acting, in fact, like a top-sergeant, trying to get some work out of these boys. But they are so *malogrados* [spoiled] that it is a full time job just seeing to it that they do what they are told to do. Well, as you know, Pete has been of no help. On the contrary, not only has he loafed and drunk himself silly every day he's been here, but he continues to set the example left by Frank and Allan, and he hinders the work of everybody. Of course, they follow his lead. They think he is the boss! I made every kind of appeal to him I could think of, from asking "please, please, please," like a supplication, to teasing, to talking frankly, to ordering brusquely, and Nothing worked. Finally, I asked him to leave, two nights ago.

Everybody was very surprised when he announced so suddenly that he was leaving. Enrique and Mario were particularly surprised, and hurt, too, because–*fíjate!*–this is what they had been planning: a five-day *despedida* [sendoff, goodbye party], during which time nobody would get a lick of work done. That means more than a dozen people would be drinking themselves blind instead of working, and meanwhile the project grinding to a standstill. When I asked him why he didn't warn me of this in advance (since he had known) he said, "You couldn't have done anything about it, anyway!" Bill and Max Blanchard are living upstairs (where I have my room), Bill being the director [actually, field director] of Allan's [Holmberg's] project. They have been so disturbed over the goings-on here, as I have, that Bill said if it didn't stop we'd all have to close up–and I don't blame him. They know how I've been struggling to get some work done, and are entirely sympathetic with my efforts and have been a great deal of emotional support for me.

Well, the night I told Pete to leave, he turned over to me his so-called accounts and what remains of the money. Our budget had been estimated, when Frank left, at a sum which turns out to be fifty per cent of what we should have estimated (their budgets have no relation to reality). The "accounts" consist of notations like: August 17–5,000 soles; August 19–4,378 soles, with no itemization whatsoever. I know we have been putting away at least two cases of beer per day, at 54 soles total, not to mention pisco, rum, gin and God knows what–and apparently that is all included under these cryptic, unitemized notices of expenditures! In addition, Pete turned over to me certain field documents, just a pile of originals and carbons, unassembled, unlabeled, unsigned, undated, the biggest mess I have ever seen! In all the time Pete has been here he has written not one field note! I know he made one interview once, because I was with him, but he never wrote it up, and as far as I can determine that is absolutely all he ever did! The same, incidentally goes for Frank. I have two documents he wrote, at my request--indeed, at my insistence! They are worth about three cents.

Well, keep in mind that for the past 15 days I have been behaving like a top-sergeant. Yesterday, when the boys found Pete was leaving (they were given no explanation as to why), they asked me very politely whether they could have a *despedida* for him, and I said that if we got through our work for the day it was all right with me. (I feel like such a bastard all the time, I was glad for an opportunity to be nice for a change.) In addition, the schoolteacher, who had also learned only that day of Pete's departure, arranged an *actuación en la escuela* [performance in the school] in Pete's honor. I gave the boys their choice of attending the *actuación* and *observing it for our study* [emphasis in the original], but also working late on the questionnaire in order to make up for the lost time; or skipping the *actuación* and not having to work late. They chose the *actuación*. *I was the only one who made a single note or recorded a single observation!* [Emphasis in the original.]

Well, I decided to skip that and not scream, because I had said "*observar* [observe]," and there was a possibility that they might have misunderstood and only thought I meant "*asistir* [attend]." And besides, I was tired of being mean.

Well, we started the *despedida* just before *comida* [dinner]. Everything went well. I attended, danced, sang, etc., and so did the Blanchards, whom Pete invited only after I told him to. I left the party at 11, made myself a cup of coffee, and turned in at midnight. At three a.m. I woke up: the *despedida* was still going strong, with more noise than you can imagine. I was utterly disgusted. I put on my storm coat and ran down to the corner room where they were and found Enrique, Alacrán (the painter) [*alacrán* means "scorpion"–a nickname?], our new interpreter, and Alirio, whooping it up. None of them is on my staff, so I told them only: "*Señores, somos acá huéspedes. Esta no es nuestra casa, y tenemos que comportarnos según estas circonstancias [circunstancias]. Yo les suplicó, este no puede ser, etc., etc.* [Gentlemen, we are guests here. This is not our house, and we have to behave ourselves according to these circumstances. I begged them, this can't be, etc., etc.] Of course they *tuvieron corage [corrage] conmigo* [they were bold with me], because they were drunk and because it was a *despedida*. I told them–*muchas veces los Blanchards me han dicho que ellos no quieren tolerar una situación así, y nosotros tenemos que irnos, etc., etc.* [the Blanchards have told me many times that they do not wish to tolerate a situation like this, and we must leave, etc., etc.], so Enrique and Alirio said, "*Mejor si nosotros mismos nos vamos mañana, etc., etc.* [It's better that we come back tomorrow, etc., etc.].

Well, as you can imagine, I was quite upset, thinking it would be my fault if they resigned. I went back to bed but couldn't sleep. Alirio, who had originally been scheduled to drive Pete to Huaraz, where he could get a car to Lima, was too drunk to drive. So at 4:00 Pete and Enrique woke Mario, to ask him to take them to Huaraz. Mario's room is directly under mine, and I heard all of their conversation. Enrique was indignant in a drunken way and, to my surprise and disgust, Pete was egging him on, encouraging him, supporting him, etc. It was a startling exhibition of direct sabotage of both projects. I heard quite a bit, until Pete said, "For

God's sake, let's get out of here. She can hear." Then, of course, I heard no more conversation, only the car driving away.

This morning, Anita, Alirio's wife, came into my room at 7:00 in tears. Between 12 and 3, while I had been asleep, this is what happened. She had left the party, had gone home, was sitting in her *cuarto* [room] nursing her youngest baby. Enrique came in and sat on the other bed and talked to her, she says. Shortly thereafter Alirio came in. He had followed Enrique because he was suspicious! There is no light, of course–the room thus was pitch black. When Alirio entered, Enrique rolled under the bed, as if hiding from a husband's indignation at finding another man in his wife's bedroom. (I found out yesterday that Alirio had grabbed a knife, but had thrown it *away*, instead of *at* Enrique, for fear of what he might do. Also, when Enrique rolled under the bed, he couldn't get all the body under because there was a big box of junk there, so there he was, his rump sticking out, and Alirio gave him a big fat vicious kick!!!) Alirio blew his top, beat his wife, threatened her. Everyone came over here and woke up the Blanchards (I slept through it all) and there was a big fuss. (I can't understand how it could happen that with such goings-on at, say two a.m, I found Alirio and Enrique palsy-walsy together at 3:30 a.m.–but no need for me to reason why, I guess.) Anyway, Anna packed up her things and asked Max Blanchard to take her into Carhuaz so she could leave Alirio, and take with her the four children and never come back. She had come to my room in the morning to tell me what had happened, and she cried all over me, etc., etc. I counseled her to forget it, told her Alirio was a good husband as a rule, that it had been the liquor talking not the man, etc., etc. But her things are in the jeep waiting to be taken to Carhuaz. The Blanchards have been stalling her all day, trying to get negotiations under way between the two, using the good offices of Sr. Picón, the *maestro*. Alirio is threatening to leave the Hacienda. Enrique hasn't showed up all day. In short, it's a bloody mess. (It's still going on this way 2 days later.)

In addition, *fíjate*! This morning I got up, had breakfast, went around to the room of every field man and woke him up. I went to Alirio's house where the new interpreter had slept, or rather had passed out, and woke him up. I told him–*a mí no me gusta cuando yo tengo que despertar a mis trabajadores. Aquí empezemos el trabajo a las ocho, etc., etc.* [I don't like it when I have to wake up my workers. Here we are to start work at eight, etc. etc.] He was hung over with a terrific *mal de cuerpo* [painful body, a hangover], but I sent him out into the field nevertheless, as I did with all the other field men. I have been after them every hour on the hour, checking their work, watching them, speeding them up, goading them. In short, I've been so busy keeping them going that I have little time to do my own work, but I shall not tolerate such a situation! (How I wish you were here to help me!) The worst thing about this situation for me is that I have such a nervous stomach that I throw up every day!

In discussing the situation with Bill and Max today, I pointed out to them that I feel the responsibility is Frank's. It was he who introduced this crazy atmosphere originally. It was he who permitted Pete to carry on the way he did. It was he who permitted everyone to think that Pete was the authority here. It was he who originally undermined my authority in a negative way, by sins of omission rather than commission. I mean that by never explaining my presence here, he made it very difficult for me to supervise anything–and by simply omitting to discuss it, he put me in a position where I could not complain because there was nothing I could say except, "you didn't do such-and-such." I couldn't say, you *did* do such-and-such." After all, it is the chief who is responsible for the conduct of his workers, and Frank never structured Pete's situation. Pete, after all, is only a graduate student in the role here of an assistant. It is just not reasonable that he should have been allowed to develop to such a point that his behavior could steer the whole project close to the edge of destruction. This should have been handled much earlier.

Naturally, Enrique (I'm not sure about Mario) is sore as hell at me, and no wonder. He has the softest job here anyone ever had, with one exception: Allan's project is so crazily run that there's no money in the budget, and he hasn't been paid for four months! But *no importa* [never mind], the fact is that nobody–but nobody–has done a day's work here in a year! And my trying to get work done means that people's drinking companions are scared away. Thank God the Blanchards understand the situation. Otherwise I would be here without a soul to talk to or to back me up!

I realize, too, that I am not entirely without fault in the matter. When George and Frank were here–at least for the first two weeks–I played along with them and did what they did. I felt that this was George's project in Vicos, he was the boss, and I could not change the way *he* lived here. I must confess, too, that my constant battles with Frank over the work, and the way he was handling the field men, wore me out. I figured what the hell, it's his project, let him handle it. I now see I should have taken over immediately. Well, there's no use crying about it. Since Frank and George have left, I have been fighting desperately, trying to whip this goddam project into shape, and by God, I'm not going to have it turn into a *fracaso* [failure]. I have too much *amor propio* [self-respect], speaking professionally, to allow this crazy *loco manicomio ambiente* to lick me now! I had no choice but to get rid of Pete, or the task would have been impossible–instead of just highly improbable, as it now is.

One thing is a little amusing in all this mess. When I told Pete he could leave, he was, of course, hurt and angry. He criticized the project severely by saying that "the quality of the data we are collecting is poor," and insinuating that it was because of me! I burst out laughing! Certainly, the quality of the data is poor but, by Christ, we're damned lucky to have any data at all, the way things are going around here.

Rosita, I can only say in summary that I have participated in field studies where people got mad at each other–and understandably, because this business of living together all in one house is very trying–and especially where things got snafued, and where there were personal conflicts, and where there were some *flojos* [lazy men] who got in the way and hindered things. But never before in my experience have I encountered anything like this! The *ambiente* here is four years old [a distortion: the Vicos Project began in January 1952], dating from the early days of the project, and as such is so deeply entrenched that it is a herculean job to fight it and get some–a little–a drop–a hint–of work done. And this four-year-old *ambiente* has been stirred up and worsened by what happened when George and Frank were here and, as the bosses, set the example that my field men now feel they are entitled to follow, to say nothing of Pete's example, since they think he was a boss too.

I am lashing the whip around here, keeping everyone up late at their work, etc., etc., and as a result I am worn out. In addition, the throwing-up every day takes it out of me (no joke intended). To add to my worries, the cook is getting impossible. I think she must be screwing a couple of the *señores* and therefore thinks she's entitled to be fresh. Yesterday she was fresh to Max. Today she spoke to me in such a way that I had to tell her: "Don't ever speak to me that way again!" And so on, ad infinitum. It is just too much for me to handle, the cook and the kitchen too, so she gets away with murder, as you can expect, because I don't supervise her.

Well, that about covers the situation. Please don't discuss this with anyone. You don't even have to know about it, as far as anyone is concerned. Just be dumb. I asked Pete to call you when he gets to Ithaca, to tell you I'm well. Don't reveal that you know he was fired, or why, or anything. I know I can trust your discretion, but I want to make it explicit, even though I know you get mad at me for making these things explicit. Love, S.

P.S. Tell Mrs. Johnson $50 monthly is okay with me (if you agree). She sent me a note lowering the price to $50.

"All hell has broken loose here." With that introduction, Levy tells her companion of her efforts, her increased pressure on the field workers, her firing of Pete, the *despedida*, the conversation in Mario Vázquez's room, the triangle of Enrique Luna, Alirio, and Ana, and her difficulties in getting her own work done. She makes it a point, twice, to tell of her vomiting episodes–a situation which would carry most North Americans to the nearest medical facility (or is it that the situation is "pregnant"?), Lima if necessary–and she ends by noting that she has asked Pete to call Rosa Sánchez, upon his arrival in Ithaca, "to tell you I am well." She continues with "nobody has done a lick of work ever" and "fiestas every night." Yet she has "taken over the reins" and she is "acting like a top-sergeant, trying to get some work out of these boys," who "are so spoiled that it is a full time job just seeing to it that they do what they are told to do." With that, Levy explains why she is so "worn out." Quiller "has been of no help" but has "loafed and drunk himself silly every day." Levy's polite "please's" have changed "to teasing, to talking frankly, to ordering brusquely," and finally to the act of discharging him several days early. The others living in the Vicos Project's house, it turns out, are "hurt" because they have been planning the kind of *despedida* that suits an alcoholic and because they desire to accompany him into the haze for several days. William Blanchard, however, tells Levy that the party has to stop, so they all settle for a much more modest fiesta than they had wanted.

Quiller gives Levy the record of the Methodology Project's accounts and "certain field documents–just a pile of originals and carbons, unassembled, unlabeled, unsigned, undated," but none-the-less "a pile." (Actually, the qualitative field notes of the three field workers, dating from June 26 to September 8, 1953, fill one double drawer 8 x 5 file cabinet.) This would convince most skeptics that *some* work had been accomplished by the project staff. However, Levy focuses on Quiller's performance–"he has written not one field note"–and Nolan–"I have two documents he wrote" which "are worth about three cents."

Levy says she feels "like such a bastard," with her insistence on work and negativity toward fiesta, that she is "glad for an opportunity to be nice for a change." She allows the abbreviated *despedida* to take place, and even participates in it (reluctantly), but retires early, is awakened by the noise and intervenes at 3 a.m. She then hears a subversive conversation, "a direct sabotage of both projects," which she does not detail, in the room below hers. Is this a punishment for relenting and allowing pleasure to occur? And, finally, she hears the noise of the car taking Quiller out of Vicos.

Next comes the incident in Alirio's house, with its libidinal implications. Levy, a mid-century feminist who seems influenced enough by patriarchal ideology to accept the image of Alirio and Enrique Luna being "palsy-walsy" after the wife-beating. Thus, while her feminism has not enabled her to deconstruct patriarchy, she has turned the gender code to her favor, instead of abolishing it (cf. Baudrillard 1975:135-136). No alternative and subversive discourse exists at the time. Levy tries to persuade Ana to stay in Vicos and then finds that Alirio threatens to leave, an action which, if carried out, would be disruptive. At this point, Levy might well say, "See where all the partying gets us!"

Levy rouses all her workers the next morning from their hangovers and sends them to their tasks, but she insists on observing them "every hour on the hour, checking their work, watching them, speeding them up, goading them," so that she is impeded from doing her own work. All of this is Nolan's fault, and the "constant battles" with him "wore me out." She realizes that she "should have taken over immediately," but "there's no use crying about it." Again, she seems herself "fighting desperately to whip this goddam project into shape," and she adds, "by God I'm not going to have it turn into a *fracaso.*" She says, "I have too much *amor propio,* speaking professionally, to allow this crazy *loco manicomio ambiente* to lick me now!"

She feels that "the *ambiente* here ... is so deeply entrenched that it is a herculean job to fight it." She continues to place both Nolan and Rogers together as do-nothings, pleasure-seekers, despite the difference between them. Nolan, as I remember him, would go off to a class of university undergraduates saying, "I wonder what I'm going to tell them today?" Rogers was always prepared, but he was a non-directive person. Levy, who had been piqued by Rogers's direct criticism and probably offended by his metaphors, and who seems to have had the kind of character that criticized too easily while being sensitive to criticism by others,–all of these conscious reactions probably floating, as it were, on a sea of abandonment feelings and fears of not conforming to patriarchal standards--must have found Rogers's non-directiveness and indirectiveness deeply irritating.

Levy's next letter, September 5, 1953, is much shorter, and she seems to be feeling easier about her life and work in Vicos:

> Just a quick note to let you know that I am making a last stand and it may turn out to be all right, although I hesitate to be overoptimistic. I held a meeting with the boys last night, told them that I couldn't continue like a *sargento del ejército* [army sergeant], that I needed their cooperation. We decided to run the house as a joint responsibility and drew up menus for a week. They decided they would cook breakfast in rotation and that breakfast would be 7 to 8. I gave them each an agenda of the tasks for which they were responsible in terms of their field work. I explained the personnel organization of the project: Frank and I co-field directors, Pete a graduate assistant. I told them that I had asked Mario to meet with us three days a week to discuss our work, since he was an expert on the culture, but I could not in good faith ask his help unless I was sure they would cooperate and not fuck off. Today I told the same things to the non-resident field men, who are not quite so *malogrados* because they just haven't been around this *manicomio* so much. I forgot to mention that last night I had a session also with the cook and Mario where we whipped her into line, and she has been as good as gold all day. Our hours are 8 to 6:30 for the non-residents, and the residents will continue working every night until we finish our jobs. (The non-residents also have homework.) It also turns out that one reason the non-residents have been fucking off is that since they were depending on *camiones* [trucks] for transportation, they had to catch their *camión* around 5:00, or so. I arranged with Bill to have Alirio pick up the non-residents at 7:30 every morning, and to drive

them all the way home at 6:30 every night, so they are not dependent on the *casualidades* [chances] of truck traffic. I also explained that anyone who had to stay–for example interpreters who needed to remain to discuss their work with their counterpart–would always find a bed and food here.

I am keeping itemized records of accounts. I bargain with all the people who sell us livestock, and turned away one man today (even though we had nothing for dinner and had to rely on *tortillas de zanorias [zanahorias]* [carrot pies]!) because he wanted 18 soles for a *gallina flaquita* [thin chicken], and I wouldn't give him more than 17.25. I told the boys about it at dinner and they were horrified because we really needed the damned chicken, but I explained that I had done it because I wanted the tradesmen to be aware that they could no longer *engañar* [take advantage of] the Hacienda, that we would no longer pay anything they ask. I bought a *carnero* [sheep] for 55 soles, beating the price down from 60. They are also taking over the care of the light plant after ten, so we don't have to pay Alirio to *cuidar* [take care of] it, and are again rotating turns at it. I explained that since we have to pay for the lights after 10, I would not tolerate their burning unless more than myself were working. If it were only me, I could use the Coleman lamp. We agreed to fix, at each dinner, what time the lights would go out, on the grounds of each man's schedule of work.

*Fernández, one of the non-residents, came to me today and apologized for his drunken behavior the night of Pete's *despedida*. I said we would forget the past–but *all* of it–and this is a new era. The meeting we held from 4:30 till 6:00 today was a real work session, and almost everyone made some sort of contribution. Moreover, before dinner tonight, Gutiérrez asked if I would be good enough to hold a brief seminar discussion, explaining to them some of the variables in the questionnaire which we had been discussing. I agreed to do so, and he asked me if I would do it as a regular feature. He said the boys had been discussing this by themselves and would appreciate it, and it was too bad, wasn't it?, that we hadn't done this in the past. Of course, he is ass-kissing to some extent, but it doesn't matter what his motivation is. The fact is that we did hold the seminar and that we have scheduled such informal talks as a regular feature, and it is real training for them.

It's just barely possible that things are looking up. Bill and Max think I have cause to be optimistic, but I am withholding judgment for a few days. Certainly the atmosphere today was (a) work, (b) friendly, and (c) respectful–and absolutely for the first time. I forgot to mention that since the dinner was so awful, and since I was still hungry after dinner, I made pancakes for everyone. Again, I think the boys appreciated it. Pepe came in to learn how to do them, since he has to make them for breakfast when it is his turn.

Well–all very nice, but all this trouble about administration means that methodology really gets bypassed. I'll give it another 8 days, and if it doesn't work out I'll close up the whole damned mess. But maybe it will work out. Love, S.

P.S. So many details about work. Tell me how are you and my animal family? Why don't you write?

Levy begins her letter with the statement that she is "making a last stand and it may turn out to be all right." Her reform consists of meeting with the field workers to organize them. They end up with a schedule for household tasks, an agenda of field work tasks, a lights-out policy, and a seminar at the field workers' request, as well as a rather vigorous respect for Levy's power and authority. The field workers are "ass-kissing to some extent, but it doesn't matter really what [their] motivation is." When her penny-pinching results in a meager dinner, and everyone is still hungry, she makes pancakes and one of them takes a cooking-lesson from her. The penny-pinching really amounts to that, for at the exchange rate of around 20 soles to the dollar in 1953 she refuses to buy the chicken because of a difference of less than five cents. Levy, now freed from the impediments offered by Rogers, Nolan, and Quiller, is showing everyone a different, and doubtlessly a quite unexpected, character. She has also managed, with Mario Vázquez's help, to "whip the cook into line." Rationality has seemingly wiped (and whipped) frivolity out of Vicos, but in the seams of this document I read an insatiable desire to have everything in order, everything working.

When Levy fired Quiller, she also left Quiller with a task to perform in Lima. This was to have the contents of the field workers' notebooks typed at the Magdalena archaeology museum, relying on the kindness of Jorge Muelle and a North American visiting scholar. Quiller reported back to her on the progress of processing the qualitative data–what Levy has repeatedly referred to as "not a lick of work"–in the next document:

Lima, September 9, 1953. Dear Sarah, I've been seeing about the note typing here. Things are complicated because *Roger Stokes [visiting at the museum] is leaving Lima permanently, and Muelle wouldn't let his secretary, Bustamante, type more than 2 notebooks. I now have B. finishing the 2 notebooks and a Sra. Barrón working on the others (she has also typed Armando's [Castillo's] notes before). Two others in the museum are working on them in a minor way. Roger bought and delivered the paper and agreed on a price of S/4 a page for the 3 copies on legal size pages. Castillo had evidently written directly to Bustamante telling her to use that size.

José Matos, whom I'd normally leave in charge of getting the stuff done, is leaving for France Saturday, so I'm leaving it in the hands of Julio Basto Girón, the new secretary of the Instituto de Etnología, with his and José's agreement. I left your address with him and told him to write you for a check or giro when he knew how much it was going to cost and when it would be finished. He's a faithful guy and I'm sure will do the necessary prodding. I told him you would write where you wanted the various copies sent. I'm afraid it's going to take so long it would be best to have them sent directly to the states. [Here Basto's address is given.] I've been having trouble getting a plane, but am now on a waiting list for Sunday and confirmed for Wednesday. I left your ticket with Braniff to have you rerouted directly to Ithaca. When you know the date you should let them know in advance, because travel is evidently heavy this time of year. You should also write Braniff in Lima telling them what you want done with your refund check. It is refunded in dollars, but the check has to come from the States and I don't know how long it takes. Better ask them and tell them according to the [unreadable word] where you want it sent.

I paid Guillén [the photographer] the S/300 and am enclosing the canceled bill. Tell Mario I left his film with Cliff: I'm taking his black and whites to the States for Zelda [Barnett] and am leaving the color for him in Lima, since I don't know whether or not he wanted me to take them. Thanks for sending the passport which I got in good order.

Tell all that the archaeologist Wendell C. Bennett was drowned in Massachusetts three days ago.

Love to all, *Chau*, Pete.

P.S. I cabled Frank to send you S/.20,000 the night I arrived in Lima.

There is nothing in this letter to suggest the tension that existed between Levy and Quiller on the latter's departure from Vicos. Quiller seems to be "in line," but probably only after imbibing enough pisco to write her. Levy continues her optimism in her next letter–in Spanish–home:

September 11, 1953. *Dear Rosita, I don't know why you don't write me but it doesn't matter. I have a lot to tell you. It's been a week that we've been working as a team here. Everything changed. I like my boys. They are working like peons. I explained to them what I wanted and they cooperated. Every day we have meetings to discuss what happened during the day. Even Celso León, a peon from the Hacienda working as interpreter and more or less as a servant, is cooperating with us, making suggestions, giving his opinions, etc. I never, never would have hoped or thought that the atmosphere could have changed so quickly and so happily. For example, today it's clear that we will have to work on Sunday to catch the peons (they're very hard to catch). And today during the meeting, they themselves made the suggestion to work on Sunday. We discussed everything–the problems, the experiences of each day. Each day the* "chairman" *is changed. I was* chairman *only twice. We also have democracy in the house. Every day another boy is* "taken" *as the breakfast cook. I'm not, because you know how I am in the morning. Every night, after the meeting of everyone, we get together as a team again. We drink* "Pepe punch"*–a very flavorful recipe that I have to* *teach you, and then we have a seminar. They asked me–the idea wasn't mine. I'm the professor about 4 nights in the week, for only about 20-30 minutes, and other nights Bill is the teacher, or rather the professor, telling them about his experiences and work.. Tonight, for example, our meeting began at 7. We drank punch. They asked me to discuss some scientific problems–the study of values, how about that!–which I did. Afterward we had dinner, and then we sang for a while. They are practicing a serenade for some girls in Marcará, because tomorrow there's going to be a fiesta, and now, at midnight, everybody is working in their rooms.*

A short while ago I spoke with Mario, and he told me that I can be optimistic and without fear. Gutiérrez told me today that he wants to write a report for me giving me his opinion about what happened here during the first weeks, because the atmosphere changed, and some suggestions and criticisms so that we could improve the next study. Truly, Rosita, I'm very pleased. It's been just a week, or about 8 days, since Pete left, and already we're working like crazy!! What good boys. Well, they have, of course, their weaknesses and errors and lacks. For example, Pepe is a loafer and a "snob." He treated his interpreter like a valet, and yesterday I found the latter sweeping Pepe's room!!! But I worked with him, Pepe, very seriously, giving him a heavy agenda, studying his reports very carefully, making notes, suggestions and demands and exactions. And today he asked me to take a walk with him for a while, and while walking he told me that up to now he did not understand very well what we wanted but now he understands everything and he would like to stay here working, if I'm agreeable!!

How much I learned–no? [Unreadable word] Spanish (I haven't had to look up a single word in the dictionary while writing you this letter) and, look, holding meetings and lectures in Spanish (bad ones but understandable). Better than language, nevertheless, are the things I learned here about how we can manage a team of workers in the field. Well, I didn't want to do more than report to you how life is going now in Vicos. Of course, we have our problems, but they are realistic problems of work, not foolishness like before.

You are proud of me? I am it of myself, without being an egotist, I think. Well, maybe it's too early to predict with conviction, but we'll see. Maybe we can finish this study without any shame. I love you, S.
I also love the rest of my family.

Levy, indeed, has "a lot to say." Everything has changed. It is now two months since she arrived in the Andes, and doubtlessly she is feeling better. All the "bad influences" are gone and she can shape the study, and her "boys," the field workers, as well, to correspond more closely with her desire. Now she can say with enthusiasm, and in truth, "I like my boys,"

who "are working like peons [i.e., hacienda colonos]." Her little group
has daily meetings and evening seminars. "The atmosphere" has "changed
so quickly and so hapily": "we discuss everything." They have
"democracy in the house." The field workers are even willing to work on
Sundays, and it is at their own suggestion. Gutiérrez wants to write an
"report," surely to reflect negatively on the previous management of the
project and positively on Levy's "new order." Benavides takes her on a
walk and confesses his former sad confusion and present happy
understanding. And Levy writes at midnight that "everybody is working in
their rooms." The field workers merit the commendation, "What good
boys"!

I do not wish to take from Levy her successful "extirpation" of the
Methodology Project's excesses, for I do not believe that the former
consumption of such copious quantities of alcohol far into the night is
conducive to serious research. Nor am I opposed to the education of data-
gatherers, and their democratic treatment. I also encourage the admission
of human desire into our work, for it will be there with a vengeance if we
foolishly forbid its approach. But there is something in Levy's letter that
nearly defies my vocabulary for conveying a feeling. Perhaps "whistling
in the dark" would describe the way in which I see her satisfaction and
pride in the work she is doing. She is going to accomplish the structured
part of the research, but she is going to do it by threatening to withdraw
her support from the field workers. This would include not only
withholding their stipends but complaining to their mentors in the
University of San Marcos. They, in turn, are abject in giving her what she
wants, like compliant children endeavoring to please a demanding parent.
It is true that the "silliness" of June and July is gone, with Nolan and
Quiller, but I have the uneasy feeling that it are merely being replaced by a
new emphasis on social "science." Levy has been molded, after all by the
patriarchs of her graduate training and squeezed by her seniors at Cornell.
She, too, can behave like a patriarch!

Levy is proud of herself, pleased that things are going so well and
hoping that she can bring the research to a successful conclusion "without
any shame." She feels so good, apparently, that she does not write her
companion again for a month. The next letter in the packet is from Lima
and dated October 10, 1953:

> Dear Rosita, I don't know what I see in you or why I ever take seriously
> one word you say. As a result of your suggestion about [meeting in a
> Latin American country], I delayed arranging for my ticket back home
> because I couldn't decide whether to return by way of [the capital of that
> country] until hearing from you. So God knows whether I'll be able to get

space now, without slipping something under the table.

What a fiasco the end of the project turned out to be. I had to fire all our anthropologists. I withheld their last week's wages pending receipt of certain reports they owe me, and here I am in Lima waiting to work with them again. I find they don't know how to write a report or a memo, so the only way to get their work out of them is to sit down at the typewriter and pull it out of them, making them dictate while I write, and questioning them like informants.

The last fracas I had with them meant I stayed up all night doing precisely this, and had to throw them out the next day (actually throw them out!) In order to avoid another *despedida*. One of them stole the portable Hermes typewriter, and I have to straighten out that little mess here in Lima.

But, in spite of everything, the study is finished. I have never worked so hard in my life, I think, nor had to improvise and do so many crazy things. You would never believe it was me lifting up a live sheep to prove to the seller that it was *bien flaco y no vale* [quite thin and not worth] 60 soles, or standing over that *cochina* [sow] of a cook and making her wash the walls with soap, and calling her back to examine the tomatoes she was giving away to see if they were really too soft for us to use, shaking eggs to determine whether they were fresh enough to buy, pinching chickens to determine whether they were *gorditas* [little plump ones]; making shelves out of planks and adobes; making the cook (again) rewashing the kitchen towels because they were dirty (she said, "I just washed them yesterday!"); preparing lunch for the *alforjas* [saddle bags] of the field men (of diced meat, sliced onions, and *ají* packed in old tin cans which I saved for precisely that purpose); chauffeuring the car over incredibly bad roads with winding curves and sheer drops without any protection at 40 miles an hour, and leaning on the horn instead of on the brake; tramping over the countryside for hours to find an inaccessible informant, and sitting on a bunch of fleabitten hides in his mud house to interview him about his attitude to new seed potatoes; checking on the work of the field men to make sure they had actually been to the informant allegedly interviewed; running the ditto machine, cutting stencils, keeping the sample straight, comparing it with census material, conducting training seminars, and God knows what else. Getting up at 6:30 every morning and turning in anywhere from 1 to 4 a.m., including a few all-night sessions. Rosita, if you and I had come here alone to do this study, it could have been done at half the cost, in half the time, and twice as efficiently. I have written to Martin [Roberts, a senior sociologist] telling him that my recommendation is to pause right here and replan the study to encompass training of field workers. I sent a copy of that letter to Art, with a personal postscript to him alone, suggesting that Frank Nolan resign. I shall make that recommendation personally to Martin, but I didn't want to write it in a letter going to the Department. I will also tell him that I want to direct this study from now on myself. No one else can do it and no one else can analyze material, for the simple reason that no one else knows what happened! I hope you have saved my letters, as I asked you to do, because they constitute part of my field notes which I didn't dare keep around the hacienda.

I have about four days' worth of work still to do in Lima, and then I plan a trip either to Cuzco and thence to La Paz and thence home. Or, if it is not the rainy season, from Lima to Iquitos by plane, and from Iquitos down the Amazon by boat to Sao Paulo, and then back to the States. I prefer the latter trip (it sounds more exciting to me) but if it's raining I'll take the former trip.

So I'll be back the end of this month. Be good and tell the animals I'm coming soon. I'll let you know arrival date and perhaps you can pick me up by car in New York for a brief *paseo* [excursion] there before getting back to the old grind. Love, Sarah.

Things are not as well controlled as Levy hoped they would be. First, Rosa Sánchez seems to have attempted to arrange for the two of them to meet in her homeland and return to Ithaca together from there, but the plan has fallen through and she scolds: "I don't know what I see in you or why I ever take seriously one word you say." Now she doubts that she will be able to get home quickly "without slipping somebody something under the table." Second, Levy sees "the end of the project" as "a fiasco." Since the Methodology Project has not ended, but is merely completing its first phase, we can well wonder if this "end" might be a goal, a desired outcome, rather than an actual termination? She has held back the field workers' wages until they produce what they "owe her" by way of final reports (a way of holding these "slippery" field workers?). One of them, it turns out, "stole" a typewriter from the project. But "fiasco" or not, she reports on her extraordinary efforts, from examining the tomatoes the cook wanted to give away, "to see if they were really too soft for us to use," to packing lunches in tin cans which she had "saved for precisely that purpose," to checking on informants and field workers, alike. She notes that she has written to Martin Roberts, a distinguished senior sociologist, with recommendations for future phases of the project, with a copy to Arthur Silver, who is currently living in California, and a postscript only to the latter suggesting that Frank Nolan resign. Levy adds: "I shall make that recommendation personally to Martin, but I didn't want to write it in a letter going to the Department." Here, too, something "slippery" is going on "under the table." She now asserts that she wishes "to direct the study from now on" herself, since "no one else can do it . . . for the simple reason that no one else knows what happened." "What happened" is unspeakable, and so Levy does not say it.

The letter to Roberts is included in the packet. Note the tone with which

Levy writes to her superior in Ithaca, so different from her letters to Rosa
Sánchez, and as if she were yet *another* person:

Lima, Perú, October 10, 1953. Dear Martin, If I have not written you
sooner, it is because I find that, in the field, every moment free for writing
is dedicated to field notes and observation. One is jealous of minutes
stolen for correspondence.
But now the Vicos part of our methodology study is finished. I say
"finished" perhaps ill-advisedly, because I am plagued by the sense of
many details un accomplished and many plans left relatively untouched.
Only consolation is that every study I have ever worked on has always left
me less with the sense of goals achieved and more with the sense of a vast,
untapped beyond.
This has been for me, in one sense, the most exciting study I have ever
handled, and in another sense the most frustrating. I have rarely worked
so hard and learned so much in such a short space of time, and against
such uneven odds. I have been field director, field worker, purchasing
agent, head of a household, secretary chauffeur, toter of heavy bundles,
and headmaster at a school for boys. I have ruined my digestion and lost
10 pounds. But I loved every minute of it.
After three and a half months of working in the field under rapidly
changing circumstances and conceptions, my conclusion is that the
character of the methodology study has changed substantially from its
original conception, and the study should be redesigned.
The most apparent need for replanning lies in the fact that our study
turns out to be at least as much a training project for anthropologists as it
is an attempt to evaluate systematically varied methods of investigating
anthropological and sociological problems. In a way I suppose this was
apparent to us as early as our planning meetings in Ithaca. But somehow
we never gave the proper emphasis to this aspect of the study. All our
early planning assumed that our investigators would somehow be on the
same level of training, competence, and experience as ourselves, and that
we could take these backgrounds as given, varying only method and
technique of securing data, and analyzing any variations in the quality of
the data gathered in terms of such alternative methods and techniques.
This assumption has turned out to be decidedly unwarranted.
For example, our staff in Vicos had as its nucleus three anthropologists,
and later a fourth. There were two undergraduates, one of whom had
changed his field three times (medicine to education to anthropology); the
second of whom has changed his field twice (education to anthropology).
There was a third undergraduate who had been writing his bachelor's
thesis for the past ten (sic) years; and the fourth is a graduate student
working for two degrees at once, in law and in anthropology, and whose
guiding ambition is to run for *diputado* [deputy, a member of the Peruvian
congress] next year. These men are allegedly the best available in Perú.
For example, all three have had from two to six years of experience in the

field. On the other hand, this experience has been entirely ethnological. They have never worked in team research; they have never worked on a study which dealt with dynamic hypotheses. Their usual procedure is to move into a community either alone or in a pair, without a director and without directives. They then take down everything that meets the eye, as amenuenses rather than as scientific investigators. These notes are never analyzed. They are typed as *"fichas"*–i.e., on 5 x 8's according to categories similar to, but not so detailed as the Yale Outline. The *fichas* are deposited in the museum archives, where they remain forever. Their work is never discussed, standards of performance are never imposed or explained, they are never trained further, they never know why they collected the data in the first place and never ask themselves why it should be significant, and they never know what ultimately becomes of it.

These men think sociology begins and ends with Morgan. They have never studied methodology in either anthropology or sociology. They have never had a course in social psychology. They are almost completely unexposed to any research in these fields during the past 20 years. Thus their professional performance, clearly, is wanting; their professional standards are inadequate; and, in addition, their professional motivation is quite different from what we expect from scientific workers and serious students in social science.

In working with these men, therefore, our main task became to define and illustrate what we meant by professional standards; to fill up the substantive gaps in their training; to cope with their lack of motivation while attempting to develop semblance of it in them. I would say that these training demands consumed more than 50 per cent of our efforts.

I foresee that unless we can work in other field stations with anthropologists and sociologists of equal training and experience as our own, we can expect to confront and equivalent situation. That is, that we will have to train our indigenous field workers right in the field in order to bring their performance up to a level where the effect of the methodological variations demanded by the study design can be evaluated.

In the field we met these needs by improvising in several ways. One was to conduct a series of informal seminars every night (with the aid of Bill Blanchard). At these seminars we discussed and explained current research, drawing as many parallels as possible between the studies discussed and our own current work. In addition, in these informal meetings, we explained in detail the aims of the methodology study, amplifying each time with reference to other works, but again always tying such works back to our own field tasks. Third, I tried to give them a broad view of the significance and development of each field task, tried to show them briefly how the material would be processed and analyzed, and how it would ultimately be related to matched material in other field stations. All this, of course, amounted to a short course in methodology, right in the field.

As far as field technique is concerned, I tried to go over each day's field notes in detail from at least three points of view: their substantive content, the sociological significance of such content, and the methodological findings. I did, of course, the best I could, but not as good a job as I should have liked to accomplish fir a number of reasons which I shall not go into here.

My recommendation on the grounds of our experience here is that the outlines of our methodology study be decidedly broadened to include training techniques in the field, and to evaluate the effectiveness of different training procedures under differing circumstances. As I see it, this is equally important as the methodological variations. Right now (before careful study and discussion) it occurs to me that we might consider gearing in with *Larry Guest's [a social psychologist at Cornell] training study, paralleling in accelerated form in other field stations, the training techniques he is developing in Ithaca, and adapting them to the demands of different cultures. At the same time it occurs to me that Larry's project might well be expanded to include more of methodology and technique, paralleling in Ithaca the sort of thing we have done in Vicos and are planning to do elsewhere.

It seems essential to me that we pause right here and analyze the materials and experiences we have collected in Perú, and on the grounds of such analysis replan and redesign our investigations elsewhere. I cannot overemphasize how important I consider this to be. I should estimate it as a four to five month full-time job of analysis.

Speaking personally, in spite of the grueling schedule, in spite of some bitter experiences, and even in spite of a great deal of self-criticisms and self-dissatisfaction, I feel very dedicated and serious about the methodology study. In many ways it has been the most rewarding job I have ever accomplished. I have always loved the feeling of reawakening that comes from travel, a new language, and a new culture; the feeling of using yourself that comes from rising to the occasion and improvising under the crazy exigencies of field work; the feeling of sharing that you get from teaching and the opportunity it presents to consolidate your own impressions; and the feeling of personal realization that you get from writing and analysis. Unfortunately, each of these four loves has all too often interfered with the others. The Vicos experience, for the first time, has happily amalgamated all four loves and has meant, for me, real vocational adjustment.

Today (Sunday) is my second day in Lima. I have about four days' worth of work here, and then I plan a brief paseo to get to see something of the country. Then back to Ithaca the end of the month. I look forward to seeing you and discussing the study in detail. Sincerely, Sarah Levy. Copy to A. S.

Here Levy presents an idealized, indeed an ego-idealized, picture of life in the field, very "slippery" indeed: she begins, "every moment free for writing is dedicated to field notes and observations." My reaction to this is, first, to assess the correspondence so far as a rather inadequate corpus of "field notes," if they can be called "field notes" at all (although, as I have stated, they constitute an excellent self-ethnography), for a period of three months in Vicos. But, second, I recall that her "free moments" are rare, so taken up is she by her obsessive-compulsive attention to small details, such as squeezing tomatoes and chickens to save a few cents, regulating the hours for electric lighting, "whipping" the cook into line, and supervising the lives of "her" field workers for twenty-four hours each day, checking their notes, informants, feeding patterns, and leisure-time activities. Although the general tone is satisfaction with the work accomplished–at least, this is the impression given by the conclusion–she notes that she is "plagued by the sense of many details unaccomplished and many plans left relatively untouched." The "only consolation," she adds, "is that every study I have ever worked on has always left me less with the sense of goals achieved and more with the sense of a vast, untapped beyond." Again, we come to Levy's uneasiness at what is left undone and unsaid, the "vast, untapped" undoable and unsayable.

She goes on to say that the work has both excited and frustrated her: "I have rarely worked so hard and learned so much in such a short space of time, and against such uneven odds." But all odds are uneven, except perhaps in some non-Euclidian region deep inside her where desire folds, enfolds, and refolds itself. She details her roles as "field director, field worker, purchasing agent, household head, secretary, chauffeur, toter of heavy bundles, and headmaster," and, she claims, "I loved every minute of it." However, "the character of the methodology study has changed substantially from its original conception, and the study should be redesigned" to include the training of "indigenous" field workers. The original study design assumed "that our investigators would somehow be on the same level of training, competence, and experience as ourselves." This was "decidedly unwarranted." The field workers in Vicos had "never worked in team research," or "on a study which dealt with dynamic hypotheses," and their production ended in a research limbo: "They never knew what ultimately becomes of it." "These men," she continues, "think sociology begins and ends with [Lewis H.] Morgan. They have never studied methodology in either anthropology or sociology," or "had a course in social psychology." Consequently, "their professional performance . . . is wanting, their professional standards are inadequate, and . . . their professional motivation is quite different from what we expect from scientific workers and serious students in social science." Levy's solution is to organize "a short course in methodology, right in the field." She does, she says, "the best job I could, but not as good a job as I should have liked to accomplish for a number of reasons which I shall not go into here." It is no great leap of the imagination to find Rogers, Nolan, and Quiller in this unspoken and unspeakable region along with Levy's other hatreds, fears, and agonies. However, her inclusion of her three abjects[13] is deliberate, while the rest is unconscious.

She concludes, "Speaking personally, in spite of the grueling schedule, in spite of some bitter experiences, and even in spite of a great deal of self-criticisms and self-dissatisfaction, I feel very dedicated and serious about the methodology study. . . . I have always loved the feeling of reawakening that comes from travel, a new language, and a new culture; the feeling of using yourself that comes from rising to the occasion and improvising under the crazy exigencies of field work; the feeling of sharing that you get from teaching and the opportunity it presents to consolidate your own impressions; and the feeling of personal realization that you get from writing and analysis." Another idealized expression which omits the agony of trying to force other people to conform to the dictates of a punitive superego. It seems also to be a bid for permanence at Cornell University.

On a carbon copy of her letter to Roberts, Levy wrote this message to Arthur Silver, who was at that time on sabbatical leave in California:

Postscript to Art: Unhappily, I have to make another strong recommendation–that Frank Nolan resign. He is scientifically dishonest (whether it is incompetence or morals is irrelevant, it amounts to the same thing). I will not say he is dishonest with budget funds, but he is irresponsible and cavalier to a point where it is hard to draw the line. He still has not the slightest conception of what this study is all about, nor the slightest interest in finding out. Not only has he made no positive contribution to the work, but in addition he has held back progress on the study and, I think, directly sabotaged it during the brief time he was in Vicos (he left around August 15). This is not only my own biased opinion–it is corroborated by the Blanchards, for example, who did not work directly with our project, but with whom I discussed work decisions simply because there was no one else around whom I could consider responsible.

Some day I shall entertain you with the full story of the Vicos experience, crazy from beginning to end. Simply the story of how you execute a survey which combines random sampling with area sampling, in an area where everyone is known by at least three names none of which bears the slightest resemblance to the others, is an evening's entertainment. Even now, having gone without more than four hours' sleep a night for weeks, living on dexedrine, and feeling utterly beat, I sometimes just sit back and laugh about the things that happened there. I wish you were coming home soon so I could tell you about it. There are so few people who can appreciate the full story, and in a few months I shall have lost the details and will have to rely on my notes–which is work instead of conversation.

After this experience, I have more respect for you and Martin and myself than ever before. With all our faults, we are serious and honest workers, and our interest in sociology and methodology is a *real* interest. And oh, Art, what a bunch of phonies! What a shocking experience! What a rude awakening!   I shall never believe a word of an anthropological study again. Most of my field notes didn't bear writing, and I took to recording them as letters home to Rosita, asking her to save them for me, because I didn't dare leave them around the hacienda.

I can imagine you, when you get this letter, wherever you are, reading it as if "through a glass darkly," feeling withdrawn and disengaged from all these problems, and saying to yourself and to Helen [Silver's wife], "How could I ever have been caught up in problems of this kind, how could I ever have thought them serious enough to stay awake over?" But you'll come back to it and to them, so save this letter somewhere.

I shall be leaving Lima the end of this week for a trip somewhere or other. I have two alternatives planned. One is to travel through Perú to Cuzco and then possibly to La Paz, Bolivia. The other (which I like but I have to check the weather) is Lima to Iquitos by plane, Iquitos down the Amazon to Sao Paulo by boat, and then plane back home. If I can miss the rainy season, that is what I should like to do.

I feel wonderful and productive, but tired. All my best to you, S.

Levy has a closer relationship with Silver because of their common training background and interests, and a Jewish understanding of another Jew,[14] but Silver is a senior sociologist and will judge Levy's movement toward tenure. In this note Levy gets right to her point which is the elimination of Nolan, her Other who represents the unspeakable for her, so she writes the phrases: "scientifically dishonest," "irresponsible and cavalier," "ignorant of the study's purpose," "uninterested," "morally questionable," and a "saboteur." "Slippery.! But not inaccurate. She then recounts some of the problems of conducting a social survey, focusing on sampling issues, in a "backward region" where "everyone is known by at least three names, none of which bears the slightest resemblance to the others." Here she holds up to ridicule an ambiguity she seems to fear because it impedes her work: she is more comfortable where each person has only one name and human affairs are more tidy, where Others are not so "slippery." Levy admits to "living on dexedrine," a drug frequently prescribed for depression a half century ago, the side effects of which may be added to hypoxia and sensory and cognitive overloading in assessing her difficulties in Vicos. She celebrates the goodness of sociologists like herself (Nolan does not fit into that category) and condemns anthropologists as "a bunch of phonies," vowing not to "believe in a word of an anthropological study again." She says, "What a shocking experience! What a rude awakening!" We can wonder what residues of earlier "shocks" and "rude awakenings," unspeakable events, may dwell in these words.

Levy imagines her friend Silver as "withdrawn and disengaged from all these problems," perhaps as Levy is herself from the unwriteable. As Levy says, "Most of my field notes didn't bear writing . . . I didn't dare leave them around the hacienda." Despite her fears of Silver's abandonment of her, Silver responds on October 25, 1953, from somewhere in Southern California, with this friendly letter:

Dear Sarah, How wrong can you be? Far from feeling withdrawn, I've been stewing over your letter, and especially the P.S. like it was all my fault. You were supposed to enjoy your trip to Peru. If I had anticipated the problems you ran into, I would have vehemently objected to your going. Your correct answer to this, of course, is that we would really have had a mess then. To that I can be more withdrawn and say, so then Nolan would be on the spot and it is his responsibility.

But, as you say, we're professionals and the project itself is important to us. What is to be done? I haven't written to Martin–my first impulse–so that you can speak to him personally first. And please don't hold back any apprehensions you have about Nolan. I know you won't about the project itself. After your discussion, let me know the result, and any way I can come into the picture. From what you say, I certainly agree that we should try to relieve Nolan of responsibility for the project, even if it is a nasty job. Every time I make a mistake like this, I realize that I knew it in advance but was too weak to do something about it.

I will leave the Nolan matter until after you discuss it with Martin. By the way, there is absolutely no mention of Rogers in your letter. What was his position?

As to the project, your report is very convincing and I sadly agree to *some* redirection toward training vs. methodology. The main thing is to end up with something–almost anything–that will make Rockefeller [i.e., the Foundation] satisfied with the way we spent the money. This means a reportable unit–probably published–on our experience. I think the worst result would be "personal" training that has no transference to the field in general. This is a *research* project, even if we switch from research on methods to research on training. And if we do switch, it should still be on at least a 50-50 basis. We add training to the project but keep at least 50% of our original methods *plan*. I could not tell from your letter just what the ratio of training to methodology results were obtained from your trip. I would appreciate a more detailed summary when you get the time. Please let me know what future plans develop from the project. I am in a good position to do some thinking about it myself–so as soon as you let me know how things stand, I'll see what I can do, even if it is to redesign the project.

Let me mention two considerations affecting a redesign. To what extent will we run into the same problem in India and Thailand? To what extent can we meet the problem rather than change the project? Could we use more trained [North] American anthropologists as field workers? How can we capitalize on field workers once we have trained them? After all, it seems to me, we are training them *so that we can use them* to move ahead with our methods research. Any training program should definitely end with the trainees going to work on the methods project. Perhaps we should return to Peru, rather than repeat the training in another area. The point I'm making is to try to meet these problems wherever possible before changing the project.

(Aside–if Nolan continues on the project, what exactly will he do in Ithaca until next year? I strongly urge that he be asked to turn out regular reports and call regular meetings. Our big mistake was in not requiring him to turn out something definite.)

As for my own experiences, they have been mixed but mostly positive. The trip [to the West Coast] was exciting and fascinating, but living 24 hours a day with the two children under circumstances they often found boring was quite a strain. But now we are settled for 3-4 months in one place, the kids are going to school, I am working 4-5 hours every day, and all is wonderful. I've done some extremely productive work on the [well known North American research on race relations] study and will mail it in next week. We'll both exchange detailed accounts when we see each other. Best regards, Art.

P.S. You may show this letter to Martin. Also, I will be in Hawaii from November 6 to November 30, so don't expect any correspondence.

There has been some questioning of Nolan's competence to undertake the study all along, and Silver admits his own misgivings. Nolan is under contract, however, and this agreement with Cornell University has, apparently, one more year to go. The problem for the sociologists is what exactly Nolan is to do during that last year. As it turned out, Nolan's personal situation changed and he was assigned courses to teach, out of the way of possible damage to on-going research. But this is getting ahead of the story of the Methodology Project. In his letter Silver brings up options for redesigning the study: good training is vital in social survey work because field workers must understand sampling procedures and their rationality. Since what the Methodology Project is about is a highly structured comparison of structured vs. non-structured methods, it is understandable that Silver would hesitate to commit resources to training issues. He even suggests returning to Peru to repeat that phase of the study–which with different directors with better preparation for field conditions might possibly have offered a better outcome.

Silver desires to satisfy the Rockefeller Foundation which gave him the resources to conduct the Methodology Project: "The main thing is to end up with something–almost anything–that will make Rockefeller satisfied with the way we spent the money. This means a reportable unit–preferably published–on our experiences." In the end, the group of researchers at Cornell gave their patron a final report of their research which looked good but meant little, if meaning resides in sharing results with other scholars. The problem was that despite Levy's protestations, many of the qualitative interviews were usable. The social survey was successfully carried out, despite Levy's concerns about sampling. And nobody could– or maybe it was because nobody *would*-- devise a technique for comparing them!

Again, I am getting ahead of events. Let us go back to October 19, 1953, a few days before Arthur Silver responded to Levy's letter. Levy had left Vicos, spent a week in Lima, and journeyed to Cuzco where she wrote this note to herself:

It's perfectly clear that once you leave off writing field notes you're sunk. You have to write them every day. I haven't written a note since I left Vicos, October 8, and the attempt to reconstruct what has happened in the interim is fruitless. It can't be done, but I'll try to reconstruct the bare outlines at least.

On the 9th, my first step was to seek out Gutiérrez. I went to his house in the morning at 8:00. (I was ready to leave at 6 o'clock but Marge [Bryson, owner and operator of the Pensión Morris where many visiting North American scholars stayed when in Lima] wouldn't let me. She said they'd throw me out.) He had already left. His brother told me where I could find him at the University [San Marcos], so I went there. Really, I was scared. I couldn't imagine how he would receive me. I came upon him in a class. (Later he explained that Castillo, Pepe, and even Sáenz [the other field workers at Vicos] had been in the same class, but it was only he who caught my eye.) He immediately came out to greet me. He was very cordial, as if there had been absolutely no unpleasantness in Vicos. He introduced me to Basto, the new secretary of the Institute, who has been arranging the typing for us. Basto is likewise an undergraduate student whose main function seems to be to hold the doors open for Valcárcel every time he enters or leaves a room. He is very polite in a *soplón*-like [informer-like] way. Basto was very deferential, and handed over the typed notes *hasta la fecha* [up to now], and I paid up. That was Castillo's notebooks 1-3. The girls were still working on his notebooks 4-6, which I collected just before I left for Lima. We decided to leave with them in Lima the last of Castillo's notebooks, 7 and 8, and also Gutiérrez's four notebooks. I took with me the few pages which remain to be typed of Sáenz's notes, and also a notebook by Fernández, containing life histories, two of which are unfinished. (I left two days' worth of salary for Fernández with Cliff, with instructions that he finish the life histories under Cliff's observations, and Cliff will send me not only the tail end of Fernández's life histories but also his own observations of how the boy works.)

After we arranged these things, I asked Gutiérrez to spend some time talking to me. I wanted to discuss two things: Castillo's taking off with the typewriter, and also the unfinished work which he and Gutiérrez, particilarly Gutiérrez, owe me. We went to a coffee joint nearby the University, and I found it difficult to proceed because I could not easily define our relationship. The last I had seen of him left me confused. On the one hand he had made a declaration of love. On the other hand, I had had to kick him out and he had behaved like a spoiled brat. I felt, however, that my best bet was to settle the Castillo affair through him. This was according to Mario's counsels, and also because I felt Castillo would be even more difficult to handle alone.

We sat in the coffee joint and Gutiérrez chattered away about how we would go out together and he would show me the real Lima, etc., while I tried to size up the situation to determine how to approach the matter. I finally decided to use the oblique approach. I told him that I had an unpleasant matter to discuss, that it concerned Castillo, that undoubtedly he knew what I was talking about, and that I hoped the situation would areglate [a blend of Spanish *arreglar*, to arrange, and English regulate?] itself without my having to take any official steps or discuss it with Valcárcel. I never once mentioned the typewriter or directly accused Castillo of having lifted it. Gutiérrez fell into the trap, referred directly to the typewriter, and said he would arrange it. We left each other around noon and I made a date to see him that night.

That afternoon Castillo called me on the telephone and I arranged a date with him too. In each case, our plans were to work on their owed reports, me at the typewriter, they dictating.

I can't reconstruct what happened day by day, but roughly it worked out like this. The first time I saw Castillo he was decidedly bitter and full of venom. He referred to the fact that I had "kicked them out" (his words). He said he had taken the typewriter as hostage for his unpaid salary. I pointed out to him that this was a stupid and unnecessary gesture since there was no doubt about our credit, and that he was damned lucky I had not discussed it with Valcárcel–that I had refrained from doing so only out of friendship, quite outside my role as director of the study. He softened considerably and by the end of the session told me the following things: that on the day in Vicos when I had insisted on an ultimatum, the boys were a little tight–they had been drinking beer, he said–and had I waited until the afternoon, the whole situation would have changed. I do not believe this is true because it was a Saturday morning and nobody had been drinking. To my knowledge, indeed, they had all been working. I feel this was only his way of being graceful, pleading non compos mentis, instead of apologizing outright. He told me that in retrospect, thinking about the study, he had decided that they had learned more in Vicos than they had learned throughout their university careers previously, and that he and Gutiérrez both wanted to specialize in methodology, that they were counting on me to send them literature, to keep in touch with them, and to return to San Marcos one day to establish a laboratory of modern social science. He and Gutiérrez both asked me to lecture at the University. (They scheduled me for three lectures, but I gave only one. I didn't feel like preparing any serious work, and didn't feel like slinging the bull without preparation, so I just summarized the methodology study.) Indeed, their attitude of leaning on me in a dependent and even affectionate fashion puzzled me no end, in the sense that they seemed to have not the slightest expectation that I would be angry with them or bitter or withdrawn or anything.

I tried to work with Castillo, getting him to be specific about his work with *Miguel Colonia [a Vicosino], but it was un unsuccessful attempt because I couldn't get him to do more than make general statements, and the concrete illustrations which I was seeking he couldn't supply. In discussion, he said that now he realizes what he should have done, how it was essential to report in as detailed a fashion on the situation, and on the method, and on the interpreter, as on the information provided by the respondent. (Castillo has done this well in his survey interviews, but not in his qualitative work.) In discussing the possible plans for the future of the methodology study, I told him that one possibility which I was considering was the possibility of returning to Vicos next year and repeating the study. I asked him: "Would you be willing to work with me again, but under *my* conditions, and you understand very well what they are?" He said yes, decidedly, without any question, he would be overjoyed, and even if he were employed he would leave whatever job to work with me again. He also offered, of his own volition, to write me a report on his present understanding of the plan of the methodology study. (I'll believe it when I see it.) Although my attempt to work with him on his report re working with an interpreter, was a fiasco (I got only two pages of broad generalizations and didn't even think it worth the trouble to finish), I told him that when Bill came down to Lima he would pay him the 480 soles we "owe" him.

Gutiérrez was a bit easier and yet a bit more difficult. He came to the house almost every day, kept protesting his love at every opportunity, in public treated me as his personal property to a point where it was embarrassing. I did a foolish thing which made it even more embarrassing—namely, I gave him my cigarette lighter as a *recuerdo* [memento], and he kept flourishing it at the slightest opportunity. I don't know whether the others recognized it, or, if they did, what they thought—I never used the lighter in Vicos—but I suppose it was kind of dumb of me.

I absolutely couldn't work with Gutiérrez. We had to work in my room at the *pensión* [boarding house], because of the typing and discussing, and it was just too difficult under the circumstances. So I told him to write me the things he owes (personal data, report on a fiesta, report on a method of working with photos, report on an interview with Adrián with photos) and send them to me in Ithaca. Whether he will or not remains to be seen, because we parted inamicably again. I got fed up with his sweet talk and no work, and refused to see him again when last he telephoned. And I foolishly paid him 400 soles out of the 480 owed, because he gave me a hard luck story about the rent and a mortgage, etc. I feel I have been engañared [a "Spanglish" word invented by Levy; the Spanish would be *engañado*, fooled; she has taken the infinitive and added an English suffix] by him, not only personally but also in terms of work. For example, in discussing the photos with him, he told me as if it were fact that the reason the Vicosinos could not perceive photos in two dimensions was because they never learned to see their images in a mirror, had no two-dimensional art forms, etc. This he reported as if it were fact that he had discovered by observation and interview. Actually, he was parroting a general discussion I had had with him early in the game, in which I speculated about these other two-dimensional perceptions and their relation to the perception of photographs.

One day at the University I went to see Valcárcel for the purpose of presenting myself, and also to discuss my evaluation of the performance of his students in Vicos. I entered his office, and no sooner had we accomplished the amenities than in came Gutiérrez, Castillo, and Pepe. They hung around and hung around (Basto was also there), so I couldn't say a word about an evaluation report. I was very irritated at Valcárcel's stupidity, and said to myself, "Well, you'll just stick it out, wait them out." We spent about an hour with everyone in turn making a conversational attempt which I would permit to hit the floor (klunk!), answering only to the point and not pursuing a topic. After about an hour of this gruesome situation, my boys left the room for a brief minute, leaving only Basto and Valcárcel, and another *catedrático* [professor], present. Even though I knew Basto, a schoolmate of the boys, will probably report what I said, I decided to take the bull by the horns and broach the subject of evaluation to Valcárcel. I told him that I assumed his university operated like ours, that when our department loans students to work in the field they usually ask for a report or evaluation of their performance, which is added to the student's docket and is relevant also to his academic standing. Valcárcel said, "Of course," as if that was what he had in mind all the time. I promised to send him such an evaluation. I will, too, without pulling any punches.

Meanwhile, I had also reported to Velasco at the Instituto in order to present myself, pay my respects, and also arrange for the Instituto to ship our stuff. Velasco was very cordial and promised to take care of everything for me. He checked cargo and also *correo* [mail], but was unable to exact a promise of delivery in New York sooner than 6 weeks earliest, possibly 2 months or more. Therefore I decided to ship the stuff air express–which will come to about $100 and change, but it seemed to me that to balk at that expense was like gagging at a hair. We have spent, and wasted, so much money already that $100 is a drop in the bucket. Moreover, I have lots of work to do on the data: index all names in the qualitative material so that we can have a docket on each person interviewed or observed by whatever method; begin to code the survey; and begin to analyze the qualitative materials. Therefore, I want the materials to arrive home when I do.

About Velasco, he pulled a gag on me. Said he was overjoyed to see me, etc., etc., but what about that article I promised to write for the Revista [del Museo Nacional]? I can recollect no such promise, and I told him so. What I had promised was only a biographical sketch of a paragraph or so. But he insisted that he was counting on an article from me, and that I had promised, so I said when I get home I would send him a descriptive summary of the Methodology Project. Must do. He was very kind and helpful, took me to dinner . . . and that was that.

For the rest, I took it easy in Lima, shopped and went around to see the sights, and then took off today at 6:30 a.m. for Cusco, where I am now.

The flight over the Andes was exciting. We flew so high we had to take oxygen, which was the first time for me. Made me gag. Arrived in Cusco, started to check in the main hotel, but decided it was too expensive, 80 soles, so switched over to a new hotel which is cheaper, 50 soles with *pensión* [here, meals] but I switched to *sin pensión* [without meals] at 20. Velasco had given me letters of introduction to the curator of the museum, the *prefecto* [Prefect], the archbishop, and two other functionaries whom I will look up tomorrow. Today, upon arrival I got collared by a tour representative who roped me into a trip to nearby ruins, in company with two youngsters who have just completed a mission (they are Mormons) in Uruguay. Very pleasant boys but, what cheek, at age 19'21 going around and telling people what is the only true belief. The ruins were interesting, but my feet hurt and I was so tired after lunch that I slept until 5:30, got up and walked around town a bit, had dinner, a bath, and now I'm ready for bed again. The tour man just stuck his head n the door again to see if I want to go to Machupichu [i.e., Machu Picchu] tomorrow at 5 a.m. again, but I politely declined. I shall look up the VIP's to whom I have *cartas de presentación* [letters of introduction] and see what they can cook up for me. I took some photographs of the ruins, but don't expect them to come out (no exposure meter), so I bought some photos too. I would like to buy some more things to take back with me. They are cheaper here than in Lima, but I'm afraid I won't have room in my bags.

I'm trying to think what are my impressions of the ruins, but they escape me. They are big and rocky, and one wonders at the engineering feat of fitting them all together and shaping them without tools. One can visualize, too, the system of communication and protection represented by the *fortalezas* [fortresses] and lookout posts, but it leaves me cold. Once you've seen a ruin, you've seen them all. I'll try Machupichu and see how it moves me, if at all.

Levy begins this unhappy account of her stay in Lima with the observation that "once you leave off writing field notes, you're sunk," and ends with "once you've seen a ruin, you've seen them all." She admits, "I haven't written a note since I left Vicos." We may assume that there were too many unwriteable events to not-write about, including the secretary who is "very polite in a *soplón*-like way," the ubiquitous field workers, the amorous advances of Gutiérrez, the bulls, and the gagging. She endeavors, nevertheless, to reconstruct her meeting with the field workers and her rescue of *their* field notes. She is very uncomfortable with Gutiérrez, who is too intimate and fawning, but needs him in order to settle the matter of the typewriter that Castillo has in his possession. She meets with Castillo whom she perceives as "bitter and full of venom," but who later "softens" and confesses that he and the other field workers "had learned more in Vicos than they had learned throughout their university careers previously." Castillo adds "that he and Gutiérrez both want to specialize in methodology." He would like to work with Levy again: "he would be overjoyed, and even if he were employed he would leave whatever job" for such an opportunity. Both "boys" asked her to lecture at the University of San Marcos, but she "didn't feel like slinging the bull without preparation." She tries to work with Castillo, to get him "to be specific about his work," but this fails "because I couldn't get him to do more than make general statements."

Gutiérrez is "a bit easier and yet a bit more difficult" because he is dependent. Moreover, his declaration of love makes her feel strange. Perhaps frightened. Levy says, "I absolutely couldn't work with him. . . . I got fed up with his sweet talk and no work." Whether or not Gutiérrez will complete the work he "owes" the project is problematic "because we parted inamicably again. Levy feels that she has been "fooled" by him both personally and professionally, what with his "hard luck story" and "parroting" of what she has said to him.

Levy goes to see Luis Valcárcel, the distinguished Andeanist scholar and is met there by three of his "boys" and Julio Basto Girón. She thus was in the position where "I couldn't say a word about an evaluation report" and "I was very irritated at Valcárcel's stupidity." Eventually, the "boys" leave and she decides "to take the bull by the horns" by negotiating a future evaluation–of which there is no record. But this talk of "slinging the bull" and taking it "by the horns" brings with it recollections of the bullfighting she witnessed in Huaraz. "Slinging" a bull would require superhuman strength, while "taking a bull by the horns" would require great courage and defiance of injury and death–unless the bull's throat had already been cut and it was bleeding to death. "Slinging the bull" consciously means "bullshitting"; and "taking the bull by the horns" means confronting a difficult situation, "rationalizing" it. Thus, "under the table" there appears an association between feces and rationality, perhaps an endeavor to rationalize elimination, to get the body "working" properly. These feelings surface again in Levy's negotiations to ship the project's materials home, where time becomes a factor and the "$100 and change" charge for air express is "a drop in the bucket." To "balk at that expense was like gagging [i.e., choking] at a hair." And then Velasco, at the Institute, "pulls a gag [i.e., attempts to trick or fool her]" on her. And finally, en route to Cusco, taking oxygen "made me gag [i.e., choke]." Is her body attempting to trick her, or is it trying to throw up something noxious so that it, and she, can "work" properly, rationally. In Cusco, her impressions of the ruins "escape" her, but "once you've seen a ruin, you've seen them all." "A ruin" among many, including her ruined relationship with George Rogers, the "*malogrado*" ruined project, the "*malogrado*" spoiled "boys," and possibly her digestion. She will try Machu Picchu to "see how it moves me, if at all."

In putting together a sub-ethnography of a woman's experience with the Vicos Project, the ethnographer cannot escape writing as a gendered knower. Helen Callaway (1992:30) writes:

What are the implications of the anthropologist as a gendered knower? . . . In what ways does rational inquiry have gendered dimensions? Since there are no ungendered lives, can there be ungendered texts? How does gender relate to the production of knowledge and its power structures (publishers' decisions, professional legitimation and so on)? These questions have been repressed, considered not worth asking, within the model of objective scientific research carried out and written up by the neutral and knower. Despite the placing of anthropology within the human sciences rather than the more positivist natural sciences and the centrality in the discipline of *participant*-observation, this image of the detached, historically unsituated observer persists.

In writing this impossible chapter about Sarah Levy, I believe I have indicated my situated gender. I have asked myself frequently: about whom am I writing? Whose ruins are being debated here? And whose digestion is being questioned? Have I used Jacques Derrida at the beginning of this chapter as a fetish, a powerful prop to cover my weakness, hesitation, and uncertainty? Or is that only a part of the truth? Is my understanding of Derrida's reading of Nietzsche's writing on women as a reading of the woman in himself a fair grasp of what he says, and a model for me in writing about a woman? So do I really see, in what I have written, the woman in me? Didn't I suggest near the beginning of this chapter, with the help of June Jordan, that the truth would be a "horrible truth?" I, a man, have my own ruins, my *cojudo malogrado* projects, my tomato-squeezing and hen-pinching, my slippery dealings under the table, my drill-sergeant pretensions, as well as my occasional wishes to lie down and play dead. But, I also have admiration for Sarah Levy, that is reminiscent of Stephen Heath's (1989:30) admiration, gazing at his mother "in a hospital ward . . . for hours and days." I have had a parallel experience, watching with mixed feelings of admiration, fear, and sorrow, a woman in hospitals and nursing homes, one with whom I shared a life for forty years, slowly turn to dust over the hours, and days, and years, but a woman who never played dead and who protested until there was silence. Sarah Levy, too, did not lie down and play dead. She refused to retire modestly, as patriarchy demands of a woman. She survived. More than that, she never ceased to struggle.

Notes

1. Clifford R. and Zelda Barnett have assisted me greatly in the preparation of these materials. We spent the day of November 11, 1997, together at their home discussing events in Vicos in 1953. They brought out field notes and correspondence which helped settle the dating of many comings, goings, and other happenings. Instead of peppering this manuscript with "personal communications" I choose to recognize their contribution here. I thank them deeply for their help and their hospitality.

2. In October, 1998, I visited the Archives of the Vicos Project, now located in the Karl Korch Library, Cornell University, Ithaca, New York, to search for data that might connect other parts of this book. I also searched the catalog for the Levy papers, to no avail. They seem to have disappeared from the collection. I have photocopies of the originals, made in the early 1970s, which I hope soon to place back where they should be.

3. Foucault (1980:133) adds to his statement on "truth" which I included in Chapter 1: "'Truth' is to be understood as a system of ordered procedures for the production, regulation, distribution, circulation and operation of statements."

Also: "'Truth' is linked in a circular relation with systems of power which produce and sustain it, and to the effects of power which it induces and which extend it." And: "It's not a matter of emancipating truth from every system of power (which would be a chimera, for truth is already power) but of detaching the power of truth from the forms of hegemony, social, economic and cultural, without which it operates at the present time."

4. But perhaps only sleeping. Not too long ago, in the aftermath of Presidential sexual scandals in the U. S. White House, the term "sexual McCarthyism" came into vogue.

5. Baudrillard (1981:85) defines "desublimation" in terms of "the deconstruction of the *ego* functions, the conscious moral and individual functions, to the benefit of a 'liberation' of the id and the super-ego."

6. Baudrillard (1975:40-41) offers a deconstruction of Marx's concept of labor, but the immediate context of this quotation is so relevant to my discussion of "work" in Levy's texts that it is worth reproducing: "Work and non-work: here is a 'revolutionary' theme. It is undoubtedly the most subtle form of the type of binary, structural opposition. . . . The end of the end of exploitation by work is this reverse fascination with non-work, this reverse mirage of free time (forced time-free time, full time-empty time: another paradigm that fixes the hegemony of a temporal order which is always merely that of production. Non-work is still only the repressive desublimation of labor power, the antithesis which acts as the alternative. Such is the sphere of non-work: even if it is not immediately conflated with leisure and its present bureaucratic organization where the desire for death and mortification and its management by social institutions are as powerful as in the sphere of work; even if it is viewed in a radical way which *represents it* as other than the mode of 'total disposability' or 'freedom' for the individual to 'produce' himself [or herself] as value, to 'express himself,' to 'liberate himself' as a (conscious or unconscious) authentic *content*, in short, as the ideality of time and of the individual as an empty form to be filled finally buy his freedom."

7. Foucault here focuses on the prison, but his point applies to many other contexts: "As it was initially conceived, penal labor was an apprenticeship not so much in this or that trade as in the virtues of labor itself. Pointless work, work for work's sake, was intended to shape individuals into the image of the ideal laborer. It was a chimera, perhaps but one which had been perfectly worked out and defined by the American Quakers, with the founding of the workhouses, and by the Dutch. But then, from the late 1830s, it became clear that in fact the aim was not to retrain delinquents, to make them virtuous, but to regroup them within a clearly demarcated, card-indexed milieu which could serve as a tool for economic or political ends."

8. *"Pendejo"* means "public hair" in Spanish, but is also used to convey an epithet like "idiot" or "jerk." As Sarah Levy uses it, I think the best translation might be "asshole," but I will leave it in its Spanish form in the text and let you be the judge.

9. Other interpretations are possible. Lacan (1988:317) says: "Behind what is named there is the unnameable. Because it is unnameable, with all the resonances that can be given to this name, it is related to the unnameable *par excellence*, that is, with death."

10. In an early definition of the term, Oberg (1960:177) says: "Culture shock is precipitated by the anxiety that results from losing all our familiar signs and symbols of social intercourse. These signs or cues include the thousand and one ways in which we orient ourselves to the situations of daily life: when to shake hands and what to say when we meet people, when and how to give tips, how to give orders to servants, how to make purchases, when to accept and when to refuse invitations, when to take statements seriously, and when not. Now these cues which may be words, gestures, facial expressions, customs, or norms are acquired by all of us in the course of growing up and are as much a part of our culture as the language we speak or the beliefs we accept. All of us depend for our peace of mind and our efficiency on hundreds of these cues, most of which we do not carry on the level of conscious awareness." Furnhan and Bochner (1986:4) add: "There is certainly evidence that culture contact can have beneficial effects on those participating in it. However, there also exists an opposing point of view, based on the central assumption that exposure to an unfamiliar culture may be, and often is, stressful and hence potentially harmful. Rather than expanding the mind and providing a satisfying and interesting personal experience, the hypothesis states that unfamiliar environments create anxiety, confusion and depression in individuals so exposed. In extreme cases, physical illness may be a direct consequence. Rather than creating better mutual understanding, culture contact often leads to hostility and poor interpersonal relations among those involved in the interchange."

11. In his first "Progress Report," Holmberg (1952:7-8) states: "[T]echnical collaboration has been offered in great abundance. The principal reason we have been yet unable to accept all offers of collaboration is that when we began our program no living facilities were available on the Hacienda. We have done all we can to remedy this situation: we have now completed two small modern apartments and will continue our building program as rapidly as time and funds permit. We have also installed a water and sewage disposal system for the plaza of the Hacienda."

12. Foucault (1980:147) defines the "panopticon principle" as: "A perimeter building in the form of a ring. At the center of this, a tower, pierced by large windows opening on to the inner face of the ring. The outer building is divided

into cells, each of which traverses the whole thickness of the building. These cells have two windows, one opening on to the inside, facing the windows of the central tower, the other, outer one allowing daylight to pass through the whole cell. All that is then needed is to put an overseer in the tower and place in each of the cells a lunatic, a patient, a convict, a worker or a schoolboy." (See also Foucault 1977a:200.) The object of the panopticon is "to induce in the inmate a state of conscious and permanent visibility that assures the automatic functioning of power" (201). The Vicos Project headquarters, of course, did not conform to this architectural model, but Levy's surveillance of her "boys" was nevertheless effective: her power was established.

13. Kristeva (1982:2) says: "To each ego its object, to each superego its abject. It is not the white expanse or slack boredom of repression, not the translations and transformations of desire that wrench bodies, nights, and discourse; rather it is a brutish suffering that 'I' puts up with, sublime and devastated, for 'I' deposits it to the father's account: I endure it, for I imagine that such is the desire of the other. A massive and sudden emergence of uncanniness, which, familiar, as it might have been in an opaque and forgotten life, now harries me as radically separate, loathsome. Not me. Not that. But not nothing, either. A 'something' that I do not recognize as a thing. A weight of meaninglessness, about which there is nothing insignificant, and which crushes me. On the edge of non-existence and hallucination, of a reality that, if I acknowledge it, annihilates me. There, abject and abjection are my safeguards. The primers of my culture."

14. This "understanding" is neither perfect nor universal. It can break down. But understanding or not, not so long ago, all the Jews that could be found in Europe, "good" ones and "bad" ones alike, observing ones and non-observing ones, Zionists and anti-Zionists, rode in boxcars headed toward the death camps. Had I been there, instead of in the United States Army in San Diego, North Africa, and Italy, I would have ridden with them, no matter what kind of Jew I was and am. Levy and Silver, minimally, had that "something" in common.

Chapter 2, Part II:

No Alibi for Endless Alibi: Sarah Levy's Fable

Within an area of discourse that has been fairly well established since the end of the seventeenth century in Europe, there are only two major types of *authorized* examples for invention. On the one hand, people invent *stories* (fictional or fabulous), and on the other hand they invent *machines*, technical devices or mechanisms, in the broadest sense of the word. Someone may invent by fabulation, by producing narratives to which there is no corresponding reality outside the narrative (an alibi, for example), or else one may invent by producing a new operational possibility (such as printing or nuclear weaponry, and I am purposely associating these two examples, since the politics of invention is always at one and the same time a politics of culture and a politics of war). Invention as *production* in both cases–and for the moment I leave to the term "production" a certain indeterminacy. *Fabula* or *fictio* on the one hand, and on the other *tekhnè, epistémè, istoria, methodos*, i.e., art or know-how, knowledge and research, information, procedure, etc. (Jacques Derrida 1989a:32.)

Yes, there are many who, suffering from what I would call premature conclusion, couldn't resist the temptation to interpret differance [i.e., *différance*] as an alibi, above all as a political alibi, an allegation destined to delay the deadline, to do everything it takes to do nothing right away.

Well, there is one thing I think I know, but it is a perilous knowledge. What remains no doubt to be thought *without alibi* is precisely a differance *without alibi*, right there where, it's true, this same difference goes on endlessly producing irreducible effects of alibi through traces that refer to some other, to another place and another moment, to something else, the absolute other, to the other to come, the event, and so forth. One has to go elsewhere to find oneself here. The here-now does not appear as such, in experience, except by differing from itself. And one trace always refers to another trace. It thus secretes, it produces, it cannot not produce some alibi. Ubiquity of the alibi. (Jacques Derrida 2002c:xvi-xvii.)[1]

How am I to trace Sarah Levy's return, a return of symbolic violence for symbolic violence? Men who write about women take a risk. As Adrienne Rich (1986:191) maintains: "By far the majority of men have written of women out of the unexplored depths of their fears, guilt, centered on our relationship to them, that is, to women perceived as either mothers or antimothers." So am I also writing about my mother? The woman who, one of my earliest memories tells me, was tall and powerful and walked so fast I was afraid I couldn't keep up, and, one of my last tells me, was frail and old, far older than I am now three years older than she, at the same age that was her last age. The mother who, needing to go to work to pay for urgent surgery and in desperation, dumped me (for a time) in an orphanage at age 4. Maybe it's an impossible task to relate or to write. In his discussion of "men's relation to feminism," Stephen Heath (1989:30) begins with the statement that such a relation is "an impossible one": for "the male position . . . brings with it all the implications of domination and appropriation." Have I then availed myself of my privilege to dominate and appropriate Sarah Levy, and have I imagined me in her body by way of avoiding the inclusion of my own body? Paul Smith (1989:37), in the same collection of articles, remarks that

we men might think that the writing of our imaginary would be exactly a pornography, the manifestation of our imaginary relation to the maternal body and nothing so much as a pure ambivalence, or an even more resilient fetishism. If the structures in which we are caught, in which our egos are constructed, are accurately described by theory and feminist theory, is our imaginary anything but a pornographic defense against the mother's body?

A pornography? Yet, at the same time, Cary Nelson (1989:157) observes:

But of course we all write our bodies all the time, at least in the sense that what we want and fear is inscribed in our language, its pauses and stresses, its periodicity, are somatically negotiated and inscribed with physical effects. Discourse is socially and libidinally constituted; gender and the life of the body are continually at issue, are continually put forward, in everything we write. Writing is at once a mediated form of bodily expression and an externalized encapsulation and rejection of bodily life.

Am I by "de/re-form[ing] a sign and write[ing] instead of phallic subtexts", as Rosi Braidotti (1989:233) says, when I write about a woman, merely writing a "pheminist" text? And, as such, do I include Andrew Ross's (1989:91-92) list of "right-thinking dictates and wrong-thinking mandates, native speakers and alien impersonators, admirers, fetishists and voyeurs, bona fide originals and flawed simulacra, gift-bearing Greeks and cultural appropriators, impulse buyers and critical cross-dressers, not to mention the multifarious discourses of authentification that serve to distinguish each from the other"? Well, what a complicated narrative if this is so! Yet John Caputo (1997b:142-143) asks and answers:

> Can a man write about women? Would this not make woman his "subject"? Can a man write like a woman? Would that not be more masculine mastery, one more usurpation or co-optation of what is properly feminine, one more move men make against women? Were a man to adopt a feminine pseudonym and were he to write in a feminine voice, and even to do so quite well, would that amount, not to the invention of a new voice, but rather to stealing women's voice, and so once again to more injustice? But if a man could not write of or in the name of women, or like a woman, or if there were no room for men in feminism, or among women, or for a womanly side of man, if all that would be reducible to more injustice, then has not woman become something powerfully proprietary and appropriative, a way of silencing new voices, with all the exclusionary, excommunicative violence that appropriation implies?
> These questions are not puzzles waiting to be solved or resolved, definitively, one way or another by some skillful and clever theoretician, but more or less permanent aporias that block our way, that divert and detour us, that cost us time, even as they give us the time of sexual difference. These aporias are not temporary roadblocks to be cleared away but undecidables that hover over and constitute the space within which the question of woman takes place, the space of "woman"—and of men, of wo/men, of the relationships of men and women.

A deconstruction of binary sexuality involves the search for a "sexual otherwise," as Derrida (1988:184) observes:

> [A] certain dissymmetry is no doubt the law both of sexual difference and the relationship to the other in general . . . , yet the dissymmetry to which I

refer is still let us not say symmetrical in turn . . . ,but doubly, unilaterally inordinate,, like a kind of reciprocal, respective and respectful excessiveness, This double dissymmetry perhaps goes beyond known or coded marks, beyond the grammar and spelling, shall we say (metaphysically), of sexuality. This indeed revives the following question: what if we were to approach here . . . the area of a relationship to the other where the code of sexual marks would no longer be discriminating? The relationship would not be a-sexual, far from it, but would be sexual otherwise: beyond the binary difference that governs the decorum of all codes, beyond the opposition feminine/masculine, beyond bisexuality as well, beyond homosexuality and heterosexuality which come to the same thing. As I dream of saving the chance that this question offers I would like to believe in the multiplicity of sexually marked voices.

Ewa Ziarek (1997:134-135) comments on Derrida's text: "In thinking the asymmetry of sexual difference, Derrida follows here the steps of certain maverick feminists: he mocks the sexual neutrality of alterity while at the same time preserving the relationship to an other beyond the predictable branding of sexual marks. . . . As a radical diachrony eluding the order of the present, the ethical asymmetry Derrida wants to inscribe within sexual relations points to the impossibility of placing the two sexual positions side by side, even in terms of contradiction." Let such a dream be our guide.

Meanwhile, in reading Sarah Levy's texts we will be well advised not to allow desire—both hers and ours—to lead us to misrecognize what is true and what is false. Paul de Man (1983:272) writes: "[N]o theory of poetry is possible without a truly epistemological moment when the literary text is considered from the perspective of truth or falsehood rather than from a love-hate point of view. The presence of such a moment offers no guarantee of truth but it serves to alert our understanding of distortions brought abut by desire." Does this not apply as well to ethnography, or autobiography. Truth or falsehood, fact or fiction? This binary opposition is "too simplistic, but the story does change in the telling" (Bruner 1993:18). Hayden White (1978:122) points out: "[A]ll written discourse is cognitive in its aims and mimetic in its means. And this is true even of the most ludic and seemingly expressivist discourse, of poetry no less than of prose, and even of those forms of poetry which seem to wish to illuminate only 'writing' itself. In this respect, history is no less a form of fiction than the novel is a form of historical representation." We can say the same of ethnography, of self-ethnography. But White is a historian, and so he speaks of his own kind:

[F]acts do not speak for themselves, but . . . the historian speaks for them, speaks on their behalf, and fashions the fragments of the past into a whole whose integrity is–in its *re*presentation–a purely discursive one. Novelists might be dealing with only imaginary events whereas historians are dealing with real ones, but the process of fusing events, whether imaginary or real, into a comprehensible totality capable of serving as the *object* of a representation is a poetic process. Here the historians must utilize precisely the same tropological strategies, the same modalities of representing relationships in words, that the poet or novelist uses. In the unprocessed historical record, the facts exist only as a congeries of contiguously related fragments. These fragments have to be put together to make a whole of a particular, not a general, kind. And they are put together in the same ways that novelists use to put together figments of their imaginations to display an ordered world, a cosmos, where only disorder or chaos might appear. (125)

We should, as White (146) suggests give full credit to our "own prodigious capacities for poetic identification with the different and strange" and have faith in our "own oneiric powers."

Sarah Levy presents us with a narrative and I, too, am constructing a narrative with her narrative. We both follow the model outlined by Susan Stewart (1980:150-151):

[N]arrative temporality involves consecutive, causal events culminating in a climax that is followed by a denouement. The triangle not only gives a horizontal order to temporality; it provides a hierarchical weighing of temporality as well. This hierarchical order implies that temporal order is a causal order, that events increase in significance through time, and that the event reaches a saturation point (climax) yet does not stop abruptly. Closure is symmetrical, events closing the narrative have a comparable significance value to those events that began the narrative. And while the quality of the denouement has the same significance as the beginning events, the quantity is reduced, for these final events lie in the overwhelming shadow of the climax.

While this model can be seen as particular to narrative events in Western fiction, it is also a model for defining the parameters of events in everyday life. It is the shape of the true story; it is also the shape of conventional historical truth

Container and content, we should not privilege one over the other but see them as alternating with each other. Interpretation of content, thus, is identical with analysis of the narrative container. They can only be interpreted/analyzed together. In a commentary on Lacan, Colette Soler (1996:44) explores interpretation in the setting of analyst and analysand:

[H]ow do we know that the interpreter is not inventing? How do we know that the meaning that appears between the subject who speaks (in general, or through his or her symptom or the failure of his or her action) and the interpreter is not invented by the latter? There can only be one form of proof, but it's decisive: The fact that symptoms are transformed when they are interpreted. The only proof of the unconscious as speech is the effectiveness of interpretation on symptoms. Here we are led to ponder over the nature of truth–not truth as exactitude. Subjective truth is only a form of truth; there are others. But the truth of a subject is not exactness concerning facts; it is something which is produced in speech. When you manage to put something into words, you transform it. That is where what we call a subject comes in. A subject is not a person or the whole reality of a man or woman. Psychoanalysis operates a cut in reality: what we refer to as a subject . . . is something implied buy what happens in speech.

Lacan (1988a:324), who tends to be deceptively simple, states that "the only real resistance in analysis is the resistance of the analyst," and proceeds to say something much more complex: "The analyst partakes of the radical nature of the Other, in so far as he [sic] is what is most inaccessible. From then on, and beginning at this point in time, what leaves the imaginary of the ego of the subject is in accordance not with this other to which he is accustomed, and who is just his partner, the person who is made so as to enter into his game, but precisely with this radical Other which is hidden from him."

What then occurs when the interpreter confronts not a living and interacting subject? If transference and countertransference take place in the space between analyst and analysand, can it likewise take place in the space between the interpreter and the written page? I think so, and I think what is going on is the interpretation of my own resistance in that space. This is not self-analysis, by any means, but some unknown partner, some other, accompanying me at the keyboard.

Alibis all over the place, all over the trace. But I'm also only repeating what Sarah Levy wrote. Derrida (1989a:51) notes: "To invent is to produce iterability and the machine for reproduction and simulation, in an indefinite number of copies, utilizable outside the place of invention, available to multiple subjects in various contexts. These mechanisms can be simple or complex instruments, but just as well can be discursive procedures, methods, rhetorical forms, poetic genres, artistic styles, and so forth. And in all cases there are 'stories': a certain sequentiality must be able to take a narrative form, be subject to repetition, citation, re-citation."

Let's resume the narrative. Levy returned to Ithaca. The first text is a letter written from home, dated November 9, 1953, from Levy to the Blanchards in Vicos:

Dear Bill and Max, This is my first day on the Campus–got back in Ithaca this weekend just in time to run into a snowstorm and have to shovel my car out!

I suppose by now everything is quite clear. I needed either $100 or 1760 soles in order to pay for air expressing my data from Lima to Cornell. The figure is only approximate since Velasco had no way of accurately weighing my package, so we could only estimate the weight and thus the cost. So far I have received no word from him nor from customs, so I can only pray that the stuff got off safely and that I will receive it soon.

After I got to Lima I spent about 8 days looking up my so-called anthropologists, wringing the last drop of reports out of them, rescuing the typewriter (I have it in my house this very minute), lecturing at the university, and arranging final details. Plus the trip to Cusco which I decided upon at the last minute and enjoyed very much. The boys in Lima were most cordial, behaved as if nothing had happened–as if we had parted the best of friends. They arranged for me to lecture to their classes, but I refused to be hijacked for more than one talk since I didn't feel like preparing anything organized, and felt even less like lecturing in a disorganized manner. They are all in love with what they consider to be methodology, all want to specialize in the field, and all think that the Vicos experience has set them head and shoulders above their fellow students (which it probably has although I don't go for their snobbish attitude.)

When I got back to Ithaca I telephoned Martin and arranged to meet him privately outside the office. We met, in fact, at the Ithaca Hotel, and I spoke to him for about an hour, summarizing the Vicos experience quite pointedly. It was much less gruesome than I had envisioned it, mainly because Martin seemed to accept everything I had to say, without being shocked or surprised or incredulous. This was unexpected since without any supporting evidence it amounted to straight slander. I should have felt better had he asked me to prepare a memo supporting my contentions, or had he asked to see my field notes. I realize of course that he doesn't have time   for that sort of thing, but it makes me feel decidedly uncomfortable not to have had the opportunity to *prove* what I had to say, even though Martin seemed to think that further proof was not necessary.

I ran into Pete on the campus this morning, and we spent about an hour just chatting in a real chummy fashion, during which chat he revealed that he expects to work on the analysis of the methodology study next semester (and that Frank and Irene have separated finally, and Frank is sharing Pete's apartment.) I haven't seen Frank yet–he has a bad cold and is staying home, Pete tells me. I spent over an hour chatting with George this morning, at the end of which [unreadable line]. He added that he had received a ten page letter from you. So I said well in that case he undoubtedly knew all that had happened and there was no point in repeating the story. He pressed me further, saying, "I understand it was all Pete's fault." I said I thought that Pete had been the precipitating agent, but that the ultimate, more general reason could be found in the fiesta *ambiente* that had been prevalent on the hacienda since the beginning. George's reaction was funny–he apparently doesn't at all remember what it was like when he was there. He said he could remember only Alirio's birthday party, and that of course such an *ambiente* was impossible for a field station, and it was too bad it turned into that sort of thing *after he left*! I didn't pursue the point at all–if he remembers his stay in Vicos as a model of sobriety and workmanlike atmosphere, let's keep his little lace-covered memory intact!

Anyway, Martin knows my summary of the situation (what he has gotten from Frank and George I don't know), and seems to have faith in my analysis of the situation. I made it clear to Robin that I did not want to work with Frank on the analysis of the data since I considered it a waste of time all the way around, that not only would it not move the work forward, but would actually move it backward–and Martin seemed to accept that too. As I say, it is gratifying to know that he trusts me that far, but I continue to feel uncomfortable at not having an opportunity to prove that my feelings are more than feelings, and are actually based on real evidence.

Well–I'll keep you informed of any developments. Meanwhile, about your questions re coding: you code the *hoja* [leaf or sheet] number precisely as read–i.e., 001, 002m etc, The unit number appears in the third column, the ten-number in the second column, and the hundred-number in the first column. If we had 100 or more *hojas*, the unit number would appear in the fourth column, etc. Get it?

Greetings to all my friends. Tell Blas I shall write to him as soon as I get the chance. Best regards, Sarah.

Levy arrives home "just in time to run into a snowstorm." She expresses concern about her field materials which are somewhere between Lima and Ithaca. She reports on her week in Lima, "looking up my so-called anthropologists, wringing the last drop of reports out of them, rescuing the typewriter." In contrast with her notes written in Cusco, in which there is more to be sent to her in Ithaca, she has "wrung the last drop" out of her "boys." Now they must be empty, and perhaps she full when the materials reach her. They have "worked," they have eliminated their valuable loads. She pictures them as "most cordial, behaved as if nothing had happened– as if we had parted the best of friends." But how can empty husks be "friends"? Not quite empty, for they "are all in love with what they consider to be methodology, all want to specialize in the field, and all think that the Vicos experience has set them head and shoulders above their fellow students," and then parenthetically, "which it probably has." They wanted Levy to lecture to their classes but she "refused to be hijacked for more than one talk." Since "hijacking" is a form of theft, it is a serious matter. What she had to be stolen from her was her methodology, her scientific instrument, but why would she not have wanted to extend her rationality beyond her "boys" in Peru? Is this not what the "modernization of underdeveloped regions" is all about, a worldwide utopia in which everyone "works"? Not if one fears one's instrument will be lost.

Levy makes an appointment with Martin Roberts off campus, at a hotel, in order to report on the persons who did "not-work" in Vicos. It had to be done stealthily, in secret (except for a very few reliable persons like the Blanchards and Arthur Silver), a rather "slippery" affair, but she observes, "It was much less gruesome than I had envisioned it." Gruesome? Perhaps her vision was that of the Huaraz bulls with their throats slit. "Slit" is also a slang term for vulva. A fatal wound? Whose? "Martin," she adds, "seemed to accept everything I had to say," even though "without any supporting evidence it amounted to straight slander." Would "straight slander" be a pure or true slander, as opposed to "crooked slander,"[2] that is, an adulterated or false slander, or queer slander? A simulated slander, worst of all?[3]   Nevertheless, she feels "decidedly uncomfortable" because she is unable to "prove" it. She "makes it clear to Martin that she does not want to work with Frank," which would be "a waste of time all the way around" because "not only would it not move the work forward but would actually move it backward." And work that is going backward, instead of forward, is painful to contemplate.

She encounters Peter Quiller on campus, and they chat "in a real chummy fashion. Quiller, unaware of the earlier meeting of Levy and Roberts, expects to continue working on the Methodology Project. (In fact, he does continue as research assistant through May, 1954, because he is the only one who can reconstruct the context of the qualitative materials.) Quiller reveals that "Frank and Irene have separated finally," and that Nolan has moved in to share Quiller's apartment. It turns out that one of Nolan's major problems has been the revival of the old extramarital affair he had with the wife of a diplomat in his former research area. Her husband died and Frank quickly placed himself at her side. I do not know when this event took place: it may have occurred before Nolan left Ithaca for Vicos. Or it may have been the principal cause of his abrupt departure from Vicos, although I think that Nolan left Vicos because he did not feel he could endure working with Levy. At any rate, Nolan finally left his wife Irene and their children and was solidly condemned by almost everyone who knew them. This did not help him out of Ithaca as much as his general incompetence, aided by his emotional turmoil and Levy's charges. His almost total inability to function insured his departure. Levy also meets George Rogers who is curious as to whose "fault" it (i.e., "the story" in a ten-page letter he had received from Blanchard[4]) was. Rogers "presses" her to reveal Quiller as the cause, and she agrees that "Pete had been the precipitating agent, but that the ultimate, more general reason could be found in the fiesta *ambiente*." Rogers's "reaction is funny" to the extent that he believes such excesses occurred only during his absence from Vicos. Levy does not "pursue the point at all": "if he remembers his stay in Vicos as a model of sobriety and workmanlike atmosphere, let's keep his little lace-covered memory intact!" Again the work ethic, but note that false memories of "working," when "not-working" was going on, are covered with lace, something a woman would wear.

The next document is a response from William Blanchard to Levy's letter. It is sent from Vicos and dated November 22, 1953:

> Dear Sarah, We went down to Lima on November 7, taking 13 hours to make the trip, the roads were so bad. After a more than busy time there, we returned here via Chimbote and Huallanca. We found the latter route very interesting indeed. There is a magnificent hotel at Chimbote—wonderful accommodations, excellent food, and the sound of the surf plus the view of a beautiful harbor. With the inevitable Peruvian complications we got the jeep on a flat-car and took the six-hour train trip up to Huallanca, passing through delightful cultivated areas until we got into the narrower part of the Santa River valley. It's too bad that you did not see that region, for the loveliest part of the Callejón is at Caraz and below, and the Cañon del Pato area is spectacular.
>
> In Lima we did a whole lot of project shopping and business, plus personal shopping, and also had a bit of time for a few shows, dinner at the Club de la Unión with Velasco, and also the accounts at the Instituto de Etnología. At the latter joint I ran into Gutiérrez and Benavides, both somewhat unrecognizable in their Lima clothes. They were quite cordial, but I do not think that I was overly effusive at running into them. Castillo I did not see, but I refused to leave any money for him until I had a signed *recibo* [receipt], so I had to go back later to finish that. I had several rewarding conversations with people in Lima–Dr. Monje, Dr. Valcárcel, and some M.D.s I'm trying to stir up to do a medical survey here.
>
> I am forwarding to you the latest accumulation of *facturas* [invoices], etc., plus the statement of your funds at present. The work at the Instituto de Etnología is not completed as yet, so there will be another bill to settle with them. Incidentally, Ciro Gil told me that the amount of red tape and running around in connection with the air express stuff was prodigious. It is my impression that a *gratificación* [bonus or tip] of some type would be

in order there, so if you want to give me authorization, I'll take care of it. Velasco also referred to the problems in connection with the shipment, but I cannot feel that a *gratificación* should be in order there. It would probably be nice if you were to write him thanking him, but I expect you have done so already if I know you.

Mario has finished all but the first 100 census *hojas*, a work that he estimates at not too much over a week or two. Then he will go over them himself to find errors. Also he is going to collect the 14 or so missing *hojas* by retaking the census, but with ages, etc., to correspond to the previous date. Could you give me any idea of the steps and time periods involved after that? I think I should communicate with Velasco, or with IBM in Lima directly to find out (when I can give dates accurately) when and if they can duplicate the cards for us, and then send them on to the University. I am wondering just when we could expect some results from them after we get them in the hands of the University. Right now we think that it would be best to try to get the medical survey arranged for April, for the rainy season plus fiestas preclude an earlier date. Census information would be invaluable in relation to such a survey.

When we returned from Lima, we found your letter of November 9 awaiting us. I was not at all surprised at the reaction given your story by Roberts, but I was very glad to find out that your alarms here in Vicos seemed to be rather groundless. Cliff relayed some of the gossip he gets, to the effect that groans about Frank's theory course are universal among the graduate students, and it seems quite possible that Vicos is not the only fiasco. Incidentally, we got chatty letter from Frank in which he anticipated a great deal of work when the methodology material arrived in Ithaca. He also told us about the separation from Irene and the rapprochement with Pete. The Ithaca hills must reverberate nightly with the merry strains of *borrachera* [drunkenness].

I shall be very interested in any developments that emerge from the situation. Also, any information you can give me on George Rogers's potential activities, as well as his apparent reactions to the situation here in Vicos will be more than appreciated. I was not amazed but I was a little disturbed to find that his memory of fiesta here is limited to the *cumpleaños* [birthday] of Alirio, for it suggests that he may feel that I encouraged such goings on.

Thanks for the dope in re coding the *hoja* numbers. It arrived just in time for them to go ahead on the first hundred. Incidentally, Mario has worked like a slave on doing the census. I never would have believed it, either, but he has kept at it doggedly, sometimes all day, and usually from six to eleven in the evening. Also, he is hard at work on the potato experiment now that the harvest is under way. He gave up a trip to Lima to keep up with his work.

People at the *pensión* spoke fondly of you, and send *saludos* [greetings]. Best regards from Max and me, too, Bill.

Blanchard's letter is another confirmation that Levy's fears for the success of her project and her condemnation of Nolan is overdetermined; that is, her estimation of Nolan as incompetent is accurate, yet her bursts of anger are precipitated by repetitions of something Other. When Blanchard tells Levy that the latter's "alarms here in Vicos seemed to be rather groundless," he is probably referring to her concern that Nolan and Rogers might undermine her relations with the senior sociologists. Rogers, certainly, had other things to occupy his attention, and Nolan either did not care any more or was too enveloped in his personal agonies. And Quiller lived in a world sanitized by alcohol.

Blanchard also confirms Levy's rather important contribution to the Vicos Project: by stimulating census and survey work, teaching the anthropologists structured methods, and setting a brilliant example of hard work and devotion to scientific duty she had quite positive an effect on the staff.

Next comes a long letter, dated November 23, 1953, from Levy to Arthur Silver:

> Dear Art, Got back to Ithaca on Friday, November 6, just in time to shovel the car out of one of the heaviest snows in years. I wrote this letter on November 9, but have been holding it to temper judgment with mercy.
>
> *Discussion with Martin.* My first day back, I phoned Martin and arranged to meet him outside the office because I did not want to discuss these matters in the department. I had not added to the letter he received from me (October 10) the postscript which I sent to you since I prefer not to have such stuff on the record. When we met, however, I told him in summary form practically the same things I had written to you in that postscript.
>
> Martin seemed to accept what I said with very little question, on the grounds of his initial misgivings about Nolan. His feeling seemed to be that Nolan should be relieved from responsibility for the study. His first opinion was that this could probably be done by making Nolan's professional position here uncomfortable to a point where he will voluntarily resign. My reaction (as usual) was that I hate to leave things unexplicit and marshmallowy–but remember, I have learned a lot, so I said: "Well, I've dumped the situation in your lap and however you want to handle it is all right with me." I did make the recommendation that one way to proceed would be for Martin (a) to ask Nolan for a progress report on the research. He cannot write a decent one because he does not know what was done, didn't hang around long enough to find out, and has made no effort to correct this gap in his information since my return. And (b) to ask Nolan for a budget analysis. Again he cannot present an adequate one since he did not keep adequate records of expenditures. Such reports are admittedly fundamental to any research project, and my feeling was that if

Nolan formally submits such crucial reports which are clearly inadequate, they would provide a point of departure for explicit discussion of whether Nolan has worked out as director of the study. Martin said he would discuss the matter with *Bascomb [Albert Bascomb, Chairman of the Department at Cornell] who, he feels, already has serious doubts about Nolan's competence.

Redesigning the Study. Your misgivings on two counts are unwarranted: first count is feeling bad that I suffered in Peru. This I will discuss in my last paragraph. Second count concerns your fears that I want to change the basic outline of the study. No. My point was–and is–thát we must *add* to the study design the training aspects I spoke of. In Peru, at least (and I have reason to believe it will be the same elsewhere) we had to raise our field workers to a level of competence where their output could be evaluated in terms of the methodology employed and not in terms of their lack of training in the methods tested. This is, if you really think about it, true of any field study: we always have to train our staff to observe before we can utilize their observations, and to interview before we can analyze their interview material, etc. We usually reserve an initial period of the field research for training purposes. Whether this period is short or long, or hard or easy, or explicit or unexplicit, may vary.

What happened in Peru, and what Bascomb assures me we can expect to confront in Thailand and India, is that with these poorly trained field workers the period is longer and the work is more exacting.. My suggestion is to build a studied training curriculum here in Ithaca (knowing full well that it will be revised and re-revised under actual field conditions) and, in the field, apply that curriculum and evaluate it and change it, according to experience. In other words, I feel we should have a two-pronged research problem: one on field training methods, and the other on the same research problem studied by a variety of methods each of which is internally varied, according to our original plan. This is, in effect, what we actually did in Peru in an improvised way. I want to take it out of the realm of improvisation. It is *in addition to*, and not *in place of* the study of methodology.

The Implications and Obligations of Emphasis on Training. I have been thinking since early in September that one feasible plan we ought to consider is the possibility of returning to Peru, conducting a study dealing with a related substantive topic, but using the same methodological variations and the same field workers, thus permitting us to evaluate the effects of the training they got from us. I am not recommending this but am offering it for our serious consideration in further planning.

You are right, too, that we ought to train our field workers *for* something. In Peru we trained our workers on the spot because it was necessary in order to get them to conduct the methodology study for us. Thus the training and methodological aspects of the project went hand in hand, of necessity. But in addition to this exploitive or self-centered rationale for training, I don't like the idea of leaving the students high and dry after we pull out, with all our work and theirs of no avail to them or to us. (This is practically the way things are in Peru: there is very little chance that our field men will ever have an opportunity again to apply what they have learned.) I'm not sure that this is precisely what you meant, but I have given this matter some thought.

The field men who worked with us are all hopped up about methodology and social research (two concepts which are utterly new to them). I lectured at the University of San Marcos, describing our project and also a little about the other studies going on at Cornell, and this lecture opened (believe it or not) an entirely new vista for the students there. Their enthusiasm gave me the idea of using the men who had worked with us as a nucleus in the University of San Marcos to develop a social science laboratory there. They, themselves, asked me about it–how it could be done, how they could get funds, etc. They have the motivation all right, but what they lack is the experience and the training. If one of us could go there for a year (as an exchange professor, or a Fulbright scholar, for example) with the aim of establishing such a laboratory there, which would then continue under its own power after we left, we would really be making a contribution. I think it's feasible and a reasonable idea. After all, that's what Paul [Lazarsfeld] did at Columbia [University] in the 30s. It could be done in Peru, too.

I am not recommending that this be made an explicit aim of our project, but it could be a tacit agreement among ourselves–that, if it's feasible, we would like to take a crack at it. In Peru it's particularly possible, I think, because such a laboratory could be self-supporting until foundation support could be secured. What is lacking there mainly is a faculty member with such interests and dedication, but if one of us could power such an enterprise I think we could groom and train someone to take over.

Nolan: Significance of his defections in this larger context. I haven't held back from you any of my impressions about Nolan. I couldn't have used stronger language to describe his incompetence and professional dishonesty. I have a moral feeling about it–not only because I feel so strongly the trust we have in administering funds which don't belong to us but also for two even more dewy-eyed reasons. Gringo specialists, all over Latin America, are immediately clothed with an aura of excessive respect and veneration. Nolan in Peru represented not only [North] American sociology in the eyes of Peruvians, but even in a sense [North] American science in general. Thus his drinking himself under the table instead of working leaves the impression that this is what *any* [North] American scientist does. If he is willing to conduct a sociological investigation without training the field workers, criticizing or discussing their work, or ensuring that they meet basic professional standards, then they think this is how all [North] American specialists operate.

The second dewy-eyed reason is this: For the Peruvian students who worked with us, this was a tremendous opportunity to learn and to train themselves to become professional social scientists. I think it was their only opportunity. I have no doubt that we actually did this–that their work with us improved their professional performance and standards and understanding of the field. I am quite proud of this and am not even complaining because it could have been even better. But Nolan's irresponsibility (had he been left in charge) would have meant that this opportunity would have been denied to these students–and actually was denied to them for the first month, until I took over. I have to use moral language because that's how I feel about it, namely that our project offers these students–whoever they are or wherever they may be–the "right" to learn and to be trained; and there is no justification for anyone to withdraw that "right" from them. The way the project has shaped up, its aims are necessarily methodological research *and* training needed to conduct the research. To louse up the training not only sabotages *our* project, but also sabotages these students' learning experience.

This fervor on my part may surprise you (it surprises me!) And deserves an analytic aside. As you know, I have always been critical of our own training and teaching, not only at Cornell but at all universities with which I have been associated. I find that, by focusing my attention on the aspects of such training which are wanting, I have tended to overlook the positive aspects. Our students, it is true, get an awful lot of what you call "eyewash." But their training is so far superior and so much more professional than the *best* in Latin America that it is impossible to draw comparisons. I know on the grounds of my own experience that this is true in [the countries in which Levy has worked], and now Peru. I have checked with colleagues working in similar training programs in sociology, agricultural economics, home economics, etc., in Latin America, and I am assured that this is generally true in related fields throughout the Latin countries. (I am referring to [North] American specialists working with the Association of American States, whom I got to know in Peru and in [a Latin American country], about which program I shall write you in more detail another time because I think we should write a research proposal for them.) Our project gives some few students an opportunity to break through this curtain of ignorance and incompetence, at least in our field, and I feel very strongly that we must recognize that responsibility and live up to it.

Nolan's Future Role in the Study. About Nolan's contribution from now on, I am at a loss. I can think of *nothing* positive he can contribute. In my opinion his collaboration holds up progress. He thinks in a muddled, obscure, oblique way. He says something is "interesting" or "very difficult," and that's that. (How many times I have said to him: "Frank, everything in the world is interesting, Our job is to specify 'interesting' for what analytic purpose?" And again: "Let's not discuss whether it's easy or difficult, just let's decide whether it's important and essential, and then we can develop ways of getting at it.") In addition, there is the further very real problem that all our notes are in Spanish– including my field notes––-and he doesn't know a word of the language. To translate all that material would take months, and I recommend immediate analysis. I also recommend against translating on scientific grounds–it would be a third filter through which the data must pass, from

Quechua into Spanish, and again into English. This linguistic barrier meant he had absolutely no real contact with the field workers or the data while he was in Vicos. Finally, since he was there about 6 weeks and absent the last and most important 7 weeks of the study, he just doesn't know what went on. To put him on the analysis of the data would be worse than picking up someone entirely new, in my opinion. Really, Art, I tried hard to make Frank work out, and subsequently Pete Quiller, but I failed in both cases. I am afraid that I will have to analyze the Vicos methodology study, or we will have to get someone entirely new, which will mean that I would have the major burden anyway since I am the only one who knows what really went on from beginning to end of the study.

George's role. You ask me about George's role in the Study. I purposely refrained from mentioning it because it requires a long explanation, and details which concern his study only and are, strictly speaking, none of our business. To summarize briefly, just for your information and not for any record, George was in Vicos approximately four weeks, spaced over a six- or seven-week period. My main work problem there, for which I have condemned Frank, was not related to his [Frank Nolan's] incompetence–which I could have countered by my competence--nor even to his drinking–which I could have countered by my sobriety. The real problem was a more tenuous one, namely the unseriousness of the atmosphere throughout the Hacienda. Not only did nobody do a lick of work, but the topic of work was avoided as if it were, say incest. A stranger wandering into the place and merely observing the situation would, I think, have been quite puzzled as to what on earth all these people were doing there, besides having a good time. This unseriousness was the hardest thing for me to combat–and it was to this atmosphere that George, too, contributed. I found out later from discussion with the Blanchards that (a) there is scarcely a field note on the Vicos project in the whole hacienda, (b) there is no discernible research design or plans for drawing one up, and (c) George's ostensible purpose in going to Vicos–to plan a two-year research program for Bill Blanchard to execute–was never approached. They never had one meeting!

Mario, the Peruvian anthropologist, and Enrique, the Hacienda administrator, have been having a picnic there for a year and a half. They have had no plan to execute, no supervision or evaluation of their work. They also have power over 350 [the correct number would have been something over 250] Indian families, which has its own corrosive effect on scientific work as you know.

For anyone to ask a direct question about George's work or theirs, or to ask to discuss a general plan of research, or even to ask to see an old field note, is a direct threat to the whole structure. I think George is baffled and doesn't know how to proceed in Vicos, and therefore he holes up in the Hacienda fiesta-ing, fixing the plumbing, and goading people in a defensive way.

Thus, what happened was that Frank's fluffing off left George unthreatened, but when I pushed to get the work done he became threatened. Frank's not doing anything, in other words, evoked positive reactions. My inquiries and attempts to get the work moving along evoked negative reactions. Therefore, I think he is actually unaware of what went on with our project–for, believe it or not, he seems to operate on the level of such feeling tones rather than on the level of research..

I find, however, in talking with him since I have returned, that he seems to have blacked out all specific recollection of what went on while he was in Vicos, or at least to have idealized it to a point where it is, to me, completely unrecognizable. So I don't know how he feels now, but I have to say that while we were in Vicos his role was obstructive, defensive, and belligerent to our work. (If you ever quote me, I shall deny having said it!)

Now, this last discussion of George is above the level of petty gossip because it is relevant to our planning elsewhere. We must be aware that when our project moves in on a host field station, such as George's, we are unwittingly in the position, in the eyes of the field director, of an evaluating commission. Keep in mind that these boys have operated like little kings in their own spheres, reporting only what *they* choose to report, with no peers on hand to criticize or evaluate their day-to-day operations. Whether we like it or not, we might as well face up to the fact that our presence was, in Vicos (and I think we can expect it to be the same elsewhere), a decided threat to George and his staff, and he reacted accordingly. In addition, by moving into his encampment, we not only cashed in on whatever positive aspects he had already established for us ("rapport," and his expert command of the area). We also inherited all the mistakes which they had made–and they were many. If only on these grounds, I am recommending in our program report that in future field stations we establish our own encampment. There is a third reason for making this recommendation (but it is not the real reason), namely, that it is a more realistic field condition to have to set up your own field station, establish your own contacts, define your own role in the eyes of the community, rather than having these things done for you by an already existing research unit. This is the reason I push in the progress report.

Specific Charges Against Nolan. I know I don't have to prove it to you, but I feel uneasy that I have condemned Nolan so roundly without giving you as supporting data any concrete ideas of what he did that was so awful. At the risk of boring you, I shall summarize here:

1) I think his casual attitude toward recruiting our staff indexes his lack of concern about our study. He hired so-called Peruvian anthropologists from the University of San Marcos without checking their qualifications, experience, or training, other than language and a general statement of approval from the Director of the Ethnological Institute. He did not specify what would be required of them, omitting mentioning even such trivialities as hours of work. (This turned out to create a real field problem when the pressure was on and they rebelled on the grounds that the extra work required in the final clean-up was never specified in the hiring situation.) He even specified salary in terms of the dollar-

equivalent rather than the sol. This also turned out to be a problem because when the sol lowered in value one of the men wanted me to recompute his salary according to the higher value of the dollar! The hiring was done by Pete Quiller, a first-year graduate student, whose role in the study was never specified, who assumed a position equivalent to director in the eyes of the students working with us. Thus Pete's subsequent defections assumed an importance far beyond the amount of the damage to the study that a graduate assistant could legitimately be expected to be responsible for.

2) He moved into Vicos without arranging for an interpreter. Thus he had to rely entirely on Pete's rather halting Spanish, and later on mine. We managed okay, Pete and I, but without an interpreter Frank remained isolated from the field men and the field work. He couldn't read or evaluate a single field report, and made no attempt or provision to do so—and, what is more important, he never even realized that it was a serious omission!

3) My arrival in Vicos was just in time to prevent Frank's putting into the field as a "survey," less than two weeks after his arrival in the hacienda, the stuff he had written at his desk in Ithaca! Those long and involved questions and situations, written so that only a Ph.D. in anthropology (and only a _____ [reference to Nolan's graduate school origin, a *very* elite, among the elite, university] Ph.D.) could understand them! The notion of capturing the frame of reference of the Vicosinos, or of specifying the variables allegedly tapped by the questions and testing whether, indeed, a given question actually tapped the variable–these were completely bypassed. Even the technical problem (which turned out to be "cute" and will make a nice story) of how you write a questionnaire in Spanish so that it can be accurately translated into another tongue, unknown to you, was completely ignored. I know the man is incompetent, but I can only conclude that his way of handling the so-called survey aspect of our study stemmed from more than his lack of understanding, and may have indicated a plan to sabotage the survey method, incredible as it may sound.

4) His only effort at "field training" was to deliver a very fancy lecture on Talcott Parsons and Robert Redfield, which even Cornell graduate students might be expected to find somewhat obscure. The lecture was filtered through Pete's Spanish, and was presumably hitched up, by the field men, to their own inadequate frame of reference. And then the men were turned out into the field and just left to wander about at random without study, review, criticism, check, or evaluation of their work.

5) For the first month our field men turned up around 9 o'clock, hung around the plaza till 9:30 when Pete or I dispatched them. They returned around 12 to wait for a 1 o'clock lunch, returned to the field at 3 (Peru customarily observes a two-hour lunch period), came back to the plaza at 4:00 to wait for someone to drive them at 5:00 to a point where they could catch a truck to their respective homes. When I explicitly took over the study (after Frank left) I discovered that this fancy schedule was partly

due to transportation and living difficulties. The problem was met by moving some of the men into the hacienda, and arranging to transport those living outside at 6:30 a.m. and at 7:00 p.m., with the out-people staying overnight when necessary. As a result, we have practically no protocols for the early period of the study (when we were ostensibly concentrating on observation and qualitative interview) that were taken outside the hours specified [sic]. How on earth we can even report this , and at the same time say we were testing these qualitative methods, is a problem which we will obviously weasel out of, but it embarrasses me. The point, however, is that Nolan made no attempt to meet this situation, scarcely recognized it as a "situation," and would, I daresay, have permitted it to continue until the end of the study, even though it could have been handled (and was handled) by simple administrative reshuffling and housekeeping arrangements.

6) Not only did Nolan do no field work himself, he also sabotaged my efforts to get Pete Quiller to do the field work we had planned in the design. Pete ostensibly translated (really, there was very little communication between Nolan and the Spanish-speakers, so there was little to be translated) and was also his drinking companion and friend. He is planning to go to India with Nolan! And they are rooming together as of the past several weeks. (Nolan is getting a divorce.) It turns out, incidentally, that Quiller, who was supposed to be our area expert, scarcely functioned as such. His previous year in Peru was *not* spent in Vicos, but in Chancos and Carhuaz. I had hoped that Pete would change and turn out to be useful after Nolan left, but he did not change, refused to cooperate with my efforts, and continued to set the pace for the fiesta-atmosphere we inherited from Nolan and Allan. After about two weeks of that, I asked him to leave. I did not do this hastily–I did it after serious consideration and discussion with the Blanchards who, as you know, are clearheaded, unemotional people, and also were uninvolved in the methodology study. Again, keep in mind that although Pete was only a first-year graduate student, in the role of assistant, in the eyes of our field men he was in a position of authority, the *patrón*, a policy maker, and set an example which they were all too eager to follow.

7) Nolan never specified to any of the field men who I was or why I was there, or what my role was. This was very important in view of the fact that he and Pete had hired them about ten days before I arrived, and also in view of the strong emphasis in Latin culture on status and formal position. The first month, while Frank was still around, I used to waylay the men whenever I could and go over their field notes on the fly, as it were. I realize I should have straightened this matter out with Frank from the very beginning, and can only excuse myself on the grounds that it took up about two weeks to realize that nobody knew who I was or why I was there, and that it took me another two weeks to realize that this was of primary importance, that I would have to take responsibility for this study myself or it would conk out or turn into a bunch of lies. For the first month I sort of wrestled with myself, sometimes saying, "It's Nolan's

study, let it flop, what do you care?", and at other times saying, "You have to face up to the responsibility, you can't let the money be wasted, you can't let the students think this is American sociology, etc., etc., etc." Well, it turned out that the decision was made for me when:

8) Frank walked out on the study. He left Vicos around August 15, when the study was not yet fixed, when it was not at all clear that we would be able to accomplish our objectives–in short, he reneged. Actually, I hesitate to include this point on my list of accusations because I think it was best for the study–but it is, for a field director, an inexcusable defection, in my opinion.

9) About budget, Nolan kept accounts while he was in Peru. When he left, he turned them over not to me, but to Pete Quiller! I have not seen Nolan's accounts, but I have seen some of Pete's entries: "August 19, 3,000 soles" is the type of entry.

I have every reason to suspect that Nolan's accounting was the same– which is important in view of the fact that we will have to analyze our budget in detail to determine ratio of subsistence expenses to salaries, to equipment, and so on, in order to be able to plan more realistically for future field work in other stations. But more important that the bookkeeping matter, to me, was Nolan's attitude toward the budget. I am, as you know, accustomed to research directors who are jealous of their research funds–that is, who plan to spread the money around in such a way that the greatest possible amount will go for actual research, and who almost plot and scheme in order to cut corners on the non-research expenditures. This means an acute awareness of budgetary matters, and an acceptance of responsibility for planning. This I did not observe at all on Nolan's part–indeed, his attitude toward the budget was cavalier and almost unconcerned.

10) I have been back in Ithaca almost three weeks now and have tried several times to meet with Nolan to discuss our next steps with him. I was against this when I spoke with Martin, but he counseled me to meet with Nolan and keep the discussion on a general level without involving him in any real work. Nolan is, apparently, as unwilling to meet with me as I was to meet with him. Considering that I have all the data on the study, and also that there are over 50 days of field work about which he knows absolutely nothing and ought to *want* to be brought up to date on, his attitude is pretty un-understandable. It leaves me in a very ambiguous position. The whole study is in my office. I have already put in four months' worth of work on it (which was all we ever planned for me to put in). I want to start work on the analysis as soon as possible, which absolutely *requires* a planning session, if only to allocate personnel, quite aside from planning procedures for analysis. Ordinarily, I would just go ahead with the work, conferring only with Martin and possibly Bascomb, using George from time to time as a resource-person. But Nolan is still director of the study and I can't pretend he doesn't exist. But apparently he has no interest or feeling of responsibility about the data–and to top it all off, my last word from him on the subject (in Vicos during the

summer) was that he plans to take off for India in February! When I got back I told him that I was recommending analysis of the Vicos material before proceeding in any other field stations–which shocked him–but I have been unable to catch him for a meeting since that casual conversation. The thing is like a caucus race and I am part amused and part fed up with the while silly, ambiguous, amorphous situation.

Well, that about summarizes the situation, but not really. I am writing the progress report in a way which will put everything in the best possible light, phrasing everything as if it were a planned variation in method or technique, or as if it luckily turned out to be such a variation. You know the technique. It will be non-controversial, non-polemical, and will sound fine, I'm sure. But I want you to know the real story.

I have told all this to Martin in summary form, with the exception of the remarks about George. I will not show him a copy of this letter until I hear from you whether you think I should let Martin know my impressions of George's role. Remember, I shouldn't even have told you, had you not asked explicitly for it. That's another thing I learned in Vicos–to be patient and somewhat more discreet.

Your Evaluation of My Role in Peru. Re your concern about my "suffering" in Peru (to revert to subtitle 2): Quite misplaced. Remember, I learned comparatively more in those four months, speaking professionally, than in any other equivalent period. I would not have missed the experience for the world. I loved the work, loved having to rise to the occasion, having to meet crises, and all the rest of it. The only really harrowing thing about the experience was my own self-doubts. Just remember that George and Frank and Pete were all behaving as if everything were going along perfectly beautifully, and as if I were completely unreasonable to worry about field notes, time-sampling, diligence on the part of the field men, training sessions for them and for ourselves, evaluation of our own work, day-by-day and week-by-week, and for serious development and pretesting of a survey instrument. I didn't get to know the Blanchards well enough to discuss such basic work problems with them until well after the first month. So I kept doubting myself, asking, "Can everyone be out of like but me–maybe I *am* the one who's crazy." Only a basic faith that at least I was handling the study seriously, that whatever errors I was making were the normal proportion to be expected in view of my limitations–and were not due to goldbricking or faking–, kept me from deciding that I must be out of my head. That self-doubt was hard on me, and to have overcome it was worth the whole experience. After I got to know the Blanchards (who had, incidentally, been fed a propaganda line about me and about you, too, for that matter), and could discuss these matters with them and rely also on their unemotional evaluations , did I get any support. But finding that I could operate relatively efficiently in that Kaffkaesque situation was what they call a real "growth-experience." So don't reproach yourself. On the contrary, I am in your debt for having had the opportunity. I feel real grown-up.

If you read a nine-page single-spaced letter about work problems at Cornell, you will have a nice measure of the strength of your identification with us, even though you are far away. I don't dare add to the burden by tacking on personal comments and gossip, except perhaps to list a few things:

   a) I feel wonderful.

   b) I feel withdrawn from social life and interpersonal relations in Ithaca.

   c) As you predicted, Rosita is staying on in Ithaca. I miss my aloneness and will have to go through the same minuet again in a couple of months to regain it.

   d) I feel productive. Since I have been back, I have been writing on content-analysis (for Core-training) and progress report (for Methodology). This coming month I shall hit Values again, and if possible continue with analysis of Methodology. I enjoy working.

   e) Have fun, relax, and my best regards to you, Helen, and the kids, Sarah.

In this long communication to her mentor, Arthur Silver, Levy does not achieve the end which caused her to hold the letter back for two weeks: "To temper judgment with mercy"--but she has x'ed out an original statement which can still be discerned, to the effect that she has been holding it back in order "to temper it with judgment." Since there is little "mercy" in the letter, we can conclude that what Levy does not desire to say is said nevertheless. She really wishes to temper judgment with "judgment," thereby demonstrating Lacan's (1978:235) maxim that "desire not to desire is still desire." She reviews her meeting with Martin Roberts. Her object, it seems, was to have Frank Nolan removed from the Methodology Project. Roberts's response was to make "Nolan's professional position here uncomfortable to a point where he will voluntarily resign." This leaves her to confront ambiguity again; she says, "I hate to leave things unexplicit and marshmallowy." However, she tells, Roberts, "I've dumped the situation in your lap." "To dump," in English slang, also means "to defecate" and immediately produces the image of a baby or small child "dumping" something "unexplicit and marshmallowy" in an adult caretaker's lap. All of Levy's judgments and condemnations are quite unnecessary, it turns out, for Roberts informs her that another senior professor in the Department also "has serious doubts about Nolan's competence."

Levy launches into a long discussion of how the need to train field workers to a higher level of competence is linked to the methodology goals of the study. She is careful not to call the field workers "native" or "indigenous," but the colonialist, or neocolonialist assumption that "natives" lack rationality is woven into the seams of the text: it is necessary to "raise" them to "our" level of competence, since they are "poorly trained." However, she employs a sexual metaphor when she balks at "the idea of leaving the students high and dry after we pull out, with all our work [accomplished] and theirs of no avail to them or to us." She recognizes that she has left her Peruvian staff overtrained for their situation, superior "rationalized" beings in a mass of "non-rational" or "irrational" inferiors. "The field men who worked with us are all hepped up about methodology and social research," she says, and she goes on to dream of a triumphant return to Peru to set up a "social science laboratory," a dream which never comes true.

Then, on to Nolan: "I haven't held back . . . any of my impressions about Nolan. I couldn't have used stronger language to describe his incompetence and professional dishonesty. I have a moral feeling about it." This feeling branches into, one, the fiscal matter of "administering funds," and two, the "dewy-eyed reasons" of representing North American social science at its best and reinforcing the "right" of students to be trained. She says, "I have to use moral language because that's how I feel about it." The feeling is one that seems strange and different: "This fervor on my part may surprise you (it surprises me!)." Here is "an opportunity to break through this curtain of ignorance and incompetence . . . and I feel very strongly that we must recognize that responsibility and live up to it." It is good to feel, to be aroused, to break free and be alive! But she loses this thread because of her desire to return to Nolan. She will not loose her hold on this abject figure: "I am at a loss. I can think of *nothing* positive he can contribute–in my opinion his collaboration holds up progress. He thinks in a muddled, obscure, oblique way." Moreover, Nolan cannot function in the language of the data, Spanish, "he doesn't know a word of the language." Nolan, thus, is dead to the study, unalive, incapable of feeling. "Really, Art," she protests, "I tried hard to make Frank work out, and subsequently even Pete Quiller, but I failed in both cases. I am afraid that I will have to analyze the Vicos methodology study . . . since I am the only one who knows what really went on from beginning to end." Why would she fear analysis of the data? Because she does know what really went on, and what really went on is for her unanalyzeable, unsayable?

Levy also does not desire to break from George Rogers; that is, she desires to cling to him as well as Nolan and Quiller as her abjects. She has repressed the feelings of abandonment and has now developed a more realistic assessment of the collective disturbance: she defines her presence in Vicos as a "threat" to Rogers. "The main work problem," "the real problem" in Vicos was "more tenuous" than Nolan's incompetence or drinking. It was "the unseriousness of the atmosphere throughout the hacienda. Not only did nobody do a lick of work, but the topic of work was avoided as if it were, say, incest." It was not enough that nobody was working, but work itself was unspeakable, much like one's worst dread, "incest." This is a tremendous load of fear and pain. A person who can work under these conditions and produce any results, is a miraculous testimony of survival in the face of doom and of the indefatigability of the human spirit! The charge against George Rogers is not incompetence but "unseriousness." I think that here Levy, because her directive, rational, and active character was of such a different nature from Rogers's, completely and deliberately misunderstands the latter's non-directive intent with regard to the Vicosinos which relied on their own Vicos rationality and called on them to act. She also ignores several years' worth of detailed field notes by Mario Vázquez and other anthropologists, which had been accumulated by 1953 and which exist today in the Vicos Project's archives. Nevertheless, Levy's observation of the "corrosive effect" of the power exercised by project staff in Rogers's absence is an acute one. But she feels that when she "pushed to get the work done," Rogers "became threatened," and she accuses Rogers of operating "on the level of such feeling tones rather than on the level of research." In her eyes, Rogers "seems to have blacked out all specific recollection of what went on while he was in Vicos, or at least to have idealized it to a point where it is . . . completely unrecognizable." This is an accurate characterization of Levy's own loss of memories of depression, feelings of isolation and being "unwelcome," and her rejection of the research as a "*cojudo* project."

Levy feels that the staff of a field station like Vicos will fear any guest project as an "evaluating commission": "Keep in mind that these boys have operated like little kings in their own spheres, reporting only what *they* choose to report, with no peers on hand to criticize or evaluate their day-to-day operations." Is this not like the state that she desired when Nolan and Quiller were gone, when she had the project all to herself, when she brought her "boys" under surveillance, and when she could "whip" them and the cook "into line," count pennies, shake eggs, and pinch hens to her heart's content? Where are her own field notes, "scarcely" discernable in her writings from Vicos which largely detail her agony, hurl epithets at almost everyone around her, avoid the unwriteable, which turns out to be "work," as if it were "incest," and crow at every petty victory?

Then back to Nolan, whom she accuses of having a "casual attitude" and "lack of concern about our study," to the point of paying the field workers in dollar equivalents, so that when the sol was devalued they wanted the same wage as before! Nolan, who spoke no Spanish, left the matter of hiring these field workers, who spoke no English, to Quiller who thereby assumed a higher position than a mere graduate assistant merited–and a mere first-year graduate student, at that--, and whose "subsequent defections assumed an importance far beyond the amount of damage to the study that a graduate assistant could legitimately be expected to be responsible for." Levy complains, "in the eyes of our field men he was in a position of authority, the *patrón*, a policy maker, and set an example which they were all too eager to follow." Nolan's lack of Spanish (for which, really, he was not to blame since those who hired him, apparently, did not believe it was important!) is again brought up: "He had to rely entirely on Pete's rather halting Spanish, and later on mine . . . but . . . Frank remained isolated from the field men and the field work. "He couldn't read or evaluate a single field report, and made no attempt or provision to do so–and . . . never even realized that it was a serious omission!" Levy arrived in Vicos "just in time" to stop the project's proceeding with a faulty survey: "I know the man is incompetent, but I can only conclude that his way of handling the so-called survey aspect of our study stemmed from more than his lack of understanding and may have indicated a plan to sabotage the survey method, incredible as it may sound." Nolan's training and interests moved him in a theoretical direction, and his experience was in qualitative, non-structured research. If you will accept my speculation here, I do not believe that Nolan desired to "sabotage" the survey, he simply did not think it was important!

Nolan's "field training" took the form of "a very fancy lecture . . . filtered through Pete's Spanish," after which "the men were turned out into the field and just left to wander about at random." The field workers kept what she calls a "fancy schedule," but she resolved the problem after she took over the study and "rationalized" things. However, she is alarmed: "How on earth we can ever report this and at the same time say we were testing these qualitative methods is a problem which we will obviously weasel out of, but it embarrasses me." Does this mean that she compartmentalizes prevarication? Is not-working, or cheating, in the field, where everyone must work at capacity, disallowed, while "weaseling out," or cheating, on a report to a research foundation allowed? She recognizes the first type: Nolan ruled himself out of any field work and also ruled Pete out. But she also ruled herself out of any serious field work, as evidenced by her field notes and her preoccupation with "rationalizing" the project and its staff. Just who is she talking about? Then, she says, "I had hoped that Pete would change and turn out to be useful after Nolan left, but he did not change, refused to cooperate with my efforts, and continued to set the pace for the fiesta atmosphere." So he had to go, with no loss but great benefit to the research..

Worse yet, "Nolan never specified to any of the field men who I was or why I was there, or what my role was." She admits that he "should have straightened this matter out with Frank from the very beginning," but "it took me about two weeks to realize that nobody knew who I was or why I was there," and then "another two weeks to realize that this was of primary importance, that I would have to take responsibility for this study myself or it would conk out or turn into a bunch of lies." She seems to have taken a passive role in all this, but some allowance needs to be made for her adaptation to high altitude and culture shock. But there is also in the text an indication of her hostility, as she says to herself: "It's Nolan's study, let it flop, what do you care?" Then "Frank walked out on the study . . . he reneged . . . an inexcusable defection." This is exactly what she desired, and so she adds, "I hesitate to include this point in my list of accusations because I think it was best for the study." It was also best for her. Nolan's "attitude to the budget was" also "cavalier and almost unconcerned." She, on the other hand, is "accustomed to research directors who are jealous of their research funds," ones "who plan to spread the money around in such a way that the greatest possible amount will go for research."

Nolan seems elusive: "I have been back in Ithaca almost three weeks now and have tried several times to meet with Nolan." But he is, "apparently, as unwilling to meet with me as I was to meet with him." She is also elusive! She desires to start working on the Vicos materials: "I have all the data . . . . The whole study is in my office. I have already put in four months' worth of work. . . . I want to start work on the analysis." However, "Nolan is still director of the study and I can't pretend he doesn't exist. But apparently he has no interest or feeling of responsibility about the data–and, to top it all off, my last word from him on the subject . . . was that he plans to take off for India in February!" Did Nolan still believe he was going to continue with the Methodology Project? Levy reports of her Ithaca encounter with Quiller: "He is planning to go to India with Nolan!" So it is quite possible that Nolan, preoccupied with both his divorce and his lover, had little attention to give to an assessment of his situation. She observes, "The thing is like a caucus race and I am part amused and part fed up with the whole silly, ambiguous, amorphous situation."

"Fed up"? Then she adds, "but not really." Because the situation allows her to operate with stealth, to "slip something under the table." She goes on, "I am writing the progress report in a way which will put everything in the best possible light, phrasing everything as if it were a planned variation in method or technique. . . . It will be non-controversial, non-polemical, and will sound fine, I'm sure. But I want you to know the real story." She denies that she "suffered, but emphasizes how much he learned: "I would not have missed the experience for the world. I loved the work, loved having to rise to the occasion, having to meet crises. . . . The only really harrowing thing . . was my own self-doubt." Her Others in Vicos "were all behaving as if everything were going along perfectly beautifully and as if I were completely unreasonable." She asked herself, "Can everyone be out of line but me? Maybe I *am* the one who's crazy." Only her faith in her serious relation to the study "kept me from deciding that I must be out of my head." She ends the letter (at long last!) proclaiming: "I feel wonderful. . . . I feel withdrawn from social life. . . . I miss my aloneness. . . . I feel productive."

Levy included in her packet no other communication from herself. There is one more document, however, which is Arthur Silver's calm reply from California, dated December 2, 1953:

Dear Sarah, I read your detailed account with somewhat mixed reactions. I agree with you completely about (1) the need to redesign the project and (2) the absolute necessity of relieving Nolan of further responsibility. I have written Martin about the above. Please show him the carbon of your letter to me. I have never withheld my problems and feelings from Martin, and I am sure he will be able to take it even better than you or I.

My mixed reaction concerns what I indelicately call none of our business. Like you, my stomach rebels at phony, irresponsible research. But I try to be content to do a good job myself, and let the other fellow live his own life. If he asks me, I'll let him have it straight, but I resist any temptation for moral condemnation or personal involvement. This means that the operation of the field stations is not my business except when it affects our research project. You've made a good case for redesigning our work to be more independent of the existing field stations, and I agree. And I had to know your story concerning Rogers in order to plan our next steps. But while I can understand your moralistic motivation, I honestly don't share it—or I should say I give it a low priority. But even if we have different reasons, we both agree that our field workers must be trained if our methodological work is to be done.

The enclosed copy of my letter to Martin [see Postscript] gives my proposed course of action. Drastic, but necessary. I wish I were there to argue the case.

Let me list my reactions as I read through your letter:

–Nolan *must* submit a research report and budget account.

–It is agreed that training becomes more or less half the project.

–I agree that we should return to Peru, provided we can arrange personnel and budget.

–Ask Martin Roberts about *possible source of funds to set up a research and training center at the University of San Marcos.* Does the Office of Inter-American Affairs have any? Or the State Department? Will Opler's [Morris E. Opler, an anthropologist at Cornell] India project with its $250,000 have any training facilities we could tie into?

–Too bad about South American sociologists, but the M.D.s they turn out are even more harmful.

–Immediate analysis is desirable, but with only you to do it, I don't see how. Let it get in line.

–Page 5 [Levy's assessment of the Vicos Project] would make an excellent article for anthropological journal, *if it could be put constructively.*

–I think you can rest your case against Nolan. The detailed facts were necessary, however. What is his excuse for leaving the field so early?

–I find it hard to believe that you thrived on adversity, but it relieves my guilt feelings no end.

–Get rid of Rosita.

–I'm beginning to look forward to getting back. It's been tough, but I too feel a lot more "grown-up." The real work . . . I did last month was a tremendous boost. Incidentally, I'm quite proud of it, and if you want to see what I consider a good design for analysis, ask Martin to let you read it. Best regards, Art.

P.S. I've decided to keep the copy of my letter to Martin for my record. Please ask him to let you read the letter.

I think that if Silver had enclosed the copy of his letter, it very well might have found its way into the packet! The action taken was "drastic," and we may assume that it left Nolan in no doubt about his future in the Methodology Project and in Cornell University.

Nolan separated from Cornell University at the end of the academic year. He obtained another academic position, the sociology chair of a minor department in a lesser private university which was more noted at the time for its football team than its scholarship. This was accomplished with the help of the senior sociologists at Cornell who were embarrassed that they had been so witless as to have hired him in the first place and therefore eager to see him gone as quietly as possible. He obtained his divorce, married his lover, and cut down his intake of alcohol. He later wrote one more book which was about a village in his original research area, based on data gathered by his two competent field assistants, and dreamed of writing a definitive text on technological change until he retired.

Levy did not "get rid of Rosita." She assisted other sociologists in preparing reports on the Vicos research which made it look good. On paper the report, "Instructions Given to Fieldworkers, Peruvian Study" (Methodology Project 1954), appears to be well organized, but it was written by Sarah Levy with both Peter Quiller's assistance and notes, before Quiller left for an extended period of research in South America. (He did not make his anticipated trip to India.) She eventually moved into a tenure track position, wrote three books, one of these as junior author, and numerous journal articles. She was promoted to tenure at Cornell University and pursued a sociological career until her death some years ago.

Quiller obtained his graduate degree and was later acclaimed, largely by scholars outside anthropology, for his brilliant anthropological journalism. He eventually was hired by a "second tier" eastern state university desperate for faculty, where the head of his department solved the problem of "what to do with a burned-out alcoholic" by assigning him a course on ethnographic film with two assistants to conduct the business of showing films and grading papers. He died in his early fifties of an alcohol-related condition.

Levy's "progress report" of 1953 is nowhere to be found, assuming it was actually written. There is a "Progress Report" which was prepared in February 1955 by the directors of the Methodology Project, which had been expanded by that time to include other faculty members of the Department. It devotes major attention to a comparison of two social surveys conducted in Vicos and at the field station in Thailand, while it successfully, I believe, disguises the failure to utilize the qualitative studies with this description of the content analysis of the field notes from Vicos:

> The processing of these data and the procedure for analysis is inductive. That is, ad hoc categories have been established, working from data to category rather than vice versa. A content analysis file has been set up. . . . Any material in the field notes which is relevant to any content analysis category, is reproduced and appears in the appropriate subdivision of the content-analysis file; and a file category has been established to provide for the classification of all materials collected. The analyst seeking to prepare an analytic memorandum on any given area of interest, for example, pulls from the file all the slips appearing behind the appropriate file-division, arranges them in logical order, and inductively arrives at his analytic conclusions. Any single item of information may have the same weight, in this scheme, as any or all other items or information appearing in this category. The file's system of cross-reference may enlarge the analyst's focus of interest as he works with the material, by routing him to related categories appearing elsewhere in the file. The character of the evidence is "judicial"–that is, the analyst relies on the convincingness of his own reasoning and the internal consistency of the data he presents, to establish the level of proof for any assertion or generalization he makes. (Cornell Methodology Project 1955:2.)

In other words, the Methodology Project's field notes were organized into a retrieval system so that a researcher could select a topic, read the relevant notes, and write about them. But certainly it puts the gathering, processing, and analysis of the materials "in the best possible light, phrasing everything as if it were a planned variation in method or technique." The "real story," however, is different from this idealized picture. Some senior sociologists desired to demonstrate the superiority of structured methods over non-structured methods, secured funds from a granting foundation to organize research for carrying out their desire, and hired a junior sociologist to take charge of the resulting project. (What could they have been thinking, or not-thinking, in choosing such an unprepared individual for the realities of field situations? And what could he have been thinking, or not-thinking, in accepting the assignment? All their desire appears to have outpaced all their wisdom.) In the field, three field workers were hired impressionistically by an alcoholic graduate student and transported to Vicos, where a drunken research director lectured to them about sociological abstractions, which lectures were translated for them imperfectly into Spanish by the graduate student. They were then sent off to find informants to interview on topics they both may or may not have understood. The field notes improve on the arrival in Vicos of another project director who alternately bribes and threatens, but who provides clearer directions for, the field workers. The notes from some three months of work are brought to Ithaca, retyped, and filed by a corps of secretaries and graduate students. The social survey is treated more considerately, and is actually used in comparative studies but never published as itself. The qualitative material is processed so that it can be reported as an accomplishment in the "progress" and "final" reports to the granting agency, but it is little valued by the researchers and only one substantive report on the acceptance/rejection of an agricultural innovation in Vicos, the new seed potatoes, is produced from all that effort; and this is a dittoed (i.e., processed on a spirit duplicator) item of fifteen pages, double-spaced, which had limited circulation.[5] And the files remain otherwise unused until a member of Cornell's sociology faculty presents them to me in 1968. The effective results of the Methodology Project are summarized elsewhere in the same "Progress Report":

> The analysis conducted up to now, and our experiences in the field, have resulted in a major extension of the theoretical relevance of the Cross-Cultural Methodology research. Establishing a framework which would permit the parallel analysis of data collected in several cultural situations, has led to the specification of a series of problems implicit in the use of the comparative method as a technique for reaching culture-free generalizations about human behavior. Its achievement, however, is dependent immediately upon certain clarifications of theory in the

concepts and methods of the behavioral sciences. For example, it assumes the conceptual equivalence of data gathered in different cultural settings. The effective use of the comparative method, therefore, prods the theoreticians in the behavioral sciences to specify more carefully the components of any analytic concept and the character of indices which define these concepts. Specifying these components and indices requires not only conceptual clarity, but terminological precision. The effective use of the comparative method, therefore, leads the social scientists to a more rigorous and mutually agreed upon terminology.

The use of the comparative method also raises problems of reliability of findings and validity of generalizations through time and space. These problems, in turn, require methodologists to specify the function of replication, comparison, explanation, generalization and prediction. . . .

Finally, the effective use of the comparative method requires the development of comparable analytic techniques which will enable the analyst to arrive at conceptually similar analytic generalizations and equivalent treatment of evidence and levels of proof. It is within this sort of framework that the findings of the Cross-Cultural Methodology Study are ultimately relevant. (Cornell Methodology Project 1955:4'5.)

In other words, the researchers found that they were not conceptually prepared for such a study, and that they lacked the tools with which to carry it out. The sociologists' inability to use the qualitative data, along with their overemphasis on the social survey to carry them to glory, made them practitioners of what Pierre Bourdieu (1993:16) characterizes as an "inhuman science . . . where the distance produced by questioning and by the buffer of the interviewer is reinforced by the formalism of blind statistics," and where a "bureaucratic sociologist treats the people he [or she] studies as interchangeable statistical units, subjected to closed questions that are identical for all." Bourdieu (1990:19-20) calls this a "microphrenic empiricism . . . whose false technological perfection conceal[s] an absence of any real theoretical problematic–an absence that generated empirical errors." The adherence of this dominant current of American social science to such"a positivist philosophy of science" explains "how the inadequacies and technical mistakes caused . . . on all levels of research" by this view, "from sampling to the statistical analysis of data, [could] pass unnoticed." In his general discussion of "a basic grammar or repertory of design imagery" in material culture, Forty (1986:12) distinguishes an "archaic," a "suppressive," and a "utopian" approach, which all demonstrate that "in the artefacts of industrial societies, design has been employed habitually to disguise or change their true nature and to play tricks on our sense of chronology." If we look at the social survey as an artefact, its "design" also fits into this scheme as a process which disguises, conceals, and transforms.

There is one more question to ask: what of the Peruvian field workers who were used and abused in the process of carrying out an impossible study? Although Levy expressed hope that what she believed to be their "superior" training might serve them in their futures, and although she expressed concern that they might be "overtrained" for what their Peruvian context offered, none of the three really distinguished himself as a Peruvian scholar. Some indication of how the study left them may be indicated by reference to the reports Levy insisted that they "owed" her. Each one typed up several pages of personal data in response to detailed questions she gave them. They are organized in sections having to do with personal history, education and experience, personal goals, what they feel they gained from work on the Methodology Project, how they evaluate the Vicos Project, and how they got along with the Vicosinos. I will not attempt to reproduce them as wholes, and I will not guess at the questions Levy asked them and which are not included in the protocols, but will, rather, attempt to focus on statements which are relevant to the substance of this essay. Let us begin with this undated report by Patricio Gutiérrez:

> The particular interest I had in working with the Methodology Project in Vicos was to obtain greater experience with techniques of social research.
> And since it happened that the Project focused on a problem that was very new to us, I felt it was a good thing to become a member of the team, and so I immediately accepted the offer that they made to me. And, truly, I learned very much.
> Even if the stipend had been small, like half or three-quarters of what we earned, I would certainly have agreed to work with the Methodology Project because my aim was to learn more
> The experience has had for me great value during my work in Vicos.
> If an opportunity came to work in this Methodology Project again, in any place that was chosen, I'd be delighted to join the team, and I think that my work would be more productive the more experience I had. Naturally, my object of continued work in this Project would be only to go on acquiring more experience and to contribute in some way to the discovery of better research techniques, that is to improve more and more the techniques utilized up to now.
> In the course of our history we have encountered many foreign researchers who have worked in Peru, rediscovering in part the huge socio-cultural, biological, and archaeological riches, and making us appreciate this good fortune of our country more and more. For it is not in vain that the "gringo" sociologists and anthropologists have come to Peru, because their social researches will result in benefits leading to the progress of the country. (The idea should not be held that here only foreigners are called "gringos," because popular speech employs that word for Peruvians who have blond hair.)

The foundations from the United States have a very noble mission which is to undertake the progress of the "less developed" peoples of the world, for which it is necessary to have a scientific knowledge of each one of them. And, in general, the foundations always support the greater development of the Social Sciences, so that in this way human harmony may occur in this vast century of ours. At least I believe it may be so from a philanthropic point of view.

It seems to me that for now it's necessary to rediscover scientifically our national reality with the assistance of foreign and national anthropologists and sociologists, so that such researches can be made in a team. I say this because we still aren't prepared and well equipped to undertake a Project like the one in Vicos. However, later when we may count on good social researchers, I think that it would be better to give the money to Peruvians to do this kind of work, although the advice of some foreign anthropologist or sociologist with experience will be necessary. And I also have said that it was important to carry out researches of this type with Peruvian social researchers, because one can't be under the tutelage of other researchers for a long time.

Similarly, I take the greatest care to master Cultural Anthropology, and I need the help of foreign anthropologists and sociologists (who have greater experience) for this, so I would like to work for a few years with the gringos who are in Vicos, like Dr. Rogers, for example, in the applied anthropological redesigning of that zone (which in my opinion is not going so well, for many reasons). For the same reason I would be delighted to continue working with the Methodology Project, with Doctors Nolan, Levy, and my friend Quiller. I like working personally with Doctor Sarah Levy. Naturally, each one of the persons I have mentioned has capacities and defects from the scientific point of view. Perhaps it would be of some use if I noted here the impression I have of each one of them, but, really, I lack the time and I also fear being indiscreet.

When there is a prior understanding of what is going to be done in the field, I think that a social researcher's work will advance further. And when work is done in a team the first task should be to establish a mutual trust among all the members of that team. The result of this trust is, on one hand, the anthropologist's or sociologist's more exact knowledge and, on the other, the same guarantee that can inspire a responsible social researcher. With regard to this last aspect, or "rapport," which has been greatly ignored by the researchers, like other research techniques in the field, I am writing a small essay which tells how the work has gone on up to now in Peru.

I think that not only my work but that of all the other members of the research team would have turned out better if relations with the Project's directors had been more personal and more appropriately a "team." As a constructive criticism I must indicate some negative aspects which I noted among the Project's directors: a) We did not know the general plan of the Project, so that our assistance in terms of suggestions, extensions, and corrections was minimal at the beginning; b) The language difficulties of the Project's directors have been another thing, when it was a matter of their isolation; c) The lack of a consistent advance plan for the field research prolonged time with delays, impairing the Project; e) The lack of systematization of the work itself dislocated at the beginning the unity of the real teamwork; f) If we indeed established "rapport" with our interview subjects, on the basis of our own experiences, I think that it is also important to do the same with the members of the whole team of researchers. I have to emphasize once more the importance of this aspect, because the success or failure of the research depends particularly on the unity of the team, and let it be understood that this aspect, which is so vital, has been largely ignored by almost all researchers when they have worked in a team. And even when one works alone, I think it's necessary to examine beforehand how we are and how we should behave ourselves in relation to every group in which we do research.

This was the first time I worked in a Methodological Project and with researchers who weren't nationals. Still, the opinion that I had formed about them was very different from the one I have now, particularly in regard to "rapport" among social researchers themselves which in its scientific aspect was quite overlooked. Here I must say that the organization or systematization of field work is vitally important, and it should originate in the head, that is, the management. I am really not suggesting that such direction be like a policeman or an army sergeant, but, rather, intelligent and harmonious. And this directive attitude should, from the beginning, proceed without dishonoring itself at any time, because otherwise the Vicos thing could happen. All members of the team should bear in mind the goals that are sought, and they should make common cause to achieve those goals. If this principle has not penetrated the researcher's brain it would seem that the latter has lost or could lose strength of character. . . .

For me it has not been something new when Indian servants eat at the table together with us, because in that regard I don't have any prejudice. I've seen similar cases in some Peruvian homes with liberal political ideas. . . . Nevertheless, with regard to Vicos, I should make note of being too generous in being familiar with servants, because that affects the respect they owe us and also diminishes their work activity. Perhaps my evaluation will not be taken as an error if we simply remember that in the Vicos *casa hacienda* there was a cook and two serving boys, and the kitchen was always dirty and the most basic hygiene was almost a luxury.
. . .

It is possible that the gringos were serious in their work, but I have the impression that their views were not in harmony. Perhaps the most eloquent testimony to this might be the team's disintegration in successive stages.

Personally I admire Dr. Holmberg and I also admire his concern with work, but I will allow myself to find certain faults in the Applied Anthropology which is going on under his direction in the Hacienda

Vicos. The faults are only in certain aspects, because I don't know the exact amount of money which has been spent to date, and I am also aware of the setbacks and problems which often occur in negotiations with the Peruvian Government. In agricultural matters I think that the innovations made aren't as promising because of the absence of the proper technical management (a person specializing in agronomy).

As for education, there is no doubt that the school building that they have had constructed is splendid, but I don't have much confidence in the body of teachers. It will always be an educational failure because they still stick to a somewhat traditional pedagogy which needs to be totally renewed and surpassed in Peru, in correspondence particularly with each one of the country's regions. . . .

As for health I think that no further comments are necessary. . . .

To make a change in work done up to now, I have much hope in that Project of Applied Anthropology which is the first to do that in a broad way and under the direction of a great anthropologist, Dr. Holmberg, whom Dr. [Alfred] Métraux praised to me. . . .

Naturally, I think that the Methodology Project is worth the money which has been spent, since its object is to go beyond research techniques without competing with the set of research methods existing up to now. Certainly we've observed in researchers the preference they have to employ a set of methods for their field work. So most anthropologists and sociologists like to study or do research according to the methods they like most. For example–as Doctor Levy said so well–some prefer to outline in their office the general variables of the study they are going to carry out in a culture. Others say that it's necessary to go to the culture itself to draw up a work plan. Even in regard to research itself, there are many who stick to the tradition of observing everything without knowing why or without taking into account their goals with enough clarity. . . .

I've already said that the Methodology Project's goals are to go beyond current research techniques, without competing in any way. In this way what the Methodology Project developed by Cornell University is going to accomplish will be of immense value for the social sciences. (It seems to me also that there will have to be some corrections in what are called "dependent and independent variables," in their function and the extension they have among themselves, because I have the impression that they haven't worked out very well in Vicos. I hope that some occasion will come for the discussion of these questions.)

A sensitive person, and more than this a lover of science, could not be so naive as to consider projects like this as aspects of what some call "North American imperialism," an expression which strikes me as mere fanciful romanticism and regional foolishness.

Gutiérrez has produced a document that is much longer than those of the other two field workers. It is wordy, opaque, and uncommitted. His critique of the Methodology Project's work in Vicos is restrained though it is to the point. We have few clues to his real sentiments, and I have the feeling that if he had been writing about his experiences in Vicos to a Peruvian mentor he would have been phrasing his responses in a different way, but as politely, responding to what he thought the other person wanted to hear. Nevertheless, he must have provoked at least a mild frustration in Levy, for he in no way provides the latter with material that can possibly fortify the charges against Levy's Others. The tone is mild, reasonable, and cooperative. Perhaps Gutiérrez, a good student who lacked funds, hoped for further employment. Whatever his motivation, and whatever his real opinions on all the topics he wrote about, he took no risks. I feel that in no way was he "left high and dry" after Levy "pulled out." Peruvians, typically, do not invest their energies in a single source of support, and Gutiérrez was no exception.

The protocol produced for Levy by Armando Castillo, and dated September 26, 1953, is much shorter and much more revealing:

> I was interested in working in the Methodology Project because I could see in advance that it would be good for me to learn working together with well prepared Anthropologists and Sociologists, because personally I'm well disposed to accept them as teachers with especially great mastery of the Social Sciences. Moreover, I understood that it was an opportunity to look closely at what the Applied Anthropological Project (Peru-Cornell) was doing because I was interested..
>
> If there had not been the stipend, which was and should have been just $75, I also would have accepted it. I mean that it was not just the stipend but above all the experience we could get, and only under these conditions I could say that I also had a certain interest in experience with Indians.
>
> If they repeated this study about Methodology, like the one that took place in Vicos, I'd very much like to participate, because I think that its of the greatest importance to achieve the greatest impact possible in the social sciences. Of course I'd want my colleagues in Anthropology to have the same interest and, if possible, to be able also to participate. In Peru I'd want for everybody to be as homogeneous as possible. It's possible that way to work better.
>
> I think that North American Sociologists and Anthropologists come to Peru because of their scientific interest, because they come to carry out the purposes that some institutions have, institutions like the Smithsonian Institution, like cooperative services, Point Four which has to do with aid to the Latin American countries; and other times it can be to achieve the objectives of a project like the present Methodological one. Also because scientific objectives can't be circumscribed in one advanced moment of their development in the national scene of the U.S.A., but it's become necessary to understand as far as possible a whole variety of different cultural situations in the world.

And foundations in the United States give money for these researches because that's the way these things are done in the U.S.A.. It's a matter of the political, economic, and institutional organization of that country, something which does not occur in Peru where there's no tradition for having institutions like foundations. Moreover, it can be the result of the good economic fortune of that country. I also think that it can be a long-term objective to take advantage of the scientific instruments of the social sciences to ward off the danger of communism. I think that in order to carry out social studies in Peru it will be necessary, at the same time, to give money for these studies to Peruvians, and that also Anthropologists and Sociologists from the U.S.A. come and that they always work in their projects with Peruvians, because that way the latter can get valuable experience and learning.

As for whether or not I'd like to work with specialists from the U.S.A. like Rogers, Levy, Quiller, and Nolan, I can say: I'd like to do it with Rogers because there is not only the guarantee of his intellectual preparation in his specialty but personally he's a very nice person and he knows how to deal with those who work with him with kindness and respect. Aside from that, he doesn't hesitate to help anyone in need. His stay in Peru has caused him to have many admirers, and he himself acts almost like a Peruvian which helps our relations with him very much. I know him personally because he was my professor in the Institute of Ethnology and because I did my field work once in his company there in the Callejón de Huaylas.

With regard to Levy . . . I've learned a lot from her and I'm sure it would have been more if we'd had to work longer. I must say that it took a lot of work to get to like her. Because . . . her manner of dealing [was] so disconcerting: what with saying so many silly things, her exaggerated gestures like her poses sometimes, and other times so irritating, she seemed like a sickly character, neurotic. Still I came to feel very friendly with her and many times I've had great admiration for her in regard to her knowledge and her great capacity for work. It's because of her stubborn, whimsical character and lack of understanding that I wouldn't feel very comfortable working with her. It's a pity, because I don't believe that there are persons who can work with her apart from us.

As for Quiller, he's a good fellow, he's very nice, he's a good friend, but he lacks much intellectual preparation. I wouldn't work with him.

About Nolan, I could say the same that I said about Rogers. It was a shame that he couldn't speak Spanish when he was with us. All the same, we are sure that we could have learned a lot from him. His personal treatment was very nice, and I can testify that he has good preparation as a sociologist, that is exactly this feature which greatly interests me.

I think that my work would have progressed more if we'd had a broad understanding of the objectives and structure of the Methodology Project as this project was developed at Cornell. This I think had to be something fundamental, because it made greater supervision necessary, and then when a thing was to be done [we should have been told] what thing to do.

I think that work would have gone along better if our relations from the beginning with Levy, Nolan, and Quiller had been more personal and the attempt had been made to treat us as colleagues rather than simple assistants. This was quite necessary because they never gave us the text of the project that had been developed in Cornell, and even more so because I suspect that various improvisations and corrections became necessary, and because of the difficulty of understanding because the project's directors did not know Spanish. Because of that there were many misunderstandings. It gave the impression that the project's directors didn't know what they were doing. One thing was said, then another, and then especially with regard to Levy and Quiller who were the ones who gave us the tasks in Spanish.

My relations with my colleagues have always been the best, in a climate of respect, friendship, and tolerance.

To make working conditions better it would have been better if social relations could have been in a climate of consideration and respect for us on Levy's part, for she has no ability to deal with people. It would have been necessary for her to understand all the time that it's necessary to respect the dignity of participants and that it's not possible to give dictatorial treatment of a penal or military type which is ruled by whim, without calm, without consideration. There are more efficient ways to deal with people. I'd recommend that either Levy change her character or not take over the direction of personnel. The fact that we may have tolerated her intemperate attitudes doesn't mean that we didn't feel affected, but by chance she was dealing with very tolerant people.

As for the fact that the Indian servants may have sat down at the table together with us, it didn't matter to us at all.

As for the work of the North American personnel in the Methodology Project, it seems to me that what they lacked was a sense of organization, a system for working, and order.

Regarding Dr. Holmberg's project, I can say that in every way it's worth the money that is being spent. Although I think that such an investment leaves much to desire, and it could be much more efficient if they tried to get out the maximum benefit and if they watched all aspects of Vicos culture at the same time as the process of the effects of technological change. I think that a project of this nature must be whole and pay attention to what is happening, and take more care in the introduction of technological elements by seeing to it that these are done in the most complete and efficient form. So it doesn't seem good to me when Enrique is left in charge, without greater control of making innovations in agriculture which, as far as I have seen, leave much to be desired. I think that these defects are due to the lack of a detailed plan where every step can be strictly controlled.

Armando Castillo, like Patricio Gutiérrez, did not provide Sarah Levy with evidence to support the latter's charges against George Rogers, Frank

Nolan, and Peter Quiller. But Castillo placed Levy's own behavior in Vicos in a spotlight. Unlike Gutiérrez who kept any anger he might have felt tightly under control, Castillo demonstrates with his denunciation of Levy that he was touched by the experience in Vicos. Whether or not Levy was as hard to get along with as Castillo suggests is problematic. Another explanation for his outburst could be, simply, that he could not easily tolerate taking orders from a woman. That his responses to Levy's questions are included among the papers of the Methodology Project is perhaps a testimony to Levy's spirit of thoroughness. Or perhaps she never read these responses. Castillo, also, is not "left high and dry," but, rather, seems to be reclaiming some of the self that perhaps he felt he had lost. Pedro Sáenz is yet another person. Here are his responses, dated September 29, 1953, to Levy's questions:

I was interested in knowing about applied anthropology from close up.

I didn't pay attention to the money when I made my personal contract. It would have been better to come to an agreement. Maybe one could work with a minimal wage if the rest of the money for wages went for the benefit of the project itself.

The experience is valuable, and likewise the experience with the Indians.

If there were another study I could work in it, but according to agreed conditions. This work ought to be planned mostly in the specialty. Other anthropologists should be brought in.

Anthropologists from other places come to study, to have experience, and to develop methods for research.

Foundations give money to improve research and do it on a large scale, or maybe because these studies require high sums of money, and because they're studies that take years and can't be done without enough money.

The foreigners' project is fine.

Work in Vicos for many years wouldn't agree with me because there are other places where I've worked which, I think, are more important to me. Otherwise, a short stay could allow the observation of the process, but not for years.

The work is fine as it's been done. It would be good to add to it in the future by providing better facilities so that the work would be efficient.

Work would have been better if the Anthropologists who are mentioned here knew how to speak Spanish perfectly. That would have made agreements easier, and there would have been better personal relations if they had known how to speak Spanish.

I don't know anything about the work of gringo anthropologists because I'm not certain how they work. As far as I'm concerned, I've given my best efforts to the work, which is because it interested me.

There'd be no need to make any change except insofar as there was difficulty in getting along personally, in regard to Spanish. The way I see it, it was fine that everybody ate together. It was just that the service wasn't so good.

I'm not certain because I don't know their work, or how they work.

Dr. Holmberg's project is worth while even with the expenditure of sums of money, because it's the first time in Peru and we're very interested in the results. We're hoping.

I don't know anything about the money spent in the methodological project, or how much was budgeted for it. In any case, I think that for this methodological project of three months, it's not necessary to spend much money. Thirty thousand soles [at 20 to the dollar at the time] would be enough.

The methodological project, as I see it, is not so valuable because in a similar way all the schools of anthropology should do it. They should put different methods into their researches so as to ascertain which of them is more useful in each case.

Projects like these, in reality, don't fit into what is called imperialism, but maybe in the future, when it's necessary to industrialize, this factor will be fully studied by Peruvian anthropologists.

Of the three field workers Pedro Sáenz seems to be the one who has passed through the experience in Vicos relatively untouched. He tells Levy so little that, in the absence of the list of questions, we can barely understand some of his answers. There is little evidence that anyone suffered a permanent disadvantage by working in Vicos. Although Levy expressed concern that through the marvels to which she had exposed them the field workers might have been "overtrained" for the work they faced, there is little evidence of her signs having been "taken for wonders,"[6] except in the case of Gutiérrez. But, then, he provides a fantastic word salad to hide behind and we really have no idea of who he is.

In its final statement (Cornell Methodology Project 1956:5), the project reported:

In all field stations, local staff were recruited and trained by Project Personnel. . . . [A]ll the professional staff employed by the Methodology Project in Peru are at present working in social science jobs. . . . Project personnel have delivered lectures at the University of San Marcos, Lima. . . . The Methodology Project will . . . contribute a . . . monograph to the volume on social change in Peru now being prepared by the Cornell-Peru Project. . . . The files of data . . . are currently being utilized . . . by students preparing theses in the Department.

There follow four pages of a list of "reports and working papers" of the project, none of which from the Vicos phase was ever published. The monograph in the volume on social change in Peru never appeared, because it was never written. No thesis on the Vicos material from the Methodology Project was ever defended at Cornell University. The only "permanent damage" we can conceive of could have been to the funding foundation, except for our faith in the likelihood that it did not really care.

The failure of the Methodology Project is really not a failure of an individual sociologist, or a failure of a sociology program at an elite North American university, but a failure of modernity itself. Zygmunt Bauman (1991:271-272) states:

> [W]e *can* now (better still, we are *prepared* and *willing to*) take a cool and critical view of modernity in its totality, evaluate its performance, pass judgment on the solidity and congruence of its construction. This is ultimately what the idea of *postmodernity* stands for: an existence fully determined and defined by the fact of being '*post*' (coming *after*) and overwhelmed by the awareness of being in such a condition. Postmodernity does not necessarily mean the end, the discreditation of the rejection of modernity. Postmodernity is no more (but no less either) than the modern mind taking a long, attentive and sober look at itself, at its condition and its past works, not fully liking what it sees and sensing the urge to change. Postmodernity is modernity coming of age: modernity looking at itself at a distance rather than from inside, making a full inventory of its gains and losses, psychoanalyzing itself, discovering the intentions it never before spelled out, finding them mutually canceling and incongruous. Postmodernity is modernity coming to terms with its own impossibility; a self-monitoring modernity, one that consciously discards what it was once unconsciously doing.

Modernity's "own impossibility." We confront here the aporia which the Methodology Project could not research, because it was unresearchable. The task defined for it, essentially, was the rationalization of ethnography. But ethnography is not rational and, in a most subversive way, it defeats its own purpose. Stephen Tyler (1987:98) offers challenging view of the monological nature of "participant observation," the key technique ("method" has no applicability whatsoever!) of ethnography:

> The fable of participant observation both reveals and obscures the presence of the native, for participation implies a "doing together" which might include speaking together, and though ethnographers make claims of fluency in the native language those claims are seldom documented by examples of dialogue. This absence of dialogue signifies the subordination of participating to observing and the use of participation as a deception, as a means of establishing a position from which to observe.

The Peruvian field workers could experience this absence of dialogue, and even write about it, but the North Americans, who spoke poor Spanish or none at all, were practicing a deception. These foreign methodologists, impressed with the "purity" of their science, engaged in monologues because they confronted cultural difference and were oblivious to it at one and the same time. And Sarah Levy's duplicity was grounded in her training by and identification with men, in a field that was dominated by men, who inculcated in her a patriarchal discourse that promoted competition and insisted that she could not compete without control of a scientific instrument, a design, a method, a fetish, a phallus. We must add that this phallus is pushed on her by her mentors. Kate Millett (2000:187) writes: "[I]t would seem that girls are fully cognizant of male supremacy long before they see their brother's penis. It is so much a part of their culture, so entirely present in the favoritism of school and family, in the image of each sex presented to them by all media, religion, and in every model of the adult world they perceive, that to associate it with a boy's distinguishing genital would, since they have learned a thousand other distinguishing sexual marks by now, be either redundant or irrelevant. Confronted with as much concrete evidence of the male's superior status, sensing on all sides the depreciation in which they are held, girls envy not the penis, but only what the penis gives one social pretensions to."

"Identification," Diana Fuss (1995:2) says, "is the psychical mechanism that produces self-recognition.   Identification inhabits, organizes, instantiates identity. It operates as a mark of self-difference, opening up a space for the self to relate to itself as a self, a self that is perpetually other." Thus: "Identification is a process that keeps identity at a distance, that prevents identity from ever approximating the status of an ontological given, even as it makes possible the formation of the *illusion* of identity as immediate, secure, and totalizable." However, Fuss (141) adds, to take identification out of psychoanalysis in order to "understand both its political usages and its conceptual limitations, the notion of identification must be placed squarely within its other historical geneologies."   To extend Fuss's discussion to my object here, then, and to deal with Sarah Levy's problem, we need to recognize how it is produced by the violence of patriarchal domination and the neurotic structure of patriarchy itself.

Sarah Levy finds herself "without words." Her "unspeakable," the doxa, is patriarchal domination.   In 1953 Levy was unable to make the connections that would have liberated her from that structure, she had no discourse of liberation.   Sarah Levy's self-ethnography is all the information we need to understand how men and women both were and are implicated in the structure of patriarchy. It is familiar. We can all read ourselves into Sarah Levy's story.

This brings to a close my endeavor to do something with the packet of letters and other documents from the guest project, ones that Sarah Levy placed with the papers of the Methodology Project's Vicos research in the archives of the Vicos Project. In her last letter to Arthur Silver, she says, "I want you to know the real story." I have kept copies of these materials for nearly a third of a century and I believe that it is timely now to release them. I have tried to interpret these documents within the limits that my capacity to understand Levy's meaning allows me to let her "real story" be known. However, if I left my interpretation to what I can make out of the collection, if I made myself into a "privileged observer," I would be doing an injustice to some residual meaning which may itself become "the real story." And I would be doing a great injustice to other readers of Sarah Levy. Paul de Man (1983:10-11) says:

> The fallacy of a finite and single interpretation derives from the postulate of a privileged observer; this leads, in turn, to the endless oscillation of an intersubjective demystification. As an escape from this predicament, one can propose a radical relativism that operates from the most empirically specific to the most loftily general level of human behavior. There are no longer any standpoints that can a priori be considered privileged, no structure that functions validly as a model for other structures, no postulate of ontological hierarchy that can serve as an organizing principle from which particular structures derive in the manner in which a deity can be said to engender man [sic] and the world. All structures are, in a sense, equally fallacious and are therefore called myths. But no myth ever has sufficient coherence not to flow back into neighboring myths or even has an identity strong enough to stand out by itself without an arbitrary act of interpretation that defines it. The relative unity of traditional myths always depends on the existence of a privileged point of view to which the method itself denies any status of authenticity. . .
>
> It is the distinctive privilege of language to be able to hide meaning behind a misleading sign, as when we hide rage or hatred behind a smile. But it is the distinctive curse of all language, as soon as any kind of interpersonal relation is involved, that it is forced to act this way. . . . In the everyday language of communication, there is no a priori privileged position of a sign over meaning or of meaning over sign; the act of interpretation will always again have to establish this relation for the particular case at hand. The interpretation of everyday language is a Sisyphean task, a task without end and without progress, for the other is always free to make what he [sic] wants differ from what he says he wants.

It is in this context that I include in this English revision some unpublished materials that were presented at the presentation ceremony held in Lima on December 8, 2000. The speaker was Professor Blanca Figueroa, a Peruvian psychologist, who has kindly allowed me to reproduce them here:

> Sarah Levy is introduced in the text as a solitary feminist of the 1950s, struggling in Vicos against other team researchers, all of them men.
>
> I would have wished to feel myself identified and in solidarity with this woman who in less than three months wrote fourteen letters to a friend and asked her to keep them as her field notes. Since Sarah Levy was thinking of using these letters later as a research document, I understand that they were not simply a matter of cathartic relief but a testimony of which she was fully conscious. Perhaps that is why the content of the letters provokes a feeling of displeasure in me which rereading does not succeed in erasing. Indeed, it was impossible for me as a feminist to identify with her.
>
> In the letters, the theme which Sarah repeats tirelessly is that of her colleagues described as drunks (which they were), and as lazy and unproductive people (which does not turn out to be as certain). In the struggle for power Sarah manages to win, showing marked intolerance and authoritarianism. This is not behavior which feminism advocates.
>
> In contrast with her long explanations about how she came to be "first sergeant" (this is the way she describes herself), in the letters there are few references to the inhabitants of Vicos. And when she speaks of them she communicates neither understanding nor sympathy. She writes twice of women: the cook and the wife of a worker; but she does not show any real approach to their lives. My question is, do there exist any other notes by Sarah Levy that indicate a more positive perception of Vicosinos? Because what she says is in no way feminist.
>
> Finally, she is very contemptuous of the Peruvian university students who help her, depreciating them as ignorant. And from their later reports one infers that, despite Levy's affirmations, she did not act as a true former of young people.
>
> In her defense I would like to say that Sarah Levy came to Peru with a deficient knowledge of Spanish, ignored the Quechua of the region, and lacked understanding of Peruvian society. She came, not because the country attracted her but because she was forced to accept the work as part of her academic career. Then she felt insecure of her position on the job, isolated by the men of the team, and confronting situations that turned out to be intolerable for her.
>
> We should recognize that Levy became very preoccupied with work and obliged the others to do it, and then preoccupied with developing the survey. However, as Stein indicates, she found it difficult to communicate with and understand the others. She found it difficult to enjoy life. My impression from her letters is one of a feeling of pity, even from the

distance of a half century.

Other professional women have come to Peru in order to take part in development projects. They contributed their small parts with a more respectful perspective on Peruvians, with greater empathy. But possibly those projects, too, presented many problems, and one could evaluate them and ask how one or another thing was done so badly. In the same way, if I wanted to delve into my own work with women over almost twenty-five years, I would find errors and incoherencies.

Therefore, finally, it happens that tolerance and sympathy for the woman sociologist from Cornell is awakened in me. I recall, for example, the Sarah Levy who wrote: "I feel as if I were in prison waiting to be liberated." It is then in her anguish, in her worries, that I feel close to her because still today in the world of work there continues to exist a most difficult field of struggle if one is a woman.

Like Blanca Figueroa we should pause before we judge Sarah Levy. As Bill Readings (1989:234) most effectively states the case: "Judgments, in that they are made without criteria, presuppose their own judgment. The justice of a judgment can only be judged, again, without criteria. Thus the just person, the judge, does not make judgments, but is made *by* them, is continually judged by and in terms of the judgments that the judge makes. Since those judgments are also made without criteria, the process is continual; the judge can never be finally judged as just (and therefore justified, described as just), since the process of judging can never reach the point where a final account can be given of it."

Levy appears to have invested heavily in "being right." As Elizabeth Grosz (1997:96) points out: "This amounts, fundamentally, and in effect, to a wish to end politics, to stop contestation, to have an answer that admits of no complications and ramifications. To know, to be right.—

Such a will to silence others, to prevent contestation, to adjudicate once and for all and with definitive status, the rightness, the appropriateness, the truthfulness or justice of any position is not a will that can be readily repudiated. In claiming a position, one must remain committed to its ability to explain, enact, produce, and outperform its alternatives; that is, in a certain sense, to its "rightness," its "truth,' its value over and above others. This is what it is to have a position. Yet at the same time, this will to overpower, to master, to control, must undermine itself, must remain bound up with the very disturbances, and to what is unsettling to, uncontainable by it, its others, The no is always committed to a (prior and stronger) yes. And in turn, the yes always contains within a maybe, a quivering of uncertainty, an acknowledgment that even as one commits oneself to a position (whatever it might be) at the same time one is also committed to its undoing and surpassing.

It would, then, be a terrible error to judge that any view we hold of Levy is "right," or even that she was "wrong" in insisting that she was "right." We are called on to deconstruct her narrative, not destroy it.

Gayatri Spivak (2000:26) provides a hint as to how we might proceed: "What would Deconstruction and Cultural Studies look like if the hospitality/*arrivant* figure were twisted [*retorse*], as a subject for historical or anthropological investigation? In other words, taking account of the earlier impulse (a fold in the fabric of hospitality), to be imaginatively hospitable to the colonizing culture, even as it contested the right to colonize, what if we ceased imagining the object of hospitality only as the begging stranger at the door, and the subject of hospitality only as the arch-European dominant, Periclean Greece or its contender, Jerusalem?" Can we then offer hospitality to Levy *and* contest her right to be right?

Deconstruction is "a way of releasing and responding, of listening and opening up," and of hearing not just "the dominant voices of the great masters, but also . . . other voices that speak more gently, more discretely, more mildly" in texts (Caputo 1997a:57). Then it would seem that I haven't deconstructed much at all, but that Sarah Levy has deconstructed what I call *me*.

There would be many other perspectives on the narrative presented here. Meanwhile, what Sarah Levy and I have struggled to articulate here is also a commentary on the Vicos Project and, more broadly, on development discourse. The question is: how are researchers, who are swayed by unconscious motives to lose control of themselves, going to control their variables? Before we intervene in the lives of others, we should try to maximize our capacity to engage in healthy and mature social relations. As I look around myself while I write this, in April, 2002, I see very little of this anywhere in the world, and certainly nowhere in the centers of power of my own country!

Notes

1. Derrida (1972:136) calls attention to the meanings of the French verb *différer*, on one hand "the action of postponing until later," and on the other "the sense of not being identical." *Defer* and *differ* are the English equivalents. It is necessary to introduce a neologism, *différance* in French, *differance* in English, to emphasize the instability of the concept–which is not a concept but a "differance"! Something that differs from itself indefinitely. See Chapter 5 for more discussion of this.

2. One would say "kinky slander" at the present time.

3. Simulated slander would challenge the separation of truth and falsity, suggesting that they might both be simulations. Baudrillard (1983:38) makes this observation of "simulation": "[I]t would be interesting to see whether the repressive apparatus would not react more violently to a simulated holdup than to a real one? For the latter only upsets the order of things, the right of property, whereas the other interferes with the principle of reality. Transgression and violence are less serious, for they only contest the *distribution* of the real. Simulation is infinitely more dangerous, however, since it always suggests, over and above its object, that *law and order themselves might really be nothing more than a simulation*."

4. The correspondence of Allan Holmberg with his field directors is not to be found in the Archives of the Vicos Project. No doubt, they would answer many of our unanswered questions.

5. Rose K. Goldsen and William W. Stein, *The Introduction of NSP in Vicos: The Story Line*. Dittoed. Department of Sociology and Anthropology, Cornell University, Ithaca, New York [1955].

6. Homi Bhabha (1994:102) uses this phrase as a title for an article on British missionary activity in India in the nineteenth century. He opens his essay: "There is a scene in the cultural writings of English colonialism which repeats so insistently after the early nineteenth century–and, through that repetition, so triumphantly *inaugurates* a literature of empire–that I am bound to repeat it once more. It is the scenario, played out in the wild and wordless wastes of colonial India, Africa, the Caribbean, of the sudden, fortuitous discovery of the English book. It is, like all myths of origin, memorable for its balance between epiphany and enunciation. The discovery of the book is, at once, a moment of originality and authority. It is, as well, a process of displacement that, paradoxically, makes the presence of the book wondrous to the extent to which it is repeated, translated, misread, displaced. It is with the emblem of the English book–'signs taken for wonders'–as an insignia of colonial authority and a signifier of colonial desire and discipline that I wish to begin . . ."

Chapter 3

Food and Fetish: The Potato
Experiments[1]

Survival is only ensured by the alteration (translation) of the original, the
differing from itself of the code (the supplement to the code), the
perpetual rewriting of history. . . . This notion of perturbation is a
common feature of what in systems theory are termed "ultrastable" or
"multistable" systems, that is, systems having a number of possible stable
states, made possible by the looseness" or indeterminacy of their
connections. Such systems are "equifinal" to the extent that while their
ostensible aim is reproduction, there are a number of ways of achieving
this aim. This potential for alternative pathways of development can, by a
process of feedback with a changing environment, actually change the
structure or program of the system. Because the code changes while
attempting to remain the same, reproduction will tend in each instance to
be the replication of the same but different. Hence similar initial
conditions may lead to dissimilar end-states. This process of divergence,
or "multifinality", is not amenable to deterministic or even statistical
calculation, its direction is not predictable in the same way that the
development of a less complex (closed) system is predictable. Evolution
is one example of a multifinal process. . . . It is precisely the play of
destination (the possibility of perturbation, noise, random fluctuation)
which makes the system work, whereas perfect transmission, perfect
reproduction, would signify literally the death of the system, paralyzing its

potential for change. (Christopher Johnson 2001:92-93.)

Holmberg and Dobyns (1965:1) begin their study of the Project's intervention in production at Vicos by stating the course of agricultural development there as a "transition by a population of Andean Indian farmers from less than subsistence production, *incapable of even feeding themselves*, to more than subsistence farming–commercial agricultural producers on a modest commercial scale" (emphasis mine). This was a joint article, with Holmberg as senior author, and so I must write "they," but it seems as though Holmberg's spirit is absent from it, an absence that carries the article to an extreme view Holmberg would probably not have chosen. Here is why. The authors choose an odd metaphor to characterize to the Vicosinos, one which seems to picture them as infants or small children who must be fed by caretakers. They soon qualify this statement, retaining the same metaphor: "Only a few of the various types of production units found in the Andes are truly subsistence farms. The types range along a continuum of productivity from those that cannot feed their resident farming population (so that members of farm families must resort to wage labor off the farm so as to earn cash with which to purchase supplementary foodstuffs) to those which produce tremendous surpluses of agricultural commodities beyond local consumption capability that are sold externally, often outside the country on the world commodity market." So it turns out that the Vicosinos *can* feed themselves, though they must do so through wage labor outside Vicos. I do not wish to challenge the motives of these authors. I believe that they had only the best intentions, but they unconsciously wrote an infantile and degrading image[2] of Vicos, one which placed Vicos people outside history. Mary Louise Pratt (1992:61) likens the task of such modernizers as one of "advance scouts for capitalist 'improvement' to encode what they encounter as 'unimproved' and, in keeping with the terms of the anti-conquest [a utopian and more innocent version of their own authority, as opposed to brutal forms of conquest], as *disponible*, available for improvement." Such an

> improving eye produces subsistence habitats as "empty" landscapes, meaningful only in terms of a capitalist future and of their potential for producing a marketable surplus. From the point of view of their inhabitants, of course, these same spaces are lived as intensely humanized, saturated with local history and meaning, where plants, creatures, and geographical formations have names, uses, symbolic functions, histories, places in indigenous knowledge formations.

The vision of Vicosinos and the vision of the improvers: from this comes the title of this chapter on the introduction of new seed potatoes, "food and fetish": an inalienable utility that is "saturated with meaning" to Vicosinos becomes, from the developers' point of view, an alienable object, a thing the meaning of which is only realized through parting with it in exchange for another object or objects. The goal of intervention is, thus, the commodification of potatoes, among other things, and the immersion of Vicosinos into a money economy, not at all a bad goal for poor and hungry people. But we confront, here, two rather different images of the land. For modernizers, inert land is a means for commodity production. For Andean farmers it is an end in itself. Peter Gose (1994:3) points to this contrast at the outset of his study of Huaquirca (Apurímac):

> These people are peasants, not just as a matter of occupational fact, but also as a matter of cultural value. The way in which they work their fields and pastures is fundamental to their sense of who they are, and this expressive dimension of their work regularly spills over into what we might want to call "ritual." Growing crops is not just a means to an end for the commoners of Huaquirca, even though they want to eat well and have abundant provisions for the coming year at harvest time. They also grow crops as an end in itself, to make the earth come alive.

The authors of the unintended insult, the developers, have also, as Homi Bhabha (1994:66) says, "employed the concept of 'fixity' in the ideological construction of otherness."[3] That is, they gazed at Vicos and saw stasis; they saw a history that began with them.[4] This corresponds with what Mary Des Chene (1997:68) calls "a feature of anthropological discourse in every period: that the ethnographer has arrived just prior to momentous changes and things will never be the same again." Thus, pre-Project Vicos is converted into Anne McClintock's (1995:30) "anachronistic space," an empty, timeless region "passively awaiting the thrusting, male insemination of history, language, and reason." These developers appear to employ Haeckel's law, "ontogeny recapitulates phylogeny," anticipating that if the Vicosinos mimic "development" Vicos will emerge from a childlike state to full adulthood, repeating thus the progression of humanity "up" from undevelopment–although they viewed Vicos as "underdeveloped." Jacques Lacan (1978:100) points out, "Whenever we are dealing with imitation, we should not think too quickly of the other who is being imitated. To imitate is no doubt to reproduce an image. But at bottom, it is, for the subject, to be inserted in a function whose exercise grasps it. It is here that we should pause for a moment." In other words, miming affects the mimers themselves in unanticipated ways.

Evolutionary discourse as narrative is an error, but hardly a new one. In his "Preface to the first edition" of *Capital*, in 1867, Karl Marx (1976:90) engaged in the same kind of "progressive," or evolutionary, thinking when he told German readers–and presumably everyone else in the world–that he was using England as a model or pattern for capitalist development in general: he quoted from Horace, "*De te fabula narratur!*" ("The tale is told of you.") "History" has *not* absolved him![5] In his early work, *Edmund Husserl's Origin of Geometry*, Derrida (1989b:65) points to "the annoyed letdown of those who would expect Husserl to tell them *what really happened*, to tell them a story . . ., can be sharp and easily imaginable; however, this disappointment is illegitimate. Husserl only wished to decipher in advance the text hidden under every empirical story about which we would be curious." It is not that Marx was "wrong"— although he *was*—but that he was unable to turn a permanent critique, the "critique of critique" which is one of his monumental contributions to world thought, upon his own texts.

Meanwhile, let us reflect on the background of the developers and the Vicos context. *Habitus* of which they are quite unaware lead them into their exercise of symbolic power, indeed symbolic violence, for they distort their construction of Vicos enough to present to us a false image. Writing over thirty years ago, they are prompted into the development discourse of the time by their very white culture, training, and experience. What I mean by "white" is conveyed in Dyer's (1997:9-10) discussion of the politics of whiteness:

> White people have power and believe that they think, feel and act like and for all people; white people, unable to see their particularity, cannot take account of other people's; white people create the dominant images of the world and don't quite see that they thus construct the world in their own image; white people set standards of humanity by which they are bound to succeed and others bound to fail. Most of this is not done deliberately and maliciously; there are enormous variations of power amongst white people, to do with class, gender and other factors; goodwill is not unheard of in white people's engagement with others. White power none the less reproduces itself regardless of intention, power differences and goodwill, and overwhelmingly because it is not seen as whiteness, but as normal. White people need to learn to see themselves as white, to see their particularity. In other words, whiteness needs to be made strange.

But let us take note, also, of an urgency to understand whiteness as metaphor.[6] Hayden White (1978:5) offers an understanding of *understanding*: "Understanding is a process of rendering the unfamiliar, or the 'uncanny' in Freud's sense of that term, familiar; of removing it from the domain of things felt to be 'exotic' and unclassified into one or another domain of experience encoded adequately enough to be felt to be humanly useful, nonthreatening, or simply known by association. This process of understanding can only be tropological in nature, for what is involved in the rendering of the unfamiliar into the familiar is a troping that is generally figurative." White's understanding supports the employment of many tropes, figures of speech, in this book, but we should not look at the familiar and the unfamiliar as opposites but as concurrences that interpenetrate each other. So I would like to aim at making whiteness, with its "ideal of white as absence [where] being nothing at all may readily be felt as being nothing in particular" (Dyer 1997:80), seem strange to you (if it does not seem so already) while making the Vicosinos seem present and familiar.

When the Project took over the Hacienda Vicos in January 1952, it was a failing enterprise. The former *patrón* was pleased not to have to complete his contract, and the Vicosinos were hungry. Successive patrons had depleted the estate's resources and its population had increased so that the land, unequally distributed in the first place, offered only partial subsistence to many residents. Vicosinos recognized and were angered by the fact that the labor rent they gave to the Hacienda was small compensation for the small plots of poor land the Hacienda gave them, so that they were attached to the estate by what Brooke Larson (1988:171), describing the colonial hacienda system far to the south, aptly calls "a web of mutual obligations (and antagonisms)." Enrique Mayer (1979:79) offers this succinct sketch of the hacienda in Perú, which helps to place the Hacienda Vicos in context:

> The hacienda, or landed estate, was owned by an upper class person, occupied a vast land area, and was worked by a resident labor force, who instead of being paid wages, received a small parcel of land to produce their own sustenance. The hacienda, a form of agrarian enterprise widespread throughout Latin America and the Andes, originated in colonial times, although its development, expansion and importance in the nation's economy came late in the colonial period and in the first century of independent republican life, when a market for rural produce began to develop. After a period of peak development, the Peruvian hacienda system began to decline. It was finally abolished by the agrarian reforms of the 1960s.
>
> The hacienda was a self contained economic, political and religious unit with limited specific types of relations with the outside world. It produced enough subsistence for all members, the resident peasant serf (colono, yanacón) and the patrón.

In addition, a marketable surplus was sold by the owner in the regional, national and international markets. The hacienda ideally owned enough natural resources, land, water, wood, and livestock to make this possible, and thus sought to expand in similar ways as communities by utilizing as many ecological zones as possible. Politically, the hacienda was also independent.

In addition to the slow decline of agriculture in Perú, from its peak after the trauma of the War of the Pacific during the 1880s, into the early decades of this century, Vicos suffered because its renters were not owners and did not seek to maintain its value. The Vicosinos were poor, felt oppressed, and expressed resentment their condition. Moreover, several crop diseases had intervened to further reduce subsistence production by Vicos households, in particular a devastating potato fungus which was taking potatoes out of production, as well as a virus and a bacterial infection, an infestation by nematode worms, and plagues of insect parasites which serve not only as disease vectors but which also eat leaves and stalks. However, potatoes appear to be a crop the extinction of which is continually threatened by these plagues yet which manages continually to produce new varieties. Potatoes diversify themselves through genetic recombination, reproducing not only by means of the tubers planted in the ground but also by seeds scattered from the potato berries. But not in Vicos. What an "observer" said of Ireland in 1852 held for Vicos: "The time was when we could hardly go wrong: no manure or any sort of manure, new soil or old soil, rich land or poor land, early planted or late planted, the tubers were all sound although of different qualities, according to the advantage each had. But how is it now? Every man has a scheme to recommend; but, do what you will, the potatoes, under every sort of management, are diseased" (quoted in Salaman 1985:165). In Vicos potatoes seemed to be becoming extinct.

Potatoes have been the second food in Vicos for generations.[7] Maize is first and potatoes are next in importance, before wheat, barley, pulses, quinoa, and minor tuber crops. Then come garden crops of peppers, onions, cabbage, pumpkins, and herbs. Potatoes constitute the agricultural product most in demand in the national market, however, since it is the staple food of the largest segments of the urban population (Vázquez 1955:48). According to Coutu and King (1969:17, 20), potatoes are by far the most important element in the Peruvian diet in terms of bulk; while tubers provide only fifteen per cent of the calories and ten per cent of the protein, they are estimated to constitute almost thirty per cent of the weight of the net yearly intake of food per person. Susan Poats (1982a:13) says of the Andes in general: "Potatoes are a primary food source and are consumed on a daily basis often in quantities of 0.5 kg/person/day or more. Per capita annual consumption levels of 100-200 kilos are common." Burton (1985:568) notes: "The potato is a source of nitrogen, vitamin C, and starch, of which the latter forms by far the greater part of the dry matter of the tuber. . . . Because of its high content of water, the potato is, weight for weight, a much poorer source of starch, of which it contains on the average some 15-20%. On the other hand the yield of potatoes, in a suitable climate, is so much greater than that of cereals that the yield of starch per acre is very much greater from potatoes than from any other source." In addition to all this, Douglas Horton (1981:29) adds: "Most people have the mistaken impression that potatoes are mostly carbohydrates with negligible or poor quality protein. In fact, the potato is one of the world's most nutritious sources of food. The ratio of protein to carbohydrates is higher in potatoes than in many cereals and other roots and tubers."

When the Project sought to intervene in potato production, it chose wisely. While inputs of labor and technology are costly, potato cropping, under optimal conditions, produce gross values two or more times that of other crops, although revenue ratios of maize are higher (Garrido-Lecca 1965:87-91). Moreover, potatoes are suited to the Vicos situation: Horton (1983:179) observes "how a traditional potato production system, employing hand implements, native varieties and organic fertilizers, can be more economical than a modern, high-input system."

At the beginning of 1952 Vicos had a population of a little over 2,000, but this was soon augmented by returning Vicosinos who had migrated to other places but who were encouraged to return by the Project's accomplishments. These farm families were located on an estate of some 14,000 hectares. However, the base of farmable land was only 1,746 hectares, of which the *patrón* customarily occupied 150 hectares of the largest and best fields near the Marcará River and on some of the shoulders (Stevens 1959:26). There is other land that could be placed under cultivation but, Garrido-Lecca (1965:125) says, "Unfortunately there is a limit to how much more land can be reclaimed for cultivation. Also the remoteness of this land and the absence of roads to these fields make transportation of inputs and produce very difficult. Four or more hours of walking are needed to reach them. If labor were idle production could be justified. Once these fields were under cultivation, farming practices would need to be performed there at the same time they are performed in the rest of the Hacienda. This would increase demand for labor at the busiest season. If roads were opened so that a vehicle could reach them the case might be very different. Road building is, however, very difficult on that broken rocky terrain." The lands the Vicos workers had for themselves, then, were scant for the expanding population. It is no wonder that most Vicosinos had to engage in work outside Vicos to supplement their meager farm production.

We now examine, utilizing mainly materials from the Methodology Project, Vicosinos' reactions to these circumstances and to the Vicos Project's interventions. In particular, the Methodology Project's "Task 2," a series of seventy-one interviews with Vicos workers by three field workers, and stimulated by Sarah Levy's arrival in Vicos, provides rich data. The three interviewers, all students in the University of San Marcos, were: Eduardo Soler Bustamante born in Huánuco, who could understand and be understood in Quechua; Juan Elías Flores from the Pacific lowlands, who spoke no Quechua and worked with a mestizo interpreter from Carhuaz, Ricardo Estremadoyro, as well as two bilingual Vicosinos, Pablo Herrera and Celso León; and Froilán Soto Flores from Huancavelica, who spoke the southern variety of Quechua and had difficulty in communication until he too began work with Estremadoyro. I supplement the materials selected from Task 2 with other data gathered by the interviewers who continued to ask their informants about the agricultural innovations, and with extracts from the work of Carlos Gómez, a mestizo from Carhuaz who was employed by the Methodology Project to gather life histories.

Here is a description of their field activities, as reported in the report on "Instructions Given to Fieldworkers (Methodology Project n.d.:7-9):

> *Introduction for all field men.* We are now going to begin a task of observation on the general subject of what happens when a person introduces a new seed in his agriculture. First, let us say something general on the subject of the diffusion of any cultural element.
>
> First of all, when a cultural element enters a community, it has to be introduced by some person. Our problem is to look for the reasons why some people accept these innovations and why other people do not accept them, after the idea has been introduced. A very important aspect of this problem is related to the sources of information and the sources of influences. The diffusion might be by personal contact and discussion or by observation only. Always, it is necessary to remember that the channels of knowledge of the diffusion of an element are not necessarily the same as the channels of stimuli to accept or reject the innovations.
>
> In the Hacienda Vicos we have the opportunity to study by observation one innovation in agriculture: the new seed potatoes which were introduced one year ago. We want to learn all about the channels of information and the stimuli to accept the new seed potatoes. This problem will be your task for this week.
>
> *Instructions given to Soler.* We want to obtain all possible information about these subjects: 1. To what extent Vicosinos have accepted the new

seed potatoes. 2. What were the sources of information about that seed. 3. What were the channels of diffusion of such information. 4. What are the stimuli for deciding to use or not to use the new seed potatoes.

It is necessary to note any information that you think is related to this problem. An important point is always to take your information in full view of the informant or the people whom you are observing. You should never try to hide your notebook. If the people notice your notebook and worry about it, it is necessary to note all the details about this. For each notation it is always necessary to register the time you started and the time you finished.

(Soler: without interpreter, unspecified situations, overt.)

Structured observation form . . . given to Soto and Flores. 1. This week Vicosinos will be in the field planting seed potatoes. You are to observe the planting of potatoes.

2. Determine how many arrobas of potatoes are being planted this year.

3. Determine the ratio of new seed potatoes to old seed potatoes being planted this year. How does this compare with last year?

4. We want to know how many of the people in this planting situation are using new seed for the first time? How many used it last year and are using it again? How many used it last year but are not using it now?

5. Try to find out what sources of information were important in informing the Vicosinos about the new seed potatoes. As far as you can determine, does the high or low status position of such a source of information have any effect on people's readiness to accept the new seed potato? Does it make any difference whether the information about the new potato comes from the administration, a mestizo, or an Indian? Explain.

6. We are interested in finding out whether the Vicosinos customarily discuss the problem of planting new seed potatoes with others. What do they say about them?

7. Indicate whether the status positions of such discussants has any effect on the willingness of the Vicosinos to use the new seed potato. Indicate also whether the fact that such discussants were from the hacienda administration, indigenous, or mestizo, had any effect on the decision to plant or not to plant the new seed potato.

8. Evaluate the relative influence on the adoption of the new type of seed potato of the following factors: a. proximity of residence. b. kinship, immediate family or extended family. c. demonstration.

9. Determine how the Vicosinos in your situation evaluate the yield of the new seed potato compared with the old. What relationship does this opinion have on their willingness to use the new seed potato?

10. We would like to know how much importance the Vicosinos attach to the introduction of the new seed potato. Does it appear to be a matter of great importance in their lives? It is a matter of a great deal of discussion? Of controversy?

11. Please describe briefly the background characteristics of the people

whom you observed in this situation, that is, sex, age, residence, socio-economic level.

Get from Mario Vázquez a list of the names of the Vicosinos who are putting in potatoes this week. Decide between yourselves whom to visit. Spend Monday (July 13) from 2-5, Tuesday, 8:30-12, 2:30-5, and Wednesday, Thursday, and Friday the same hours. We shall meet Saturday morning to discuss your work.

The field team as a whole operated as what Mary Louise Pratt (1992:135) calls "transculturators," transporting to North America knowledge that originated in Vicos, and producing North American knowledge infiltrated by Vicos discourse. Vicosinos told the field workers what they believed the latter wanted to hear but their accounts, filtered through translation from Quechua into Spanish, and now from Spanish into English, are at the same time representations of Vicos. The development discourse of the designers of the study flowed past the interviewers and the informants because the North Americans appeared to be intent on the ultimate conversion of potatoes into commodities. That is, they sought career enhancement by way of the success of the experiment, that is, raising production and fomenting commerce. The interviewers, both as instruments of the Methodology Project and as Peruvians searching to piece together a livelihood from the resources at their disposal, appeared to be intent on satisfying the North Americans and developing useful methodological skills. And the Vicosino informants were surely intent on viewing potatoes as food. However, the field activity allowed some of the Vicosinos to speak about their situation and about the Vicos Project's interventions. Let us begin with the Vicosinos' perceptions of their situation. Vicos interest in the potato plagues and alternatives for dealing with them are illustrated in these interview extracts:

> Hermenegildo Gutiérrez: The disease we call *mañuco* arrived here about three years ago and attacked the potatoes, *ocas* [tubers], and *habas* [broad beans]. This disease comes with the rains and the clouds, so now we plant potatoes ahead of time in May. . . . We don't cure it because we can't buy the medicines. They cost a lot. We just treat the plants with ashes which we sprinkle over them. Sometimes the ashes overcome the disease. We do the same with *ocas*, *habas*, and wheat. With wheat it's against the *polvillo* disease, and also so the birds won't eat it. (Soler, July 10.)

> Santiago Basilio: In these last four years our crops have been suffering badly. We don't know what sickness it is. I think it may come from the mist that settles in the Quebrada Honda [an upland gorge where frost resistant varieties of potatoes are planted]. Let me tell you, that sickness

withers the plants almost completely. The roots get hard and the leaves shrivel as though they had been burned. The potatoes themselves can't be eaten because they're too hard. Not even the pigs want to eat them. They're nauseating. We can't use them for *toqosh* [fermented potatoes] either. . . . We never treat the crop with medicine because we don't know how to do it. The Hacienda has brought some medicine, but only a little and it's expensive. You know, with only a little bit we can't treat a whole field. Sometimes we put a cross in the middle of a field to protect it against sickness, so the sickness won't get to it. . . . Long ago, when my grandparents were alive the sicknesses that are here now didn't exist. In these last few years things have gotten bad. Surely the sickness is here because God lets it in. Everything happens because God wants it and orders it. (Soler, July 21.)

Víctor Evaristo: When relatives marry each other then sickness comes to the things we eat. All the potatoes go bad. It's God's punishment. When things like that happen, the *varayoq* [community authorities[8]] learn about it and punish them. (Soto, with Ricardo Estremadoyro, August 12.)

Alfonso Cruz: (What is the potato disease?) I don't know what it is. It shows up quickly in the maize, potatoes, and *ocas*. It's like a scorching, as if it had been by fire. The student engineers ought to know about it. . . . Maybe it comes from the air, or maybe it's a punishment from God. (Why a punishment from God?) Sometimes there is some transgression by Indians or *mishtis* [mestizos]. (What transgression?) When somebody gets drunk and beats on his family, or when people exchange bad words. (They tell me that those sicknesses come from having sexual relations inside the *casta* [lineage]. Is that so?) Sometimes, when people are close relatives. When people fight with their *comadres* [co-mother, baptismal sponsor of one's child] or *compadres* [co-father]. It's thought that the *viento* or *aire* [supernatural wind or air] comes from that and damages the crops.

I think that punishments, those *vientos*, come from the people themselves. Because there was a case in Recuayhuanca [a community across the river from Vicos]. A woman hit her mother and it [the sin in the form of a *viento*?] went out into the field. Her mother had come to the house and found her grandchildren crying, so she began to cook for them. The daughter came home and asked her why she had come into the house and taken over her things. The mother hit the daughter with a stick, and then the daughter hit her mother. Two days later the daughter went off to Paramonga [sugar plantation on the coast where men went in those times to cut cane] where her husband was. Then a *viento* came into the place across from the house. The *viento* was there in that place. A woman told us abut it. I found out because I am a *Campo* [a member of the *varayoq*]. It was a woman from here, Vicos, who knew about what happened and came before the authorities here. We didn't know anything about what caused the *viento*. We sent to have the daughter appear and tell because she was the one who had to know about it. She told about it, and then the authorities took her prisoner to Carhuaz. And, like that, the *viento* disappeared in three days. But it damaged the fields and the houses. So I believe in God and in those punishments. The sicknesses are the people's fault. . . . We ignorant Indians know that sicknesses are produced by the people themselves. But mestizos don't believe that. They say that sicknesses come by themselves, and they don't believe that they come because there are bad people. (Flores, with Celso León, August 17.)[9]

Eugenio Leiva: (Why are the plants getting sick?) It must be a bad time. I don't know why. (What is the potato sickness?) The leaves dry up. (Why does this sickness happen?) I don't know. Maybe it's a bad *aire*. (Why would it be a bad *aire*?) I don't know. People say it's because sometimes family members fight, and then the *viento* comes. (Is that true or not?) They say that it's from fighting with a *compadre* or a *comadre*. However it may be, the *viento* comes. I don't know if that's true or not. (Can that *viento* make *paltaq* [a variety of *papa común*, ordinary potatoes, planted by Vicosinos] potatoes sick?) It must be a sickness that floats in the *aire*, but a person can't see it. It will make any crop sick. It's the same in Marcará. When they planted late, the sickness finished it off. They didn't harvest anything. (Flores, with Celso León, August 18.)

In Vicos discourse a sin seems to be a kind of inverted "inalienable possession"[10] which blows into fields in the ghostly shape of a metaphysical wind in a negative reciprocity with supernatural beings,[11] and in which the offense that is given is kept (cf. Weiner 1992). These materials suggest, moreover, that in crop-"curing,"–as in people-"curing" which we will examine in Chapter 5–what is indicated from the Vicos point of view is what Claude Lévi-Strauss (1963:201) would call "living out a myth." He adds:

[W]e should ask ourselves whether the therapeutic value of the cure depends on the actual character of remembered situations, or whether the traumatizing power of those situations stems from the fact that at the moment when they appear, the subject experiences them immediately as living myth. By this we mean that the traumatizing power of any situation cannot result from its intrinsic features but must, rather, result from the capacity of certain events, appearing within an appropriate psychological, historical, and social context, to induce an emotional crystallization which is molded by a pre-existing structure.

Vicosinos' views of time and space, sin and redemption, and the profane and the sacred are thrust into the Methodology Project's interviews despite the designers' interest in rationality, science, and development, all of which relegate religious concepts, as Marc Augé (1998:115) notes, "in the name of progress to the pole of fiction." This occurs, also, despite the Peruvian interviewers' distance from this Andean discourse. I employ the term "Andean" here with the same reservations as those offered by Jeanette Sherbondy (1992:48) who writes of the Central Andean region:

> Given the variety of cultural expressions in the past as well as in the present, it seems very limiting to focus only on traits that appear to persist in order to define what is Andean to the detriment of all the forms that may or may not have persisted but should be considered equally Andean. After all, the term *Andean* itself is a fairly recent invention by non-Andean observers. . . . In an attempt to define culture areas anthropologists have applied *Andean* to this area, especially to the area occupied formerly by the Inca state; and then they posed themselves a problem of identifying what *Andean* meant in terms of the cultures of the peoples of that geographical area. Although the Inca state covered a good part of this area, the cultural and geographical term extends far beyond its boundaries, so that the problem is posed of trying to identify the traits that define a concept that has no real foundation on any single cultural reality. It is essentially a concept that has meaning primarily for non-Andean anthropologists, and so it is, on a smaller scale, a sort of "Orientalism," a product of neocolonial intellectual nomenclature."

Sherbondy refers to Edward Said's influential work on Orientalism which I have cited in Chapter 1. Said's (1978:5) point is that the "Orient" is a construct, but "to believe that such things happen simply as a necessity of the imagination, is to be disingenuous," for: "The relationship between Occident and Orient is a relationship of power, of domination, of varying degrees of a complex hegemony." Like Orientalism, Andeanism exercises a certain "intellectual authority" over the Andean in the North American and European milieu, which is not really Andean but Andeanist, or Andeanist discourse. I will hereafter separate these two terms. But let us not leave the matter there. Said (24) raises the strategic question of "how one can study other cultures and peoples from a libertarian, or a nonrepressive and nonmanipulative, perspective."[12]

What should be—but is not—the last word on "the Andean" was written by historian Alberto Flores Galindo (1989:150, quoted in Hurtado 1997:86, n.) in a discussion of cityward migration from the Andes, in which he wrote about an "Andeanization of cities":

> All this has to do with the fact that Andean culture is, in reality, a colonial creation which, since the 16th century, absorbed a series of Western elements and, at the same time, created others. A great part of its vitality

is rooted in such a capacity to take new things and incorporate them in its universe. Thus, the Andean is no longer only identified with the rural or restricted to the highlands. The Andean is now found in Chimbote [a coastal city] or in Lima. Moreover, a process of cultural boiling-over is being lived and new things are appearing.

This is no longer "Andeanist" but Peruvianist, as Peruvians take José Carlos Mariátegui's advice and "Peruvianize" their country.

Meanwhile, the Vicosinos interviewed spoke about sacred things in spite of their awareness of outsiders' contempt for their views on a world order of repetitive, rather than lineal, change. David Gow (1976:179), in an outstanding statement of the Andeanist perspective, observes in regard to Pinchimuro and Lauramarca, the comunities he studied in the Cusco region:

> Each stage [of history] ends in a cataclysm to be followed by a new creation which, in turn, also ends in a cataclysm to be followed by yet another creation. But it would be mistaken to say that the peasants regard their history as purely cyclical, for they see each stage as fusing with the ones that preceded it and the ones which will follow it. The past is always alive and part of the present; the future exists now and existed long ago. Thus their vision of history is both cyclical, in that a cataclysm or catastrophe ends one stage and creates the next, and cumulative in that the previous stage has not been destroyed but only driven underground, where it continues to exert a powerful influence through its frequent surfacings into everyday life and also through myth, ritual and symbol.

Sigmund Freud could not have illustrated the psychoanalytic conception of the repetitive acting-out of repressed desires any better than this enthusiastic expression of Andeanist discourse which struggles to articulate an autoethnography along with its struggle to master an Andean discourse.[13]

This said, let us now take up again the background for the potato experiment. Even in the best of times, most Vicosinos were micro-holders whose household production needed to be supplemented by other sources of income. People saw themselves as poor, at the mercy of powers greater than their own, and with access to few alternatives to improve their situation:

> Simón Díaz: Before, when we used to plant in our little bit of land we got out a good harvest in the end that was enough for all of us. Now in these times we have to plant a lot and then the harvest isn't any good. That's why we have to spend our money buying produce. I'm not sure

that those past times will come back in the future. In the old days, when there was a good harvest, people had enough even to spend, but now there's not enough. So I'm tired of it. I don't understand why times have changed so much or why the land has become poorer and the sicknesses have appeared. It's surely people's bad faith. Other Vicosinos are the same as I am. They don't know what's going to happen. God must be punishing us and that's why there's no food. It's because there are women with more than one husband. They've become corrupted and so our God is taking revenge. If he would punish just those bad people, that would be good, but I don't understand why it is that everybody is punished. (Soto, with Ricardo Estremadoyro, August 21.)

José Santos: After I'm finished with my Hacienda *tarea* [Mondays, Tuesdays, and Wednesdays of work for the Hacienda] every week, I usually go to Marcará or Carhuaz to work for people there. With the wages I get I buy food supplies and other things we need at home. Sometimes I hoe maize or potatoes, make *tzaqma* [break sod], make adobes, work in construction, cut wood, or anything. I do any kind of work that's offered. I like to work that way because it's the only way I know how to make the money we need. (Gómez, undated.)

Gregorio Vega: What we plant doesn't satisfy our needs. It doesn't get to last through the year. So we have to buy things in other places, especially Marcará. When we work in those towns they pay us two or three *soles* and other times they pay us in grain. . . . When we get sick we don't buy medicines from the store because we don't have the money. We just use home remedies. It's a good thing we don't get worse. Surely God wouldn't allow that, or it's because he hasn't abandoned us yet. (Soler, June 27.)

Estenio Meza: I don't have anything to sell because things are scarce. I'd like to eat more. Sometimes the harvests aren't enough and so we've gone to work down below to earn money to buy grain, maize, cornmeal, or *habas*. (Flores, with Pablo Herrera, July 18.)

Alfonso Cruz: (Why is life getting worse?) The crops are getting tired and the land has less strength, and so harvests are bad.

Before, in the heights when I was young, we cropped enormous potatoes. Those aren't to be seen any more. That's the way these lands are, and that's the way the heights are, and it's not the way it used to be. Now the potatoes are small, and they're full of worms. It must be the seed. Seed will last two or three years with manure, but then time will take the force out of them and they'll be the same as the oldest seeds. With livestock the first animals born are good and then they get worse. The last one comes out very feeble because the mother is old. Year by year they lose their strength. . . . (Are there other reasons why the times are getting worse?) It's according to the times. The world is tired from wickedness and punishment. The land also gets tired because irrigation and the rains are strong and carry off its strength. (Flores, with Celso León, August 18.)

Expectations are low. People believe that poverty is their destiny. When Vicosinos were asked what they would do if they had a lot of money, most were hard put to dream of anything beyond food and clothing. This affirmation represents many Vicosinos:

> Manuel Cruz: If I had lots of money I'd do what you do, I'd put it in the bank. I'd like to have it like you do. We work more than we should and so we ought to have more than you. You are lazy people who spend your time writing papers, and they pay you a lot. If I had a lot of money I'd take good care of my relatives. Since I've never had so much money, I wouldn't know how to use it. So I don't want anything. If I had it I'd buy everything I need, like grain, clothing, cloth. These days the little we have we spend because everything costs a lot. (Flores, with Ricardo Estremadoyro, July 9.)

The hacienda system leaves few opportunities for the hacienda worker–referred to by mestizos as a *colono*, which means "serf"–to produce surplus on the family's holdings for saving or sale. In the hacienda system workers receive no wages in return for their services. Rather, workers are granted land and other privileges (in Vicos, pasturage and access to clay pits). Before workers can work their own allotted household land they are obliged to complete their duties (*tareas*) to the estate or other tasks to which they may be assigned. In Vicos the Hacienda *tarea* was three days a week for approximately 250 workers, 160 of whom performed agricultural service while the others served as shepherds, gardeners, field and warehouse guards, *mayorales* (foremen) and other minor specialized occupations.. In return for these labors workers received house sites with their gardens, some pasturage rights in the grasslands located above the farmed parts of Vicos, and "three fields," that is, land in the three major ecological zones, traditionally "for maize, wheat, and potatoes" (Stevens 1959:25). Distribution of land among the Vicos workers was quite uneven, with a few privileged families and many deprived ones. The pattern of equal inheritance by all children had severely divided holdings into increasingly smaller plots, so that many workers did not possess the ideal three allotments. Moreover, there were in 1950 about one hundred families with house sites but no other land holdings. In these cases the household head served as "colono," *peón* in the Vicos sense, to another worker with land, laboring in the latter's fields for a share in the produce and working that person's tarea in the Hacienda. Compliance with the system was obtained under the threat of *embargo* (confiscation) of moveable property: animals, tools, utensils, or clothing. For a disobedient worker, the final resort of a *patrón* was expulsion from the Hacienda. A jail existed in Vicos up to the time the Project entered the community, and in the last century it is recorded that a whipping post existed and was used. In 1950, workers were receiving the token payment demanded by the Republic of Perú's Constitution, twenty centavos per Hacienda work day, but even this could be withheld if the worker defaulted, even though he or she made up the work later.

Barnett (1960:81) has outlined the dysfunctions of the hacienda system: it isolates the workers from the outside world, prevents effective community action, limits family and community authority through its system of outside control, keeps the workers impoverished, and encourages them to maintain a "double standard" or morality relating to work and honesty. In traditional Vicos, appropriation of Hacienda produce was an alternative in the workers' definition of subsistence activity. Vicosinos knew that mestizos stereotyped them as "thieves." And certainly they had listened to priests' sermons regarding appropriation of another's property as "sinful." How they felt about it is not revealed in the interview materials I am examining here. But Vicosinos are skilled in the art of telling strangers what they believe these strangers want to hear. Ricardo Godoy (1990:97) says of Bolivian "*jukeo*," the appropriation of tin by peasant miners, that "it does not represent a breach of contract so much as an understood part of the silent agreement by which workers are hired and kept in the mine." I believe that the principle applies to Vicos, and many other haciendas, as well.

Appadurai (1986:26) calls such appropriation "the humblest form of diversion of commodities from preordained paths." James Scott (1985:290) raises the question of whether the act of a poor worker in Malaysia who leaves paddy in a rich man's field for his family to glean should be called "an act of petty pilfering or an act of resistance." Alternatively: "A harvest laborer who steals paddy from his employer is 'saying' that his need for rice takes precedence over the formal property rights of his boss" (301). And Frantz Fanon (1963:308-309) reports for Algeria: "Under the colonial regime, anything may be done for a loaf of bread or a miserable sheep. The relations of [people] with matter, with the world outside, and with history are in the colonial period simply relations with food. . . . To live means to keep on existing. Every date is a victory: not the result of work, but a victory felt as a triumph for life. Thus to steal dates or to allow one's sheep to eat the neighbor's grass is not a question of the negation of the property of others, nor the transgression of a law, nor lack of respect. These are attempts at murder."

Vázquez (1955:57-58) characterizes the Hacienda harvests of 1951 and 1952 as a "battle" between the administration and the workers who took potatoes from the fields from the time of planting, when they would return to the fields to dig up what they had planted the day before, to the harvest when the workers would deliberately hide potatoes in the field and recover them when the harvest was formally "over." Potatoes were even taken from the Hacienda warehouse. When the Hacienda appointed additional guards to watch the potato fields, the workers staged a mass raid to recover their gleaning rights:

> The harvesting of Hacienda crops took the form of a battle between the administration, which tried to save its investment, and the people who were trying to make off with most of the yield. To enumerate the robberies which were committed by the Vicosinos at that time would fill many pages, but as a single illustration we mention the thefts of potatoes discovered in 1952. Thefts began from the very time of planting. Several thefts by persons responsible for planting were discovered. The workers had remembered the position of the seed which they had hidden and, returning the following day, had dug up the seed to use it for food. Thefts again began to occur about four months after planting and continued until the harvest. These thefts were committed when workers were in the field irrigating or weeding, or when they were pasturing oxen in neighboring fields. In addition, nocturnal thefts were discovered in which the plants were torn up and the soil turned to find the potatoes.
>
> At harvest time ingenious thefts took place. The Project harvested potatoes which had been planted by the previous renter. Often the harvester's basket of potatoes would be emptied into a break in the ground and the tubers covered with earth. An accomplice, being advised of the location of the cache, would later go out to the field to complete the theft. Harvesters would also take advantage of the least slackening in vigilance on the part of supervisors to empty their baskets into the brush or throw the potatoes there like stones.
>
> When the harvested potatoes were at last in the storehouses, the thefts continued. In a period of two months, January to March 1952, eight cases of theft were discovered. A Vicosino caught stealing a sack of potatoes would excuse himself through the intermediation of his *padrino* [godfather], who would report that the man had been obliged to steal out of poverty and in order to feed his children.
>
> The continuing thefts forced the administration to select persons to stand guard over the potato crop. This action caused the workers to protest, and on December 29, 1952, they carried out a mass raid on the potato fields belonging to the Hacienda. Interviewed about their motive for such conduct, they answered with many varied explanations and evasions, the most significant among them being: "We stole because we

were not allowed to take even the rotten potatoes from the harvest."

Peter Gose (1991:46) reports on an Andean pattern of "private appropriation" in Huaquirca:

> Once the crops become officially consumable after Carnival, they undergo a radical change in status from an object of interhousehold cooperation to an object of private appropriation by individual households. In many parts of the Andes, this is vividly expressed during Easter, which corresponds approximately to the onset of the killing frosts. Andean people say that both the earth and God die during Holy Week, and that it is permissible to steal crops from their neighbors at this time because God does not see. While such theft may become particularly intensive and almost ritualized during Holy Week, it in fact continues right up until the harvest. Indeed, institutionalized crop theft at this time of year has been reported widely throughout the Andes, and is (paradoxically) every bit as much a social fact as is the intensive cooperation that precedes it. During April and May, property consciousness rises to a crescendo, and households even send one of their members to sleep in the fields at night in order to maintain constant vigilance over the crops. People who short weeks ago had been linked in a harmonious productive effort now greet one another with suspicion on the paths to the fields, and acrimonious accusations of theft abound.

Orin Starn (1999:44) reports on the people of northern Peru:

> I was not always able to pin down the "facts" of theft. Although everywhere I went in the northern mountains villagers admitted in the abstract that "just about everyone" was involved. I did not find anyone who wanted to talk about his or her own role. Too many people believed such admissions would expose them to damaging gossip and perhaps even sorcery, if not prosecution.

In the case of Vicos, I view the taking of produce, and anything else moveable, from the Hacienda as a kind of "foraging" which contrasts with other modes of production[14] engaged in by Vicosinos, such as farming, wage labor, or cattle trading. If it is to be seen as petty theft at all, it constitutes a valiant effort by most Vicosinos to mime the grand theft practiced daily by their patrons. But I would rather look at it with Scott's (1985) vision as a "weapon of the weak"; that is, as a manifestation of resistance to the hacienda system, minimally, and maximally as rebellious assertion of what Taussig (1997:250) characterizes as "the power of the copy to influence what it is a copy of." In Vicos the Hacienda administration in past times accepted theft but exercised vigilance that it not exceed conventional limits, while the Vicosinos undoubtedly enjoyed watching patronal discomfort. With the coming of the Project, these war games intensified. Jacques Lacan (1978:99) observes, "Mimicry reveals something in so far as it is distinct from what might be called an *itself* that is behind. The effect of mimicry is camouflage, in the strictly technical sense. It is not a question of harmonizing with the background but, against a mottled background, of becoming mottled–exactly like the technique of camouflage practices in human warfare." And Bhabha (1994:90) adds to Lacan's brief statement that the "threat" of mimesis "comes from the prodigious and strategic production of conflictual, fantastic discriminatory 'identity effects' in the play of a power that is elusive because it hides no essence, no 'itself.'" The Project's designers wished the Vicosinos to mime their design *up to a point,* that is to mimic their conception of development by commercializing potato production but *not* to mime other aspects of their intervention, e.g., *their* desire (lust) to desire "experimental" success, *their* contractual obligation to maintain the authority of the hacienda system, albeit a reformed one, *their* inability to redistribute private property in Vicos, *their* deprivation of Vicos families by their ultimately increased surveillance of the Hacienda's potato fields, or *their* ambivalence in the face of the Vicosinos' subversive and disruptive challenge to their authority.

Workers' attitudes toward the hacienda system and the Hacienda are illustrated in the following extracts:

> Juan Coleto: I'm not a *peón* in the Hacienda, but I certainly am an Hacienda man. A *"peón"* is a person who works for wages, who is paid, like for example when we go to work in other places. I work in the Hacienda by *tarea,* three times a week. We trade work for the fields we plant, as if it were payment of rent. . . . It's an established custom in this Hacienda to work three days a week. That way we always are thinking about work for the Hacienda. If they charged us half the money we earned in other places for all the days we work during a year, we'd rather pay in money, for which we could go out to any place to work. In past years we've negotiated to rent the Hacienda ourselves, for which everyone gave 16 or 19 *soles,* but they say the money wasn't enough and so Huachón [Watson, the renter from whom the Project subleased the Hacienda] won.[15] In any case, I think that it wouldn't be good now for us to rent it because the leaders would be the ones who would take over the fields and we'd waste our time. (Soler, August 8.)

> Eugenio Leiva: Work for the Hacienda is not good. We work three days for the Hacienda and we're left with just four days for our personal work, and that includes Sunday. That's why we don't make progress with our own work. Other people have sons and so they can get on. But those

of us who are single can't do that.

In other places they pay from three to four *soles* a day, with full *temple* [a gratification consisting of a few cents]. And they also provide *chicha* [home brew], alcohol, coca, and cigarettes. That happens in Marcará. Here they don't pay anything. All the work we do in the Hacienda is payment that we make in order to plant fields, ones in the heights. That's why we have to work.

Sometimes when I have friends or relatives to work in my place I'd rather pay three *soles* a day. That's when I have a lot of things to do and I have money. But generally I have to work in the Hacienda because I don't have the money to pay them. It's better for me to go to the Hacienda than pay, because in some years the harvest isn't good, and even if a person puts in manure the yield is small. In other words, if I busy myself working my fields personally, and paying a wage for someone to work in the Hacienda, it wouldn't turn out well for me because besides paying, and my own work in the fields, I wouldn't get a crop to harvest. And if a person doesn't work for the Hacienda they take an *embargo*, his *lampa* [hoe], *barreta* [utility bar], rope. And if you miss one day, they don't give you *temple*. They refuse and tell you and ask you why you missed. Then a person has to make it up on the next day, Thursday, and if you miss two days you have to make it up with Friday too. (Soto, with Ricardo Estremadoyro, August 17.)

Lucas Díaz: I don't make many trips out of here because I have to work my *tareas* for the Hacienda. Here if I miss a few days they demand that I make up the lost days. Since I plant the fields they give me, I'm forced to work for the Hacienda. And it's not a great thing that they give us for those three days we work, but just twenty *centavos* [cents] a day which we call "*temple*." We can't even register a complaint because we don't know how to read or write. Surely they could tangle us up with their papers.

Now and then I go to Huaraz, Carhuaz, and Caraz where I buy things like coca, cloth for shirts, salt, bread, and sugar. I only go once or twice a year. I go to Marcará more frequently when I need to get salt, coca, or *ají*. Most of the time I spend working in my fields or working for the Hacienda. (Soler, June 27.)

Pablo Reyes: *Temple* is the pay the Hacienda gives to the Vicos workers. It is twenty *soles* each day for our coca. We work three days, and on Wednesdays we receive sixty centavos. We're poor and our crops don't last us through the year. The *temple* money isn't enough. It doesn't even equal the price of the coca we use during those three days of work for the Hacienda. And the Hacienda doesn't want to increase the pay. That's the way it is. (Soler, June 27.)

Jorge Reyes: I've gone to Chacas [a town on the other side of the mountain range east of Vicos] to buy eggs. I've gone there many times, maybe ten times. It's the Hacienda's fault that I don't go now. I used to buy wool in Carhuaz and in Collún which is near Huaraz. Now I get wool from my animals. I bought grain in Collún and Marcará. I've bought potatoes from the Hacienda Vicos, and also from Collún. I've worked for wages in Marcará when my salt and *ají* were gone. I'm poor and so I lack everything. I've gone to the Cañón del Pato [the Santa River gorge in the north] for wage work. I was there a month. Now I don't go away to any place because I'm with the Hacienda Vicos. It's the Hacienda's fault that I haven't wanted to *enganchar* [take a work contract outside Vicos]. I give a good account of myself and I don't want to miss days in the Hacienda. I've been in the Hacienda twenty years. I don't steal anything from the harvests. Rather, when they want to the *patrones* make me gifts, and when they don't want to they don't.   (Flores, with Ricardo Estremadoyro, July 1.)

Sebastián Sánchez: Whether I like it or not I have to work for the Hacienda, and because I'm poor I have to live like that. The Hacienda doesn't want us to miss work at all, and they pay us very little. It's not even enough for our salt. They hardly help us, either. We have to go out to other places to look for work or sell our chickens, and if we don't show up on those days, the Hacienda takes our things as *embargos*. The Indians in Recuayhuanca and Chacas are different from the Vicosinos because they have their own lands, while here we don't have land and we have to work for the Hacienda. That's why the others can go off to the coast, even for two months, while here we can't move because we have to work for the Hacienda. All those others aren't more strong or less strong. They're the same, although the Recuayhuanquinos [people from Recuayhuanca] feel a little more proud because they have their own land. (Soto, with Ricardo Estremadoyro, August 5.)

Manuel Sánchez: I dpn't know what I'd do with a lot of money. To get money I have to sell my animals, and I'd use up all of it eating. Or I'd bury it. I've become poor and that's the way it is for us. If I were *patrón* of the Hacienda I wouldn't know what to do. I don't think I'd want anything. All *patrones* are the same. They lie and cheat and they don't give us what they promise. . . . We'd like it if they helped us, but they never do. Everything we harvest for them they haul away. (Flores, with Ricardo Estremadoyro, July 9.)

Antonio Reyes: I wish I could read everything that you're writing! It's a shame to be blind. We're only fit for working in the fields. We haven't had the opportunity to learn things like you people. If we had, things would have been quite different for us. We wouldn't have had to work every week for the Hacienda. At least we would have known about other places and we would have learned many things. Since we don't know how to read or write it's like we were chained here, unable to leave for any other place. (Soler, July 15.)

People were used to the idea of losing harvests. They tell many stories of famines, even of circumstances in which people ate burro meat, which is ordinarily taboo. When there is famine, people eat the seed which they have stored, and then they sell their livestock in order to obtain food. This story was told by an old woman who remembered hard times:

> Juana Valerio: When I was around twenty-five years old there was a famine in all these places. I think it was because that year there was no harvest from the frost and from different diseases which attacked the crops. I remember that when my husband saw that we didn't have anything to eat, he went off with our pigs, sheep, goats, and chickens to Carhuaz to trade them for different kinds of grain like wheat, maize, barley, and *habas*. But those rich people gave us such a miserable amount for so many animals that it didn't last us two weeks. I and my husband went to work in Marcará and Carhuaz. I worked as a cook in rich families' houses and he went to do other things. They gave us a little grain for our work. Once when my husband came back from Carhuaz, after having taken our animals to trade for grain, my son who was already a big boy, when he saw what a small amount my husband brought back, began to cry, saying: "Papa, our pig was a big one. Why did they give you so little for it?" I remember that once my children, my husband, and I went hungry for three days because that week we didn't find any work in Carhuaz or in Marcará, and we'd already sold all our animals. My children cried and went to sleep, and then cried and went to sleep again. We suffered because we didn't have anything to give them to eat. (Gómez, undated.)

When the Hacienda was expropriated from the Beneficencia and subleased to the Project, most of the abuses of the hacienda system were immediately abolished, although the sublease mandated the continuance of labor rent. The Hacienda no longer practiced the custom of *embargo*, the confiscation of personal goods as punishment for failure to perform duties or any other infraction of the rules. The many unpaid personal services rendered to the *patrón*, at the *casa hacienda* and in fields outside Vicos, were terminated.

Thus, the estate fields continued to be worked by representatives from Vicos households, and this was accepted by the Vicosinos who related to members of the Project as *colonos* to *patrones*. The estate's fields, under these circumstances could be converted into agricultural demonstration centers (when they were closely supervised!), affording exposure of any innovation to a majority of Vicos households. The introduction of disinfected potatoes, together with other items designed to improve production was not only calculated directly to provide more food for

Vicosinos through diffusion, but also indirectly to benefit the community by the sale of surplus potatoes regionally and the reinvestment of the proceeds in Vicos, in the construction and outfitting of the school, teachers' quarters, a clinic, and the Project center itself. The Vicos workers were required, as part of their Hacienda duties, to put in the new potato crop according to directions from technicians.

Customary potato planting in Vicos is associated with two distinct agricultural seasons: the rainy season, which is the main planting and begins a month or so before the first rains that come in October or early November; and the dry season planting in June and July which is watered by means of irrigation channels. The latter is known as the *mitzka muruy*, advance or early planting, and takes place in the lower parts of Vicos. The *qaypa muruy*, late planting before the rains, is conducted in the heights, on the *puna* (high altitude grass land), or in the Quebrada Honda, a spacious gorge which extends deep into the range of mountains behind Vicos on the northeast. According to Stevens (1959:13-14), the earliest plantings can occur in April and the latest in November, before the rains have ended and after the new rains have begun, probably as a consequence of the necessity of "fitting potatoes in with the maize season and the times of greatest food need, rather than to a consideration of the conditions which would give the best potato crop."

Fields are fertilized in advance of plowing by enclosing livestock on the land to deposit manure, and by adding additional manure gathered elsewhere. Fields are surrounded by fences of stones which are available in the soil in quantity, or plantings of thorny bushes. In order to achieve even manuring, larger animals are staked and moved daily while smaller ones are penned up with thorny branches which are also moved daily. The herder takes shelter in a small and portable brush hut which can be shifted about the field as the livestock is moved. Vicosinos lacking in livestock either borrow them, preferably from relatives, or plant with inadequate fertilization or none at all.

Land that has been fallowing and has built up a layer of sod is broken up by hand with a utility tool, the *barreta*, a bar of steel which is pointed at one end and flattened at the other so as to form a sharp blade two to four inches in width. The backbreaking process of turning over the sod is called *tzaqma*, and must be done before plowing because the simple scratch plow cannot easily be drawn through sod, especially if, as is the case with many poor families, the plow is equipped with a wooden point. After the ground-breaking, the clods are separated with hoes and then the field is plowed with a team of oxen. In the case of a field which has previously been cropped, animals have been permitted to graze on the stubble. If the stubble is heavy, the field may be burned off before plowing and possibly broken up with *barretas*. Plowing is done two or three times, depending on the condition of the field, but the first pass over the field is made a few weeks before further plowing in order to permit the vegetation which has been turned under to rot. Meanwhile the soil is beaten and pulverized with hoes. The final plowing is done just before the seed is put in.

At the time the Project intervened and Vicos agriculture veered toward the commodity form of production, technology was impoverished. Vicosinos found it difficult to adapt to some of the innovations. Currently, a wide variety of customary and newer tools is used. It would be difficult to locate a plow with a wooden point, if such still exists at all. In 1953, however, changes had barely begun. Here are some Vicosino reactions to new technological items:

> Delfin Coleto: We don't use mattocks or picks in our own fields because we're not used to working with tools like those. The Hacienda uses them now, however, and so we're forced to work with them during the three days we work there. Let me tell you, we certainly feel more comfortable with our own tools!
>
> We can't get wheelbarrows because, in the first place, they wouldn't be much use to us because wheelbarrows are good for big jobs. Since our fields are small, why would we want them? And even if we wanted them, we couldn't get them because they must be very expensive and we don't have the money to spend on such things. (Soler, June 30.)

> José Coleto: In Carhuaz I've seen them plant with a tractor. If Vicos were a *pampa* (a plain) one could be brought in, but my land is all stones. A tractor couldn't work here. I'd like to drive one but I don't know how. I plow with a *yunta* [a team of oxen] and I use a wooden plowshare with a shaft made out of a eucalyptus log. I don't use a metal point because I haven't bought one. It's the custom to use just the wooden point. Some people use a metal point. The crop comes out the same with either one. (Soto, June 30.)

> Teodoro Celio: (Could the tractor be introduced for farming?) That would be useful on *pampas*, but not for hills like my fields in Wicushpachán [a Vicos neighborhood]. Also the field is small. Cropping couldn't be done. (Do you use metal points in your fields?) I use wooden points, not metal ones, because the metal ones spoil the seed. (Soto, July 1.)

> Eugenio Leiva: I wouldn't like to have a tractor because the soil is hard and there are large stones. It's good for the coast where the soil is soft. Here everybody plows with a *yunta* and wooden points. We're not used to a metal point. The *yunta* is weak and the work wouldn't get done. If

the metal point were used, the *yunta* would walk in a different way. We also use *lampas* and *barretas*, but usually not picks. We use curved *lampas*. Only people in the valley use flat ones. Here that kind of *lampa* hits the stones and the edge curls. (Soto, July 4.)

Tomás Colonia: I don't use metal points because I don't have the money. They're expensive, about twelve *soles*. Both kinds of point can be used (Soto, July 1.)

In the act of planting, two furrows are plowed. The potato seeds are put in one at each step by the planter who alternates between the furrows. Then the original furrows are closed by plowing two more furrows. Since customary Vicos agriculture is labor intensive, potato fields receive much attention. In the dry season a potato crop is irrigated for the first time when the seeds germinate and once a week, or oftener, thereafter. After the plants have attained a certain size, at around two months, the soil is hoed to stir it up, remove the weeds, and form hills for the plants. This is called the *ishun*. A second cultivation, the *unkun*, takes place around two months later. The crop takes about six months from planting to maturity, although early potatoes begin to be taken out at four to five months as they ripen. When a crop reaches the final and edible stage, a member of the household is sent to watch over the field from a portable brush hut. Because of the removal of early potatoes, households find it difficult to make a precise accounting of potato production. However, Vicosinos are quite sensitive to fluctuations from one crop to another. The harvest is a family affair which extends beyond the boundaries of the household and involves people of both sexes and all ages. The potatoes are dug up, placed in baskets, and then sacked at the field border. Before sacking, the tubers are sorted according to size. First class potatoes, the largest, are set aside for festive dishes. Some second and/or third class potatoes, middle-sized and small, are saved for seed. Fourth class potatoes, ranging in size down to that of a marble, can only be eaten. After sacking they are carried home for storage, in the sacks themselves or in ceramic containers. At larger harvests, the men race each other to the store rooms with potato sacks weighing well over one hundred pounds strapped to their backs.

Vicosinos employ a great variety of techniques to maintain potato production. Crop rotation and fallowing are customary. Potatoes are planted after a field has rested for a year or two, and then in succession, maize, wheat, and finally barley are planted. The cycle may be repeated a second time in bottom lands before fallowing, but in the heights the land is allowed to rest after one cycle. This patterning is ideal but, as Stevens (1959:32) points out, few Vicosinos can afford to conform to it. Similarly, everyone knows the value of fertilization but many Vicosinos cannot afford it. A family fertilizes its fields according to the size of its herds, but domestic units which lack cattle request the loan of livestock from relatives in order to fertilize their fields at least a little. According to custom Vicosinos occasionally import new seeds in order to guard against the deterioration of the old, even if it is of the same variety. Most Vicos farmers name from ten to fifteen varieties of *waska*, known in Spanish as *papa común* or *papa variada*, with which they are personally familiar.[16] Before the Project came to Vicos, people did not purchase potato seed. The usual method for obtaining them was day labor outside Vicos for payment in cash and/or produce. Most Vicosinos are ready to use new seed but are wary of unfamiliar items with uncertain production. The following illustrates a more change-minded Vicosino, an army veteran, with the ecological sensitivity that is typical of Vicos farmers:

> Eugenio Leiva: (Do you like to plant what other Vicosinos plant?) Of course! I plant according to custom. It's because I like it that way. I always hope the crop will turn out all right. I plant the *warqa* seeds or I plant new ones when I get them in Marcará. (Would you plant a new kind of seed even if other Vicosinos weren´t planting it?) I guess I'd try it if I had the opportunity even if I wasn't familiar with it, even if other people didn´t know about it. I have patience for making experiments to see if something would turn out all right even though it isn't produced here in Vicos.... I'd plant something so as to try out my land. (Do you do what others do or do you try to be different?) I don't follow the others. I have my own ways of planting fields, my own ways of working. Each person here has his own ways of planting, because every field is different. Even though I only have a few fields to plant, I don't lose out because I have my own ways of planting them. (Soto, with Ricardo Estremadoyro, August 26.)

Planting takes place on saints' days with the object of securing supernatural protection for the crop. However, with their characteristic practicality, Vicosinos say that if the crop yields well one should keep the same date every year, but otherwise one should change to another saint Planting, like weeding and hilling, is done according to the phases of the moon:

> Eugenio Leiva: (When do you usually plant your fields?) I plant in September and October. I plant potatoes in August. (Which days? With what fiesta?) I plant maize on August 15. That's Asunciana's day. Then on August 30 is Santa Rosa. September 8 is Notocha, and that's good for planting maize. September 14 is Santa Cruz. September 24 [feast day of the Virgen de las Mercedes, patron saint of Vicos] is a good day for

planting. All Saints' Day is good for hilling up maize. *Mitzqa* potatoes can be planted from April to July. The day before the Corpus Christi fiesta is a good day for getting a harvest. If the day when a person plants doesn't yield a crop, then the date must be changed. However, if it yields well a person should stick to it. (Won't the *paltaq* potato yield well if it's planted on any day?) When it's planted in quantity, it's planted on any day from April to July. On any day, at any time. That's for harvesting in January or February at Carnival time. (Can *warqa* potatoes be planted on any day?) They're planted in August, but if there's no time they're planted on any day. Sometimes the yield is good and other times it's bad, and so the date is changed. When there are people to help one can even plant up to Sunday a week later, or four or five days after the appointed day (Flores, with Celso León, August 18.)

Alfonso Cruz: (On what fiesta days are you accustomed to plant your fields?) I plant maize on August 30 for Santa Rosa, and also on September 14 and 24 for Santa Cruz. The 24th is in Marcará and the 25th is in Huapra [an hacienda across the river from Vicos]. September 24, Merced, is good for maize. All Saints' Day is for maize and potatoes. (On what fiesta is the *mitzqa* planted?) On June 1, or the whole month of June. June 30 is San Cayetano. For San Pedro, too. Those who plant in quantity do it the day before the fiesta. (On what day do you plant *paltaq* potatoes?) On San Juan, or the day before. That's the first planting. (Why do you plant on fiesta days?) It's the idea and the custom of planting on saints' days because they make miracles. (Even with the new seeds?) With any seed.

(What are the beliefs about planting with the moon?) The new moon is good for planting potatoes and maize. (Why?) Production is good that way. If it's done in the first quarter it won't yield well, the crop won't develop. The first quarter is good for *habas* and wheat. When people plant while the moon is waning the crop comes out bad. It turns green and the potatoes disappear in roots and flowers. The plants won't produce tubers. . . . (For hilling and other cultivation do you watch the moon?) It's not done with a waning moon, even though it needs to be done. Only fences can be made, and a person can plow. The waning moon is no good for hilling and weeding. (When is it good for that?) The full moon is good. Also the new moon and when it's waxing. (Flores, with Celso León, August 19.)

Some informants discussed other methods of protecting the crops:

Ciriaco Evaristo: People put up crosses in their fields so as to have better protection, because Our Lord Jesus Christ died on the cross and that's why it's miraculous. Only some people put up the crosses because it's expensive. It's necessary to have a special fiesta in order to carry out the ceremony. Every year the crosses are put in place during Carnival.

They celebrate with feasting and dancing. Well, some people aren't in condition to go to a lot of expense and so they've stopped doing it. They don't put up the crosses, even though their parents used to do it. The *tzaqpa* plant is put in potato fields to protect them from the frost. Still, last year I set *tzaqpa* up in my fields but the frost withered the crop completely. This year I'm getting ready to put *tzaqpa* in my potato fields, too, but just to satisfy my wife because I don't believe in it any more. (Soler, July 22.)

Félix Tario I: It's the custom to put plaited crosses in the fields at Carnival. We've done this since our grandparents' time. As I say, it's the custom. Some say that it holds back the sicknesses and that it's very good for keeping frosts from the crops. However, from my experience I don't believe it. I've seen crops with their crosses, but they've gone bad with the rot, or they've withered from the frost. If God wills it, the crop is saved. Otherwise, nothing is saved. Putting *tzaqpa* plants in the fields is a way of protection that has been followed since our grandparents' time, too. *Tzaqpa* is a bush that grows in the *puna*. It's used for making baskets as well as protecting potatoes from the frost. (Soler, July 24.)

Justo and Alejandro Colonia: (Justo) As a form of preventing frosts we use *tzaqpa* and *tzeqaq*, which are small bushes that grow in the heights. We put branches from those bushes in each one of the plants for the purpose of protecting it from the ice. (Alejandro) I'm not very sure if it's only these plants that have the ability to save potatoes from the frost. I think it can be done with any one of the plants or bushes, because naturally by putting those plants or any others on the potato shoots the first thing that has to be affected by the frost has to be those plants which are out in the open. (Soler, August 26.)

Santiago Basilio: God exists and is all powerful and lives in heaven, just like our Government lives in Lima. God created us like all things in nature. If he hadn't willed it, nothing would exist. We wouldn't be here. God surely has his mother and his father. They say that his mother is the Virgin Mary or the Virgen de las Mercedes. The saints must also be his relatives. All the virgins and the saints live inside churches, and because they are there they make miracles. So if we ask them with faith they help us in our fields or they give us good health. (Soler, July 30.)

Vicos farm production averaged below what would be required to reproduce the Vicosinos. Together with variation in production, from one household to another and from one season to another, this means that while some redistribution occurs within Vicos some quantity of subsistence goods must be fed into the system from outside. The circulation of potatoes takes place by means of foraging, gift, gleaning, loan, trade, payment for services, and purchase. Thus, Vicosinos are foragers, farmers, and rural proletarians. Potatoes play a part in generalized reciprocity[17] in which households provision each other. They also constitute wages for services performed:

> Nicolás Herrera: The Hacienda is the same. Only they change renters, one after another. Some renters are good and others are bad. And some are good when they first get here and later they turn bad. Some *empleados* [the Peruvian word for "white collar workers," here used in reference to mestizo overseers] beg the renters not to be good. The *empleados* are bad. Sometimes the renters give out food, like they do on the coast. But then the *empleados* tell them not to give out anything, that they have to stick to old customs when they didn't give anything. The present renters are good. The gringos are the best because they're rich. Dr. Holmberg is good. Enrique is the worst. Mario is better. At the potato harvest other *empleados* used to give free potatoes to the workers. These days Enrique doesn't want to give anything so that people won't get used to it. (Flores, with Ricardo Estremadoyro, June 30.)

> Víctor Sánchez: When I'm out of seed I go around helping my neighbors, my relatives, in Vicos. From that I bring back a few potatoes, sometimes to plant and otherwise to eat. All my crops are from my own seeds. I don't buy any. (Soto, July 13.)

> César Sánchez; At times when the harvest is bad, or when it isn't enough to cover household needs, we have to resort to borrowing among ourselves. I have an understanding with my *compadre*, Don Juan Coleto, from whom I borrow when we're out of seed. Sometimes I borrow a sack or a few pounds, and when the crop comes in I return it. It can be a year, or whenever the harvest is. . . . Years ago I was used to planting with my own seed. But last year when the potatoes went bad I had to turn to Chacas for a supply. I bought about a sack of potatoes in Chacas, but I only used two *arrobas* [at twenty-five pounds each] for seed. We had to eat up the rest at home. (Soto, July 18.)

> Andrés Cupitán: Last year's harvest came in well, because it always yields when God wants it. If he doesn't want it, it goes bad and there isn't anything. I gave potatoes from my harvest to my relatives, to my mother, Lucía Bautista, and my father, Benjamín Cupitán, and to my cousin, José Cupitán. I didn't give anything to my in-laws because they weren't there at the harvest. Before the harvest I talked with my wife and she told me that would be alright. I also talked with my relatives who offered to help me with the harvest. I was very happy with that. (Soto, July 14.)

> Nicanor Sánchez: Some years, when I'm out of potatoes at home, I buy them in Marcará if I have the money, an *arroba* at a time. When I don't

have money I don't buy them. Those purchases are just for eating. . . . At harvests, relatives and friends offer each other potatoes, and they return in kind. When Vicosinos don't have potatoes they borrow them, a bag or a basket, depending. (Soto, July 16.)

Alejandro Quijano: When harvests don't provide potatoes for us at home I do *taripakushun*, that is, I go to places where they're harvesting to help them in return for potatoes. I don't buy them. When my harvest yields a lot of potatoes I offer them to my relatives, and when the harvest is bad I don't offer potatoes to anyone. When the neighbors come to visit my house they bring me a present of potatoes. We don't borrow or lend them because we don't have potatoes to give or give back. (Soto, July 16.)

Manuel Mendoza: In times of scarcity, when I'm out of potatoes at home, I have to buy them down below, wherever I can find them. I buy about an *arroba* and that's enough to eat with a little extra to plant. I generally get this seed in other places. (Soto, July 17.)

Alejo Valerio: Here we don't buy potatoes. Here the custom is a gift. People won't give you anything for money. If you need *ocas* you buy some bread, sugar, salt, or *aji* and take it to a friend. My sister or my mother takes it to somebody, and that person says, "What's that for?" "It's a present, it's for *ocas*," she says. Then the person gives her one, or two, or three little baskets of them. When people are harvesting wheat, they go to the harvesting floor with lunch in a *mate* [calabash bowl] and the people give them some wheat. They give them big *mates* of wheat. Maize is given by the ear or in a basket. Barley is given like wheat, and it's the same with *habas* and peas.
Meat can be given away by the piece. When somebody's sheep or beeve dies, they give us a piece. When they kill pigs they give presents of *chicharrones* [fried pieces of fat] to their neighbors, their relatives. We don't return it immediately. We return it when we kill a pig, the same way. If they give me meat, I return the same, meat. If it's *chicharrones*, they I give back the same when I have them. (What do you think of this way of exchanging?) It's good that way here. If you're hungry, they always give you something to eat. But in town if you don't have any money you can't get anything to eat. (Flores, with Pablo Herrera, July 23.)

You should take note of the fact that here the circulation of potatoes is the circulation of people who come to each other's harvests to help in return for a share of the produce, establishing and re-establishing social bonds. And such recipients themselves share their shares with others in such a way that potatoes and people are in constant motion, for, as Maurice Godelier (1999:102) so brilliantly points out:

Things do not move about of their own accord. What sets them in motion and makes them circulate in one direction, then another, and yet, another, is each time the will of individuals and groups to establish between themselves personal bonds of solidarity and/or dependence. Now the will to establish these personal bonds expresses *more* than the *personal* will of individuals and groups, and *even more than what comes under the heading of will*, of personal liberty (individual or collective). What is produced or reproduced through the establishment of these personal bonds is all or part of the social relations which constitute the foundations of the society and which endow it with a certain overall logic that is also the source of the social identity of the member groups and individuals. In short, what appears in the goals pursued, the decisions taken, the actions voluntarily performed by the individuals and groups which make up a given society is not only their personal wills but a-personal or impersonal necessities having to do with the nature of their social relations, which spring up again and again in the process of producing and reproducing them (whether relations of kinship, power, with the gods and spirits of the dead).

Nevertheless, for many poor families the outlook is bleak:

Rosario Celio: I don't buy potatoes in other places because I don't have the money. I'm poor. Where am I going to get them? The potatoes I planted I lost with the sickness. (Soto, July 14.)

Gregorio Vega: When I'm out of potatoes I don't buy them but I eat *kamtza* [toasted maize] or I chew coca. (Soto, July 14.)

When the Vicos Project took over the operation of the Hacienda in January, 1952, one of its first efforts was to intervene in agriculture in order to alleviate the desperate nutritional situation. This more immediate and specific goal was also related to the general and longer-range goals of conserving natural resources, maximizing land use, diversifying and broadening the economy, and creating new sources of income (Vázquez 1955:56). The Project was instrumental in getting the Peruvian Ministry of Agriculture to open an experimental station of SCIPA (Servicio Cooperativo Interamericano de Producción de Alimentos)[18] in Vicos. Project staff members in collaboration with agricultural technicians worked out a program which was adapted to the agricultural problems and needs of the region. Vázquez (1955:47) reports that SCIPA "personnel spent two days of each week at the Hacienda during the first year of the experiment." Before the early planting of 1952, two varieties of seed potatoes were obtained from another agricultural experimental station which SCIPA maintained in Tarma, in the central highlands. One variety was the *paltaq* potato, also known as the *papa marcos*, a leaden-colored flat tuber. The other was the white potato, a rounder and slightly larger variety. Both were similar to the *papa común* of Vicos. Accompanying these seed potatoes was commercial fertilizer (*guano de la isla* or *guano de chincha*) which had previously been used in Hacienda agriculture and was widely known in the region–although it was not customarily used by Vicosinos in their household farms because of its cost--and crop disinfectants to combat the potato fungus, worms, and insect pests: copper compounds (e.g., "Dithane") in which to soak the seeds, "Aldrin" powder for the soil, and DDT spray for the plants. The agronomists advised new planting arrangements in which rows of plants are set 70 to 90 centimeters apart, the plants themselves being placed at 45-centimeter intervals in the rows, yielding ideally about 30,000 plants per hectare (Stevens 1959:14).

Holmberg and Dobyns (1965:44-45) discuss the Project's rationale and its problems:

> [S]erfs were required to continue working the obligatory three days a week, to which they did not especially object, in order to carry out a gradual transition and to provide a demonstration and training experience in new agricultural and social practices; and to produce new investment capital. Thus, when innovations in agricultural technology were introduced on the manor's commercial fields, the serfs had to adjust to them.
>
> On the other hand, the Cornell Peru Project resorted to persuasion to insure that these innovations would be applied by the serfs to their own fields, and not simply be ignored as things the rich and slightly crazy gringos understood and could afford to do, but that poor, ignorant, Indian serfs could not. The Cornell Peru Project offered to make improved seed, fungicides, insecticides, fertilizer, etc., available to those serfs who wanted to try them on their own subsistence plots, through a sharecropping arrangement. The serfs, subject to repeated crop failures, were accustomed to obtaining new seed from local merchants upon fairly disadvantageous terms. The Cornell Peru Project offer permitted them to keep a considerably larger share of the harvest, but charged them enough to convince them the Project was making a serious offer, and was not foolish.

The arrival of the new items, and plans for the demonstration in Hacienda fields, were discussed with the *mayorales*, the Vicosino foremen and other community authorities and then announced at a meeting of the Hacienda labor force soon after the Project had taken the role of *patrón*. The Project also offered the items to the Vicosinos at that meeting and in subsequent meetings. Vicosinos could obtain them in two ways: 1) purchase at cost of disinfected new seed potatoes, commercial fertilizer, and pesticides; and 2) anticipating that most Vicosinos would not have the money to purchase these items, a system of share-planting with volunteers who would furnish the land, draft animals, tools, and labor, while the Hacienda would provide the disinfected seed, fertilizer, and pesticides, as well as direction of cultivation from ground-breaking to harvest, each receiving half the crop. Few Vicosinos took advantage of the first method of obtaining the innovations, and those who purchased the potatoes tended not to buy the other items. The method of share-planting was not alien to Vicosinos, though it was associated with gross exploitation of workers by landowners. However, the unconventional directions, restrictions, and control were awkward from the Vicos point of view. Despite the Project's efforts to make it possible for Vicosinos to maintain or increase potato production, and despite the successful demonstration in Hacienda fields, where production of good potatoes more than doubled during the first new planting, a variation far outside the range of Vicosinos' expectations,[19] Vicosinos were slow in responding. Finally, Mario Vázquez conducted a series of interviews with Vicosinos in which he endeavored to persuade people to take up the Project's offer. Out of 196 workers inscribed in the Hacienda's roll, only 40 finally signed up to plant the new seeds on shares, and only 17 of these actually carried through with the planting in the first year of intervention. During the second season, at the time of the Methodology Project's research in 1953, 87 Vicosinos were planting on shares with the Hacienda (Vázquez 1955:6). After the Project adapted its program more closely to their needs by instituting a credit program, most Vicos farmers adopted the innovations in view of their need and the compelling results of the demonstration plantings.[20] Vicos became the biggest potato producer in the region, and potatoes became a source of commercial activity as well as a subsistence crop for many Vicos households. Under some conditions yields doubled, redoubled, and more. A decade later it was hard to find Vicosinos who were still planting by customary methods (Holmberg 1960:86). In the intervening years the Vicosinos used the potato profits to make a down payment on the purchase of the estate from the Beneficencia in 1962, pay off the latter and make payments on the government loan with which the transfer was accomplished.[21] As a token of its liberation, the community of Vicos acquired a truck to haul its potatoes to market.

By 1971, at the time of my visit in September and October, production of commercial potatoes had ceased in the commons. An agricultural cycle had come to completion through the intensive farming of one crop leading to exhaustion of both soil and seed, and with the appearance of new potato diseases. A regional bacterial infection was serious enough to cause the government to forbid the export of potatoes from Ancash to anywhere else in Perú. With the vision of the 90s, Ploeg (1993:222) comments that new types of potato quickly degenerate: "Within three or four years they become incapable of generating even low levels of production. The new stock is 'done' or, as farmers in the highlands state, 'Ya no tiene fuerza' (It has no power any more). That is to say, the claim of 'superiority' provokes a reaction that is equally formulated as a magico-religious statement: the power which was once claimed turns out to be rather ineffective (to be lost)." Ploeg (223) continues:

> "Magic" and "misery": these are the clues that explain the increasing adoption of improved varieties by Andean farmers. "Magic": because a cultivar intentionally constructed to be superior, effectively functions as a spell. It is introduced and perceived as an emanation from another, more powerful world. The new varieties are also represented (and accepted) as a gift; this association is made especially at the level of direct encounters between technicians and *promotores* [promoters, or extension agents] on the one hand and farmers on the other. The problem is only that after some time the gift seems to have lost its power. But then, in the mean time other things have changed too. Through the adoption of the gift, the genetic stock normally conserved carefully by these farmers may have been eroded. And then the "misery". . . .

In 1971 the commons were planted with wheat and barley. Some households were still planting potatoes for sale in the region and I saw many potato fields which appeared to be in good condition. People were also planting varieties of the *papa común*, in accord with what Karl Zimmerer (1996:34) writes of as the "diversity-rich farming for subsistence and diversity-poor cropping . . . destined for nonsubsistence, or so-called 'surplus' purposes" which has existed in the Andes since at least Inca times–and probably longer. Biodiversity had not been lost in Vicos but, as Stephen Brush (1999:535) reports for the Tulumayo Valley in central Peru, the non-commercial sector consisting of the poorest farmers had retained dozens of varieties of potatoes which were being planted at different times in a variety of eco-zones. Zimmerer (1996:231) concludes his study of farming in Paucartambo, in the Cusco region, with these words of hope for an informed and reflexive agricultural development:

> Quechua farming of diverse crops . . . makes clear that in situ conservation will depend on the enabling of certain development rather than attempting to constrain it altogether. Peasant farmers are eager to

pursue the planting of improved high-yielding varieties and other income-generating activities. Their aspiration to improve their livelihoods indicates that efforts at sustainable development and in situ conservation will need to involve social, economic, and political sectors that reach well beyond the pleasantries of rural regions. While Paucartambo farmers have selectively and ably combined the improved varieties with their diverse crops, they are evermore subject to the propagandistic promotion of agricultural modernization involving scant biodiversity. To moderate the effects of this governmental and private sector propaganda, information campaigns in favor of in situ conservation could be waged by respected sources such as a small but growing number of sustainable agriculture research organizations.

In the case of the Vicos Project, these early modernizers could not foresee the research which would inform development work a half century later. In 1963, having spent all its reserves on the purchase of the estate, the community still wished to add thirty-one hectares in the lowest and warmest part of Vicos, Chancos, which provided more maize fields as well as the remains of a tourist hotel at the hot springs there (Dobyns, Doughty, and Holmberg n.d.:51-59), which it did with a loan from the North American Ottinger Foundation (Garrido-Lecca 1965:47). Maize production soon came to rival potatoes in importance. In addition, stands of eucalyptus trees were maturing and Vicosinos hoped to diversify their economy further through lumbering. By 1971 Vicos had acquired a small herd of dairy cattle and were raising alfalfa, rather than potatoes, in the community's fields with the expectation of producing milk and cheese commercially. Héctor Martínez (n.d.:10) reports that officials of the Ministry of Agriculture persuaded community leaders in 1973 to participate in a larger-scale dairying enterprise with a loan from Peru's Agrarian Bank, but that when the cattle arrived they turned out to be of inferior quality. The Vicosinos had been defrauded, but when they refused to accept the cattle and tried to reject the loan the Bank insisted that the loan be repaid.

Another significant failure was the truck, which had been sold at a loss before my visit. Garrido-Lecca (1965:48) reports:

> The community . . . bought a heavy duty Ford truck to transport its potatoes to Lima's wholesale market and the needed agricultural inputs back to Vicos. In this manner it was hoped that the Vicosinos would retain at least part of what they were paying for transportation. . . . Unfortunately, the fact that the volume of transport business is insufficient to cover the expense they had to incur was overlooked. Potatoes are perishable and since most of the harvest comes at once, during January, February, and March, their truck could handle only a part of the total

harvest and they still had to hire other trucks. After the harvest season, the truck was idle until July when they started shipping in their supplies. Then it was idle again until December. They also overlooked the fact that on many trips the truck must go one way empty. In January, for example, it goes to Lima with potatoes but has little or nothing for the return trip. Therefore, the truck has caused losses which have increased instead of reducing shipping expenses.[22]

Earlier, in 1956, the Project's contract was renewed. At the same time, the tasks of agricultural development in Vicos were taken over by the Programa Ancash, a cooperative effort by the Ministries of Agriculture, Labor and Indigenous Affairs, and Education, together with the Agrarian Promotion Bank (41). An elected community Junta de Delegados was formed to govern the community, thus transferring control of the estate from the Project to the Vicosinos themselves. One of the first decisions of the Junta in 1957 was to operate the former Hacienda fields collectively with the understanding that the householders of Vicos would contribute the necessary labor. In 1958, increased control over the means of production led to a doubling of potato production (Holmberg 1959:9). At the same time, Vicosinos informed me, the former Hacienda *tarea* of 156 days per year was reduced to 40 to 60 days of labor annually for the community, freeing people to work more intensively on their household fields, to work for wealthier Vicosinos, and to seek wage labor outside Vicos.

I now shift focus back to the situation regarding the Project's innovations as informants experienced them in 1953, the second year of the Project's intervention. You should keep in mind that at this historical moment the intervention had barely begun. Vicosinos had no reason to believe that their present situation and future prospects would improve. Rather, they expected continued exploitation. The typical Vicosino believed that the Project *patrones* would, like other *patrones* before them, skim off the estate's profits for themselves. An illustration of this attitude is the 1953 effort to build a school, the construction of which was carried out by the Vicosinos in their *tareas* to the Hacienda. Until the school was completed and in use, people believed that the building was being put up for the sole benefit of the Project and its staff.[23]

Vicosinos were also skeptical regarding the agricultural innovations. The materials generated by the Methodology Project reveal a mixed opinion of the two new types of potato, a desire for commercial fertilizer, misunderstanding of most of the other innovations, and rejection of or strong resistance to the share-planting system. Several factors appear to have conditioned rejection or hesitation by Vicosinos: poverty, misunderstanding and suspicion of outsiders' motives, hostility toward the Hacienda, conflict with customary agricultural practices, and the appearance and taste of the tubers. Let us look at these in order, beginning with poverty:

> Marcos Quinto: I learned about the seed potatoes the Hacienda brought because I was watching when they unloaded them here. Don Enrique [Luna] told us that they were brought all the way from Huancayo. I and the other Vicosinos didn't believe that. We thought those seeds probably came from closer, maybe the *Vertientes* [Pacific slopes of the Andes, on the other side of the mountain range on the western side of the Callejón de Huaylas] where they produce good potatoes. We couldn't get those seeds because we didn't have the money. We are the workers [note this self-reference as *obreros*, workers, rather than "serfs," "*colonos*," or "Indians"!] in this Hacienda, and we're poor. . . . I found out that they were really potatoes from somewhere else when they began to produce very good potatoes in the Hacienda's fields, and that other Vicosinos were planting on shares with the Hacienda.
>
> When some Vicosinos planted on shares with the Hacienda they first had to put guano in their fields, guano given out by the Hacienda itself. They also cured the plants with DDT and maybe with other medicines that we don't know anything about. Then the harvest was very good. Other men and I thought then that the good harvest depended on good curing and good guano, and mainly good seed. So everyone thought about planting this year on shares with the Hacienda. I couldn't plant under those conditions because I only have a few fields. Some people have more land and others have less. It's because they gave a good portion of the land to people in the old days, while they only gave a few fields to those of us who came in recently. That's why we're ready to ask them to give us as good a portion as they gave to others. Otherwise I think we can't plant potatoes on shares with the Hacienda like others have done. And then we can't even buy them from the Vicosinos who have planted them here, because they sell them at a good price to traders from outside this place. They already have them contracted, so that they come with their trucks and they take everything away. And since they charge us the same as they do those traders we don't have the money to buy them because we're poor.
>
> When we plant potatoes we don't get a harvest like that. The potatoes turn green, or they rot, or they're tiny. Meanwhile, others are having good harvests. Maybe it depends on the guano. If you put in a small amount it yields less. I've seen that guano de la isla [island guano, produced in Peru] is very good. Last year Emilio Flores planted potatoes and harvested 16 sacks. Alfonso Cruz got 30 sacks. Alejo Valerio got 9 sacks. Herminio Colonia got 16 sacks. Daniel Ferrer got 6 sacks. And Víctor Valerio got 12 sacks. These last ones were not happy with their production. They wanted it to be more. On the other hand, Alfonso Cruz

and Emilio Flores were happy.... I could plant too in my tiny little fields but I'm afraid the plants could get sick and that way I'd lose everything, that is, if I planted on my own account. Still, I'm thinking of planting next year by buying seeds from the Hacienda or from Vicosinos who have better seed.
(The informant is 30 years old. He has been to Huaraz. He has gone there at least ten times. He used to stay there for a week. He did not earn anything because he worked for this Hacienda when they were sent to Huaraz to [work in] the house of *patrón* Bravo. He has also been in Caraz and Yungay. He just went there to see those places. He goes to Carhuaz now and then to make purchases. He has been in Chacas. He went there three times to visit and to buy wheat and wool. They bartered and they also used money. At the close of the interview the informant asked me where I was from. I answered that I was from Huánuco. Then he said that maybe I had been to all the places on the coast, but that he unfortunately had not had the same luck that we have because he is an Hacienda worker and they have the obligation of working there every week. He also told me that he had much desire to visit other places. (Soler, July 12)

Juan de la Cruz: We're almost all interested in the new seed because we've seen that it produces well. That's why many people signed up to plant on shares with the Hacienda. Still, we have to keep on planting our own seed in August, September, and October. We barely plant it and the sickness hits it, but we keep hoping that we will be able to harvest even a little. We also think that the sickness has to end. I've heard in the Hacienda that the sickness only lasts five years. We've noticed, too, that the effects of the sickness are diminishing every year. Because we see that some people's crops are saved, we don't want to lag behind. We don't want to feel bad because their yield is totally good. (Soler, July 15.)

Manuel Sánchez: The Hacienda has guano de la isla and DDT, and so it has good crops. But we don't have those things and so we can't improve our crops. In the Hacienda everything yields well, but we don't get anything out of ours We can't get guano because we don't have the money to buy it.... Manure is good, but since we don't have many animals we don't have that fertilizer. We scatter the little manure we get from our *cuyes* [guineapigs],[24] and we look for places where we can gather manure. We wish they'd send us guano chincha [same as guano de la isla]. (Flores, with Ricardo Estremadoyro, July 9.)

Víctor Sánchez: Last year I didn't plant the new potatoes. Not with the neighbors or on shares with the Hacienda. This year I've planted them, but I don't have more fields and I only have one piece where I plant maize. What am I going to do if my field is small? I don't use guano de la isla either for crops like maize and potatoes. I don't have money and I don't have fields. I've talked with my wife about whether or not we should buy guano de la isla. She said, "*Allim* [that's good]," but "*kanan mana* [not today]." We just fertilize with manure from our sheep.

Víctor Valerio planted with the Hacienda's potatoes and they put in guano de la isla. This was last year. He planted this year, too, but I don't know how many *arrobas*. I haven't seen any other neighbor with the new seed potatoes. I haven't seen anybody planting with seeds from somewhere else. When I'm out of potatoes I don't buy them because I don't have the money. The Hacienda itself sells the seed potatoes at a very high price. I asked Enrique Luna. I haven't planted potatoes yet this year, but next month I'll just plant a small amount in the Quebrada Honda. Last year I planted about an *arroba* and the harvest was good to me.

I saw that when Valerio harvested he got out about ten bags, and after dividing them with the Hacienda in equal parts he had five bags. He used an *arroba* and a half of seeds. . . . I don't know if Valerio has money. He only has two oxen and he knows how to make baskets. With that he certainly ought to make money. Valerio doesn't talk to me about the seed. In the Hacienda they told me I should plant them, but since I didn't have a field I couldn't do it. I told Enrique and Mario at the *mando*.

I haven't talked with other people about the seed potatoes that came to the Hacienda. I've also seen Antonio, Colonia, Nicanor Coleto, and Sebastián Coleto planting them. Also my brother, Manuel Sánchez. He just planted them, like all the others.

I'd also like to plant them. I don't do it, not because I don't have money but because I don't have a field. My crops don't produce well, and of course I've seen that those who plant on shares with the Hacienda get out a good harvest. That's because they cure the crop with medicines from the Hacienda. If they'd give it to me I'd save my crops in the Quebrada Honda.

I've seen the *papa blanca* in the harvest. It grows big and beautiful. The old seed is big but it's rotten. Valerio gave me a basketful when I went to help him, and I'm keeping it in my house for seed. I'll plant it together with maize in a corner of my field.

(The informant and his wife both dress in Indian style, and they are old. They have some sheep and little goats with them. . . . The informant is completely ignorant of Spanish. When we talked he sat down beside me and listened to what I was saying. While he was talking and I was writing, he looked at me. When I asked him if he didn't want to plant those potatoes, he answered that maybe he would next year. . . . He does not use guano de la isla, just manure from his sheep. He has not eaten any of the potatoes he has saved, except for the few they ate on the day he received them. He says they are good and better than the old potatoes. He says they are "*machkapa*," grainy, and both his wife and his son ate them. His cousins, Manuel and Daniel Sánchez, and some woman named Leandra Sánchez came and shared the meal. They all talked about the potatoes and said they were good and grainy, but they didn't say that they would asked the Hacienda for them, and they didn't ask the informant to sell them any.

When I asked him if he wanted new tools for working his fields, like *lampas* or *barretas*, he told me yes and that he would pay for them little by little for three years. He asked me how much it would be, and I told him about sixty *soles*, which frightened him. Then he laughed and said that he could not pay that, maybe not in three years' time, that he was a little sickly. Then he went into his house and brought out a curved *lampa*, and asked me if that kind of a *lampa* cost sixty *soles*. I told him no, it was another kind, a long one. Then he asked me the price of the curved ones.

He is an old man with a friendly, patient, and good manner. He asked me if I had written about several people, and what I had written about them. I answered that each was different.) (Soto, July 13.)

Gregorio Vega: I didn't get seed potatoes from the Hacienda to plant. I haven't yet planted my own seed this year from the half sack, about three *arrobas*, which Alejandro gave me. I'll plant a sack and a half. I use guano de la isla. I bought half an *arroba* last year. This year I'll buy an *arroba* and a half. When I'm out of potatoes I don't buy them in other places. I eat *cancha*, I chew coca, and so on. I haven't seen my neighbors planting with the new seed. I haven't talked with them. I don't ask for the seed because I don't have enough land. I haven't spoken with my wife about getting seed from the Hacienda. I was there at the *mando*, but I didn't sign up because it's too much work to plant and take care of the crop.

I plant more maize than potatoes on my land. I use up two *arrobas* and a half of maize and sometimes the crop doesn't come because we don't cure it with medicines. I don't buy guano for maize. I don't have the money. I'm poor.

I don't ask the Hacienda for potatoes to plant, even though other people are planting on shares, because I don't have a field. So where am I going to plant?

(When I found him he was working in his relative's house together with others. His clothing is Indian. Maybe it was for the work he was doing that he asked me to buy *huashco*, or that otherwise I give him cigarettes. I offered him two of the latter. He knows how to speak a little Spanish. He does not speak it with others from Vicos, either, but only in the Hacienda when everybody is together on work days. He says that at harvest time people offer produce to others, but they haven't offered him anything. He pointed up and said that single women live there, and then across the way saying "*apallanshi* [a single woman, they say]." He says he does not go there. Then he was busy and I could not ask him more.) (Soto, July 14.)

Alejandro Quijano: I want to plant on shares with the Hacienda, but I just don't have the money for the expenses. I plant one or two *arrobas* of maize in the same place and sometimes I get a sack, but in a bad year the crop isn't good. I don't plant *ocas* because I don't have seed. I don't buy any because we don't have any money. I don't cure maize when it goes bad, and likewise I don't cure potatoes because I don't have the money to buy those medicines. I know about the potato medicine.

Nicanor Coleto is my only neighbor who plants the Hacienda's potatoes on shares. I don't do it because it's very difficult to irrigate and it's a lot of work. I know about guano de la isla but I don't know where it comes from. I'd like to have a little but since I don't have any money, what am I going to buy it with? Other people aren't planting on shares. I've only seen Sebastián Coleto planting potatoes, but I don't know if it's with seed from the Hacienda. I've planted potatoes in the past, about the same quantity that I've planted now. There's just been a small variation.

I've seen them plant with the measure, but I plant without it. I also thought about planting potatoes, but I'll plant maize. . . . I know about the new seed potatoes because I saw them in the Hacienda, and I also saw them harvested. I don't know how to tell if the old seed is better than the new seed in the Hacienda.

(The informant no longer has a father or mother. They died and now he lives alone with his sister. They are both still single. He wears a shirt purchased in Marcará, and he says he bought his jacket in Huaraz. He is still young. He answered everything he was asked. He does not know how to speak Spanish. When I found him he was helping Nicanor Sánchez on the threshing floor. He is a little humble and seems uncommunicative.) (Soto, July 16.)

Ciriaco Evaristo: Very few people use the medicines the Hacienda has brought. There are very few who have the funds to buy them to cure their potatoes. The rest don't buy them because they don't have the money. It's because they cost a lot. If they were cheap we'd all buy them. They say that for one cure it's necessary to invest at least eight *soles*. (Soler, July 22.)

While many Vicosinos found it difficult to account for the presence of outsiders, some were receptive to them:

Félix Tario I: I think that the gringos are better as *patrones* than the *mishtis*. It's just that with time they'll turn bad because of the administrators who are surely telling them false things about us. Some *mishtis* are also good as *patrones*, like that Señor Estremadoyro who was always concerned about us and used to give us one thing or another. Maybe the gringos are *mishtis*, although others say that they aren't but that they're from a different *casta* [lineage]. You ought to know more about that than I do because we don't read. We only talk about what other people talk about. We call other people *mishtis* for different reasons, because they're from the city, because they wear store clothing, because they know how to read, write, and speak Spanish, and because the color of their skin is lighter than ours. People who aren't *mishtis* are known by their woolen clothing, because they chew coca and work in the fields all the time. But the fact that a Vicosino may put on store clothing doesn't mean that he is then a *mishti*, even though he may know how to read, write, and speak Spanish. We call all those who were born here our fellow residents even if they live in other places.

Among the Vicosinos there are two tendencies in deciding about the presence of you people. Some think that you're here just to fool with us. It's because you ask us about our life and our trips to other places. Others say that you're not here in vain. Just like Don Mario is working, you're interested in our problems so as to take care of our agricultural hardships.

I think you've been sent by the Government to see how we live and then give an account of it so the President can send us medicines for the potatoes or do something else for us. (Soler, July 24.)

Many more expressed suspicion and fear:

> Carolina Mendoza: What I'd like to know is why and for what purpose so many gringos are coming to this Hacienda. Is it true that they've come to *pishtar* [slaughter or cut throats] the people and to evict us from this Hacienda? . . . Would it be possible for the gringos to speak with us in Quechua? Up to now we don't know what their object is. That's why we're uncertain and mistrustful. . . . Rumors are going around that more gringos are coming, and such bad news has made us shiver. (Gómez, undated.)

In the light of nearly five centuries of Andean history it is understandable how people in thousands of rural communities might fear strangers and believe the worst of them. In this last statement by a Vicosina, the gringos are suspected of being *pishtacos*, supernatural cut-throats.   Mary Weismantel (1997a:10-11) characterizes these well-known figures in Andeanist literature:

> The tale of the *pishtaco*, an evil white man who seeks out Indian victims in order to kill them through evisceration, mutilation, or by draining their body fluids, offers an obvious indictment of the racism that pervades the Andes–and of sexual predation as well. The further atrocity committed when the *ñakaq* [the term for "slaughterer" in southern Peru] turns his victims' fat into a commodity for sale on the international market, locates this violence in the exploitative relationships of labor and commerce that bind Andean communities to the world economy.
>
> In calling us *pishtacos*, the tellers of the tale confront us with the material differences of class, race, and nation separating us from those about whom we write–and challenge us to do something about them. These stories impart a moral imperative that extends to anthropologists no less than to others; and as with the ghost of Jacob Marley, the very

ghastliness of the *ñakaq* compels us to listen when we would rather not.

"This terrifying white bogeyman . . . takes the Indian fat he has accumulated and sells it to other whites, who use it to manufacture industrial goods ranging from pharmaceuticals and processed foods to rocket fuel, skin creams and scented soaps. . . . Within Andean Communities, stories about the pishtaco remind Indians to fear whites, and the poor to fear the powerful" (Weismantel 1997b:2). Peter Gose (1986:296-297) calls the *ñakaq* "an image of terror and power that constantly recreates itself in the Andean imagination."[25] Weismantel (2001:194-195) says: "The pishtaco is a kind of tradesman, like a butcher; the things he owns, wears, and carries are the tools of his dreadful occupation." These tools include knives, guns, needles, machetes, "things that can penetrate the body and inflict a deep wound." She adds:

> The sexual symbolism of the pishtaco's tool is hard to miss. He always has something big, hard, and dangerous in his hand or hidden beneath his clothing . . . . Often it dangles ominously from his belt. This terrifying thing is overtly phallic, the sign and instrument of a vicious masculinity. Even the pishtacos's genitals are said to be a weapon–not only does he use them to rape his victims . . . but to kill as well. (220.)

With this monster "Andean peasants continue to see their connection to more global structures of power in terms of sacrificial tribute."[26] Like so many anthropologists in the past (including myself), neither the personnel of the Methodology Project nor of the Vicos Project chose to see anything more in such tales beyond amusing folklore that illustrated how "backward" peasants were! Bruce Mannheim and Krista Van Vleet (1998:332) comment: "The celebrity that such stories have obtained among scholars of the Andes (anthropologists, in particular) is probably a mixture of a nervous self-doubt that our monographs are the church bells that resonate beautifully with the life force of our Native Andean interlocutors and misplaced self-importance of the role of scholars in mediating the relationships between Native Andeans and others."

The newcomers to Vicos were also thought to be *gamonales*,[27] land-grabbers who would evict people, tax collectors, army recruiters, and poisoners, among other things. The expectation of the worst from the Hacienda and its personnel was a fact of the world in which the Project endeavored to carry out its program of development:

> Narcizo Meza: Sure I think that the Goverment sent the medicines to help us out, but just the same here in the Hacienda they sell it all to us,

and then the administrators account for it possibly by letting the Government believe that they're giving it to us for free. In the Hacienda they've forgotten to help us like other *patrones* used to do. In the Hacienda they always tell us: "If you want to eat well, you've got to work hard." (Soler, July 16.)

Teodoro Cilio: I don't use DDT for potatoes, but I know that they get a good crop with it in the Hacienda. I don't use it because it's very expensive. DDT has been good for houses and clothing, so there wouldn't be lice and fleas. When they first brought it, people said that it was for killing them. They didn't want it because it wasn't the custom. Now we all want DDT for our houses. (Flores, with Ricardo Estremadoyro, July 8.)

Estenio Meza: I've tried the two kinds of potatoes. I bought some from the Hacienda. They sold the small ones at three *soles* for half an *arroba*. . . . I bought two *arrobas* from the Hacienda for twelve *soles*. I planted them this year. I manured with my animals and if the sickness hits I'll have to buy medicines from the Hacienda to cure the crop. I hope they sell them to me cheap, because some people are saying that they are selling them for a little too much. They're also saying that the administrators are the ones who are selling them for more than the *patrones* charge. (Soler, July 12.)

Izaquel Sánchez: I've planted my field with the *papa común* that we have. I probably won't plant *paltaq* potatoes because I don't have enough money to buy the seed. In any case I'd rather get the ordinary seed potatoes from my neighbors because they sell more of them to us, and cheaper, while the Hacienda sells them to us at a high price and measures the amount exactly. (Soler, July 17.)

Ambrosio Evaristo: *Paltaq* potatoes are good for them in the Hacienda because they can buy the DDT, but they're not good for us because we can't buy it. . . . The crop is very good in the Hacienda and we're jealous just because they never give any to us. . . . The most abusive *patrón* is Don Enrique because when our animals get out and damage the crop, he takes them away and works them himself. Then he uses bad words when he scolds us. (Flores, with Ricardo Estremadoyro, July 10.)

Eugenio Leiva: For the maize crop each person works with his own tools. We only ask the Hacienda for *barretas* and picks to turn over the soil. The rest are brought by each person himself. We've told the Hacienda that they ought to provide the tools, but the Hacienda is against it. I wonder where we're going to get tools when they cost so much. . . . A sickle costs 6.50, and *lampas* cost 15 *soles*, according to size. The Vicosinos haven't gotten together about this. Everyone is used to working in silence. So an *empleado* of the Hacienda could say to me: "You, why are you complaining when everyone else works with their own tools? You're just making a lot of noise and being bothersome. The others are satisfied and they don't ask." When we told the *mayoral* about the need for the Hacienda to provide tools, the *mayorales* told us: "It doesn't matter because everybody else is working with their own tools. It still is not customary for the Hacienda to provide them." That's what they told me. How are you going to make them if they're continuing customs of our ancestors? Besides, some have cows and they've purchased tools with the proceeds from the milk. So they are content, but where are poor people going to get the money? They have to go to work. These days a *barreta* costs 75 to 85 *soles*, according to size.

(Why doesn't the Hacienda give a gratuity on the Fiestas Patrias [Peruvian Independence Day, July 28]?) That? What do you expect? Enrique Luna is a *conchudo* [a fool, a dumb-ass]. Mario is another. Maybe they give that in other places, but here they don't. I think Luna is a bad person. Once he came into the vegetable patch [this informat's Hacienda duty was to take charge of one of its vegetable gardens] and saw that I was taking care of a lot of buyers. He told me: "Leiva, you're doing too much business. I want you to sell a single head of cabbage for 60 *centavos*:" That's very dear. It won't satisfy a family. So I told him: "I'm just selling a little. It wouldn't be good to sell it like that. We should give more." Luna answered: "That's not right, *tayta* ["father," a polite form of address[28]], it costs money. There's no seed." So I answered him: "Well, it makes no difference to me." When Mario comes in he doesn't say anything. He doesn't bother me. But others have told me that he's nasty.

They pay me two *soles* a weekfor working as a gardener. My helpers get the same. I came to work in the garden when Don Mario had me appointed by a *mayoral*, after I'd been working outside for just three weeks. When Mario asked me, I told him: "Don Mario, I don't know anything about working in gardens." But then I learned how. Another gardener taught me in two days. (Soto, with Ricardo Estremadoyro, August 17.)

One of a very small minority of bilingual and literate Vicosinos, who in 1953 had much experience outside the community, a man who identified himself with the Project and its personnel, understood the current administration as different from former Hacienda regimes and from the regional social system. (Perhaps the term "overunderstood" would capture his grasp of the situation, given his transferences to Project personnel.) Here is his response to questioning:

Hilario González: It's good. That's the way the new things that the Hacienda has brought seem to me. I'm happy with all of it. At least they're going ahead with the school. I like the new things because that way we'll get to be a little more civilized. Certainly, when new things arrive I like them, but people here still need to have them explained. But I travel outside. It would be a great thing for Vicos to progress. People are getting civilized a little better with the gringos. As long as the gringos are here Vicos will move forward. Of course! But Peruvian people are *fregados* [pests], *carajo* [untranslatable expletive, "shit!"]! The Peruvians ought not to stay on. They haven't built schools. In all that time they haven't found a single teacher. . . . If Vicosinos knew how to read, if they were educated, then they could be gentlemen. They'd know how to manage. In all this time, all the renters haven't set up, *carajo*, a single school. They only wanted us to serve them. . . . Vicos will make progress if the gringos stay on as *patrones*. Some of the *patrones* didn't do anything. They wanted to keep the Indians the same as ever, not knowing how to read or write, so that they'd keep on doing everything for them. The Indians can't make Vicos progress by themselves. How are they going to do it? Indians don't think about those things. (Flores, without interpreter, August 7.)

Vicos farmers are customarily cautious. A number of the informants initially feared to risk planting the new seed. They expressed concern that the potato sickness would still attack their fields, that the commercial fertilizer would be too strong, or that the medicines would injure the potatoes, and that they would end up with less food than if they had planted other crops:

Estenio Meza: Last year some people planted on shares with the Hacienda. This year many more have done it because they saw that last year's harvest was very good. Others had planted on bad days, and the harvest was also bad. That's why even though the Hacienda planted with a lot of guano, and took the trouble to cure it with medicine, it also went bad. That's why I say there surely are bad days. In any case it depends on God's will.

(Here the informant asked me why I was writing all this. I answered that it was to write a book. At my response the informant asked me no more questions. Rather, he seemed to follow with his eyes everything that I was writing, as though he wanted to discover the truth in all those mysterious signs that writing consists of. Finally, the informant asked me if it was easy to write, and than he said he was sorry that he could not do it like me. He said, "I'm blind." When I answered that there was still time for him to learn, he appeared to be contented. Then he said that maybe it would be possible for him to study at night.) (Soler, July 12.)

Justo Colonia: The medicine that the Hacienda uses and sells came almost at the same time as the new potatoes. The Hacienda administrators told us about it. Possibly the medicine is good because most of the time the crops the Hacienda has planted have been saved, but there also have been cases where the Hacienda's crops have almost totally gone bad, even though they used those medicines. Because of that we say that maybe it depends on God. If he wants it, the crops can go bad even though they are cured [see Chapter 5 for an exploration of the double meaning of "cure"], and also if he wants it, the crops don't go bad even though medicine is put on them.

When people are bad God punishes them in different ways. Sometimes we get sick ourselves, or our relatives do, and other times our crops go bad, like what is happening now with our potatoes and *habas*. "Bad people" are those who are always quarreling with their relatives and friends,, and so too are those who are nasty, selfish, jealous, or when men live with another woman. People are good when they live in harmony with their relatives and friends, when they are generous and always try to help other people. (Soler, August 26.)

Dionisio Quinto: The potato disease called *mañuco* came here in 1948. Everything that was planted in September and October went bad almost completely. That's why many people prefer to plant in May and June because those crops are saved. The Hacienda cures the *mañuco* disease with nitrate. We can't cure it because we don't have the money to buy it. I think that the medicne is not so good because, according to what other people have told me, that medicine doesn't cure as well as was expected. Sometimes the disease tales hold of the crop and ruins it completely. (Soler, July 16.)

Eugenio Leiva: They say that in 1949 they put DDT in the Vicosinos' houses. The women and children ran away to the hills, saying that the technicians were going to kill them. Then when the technicians went to the houses , they didn't find the owners there. Those DDT people began to spray powder over the clothing and bedding. When the owners came back they found their things full of DDT. Some chose to beat their things and others said they would take them to the river to wash them. They soaked their things there so the DDT would be gone. They said it was poisonous and it smelled bad. . . . Some people have said that when DDT is put on the crops, the earth gets damaged and the livestock won't eat the pasture. The DDT technicians said when they were spraying that care was needed because it was poisonous to animals. (Soto, with Ricardo Estremadoyro, August 17.)

Alejandro Colonia: Using guano de la isla has many advantages but sometimes we can't get it because we lack the wherewithal. In that case the only thing we can do is to fertilize our fields the way we've always done, by borrowing livestock from our neighbors and manuring. We know it isn't enough but there's no help for us. The same thing happens when we want to use the medicines that the Hacienda sells. Then, even more than because we lack the money that needed to buy those things, we don't use them because we don't know how to apply the treatments. (Soler, August 26.)

Alejo Valerio: (Is your form of working the land old or modern?) It's modern because I clean the fields, manure them, and plant. I use both old and modern forms. The old forms are without making ridges. A line is made with a *yunta* and potatoes are put in. Another line is made to cover them, and then another line close to it. With the modern kind of ridges, the distance between furrow and furrow is smaller, and it's done with a measuring stick. To hill potatoes in the modern way both edges serve to carry the soil toward one line of plants, and toward the other. In the old form of planting potatoes, the plants often come up together. Other times they don't come up and are lost. To hill we make basins up to a radius of a meter's distance. When the plants are together, they're not divided during hilling. They're just considered one plant.

Planting with ridges is better when it's with the new *paltaq* seed. However, with the old seed it's better the old way, without ridges, by making hills. It's because the old seed has more roots and needs more room. With the old way of planting, and the old seed that we plant in September and October, there's no longer the need for irrigation because the crop is watered by the rains. We do the *mitzqa* with ridges and the new seeds. Irrigation is easier with ridges, but with big ridges a person gets very tired in hilling. With basins it's easier, lighter. That's why a lot of people aren't interested in ridges, because they get tired hilling and they say that the fields are wasted. I like the new method with ridges because it's easier to irrigate, to hill, and to put in medicines and guano. When the crop is with basins, many times some plants remain unfertilized. (Flores, with Pablo Herrera, July 23.)

In general, the use of commercial fertilizers and plant medicines did not conflict directly with customary agricultural practices. Most informants were aware of the existence of guano and, despite some concern at possible dangers, accepted the idea that crops could be treated and cured. In the demonstration fields, the Hacienda imposed strict surveillance which, along with its interference with customary gleaning practices, aroused Vicosinos' latent resentment. While the Hacienda had abolished what *it* chose to view as abuses characteristic of the hacienda system, the new precautions designed to assure a fair demonstration as well as income for the community were viewed by *Vicosinos* as new abuses. Thus, the Project was required by its own desire to circumvent the people's desire in order to commodify potatoes. The vigilance which prohibited the taking of produce from the Hacienda's fields by the workers, and the denial of gleaning rights were perceived as threats to well-being:

Rosario Celio: The Hacienda isn't supervising well because it doesn't favor many Vicosinos. Other renters were better in this regard. They had better consideration for us when they told us to plant in one or another field. Now it isn't that way any more. They don't allow people to dig potatoes from the Hacienda's fields. (Soto, July 14.)

José Vega: The present *patrón* buys products from the State at low prices, saying it's for the Vicosinos when in reality he gets them for himself. And he doesn't want to give us anything. He says that we'd get used to it.

The last *patrón* was very good. That one just didn't make us go without supplies for our homes. After the harvests he allowed us to collect products left in the soil, but this one now searches us, even our pockets. The new one doesn't want us to take anything at all from the Hacienda's fields. I think they've told him everything that we've been producing and they've told him that we've gotten into the habit of stealing from his fields. With luck like that, I don't know what's going to become of us. And the worst of it is that our fields aren't producing enough. (Soler, July 2.)

Ciriaco Evaristo: Both the *mayorales* and the *tápacos* [watchmen] are more demanding these days than they used to be, because they're earning wages and they don't want to lose their jobs. They're always on the Hacienda's side, which makes us quite angry. They always worry us that they're going to tell the *patrón* if we don't finish the assigned work or if some men want to take home some of the produce from the harvest. (Soler, August 5.)

Dolores Cruz: They're mean, greedy, and avaricious in the Hacienda. They never give anything away. They won't even sell me anything. I plant a little land and the Hacienda doesn't want to give me more. I wish they'd give me some more fields so I could plant potatoes and wheat. They're very manly in the Hacienda when the women come for the *kallpa* [gleaning]. They throw them out of the fields and whip them. They take their *llikllas* [carrying cloths] away from them. The *patrones* were better in the old days because when we would bring them chickens and eggs as presents they'd give us presents of wheat, maize, *habas*, and barley in return. The *patrones*' wives would give us food. They used to feed the grooms right in the Hacienda. Now they've stopped all that. In the old days they used to feed us potatoes, cabbage, wheat hominy, and pudding. I wish they'd throw Don Enrique out because he's bad, but he's very obsequious with the *patrones* and that's why he does't leave. Don Enrique runs down women with his horse. He whipped one of the women at the potato harvest when she went into the field for *kallpa*. Don Enrique is greedy because he is from another place. That's why we hate him. . . .

Women shouldn't be treated that way at *kallpa* because when they throw them out God won't give us good harvests. (Flores, with Ricardo Estremadoyro, July 3.)

In the case of share-planting, Vicosinos tended to expect that, despite the Project's announcement that the crop would be divided in half, somehow the Hacienda would end up with a larger share and leave its partners with little return for their labor. Several informants believed that the Hacienda was supposed to give the new items to the Vicosinos, rather than sell them. People generally maintained the impression that the Hacienda was making profits from the sales. The strict accounting required by the Hacienda interfered with the custom of taking potatoes out early. Moreover, a field of ripe potatoes is tempting to others, and so it requires extra vigilance on the part of its owner. Vicosinos were not happy with this arrangement:

Víctor Sánchez: I'd like to plant with the new seed but I don't have land. I just plant potatoes on a small scale in the Quebrada Honda. I don't plant with the new seed from the Hacienda there because I don't have a fence, and it's a lot of care because cattle get into the field. The Hacienda *patrones* get out good crops, but the ones who planted on shares with the Hacienda lost out, almost all of them. (Soto, July 13.)

Narcizo Meza: It's about two years since the new seed potatoes arrived at the Hacienda. Don Enrique told us about it and had us plant them in Atashpampa [the location of the Hacienda's field]. The year after that, we planted in Wicushpachán. The one we planted first was the *papa marcos* and then we planted the *papa blanca* here in this big field that is Wicushpachán. The year that the *papa marcos* arrived no Vicosino planted it because the Hacienda had brought in a small amount and they were only going to try it out. At least that's what people said. It was during the second year that Vicosinos began to plant the seed from the first harvest. Don Enrique offered that seed to us. That year few Vicosinos planted on shares with the Hacienda. I didn't plant any because I have little land. This year many Vicosinos have planted on shares, and maybe others have planted seed they bought on their own account. . . .
It's not very convenient to plant on shares because when we divide the crop in half at the harvest, the seed, guano, and medicines the Hacienda puts in is not in proportion to our work. It's like this–we put up our fields, and then we work getting the soil ready, we cultivate, irrigate, and take care of the crop up to the harvest. Then we have to go without sleep and watch at night so as not to get robbed, or stay up to irrigate, so that it takes up almost all of our time. Then, if the harvest unfortunately turns out bad, all our sacrfice is lost. All this doesn't influence in any way the Hacienda's life like it does ours, because the Hacienda plants a lot and small losses can't affect the Hacienda's share. The Hacienda takes off

half the crop by the single fact of having given us the seed, guano, and medicines. (Soler, July 17.)

Alfonso Cruz: (How would you like the Hacienda to improve that form of planting on shares?) I'd like what I've seen on other haciendas. In Macate they give those who plant on shares food and coca. The one who puts up the seed does that. In other places they pay for sharecropping. If the Hacienda here would help like that it would be comfortable. That way the both of us would come out ahead, the Hacienda and the worker. For example, if I planted a half sack I'd have to fence the field. When my turn came up to work in the Hacienda, they should recognize those days and consider them on the Hacienda's account. Just like that we'd come out ahead. (Flores, with Celso León, August 18.)

Estenio Meza: I knew that the Hacienda brought in new seed potatoes last year. They were from Huancayo. Don Enrique Luna told me about it. . . . I was there when they brought them. They brought two kinds, the *blanco* and the *marcos*. The *blanco* has a hole inside it and the sickness gets to it faster. It's weaker. On the other hand, the *papa marcos* is stronger. (At this moment the informant asked me how much I earned. I told him that I was a student and was going around learning how to be a professional and earn money later.)

It's more convenient for a person to plant himself, because then we don't wait for the crop to ripen in order to eat potatoes, but we take them out as they ripen without thinking that someone is going to ask us to account for them. Even when the Hacienda puts up the medicines and the guano it doesn't equal our work and sacrifice. (Soler, July 7.)

Ambrosio Evaristo: I know that a year ago the Hacienda brought seed potatoes called "*paltaq*" in Spanish. We call them "*marcos*." We used to have that same potato in our grandfathers' times. I plant potatoes every year. It's just that each *patrón* who comes to the Hacienda always brings his own seeds. For example, now the *patrón* has brought seeds, and according to what Don Enrique and Don Mario say they're from the United States. But I say again that it's the same *paltaq* seed, except that it ripens faster. It seems better than ours. It produces a larger quantity of potatoes and they're more developed. Also, the worms don't eat them like they do ours.

I've planted my own seeds because I couldn't buy the seed potatoes the Hacienda has, because I didn't have the money. They're expensive. An *arroba* of small ones costs six *soles*. Vicos people say that the seed is expensive and besides they are very little. In the end the people who have money bought them and planted them in their fields. My cousin, José Francisco did that. People who plant on shares with the Hacienda have to divide the harvest in half, according to the yield. I haven't planted on shares because it's not convenient for me. It's the sacrifice of my personal labor as well as planting in my own field. Even if they put up the seed, guano, and medicines, in reality it doesn't equal, it doesn't make up for our personal labor. Besides, I don't plant on shares because I have so little land. I have to divide it to plant maize and other products. If I planted with the Hacienda and they took away half the crop, there'd be very little to eat. If, on the other hand, it was a share like a third or a fourth, those of us who have little land would be fine.

Alfonso Cruz planted on shares with the Hacienda last year. He planted two sacks of seed and harvested thirty. He told me so himself. That's why this year other people have planted like that. Another person who planted on shares was Daniel Herrera. He only planted a half sack and he harvested three. I don't know what happened. Maybe there wasn't enough medicine, but more likely it was because of the poor quality of the land. Because of that, this year he hasn't planted on shares with the Hacienda but he's gone back to planting his own seed, that is, seed that he got from that harvest. The reason Alfonso harvested thirty sacks was because he had manured his field with his animals, and then he put in guano from the Hacienda. The others didn't do that.

Another one who planted was Emilio Flores. With two *arrobas* of seed he harvested fifteen sacks. He planted in a wheat field without manuring with his animals. He probably liked his potatoes and worked hard on them. Víctor Valerio planted one sack and an *arroba* and harvested fifteen sacks. Another was Alejo Valerio. He planted two sacks and harvested eight. I know about it because I worked there. Most of the potatoes had gone rotten and green. It was probably caused by much rain, principally because the land was very damp. Water comes out of the ground there. Despite that, he planted again on shares with the Hacienda but in another place. He told me that. He says he was curious to see who would win, he or the potatoes. Herminio Colonia also planted two sacks and harvested sixteen. I also worked in his field as part of my *tarea* [i.e., workers were assigned to fields planted on shares as part of their Hacienda duties]. I knew that Delfín Coleto also planted on shares. He put in two sacks and harvested twenty. I know that, too because I helped him at the harvest on the Hacienda's account. They didn't give us a single potato. They're mean in the Hacienda. We didn't ask them to roast potatoes for us. But when we harvest ourselves we always roast them. We make a *pachamanca* [a festive barbecue]. That way people are happier in their work.

Now I'm planning to buy seed potatoes from other Vicosinos who've planted on shares this year. I think that they'll sell them cheaper during their harvests. Next year I want to plant the same seeds the Hacienda has because they're better than the ones I've always planted.

(At this point the informant asked me why we were writing all these things down. I answered that we were planning to write a nice book about their life and the ways they worked their fields, what medicines they needed for when their crops got sick, and why engineers who read about these things come to cure their plants. The informant seemed comfortable. Then he told me that we were making a lot of money. That's what the young man who has come from Carhuaz told him. He said he was making two thousand *soles* a day. I told him that the three of us were students and that we weren't earning anything. We were studying their problems like young Mario did before. The informant was comfortable with my response. (Soler, July 12.)

Antonio Reyes: When the sickness still hadn't arrived our potatoes were better than *marcos* potatoes. They produced a lot and they were well developed. Since the sickness arrived, our potatoes have almost disappeared, and now they are of lower quality. They almost don't produce anything. They are little and they soon fill with worms. In the first year the Hacienda only got to plant *marcos* potatoes. The year after that some Vicosinos planted them as a result of Don Enrique Luna's offer, and because they saw that the potatoes were producing very well. A lot of people have planted them this year. I haven't, because the guano ran out. Now I'm planning to plant them and I'll talk with Don Mario. It's more convenient to plant for oneself and not on shares with the Hacienda, because if the crop is one's own one can consume it as it ripens. And also, we work more and are on the go day and night till our health is in danger. When people steal from the crop, or when animals damage it, we have to account for that ourselves because the Hacienda thinks we ought to be on the go day and night looking after the crops, without taking into account that we have to show up for our *tareas* or work in our other fields.

(After he answered my questions he asked me about my clothing, eyeglasses, if I were single or not, and why I didn't look for a woman so that I could work more happily, and a whole lot of other questions. All of that did not let me write carefully because I had to satisfy him with adequate responses. . . . . From time to time he looked at what I was writing, and then he said to me bluntly: "How I wish I could read all that you're writing. It's a pity to be blind. We're only good for working in the fields. We haven't had the opportunity to learn things like you people. If it had been different we'd be in that condition. We wouldn't have had to work every week for the Hacienda. At least we would have gotten to know other places and learned many things. Because we don't know how to read and write we're here as if we were chained to it.") (Soler, July 15.)

Eugenio Leiva: When they told me to plant potatoes with the Hacienda I obeyed, but I didn't like it because I had to watch it constantly, even at night. There were nights when I was thinking about water and other things relating to the potatoes I'd planted with the Hacienda that I couldn't even sleep. But the Hacienda doesn't think about anything at all relating to the worker. They don't given even a package of cigarettes. They're satisfied when they give potatoes and guano, nothing more. They don't worry at all. But we have to be there in the field at six in the morning already to look for water. Now when everybody has planted with the Hacienda's potatoes we all need water, and in such conditions the water doesn't go around. So at times we have to get there early and take it- We have more work than the Hacienda. The only thing the Hacienda wants is to harvest. That's what they wait for. When a person has to irrigate at night because there isn't enough water, the Hacienda doesn't give us anything. We have to get up without alcohol, without cigarettes and coca. There's no use like that. . . . With our own potatoes, we can be eating them while the crop is ripening, but with the Hacienda we have to harvest all at once. We can't take them out little by little. (Soto, with Ricardo Estremadoyro, August 25.)

If I were the one in the Hacienda I'd give ten *soles* or a package of cigarettes to the ones who plant potatoes on shares. I'd tell them, "Take this, you're working hard." I'd also buy them boots for when the irrigate. You need to think about it because those expenses can come out of the next harvest. If you don't do those things, how are you going to get the people's love? How are you going to take care of people? (Soto, with Ricardo Estremadoyro, August 17.)

Alfonso Cruz: (What do you think of the Hacienda's system of giving seed, DDT, fertilizer, and the form of ridge-planting to the workers on shares?) As far as I'm concerned it's all right. It's just that they don't help with the work. It takes a lot of work to plant and cultivate the *paltaq* seed that they give out. When the Hacienda gives potatoes they want us to take out the stones and turn over the soil with a *barreta*, and that we go over it five times with the *yunta*. This is very expensive for the operator. The Hacienda gives seed, fertilizer, and DDT, but sometimes nothing comes out. Everybody has accepted it in this form but the Hacienda doesn't want to help even with a day's work for the crops. I've gone to great expense and so it isn't convenient for me to plant on shares with the Hacienda. I paid for six men, one to open furrows, another to put in guano, another to put in the seed, another to cover it, and others who brought the seed. Then the *yunta* has to be driven by another, and one to put in stakes for it to follow. They require a lot of cultivation in the Hacienda. The Hacienda is obliged to send workers for the harvest, the same as the operator. The ones from the Hacienda were paid wages [was it part of their Hacienda *tarea*?]. On the other hand, I had to pay my own workers with potatoes. Nobody wanted to take money. This way the Hacienda doesn't lose but it gets much more. So the Hacienda gets people excited because it's convenient. Otherwise it wouldn't give anything to people who plant on shares. (Flores, with Celso León, August 18.)

Workers who planted on shares were required to plant under the same kind of supervision as in the case of the demonstration fields. Directions included specific requirements for the preparation of the fields for planting, as well as for the act of planting itself. The seed tubers were placed in the soil with a measuring stick a little closer together than in the customary way of planting by paces, and they were set in ridges with the rows farther apart.

Informants complained that all this made for more work and more expense, since the relatives who came to help the share-planters might not themselves be planting on shares and their extra labor in following the Project's directions had to be reciprocated. Several informants perceived in the close supervision a criticism of customary agricultural practices. They resented the implication that they were less qualified to farm than the mestizo technicians who were ordering them about in the fields. Vicosinos believed that urban and educated mestizos did not engage in agricultural labor and knew far less about farming. The need for so much attention and work at night was worrisome to many people because they said that the night air was dangerous to their health, a concept widespread in the region and shared by both mestizos and workers.

In the recent symposium on Andean irrigation, and with regard to Andean rituals and narratives concerning water management and mountain spirits, Paul Gelles (1994:260) makes some comments about the relations of peasants and mestizo bureaucrats that would fit, by changing the content slightly to deal with Vicos farming and health discourses, what I have been writing about here:

> [T]he maintenance of local models of irrigation is a form of cultural resistance, one that questions the power and legitimacy of the Peruvian state. . . . Andean peasants are dominated peoples within a nation-state that neither shares nor respects highland cultural values. National power-holders who determine the state's policy toward Andean communities, live an urban *criollo* [monolingual Spanish] life-style in coastal cities and emulate Western lifeways. They generally disdain "indigenous" culture and view Andean peoples as backward, dirty, lazy members of an almost subhuman caste. Unfortunately, these attitudes find institutional and increasingly violent expression. Bureaucratic attacks against the beliefs and rituals surrounding irrigation water and mountain worship must be examined in this context. State officials who denigrate and ignore Andean ethnohydrological principles are actually carrying out the agenda of domination. . . . Andean peasants resist new forms of distribution not only because of their potential for greater inequalities in water use but because they constitute a form of cultural hegemony.

There can be no questioning of the Project's sincere effort to bring potatoes back into production, and to benefit Vicosinos from the sale of the Hacienda's and their own increased crops. The Project's design included the empowerment of Vicosinos, at least locally and subregionally (see Chapter 1),[29] but the direction of the Hacienda was given over to two mestizos, Enrique Luna and Mario Vázquez,[30] who, as Laura Macdonald (1995:206) puts it, saw local practice as dysfunctional and whose "version of participation ha[d] a strongly instrumentalist and technocratic character." The agronomists who were consulted and who assisted with the implementation of the Hacienda's program had been educated in an urban context of racism. We can interpret Vicos resistance in terms similar to those so eloquently stated by Gelles. At the same time, it would appear that Vicos agriculture was in need of technical assistance. Seligmann and Bunker (1994:217, 225) suggest that the fragmented knowledge of Andean peoples may now be inadequate for managing their habitat. Technical intervention was, then, appropriate. Could the program have been implemented in a libertarian, instead of an authoritarian, way? I believe so, but I do not know for it was never tried.

However fragmented Vicosinos' knowledge may have been, in 1953 they were successful survivors. They reacted to the new directions:

Pablo Celio: Last year I planted two and a half *arrobas* and only two sacks came out of it. We divided it up, one sack for each of us. The *patrón* was angry and asked me: "What did you do with the potatoes?" I told him that they didn't yield. I'm not going to plant this year because there was no yield last year and the *patrón* told me that I hadn't dug enough. (Soto, July 15.)

Alfonso Cruz: (Is it good that the Hacienda requires so much care in cultivating this crop?) It would be good, but the Hacienda says for us to turn over the soil from below to get new soil on top. And then when a good harvest doesn't come they say that we don't know how to farm. (Is it good that you have to turn over this new soil?) I don't think it would need much more cultivation than to plow it with a *yunta* two or three times, but the *patrones* aren't content with that. First they look at the field and they say to turn it over with a *barreta*, to take out the stones. To bring the *yunta*, the *patrón* has to look at what we've done, and then we give it four or five plowings. Then we notify the Hacienda. They look over the field to see if the soil is well stirred, but if they find it's not done they refuse to give the seed. They say that we're going to lose it, that the crop is not going to yield. This year a lot of people have planted with the Hacienda. I don't know why. Last year just a few planted, the ones who knew about it. But because they didn't cultivate enough, this year they haven't wanted to give them seed. (Flores, with Celso León, August 18.)

Eugenio Leiva: When we planted potatoes in the Hacienda fields I told Don Enrique that we wouldn't plant with the measure. But Don Enrique answered just to plant, and I had to obey. Now Don Enrique wants us to turn over the soil with a *barreta*. He told me it was no good with a *yunta*. So I asked him why we were going to turn it over like that, and he said it was so the new soil would come up. If the plow is no good, then, we'll just use the *yunta* for planting. That's why all of us had to work with *barretas*. We did the work with some sixty or seventy men for a day. . . . I think the *yunta* does it faster. With the *barreta* it takes more time. I use the *yunta*. When a person is alone it's even worse, and he has to take more time than he should. When I asked Don Enrique why it was they told us to do that, he said it was so the crop wouldn't fail. I've turned over the soil with a *yunta* and the crop comes out the same. . . . All the Vicosinos prefer to work with the *yunta*. If we did it with a *minka* [persons who come to help[31]], it would be more expensive, and we'd have to furnish coca and cigarettes. To work with a *yunta* we need less. With seventy *centavos* it's done. So we use the *barreta* only when they order us, but afterward we all use the *yunta*. (Soto, with Ricardo Estremadoyro, August 17.)

Alejandro Colonia: We know that the Hacienda is planting with ridges and the measure. But we don't make ridges, we just plant as we go. It's certain that when you plant with ridges it produces a larger crop of potatoes. When we plant in the customary way it doesn't yield as much as in the other case. Just the same, it's not convenient for us to plant according to the Hacienda's system because for that we need a greater number of people. The work goes more slowly because we have to make ridges and do it with the special measure. Sure, it can be done, and we know that it produces more, but in our case we have the problem that we are just two brothers who have to divide up all the work, besides having to perform our *tareas* in the Hacienda. The Hacienda doesn't remember the work when a Vicosino plants on shares. It's the people themselves who perform all the work from planting to harvest, and with the danger than we could get sick watching at night or in irrigating, and still the division is by halves. (Soler, August 26.)

It is clear that in general Vicosinos rejected the share-planting system proposed by the Project. They complained about the extra expense, labor, and time. They tended to agree that it was inconvenient to wait until the whole crop was ripe to harvest all at once and divide the product at that time, not only because people like to begin eating the new crop as it matures, or even eating it before it is really ripe from hunger, but risks of damage to the crop by other people or animals. If the crop is left in the field it is necessary to protect it from such threats, and this requires additional inputs of household labor. Two responses were frequent: 1) "I'd like to plant potatoes on shares but it's more expensive like that"; and 2) "I can't plant on shares because I don't have the land to spare." Vicosinos felt that they were being obliged to work harder and to take more than their share of the risk. As I have noted, for the 1954 planting, the Project adapted its program to Vicos needs and instituted a method whereby people could get the new items on credit. The innovations were offered at low interest, with repayment either in cash or in produce (Vázquez 1955:61). This adaptation was achieved when the Project finally understood how unsuited the original plan was to conditions at Vicos. Share-planting ceased entirely with the coming of the Programa Ancash and its Crédito Rural Agrícola Supervisado, Rural Agricultural Supervised Credit (Garrido-Lecca 1965:41).

Almost all informants were satisfied with the *paltaq* potato which appears to have been so much like one variety of *papa común* that several persons claimed to have been familiar with it for years. In contrast, the white potato was an object of some concern and discontent. Its principal defect was a small hole at the center of the tuber, about which most of the men interviewed[32] expressed themselves negatively. They said that the hollow place made it look like a rotten potato. Some interpreted the hole as an indication of weakness and said they believed that the sickness would get to it more easily. Some pointed out that the white potato had less flavor, or that it tasted bad around the hole, or that it was not as grainy as the *paltaq*, or that it broke apart on cooking. Several people refused to have anything to do with it, while others planted it as a last resort when the supply of paltaq potatoes ran out. For the Vicosino the ideal potato is grainy, large, plentiful.[33] Here are some examples of the Vicos response:

José Basilio: I learned about the new potatoes from Don Enrique when he told us that the new seed had arrived. He offered to sell it to us or let us plant it on shares with the Hacienda. It was on a Wednesday during the *mando*. When I saw the potatoes they were really good. I tried them after the first harvest and they were very tasty. They were grainy and they produced well, possibly better than our own. I couldn't plant on shares with the Hacienda because I have a few small fields that are barely enough to plant our own seed.

(I found the informant breaking stones with a drill at the construction of the new school. I took advantage of a break in the work to interview him. It was late in the afternoon. I did not continue my work with him because it was time for him to leave work. However, we agreed to continue the interview tomorrow.) (Soler, July 16.)

Izaquel Sánchez: The new seed potatoes came to the Hacienda from Tarma two years ago. The first potatoes were the *paltaq*. We also call that potato the *marcos*. They planted this potato in Atashpampa for the Hacienda. No Vicosinos bought the new seed because the Hacienda had them brought just for itself. Vicosinos talked about this white potato they also brought from Tarma, the one that came after the *marcos*. I think that the Hacienda's potatoes are better. They grow and produce more and it has a better flavor. That's why I'm planning to buy them from my neighbors who planted them this year. Almost everybody says that the new seeds are good. I proved it to myself when I tasted them at the Hacienda's harvest. The sickness has hurt almost all our *papa común*. Some of us are almost completely our of potatoes. Only a few still have this seed, and we get them from those people to make them produce. Both the *marcos* and the white potato are very good potatoes. The *paltaq* tastes better. It's grainier. But the white potato produces more and the tubers are well developed. Still, the white potato has its center with a hole. It's like it was rotten. We plant both kinds of potatoes here and each one of them has its advantages and its disadvantages. (Soler, July 17.)

Alejandro Colonia: We're buying the new potatoes from the Hacienda at fifteen *soles* an *arroba*. This is the way we're trying out those potatoes, and so we can say that both kinds are the same. The *paltaq* potatoes are better because they grow to the same size, while the white potatoes grow unequally. And the *paltaq* potatoes are grainier. They cook more quickly and so it's necessary to take a lot of care because they open like a rose and they can fall apart. Another of their benefits is that their center is not *toqtu*, has no hole in it, like the white potatoes. (Soler, August 26.)

Francisco Copetán: We've known about the new seed potatoes for two years, since they arrived at the Hacienda. The *marcos* potatoes came first. Those of us who were working in the Hacienda saw it. We planted that seed on the plains [*llanos*, level bottom lands] and Don Enrique offered them to us on sale and for planting. That year the white potato, or the *tarmeña* [from Tarma], also came here. We planted that seed in Wicushpachán and, like I said, some bought it to plant on their own account. The potato harvest was good, because it produced well and with large sized potatoes, but it had the problem of being weaker with the sicknesses and it had a hole in its center. It was *toqtu* or *qaptu*, and that part had a bad taste. Just recently, according to what people say, the Hacienda has brought a new kind of white potato seed, possibly from another place. Let's hope that seed is of better quality than the other.

When the Hacienda got the produce from the first planting of the new seed, they lowered the price which was very, very high at the beginning. They first wanted to sell it to us at 80 *soles*, but then they lowered the price to 60 *soles* a sack, and it was then that some people were willing to buy it and others planted it on shares with the Hacienda. . . .

The former *patrón* had another kind of seed. It was the *papa colorada* [red potato]. That potato was good too, but it was small. Even now we plant that potato and the Hacienda also sells it for people to eat. So we've tried all those potatoes. The Hacienda used to sell them or lend them to us, for example, 6 *arrobas* of the small ones would be returned with 3 *arrobas* of big potatoes when we harvested them. I can tell you that the best quality potato is the *paltaq*, because it's stronger against the sickness, has a better taste, and is grainier than the white potato. That's why I planted a sack of *paltaq* on shares with the Hacienda on June 22. (Soler, July 18.)

Marcelino Cruz: I haven't planted on shares with the Hacienda because we're barely two with my father. In our case the work could get the better of us. Just the same, I wanted to buy the new seed for planting, but they told me they were out of it. I'm planning to plant it next year because the seed is good. Now all I can do is to plant my own seed, the *común*. I'm going to plant tomorrow. I'm preparing the soil now. Maybe this crop will ripen. Our potatoes are just as good as the Hacienda's. The colors of our *papa común* are white, black, and red.

The two kinds of potato are just about the same. Still the *paltaq* potato seems better to me than the white one because it's grainy and has a better taste. The white potato is *toqtu*. It has a hole in its center, but it's bigger than the *marcos* potato and it produces plenty. Compared with our own potatoes, I'd say they were the same. Our potatoes are also tasty and grainy, it's only that we don't have medicines to cure them. Maybe the Hacienda's potatoes are a little better than ours because they resist the sickness, and even when they get sick they don't get attacked completely, only certain parts like the leaves which shrivel. In any case, I'm ready to get that new seed from the Hacienda so I can plant it myself. I think that's more convenient.

Other people are also happy with the new seed because it's saved from the sickness, and it also has a good taste and it produces well. Just the same, people say that it's better to plant the *marcos* potato than the white one, and if this time some have planted the white potato it's been because they were out of the *marcos* seed

(During the course of the interview he asked me why I was writing down all these things. I answered that it was in order to write a book about their lives, their agricultural problems, and the ways of curing their potatoes when they were attacked by the sickness. At the beginning the informant was a bit incredulous, but as I explained things with examples he became satisfied. He chewed coca and smoked a cigarette all through the interview. Now and then he looked at my notebook as if he wanted to read everything I was writing, and then he lowered his gaze, tired, as though he were defeated by ignorance because he could not make out anything in the notebook.) (Soler, July 17.)

Natividad Tario: The harvest of the first seed, the *paltaq*, turned out well, so Don Enrique offered it again to the people to plant on shares with the Hacienda. Several Vicosinos were willing to plant in these circumstances. . . . This year many others have planted it because the harvests from the first planting have given good results. Some planted the *marcos* potato and others the white potato. Almost everybody prefers to plant the *marcos* because its quality was better than the other, but some have had to accept the white one because the *marcos* seed ran out. They knew, too, that the white potato has a hole in its center, and that part doesn't taste good. It looks like a rotten potato. But they didn't want to be left behind the others who planted, and so they had to make up their minds to plant the white potato. In the Hacienda they asked my son how it was possible that I wasn't planting potatoes like other Vicosinos, and did I expect to starve? That was the reason why I'm planting on shares with the Hacienda.

They gave me a sack of small white potatoes mixed with rotten potatoes and some of another color, like the red potato. They also gave me half a sack of guano. When the plants were already beginning to grow they gave me medicines for curing the plants. We divided the crop in halves. Many people have planted under the same conditions this year. I would have liked to plant the *marcos* potato too, but like I told you they were out of seed. So instead of planting nothing I was glad to plant the seed they gave me. Now we've been told that this white potato seed is of better quality. Well, we'll see at the harvest if this information is true. (Soler, July 18.)

Estenio Meza: I saw that the *paltaq* potato harvest in the Hacienda was good and so I decided to plant it myself. Before they brought the *paltaq* to the Hacienda I saw in Marcará that it was producing. When I saw it there I didn't want to buy it because I thought it wouldn't yield a crop here. Nobody among the Vicosinos made me want to plant it. I planted it when I saw it in the Hacienda and there were other people here who were planting it. . . . The *paltaq* potato is grainier than the *waska* and it produces better. The potato is more developed, larger.

I don't get together with many friends, but people say that the *paltaq* potato is good. On my part I take a great interest in planting because I think it's a blessing when I'm given a good harvest. I haven't heard anyone say it's bad. Everybody is content. They've said it's a good potato. I'm very interested. I don't think it's an ordinary thing. (Flores, with Ricardo Estremadoyro, July 18.)

Antonio Bautista: I already planted an *arroba* of *paltaq* potatoes. I bought them from the Hacienda. I'll plant more in October. . . . When the *paltaq* yields it's better than the ordinary potatoes. . . . I learned about it when I went to Marcará to work in a harvest. . . . I decided to plant it because I saw that it was producing well in the Hacienda, and I was envious. So I said to myself, "Why are just they going to have good crops? And so I planted it myself. . . . I'm happy with the *paltaq* potato because it's pretty, because the Virgin fixed it so that potato would come here. I used it for food. I make dried potatoes.

(The informant answered the questions in good humor and only when we finished said he would go on working. We had told him that we would finish soon. He asked what the questions were for, if we were from the Government. Estremadoyro had told him that we were from the would finish soon. He asked what the questions were for, if we were from the Government. Estremadoyro had told him that we were from the University and that we wanted to help them with their crops. During the interview, and at the end, I gave him cigarettes.) (Flores, with Ricardo Estremadoyro, July 13.)

Although no extreme negative response was recorded by the interviewers, there were some Vicosinos who maintained neutrality. A few informants favored customary approaches to agriculture:

Alfonso Cruz: (Which do you prefer, the new seed potatoes or the old ones?) The only thing is that a good harvest depends on the day and the phase of the moon when it's planted. If a person doesn't know that, no matter how much he plants it won't get results. (Flores, with Celso León, August 18.)

José Francisco: I plant the *papa variada*. If the Hacienda happened to give me the *paltaq*, I'd plant it. The *papa variada* yields better in the heights and the *paltaq* does better in the Hacienda. (Flores, with Ricardo Estremadoyro, July 11.)

Emilio Lázaro: The *paltaq* potato is good because it's grainy, but it yields a very small harvest. It's good in a boiled dinner, boiled alone, and in *papakashki* [potato soup]. The *papa variada* is good if we do enough manuring. If we don't spread manure the *papa variada* won't yield a harvest. The white potato is good because it grows big. When the *papa variada* is manured it also grows big, and if not it stays small. I'm content that the *paltaq* seed is here because it's good. I plant if there's seed, and if there isn't I don't plant. Sometimes if a seed doesn't yield I'm not going to plant it, but when I see that other people are planting it I also plant it. I like all kinds of seed. (Flores with Pablo Herrera, July 17.)

In addition to judgments about the potatoes themselves, attitudes toward the Hacienda played a part in the decision whether or not to take up the Hacienda's offer. Some Vicosinos expressed a wish for caretaking on the Hacienda's part:

Ildefonso Tario: The seed that the Hacienda brought is better than ours. It produces more and has a better taste. The sickness attacks our potatoes faster even when we manure the fields. We plant for nothing. We don't buy medicines from the Hacienda because there's no money and they're expensive. I think that planting on shares with the Hacienda won't turn out well because we'd spend a lot of time and money. Besides taking care of our own crops we'd have to plant, irrigate, cultivate, and take care of the potatoes, and we'd get sick from all of that. So that form of planting won't do. If the medicines were cheaper than what they're now selling them at, we'd buy them to cure our plants and that way we'd plant more. We all want to plant the new seeds that the Hacienda has brought. If they gave us the wherewithal we could plant them on most of our land. But now when our crops go bad we find ourselves obliged to buy seed from the Hacienda or in other places where they're sold for less. In the old days, the Hacienda gave us presents, a measure to each one of us, and we could gather the small potatoes. Now they don't give us anything, not even the small potatoes.

(He told me that he did not know the name of the President or of the country. He only remembered the name of Leguía. He asked me how much I was earning. I told him that I was a student and that I was learning in order to make a living when I received the doctorate. Then he asked me if I could eat without being paid. I told him yes. The informant said no more to me.) (Soler, July 13.)

Manuel Cruz: The *paltaq* seed that the Hacienda has brought is good. I haven't planted it because the Hacienda doesn't want to give it to me. I'm planting *habas* and maize. . . . We'd like to plant *paltaq* potatoes, but what would the Hacienda charge us for an *arroba*? (Flores, with Ricardo Estremadoyro, July 8.)

Some Vicosinos took a wait-and-see approach, becoming interested as they observed a succession of good crops in both Hacienda and share-planting demonstrations:

Manuel Mendoza: In regard to potatoes, last year I was already thinking of planting them but I wasn't sure a good harvest could come of it. So I waited for other people to plant. Now that people have got out a good harvest, this year I'm ready. I saw the potato harvest in Alejo Valerio's field. Of course many Vicosinos are talking about the good harvest. (Soto, July 17.)

Juan Coleto: I've heard from Vicosinos that the Hacienda's way of planting potatoes is good because that way the products are bigger and there's more of them. I'm still not so sure about that because I personally haven't tried it yet. Just the same, I'm planning to plant next year the same as the Hacienda's crop. (Soler, August 8.)

Jualián Vega: The Hacienda's first crop had good results. Sure, because they used a lot of guano and they cured the sickness continually. All of us who were there at the harvest noticed that the potatoes were really of good quality and they produced more than ours. Also, they were more resistant to the sickness, whereas ours died sadly. That's why some people planted on shares with the Hacienda, proving it. And this year, with the good results of that first harvest, more Vicosinos have become interested in planting them. Among them I count myself.

In order to plant next year, I have to save seed from this first harvest from planting on shares, for the purpose of planting on my own account. If the crop gets sick the only thing is to have patience. I'll keep on planting until it gives me a harvest in the end.

I think that planting on shares has good results because that way we have the opportunity to cure the plants with the medicines the Hacienda gives us. Still, judging it carefully, we are the ones who do almost all the work, in addition to planting in our own fields, and in the end we have to divide it in half during the harvest. As I said, judging it carefully, it isn't fair. (Soler, July 17.)

Generally, informants were interested in the innovations, even if they did not use them in their own farming:

Nicanor Sánchez: Last year I planted *mitzqa* potatoes in Cullhuash [a Vicos neighborhood] with a half sack of my own seed. I got out between five and six sacks. It depends on the year. Sometimes it comes out well and other times not. This year the sickness has damaged it. This year I planted on June 24, the same as ever. I always plant in Cullhuash.

I know about medicine for the potato sickness but because I don't have any money I can't buy it. I plant according to the old custom and not with the measure. Two years ago they started with planting by the measure. Enrique taught me. Before that, they didn't plant in ridges, but now they're planting like that. I didn't ask for it because I don't have the land to plant it. Besides, that calls for a lot of attention and we don't have sons who can help us. . . . I've seen the potato seed in the Hacienda when we were planting in Soqyacucho [the name of one of the Hacienda's fields]. The Hacienda's seed came out the same as the old, as I see it. . . .

Among Vicosinos, when people are out of potatoes they borrow them. Between friends, they return them little by little until they're even. I've talked with other Vicosinos about the new seed potatoes, and some want to plant them while others don't. Some don't have the land and others don't want to be attending it constantly. Nobody says that seed is no good. Everybody speaks positively about it. If I were to plant it, it would produce well for me. (Soto, July 16.)

In summary, Vicosinos who had the money bought the new seed potatoes from the Project and used them in customary ways. Many who did not have the money, and did not have the land for planting the potatoes either, went without. Others did not trust the share-planting arrangements, and many of these were fearful of the extra labor and attention that these would entail. Some planted on shares, despite what they saw as an unfavorable terms, because they had no other way of obtaining the seed and had no supplies of the old seed:

Manuel León: I already planted five *arrobas* of *paltaq* potatoes. This year I planted on shares with the Hacienda. I didn't plant any *papa variada*. I don't plant them because I don't have seed. I watched the people who planted a lot and got a big harvest. I just got interested and I spoke with Mario about planting on shares. Nobody told me to plant like that. I saw the *paltaq* potatoes planted here in the Hacienda. I've seen other kinds of potatoes planted in Marcará. It took the *paltaq* potato three weeks on the road to come here. That potato didn't exist here. It must be from the *mishtis*. Vicosinos talked about the *paltaq* potato and said it was good. Nobody says it's bad. It's good because it ripens quickly. It's good to eat because it's grainy. It cooks quickly. I'm satisfied. I'm very glad I planted this potato because I'll get a harvest, no matter how small it is. (Flores con Pablo Herrera, July 18.)

Narcizo Meza: There are many people who planted on shares with the Hacienda. The only advantage in that was in harvesting by some good fortune at least a small number of potatoes. That was by using the guano and the medicines from the Hacienda. Others planted so as not to remain behind, because many Vicosinos planted that way. Maybe they all knew the consequences, and even though they were aware that the results were not always favorable for the planter, the land operator, they wanted to eat a few potatoes. So they planted anyway even though it was unfavorable. (Soler, July 17.)

Tomás Modesto Colonia: This year I planted on shares with the Hacienda. I planted two sacks and some *arrobas*. They also gave me a sack of guano plus an *arroba*, which I put into the field while I was planting. It's not convenient to plant on shares with the Hacienda because they only give the seed, guano, and medicines. On our part we use up more time in the work we do and in guarding the potatoes. Even though it's not convenient for us, when we look at others planting we want to plant so as not to remain behind, so as not to look and see that only they have potatoes. Just the same, we're now thinking about planting on our own by buying the seeds and the guano. We'll do that next year.

We planted on shares because they agreed to cure the crop. That way we can save what we can't do by ourselves. We also plant our own seeds which haven't stopped being good. We can't cure them, though, because we can't buy the medicines. They're expensive and sometimes, even though it's cured, the crop goes bad. The plants don't resist.

(At this moment the informant asked me why I was writing. I told him it was to make a book, because if other people don't know about a book on how they live and the sicknesses of their crops they will believe that you live very well. "Sure," said the informant.) (Soler, July 15.)

The Project's efforts to improve potato production in Vicos were successful. Potatoes became an export commodity as well as a staple food. The community used potato profits, as I have noted, to purchase its own lands from its former owner and to add some additional agricultural plots to the total. It also used its income to invest in the Vicos school and other community endeavors. The intervention was a technical success. A number of Vicosinos, who were fortunate enough to have sufficient land, became commercial producers of potatoes, employing poorer Vicosinos as laborers in exchange for cash and/or produce. And as people became more productive and more involved in the shipment of potatoes to places outside the community the circulation of potatoes within Vicos undoubtedly slowed. As the Vicos population increased to 3,000, and then over 4,000, pressure on the land resulted in the parceling out of communal fields, so that the community's resources have lessened while those of individuals have increased. Parcellation occurred as soon as agrarian reform decrees were lifted, and even before, in accord with trends in Peru (see Lastarria-Cornhiel 1989, Carter and Alvarez 1989). This should come as no great surprise in view of the problems of collective agriculture. Peter Dorner (1992:54) writes of land reform in Latin America:

> The cooperative form of organization in agriculture is very complex. Even with supportive efforts by government agencies, problems of effective internal organization and of member commitment and morale will arise in group farming. It is a delusion to expect that group farms have such obvious benefits to members, or such decisive economic advantages, that organizational problems are easily overcome. These organizational problems arise largely because of ambiguities in the roles of both managers and members of group farms. Members are supposed to be both workers and participants in policymaking: managers are supposed to supervise the workers and at the same time be responsible to them. A common outcome of dilemma is ineffective management on the one hand and poor work discipline and absence of effective participation in policymaking by the members on the other.

However, factors like members' commitment and *esprit de corps* are relevant. Collective farming works in Israel. Tanya Korovkin (1990:136) begins the conclusion of her study of cotton cooperatives on the Peruvian coast with these words:

> The co-operative movement in Peru developed on a national scale during military populism characterized by increased state intervention in national economic development. Most agricultural production co-operatives were created directly by the state, on which they came to depend administratively, economically, and politically. Such state-sponsored

production units certainly had little in common with independent grassroots forms of co-operation generally identified with the concept of co-operativism. Their emergence and operation were determined by state policies rather than by the spontaneous actions of direct agricultural producers who had opted for co-operation of their own free will. As a consequence, an analysis of state policies for the co-operative agricultural sector is extremely important for understanding its functioning.

In her work Korovkin shows how the Peruvian military government of the early 1970s sabotaged its own creation by its inability to judge what was appropriate, its arbitrary regulation of the cooperatives, and its decapitalization of the agricultural sector in favor of import substitution industrialization. Much of this commentary can be applied to the Vicos Project's interventions.

With agrarian reform, which was decreed in 1969, by 1971 the hacienda system had disappeared from the Marcará River valley, except for the Hacienda Pachín, opposite Vicos, owned by Enrique Luna, who employed a number of Vicosinos there. I later learned that Pachín had been expropriated and its lands given to a community on that side of the river. Life was changing. Fluency in the Spanish language had diffused throughout Vicos and the neighboring communities, and everywhere I went I found *leídos* who were eager to speak with me. Some Vicosinos had graduated from secondary school and normal school, and two with professional certification were teaching in the Vicos school.[34] Vicos voters now constitute the majority in the District of Marcará, as I reported in Chapter 1, and have influenced the political structure of the micro-region. Mestizos in Marcará, and other towns and cities of the Callejón de Huaylas, now hesitate to employ the word "*indio*" openly, although in conversations with them in 1971 and 1977, the date of my last visit to the region, I could not read their minds. What does the potato experiment have to do with all that?

Henry Dobyns (1971:142-144) writes of "potato power" which "provided Vicosinos greater equality with nearby mestizo trading-town merchants," "permitted Vicosinos to escape from the local market to sell produce on the regional and national markets for cash," elevated the status of those Vicosinos who as "large-scale potato shippers" could "demand cabin space" in trucks, and "converted Vicos from a large exporter of unskilled labor to a steady small hirer of skilled labor while it cut local labor outflow to a comparative trickle." Dobyns views people's "power" as their "ability to influence others," adds that the Vicos people "acquired 'potato power' with the farming skills that they learned from . . . the farm practice change program," and notes, moreover, that this "potato power provoked many changes in dominant group behavior toward" the Vicosinos. His intention, without doubt, is to carry the notion of "potato power" no farther than this, but the idea captures my attention and my intention, insists on my extension and my invention beyond convention. Or maybe it is that my intention captures it. I can say that it exerts a power over me; indeed it hexes me. It asks me to interpret and to overinterpret. Because it awards a degree of economic power to Vicos and significant symbolic power to the Project.

The invention of "potato power" is the invention of a narrative. The potato has been transformed from food into a commodity, but not merely "a commodity," rather, a fetished[35] one with "power" to intervene in people's lives. What should impress us, though, is the utilization in a text of one story to hide or suppress others. "Potato power" can be viewed as only a mask for "money power," which is itself a mask for human relations in which some fortunate Vicosinos become potato merchants while other unfortunate ones become poorer and more dependent on such wealthy and powerful persons. It is this hidden text, folded into the text, that is present while it is absent. Pietz (1987:23) defines "the idea of the fetish" in terms of four themes:

(1) the untranscended materiality of the fetish: "matter," or the material object, is viewed as the locus of religious activity or psychic investment; (2) the radical historiality of the fetish's origin: arising in a singular event fixing together otherwise heterogeneous elements, the identity and power of the fetish consists in its enduring capacity to repeat the singular process of fixation, along with the resultant effect; (3) the dependence of the fetish for its meaning and value on a particular order of social relations, which it in turn reinforces; and (4) the active relation of the fetish object to the living body of an individual: a kind of external controlling organ directed by powers outside the affected person's will, the fetish represents a subversion of the ideal of the autonomously determined self.

But whose fetish? I have described here the Project's cathexis[36] of the potato. By now you can grasp the origin of this cathexis, its identity, and its power to affect lives. What remains for me to do is to elucidate the social relations it depended on. When we write of "commodity fetishism," we need to recall Karl Marx (1976:164-168) who employed the term in his analysis of capital. (We might very well read his text also as a highly personal statement):

The mystical character of the commodity does not therefore arise from its use-value. . . . It is nothing but the definite social relations between [people] themselves which assumes here, for them, the fantastic form of a relation between things. In order, therefore, to find an analogy we must take flight into the misty realm of religion. There the products of the human brain appear as autonomous figures endowed with a life of their own, which enter into relations both with each other and with the human race. So it is in the world of commodities with the products of [people's] hands. I call this the fetishism which attaches itself to the products of labour as soon as they are produced as commodities, and is therefore inseparable from the production of commodities. . . . [T]his fetishism of the world of commodities arises from the peculiar social character of the labour which produces them. . . . To the producers, therefore, the social relations between their private labours appear as what they are, i.e. they do not appear as direct social relations between persons in their work, but rather as material relations between persons and social relations between things. . . . Value . . . transforms every product of labour into a social hieroglyphic. . . . [Magnitudes of value] vary continually, independently of the will, foreknowledge and actions of the exchangers. Their own movement within society has for them the form of a movement made by things, and these things, far from being under their control, in fact, control them.[37]

"Potato power" conceals the unequal relations of small farmers and micro-holders in Vicos and commodity exchange with buyers outside the community. It conceals class variables which intervene to benefit some producers but not all. As a celebration of the Project's achievement it would be, thus, perverted, inverted, an upside-down monument. But let us penetrate deeper into the fetish. Michael Taussig (1992:4-5) comments on Karl Marx's conception in which "things acquired the properties of persons, and persons became thing-like":

The matter of factness of production becomes anything but matter-of-fact, and facticity itself is rendered marvelous, mist-enveloped regions of frozen movement, projections at a standstill, in which things that come from the hands of people change place with persons, the inside changes place with the outside as commodities erase the social nexus imploded within and become self-activating spirit, even Godlike, 'things-in-themselves.'"

Following Derrida, John Caputo (1977b:143) comments:

Marx is both for and against ghosts. He both exorcises them and believes in them—since an exorcist is someone who believes in ghosts, who takes them seriously—but without quite being able to monitor these operations. Marx is in a double bind. On the one hand, he exorcises the ghost of the commodity, the spectral table that stands up on its feet and discourses with other commodities. He reduces that specter back to the artifactual, technical body that is constituted by labor. But, on the other hand, he founds this exorcism of the ghost on a pre-deconstructive "critique," on an "ontology" of the presence of what is really real that aims at dissipating this phantom into thin air, conjuring it away inasmuch as the real forces of production have no more to do with these fantastic beings than does a railway with Hegelian philosophy.

Baudrillard (1981:88-93) offers a critique of Marx's concept which outlines the "process whereby the concrete social values of labor and exchange . . . are erected into transcendent ideological values" which regulate "all alienated behavior." It is a "successor to a more archaic fetishism and religious mystification ('the opium of the people')." Marx attached the concept of commodity fetishism to money but it has been expanded into a "diffuse, exploded and idolatrous vision of the consumption environment . . . in the guise of a disturbing attack on the system." Baudrillard feels it is a "dangerous" term "because it short circuits analysis" and "because since the 18th century it has conducted the whole repertoire of occidental Christian and humanist ideology, as orchestrated by colonists, ethnologists and missionaries." The metaphor of fetishism has not rid itself of "this moral and rationalistic connotation" but has continued as "the recurrent leitmotiv of the analysis of 'magical thinking,' whether that of the Bantu tribes or that of modern metropolitan hordes." It is extended into the modern social context by enmeshing "critical analysis . . . within the subtle trap of a rationalistic anthropology." Marxism refers "all the problems of 'fetishism' back to superstructural mechanisms of false consciousness" and thereby prevents analysis of "the actual process of ideological labor." Baudrillard quips, "The term 'fetishism' almost has a life of its own." In place of serving "as a metalanguage for the magical thinking of others, it turns against those who use it, and surreptitiously exposes their own magical thinking." Psychoanalytic theory, Baudrillard continues, returns "fetishism to its context within a perverse *structure* that perhaps underlies all desire," and thus "it becomes an analytic concept for a theory of perversion." Meanwhile, the word "fetish" has become semantically distorted: it refers to a force, a supernatural property of the object and hence to a similar magical potential in the subject," but it originally "signified exactly the opposite: a *fabrication*, an artifact, a labor of appearances and signs." If we use the concept of fetishism we need to recognize that it is "not a fetishism of the signified, a fetishism of substances and values . . . but a "fetishism of the signifier . . . not the passion . . . for substances" but the "passion for the code," which makes it possible to manipulate them abstractly. Consequently, fetishism, rather than sanctifying objects or values, "is the sanctification of the system as such, of the commodity as system." Thus, it is not that money "grows" or "talks," popular metaphors in our society, or that there is "smart" money and "mad" money and "bad" money, or that money is said to "work" for one, but that money is said to dissolve everything, including love and hate. Nowhere does Baudrillard suggest that we should stop using the term "commodity fetishism," but his discussion is aimed at showing how tricky it is to use it. Of all that he has to say here, the point that I think has significance for the Vicos case we have been exploring is that fetishing is not a permanent human condition, that fetishing is not a human mental "structure," and that Vicosinos are not caught on the binary horns of the dilemma of choosing between "God, the saints, and the mountain spirits" on one hand, and "potato power" or "money power" on the other. This is Taussig's (1980:230) aim in calling for "a nonfetishized mode of understanding human relations and society." Thus, Vicosinos would not have to mime the fetishing of the developers but could grow and develop on their own.

Bhabha (1994:91) points to the resemblance between fetishing and mimesis: "Under cover of camouflage, mimicry, like the fetish, is a part-object that radically revalues the normative knowledges of the priority of race, writing, history. For the fetish mimes the forms of authority at the point at which it deauthorizes them. Similarly, mimicry rearticulates presence in terms of its 'otherness,' that which it disavows." This is more than tricky; it is a downright danger. Taussig (1997:16-18) points out "the magic of mimesis wherein the replication, the copy, acquires the power of the represented." He says of "Enlightenment": "By their little bonfire on the edge of the forest, how ardently these gringos labor for the abstract universal! But what of the pestilent and uncontrolable spirit gringos thereby released, dancing wildly through the flames? Where will their power, the power of magical mimesis reemerge?" Stephen Tyler (1987:55) writes:

> Mimesis does not ensure automatic communication;   it fosters idiosyncrasy. The idea of mimesis harbors an inherent contradiction. While it provides the means of knowing whatever it mimics–even if that is only itself–it reveals itself as a trick, a sleight-of-hand, it gives and takes away at the same time. . . . A better mimesis, then, is a better trick, a better piece of illusory play that points to the mastery of magical means by a trickster, sorcerer, demon, a knowing consciousness. The master of tricks is the one who plays tricks best, whose technique and style produce illusions so brilliant and captivating that they are valued above the reality they both obscure and reveal, not because they are understood but because they seem to be just beyond the limit of understanding at the same time as they are within it.

Timothy Mitchell (1991:18-21) comments: "To the mechanism of misrepresentation by which power operates, Marx opposed a representation of the way things intrinsically are, in their transparent and rational reality. . . . The problem with such an explanation was that, in revealing power to work through *mis*representation, it left representation itself unquestioned. . . . Marx himself, although he wanted none of the accompanying political passivity, conceived of an essential separation between the person and an object-world in the same way, in terms of a structure or plan existing apart from things themselves." We can take another, de-essentialized look at Vicos, perhaps a "de-fetished" (cf. Miller 1997:16-17) one at the commodity.

Money was not something new to Vicosinos in 1953, although people did not have much of it. The interview materials I have examined here indicate that informants were quite sensitive to commodity prices. This has also been my personal experience as well, in both Hualcán and Vicos, where friends and acquaintances would strike up conversations by asking me how much everything associated with me cost, from hat to shoes and including notebook, pencil, camera, film, candle, canteen, primus stove, soap, toothbrush and toothpaste, toilet paper, etc., etc. At the beginning of my stay in the Callejón de Huaylas, this seemed intrusive to me, and even obscene, for like Freud in nineteenth-century Vienna I grew up believing that money was dirty and that I should wash my hands after touching it. In the Andes I came to learn that the topics of money and prices were not only ways of being friendly but that they were of great interest, relevance, and fascination, much like the weather in North America, and especially in West Texas! Then, what if money were neither good nor bad but neutral as Olivia Harris (1989:244) suggests?[38] Just as in her Aymara example, in Ancash Quechua the word *rantin* applies to both market exchange for cash *and* reciprocity and one can make a ceremonial gift as *qellay*, the supporter of a festive sponsor, in either cash or festive supplies. Maurice Bloch (1989:167) observes that: "It is in European culture that money is far from morally neutral and its moral charge hinders conversion from one sphere of activity to another." And he adds, with regard to the "received wisdom" of anthropological discourse which "contrasts commercial exchange and gifts" as antithetical: "In societies where only gift exchange prevails, there is no money, but with the coming of commerce money makes its appearance. As a result the introduction of money comes to signify almost automatically an assault on a disinterested autarchic society dominated by pure morality" (169). Arjun Appadurai (1986:11) writes:

> The exaggeration and reification of the contrast between gift and commodity in anthropological writing has many sources. Among them

are the tendency to romanticize small-scale societies; to conflate use value (in Marx's sense) with *gemeinschaft* (in Toennies's sense); the tendency to forget that capitalist societies, too, operate according to cultural designs; the proclivity to marginalize and underplay the calculative, impersonal and self-aggrandizing features of noncapitalist societies. These tendencies, in turn are a product of an oversimplified view of the opposition between Mauss and Marx. . . .

Olivia Harris (1989:236) similarly focuses on the binary opposition of these two kinds of society:

The contrast between non-monetary and monetary economies is also built into the very structure of anthropology as a discipline, whose theories are so often articulated around a play of opposites: primitive and civilized, traditional and modern, pre-capitalist and capitalist, non-literate and literate. Money and markets, their presence or absence, have provided a central axis along which historical reality has been divided into two polarized and contrasted fields. The appearance of money then becomes an index of inexorable transition . . . from a previous state, subsistence-oriented and based on use-values, to the economy that we know, based on exchange-value, dominated by money and the market.

Harris (237) then points out that Marx's conception of "natural economy" implies "that there is something *unnatural* about exchange," and that "lurking in his writing is an implicit critique of money itself, and thus, since his concept of exchange relies so heavily on *monetary* exchange, also a critique of exchange." Jonathan Parry (1989:64-66) also challenges a discourse based on the radical opposition of two types of exchange, for gifts, too, may "embody evil and danger," and "it becomes clear that this picture must be qualified, for neither gift exchange nor commodity exchange constitute morally homogeneous and undifferentiated categories." And Alfred Gell (1992:142) comments that prestation has "had a favorable press in anthropology" while "'commodities' an unfavorable one," and he notes: "Objects are alienated in gift exchanges. . . . What is not 'alienated' in gift-giving is not the gift-object itself, but that which *cannot* be alienated, namely, the social identity of the donor, which still attaches to the object after it has been given away."

Derrida (1992a:7) allows the gift to deconstruct[39]: the "gift" is "aneconomic," it is, indeed, not simply an impossibility but "*the* impossible. The very figure of the impossible. It announces itself, gives itself to be thought as the impossible." And: "For there to be a gift, there must be no reciprocity, return, exchange, countergift, or debt. If the other *gives* me back or *owes* me or has to give me back what I give him or her, there will not have been a gift, whether this restitution is immediate or whether it is programmed by a complex calculation of a long-term deferral or difference" (12). Consequently:

> For there to be a gift, not only must the donor or donee not perceive or receive the gift as such, have no consciousness of it, no memory, no recognition; he or she must also forget it right away and moreover this forgetting must be so radical that it exceeds even the psychoanalytic categoriality of forgetting in the sense of repression. It must not give rise to any of the repressions (originary or secondary) that reconstitute debt and exchange by putting it in reserve, by keeping or saving up what is forgotten, repressed, or censured. Repression does not destroy or annul anything; it keeps by displacing. Its operation is systemic or topological; it always consists of keeping by exchanging places. And, by keeping the meaning of the gift, repression annuls it in symbolic recognition. However unconscious this recognition may be, it is effective and can be verified in no better fashion than by its effects or by the symptoms it yields up for decoding. (16.)

We may well ask at this point: which, really, is haunted, money or the gift or the impecunious Marx supported by Engels? The latter relationship, an oral dependency, between the two nineteenth-century revolutionaries was "natural" enough. Would any other have been "unnatural"?[40] Andrew Parker (1993:23) proposes, irreverently and intriguingly, "a *sexual* reading of Marx's texts, a reading that could map the (de)structuring effects of eroticism even–or especially–in works whose subjects seem utterly unsexy." Parker (34) concludes, after examining the Engels-Marx correspondence: "What Engels's and Marx's letters both put into play . . . is a way of safely raising something filthy between themselves. While many scholars have noted (how could they not?) that their correspondence is smeared liberally with excremental imagery, these same readers never acknowledge that shit can acquire significance only by activating an economy of anal pleasures, desires, and attachments." There is nothing to suggest that Engels and Marx were anything but homophobic and heterosexist; indeed, the heterosexism in Marx's emphasis on production and reproduction "is not to be dismissed as merely figural, for Marx views labor invariably" as productive of human life (35).[41]

My purpose is neither to critique a theory of commodity fetishism that is well over a century old and well established, nor to defame sacred texts or their authors. Marx's analysis of the excessive cruelty, obsessive accumulation, ruthless destruction (its poisoning of our atmosphere and waters may well put an end to the human race before scholars finish debating whether or not Marx's prediction of the demise of capitalism was "correct"), and self-satisfied rationality of capitalism in modern times was, is, and will continue to be a monumental achievement and very libidinal as well. I think it was also overdetermined to the extent that it reflects his obsession with his work, his ruthless creativity, his identity crisis,[42] and the harm inflicted on persons close to him by the poverty he put them through. We can also look at the twentieth-century consequences of Marxism which Bourdieu (2000a:41) aptly characterizes as "irresponsible utopianism and unrealistic radicality": the "communist" dictatorships of Stalin, Mao and others, years of "cultural revolution," the invention of "socialist realism," the international paranoia resulting in the Cold War, and the bullying of small and weak countries by both sides, not to omit mention of the intellectual stagnation induced by the essentializing of concepts like "capitalism,"[43] "class," "mode of production," "surplus value," and "labor power." It even seems, now, that "Marxists," like capitalists who preach the sanctity of private property, "own" Marx and Marxism. Derrida (1999a:222) is eloquent concerning one author's "proprietorial" claims which fetish Marx's work:

> What will never cease to amaze me about the jealous possessiveness of so many Marxists, and what amazes me even more in *this* instance, is not only what is *always* a bit comic about a property claim, and comic in a way that is even more theatrical when what is involved is an inheritance, a textual inheritance, and still more pathetic, the appropriation of an inheritance named "Marx"! No, what I always wonder, and even more in *this* instance, is where the author thinks the presumptive property deeds are. In the name of what, on the basis of what claim, exactly, does one even dare *confess* a "proprietorial reaction"? Merely making such a confession presupposes that a title deed has been duly authenticated, so that one can adamantly continue to invoke it in defending one's property.

Yet we all possess Marx as he possesses us. Derrida (2001b:549) points out, "[W]e are, amongst other things, inheritors of Marx and marxism. . . . [T]his involves an event which nothing and no one can eradicate, not even–in fact, especially not–the monstrosity of totalitarianism (all the various totalitarianisms, and there were several of them, which were in part linked to marxism, and which cannot be seen as mere perversions or distortions of the inheritance). Even people who have never read Marx, or so much as heard of him, are Marx's heirs, and so are the anti-communists and anti-marxists. And then, you cannot inherit from Marx without also inheriting from Shakespeare, the Bible, and much else besides." Caputo (1977b:146) points to the relevance of Marx's messianism:

> The ghost, the *revenant*, is the ever recurrent specter, the messianic

prospect of the *tout autre* who haunts our self-presence, our self-sufficiency, who disturbs the order of the same, who comes to us as the voice of the dead to whom we bear a responsibility, and as the voice of the ones still to come, as those others, other-than-the-living present who lay claim to us. That coming, that *à venir*, that coming messianic figure, is the religious automatism that Marx knew but did not know, that he would not let himself know, the specter with a life and operation all its own.

But let us focus again on Vicos. I end this chapter simply by observing that if indeed the slowing of the circulation of potatoes in Vicos is the slowing of the circulation of people, I have the strong conviction that the Vicosino imagination will invent other ways of cementing social bonds. Certainly, the strong links which Vicosino migrants maintain with their kindreds in Vicos, a phenomenon which has been observed in many communities by countless researchers in Peru for the last forty years, is not what we might expect if commerce, or "potato power," really had eroded them. For example, Karsten Paerregaard (1997a:55) demonstrates for Tapay, in the Colca Valley, "how cultural creativity and invention come into play in a deterritorialized culture" among migrants in urban areas who "create new individual livelihoods and establish different forms of communal life." In "the encounter between imagined place and lived space . . . [a] strong sense of attachment to the native village . . . persists among most . . ., evoking different notions and images of rural life." This can be said of Vicos, and so I think that the future of Vicosinos is not something to be feared, decried, or put off, but rather something to be celebrated. At the same time, we may also ask: what else is "potato power" hiding?

Pierre Bourdieu (1984:164) suggests that "what the competitive struggle makes everlasting is not different conditions but the difference between conditions." In other words, it is not only Vicosinos who are changing. While they become teachers, mechanics, and merchants, Enrique Luna is busy assembling a modest fleet of trucks and becoming a regional beer distributor. Conditions in Vicos have indeed changed, but while much has improved, much is reproduced. Bourdieu (165) continues: "Competitive struggle is the form of class[44] struggle which the dominated classes allow to be imposed on them when they accept the stakes offered by the dominant classes. It is an integrative struggle and, by virtue of the initial handicaps, a reproductive struggle, since those who enter this chase, in which they are beaten before they start, as the constancy of the gaps testifies, implicitly recognize the legitimacy of the goals pursued by those whom they pursue, by the mere fact of taking part." Thus, no amount of "potato power" will extend the "trajectories" of Vicosinos in such a way as to reverse their subaltern status in relation to those who dominate them. That is, until the field changes or is changed. Because power is not a "thing" but a social relation. Foucault (1990:94) writes: "Power is not something that is acquired, seized, or shared, something that one holds on to or allows to slip away; power is exercised from innumerable points, in the interplay of nonegalitarian and mobile relations." So the same things always already change and everything remains different. Difference is another face of resemblance.

Notes

1. The materials presented in this chapter originally appeared as "Nuevas semillas de papa para Vicos: cambio agrícola en los Andes," *América Indígena*, 31(1):51-83, 1971. It appeared in monograph form, revised and augmented by the results of two months' field work in Vicos later in 1971, as *Changing Vicos Agriculture*, Special Study No. 15, Council on International Studies, State University of New York at Buffalo. Buffalo, New York, 1972. It is further revised and expanded here. I am glad to acknowledge the generosity of Professor Rose K. Goldsen who passed along the Methodology Project files to me in 1968. The original field notes of the interviews reproduced here are on file in the archives of the Vicos Project, Karl Korch Library, Cornell University. I also want to thank Profesor Urbano Sánchez for his many kindnesses, hospitality, and assistance while I was in Vicos in 1971. Parts of this chapter appear in elaborated form in Stein (2000b, n.d.a).

2. This is nothing new. Charles Walker (1999:78) writes of Peruvian history: "From the conquistadors in the sixteenth century to the caciques interinos [local officials] in the final colonial decades (and into the republican period), officials argued that because Indians were irrational and infantile, they needed the guidance or prodding of outsiders."

3. In the same passage, Bhabha continues: "Fixity as the sign of cultural/historical/racial difference in the discourse of colonialism, is a paradoxical mode of representation: it connotes rigidity and an unchanging order as well as disorder, degeneracy and daemonic repetition."

4. Cf. José Carlos Mariátegui (1970:117) who said: "True revolutionaries never proceed as if history began with them."

5. Hayden White (1978:66) comments on Marx's method: "Marx . . . purports to be able to predict the specific form of the next phase of the whole process by a[n] . . . organicism integration of all of the significant data of social history. But he claims to justify this predictive operation by virtue of the mechanistic reduction of those data to the status of functions of general laws of cause and effect that are

universally operative throughout all of history."

6. I have elaborated on this topic in Stein (n.d.c).

7. Potatoes are first in importance at higher altitudes in the Andes. Maria Lagos (1994:79) writes of Sank'ayani, a community located at 3,500-4000 meters above sea level in the Cochabamba mountains of Bolivia: "The importance of potatoes in the household economy cannot be overemphasized. Campesinos take particular interest and care when farming potatoes, since it requires the largest investment of labor and inputs. Potatoes are their main staple as well as their principal means of market and barter exchange." She follows this with an excellent discussion of potato-cropping (79-86) which offers data that suggest many comparisons and contrasts with Vicos.

8. Varayoq means "envarados" in Spanish, "those who hold staves of office." These consist in Vicos of a body of seventeen ranked community authorities who regulate water management during the dry season, supervise corvée labor, direct the performance of religious rituals through the year, and settle land and other disputes. In the last century they collected the head tax which funded both regional and national government. They carry whips which in former times were used to punish wrong-doers. They also intervene in cases like the one discussed here, which combines physical aggression with family crime, where sinful behavior affects the well being of the community. (See Vázquez 1964.) They accumulate "symbolic capital"–which Pierre Bourdieu (1990:120) says "is always very expensive in material terms"–by engaging in progressively more costly festive celebrations as they rise in rank. Varayoq authority has, in recent years, been stripped from them by the formation of a producers' cooperative in Vicos, after the abolition of the hacienda system, as well as by Peruvian governmental intervention in and regulation of registered "comunidades campesinas," rural communities. In the late 1950s a system of delegados was installed for the ten zones of Vicos, a new set of elected leaders who took over most varayoq functions, except the festive ones. Ghersi (1961, III:156-158) provides a brief description of the varayoq in the District of Marcará. For the functioning of the authorities in Hualcán and the District of Carhuaz, a region just to the north of the District of Marcará, see Stein (1961). See also Mayer (2002:125-126) for a description of this "civil religious hierarchy in Tangor, a community located south of the Callejón de Huaylas.

9. A more extended discussion of this interview protocol is to be found in Stein (n.d.a).

10. Annette Weiner (1992:33) writes: "Whereas other alienable properties are exchanged against each other, inalienable possessions" as "symbolic repositories of genealogies and historical events, their unique, subjective identity gives them absolute value placing them above the exchangeability of one thing for another."

She concludes that "it is the tenacious anthropological belief in the inherent nature of the norm of reciprocity that impedes the examination of the particular cultural conclusions that empower the owners of inalienable possessions with hegemonic dominance over others. It is, then, not the hoary idea of a return gift that generates the thrust of exchange, but the radiating power of keeping inalienable possessions out of exchange. For even in the most mundane exchanges of greetings or Christmas cards, the social identities of the participants–what they have that makes them different from each other–color the styles, actions, and meanings that create the exchange."

11. The Vicos materials, especially Alfonso Cruz's narrative, resemble myths from other parts of Peru. My reading of Billie Jean Isbell's (1998:287) account of *arpilleras*, pictures on cloth, made by Lima refugees from the war in Ayacucho, gives me a feeling of familiarity with the structure of this new content in which surveillance of people is carried on by a radio tower instead of God and helicopters take the place of *vientos*: "Two icons of power predominate in their depictions of violence. One of these is a large, orange radio tower, placed at the center of many scenes. For arpillera makers, the tower is something like a 'postintramodern' version of Foucault's panopticon. Women told me that the tower is always listening. It transmits messages that bring the helicopters and troops. The helicopter is the other predominant icon. Like motorized condors, helicopters are shown snatching victims away. In one scene, for example, a green helicopter is in the foreground, and armed men are loading bound captives; two helicopters hover overhead, one with a man, also bound, dangling by a rope underneath. The creator of this arpillera explained: 'The helicopters then fly over the mountains and the soldiers cut the rope; the man falls into a ravine, never to be found . . .'" Perhaps what is familiar is an Andean theme: *poor people are punished and suffer for sins that others commit.* This is rather different from the guilty self-punishment of the West.

12. Orin Starn (1994:19) suggests that "the absence of the term 'Andean' in the self-description of most inhabitants of the [Andes] mountains should be a clue to its origins in the imagination and usage of outside observers. Depending on the situation, peasants identify themselves by their nation, religion, province, village, or family." True in a way, but I do not think that if I refer to Vicos as an Andean community, or Vicos discourse as an Andean one, that I am imagining communities and discourses that do not really exist. In her reply to Starn, Olivia Harris (1994:27) states: "The concept of 'the Andean' as developed within the subfield is grounded in the archaeological horizons, especially the Late Horizon of the Inca state. The reaches of Andean anthropology in this sense are those of Tawantinsuyu [the Inca polity]. The effects of Inca policies were profound and in their turn shaped the policies of early Spanish administration. There is a striking parallelism with the concept of Europe; there is general agreement that the effects of the Roman empire–both the Classical polity and medieval Christendom–were

decisive in establishing a level of shared meanings that accompanied the play of diversity." Starn (1999:20) has modified his position: "I was wrong as well as right. Not all of the many studies were as guilty of the sins of stereotyping and exoticism as I had assumed. Yet many anthropologists indeed failed to reckon with the full extent of flux and mixture in the Andes. . . . If a negatigve view had coded the culture of the Andes as a drag on development and progress, anthropologists inverted the equation to present it as a storehouse of strength and dignity . . . . Such scholarship countered the stigmatization of the peasantry as backward and savage, but left intact and even furthered the presumption of a radical split between the rural and the urban, the United States and Latin America, and the Andes and the West."

13. David Gow's (1976) dissertation has, and most regrettably, never been formally published. It is both an excellent ethnography and a touching autobiography in which the author does not hesitate to reveal himself.

14. Leacock and Lee (1982:7-9) define a "foraging mode of production" for "band societies." It in no way resembles what I am discussing here, although I think the two cases share a basic element which is the exploitation of the habitat for subsistence purposes without the accumulation of what Eric Wolf (1966:8-9) would probably call a "replacement fund," or any other kind of fund for that matter!

15. The informant appears to be confused as to events at an earlier time when a number of Vicosinos, with the help of some mestizos in Marcará, negotiated with the Beneficencia Pública de Huaraz with the object of renting Vicos. The Beneficencia, composed of course by regional landed interests who had no wish to see workers in control of any hacienda, refused. See Barnett (1960) for accounts of several protest movements, including this one, over the last century. I discovered an earlier one in the archives of the Beneficencia Pública de Lima, an earlier owner of Vicos. See Stein (1991b).

16. There are literally hundreds of varieties of potatoes in the Andes. New ones are constantly coming into being through genetic recombination and hybridization with wild species of *Solanum* (see Salaman 1985:159-187).

17. For a recent and excellent study see Enrique Mayer's (2002:105-142) essay, "The rules of the game in Andean reciprocity."

18. The Inter-American Cooperative Food Production Service was founded in 1943 through the U. S. Embassy as an autonomous unit of the Peruvian Ministry of Agriculture in response to the critical wartime shortage of food in the country due to curtailments of imports. (See Ford 1955:139-141 and Mosher 1957:47.) The role of the agronomists was strategic. Whyte (1965:42) points out that the

Vicos Project anthropologists had little knowledge of agriculture: "Their spectacular success depended upon helping the Vicosinos to reorganize their ways of working and thinking *and* establishing effective communication between the community and the men who possessed the technical knowledge of agriculture."

19. Stakman, Bradfield, and Mangelsdorf (1967:202) point out that effective demonstration consists of extraordinary yields: "A demonstration showing a rise of 20 to 30 per cent resulting from a single practice [has] much less impact, because farmers [have] often seen variations of this magnitude occur from year to year as a result of natural causes."

20. 135 Vicosinos participated in share-planting during the third season, 1954 (Vázquez 1955:6), and 158 during the fourth season (Garrido-Lecca 1965:39), after which share-planting was abandoned. For survey research results relating to agricultural innovation in Vicos and changing attitudes over the decade, 1953-1963, see Alers 1966:109-126.

21. Garrido-Lecca (1965:47) provides details of the transaction on July 13, 1962: "A down payment was made to the Beneficencia Pública de Huaraz of one and a half million soles ($55,865), of which the community contributed one half million ($18,620) and the remaining million ($37,245) was covered by the Peruvian Government in a twenty-year interest-free loan. The community owed another one-half million to the Beneficencia payable during the following three years. The community is paying S/ 166,666.67 per year to the Beneficencia and S/ 50,000 per year to the Government."

22. In addition to these factors, the truck also failed because it, plus a jeep and an unused tractor that had been donated by North Americans, did not constitute a motor pool large enough to keep a full-time mechanic busy. A member of the household in which I lived in 1971, Francisco Sánchez, worked as a mechanic in a shop in Huaraz and came home to Vicos only on weekends. I was told by Vicosinos that repair shops in Huaraz overcharged them for work done on the truck, and that the sale of the truck was economically an advantage to Vicos.

23. In his first "Progress Report," Holmberg (1952:9) states that as f June 22, 1952: "[W]e had hoped to have a new school in operation by May of this year. However, due to an exceptionally long rainy season which prevented us from making adobes, tile and other necessary materials, we are only now getting underway in the construction of the new school in collaboration with the Indians. . . . At present educational and teaching facilities are extremely inadequate. Despite this fact, we have made a number of innovations which have helped to raise the enrollment from about 20 to 60 students. In part this may be due to the providing of a hot plate at lunch time." The new school was completed in 1953, and when I visited in 1971 its enrollment was over 300 pupils.
    Dobyns, Doughty, and Holmberg (n.d.:61) note that the building of the school

led to other development in Vicos: "The school construction program launched in 1952 was used by the Project to lay the foundations of a specialized construction industry in Vicos. The Project hired mestizo journeymen masons and carpenters to act as foremen on the school building effort, construction of quarters for Project personnel, warehousing, teachers' quarters, etc., and to teach the [Vicosinos] their skills. No significant degree of specialization in the building trades had existed previously in Vicos. Each Vicos farmer was approximately as skillful as every other Vicos farmer at building the traditional local house, and such unspecialized labor was readily exchanged between relatives in the reciprocal ceremonial labor exchange institutions that built houses. The intervention of the Project quickly created a competent carpenter and a competent mason. Later, another Vicosino hired out to a mestizo roof tile maker until he learned to make and bake tiles, and could purchase the appropriate tools. Within a few years, Vicosinos learned that contracting a construction job to these specialists cost less than sponsoring the traditional labor exchange bee [the *minka*], and produced a higher quality building because of the greater skill and soberness of the new specialists."

These are indeed accomplishments, but I cannot resist the sad comment, "No more partying, boys and girls!" Alberto Cheng Hurtado (1958:20-21) writes of the *minka*: "It is a source of social integration because its regular practice establishes strong ties of cohesion in the group which carries out a *minka*. . . . It is also a source of social tension and insecurity. The host's "obligations" require a large supply of food and money because if his "attentions" are bad he will be considered stingy, someone who does not know how to appreciate the work of those who attend. . . . It is a source of recreation and relaxation. When the work is done intimate gatherings take place which are characterized by the drunkenness of those present."

24. When I first encountered statements regarding the use of guinea pig manure I believed that they were a reflection of Vicos wit, rather than agricultural practice. How could those pathetic specks of fecal matter be of service to anyone? In his study of Andean guinea pig production Morales (1995:21) describes an Ecuadorian family thus: "This family has about twenty-five cuys that are kept under one of the beds. When the food waste and manure under the bedstead in the bedroom make up a thick layer of humid fertilizer, the cuys are removed to the kitchen. The cuy fertilizer is shoveled out into the yard to be dried and used in the corn plot or the orchard in the backyard."

25. To bring Andean fat-stealing up to date, Andrew Orta (n.d.:3) reports that in Bolivia, where the frightening figure is known as a *kharikhari*: "[W]hile the colonial fat extractor is a robed monk, contemporary kharikhari appear as development workers and engineers, schoolteachers and politicians, working the will of such distant powers as the World Bank. In the mines, kharisiris [another term for fat-stealers] operate out of laboratories and concentration plants and may use pumps and picks to extract their victim's fat. . . . The modern-day kharikhari has traded in his black mule for a red Toyota land-rover."

26. According to Shane Greene (n.d.), vampire stories about outsiders are found not only among Andean farmers and tropical forest people (his case is from the Aguaruna in northeast Peru) but constitute a global phenomenon.

27. Deborah Poole (1988) provides a more extended discussion of these local bosses. See also the relevant portion of Stein (n.d.c).

28. But impolite when Luna, a mestizo, uses it to address Leiva, an army veteran who knows some Spanish. A mestizo would never use terms like *señor* or *caballero*, both variants of "sir," with a worker. Luna *could* have addressed him as "Don Eugenio."

29. Laura Macdonald (1995:203) characterizes "progressive" international non-governmental organizations as ones with "[a]n explicitly political strategy of empowerment, involving not only greater control by community members at the local level but also their involvement in broader social movements seeking increased political participation by excluded groups in national decision-making processes." A half century ago, early development discourse could not conceive of such a possibility.

30. Dobyns and Vázquez (1964:30-31) have this to say about Enrique Luna: "He was the overseer of the Vicos manor for many years prior to the intervention of the Cornell-Peru Project. With unusual vision, he grasped the aims of the scientific experiment in cultural change, and participated whole-heartedly in the process. He stayed on as . . . foreman until the Indians of Vicos assumed responsibility for directing their own affairs in 1956. He operates a store in Marcará and owns mining and livestock interests." Vicosinos expressed rather different opinions of him. I believe that he was kept on the Project staff in large part to provide a useful connection with mestizos in Marcará and Carhuaz. This may have been highly relevant to the survival of the Project but his continued presence as a "master" may have defeated many of its purposes during its early years. Luna was fluent in both local Quechua and Spanish, a condition that no North American Field Director of the Project ever achieved.

The late Mario C. Vázquez grew up in Aquia, a small town in the Province of Chiquián. His Quechua, although it could be easily understood, marked him as a stranger to Vicosinos. He engaged in ethnographic work there, beginning in 1949, but I think he was never able to shift completely away from the *Indigenista* (i.e., "Indianist" who is not "Indian") discourse of his populist political past.

31. Alberto Cheng Hurtado (1958:19-20) defines the *minka* in Vicos: "It consists in the giving of services in exchange for food and comforts [i.e., alcoholic beverages and coca] during the time the job lasts. The host or "owner" of the *minka* also feeds the relatives of his guests when the latter request it. . . . It is not practiced only by men. Women heads of family (independent single women, separated married ones, and widows) also participate; it includes as well the

feeble and handicapped, like young orphans, sick people or invalids, and old persons whose existence is thereby assured. . . . It does not necessarily imply *rantín*, reciprocity, even when a person responds to an invitation with the feeling of settling a debt and indebting the host to the guest. . . . It takes place when the labor required for a task demands greater force than a person or household can provide."

32. It is regrettable that the three student interviewers did not ask women their opinions of the new potatoes, especially in view of the symbolic significance of the hole. At the same time, it is possible that men's responses also reflected family discussions.

33. Susan Poats (1982b:11) says of her taste-test sample: "The "ideal" type of potato for these Peruvian consumers is high in dry matter content, giving it its 'floury' taste. This taste is sought out in potatoes and those which come nearest to the "ideal" type of 'floury' taste the best. However, along with this 'ideal' type is a recognition that certain potatoes should be prepared in certain ways. For boiling . . . the preferred potato is one that is 'floury.' For frying, however, a less 'floury,' more 'aguachenta' potato is desired since they normally absorb more oil. These same 'aguachenta' potatoes are not usually prepared by boiling."

34. One of these teachers was the object of controversy in Vicos during my visit. A group of parents was petitioning the Ministry of Education in order to effect his removal. They charged he was rude to his pupils and used the epithet "*indio*" with reference to them and their families.

35. I am using "fetish" as a verb, "to fetish," as it was used in the fetish discourse of the eighteenth century. See Pietz (1988:111). I prefer the term "fetishing" to "fetishism" because the "-ism" in the latter simply does not place it with other "-isms" like communism, patriotism, and sexism–because communists are not always communal, patriots are not always patriotic, and sexists also pretend to be what they are not, whereas a fetisher always fetishes.

Vitebsky (1992:244) makes a most interesting observation of Native Siberians as the Soviet Union was dissolving: "what has certainly disappeared from shamanism is its -ism," and "the move toward a post-socialist society may include an element of re-shamanizing." I also eschew "fetishist" and lean toward "fetisher" for the same reasons. I retain the older vocabulary in quotations, however.

36. "Cathexis" refers generally to an emotional investment in something. Exaggeration is not pathology but nevertheless it may assist readers to include here a statement by Laplanche and Pontalis (1973:65): "There are certain pathological conditions which seem to leave us no alternative but to postulate that the subject draws on a specific quantity of energy which he [sic] distributes in variable proportions in his relationships with objects and with himself. In a state such as mourning, for example, the manifest impoverishment of the subject's

relational life is to be explained by a hypercathexis of the lost object, and from this we can only infer that a veritable balance of energy holds sway over the distribution of the various cathexes of external or phantasies objects, of the subject's own body, of his ego, and so on."

37. White (1978:185) comments on Marx's method: "Marx applied nothing less than logic which he called 'dialectical' but which I would call a logic of metaphor, which he took to be the key to the understanding of all forms of fetishism and to that process of alienation by which men [sic] psychologically distanced themselves from those things that were ontologically closest to them and turned into idols those that were most removed from their own natures as men. Prior to his analysis of the logic of commodity exchange, Marx set forth a logic of men's thought *about* commodities, so as to demonstrate how what had started out as a perfectly understandable and commonsensical equation of one thing with another ended up in the fetishism of gold that was characteristic of the most highly advanced system of exchange, capitalism."

38. Maurice Godelier (1999:166) states: "Money is neither moral nor immoral. It is neutral. Let us say it is useful."

39. Maurice Godelier (1999:248, note 13) has more recently commented on Derrida's work: "The task of deconstructing an object in order to make it more intelligible before reconstructing it on the basis of new hypotheses is here carried to absurd lengths because, in the end, the deconstructed object has been entirely dissolved." I can only view with sadness this stubborn refusal to part with a valuable, in the light of Derrida's clarification of the nature of exchange.

40. Inspired by Donna Haraway (1991:149), I remind readers: "Blasphemy has always seemed to require taking things very seriously. . . . Blasphemy protects one from the moral majority within, while still insisting on the need for community. Blasphemy is not apostasy."

41. In *Double Talk, The Erotics of Male Literary Collaboration*, Wayne Koestenbaum (1989:3) says of the uneasy relationship of male co-authors: "When two men write together, they indulge in double talk; they rapidly patter to obscure their erotic burden, but the ambiguities of their discourse give the taboo subject some liberty to roam." He adds that "men who collaborate engage in a metaphorical sexual intercourse, and that the text they balance between them is alternately the child of their sexual union, and a shared woman." Of Marx and Engels, he states: "I lack the temerity to venture a gay critique of *The Communist Manifesto*, but it is tempting to compare Marx and Engels forging communism, and Freud and Breuer laboring over psychoanalysis" (12-13).

42. Marx was a Jew who had been converted as a child, but always thought of

by others as Jewish no matter how he endeavored to distance himself from Jews. Sander Gilman (1986:194) points out that in his 1844 essay, "On the Jewish Question," Marx "sees himself as the antithesis of the money Jew." Gilman (202) deconstructs Marx's use of the term "language of commodity" in *Capital* to reveal the "language of haggling, the language of the Jews," which I interpret as a reference to Yiddish, at the time widely viewed as a "corrupt" form of German. Gilman (207) says: "Marx is a convert, not to Protestantism, but to a world view where even the external signs of the Jew would vanish, the ideology of revolution. Marx, as an adult, still believes in that instant of conversion when all the outward signs of the Jews, such as the system and language of capitalism, will suddenly vanish."

43. Fredric Jameson (1991:xxi) writes: "*Capitalism*" was itself always a funny word in this sense: just using the word--otherwise a neutral enough designation for an economic and social system on whose properties all sides agree--seemed to position you in a vaguely critical, suspicious, if not outright socialist stance: only committed right-wing and full-throated market apologists also use it with the same relish." Later Jameson (47) points to Marx's "dialectical" intent in thinking the history of capitalism: "Marx powerfully urges us to do the impossible, namely, to think this development positively and negatively all at once: to achieve, in other words, a type of thinking that would be capable of grasping demonstrably baleful features of capitalism along with its extraordinary and liberating dynamism simultaneously within a single thought, and without attenuating any of the force of either judgment. We are somehow to lift our minds to a point at which it is possible to understand that capitalism is at one and the same time the best thing that has ever happened to the human race, and the worst." Again, we can read this as Marx's unconscious reflexivity and, no doubt, a personal statement by Jameson as well.

44. It is neither appropriate nor possible to elaborate here on what Bourdieu means by "class," which is in his work a multi-dimensional position structured by much more than "economic capital." See Bourdieu (1984, 1998).

Chapter 4

The Case of the Missing Hacienda Worker: A Dismemberment[1]

What remains concealed and invisible in each law is . . . presumably the law itself, that which makes laws of these laws, the being-law of these laws. The question and the quest are ineluctable, rendering irresistible the journey toward the place and the origin of law. The law yields by withholding itself, without imparting its provenance and its site. This silence and discontinuity constitute the phenomenon of the law. To enter into relations with the law which says "you must" and "you must not" is to act as if it had no history or at any rate as if it no longer depended on its historical presentation. (Jacques Derrida 1992b:192.)

How is one to hear [the silence between ethics and politics, ethics and law]? . . . As always, the decision remains heterogeneous to the calculations, knowledge, science, and consciousness that nonetheless condition it. The silence of which we are speaking, the one toward which we are above all attentive, is the elementary and decisive between-time, the meantime, the instantaneous meantime of decision, which unsettles time and puts it off its hinges ("out of joint") in anachrony and in contretemps: that is, when the law of the law exposes itself, *of itself,* in the non-law, by becoming at once host and hostage, the host and hostage of the other, when the law of the unique must give itself over to substitution and to the law of generality–without which one would obey an ethics without law–when the "Thou shalt not kill," wherein both the Torah and the law of messianic peace are gathered, still allows any State (the one of Caesar or the one of David, for example) to feel justified in raising an army, in making war or keeping law and order, in controlling its borders–in killing. Let's not insist too much here on the obvious, but let's not forget it to quickly, either. (Jacques Derrida 1999b:115-116)

Margaret Davies (2001:219) comments on Derrida's work: "When it recognizes us as legal persons, the law does not give us any choice about accepting it: We stand before it, but are not empowered to see behind it, or to question its history, its source, or its authority. Although it may hold out a promise of transparency and accessibility, the authority of the law is absolutely beyond criticism, meaning that in all practical instances it is pointless to question any law without passing through the channels of reform which the law itself lays down: if we find the law unreasonable, unfair, irrational it is, nonetheless, the law. . . . *Every* moment of founding and conserving law is politically charged, and has implications for power relations in society, despite law's claim to a grounded neutrality. In this way, the question of what the law is, and the quest for the law itself are irresistible, yet their fulfillment is endlessly deferred and ultimately impossible." However, "to articulate the foundation of authority in this way does not amount to a celebration of violence or force. I understand it more as a *revelation* or *exposure* of the fact that the law as we know it is not ultimately justifiable, and a reminder that positive law masks its own violence by reference to some justification which it can never find" (227).

When "the law of the law exposes itself," when it reveals the violence that sustains "law and order," we come to the understanding that a punitive social system not only designs and produces its code of capital offenses and their punishments but it designs and produces its capital offenders as well. This applies to modern states, but it also applies to Peruvian haciendas whether they are operated by *hacendados* or by North American research and development teams. Workers who do not work are subjected to the cutting-off of their livelihood. Capital offense is thus followed by capital punishment. The secret violence of "the law of the law" is thus revealed. Proponents of "law and order" tend to react negatively–and sometimes violently–to such a revelation. The violence of the law is not only a secret which must be kept, but it must be kept so secretly that they must not be conscious of it, an absolute secret which makes capital punishment possible despite the injunction, "Thou shalt not kill." Derrida

(2001c:57-58) says of the "absolute secret": "[I]t is the *ab-solutum* itself in the etymological sense of the term, i.e., that which is cut off from any bond, detached, and which cannot itself bind; it is the condition of any bond but it cannot bind itself to anything–this is the absolute, and if there is something absolute it is secret. . . . Clearly, the most tempting figure for this absolute/secret is death, that which has a relation to death, that which is carried off by death–that which is life itself." I try here to let the secret deconstruct itself.

This chapter is also about irrationality and misrecognition. It continues analysis of the Vicos Project's interventions and utilizes data on the case of *Pedro Cruz,[2] a member of the Hacienda work force who was dismembered. Cruz had consistently accumulated *faltas*, failures of a registered worker to attend Hacienda labors. These absences– suggesting voids or lacks or gaps or faults–may resonate in an observer *unconsciously* like some uncanny loss of consciousness.[3] There can be no doubt that the Project saw Cruz as a bad example for other Vicosinos, but what deserves emphasis is that the Project appears also to have identified with him as a bad example for itself. Thomas Keenan (1997:45) writes:

> What would we humans do without bad examples–without the example of the bad example, and without our regular innoculation by and against it? Responsibility begins in the bad example: one could even say that the only good example, the only one worthy of the imitation, interiorization, and identification that the example calls for, is the bad example. The classical subject is installed in its stance of responsibility and the safety of identity after the passage through the bad example, after the security failure that reaches the fragility of identity and the defense against the other. And yet there could be no experience of difference, no change, and no relation to the other without the adventure of the comparison and its failure . . . precisely because it is not always safe.

The Project became itself a bad example in order to counter the bad example. The Project's staff reacted to Cruz's absence with fear of their loss of control–*their* dismemberment–not only of the Hacienda work force but of their science. They abandoned their method and chose power. What happened then was that they became critically involved in exactly what they criticized, undeveloped Vicos. Their fear was *their* secret, and they did not share it with the Vicosinos. Derrida (1992c:86-87) points out: "In certain situations, one asks oneself 'how to avoid speaking,' either because one has promised not to speak and to keep a secret, or because one has an interest, sometimes vital, in keeping silent even if put to the rack." Animals do not keep or have secrets "because they cannot *represent as such*, as an *object* before consciousness, something that they would then forbid themselves from showing." Thus, he continues, "one would be tempted to designate, if not to define, consciousness as that place in which is retained the singular power not to *say* what one knows, to keep a secret in the form of representation. A conscious being is a being capable of lying, of not presenting in speech that of which it yet has an articulated representation: a being that can avoid speaking. But in order to be able to lie, a second and already mediated possibility, it is first and more essentially necessary to be able to keep for (and say to) oneself what one already knows. To keep something to oneself is the most incredible and thought-provoking power." How to avoid thinking is a related question which deals with an even more awesome power, but we will deal with that later.

Stephen Tyler (1991:91) writes: "The discourse of critique is already and inextricably involved in what it criticizes. It is not . . . an outer way existing outside and independently of what it criticizes as an objective step-back, or step outside its object. It is already inscribed as power, is committed to it, involved in it, and emasculated by its own desire to expose and correct, to prescribe and domesticate." The Project confiscated Pedro Cruz's land. (As I, without a shred of innocence, confiscate the Project's texts for the purposes of this book.)

Cruz, a man who had, in effect, separated himself from Hacienda labor was dispossessed of–separated, voided, parted, severed, or cut off from-- his land in consequence. In thus disciplining one of its wards, the Project took on a patriarchal role. Like Jehovah. An absence for an absence. A cutting off for a cutting off. Indeed, one might say that Pedro Cruz became a fetish to the Project, a ghost that absorbed its secret fears, and a mirror in which it could look to gaze on its own failure. But let us keep in mind, with Samuel Weber (2001:140), that "to see one's mirror image and to arrive at self-knowledge are . . . not necessarily identical."

Lacan (1978:218) speaks of a "unary signifier" emerging "in the field of the Other," representing "the subject for another signifier, which other signifier has as its effect the *aphanisis* of the subject"—thus, "the division of the subject—when the subject apperars somewhere as meaning, he [sic] is manifested elsewhere as 'fading', as disappearance." In other words, Cruz, who so occupied the Project with meaning, does not appear at all as a person—not only in Hacienda labors but in the Project's texts where he does not speak but is only spoken about.

Here we look at this missing member–the Project's castrated castrator– of the Hacienda's work force both in terms of what was said and of what was not said, in order to explore its significance, what it meant, what it wanted to say and what it did not want to say. This will take us away from Vicos to a theoretical consideration of fetishing, ghosts, mirrors, castration, and even patriarchy itself. In this way the Vicos Project becomes a more exotic object of study than was initially apparent.

Deconstructing Secrets

A fetish is a replacement for something that is missing. Donna Haraway (1997:136-137) writes: "Curiously, fetishes–themselves 'substitutes,' that is, tropes of a special kind–produce a particular 'mistake'; fetishes obscure the constitutive tropic nature of themselves and of worlds. Fetishes literalize and so induce an elementary material and cognitive error. Fetishes make things seem clear and under control. Technique and science appear to be about accuracy, freedom from bias, good faith, and time and money to get on with the job, not about material-semiotic troping and so building particular worlds rather than others. . . . [P]erhaps worst of all, while denying denial in a recursive avoidance of the tropic–and so unconscious–tissue of all knowledge, fetishists dislocate 'error.' Scientific fetishists place error in the admittedly irreducibly tropic zones of 'culture,' where primitives, perverts, and other laypeople live, and not in the fetishists' constitutional inability to recognize the trope that denies its own status as figure. In my view, contingency, finitude, and difference–but not 'error'–inhere in irremediably tropic, secular liveliness. Error and denial inhere in reverent literalness."

Hayden White (1978:184) presents us with three senses of fetishing: "Belief in magical fetishes, extravagant or irrational devotion, and pathological displacement of libidinal interest and satisfaction to a fetish."

E. L. McCallum (1999:112) gives this definition: "When one fixates on a thing, be it material or immaterial, in order to maintain a belief in opposition to one's knowledge, ambivalently choosing neither one nor the other, one is a fetishist. Both the fetish object and the fetish subject are constituted through this ambivalent relation to the thing and the loss–of either belief or knowledge–that it staves off." In the last chapter we saw how "potato power" became a substitute for operations the Vicos Project could not perform in order to change the structure of the field of power in which Vicos was situated. In the present chapter we will review how the Project made a mistake through devotion.

The matter of fetishing is anything but matter since it deals with spirits, ghosts, and other imaginary beings. William Pietz (1993:137-139) traces the concept of "fetishism" to post-Enlightenment philosophy:

> The term was adopted . . . because its discourse displaced the problem of religion from a theological to a materialist problematic congenial to the

emerging human sciences and to anticlerical activism alike. . . .: it offered an atheological explanation of the origin of religion, one that accounted equally well for theistic beliefs and nontheistic superstitions; it identified religious superstition with false causal reasoning about physical nature, making people's relation to material objects rather than to God the key question for historians of religion and mythology. . . . Fetishism was the definitive mistake of the pre-enlightened mind: it superstitiously attributed intentional purpose and desire to material entities of the natural world, while allowing social action to be determined by the (clerically interpreted) wills of contingently personified things, which were, in truth, merely the externalized material sites fixing people's own capricious libidinal imaginings ("fancy" in the language of the day).

Karl Marx, resonating with the spirit of this philosophical movement, brought fetishing out of metaphysics and into social relations. Marx deconstructed himself to the point where he allowed the mystical (and secret) nature of commodities to deconstruct itself. He showed that private property is dying, and also (though he may not have been aware of it) that dying is private property (such is the nature of the copula). He thereby earned himself the eternal wrath of all "defenders of private property." But, Christine Britzolakis (1999:72) suggests, "Marxist science" does not adequately "deal with the questions of subjectivity and aesthetics thrown up by modernist practice." Indeed, "[e]nlightenment notions of modernity are based on a refutation of specters, but are haunted, as so much modernist literature attests, by the return of premodern, animistic, or magical modes of thought." It is precisely this that leads Jacques Derrida (1994:46-47) to comment: "Marx does not like ghosts any more than his adversaries do. He does not want to believe in them. But he thinks of nothing else. He believes rather in what is supposed to distinguish them from actual reality, living effectivity. He believes he can oppose them, like life to death, like vain appearances of the simulacrum to real presence. He believes enough in the dividing line of this opposition to want to denounce, chase away, or exorcize the specters but by means of critical analysis and not by some counter-magic. But how to distinguish between the analysis that denounces magic and the counter-magic that it still risks being?" Thus, "Marx loved the figure of the ghost, he detested it, he called it to witness his contestation, he was haunted by it, harassed, besieged, obsessed by it. In him, but of course in order to repulse it, outside of him. In him outside of him: this is the place outside of place of ghosts wherever they feign to take up their abode. More than others, perhaps, Marx had ghosts in his head and knew without knowing what he was talking about" (106). Marx uncovered the theatrical secret of the commodity in a "quid pro quo":

Here the theatrical *quid pro quo* stems from an abnormal play of mirrors. There is a mirror, and the commodity form is also this mirror, but since all of a sudden it no longer plays its role, since it does not reflect back the expected image, those who are looking for themselves can no longer find themselves in it. People no longer recognize in it the *social* character of their *own* labor. It is as if they were becoming ghosts in their turn. The "proper" feature of specters, like vampires, is that they are deprived of a specular image, of the true, right specular image (but who is not so deprived?) How do you recognize a ghost? By the fact that it does not recognize itself in a mirror. (155-156.)

Let us keep this in mind as we move from Marx to Freud. If Marx is to be credited with opening the fetish to a new scrutiny, then Freud might be credited with opening scrutiny to a new fetish. Freud is also to be credited with saying what Marx did not say by libidinizing the fetish, but he did not establish a connection between materialistic and erotic desire.[4] McCallum (1999:156) calls attention to "the uniqueness of Freud's interpretation . . . as it goes against the grain of fetishism's cultural history, which turned a socially shared object relation into an individual idiosyncrasy." Still, as Roger Luckhurst (1999:52) says, "what haunts Freud is *haunting itself.*" He continues:

Ghosts haunt borders. As in the stories of Henry James, they stand on thresholds, monitory absent presences that forbid entry, or contemptuously turn their backs; when they show their face, barring the door, it is enough to make you lose your self-presence. Monitoring borders, the ghost also breaches boundaries (life versus death, presence versus virtuality), thus necessitating an anxious restatement of the border with each passage. Freud, as is often remarked, was repeatedly compelled to re-draw the limit around that which was proper to psychoanalysis, to mark out a circle and bind the inner committee to this ring. External attacks were perhaps less significant than those which arrived in the sunderings of this inner circle, the Secret Committee formed to perpetuate the institution. . . . The re-narration of the history of the origins of psychoanalysis is a compulsive activity, undertaken by Freud at each departure, working also, in a logic of restitution, to attach and detach simultaneously psychoanalysis from the complex weave of filiation and disinheritance from nineteenth-century and contemporaneous psychologies.

So Freud had ghosts in his head, too, since his analysis was interminable and indeterminable. Nicolas Abraham and Maria Torok (1986:103) write: "Freud himself carries a crypt" the revelation of which "combats the canonization of Freud's theories or person and holds out the hope of one day rooting psychoanalytic theories in their own (human) sources of meaning." What, then, did Freud have to say about fetishing? He stated, after having studied "analytically a number of men [perhaps including himself] whose object choice was dominated by a fetish":

> In every instance, the meaning and the purpose of the fetish turned out, in analysis, to be the same. It revealed itself so naturally and seemed to me so compelling that I am prepared to expect the same solution in all cases of fetishism. When now I announce that the fetish is a substitute for the penis, I shall certainly create disappointment; so I hasten to add that it is not a substitute for any chance penis, but for a particular and quite special penis that had been extremely important in early childhood but had later been lost. That is to say, it should normally have been given up, but the fetish is precisely designed to preserve it from extinction. To put it more plainly: the fetish is a substitute for the woman's (the mother's) penis that the little boy once believed in and–for reasons familiar to us–does not want to give up.
>
> What happened, therefore, was that the boy refused to take cognizance of the fact of his having perceived that a woman does not possess a penis. No, that could not be true: for if a woman had been castrated, then his own possession of a penis was in danger; and against that there rose in rebellion the portion of his narcissism which Nature has, as a precaution, attached to that particular organ. In later life a grown man may perhaps experience a similar panic when the cry goes up that Throne and Altar are in danger, and similar illogical consequences may ensue. (Freud 1961:152-153.)

Narcissistic self-protection is human,[5] but can be carried to fantastic extremes. If one believes unconsciously that one is threatened by castration, then, if one plays as if one were castrated, perhaps the real castration will not happen. Derrida (1986:210) points out, that in Freud's "very subtle cases . . . the structure, the construction of the fetish rests at once on the denial and on the affirmation, the assertion or the assumption of castration." Thus, one pretends "to lose, to castrate oneself, to kill oneself in order to cut death off. But the feint does not cut it off. One loses on both sides."

Emily Apter (1991:x) points to the need for "a broader, less gender-restricted conception of partial object substitutionism in sexuality, thereby culturally and historically relativizing those all-purpose referents, the surrogate male phallus and the phallic mother." Lacan (1977:282) attempts to resolve the ambivalence outlined by Derrida and achieve the goal set by Apter by establishing a "relation of the subject to the phallus that is established without regard to the anatomical difference of the sexes," but notes that "this very fact . . . makes any interpretation of this relation especially difficult in the case of women." He writes: "The idea of phallicism implies that by itself it isolates the category of the imaginary" (Lacan 1994:33). And: "The phallus is not at all the masculine genital apparatus, it is the masculine genital apparatus with what goes with it left out, the scrotum for example. What is fundamental is the erect image of the phallus. There is just the one. There is no choice other than a virile image or castration" (52). Moreover, "we are absolutely not dealing with a real phallus which, as real, exists or does not exist, but with a symbolic phallus which by its nature appears in the exchange as absence, an absence which functions as" (154). He continues:

> The woman does not have this phallus symbolically. But not having the phallus symbolically is announcing it by way of absence, and so it is having it in some way. The phallus is always beyond all relations between man and woman. It can be at times an object of an imaginary nostalgia on the woman's part, since she only has a tiny phallus. But this phallus which she can feel as insufficient is not the only thing that intervenes in her case, for on being implicated in the intersubjective relation, there is for the man, beyond herself, the phallus which she does not have, that is, the symbolic phallus which exists here as absence. This is completely independent of the inferiority that she may feel on the imaginary level, due to her real participation in the phallus. (155.)

Lacan (72) defends Freud: "On his part, Freud tells us that the phallus is included among the woman's lacks of essential objects, and that this is intimately linked to her relation to the child. For one simple reason–if the woman finds a satisfaction in the child, it is exactly to the extent in which she finds in him something which calms, something which saturates, rather well, her need of a phallus." Lacan (1982:79) adds: "In Freudian doctrine, the phallus is not a fantasy, if what is understood by that is an imaginary effect. Nor is it as such an object . . . insofar as this term tends to accentuate the reality involved in a relationship. It is even less the organ, penis or clitoris, which it symbolizes. . . . For the phallus is a signifier, a signifier whose function in the intrasubjective economy of analysis might lift the veil from that which it served in the mysteries. For it is to this signified that it is given to designate as a whole the effect of there being a signified, inasmuch as it conditions any such effect by its presence as signifier." In Lacan's reanalysis of the case of Little Hans, the little boy whom Freud studied a half century earlier, he notes that the boy was for his mother "the metonymy of the phallus" (1994:244). In the subtleties of this relationship:

The demand for love can only suffer from a desire whose signifier is alien to it. If the desire of the mother *is* the phallus, the child wishes to be the phallus in order to satisfy that desire. Thus the division immanent in desire is already felt to be experienced in the desire of the Other, in that it is already opposed to the fact that the subject is content to present to the Other what in reality he may *have* that corresponds to this phallus, for what he has is worth no more than what he does not have, as far as his demand for love is concerned because that demand requires that he be the phallus.

   Clinical experience has shown us that this test of the desire of the Other is decisive not in the sense that the subject learns by it whether or not he has a real phallus, but in the sense that he learns that the mother does not have it. (Lacan 1977:289.)

Judith Butler (1993:82) comments: "Lacan seeks to relieve the term of its catachrestic wanderings, to reestablish the phallus as a site of control (as that which is 'to designate as a whole the effect of there being a signified') and hence to position Lacan himself as the to control the meaning of the phallus."

   In all of this where is the father? (We should highlight this because, during the events reported here concerning the absent worker, Holmberg, the principal investigator of the Project [i.e., the Project-s "father"], was absent from Vicos.) Lacan (1994:206-207) asks: "*What is it to be a father? . . . .* This question is one way of approaching the problem of the father as signifier, but let us not forget that it also has to do with subjects who end up becoming fathers in their turn. To pose the question *what is a father?* This is still something different from being a father oneself, taking over the paternal position. Let us see. If it is so that the paternal position is wholly a quest, it is not unthinkable to say that truly, from beginning to end, nobody has been it completely." The oedipal problem, then, is that:

The symbolic father is the *name of the father.* It is the essential mediator of the symbolic world and its structure. It is necessary for weaning, more essential than primitive weaning, by which the child passes from its pure and simple union with the maternal omnipresence. The name of the father is essential to it for all articulation of human language, and for this reason Ecclesiastes says–*The fool has said in his heart: God is not.*

   Why does he say it in his heart? Because he cannot say it with his mouth. On the other hand, it is foolish, strictly speaking, to say in one's heart that God is not, simply because it is foolish to say something that is contradictory to the articulation of language itself. . . .

   There is the symbolic father. There is the real father. As experience teaches us, on taking over the virile sexual function the presence of the real father plays an essential role. In order for the subject truly to live the castration complex, it is necessary for the real father really to play the game. He must assume his function as castrating father, the function of a father in its concrete, empirical form, I was almost going to say degenerate, thinking of the personage of the primordial father and the tyrannical and more or less horrible form with which we are presented with the Freudian myth. To the extent to which the father, such as he exists, fulfills his imaginary function in which he has what is empirically intolerable, even infuriating when its castrating implication is allowed to be felt, only in this perspective is the castration complex lived. (366-367.)

In other words, and perhaps not exactly Lacan's conscious intent, this is the way the growing son joins up with his father in a patriarchy which views women as "castrated."

How are we to read such exotic texts as those of Freud and Lacan? The place to start might be Theodor Adorno's (1978:49) ironic statement: "In psycho-analysis nothing is true except the exaggerations." In his commentary on Freud's *Interpretation of Dreams*, Edward Said (1988:165-166) suggests that we read the text as a palimpsest:

Thanks to James Strachey's precise editing, we can see physical signs of how, in each of the eight German editions, Freud interpolated new or revised material, sometimes to make new or revised points, sometimes to clarify old ones. The palimpsest goes beyond this sort of intervention. Since Freud's subject matter and his attitude toward it can be grasped only in verbal fragments (whether of dreams or of language--i.e. sequential prose), they must be able to accommodate important changes. Usually the reason for these changes is that the fragment as first apprehended was necessarily incomplete--that is, its intention, while present, was not visible. Therefore, none of Freud's sentences at a given point in the text is a final statement, not even in its immediate context.

Thus the way to read these texts is as palimpsests with layers of meaning between which exist the work of the primary process[6] which is not directly available to language, i.e., the unspeakable and unwriteable (and unthinkable). But then, how to avoid speaking?, how to avoid writing? (and how to avoid thinking?)

Although, it seems to me, we should read Freud's work as a dream, or a daydream, it still holds shock value for some readers. To the extent that Freud's conception of fetishing constitutes a mirror image we are not prepared for, our indignation, consternation, and perhaps even panic, allow many of us only to see ghostly absurdity, unlikelihood. A recent example of a reading of "silliness" in Freud is Pels's (1998:116, note 14) thought-provoking article on fetishing, in which he writes: "To interpret

Freud's theory of fetishism as saying first of all that the fetish represents the mother's phallus is, I feel, as silly as saying that the fetish is a typically 'African' thing." In a different manner, but still unable to suspend disbelief, Charles Bernheimer (1993:83) maintains: "The massive authority of Freud's thought (whose historical roots in the decadent soil of the fin de siècle are too often overlooked), the close link between decadent aesthetics and modernism, the systematic fetishism that underpins our consumer culture--these are important factors. But there is also the fact, not to be neglected, that castration appeals to theory because it privileges the theoretical. Indeed, it could be said that castration produces female sexuality out of (male) theory. Woman lacks because theory is full, woman is mutilated because theory holds to its erection despite evidence of the monument's collapse. Castration is theory's decadent fetish. It is high time to discard it on the compost heap of history."

Freud (1961:157) concluded his brief article on "Fetishism" with the words: "we may say that the normal prototype of fetishes is a man's penis, just as the normal prototype of inferior organs is a women's real small penis, the clitoris." Feminists read this statement, with much more than a little justification, as sexist. It clearly reveals the value Freud (and apparently Lacan as well) placed on the size of his sex: he could have selected intensity of feeling, for example, or the capacity to give pleasure to someone else. In his self-analysis Freud was not able to touch the fear which plagued him, a patriarchal crypt which some readers have attributed to a blind spot. Adrienne Rich (1986:201-202) observes:

> But in fact there is no such thing as an intellectual "blind spot" surrounded by an outlook of piercing lucidity–least of all when that spot happens to cover the immense and complex dimensions in which women exist, both for ourselves and in the minds of men. Freud need not have been a feminist in order to have had a deeper sense of the resonance and chargedness of the figure of the women–especially as mother–in patriarchal thinking. But, even in terms of his own proclaimed methods and goals, he, as it were, lost his nerve and drew back where women were concerned. And this affected not simply his attitudes toward women but, of necessity, his speculations and observations about men, and about the significance of the penis for both sexes. The Freudian view of the son is saturated with the Freudian hostility–and sentimentality–toward the mother. . . . Freud meant female castration as a metaphor. But precisely because he did not pursue the psychic meaning of this *social* mutilation of women (which would have forced him to go deeper into male psychology, also) his work, both on women and on men lacks a kind of truth which has been called political and which I would call poetic and scientific as well.

Hélène Cixous (1994:41) looks at Freud in stronger language: "[M]an has been given the grotesque and unenviable fate of being reduced to a single idol with clay balls. And terrified of homosexuality, as Freud and his followers remark. Why does man fear *being* a woman? Why this refusal (*Ablehnung*) of femininity? The question that stumps Freud. The 'bare rock' of castration. For Freud, the repressed is not the other sex defeated by the dominant sex, as his friend Fliess (to whom Freud owes the theory of bisexuality) believed; what is repressed is leaning toward one's own sex."

Daniel Boyarin (1998:218, 224)) notes Freud's hidden wish "to be uncircumcised" and an unanalyzed self-image as a clitoris, the understanding of which "might have generated a powerful critique of gendered and sexual meanings" and might have revealed his homophobia.

We can thus ascribe this flaw in psychoanalytic theory to the patriarchal *habitus* in which it was developed. At present, feminism has indeed provoked a revision of the way in which we think and write of fetishing. For example, in her analysis of female fetishing in the work of George Sand, Naomi Schor (1985:303) asks: "what are we to make of an episode imagined by a woman author which so clearly, so prophetically rehearses the gestures of what has come to be known as fetishism?"--when "it is an article of faith with Freud and Freudians that *fetishism is the male perversion par excellence*," and when "traditional psychoanalytic literature on the subject states over and over again that there are no female fetishists; female fetishism is, in the rhetoric of psychoanalysis, an oxymoron." Actually, Freud (1988:156) had, in a lecture recently discovered, stated in 1909 that "half of humanity must be classed among the clothes fetishists. All women, that is, are clothes fetishists," but by the time he published his better known works on the subject, including "Fetishism" in 1927, he had changed his mind.

Gamman and Makinen (1995:111) suggest revisions of the psychoanalytic theory of fetishing which "point strongly towards another model . . . that . . . opens up a space to include women as both sexual fetishists and fetishists of food." These revisions state "that fetishism is as much about the disavowal of *individuation* (separation from the mother) as it is about sexual difference"; "that fetishism carries a strong oral component"; "that a narcissistic blow to the body image of either sex can develop the fetish at puberty; and "that fetishism is in fact a highly creative compromise which, through its doing-and-undoing oscillation, enables the subject to cope with unconscious menace, while still allowing the gratification of pleasure."

Thus psychoanalytic theory has not managed to resolve its patriarchal tilt. Luce Irigaray (1985:69-70) comments: "The fact that Freud himself is enmeshed in a power structure and an ideology of the patriarchal type [and can this not be said of Lacan as well?] leads, moreover, to some internal contradictions in his theory":

> [I]n the process of elaborating a theory of sexuality, Freud brought to light something that had been operative all along though it remained implicit, hidden, unknown: *the sexual indifference that underlies the truth of any science, the logic of every discourse.* This is readily apparent in the way Freud defines female sexuality. In fact this sexuality is never defined with respect to any sex but the masculine. Freud does not see *two sexes* whose differences are articulated in the act of intercourse, and, more generally speaking, in the imaginary and symbolic processes that regulate the workings of a society and a culture. The "feminine" is always described in terms of deficiency or atrophy, as the other side of the sex that alone holds a monopoly on value: the male sex.

Elizabeth Grosz (1993:114) writes that "insofar as psychoanalysis can be seen as an active participant in patriarchal social values, we need to show how its terms do not adequately accommodate women's specificities and differences from men. The categories that Freud proposes as universally relevant–the function of the phallus, the Oedipus complex, the ubiquity of the castration threat and women's status as passive–surely need to be contested in order that social relations themselves can be transformed." But we are not yet ready to do without the theory and its terms. Marcia Ian (1993:176-177) points out that "the castration anxiety, which fetishism seeks to relieve, is less a male fear of damage to the penis than the fear in either sex of narcissistic injury associated with the sudden, uncontrollable, unbearable loss of body integrity or beloved object." This expresses well the associations that operated behind the Project staff's reaction to absenteeism in Vicos.

Shoshana Felman (1993:5), in her address to women, best elucidates our dilemma when she asks from where we might exorcize patriarchal mentality "if we ourselves are possessed by it." Felman's words are as appropriately directed at the minds of men, which also need a place to stand in order to exorcize patriarchal thinking. As Pierre Bourdieu and Jean-Claude Passeron (1990:37) suggest, finding that place is not easy: people who can critique their culture are already enculturated, and those who can question the way they are brought up still have roots in that upbringing.[7] We need a new discourse but until we have one we seem, *a faute de mieux*, faced with the continuing use of these terms, "phallus," "fetish," "castration," each one of which is overdetermined. Like other signs, they are polysemic. Beyond that, Nicolas Abraham (in Abraham and Torok 1994:85) asserts that psychoanalytic terms "literally rip themselves away from the dictionary and ordinary language":

> The allusion to the nonreflexive and the unnamed in fact induces this unprecedented and strange semantic phenomenon. The language of psychoanalysis no longer follows the twists and turns (*tropoi*) of customary speech and writing. Pleasure, Id, Ego, Economic, Dynamic, [and I believe we can add Castration, Fetish, and Phallus] are not metaphors, metonimies, synechdoches, catachreses; they are, by dint of discourse, products of designification and constitute new figures, absent from rhetorical treatises. These figures of antisemantics, inasmuch as they signify no more than the action of moving up toward the source of their customary meaning, require a denomination properly indicative of their status and which–for want of something better–I shall propose to designate by the neologism *anasemia*.
>
> Thus, psychoanalytic theory speaks in an anasemic discourse. What justifies such a discourse? At first nothing except its sheer existence. The very fact that, running counter to the known laws of discursive ratiocination, such a discourse actually occurs–that it evidences genuine impact and fruitfulness–amply confirms that its allusion meets a resonance in us capable of founding the discourse and allowing it to reveal, by its advance toward this nonpresence in us, the place from which all meaning ultimately springs.

The meaning of these terms is, then, undecidable.[8] Abraham (88, 142) points out that "anasemic Castration does not imply the excision of the genitals." And fetishing is an "invention of the mind" which rests on "some 'gaping wound' opened long ago within the ego and disguised by a fantasmic and secret construction in place of the very thing from which, through the loss, the ego was severed. In all cases, the goal of this type of construction is to disguise the wound because it is unspeakable." To the extent that these concepts constitute a patriarchal mirror that Freud, Lacan, and others hold up to us, our indignation, consternation, and perhaps even panic, allow many of us only to see ghostly absurdity, unlikelihood.

Robert Scholes (1982:127-129) refers to a "Freudian myth of human socialization." This is "not a testable hypothesis so much as an intuitive narrative with explanatory power." What is "crucial" is "a binary opposition, so characteristic of human thought–in both logic and mythology" in which "male and female have been defined as a fullness and a deficiency, a presence and an absence, a plus and a minus, an 'on' and an 'off.'" This binary opposition would be perfect were it not for "a part left over . . . which does not fit into the neat binary scheme." It is the clitoris, a "masculine feature attached to the female body," which "becomes a great burden for Freud" who "does everything he can to trivialize it, to criticize it, to erase it from the discourse of sex." Scholes (130-132) goes on to discuss the etymology of the word "clitoris" and discovers the Greek meaning, "precious gem." He comments that such an evasion of meaning suggests: "We are dealing . . . with a widespread process of censorship–not a political conspiracy but a semiotic coding that operates to purge both texts and language of things that are unwelcome to the men who have had both texts and language in their keeping for so many centuries. This code is both unconscious in its operation and powerful in its action, for it derives its energy from a deeply felt male fear of feminine sexuality." He goes on:

> There is a male awe at full female sexual response, an awe which is often ready to turn nasty. This feeling is expressed in a classic form by a remark actually made to a woman by her British lover during the quarrel that terminated their affair. Speaking of their lovemaking he said, "I would have enjoyed it more if you had enjoyed it less." One suspects that a significant portion of the whole male sex would endorse that proposition. . . .
>
> Is there a reality behind the myth? Do women have more pleasure? We cannot know and it does not matter. What matters is the male fear that this is the case.

Scholes (133-134) then discusses clitoridectomy and notes: "[T]his ritual, whether sanctified by custom or justified as clinical practice, is in fact an acting out of male fears and wishes that are widely distributed, if not universal." As for Freud, he "himself has become the prisoner of his own binary code" (138).

Meanwhile, we are confronted by the all-too-human feeling that "something is missing." Why do I, when I misplace something–a book, some notes, an implement, whatever–anxiously and restlessly search for it? Why do I find so much meaning in the Vicos case that is the subject of this chapter? Why did the staff of the Vicos Project react as it did? Why did Sarah Levy interrupt the activity of her field workers in order to concentrate on Pedro Cruz? If you are also possessed in similar ways, you have much company. Derrida (1996b:85) comments: "It is known that Freud did everything possible not to neglect the experience of haunting, spectrality, phantoms, ghosts. He tried to account for them. Courageously, in as scientific, critical, and positive a fashion as possible. But by doing that, he also tried to conjure them. Like Marx. His scientific positivism was put to the service of his declared hauntedness and of his unavowed fear." Under psychoanalysis, delusion's unlikelihood appears to disappear:

So here is a lack of verisimilitude which seems to dissipate with explication, *at least in large part!* What is this part? What is it due to, this piece which resists explanation? Why this insistence on the part, the parting, the partition, the piece? And what does this partition have to do with the truth?

We know the Freudian explanation. Announced by this strange protocol, it mobilizes the whole etiological machinery of psychoanalysis, beginning, obviously, with the mechanisms of repression. But we should not forget that if the psychoanalytic explanation of delusion, of hauntedness, of hallucination, if the psychoanalytic theory of specters, in sum, leaves a part, a share of nonverisimiltude unexplained or rather *verisimilar*, carrying a truth, this is because . . . there is a *truth of delusion*, a truth of insanity or of hauntedness. . . . Delusion or insanity, hauntedness is not only haunted by this or that ghost . . . but by the specter of the truth which has been thus repressed. The truth is spectral, and this is its part of truth which is irreducible by explanation. (86-87.)

Thus, spirit is always haunted by its spirit: "A spirit, . . . a phantom, always surprises by returning to be the other's ventriloquist" (Derrida 1989a:40). Thus, castration, the *missing member*, is itself haunted. Derrida (1986:209) offers this summary of fetishing:

What is it to speculate concerning the fetish? For such a question, the headless head is undecidability. Despite all the variations to which it can be submitted, the concept fetish includes an invariant predicate: it is a substitute–for the thing itself as center and source of being, the origin of presence, the thing itself par excellence, God or the principle, the arçhon, what occupies the center function in a system, for example the phallus in a certain phantasmatic organization. If the fetish substitutes itself for the thing itself in its manifest presence, in its truth, there should no longer be any fetish as soon as there is truth, the presentation of the thing itself in its essence. According to this minimal conceptual determination, the fetish is opposed to the presence of the thing itself, to truth, signified truth for which the fetish is a substitutive signifier (from then on every fetish is a signifier, while every signifier is not necessarily a fetish), truth of a "privileged" transcendental, fundamental, central signifier, signifier or signifiers, no longer belonging to the series. Something–the thing–is no longer itself a substitute; there is the nonsubstitute, that is what constructs the concept fetish. If there were no thing, the concept fetish would lose its invariant kernel. What is called fetishism should be analyzed in a completely different place. If what has always been called fetish, in all the critical discourses, implies the reference to a nonsubstitutive thing, there should be somewhere–and that is the truth of the fetish, the relation of the fetish to truth–a decidable value of the fetish, a decidable opposition of the fetish to the nonfetish.

McCallum (1999:107-108) seeks a poststructuralist mode of turning our conception of the fetish around:

> Where the fetish provides a different version of the phallus in the individual's development as the thing through which all meaning is mediated, it opens up new possible directions for diverse subjects to emerge and grow. Yet it does so without rendering the subject as a boundaryless and disoriented entity altogether, which is the spectre that narrowly binary logic posits as the result of doing away with a singular, transcendent signifier. In other words, we should reverse our thinking about the relation between the fetish and the phallus; no longer should we view the phallus as a fetish substitute, whose centering services are now more hurtful than helpful. Reconceiving the phallus as the fetish decenters and disperses the dominance of sexual difference culturally associated with the phallus, allowing individuals to negotiate their differences based on particular and local interests rather than as mediated through an ahistorical, atemporal standard. Since the hallmark of postmodernism is the loss of a center which can arbitrate meaning, fetishism, which has played a significant role in modern conceptions of the subject, becomes in its reinterpretation even more important in postmodern subjectivity.

All of this said, let us try to bring it into our understanding of the Project in Vicos. What was the Project doing, or trying to do, in Vicos? What did the Project want? Holmberg's (1960) article on "Changing community attitudes and values in Peru: a case study in guided change" summarizes his conception of research and development and provides a first step toward an answer. After a discussion of resistance to modernization by the people in rural communities and their current disorganization, pessimism, and fear of the outside world, he states:

> Changing this state of affairs, without a large investment of resources or without a revolution, would seem at first glance to be an almost insoluble problem. To be sure, it was and still is no easy task. Yet it is not as hopeless as it might seem. In the case of Vicos, at any rate, it has been possible, on the basis of careful studies carried out in advance of initiating any action, to design a modest program of technical assistance and education which has gained fairly wide acceptance and has helped to awaken most members of the community to new opportunities for improving their lot through their own efforts.

Dobyns (1974:204-205, 209), who knows how not to write self-interest, offers this rational image:

> First, the Project sought to improve the standard of living of the Vicos population. Second, it set out to determine scientifically what actions would be effective in increasing agricultural and human productivity among Indian serfs. . . . [The Project] might have instituted sweeping innovations by employing the coercive power that manorial managers wielded at the time. . . . In contrast, members of the Project seldom directly coerced anyone. Power of another kind constituted the key to the Project's success. . . . The Project eschewed power that was backed up by severe deprivation and instead relied on the power of persuasion. . . . The Project director chose to persuade serfs to change by enlightening them, educating them, and giving them new experiences. The Project exposed Vicosinos to egalitarian and decision-making experiences that afforded them new knowledge with which to perceive new needs and desires and fashion novel ways of satisfying both. . . .
>
> Were the sort of social and economic transition that experimental intervention by social scientists triggered in Vicos to spread widely over the Andean region, many of its gravest political and social difficulties would be likely to disappear.

In the statements by Holmberg and Dobyns lurk silent Cold War ghosts, spirits, and specters in the form of signifiers with multiple signifieds. Both authors attend to the prospect of revolution,[9] Holmberg more directly and Dobyns more indirectly with reference to the "gravest political and social difficulties." The gravity of the "gravest" difficulties seems likely to draw us, who would otherwise be standing erect and free, down into the grave where we ourselves might exist as ghosts. But let the latter disappear so that we may look at the word "revolution," the various meanings of which have their way with it, tease it, mime it, and drive it insane. And let us think of "revolution" as a mirror. Susan Stewart (1980:129) comments on "all play with mirrors":

> The mirror both confirms and questions identity in a single stroke. When one looks into a mirror, there is a splitting of subject and object, watcher and watched. One can look at one's self as an object, from more than one point of view, as others do. Yet there is also the terrifying possibility that the repetition will go on, that the splitting will occur in reverse and the self will break off towards infinity. And even more frightening is the possibility that all one will see in the mirror is another mirror, a doubling of reflexivity that cancels into nothingness.

To those who see revolution as the permanent erection of the "expropriation of expropriators" or the "socialization of surplus value" it may be a welcome spirit. To those who view revolution as a dictatorship of party or class it may be applauded or hissed at, depending on how one looks into the mirror, whether one sees avenging angels or angry ghosts. To those who see revolution as permanent castration (the "upside-down erection"), chaos, loss of control, or liberation of repressed desire, it may be a fearful specter, the object of exorcism. And to those who discern in revolution nothing more than a hall of mirrors, it is a path to bloodshed, terror, madness, and death. "Revolution," a term borrowed from the science of mechanics, turns out to be not a social event, or a social process, or a social condition, but a metaphor. As Bruno Latour (1993:40-41) suggests, people use the term to make what is happening to them "modern" and rational, to give themselves courage to make decisions, and to move people and things. Thus, the meaning of the sign is undecidable, endlessly deferred.

If the Project was in Vicos not to make a "gift" but to arrest social unrest, the kind of unrest that threatens the socially rested, the rest of humanity, also with unrest, it aimed to do this by "determining scientifically" how people may be made more productive, thereby satisfying their needs and losing their restlessness. With its goal of science, the Project gave up "coercion" in favor of "prediction and control," so that it "seldom directly coerced anyone" as long as it could persuade people to be dependent variables in social experimentation. The secret that is not said, that goes without saying, that does not need to be said is that career maintenance, development, and enhancement motivate "scientists," and when events conspire to block scientific endeavor, scientists behave unscientifically. In Vicos, Project staff resorted to coercion

Anthropology is a life science, one which Derrida (1988b:6) defines in terms of "biology and biography" as a different kind of science. Derrida continues:

> It is *painfully difficult* for life to become an object of science, in the sense that philosophy and science have always given to the word "science" and to the legal status of scientificity. All of this–the difficulty, the delays it entails–is particularly bound up with the fact that the science of life always accommodates a philosophy of life, which is not the case for all other sciences, the sciences of nonlife–in other words, the sciences of the dead. This might lead one to say that all sciences that win their claim to scientificity without delay or residue are sciences of the dead; and, further, that there is, between the dead and the status of the scientific object, a co-implication which *interests* us, and which concerns the desire to know. If such is the case, then the so-called living subject of biological discourse is a part–an interested party or a partial interest–of the whole

field of investment that includes the enormous philosophical, ideological, and political tradition, with all the forces that are at work in that tradition as well as everything that has its potential in the subjectivity of a biologist or a community of biologists. All these evaluations leave their mark on the scholarly significance and inscribe the bio-graphical within the biological.

How to carry out a successful *scientific* study in Vicos with unwilling workers? How to persuade with coercion? How to overcome fear with threats? How to open minds with closed minds? How to enlighten in the dark? It is possible to ask these questions now in the context of what we already know. It is time to review and broaden our understanding of the Hacienda Vicos at the time of the Project's intervention.

The Hacienda Vicos

When the Project took charge of the Hacienda Vicos in January, 1952, as I have noted, the terms of the contract required the continuation of the hacienda system. Thus, as it introduced experimental reforms during the five years in which the Project's personnel acted as *patrones*, the Hacienda's workers continued under certain customary conditions of control. At the beginning the Project had to confront serious problems with this control, especially absenteeism and the evasion of work obligations. All of this was related to matters of respecting the terms of the contract, avoiding organizational disorder, and–perhaps the most important–creating and observing a set of demonstration effects from its technical innovations.

Until Vicos was recognized as a *Comunidad Indígena*,[10] "Indigenous Community," its organization corresponded to the customary rural power structure known as *hacienda*. By saying that this structure was "customary," we should keep in mind that this was not a legacy passed down from immemorial times but one which took shape in the nineteenth century Republic. Certainly the hacienda system has its roots in Spanish colonial rule, a polity which provided a reserve of human resources for the great mining enterprises. Both haciendas and "free" communities were formed in different ways.[11] Individual "liberty" derived from the establishment of independence from Spain favored a greater exploitation of the land when the former intermediaries became landlords. Later in the nineteenth century, when guano wealth allowed large-scale importation of food and luxury goods, rural property which had up to then been producing for regional and national consumption began to decline. Only export agriculture of cotton and sugar was profitable.[12] Toward the end of the century the period of *caudillismo*, dictatorial leadership, came to an end, after the War of the Pacific, 1879-1885, with the consequent reduction of private military (or para-military) forces. Despite the effort of the *civilistas*, Civilists, who sought electoral government by civilians, to centralize control in order to assure a more efficient exploitation of guano and nitrate deposits, such private forces were largely constituted by armies of clients and retainers until after the war (North 1966:21-25), which signaled the declining power of the Andean *hacendados*, landlords.[13] Demographic growth reversed the ratio of labor to land. The labor scarcity with an abundance of land during the nineteenth century became an abundance of labor with a scarcity of land in the twentieth.[14] In the case of Vicos this tendency, for an estate of 1,746 hectares farmed by the *patrón* and the Vicosinos, appears clearly in demographic figures:

Year	Population
1593	99
1774	301
1850	512
1876	683
1901	800
1940	1,617
1950	1,785[15]

Tannenbaum (1962:80-81) views the hacienda as a socio-economic system "that seeks to achieve self-sufficiency and autarchy on a local scale," the aim being "to buy nothing, to raise and make everything within the limits of its own boundaries." Wolf and Mintz (1957:380) define the hacienda as "an agricultural estate, operated by a dominant land-owner and a dependent labor force, organized to supply a small-scale market by means of scarce capital, in which the factors of production are employed not for capital accumulation but also to support the status aspirations of its owner." With cheap land and scant equipment, plus intensive labor, it needs "only enough capital to maintain [itself] in a state of stability" (387). It directly supports the people who comprise it, the labor force and the dominant group (the *patrón* and the overseers), by providing what is necessary for the reproduction of their distinct life styles, including the status needs of the dominant group. For the subordinate laborers it furnishes subsistence through the allocation of productive resources: "Such perquisites take the place of wages which must remain limited due to the scarcity of capital" (389). The hacienda binds its labor force through its monopoly of land which deprives the subordinates of economic alternatives, its provision of the resources with which they may produce their own subsistence, its private use of force, and the reciprocal relations between the two groups which range from mutual service to ceremonial bonds (390-391).[16]

When we use the term "hacienda system" we should keep in mind that, far from consisting of the structure of one estate, it involves a whole region, haciendas, small-holdings, market towns, free-holding communities, wage-laborers, sharecroppers, merchants, professional persons, members of the State apparatus, and so forth. This regional social system, known as *gamonalismo*, undoes what a centralized system does, as José Carlos Mariátegui (1959:33-34) so eloquently pointed out nearly three-quarters of a century ago: "'*Gamonalismo*' inevitably invalidates all laws and ordinances which protect the Indian. The *hacendado*, the landlord, is a feudal lord. Written law is impotent against his authority, supported by milieu and habit. Unpaid labor is prohibited by law but, nevertheless, unpaid labor, and even forced labor, survive in the landed property. The judge, sub-prefect, commissioner, teacher, tax collector are enfeoffed to property. Law cannot prevail against *gamonales*. The official who stubbornly imposes it would be abandoned and sacrificed by central power, upon which the influences of *gamonalismo* are all powerful and act directly or through parliament, one way or another with the same effect."[17]

As I have noted, the Hacienda Vicos was owned by the Beneficencia Pública de Huaraz, a charitable enterprise controlled by landed interests in that capital city and in the region. The rental of Vicos was assigned periodically, at public auction, to the highest bidder who, for all intents and purposes, had complete control of the estate during his tenure. This renter was the *patrón*. It was he who could draw on the estate's labor force to earn his rental fee plus a profit. However, in addition to providing for the Beneficencia and the *patrón*, the Vicos people also served mestizos in Marcará, Carhuaz, as well as a few other urban centers, as day laborers on other estates, on construction projects, and as servants in country and town houses. In addition to that, the Vicosinos made up labor gangs on public works projects in the District of Marcará, in corvée labor. Thus, the contract signed by the Project and the Beneficencia reflected the mestizo sector's interest in maintaining intact–we could say erect–the hacienda structure in Vicos. I have already said that one of the clauses of the contract stipulated that "established customs" be respected. My emphasis of this point calls attention to a fact which the Project had to live with, one which impeded it from changing any of the rules which governed labor on the estate.

In the Hacienda the basic labor relation was that of *patrón* and worker [18] The Vicos workers were known as *colonos*, the traditional term for serf, but also *hacienda nuna*, hacienda people, which refers to people who are inscribed in the Hacienda rolls with the obligation of providing a certain number of *tareas* per week (from one to three days of labor). Mangin (1954:II, 20) says, "The word 'peón' is rarely used." This accords with my experience in the Callejón de Huaylas, so that the frequency of its use by the staffs of both the Vicos and the Methodology Projects is indeed curious.

Most of the workers worked three days, for which they were allotted pieces of land for "maize, wheat, and potatoes," that is, lands in the appropriate eco-zones. Persons who held small parcels owed less labor, although this does not imply that land was distributed evenly among the workers. Also, in exchange for the *tareas* generally performed by labor gangs in the different subdivisions of Vicos from Monday to Wednesday, the worker was allowed to pasture his livestock on the *puna*, to utilize the Hacienda's irrigation system, to gather firewood, and to mine clay from deposits on the estate. The worker had to appear for his *tareas* with his own tools, and if he possessed cattle the Hacienda also took advantage of the labor of these animals for plowing its fields, reasoning that the Hacienda's pastures were open to them and so they too should contribute to Hacienda labors. The worker received no wage except for *temple*, a gratification of a few cents for each week of work. One who brought a *yunta*, a team of oxen, received a bit more for each day of work with his animals.

Theoretically, each worker represented a family. And, theoretically, all the Vicos families had to supply an active person for Hacienda work, preferably a male. William Mangin (1954:II, 18-19) reports that around 1950 there were 349 families in Vicos, but only 252 workers were inscribed; the *tareas* of these 252 were carried out by a total of 372 persons; and actually only 140 workers were working for themselves, while the rest alternated or shared *tareas* with other members of their families. 47 families did not ever send anyone. Clifford Barnett (1960:29-30), who conducted research in Vicos around the same time, says that some workers had their *tareas* permanently filled by a substitute and never attended Hacienda labors; others did not appear because they were away on military service, too old or infirm, or engaged in "more profitable work elsewhere." Of the substitutes, Barnett (30) continues: "In addition to those who regularly alternate with someone else or have a regular substitute, [on] any one day of work many others may send someone in their place. Particularly near the date of a major fiesta or when the [workers] are busy harvesting their own fields, as many as 100 women and children (from 10 years and up) will appear." The Project's archives contain a report by Norman Pava[19] which illustrates the utilization of women and children:

> The Hacienda accepts children from about ten years old and up to work *tareas*. The smaller or younger children do lighter tasks–shelling corn, tending animals, working around the Hacienda, or spreading fertilizer. These peons receive the same *temple* as other peons, and come forward to receive their *centavos* at *temple* time. In many tasks, such as cutting weeds out of corn, where a small body is advantageous, all the child-peons, known as "*los huamra,*" are assigned as a group.
>
> The Hacienda does not like to accept school-age boys because they cannot do a man's work. If the man of the household is dead or ill–if the child is the only available member of the family–then the Hacienda accepts him to fulfill the family responsibility. Parents often go to work in Marcará or malinger at home and send their children to work in the Hacienda. When Enrique [Luna] suspects this, he sends the child home and the peon has a default for the day.
>
> If there is no man available, and the Hacienda will not accept a child, a family sends a woman. They mill fertilizer, shell corn, and generally do the same things a child does.
>
> Several children and women are inscribed in the Hacienda records as regular peons, which means that they have rights to the land they live on and are working their own *tareas* rather than substituting for their parents or relatives. This happens when the father has died or has deserted the household: the mother or relatives come to the Hacienda on the child's or the woman's behalf and ask to have that person inscribed.
>
> Children also come to work in the Hacienda to help their fathers or relatives make up defaults. [In this case] the Hacienda often does not accept them. (AVP, January 16, 1952.)

Pava gives this description of substitution customs:

Peons often get substitutes to work their *tareas* in the Hacienda. The substitute fulfills the other's work responsibility. He answers for the other man at roll call. Substitutes seem generally to be relatives: sons, in-laws, grandsons, nephews, or *ahijados* [godsons]. Son-for-father substitution seems the most common. If the substitute is to get the *temple* of the other, the substitute answers for the other at *temple* and collects it when the other's name is called. This is an arrangement between the two parties. The Hacienda owes the *temple* only to the person who is responsible for the *tarea*. Thus, at *temple* today, Marcelino León came forward when his father, Alejandro León, was called. Francisco Tafur answered for his step-brother, Víctor Maihue. Occasionally a father sends his son to pick up the *temple*, although the son has not substituted but is simply doing an errand for his father.

Delfín Coleto's sister is married to Andrés Cruz. Andrés has two sons of working age. One works for Andrés, while the other occasionally works for José Baltazar, Delfín's son-in-law. José does weaving and other favors for his substitute, and gives him extra money for coca, generally 10 cents per day which is the amount the substitute consumes while working for the Hacienda. (APV, January 17, 1952.)

The roll of the Hacienda Vicos work force for 1954 contains a list of arrangements for substitution. I present it here as an indication of family relations in the community:

Workers who work for themselves	131
Worker who alternates with a son	22
Worker who alternates with more than one son	3
Son who works his father's *tarea*	13
Sons who work in place of their father	7
Daughter who works her father's *tarea*	5
Stepson who works in place of his stepfather	5
Total	51
Worker who alternates with a brother	25
Worker who alternates with brothers	1
Worker who alternates with sisters	1
Brother who works the *tarea*	2
Sister who works the *tarea*	2
Total subnstitutions by siblings	31
Worker who alternates with a nephew	6
Worker who alternates with nephews	1
Nephew who works the *tarea*	1

Total substitutions by nephews	8
Worker who alternates with son-in-law	6
Worker who alternates with brother-in-law	1
Brother-in-law works the *tarea*	1
Total substitutions by in-laws	8
Worker who alternates with his father	2
Mother who works the *tarea*	1
Total substitutions by parents	3
Uncle who works the *tarea*	1
Uncles who work the *tarea*	1
Aunt works the *tarea*	1
Total substitutions by aunts/uncles	3
Niece's husband works the *tarea*	1
Grandson works the *tarea*	1
Son and nephew work the *tarea*	1
Wife works the *tarea*	1
Total substitutions by other relatives	4
Unknown	3
Total	245

(AVP, Masrio Vázquez, 1954.)

It must not be assumed that land was distributed to workers according to the work they performed. Holmberg and Dobyns (1969:405) characterize subsistence production in Vicos as "minuscule agriculture" or "gardening," with "upwards of 10,000 individual identifiable cultivated plots," the individual farmers cultivating "a few square meters in four, five, or six areas, at distances of from a few yards to several kilometers from their farmsteads." Thus, the three customary fields for "maize, wheat, and potatoes" became under conditions of demographic growth an inequitable distribution of very scattered plots the size of which was not relevant to the performance of *tareas* (Vázquez 1952:96, Stevens 1959:25, Garrido-Lecca 1965:20-21).[20] Barnett (1960:31, note) says that a few workers work only one or two *tareas* per week but concludes: "This does not mean that the remaining peons who work three days per week have the same amount of [land]. There actually is great variation, but no exact figures are available. There is a great deal of resentment over this situation, directed more against those with a great deal of land than against the *patrón* who has the power to change the situation." Mangin (1954:II, 17) offers this contrast: "A man with one hundred acres under the control of his family and with one hundred cattle on the *puna*, may work the same three days as a widow who has only a half-acre field adjoining her house and a few sheep on the *puna*." Vázquez (1952:96) notes that around 1950 there were over one hundred *vacos*, able-bodied men who worked the *tareas* of others, alternated with others, or worked for others apart from Hacienda *tareas*.

Individual land holdings were passed down in the family by inheritance and there existed no records of original grants, nor did land transfers ordinarily come to the attention of the Hacienda administration if there were no contestations of title. The patrón cound make a grant if he chose, but this custom had practically ceased by the time of the Project's arrival because the Hacienda´s land had been reduced to a minimum for profitable operation. A few wealthy and powerful families, especially those with special access to *patrones*, had taken advantage of their position to extend their holdings. Mangin (1954:III, 4) writes: "Several wealthy men acquired their large holdings, it is reported, through currying favor with past *patrones*, robbing a widow or a weak man with no strong family connections, and being supported in the ensuing conflict by the *patrón* and his hand picked native field bosses [the *mayorales*]. . . . The holdings vary in size from one family with a field of less than two acres to several families with at least 300 acres. Wealthy Vicosinos acquired power over their poorer neighbors by lending them money, providing them with draft animals, sponsoring fiestas, serving as fictive kinsmen, and acting as intermediaries between poor Vicosinos and mestizos. Such individuals had *peones* of their own to fulfill their Hacienda *tareas* and work their household fields."[21]

Mangin (1954:II, 20-21) shows how individuals can better their lot by becoming *mayorales*,[22] the leaders of work teams in the several Vicos neighborhoods:

> There are six *mayorales*. These men are field bosses and assistant foremen to the administrator. All are relatively wealthy and powerful men in local society and men of considerable local prestige. Four of the six have held the highest local political office, and the other two have participated in the political system. Four are over sixty, one fifty-seven, one thirty-eight. These men are chosen as *mayorales* by the *patrón* and, in the past, have used their position to curry favor with the *patrón* and increase their land holdings and privileges at the expense of some of their fellows. Five of them represent quite powerful families. They act as an informal court in land disputes among the peons.

Most workers attended Hacienda labors in gangs led by *mayorales* and were assigned a variety of tasks according to the season and crop, or other profitable activity for the *patrón*. In addition to their work in the fields they repaired irrigation ditches, fences, and Hacienda buildings. The renter who was operating Vicos at the time the Project took over had been planting flax and had built a linen factury near Carhuaz to which he transported some of the Vicos workers daily. Previous *patrones* had assigned workers to tasks such as spinning and weaving, charcoal making, and hauling produce to markets. On occasion, *patrones* even sold the labor of Vicosinos to contractors, miners, and other *hacendados*, and the workers were required to spend a fortnight or a month, in rotation, away from Vicos. Truly, as specified in the Vicos rental contract, the workers were "at the disposal" of the *patrón*.

According to Mangin (1954:II, 20), only 213 of the 252 registered workers engaged in the common labor of field hands. The others were assigned permanently, semi-permanently, or rotationally to a variety of other tasks and services. To begin with, six workers with influence in the community were assigned as *pampa mayorales*. These Vicosinos supervised the labor of the workers in their respective parts of Vicos, called rest periods, reported attendance, and advised the Hacienda administration on agricultural operations. They served the *patrones* as enforcers by checking up on absent workers and confiscating the moveable property of defaulters, a punishment known as *embargo*, which was kept by the Hacienda until defaults were made up. They also performed judicial functions in cases of land disputes among the workers. One additional *mayoral*, the *ruri mayoral* or "inside boss," worked at the *casa hacienda*, supervising the tasks of the Hacienda servants. He was also in charge of the Hacienda's grain mill and collected a fee for its use. The *mayorales* were named by the *patrón* and served at his pleasure.

Parallel with the *mayorales* were the *varayoq*, a complex organization of seventeen politico-religious offices, who led the community in rituals, water management during the dry season cropping, communal and corvée labors, the settlement of disputes, and as arbiters of morality in the regulation of conduct. They were called on when necessary to aid the *mayorales* in enforcing Hacienda rules. In former times they collected the poll tax known as the *contribución personal*.[23] In return for his service, a *mayoral* received a cash bonus of S/. 1.00 per week instead of the .60 received by workers, and he might have his household fields cultivated by them. The lesser tasks and services to which Hacienda workers might be assigned, as they existed around 1950[24] were:

Hortelanos. Eight workers in two groups of four were assigned to the Hacienda's vegetable gardens in alternating day and night shifts weekly. The gardeners were exempted from all other Hacienda duties and received the standard weekly bonus, like other workers. They might, in addition, gather greens from their gardens.

Tápacos. Ten or twelve workers were assigned to guard the Hacienda's crops. During the planting season they watched for livestock that might enter and do damage. They irrigated the crops and guarded against theft when the crops were ripe. At crucial times during the agricultural cycle they were given temporary helpers from the Hacienda labor force. When there were no crops in some fields, the *tápacos* let in plow oxen to graze the stubble. They received the standard bonus.

Repunteros. Four workers were assigned semi-permanently to herd livestock on the *punas* in the high mountain canyons. The animals belonged both to Vicosinos, who had free use of the high grasslands, and to mestizos who paid pasturage fees to the Vicos renter for the service. The *repunteros* received the worker bonus but also had the opportunity to take milk from the cattle with which they made cheese to sell or barter with transients from the other side of the mountain range coming or going through the pass.

Portero and *Preñadero.* Two or more workers were assigned by turn for a period of a month to assist in supervising the livestock on the *punas*. The *portero* worked for the *capataz*, assistant steward, a salaried mestizo member of the Hacienda administration, who was assigned the task of *cobrador*, collector of fees for the use of the pass. Both the *portero* and the *preñadero* guarded the pass, guarded the livestock from rustlers, and collected pasturage fees for the animals that came through. The *preñadero* made a daily count of the livestock. They received the bonus and might, like the *repunteros*, take milk from the cattle. In addition, they were able to collect fees from Vicosinos with herds in the area. Since cattle rustling occurs from time to time, people with livestock in the uplands were glad to have friendly eyes look on their property.

Ruritápaco ("inside *tápaco*") or *semanero.* One worker was appointed monthly, by turn, as night watchman and to serve the administrative staff at the *casa hacienda.* He assisted the *mulero*, chopped firewood, fed the domestic animals, served food, and the like. He received the bonus and one week of rest after his month of service.

Hacienda huarmi ("Hacienda woman") or *cocinera.* Widows took turns serving as cooks for the administrative staff, the number depending on which members of the staff lived in Vicos. They received the worker bonus and were allowed two weeks of rest when their service was over.

Cuchimitzeq (pig herder). One woman was appointed from all the widows who lived alone to take care of the Hacienda's pig herd. She worked for two weeks and was followed by another woman in the same condition. She received no compensation for her work.

Mitaq ("one who takes a turn"). Single women served weekly in the Hacienda as servants and assistants to the cook, also without compensation. It is said in the Hacienda that the service was instituted because single women consume Hacienda resources, like wood and water, and therefore should be of some use to the Hacienda.

The patrón was the maximal authority who enjoyed total power. He directed the use of the Hacienda's land and people. He was the supreme judge and there was no appeal of his decisions (Vázquez 1963a:24). Many'of the Vicos renters did not live in the *casa hacienda* themselves but only visited now and then, especially in more recent times when roads made the towns of the Callejón de Huaylas more easily accessible and more pleasant accommodations were to be found there. Therefore, much of the time, the estate was in the hands of a second-in-command, the *administrador* or *mayordomo*, with his staff of *capataces*. The *mayordomo* kept the Hacienda's books: accounts, records, and the roll of workers. He had three assistants, *capataces*, one on the *puna* at the pass, and two others who supervised the *pampa mayorales* and their work gangs. All these administrators were called *"patrones"* by the Vicosinos. They received salaries as befitted their mestizo status, as well as service from the workers, their families, and their mounts. The renter did not interfere with the running of the Hacienda, as long as an appropriate profit was forthcoming. The rental fee was around S/. 14,500, slightly under $1000 in the early 1950s, and the renter could do as he wished within the broad limits of his contract and local usage. Garrido-Lecca (1965:23) notes: "Very little, [if] any at all, of the 'profits' obtained by the *hacendado* were reinvested. He not only exploited the Indians but also the already somewhat poor agricultural resources. Thus the productive capacity of the Hacienda was not being increased or even held constant. It was slowly but steadily declining."

Workers did not work enthusiastically under these conditions. Their slow start, numerous rest periods, and general lack of industry were noted by all observers. The schedule of the Hacienda work day at the time the Project came to Vicos, according to Vázquez (1952:103) and Barnett (1960:32), was this:

> 8:00-9:00 a.m.: A worker leaves home and gathers with others at the assigned work location. They chew coca and converse.
> 9:00-9:15 a.m.: Work begins.
> 10:00-10:15 a.m.: First rest period of fifteen minutes for chewing coca.
> 11:30-11:45 a.m.: Second rest period.
> 12:30-2:00 p.m.: Mid-day rest period begins.
> 3:00-3:15: Third rest period.

4:00-4:15 p.m.: Fourth rest period.
4:30 p.m.: Work stops for the day and the worker goes home.

Barnett (33) says that with this schedule the worker worked only five hours of the seven-and-one-half he spent in the field..[25]

It was the custom at the close of the Hacienda work week on Wednesday afternoons to hold a *mando*, a meeting of all Hacienda personnel, in the patio of the *casa hacienda* or in the fields. At this meeting the workers were given their assignments for the coming week, announcements were made, and the cash bonus, *temple*, was passed out. This bonus was instituted in the late 1940s to replace the coca and *chicha*, home brew, which had been provided by earlier *patrones*. If a worker missed one day he lost the bonus for the entire week even when he made up the default.

Workers or members of their families were obliged to make up absences or defaults, *faltas*, no matter for what reason, except for military service in recent years. Extreme cases of invalidism and poverty were overlooked. If an able-bodied worker became sick he had to make his absence up when he was well again. Ordinarily, the administration did not act until a worker had been absent for a month, at which time the *mayorales* were sent to investigate and take punitive action, or threaten it. Absenteeism was common, however. Mangin (1954:II, 24) observes: "Eviction is not common in the area. . . . Most *patrones* realize that labor is their main resource so they do not press their peons too hard." Barnett (1960:30-31) reports: "On April 3, 1953, there were 1,362 *faltas* recorded for the 251 peons, ranging in individual cases from 1 to 81, with the median at 36 *tareas*." William Blanchard included in the Project archives an account of the Hacienda's manner of keeping the roll of the workers, as explained to him by Enrique Luna. These field notes are dated August 29, 1953. They were recorded less than a week after the field of the *missing member* was confiscated by the Hacienda, an action we will soon review. The notes illustrate the operation of the reformed hacienda system of 1952-1957:

> This afternoon, Enrique [Luna] was checking off *tareas* and men prior to payment of *temple*. He uses a four-drawer file. Each man on the labor force, representing each holder of land known to the Hacienda, has a card. Most cards bear a "3" at the top, although there are some exceptions where "2" is seen, and I think there is a case or two of "1". The numbers refer to the number of days' work per week the men owe the Hacienda. The reductions are made on the basis of the smallness of fields. Down the left side of the cards are the names of months, almost all starting with September 1952. . . . Across the tops of the cards are the weeks in each month. In the squares which result are placed "1" or "Y" in reference to each day's *tarea* worked or *yunta*-day. If the card has a "3" at the top,

there should be three marks in each square. If a man is sick, an "e" [for *enfermo*, sick] is placed in the square. . . . Other cards have "*cárcel*," jail, written on them for time spent in jail. . . . In other cases a notation "d" indicates *dispensado*, excused.

Enrique said that sometimes men with good records come and say that thy just simply have to work in their fields, or that something has come up and they are in a difficult position. Sometimes, too, they go to Mario [Vázquez] and he excuses them. Enrique indicated that he believed they pulled the wool over Mario's eyes as often as not.

On the right margin of each card was indicated the amount of *temple* that had been paid. Thus the cards are also a record of the money the Hacienda has given each man.

I estimated the total number of cards at 249. This gives a theoretical total of 747 *tareas* per week owed the Hacienda, but since there are some on reduced rates the number is less than that.

Men get in arrears in their Hacienda obligations. Men can also get ahead in their obligations. This is possible in two ways: 1) when they actually work more than the three days in some weeks, or 2) when they bring someone with them to work–usually a relative but not necessarily one–and the men are credited with the number of *tareas* put in. Thus a man can have five or six days' work credited to him in a three-day period. Enrique says there are people who are ahead and can take time off later.

Enrique calculates the *faltas* by the blanks or incomplete weekly squares. The record is transferred from his notebook to the cards and then the notebook entries are checked off. . . .

I asked Enrique how many people had *faltas*. He began to go through the cards while I took down only the flagrant cases along with some of the remarks he made:

No. 1: 13 *faltas*

  2: 21

  3: 16

  4: 20   This is one known to the administration as "the laziest man in Vicos." Enrique says he does fairly well when he is working by himself. However, now he is working with his brother, who is a bad influence, and he has been getting *faltas*. His brother is supposedly worse.

  5: 25

  6: 13

  7: 30

  8: 21   This man was in jail a spell, and the 21 *faltas* were from before that. Men in jail are excused. Enrique spoke of him as though he were rather good for nothing. The jail term was for theft.

  9: 30   He has been sick and now his son is working in his place.

  10: 27   Sick. His girl is working now, shelling maize, in his place.

  11: 16

  12: 16

13: 46   Members of the family have guaranteed that he will make them up in order to forestall the confiscation of his land by the Hacienda.

14: 15

15: 12

16: 9

17: 9

18: 14   He had 23 *faltas* two weeks ago, but he too has been guaranteed. He has made up 9 and kept current.

19: 70   (Pedro Cruz) Enrique told me yesterday that he had 70 *faltas*. Today I did not try to count the many blanks on his card.

20: 10   He spent six months in jail and has the *faltas* since then.

21: ?   He has endless *faltas*. Enrique says he was given a field last September but shows no evidence of responding by working.

22: 11

23: 11

24: 22   This man is an ex-soldier and #8's brother. Both are lazy more than anything else, Enrique said.

The whole list represents about 400 *faltas*. . . . The regular workers, those who may be assigned to any job, are first in the file. At the end of the file appear cards for the *mayorales*, *tápacos*, and others who have special assignments. The ones who go off special duties are given time off from Hacienda work, so that they have what Enrique referred to as a "vacation." (AVP.)

Before the Project came to Vicos, as I have noted, the ordinary sanction which was applied when workers did not fulfill their obligations was the *embargo*, the confiscation of goods. This was, and I believe is today, the practice on various administrative levels to force the owner of the goods to conform to the mandate of some authority: for example, failure to heed a summons from judicial authority, or an order to satisfy a judgment; absence from communal work projects; to oblige the payment of taxes or fees; or theft and the flight of the thief. The Hacienda used confiscation not only for absence but for damage to or theft of its crops, as well as other forms of disobedience. The goods taken were livestock in cases of serious delinquencies or *faltas*, and household animals or tools for minor ones. They were kept at the *casa hacienda* until they were redeemed by the fulfillment of whatever the obligation was (AVP: Mario Vázquez, March, 1953, IV, 39-40).[26]

The Vicos *patrón* had at his disposal a number of other means of social control. According to Barnett (1960:49), he could reward workers with liberal excuses of absences or by giving aid to people in personal difficulties. When there were bad harvests he could provide food products. *Patrones* might contribute to baptisms, weddings, funerals, and might inscribe themselves as *devotos* for fiestas, that is, persons who contribute funds or goods toward the celebration of saints' days. The *patrón* had great power because his judgment was final in matters of land disputes, the transfer of land, and the granting of land to new workers. Barnett (50-54) lists of six negative sanctions which the *patrón* might use to control his workers: 1) Difficult workers could be assigned uncomfortable tasks such as, for example, one of the special duties on the *puna* for an extended period. The *puna* is a cold eco-zone and a long stay there can be quite unpleasant, especially in the rainy season. 2) *Capataces* and *mayorales* customarily employed whips to convince reluctant workers and speed up slow ones, until early in the twentieth century, and a public whipping post existed in Vicos until the 1920s or 30s.[27] 3) Since mestizo authorities in the towns supported the existing hacienda system, the *patrón* could always have recourse to their intervention with troublesome workers, who were on occasion jailed or fined for real or fictitious infractions. 4) From the early part of this century to 1926, some *patrones* sold Vicos labor to contractors outside Vicos, which required workers to leave their homes to carry out their work obligations. 5) The *patrón* could see to it that a worker was drafted into military service. 6) The worker's land could be confiscated, forcing him to choose between leaving Vicos or serving as what Barnett calls a "sub-*peón*" to a relative or a wealthy person who would support him. Holmberg (1967:5) mentions capital punishment as a possible sanction as well, in citing a case where in 1960 the workers of a neighboring hacienda were shot by the police, with three killed and five wounded, when the *patrón* of that estate called for assistance in removing them from some land they were planting.

Barnett (1960:81) provides a summary of the major effects of the hacienda system on the Vicos community:

1. It has isolated the community from the national culture.
2. It prevents Vicosinos from leaving the community for any extended period of time.
3. It fosters a dual set of values regarding work and honesty; and the careless work and stealing encouraged and facilitated by the system, dominates non-Hacienda life and work.
4. It is an inefficient economic system that helps to keep the people impoverished.
5. It provides aid to the people during time of famine and thus preserves the community; but at the same time,
6. It fosters and forces an acceptance of authoritarian, paternalistic outside rule.
7. It undermines the authority of the community leadership and co-opts

all potential Vicosino community leaders.
  8. It undermines the customary authority of the father of a family.
  9. It has prevented the development of positive values toward community activities.
  10. It has fostered the development of utilitarian values in social relationships.

The only restraints on the hacienda system *within* Vicos were those imposed by the regional hacienda system *outside*, a field of power which provided mestizos with access to a cheap and docile labor force. As I have noted, land distribution within Vicos was not such as to distribute resources evenly in the community, or even according to need. Most Vicosinos were forced by their circumstances to seek supplements to what their limited household fields could provide by working for outside *patrones* for wages in cash or produce. Mangin (1954:III,29) reports for the early 1950s that daily from five to fifty persons went to the main valley to work.[28] Occasionally Vicosinos would leave for work farther away than the valley towns, sometimes on a labor contract or "*enganche*," the "hook,"[29] but in general their obligations to fulfill Hacienda *tareas* and their "asymmetrical reciprocities" (Mayer 1974:222) with the other mestizo *patrones* for whom they worked kept them in the Province of Carhuaz.[30]

There was ambiguity and potential conflict for Vicosinos, the administrators of Vicos, and the mestizos of the valley towns in the existence of multiple *patrones*, that is, the Vicos *patrones* and other mestizo *patrones* for whom Vicosinos worked outside Vicos. As long as the balance between the internal needs of the Hacienda and the requirements of the owners of the smaller estates near Marcará and Carhuaz was maintained, the order of things was maintained. On those occasions when Vicos *patrones* acted to interfere with the access outside *patrones* had to Vicos produce and labor power, disturbances were fomented which put an end to the regimes of those Vicos *patrones*, and the balance was reestablished. Three such collective disturbances during this century are reported in Barnett (1960); and one nineteenth century disturbance is reported in Stein (1991b). A similar occurrence was connected with the expulsion of Peace Corps volunteers by the Vicosinos in 1964.[31]

How did the Vicosinos view this system? We are fortunate to have some record of their feelings in the interview protocols provided by the staff of the Methodology Study in 1953. Before the events connected with Pedro Cruz took place, the interviewers were required to ask about past and present operation of the Hacienda, and possibilities for transforming it. In their responses, Vicosinos talked about many aspects of their condition as workers and the conduct of Hacienda labors. At the risk of repeating something of what has been said in Chapter 3, I present these interview extracts. I think you will find more in them after having read the extended discussion of the hacienda system just provided.

First, here are some Vicosinos views on the subject of being an Hacienda worker:

> Alejandro Leiva: I just work in this Hacienda. We don't earn anything. We work in the sense of rent for occupying the Hacienda's *chacras*, [fields]. Every week we work three days for the Hacienda, and we receive only *temple* which consists of 20 *centavos* for buying our coca. We don't sell our produce. Rather, we buy things from other places like Marcará, Carhuaz, and Chacas, so as to supply our needs during the year. To get the necessary money for buying food products we must see ourselves obliged to work in the places I've mentioned for two, three, or more days, earning more or less S/. 4.00 each day. (MP,[32] Soler, June 26.)

> Pablo Reyes: *Temple* is the pay that the Hacienda the Vicos workers. It's for their coca. We're poor people whose fields don't provide enough for us to last through the year, and the money from *temple* isn't even enough to buy the coca we use during those three days of work for the Hacienda. And the Hacienda doesn't even want to give us a raise in pay. That's their style. (MP, Soler, June 27.)

> Lucas Díaz: We must work for the Hacienda. It's no great thing that they give us for those three days that we work. We get 20 *centavos* and we call it *temple*. We can't even register a complaint about it because we don't know how to read and write. Surely the ones with their papers could tangle us up. (MP, Soler, June 27.)

> Víctor Sánchez: I've gone to Huaraz since I was a child. Sometimes I went on foot, and other times in a truck. I went there to work making adobes when I was young. They used to pay me S/. 3.00. . . . I've also gone to Carhuaz. I've gone there, too, since I was a child. I always go when I'm out of things at home. I go on foot, because going in a truck is expensive. I don't sleep there. I just stay as long as I need to buy bread, *aji*, lard, and sometimes cloth for shirts. I went one time to work hauling logs. They paid me 3 *soles* a day. I was there for a week. I also go to work in Marcará, but I almost never stay over. I do everything possible to return the same afternoon. The pay is the same, but some pay a little less, maybe S/. 2.00. For the fiesta of our patron [the Virgen de las Mercedes] we go out to work more often, as much to buy new clothing as to buy victuals so as not to be needy. So we can be content at least for those days. (MP, Soler, July 1.)

Marcos Quinto: I haven't been able to plant [on shares with the Hacienda] because I have little land. Some have a greater extension of land while others have less. That depends on whether or not men in the old days gave them more land, while they gave others less, so that they've given little land to those of us who went in more recently. That's who we'd like to register a complaint so that they give us as much land as they've given to others. (MP, Soler, July 12.)

Alejandro Reyes: The *patrones* used to worry that the Hacienda's crops would be good, but the Hacienda didn't worry much about us. It was like we couldn't even miss one day, because if we did they'd come for an *embargo*. We couldn't even get sick, because they made us work all the days we were sick. (MP, Soler, July 12.)

Alejo Valerio: (Have you ever refused to work for the Hacienda?) Never. . . . If I work for the Hacienda I have to obey until it's rest time. (Have you always respected the *mayorales*?) Yes, but when the *mayorales* or the *empleados* [white collar workers in Peru, here the *capataces*] have treated me bad I've gotten angry. Then I've told them, "Why do you treat me like that? Can't you deal with people an other way?" So we've had arguments. For that reason, when I was 17 or 18 years old I had a fight with Ernesto Vidal who was an *empleado* of the Hacienda. He was quite an idiot. He used bad words when he talked. So we didn't like him. He also punched and kicked. So I answered him back. (MP, Flores, with Celso León, July 25.)

Alejandro Quito: (You've worked all your life. What for?) When my father died I went into the Hacienda to work. . . . (Don't you think you should have worked more when you were young for now when you're old?) It's just because we've been the Hacienda's people that we've worked there. There wasn't time to set up my home for when I'd be old. It's because I've been the Hacienda's since I was a boy that I've come to have nothing. Now I work so I can plant. Now that I'm old, who's going to take my place in the Hacienda? And if I don't go to work maybe the Hacienda will take everything away from me and I'll have no place to plant. (Don't you work, thinking it will be for your children?) How are we going to do that when we work every week for the Hacienda? I'll just leave them my animals. The house and the land will be for my children as long as they work for the Hacienda. Otherwise, the Hacienda would take the house and the fields. (MP, Flores, with Celso León, August 3.)

Sebastián Sánchez: Whether I like it or not, I have to work for the Hacienda. Because I'm poor I have to live like that. The Hacienda doesn't want us to miss work, and they pay us very little. It isn't enough to buy salt. They don't help us at all, and we have to go out to other places to look for work or to sell our chickens. And in the old days if we

didn't obey, the ones in the Hacienda would take *embargos* of our things.
. . . I'm good natured and if I don't show up I get worried. Even though I
have a lot of my own work, if they order me I have to obey. (MP, Soto,
with Ricardo Estremadoyro, August 5.)

> Eugenio Leiva: Hacienda work isn't good. . . . We work three days for
> the Hacienda, and they give us only four days for our own work, and that
> includes Sunday. That's why our own work doesn't go well. If a man is
> single, how is he going to get his work done? On the other hand, other
> people have their children and that way it gets done, but those of us who
> are single can't do it. In other places they pay three or four *soles* a day,
> with full *temple*. They also hand out *chicha*, alcohol, coca, and cigarettes.
> That happens in Marcará. Here they don't pay anything. All the work we
> do in the Hacienda is the payment we make for planting in the fields up
> above. (MP, Soto, with Ricardo Estremadoyro, August 17.)

The hacienda system restricts movement. This leads me to think of the
tight swaddling sashes with which Vicos mothers, along with other
campesinas, wrap their infants so that the latter can be carried in their
llikllas or placed safely on the ground. While swaddling cannot be shown
to affect character in later childhood or adulthood, I only want to suggest
here that restriction on the movement of adults constitutes a metaphor for
Vicosinos. It signifies their reduction to infantile condition, as does the
helplessness of illiteracy, and a condition in which the Project tended to
view them (see the opening paragraph of Chapter 3):

> Lucas Díaz: I don't travel much because I have to carry out my *tareas* in
> the Hacienda. Here if we miss a few days they nag us to make those days
> up, and because we're planting crops in the fields they've given us we
> have to work for the Hacienda. . . . We can't even register a complaint
> because we don't know how to read and write. (MP, Soler, June 27.)

> Félix Tadeo I: When I was a boy I traveled one time with my father to
> Recuay to buy wool. I've gone to Chacas to buy eggs for trade. I got
> money from a man in Marcará and with that *enganche* I went to look for
> eggs. I've also gone to the lake [unidentified] to work hauling stones and
> digging as a *peón* for the government.
>   I don't consider trips to Marcará to work as travel. I went to Huaraz on
> the Hacienda's account to do my service [in the *patrón*'s house]. I go to
> Marcará two or three times a month to work and to buy things. I've gone
> to Carhuaz about four times to buy wool, *ají*, salt, and sugar, because in
> Marcará they sell those things with short weight. In Carhuaz they give
> you full weight.
>   I don't like to go out to other places. Here I was born and here I am. I
> don't like the idea of going out. When I was a young boy I didn't leave

here. I don't want to go. I don't like to travel. Since I'm the Hacienda's person I can't leave for anywhere because the Hacienda won't give me permission. They always complain if I miss a day. (MP, Flores, with Ricardo Estremadoyro, June 26.)

Andrés Copitán: When we go out of Vicos to travel to the coast we can ask leave of one to five days, and if we don't return on the days they indicate they make us absentees, and then they punish us. (MP, Soto, with Ricardo Estremadoyro, August 26.)

Marcos Quinto: Where are you from? (I answer that I'm from Huánuco.) You probably know all the places on the coast. Unfortunately, I'm not as lucky as you people because I'm a worker in the Hacienda and I'm obliged to work every week. We greatly want to get to know other places. (MP, Soler, July 12.)

Jorge Reyes: It's the Hacienda's fault that I haven't wanted to get an *enganche*, because I give a good account of myself and in the Hacienda they don't want anyone to miss. I've been a good *tápaco* for twenty years, and so the other workers hate me because the *patrón* likes me. They tell me, "You're very obedient, you're bad." That's why I don't get together with people, because they could kill me.
When I'm not working I cry. I work day and night, and at night I don't get sleepy. I like to work more at night than in the daytime, because it's not warm at night. (Pablo Herrera says that when there's a moon at night almost everybody works. They work till midnight, until they get sleepy. They have to work like that, because if they're single or when they're working in the Hacienda they don't do their own work. The day is not long enough to do all the work their fields need.) (MP, Flores, with Pablo Herrera, July 7.)

Alfonso Cruz: Now I've got a greater obligation because I'm a *campo* [a member of the *varayoq* organization] and I have to make many expenditures: liquor when they have *la república* [corvée labor] and food for Easter. I have to spend for all that. In *la república*, everything is expense. I haven't even planted wheat yet for attending to people. My fellow *varayoq* are planting more and they give better attention than I can, and so like that I'm falling behind in my obligations. There are expenses for all the fiestas, and the Hacienda doesn't excuse anything if I miss work here because I'm going to look for it somewhere else. Certainly then they would order an *embargo* taken from me. (MP, Flores, with Celso León, August 17.)

Vicosinos are proud of their physical prowess, their ability to carry heavy loads, and their resistance to fatigue. Mangin (1954:V, 64) says that one of the five basic values of Vicos culture is "the positive evaluation of agricultural labor." Vázquez (1952:44) reports of the Vicosino that he/she is a "lover of work; he/she lives all year dedicated to agricultural activities. Price (1961:9-11) emphasizes that sexual roles are quite clearly defined, which explains a certain aggression between them. These relations are more physical than romantic, the best way young men and women can display their desirability. His description of a "mock battle" between a group of young men and women is worth transcribing here:

> One day last summer, high in the puna up above the inhabited area of Vicos, I witnessed a mock battle between about fifteen girls [sic], all in their late teens or early twenties, and an equal number of young men. After having spent the day working together preparing the soil for planting by breaking oversized clods of earth, in the late afternoon they separated by sex into two groups which sat down in the field perhaps fifty feet apart. The men began chewing coca while the girls gossiped quietly among themselves. After a few minutes had passed, one of the men lofted a large clod of earth in the direction of the girls. Soon the "war" was underway, with the girls moving into a tight defensive huddle, presenting as little area as possible to the arching trajectories of the men's missiles. The men remained somewhat separated and fired away at the girls stopping occasionally to add lime to the wad of coca in their mouths. The girls teased and shouted at the men, and their accuracy and force in throwing at least equaled that of their male friends. Woman in Vicos learn to throw rocks at their flocks from the age of five or six years and develop what appears, to a male North American, to be a remarkable throwing arm. After several minutes of long range bombing, one of the girls sprang up and made a charge at the nearest boy, throwing clods as she ran. He, feigning helplessness, ran in the other direction at full speed but was clipped by a number of projectiles before he got out of range. Later, the same girl who was the oldest, most provocative, and ringleader of the girls, made another charge which ended with a flying tackle in a cloud of dust as she brought down the man she had been chasing. The man rolled over on top of her and forced her to eat some dirt, to the great amusement of his friends. She continued to pummel him with her fists, kicking her foot and squealing as he fed her. After about fifteen minutes of bombing and chasing, a spontaneous truce was declared.

The value of work in Vicos, rather different from the rational work ethic mentioned earlier, is described by Vázquez (1952:101):

> Work is considered to be an unavoidable fact in life, the practice of which dignifies one, while laziness is denigrating. Therefore, in Vicos, it is offensive to call a person "*weqlla*" or "*qella*," that is, a "lazy one." When the Vicosino speaks of work he does it with a certain air of pride, and he considers himself to be superior to mestizos and whites, who are referred

to disparagingly as people who only know how to give orders and do not know how to haul loads, take hold of things, and work with a plow. . . . The theme and daily concern of Vicosinos is: "Work." Still, their performance is not uniform. There are poor people with great worries and aspirations, who devote themselves to obtaining the maximum productivity of their scanty lands, and next to these there exist others, without aspirations, owners of large extensions of land, who barely plant small parts of them, and often harvest nothing because of their lack of care. Such people prefer to live as day laborers in neighboring towns, depending on the good will of their neighbors or on thievery. They are objects of compassion and contempt, while the former, whose social status rises daily, enjoy esteem and consideration.

But what Jorge Reyes said touches me: *when I'm not working I cry.* The complement to this statement is: *when I'm working I'm not crying.* The significance of work, then, has to do with the reestablishment of bonds with the *missing object*, for this work is work on the land, on Mama Patza,[33] Mother Earth. Work is, in this way, a shelter from loss, separation, being cut off, castration.

However, all this has little to do with the Vicosino attitude toward Hacienda work. The notoriety of Vicosinos as being inefficient in their *tareas* is only the echo of the "double standard" characeistic of the hacienda system in which workers have neither access to the means of production, in any permanent sense, nor to the product of their labor. Vicosinos' love of work indicates an attachment to their own enterprises, something quite alien to the mestizo elite of Marcará and Carhuaz who see neither dignity nor value in labor.[34] Vicosinos expressed themselves:

Alfonso Cruz: (How long have you been an Hacienda peon?) Since I was a little boy. When my father died I had to go in as a worker in the Hacienda, because there was nobody else to work. It was so as not to let others come in to work the fields that belonged to my father, and before that to my grandfather. (Do you think you're a better worker in your fields or as a peon?) I'm proud of being a good worker. That's why I don't like it when work goes poorly for me. When I'm working for somebody else I do it well. I work conscientiously, with good will. A person accepts it so as to do good work and not work badly. (In your fields, do you try to do the best you can, and not carelessly like a lazy man?) I work calmly and in peace, with patience. Others do it too fast and so the work ends up poorly. (When you work for the Hacienda, do you do it the same way you work in your fields?) It's my custom to work the same. If a person is used to working hard, he works the same. Then the owners of the Hacienda see that a person is working well, that he's a good worker.

(Are there peons who work well in their fields and don't work the same way in the Hacienda?) Yes, there are. Each person has his way of working. (Why do they do that?) It's because there are times when a person works willingly in the Hacienda. It's like this–on the homestead a person works, and then he says, "Why should I work so hard in the Hacienda and then be tired out for working in my fields?" That's why they get confused. (Are there peons who are lazy in their work?) Yes. (What do you think of such lazy men?) I don't like those men. (Why?) Because the work doesn't get done. (What do you think of a peon who is lazy when he works for the Hacienda?) If I work with five or six men and one of them is lazy, I say that we all should work the same in all the *tareas*. Those lazy men make the rest lazy. They ought to choose people who work the same in a work group and that way get the job done and then rest. (Why are lazy men like that?) It's the habit of their bodies. Sometimes laziness dominates them. Sometimes they're like animals. Some *yuntas* take big steps and others take little ones, and no matter how much you whip them they veer and don't go in a straight line. That's the way they are.. (MP, Flores, with Celso León, August 19.)

Eugenio Leiva: (Have you ever not wanted to work for the Hacienda?) I've worked all my life. How am I not going to work if I'm the Hacienda's worker? I'll work all my life till I die. How are we going to get along in life without work? . . .
(In the weeks that you don't work in the garden [the informant is an *hortelano*] do you visit? No, because we're not like *mishtis* who walk around when they're not working. We always have something to do at home. . . .
(Do you like to work more with Vicosinos or with *mishtis*?) I get lazy with *mishtis*. With Vicosinos a person works as well as he can. The *qarakos [mishti* gentlemen] make me lazy hoeing maize when they don't like the *lampas* we use here. They sit down and I also get lazy. On the other hand, with Vicosinos, we chew coca, talk a while, and then we take hold of the work till it's time to chew coca. (MP, Flores, with Celso León, August 11.)

Simón Díaz: *Minka* [festive labor] work is the best, I think. Most of the time I plant in my fields alone, and sometimes the neighbors come to help. I don't do the work another way because I have no money. If they don't come to help me, I have to do the work even if I'm alone, even if it takes more days to do it. Wage labor is the same as *minka*.. If I earn three *soles* a day for work I do, and then if I have someone come to do it I have to pay out three *soles*. The problem is that we don't have the money to hire people. In *minka* work I spend for *chicha* and alcohol, and if it goes on into the night I can spend more. Otherwise, those who come to work can agree on compensation in advance.
I'm the Hacienda's person. In my work I can do it with others or alone.

It's the same to me. Vicosinos work well. I work as willingly for myself as for the Hacienda. But other people work for the Hacienda unwillingly. Then, when they [in the Hacienda] see these things they get angry in their hearts and they call us lazy and weak. If a Vicosino worked unwillingly in a field of mine, I'd tell him, "Now, you've come to work in a *minka*, fellows, let's do it well!" (MP, Soto, with Ricardo Estremadoyro, August 22.)

Most Vicos workers appear to hold an ideal model of the hacienda system in which the *patrón* is good and kind to his clients. The changes which were suggested by some informants seem to take the direction of a more liberal regimen:

> Alejandro Quito: (How could life be better here?) The best life would be if the Hacienda provided us with better seeds and if the *patrones* helped us in other ways. (How?) It would be better if they helped us in times of scarcity with maize, potatoes, and grain. Sometimes we can't get what they produce all year long. We'd like them to sell produce to us. We'd also like them to give us tools. Wherever I've gone I haven't observed that workers have to bring their own tools. . . . It would be good if there were more help. (MP, Flores, with Celso León, August 4.)

> Alfonso Cruz: (How would you like them to pay *temple*?) Twenty *centavos'* worth of coca daily isn't enough. Sometimes in work people spend 40, 60, or 80 *centavos* for coca–and the 20 *centavos* that they pay isn't enough. Even 50 *centavos* as *temple* would be good. That way people would work with good will. We work like in any other place. They could even increase *temple* in February and March, because it rains a lot, and in November and December, which is a time of great hunger. The Hacienda ought to help poor people who haven't had good crops. But here in Vicos we eat just to live. Later, in January and February, there's *choclo* [green corn], and then even if the Hacienda doesn't help out with victuals everyone can get along with what they take out of their fields, but in November and December they ought to help people. (MP, Flores, with Celso León, August 19.)

> José Francisco: The present *patrones* are good. They treat us well. But we're sad that they don't give us help. In the old days, the *patrones* gave us help from their crops. Now they don't give that out because they carry off the produce to other places. (MP, Flores, with Pablo Herrera, July 11.)

We should not assume that all that is meant by this image of the Hacienda as protector is an attitude of passsivity and dependence on the part of the worker. The image of the Hacienda is overdetermined.

Another possible interpretation of the desire for assistance from those who are powerful is the the Vicos model of the leader as a redistributor. We may keep this in mind in order to understand Vicosinos' responses to the proposal: "What would you do if you were the *patrón*?:

> Antonio Padua: If I were the *patrón* of the Hacienda I'd have the people work. I'd pay wages, what the workers asked for. I'd have them plant potatoes, maize, and wheat to sell. If I were rich I'd sell everything I have. I'd have a house built, a beautiful one like the school. I'd buy a truck to carry cargo. I'd be a good patron. (MP, Flores, with Ricardo Estremadoyro, June 30.)

> Manuel Tafur: If I were the *patrón* of the Hacienda, I'd have the people work. I'd write things down on paper. I wouldn't plant the same way. I'd buy tools, *lampas, barretas,* sickles, picks, clod-breakers. I'd pay my workers more, S/. 3.50 or 4.00, according to their work. That's the way they pay in Marcará now. Here in the Hacienda there are no wages. Everything is for the Hacienda. (MP, Flores, with Pablo Herrera, July 2.)

> Dolores Cruz: I don't have a head. How am I going to be *patrón* of the Hacienda? If I were *patrón*, I'd just sit and I wouldn't do anything. I'd plant a few pieces of land. If I were the head, I'd plant a lot of potatoes, barley, *ocas, mashua, ollucos,* maize, and *chocho.* I'd plant lots, with many workers. I'd be good to my people, to everyone. If the people wanted to cook food, I'd give it to them. (MP, Flores, with Pablo Herrera, July 3.)

> Agustín Reyes: If I were *patrón* of the Hacienda, I'd do the same as they are doing now. I'd build houses and give orders to the people. I wouldn't be bad to my people. When these *patrones* first came they said they were going to give help and presents to the people. Now they're giving nothing. A person eats in his house, even though there isn't anything to eat, and we keep going to work. (MP, Flores, with Pablo Herrera, July 3.)

> Manuel Sánchez: If I were *patrón* of the Hacienda I wouldn't know what to do because I think I wouldn't want anything. All the *patrones* are the same. They lie and cheat, and they don't fulfill their promises. . . . We'd like them to give us help, but they never give it. They took away everything that we harvested. And with the money that they give us we have to be going around to buy grain. (MP, Flores, with Pablo Herrera, July 9.)

> Manuel Cruz: If I were *patrón* I'd know how to do what I promise. All of those who come promise us and then they don't do it. If I were *patrón* I'd plant all the fields. The *patrones* before looked to our needs. Now

they give to those who need it less. (MP, Flores, with Pablo Herrera, July 9.)

Eugenio Leiva: If I were the *patrón* of the Hacienda I'd give 10 *soles* to those who plant on shares. I'd give them a pack of cigarettes saying, "Take this, you're working hard!" I'd also buy them boots for irrigation work. It would be necessary to think, because these expenses would be taken from the harvest before. If a person didn't do these things, how would he earn the love, how would he take care of the people? (MP, Soto, with Ricardo Estremadoyro, August 17.)

Eloy Neira and Patricia Ruiz Bravo (2000:214) suggest that the word *patrón* has many meanings: "The density of this personage's presence in collective memory leads us to regard it, rather than a literal term—one which designates a concrete object—, as above all a metaphor which allows a sense of a field of significations which refer to several aspects of people's identity, and as well to relations among them. Moreover, the reiteration of certain ways of talking (of remembering) about the *patrón* allows us to us this metaphor as an entry—a point of condensation—to the social construction of local imaginaries, to the magma in which are interwoven factors which we recognize analytically as class, ethnic-racial, estamental, and, certainly, gender."

Most workers really did not think in terms of personal mobility for themselves into the position of *patrón*. Rather, when the proposal for change was put to them, they visualized replacing the hacienda system with a kinder order of things. They readily grasped the fact that the Project was not changing it:

José Vega: The last *patrón* was very good. He didn't let us go without victuals for our families. After the harvests he let us collect the products which had fallen to the ground. The *patrón* here now searches us carefully, even our pockets. He doesn't want us to take anything at all out of the Hacienda's fields. I think they've told him that we were in the habit of stealing from his fields. With such luck I don't know what's going to become of us! (MP, Soler, July 2.)

Narciso Meza: The *patrones* have forgotten to give us the help or the victuals that other *patrones* used to give in the old days. Now in the Hacienda they're always telling us that if we want to eat well we have to work hard. (MP, Soler, July 17.)

Nicolás Herrera: The Hacienda is the same as it was. It's just that the renters have changed, from one to another. There are some renters who are good and others who are bad. When they are newly arrived they are good, but later they become bad. The *empleados* request the renters not to be good. The *empleados* are bad. There have been times when the renters have provided food, like on the coast, but then the *empleados* have told them not to give out anything, that it's necessary to keep to old customs and not give anything.

The present renters are good. The gringos are the best, maybe because they're rich. Dr. Holmberg is good. Enrique is the worst. At the potato harvest other *empleados* used to give presents of potatoes to the workers. Now Enrique doesn't want to give them so that people won't get used to it. (MP, Flores, with Ricardo Estremadoyro, June 30.)

Dolores Cruz: They are mean, greedy, and avaricious in the Hacienda. They don't give anything away. They don't even sell it to me. They ought to sell to those who want it, when they want it, and otherwise not. I plant a few fields. The Hacienda doesn't want to give me more. I'd like them to give me more land for planting potatoes and wheat. . . . The *patrones* in the past were better because when we used to bring them presents–guineapigs, chickens, eggs–they'd give us grain–wheat, maize, *habas*, barley. The *patrones'* wives would give us food. In the old days the *mulero* ate in the Hacienda. Now he doesn't eat there. They used to feed us potatoes, cabbage, and wheat hominy. (MP, Flores, with Pablo Herrera, July 3.)

Alejandro Tapia: Now that the *forasteros* [outsiders] are here I don't like it because they don't give me anything. . . . The Hacienda's *patrones* in the old days were better. They helped us out with grain, and even food. That used to exist here. Now it doesn't. . . . In the old days the *patrones* gave presents of food. Grain cost less. Now it's very expensive. In the old days the *patrones* gave grain out to poor people. Now it's nothing, not even food. (MP, Flores, with Pablo Herrera, July 4.)

Simón Díaz: In the old days the *patrones* didn't give us *temple*, but when they harvested crops in the Hacienda they gave us potatoes and maize. We used to go with our baskets to get those things. Now the ones in Vicos don't give us anything. . . . The *patrones* were better then. Now Don Enrique isn't good. He's not abusive to me, but he abuses other people. (MP, Soto, with Ricardo Estremadoyro, August 21.)

Antonio Padua: (What do you think of Enrique Luna?) He's so restless! When is that Enrique going to leave? He keeps getting the gringos' confidence, but he's deceiving them. (Why don't you like him?) He stuffs every *patrón* who comes in with stories about the Vicosinos. He tells them what the Vicosinos are like. The new *patrones* who are coming in are good, but if they start giving presents to the Vicosinos he fixes it so they don't keep it up. He wants to take advantage of the Hacienda for himself. (What does he tell the *patrones*?) He tells them not to give presents to poor old people. He says it's not the custom to give things away like that. The *patrones* listen to him. The gringos made an agreement that the poorest people, ones like me, wouldn't have to work three days for the Hacienda and that they would plant their fields anyway. If they did work for the Hacienda, they'd get paid for it. Enrique told them not to do it because everybody would want to have it like that, and to go on like before. (MP, Flores, with Celso León, August 17.)

The Missing Member: *The Case of Pedro Cruz*

In August 1953 the administration of the Project (and the Hacienda) consisted of Dr. William C. Blanchard, Project Field Director,[35] Enrique Luna, a resident of Marcará who had been an assistant administrator of the Hacienda under the previous *patrón*, who was retained by the Project in the capacity of capataz,[36] and who represented the dominant mestizo sector of the Callejón de Huaylas in Vicos, and Dr. Mario C. Vázquez, Project Anthropologist, who had been conducting intensive ethnographic work in Vicos for several years.[37] Also resident in Vicos was Dr. Sarah Levy, of the Methodology Project, and her staff, and two North American anthropology students, Clifford Barnett and Norman Pava. All these persons appear to have been touched by the case I discuss here.

Earlier, when the Project took charge of Vicos, a series of significant reforms were quickly instituted. Plans were made in advance and the new regimen was announced to the Vicosinos at *mandos* and other meetings of the *mayorales* in late 1951 and early 1952. Here is what the Project told the people of Vicos:[38]

1.–The principal goal of the Project is to maintain good relations with the Vicosinos. It seeks no economic gain.

2.–The custom of *embargo* is discontinued. *The Project will no longer take from the Vicosinos their moveable, semi-moveable, or non-moveable goods.* [Emphasis mine.]

3.–Only food products will be planted in Hacienda lands. Those products will be sold preferably to Vicosinos and at special prices.

4.–Profits from the sale of these products will be invested in the construction of public buildings in Vicos, in salaries for administrative *empleados*, technicians, and for the payment of *temple*.

5.–*Temple* will again be paid (and brought up to date), with increases for *yunta*-days worked and special services.

6.–*Capataces* will not be employed and additional *mayorales* will be hired.

7.–All unpaid services will be abolished: *mitaq, cuchi mitzeq*, cook, and *ruritápaco*.

8.–Workers will no longer have to carry out *tareas* outside the Hacienda.

9.–Before making changes the Project will consult the Vicosinos so as to take their opinions into account.

10.–The new renters will live in the Hacienda and they are willing to listen to complaints and grievances from all the workers.

Before the transference of the estate was made to the Project, Hacienda work in Vicos was much reduced because the enterprise of the previous *patrones* to make linen from flax had ceased to function. At the end of December, 1951, according to the Project archives the situation was this:

> Attendance of the *peonada* [the body of Vicos workers] at work has diminished at an alarming rate. The number of 240 *peones* is reduced to 60 a day, which has caused a serious setback in Hacienda work. In view of this, it was agreed with the *administrador* to pay *temple* which has not been paid for two months, the payment of which we offered at the last meeting. The *peonada* attending work yesterday was notified that the *temple* which was owed them would be paid on Saturday and that all the *faltos* [i.e., those with *faltas*] should come to work to make up their absences.
>
> Attendance today increased. The planting of maize which ought to be paralyzed today from the lack of peons will be continued till Saturday. (AVP, Mario Vázquez, 27-xii-51.)

I hope you will take note of the use of the term *peonada* by one of the Project's persons– although, as I have pointed out, the term "peon" was in general use. The first term is hard to translate. It carries the connotation of a "crowd" or "mob of peons," and as such distances the one who employs it from the Vicosinos, as a way of establishing his "here and now" from their "there and then." That is, a *peonada* is an object from the Peruvian past, a "primitive" survival, shameful relic, and something that must be "disappeared." Johannes Fabian (1983:30) identifies this as "typological time":

> As distancing devices, categorizations of this kind are used, for instance, when we are told that certain elements in our culture are "neolithic" or "archaic"; or when certain living societies are said to practice "stone age economics"; or when certain styles of thought are identified as "savage" or "primitive." Labels that connote temporal distancing need not have explicitly temporal references (such as *cyclical* or *repetitive*). Adjectives like *mythical*, *ritual*, or even *tribal*, will serve the same function. They, too, connote temporal distancing as a way of creating the objects or referents of anthropological discourse. To use an extreme formulation: temporal distance *is* objectivity in the minds of many practitioners.

Fabian (32) suggests that we do not condemn such usage morally, for "bad intentions alone do not invalidate knowledge. For that to happen it takes bad epistemology which advances cognitive interests without regard for their ideological presuppositrions."

A special effort was made by the Project to obtain attendance at Hacienda work, and at the *mando* held on January 12, 1952, the issue was raised before the Vicos labor force:

> A call was made to the *peonada* for a greater attendance at work. They were told that there would be no exceptions except for illness or misfortune, in which case peons would be freed from the *tareas* that they otherwise would have been required to perform. They remained silent.
>
> A list was read of those excused for last week and the present week. Then they were warned not to abuse excuses, because if dishonesty in claims was proved excuses would be abolished. They expressed their agreement.
>
> A list was read of habitual defaulters. They were notified of the necessity for their appearance at the Hacienda to arrange with the *patrones* and *mayorales* for the best way of settling the matter of their absenteeism. Similarly, a list was read of fairly frequent defaulters who have more than 20 *faltas* to date. In response to this, many peons pointed out that they had missed work through illness, or that their names had been omitted from the list of workers by the old *empleados*. All the ones named were urged to attend next Tuesday to talk with the *patrones* and *mayorales*.
>
> The need for reliance on stable people in construction work was emphasized, for which purpose people who attended every week were selected to alternate. The names of those selected were read. For the selection, it was announced, frequent defaulters who had returned to work in the Hacienda were taken into account, as well as the complaints of some *mayorales* that certain peons were insolent and wished to take frequent rest breaks. There was silence.
>
> The names of women-peons were read, and it was announced that women would not be accepted in place of men. The total of women was 8. (AVP, Mario Vázquez, 12-i-52.)

Although, in the same month, a "second and last call for habitual defaulters" was made (AVP, Mario Vázquez, 16-1-52), the problem did not disappear. It is constantly mentioned in the *mandos* held throughout the presence of the Project in Vicos. At the end of 1952 the problem of absent workers became serious because the rainy season, the time for planting, was approaching. It is true that the Project had no interest in obtaining profits from Vicos, but there existed, as I have noted, the concern with conducting research and developing a program of agricultural experiments, observing and analyzing the effects of these in the community. It was particularly difficult to be able to rely on the attendance of workers with *yuntas* for plowing:

In the last two months, November and December, the period of the greatest agricultural activity in ground-breaking and the planting of potatoes, wheat, barley, and *tauri*, the absence of *yuntas* in the work has been noted. The owners of *yuntas* avoid work, sometimes not coming to work on the first three days of the week but after Thursday. Others make up their *faltas* by attending one week with a *yunta* and a peon, and then after that they stop coming the next week and the week after that.

When the owners of *yuntas* were asked the reason for their absences, they justified themselves with one or another of the following excuses: the lack of pastures for feeding the *yuntas*, lameness of the animals from excessive work, thinness and infestation with lice, diarrhea, the fear that young animals would be injured by making them engage in heavy work like that in the Hacienda, and the loss (or straying) of the animals.

Many of these excuses were true, but the truth as we saw it was: the distance of the fields to be worked, because this required much work in driving the animals there as well as in the transportation of implements. Nevertheless, these were not mentioned.

The *mayorales* reported the following at their meeting of December 9: the owners of *yuntas* had a rebellious attitude. Some of them, on being asked to attend work with their *yuntas*, were insolent, while others offered to come but did not do so. The *mayorales*, after a long discussion and in the form of a petition by the group, requested that the *embargo* be reestablished because they believed it was the only way to oblige attendance. Otherwise, work would continue to lag and their orders would be mocked.

This petition of the *mayorales* was accepted and it was proposed to communicate it to the peons at the next *mando*. On the day of the *mando* it was announced that the *mayorales* had requested the reimposition of the *embargo*, because their orders were not being obeyed by the peons. At the same time, it was emphasized that the reimposition of the *embargo* was going to be considered at the next meeting of the *mayorales*, since at the moment it was only being discussed by the *mayorales* and not by the Project.

On the Monday after the *mando*, a record attendance at Hacienda work by *yuntas* was registered, a total of 50 out of 60 pairs, while during past weeks only 18 or 21 appeared. The reimposition of the *embargo* was not mentioned again. (AVP, Mario Vázquez, xii-52.)

The Project offered to reward workers whose attendance was perfect, and later festive moments were introduced in Hacienda work. In the Project's archives there is this note, entitled "Distribution of prizes on the completion of the first year's work of the Cornell-Peru Project in Vicos":

> Last year, when the purposes of the Project were announced to the peons, among other changes offered was the awarding of prizes to the peons who had no *faltas* during the year's Hacienda work. On the 24th of this month they were reminded during the *mando* that the requirement for the award of one of the prizes was having carried out all the *tareas*. The announcement of the prize winners, in order of importance, was:
>
> Among the peons with *yuntas*: First prize to Juan L. Lázaro, a peon without *faltas*, except for 6 excuses justified by illness. He worked alone all year, without alternates. He performed 70 *tareas* with his *yunta*. The prize awarded him consisted of a sack of small potatoes and a steel point for his plow. Juan L. Lázaro was not present at tie time he was called on to receive his prize during the *mando*. He picked it up two days later. He said that he did not believe about the prize, and also he was ashamed to come to get it because people would be criticizing him for eating gifts from the Hacienda. He got up the courage to claim his prize, he said, from the insistence of his wife and other relatives, who reproached him, asking him why he did not go to get it when others had done so.
>
> The second prize was given to Toribio Salas, for whom his two sons worked alternately. Without *faltas*, because those they had they had made up last week and this week with the father and the two brothers all working. They accumulated a total of 63 *tareas* with *yunta*. The prize was 5 *arrobas* of potatoes, picked up during the *mando* by one of Toribio's sons. At first he seemed timid, but encouraged by the other peons, and especially by the *mayorales*, took courage and silently took his sack and left the *mando*.
>
> The third prize was awarded to Liberato Colonia, who has practically been replaced by his son Antonio. When they have had *faltas* they have alternated with his son Elías, and Liberato himself has come. They have two *faltas*, both excused. The number of *tareas* with *yunta* was 64. The prize was 4 *arrobas* of small potatoes. It was picked up immediately by Antonio who complained that it was very little. When Antonio indicated that it was little, in an ironic work, the other peons answered him, "Shut your mouth. It's something instead of getting nothing!"
>
> Among the peons in construction the following were awarded prizes: First prize to Alejandro Reyes Segundo, the only one who worked without alternating. He had no *faltas* and no excuses. The prize was a sack of small potatoes. The prize was picked up two days later because, according to what Reyes said, he hadn't come before that. Alejandro expressed thanks at the time he took his potatoes away.
>
> Pedro Meza was the second. He is a rich man and sometimes worked with *minkas* [here the word is used in the sense of "helpers" or *peones*, a word which is used by Vicosinos]. With no *faltas*, but with three excuses for illness. The prize was a mason's plumb. It was picked up during the *mando*, and Pedro appeared very happy, for the prize was selected

knowing that he was desirous of acquiring one. People reacted favorably, and some said to Pedro that they hoped the plumb would be used in the construction of their houses. Pedro answered, "Let's see if it lasts."

The third was Daniel Herrera Primero, peon without alternates, and without *faltas* and excuses. (The one he had he had made up today.) The prize was 3 *arrobas* of potatoes. They were picked up at the end of the *mando* without comment. It appears that Daniel expected a larger quantity.

Alejandro Tafur was the fourth of those who worked on construction. This prize was created, it can be said, by Alejandro's force and strength. He claimed not to have any *faltas* and thus had the right to receive a prize. However, there were two *faltas* registered in the *tarea* book, and after much argument he finished the *faltas*, and so he had to be given his prize which consisted of 3 *arrobas* of potatoes. He is a peon by himself, without *faltas* and excuses, and he works permanently like the others in construction.

Among the *pampa* peons [the field hands], the first prize was awarded to Pablo Cruz Primero, a rich peon practically replaced by his son Jacinto in Hacienda work. He had no *faltas* and excuses. He was awarded a mcahete. The prize was picked up by Jacinto during the *mando* and caused no surprise or special commentaries.

Asunción Valerio was the second. He is a single peon, without *faltas* and excuses, but approximately twelve *faltas* were completed by his sister and daughter who shelled maize during the harvest. The prize was 4 *arrobas* of potatoes which were picked up during the *mando*.

Pablo Tadeo Segundo was next. He alternates with his brother Asunción. They have no *faltas* and no excuses. The third prize consited of 4 *arrobas* of potatoes. Later I was informed that the potatoes had been divided into equal parts.

Next was Hermenegildo Reyes, a peon who alternates with his step-son. His *faltas* were made up today, and he has no excuses. The prize was 4 *arrobas* of potatoes which were picked up several days after the *mando*.

Then came Natividad Tadeo, a peon who alternates with his son. This fifth prize was not announced during the mando. It was necessary to create it afterward, in view of the constant complaint by Natividad who claimed he had no *faltas*. He was told that he had three *faltas* in the register, so he offered to complete them on condition that he be given an appropriate prize. That was what happened.

The prizes awarded caused a certain jealousy among the peons, some of whom complained that the winners had been rich people. Others said that some had better opportunities than others, if they had sons to help them, but this argument has no basis. A few recognized that they had missed work and that next year they would be candidates to receive prizes. (AVP, Mario Vázquez, 31-xii-52.)

One year later, William C. Blanchard recorded comments on problems of obtaining labor. He discussed providing incentives in connection with his description of a meeting of the Project staff with the mayorales:

> Enrique started the meeting. He brought up the problem of all the children and women who show up to work in place of peons. He had counted one day and said that fifty-five boys and women had worked one field with hardly a man among them. There was discussion about this which, of course, arrived at no conclusion, as usual. I asked if there were any possibility of setting a quota on the number of days in a given period that would be counted when worked by such substitutes, but this was dismissed at once. . . . I noted down the need to study the possibility of giving some kind of incentive to the people with good work records, only to find out later that this was done last year. . . . After the meeting, the Project staff talked about an earlier warning that the Vicosinos would ask for something like an increase in temple, a thing we would not want to do.
> (APV, December 15, 1953.)

Two months later, this account of the potato harvest was filed under the heading "Harvesting potatoes and the attitude of peons toward work":

> It was time for the potato harvest in Campanilla [a sector of Hacienda land] and we had in mind the convenience of finishing it this week. This was something which was not going to take place under the conditions in which harvest labor is developing. At lunch it was agreed with the *mayorales* how we would finish the harvest today. The only way was to urge people to work with greater enthusiasm and speed.
>
> When the *mayorales* were asked about the way in which we could obtain people's cooperation for finishing the harvest today, they answered: "We promise to finish the harvest today as long as you will provide alcohol for the people." We accepted the *mayorales*' point of view, and they immediately notified the people of the agreement they had reached with the *patrones*. To reinforce the offer they said they would personally see to it, they would guarantee the *patrones*' offer, that is, the supply of alcohol for all the people.
>
> Most of the peons at the beginning appeared to be pessimistic and incredulous, and they answered the *mayorales*, telling them: "Well, it's not the custom for the *patrones* to pass out alcohol or any other drink to their peons during harvests, like it used to be years ago." And there were others who protested: "When the work is finished the *patrones* won't do what they promise," and so on. It appears that people's disbelief was conquered by my intervention and the assistance of the *mayorales* who kept repeating that they would guarantee the good faith of the offer. In the second act, the harvest was begun with an accelerated rhythm. The peons were divided into four groups, each group with its own *mayoral* who directed the work. The work progressed in the form of a competition

among the four groups. During work enthusiasm and humor were observed. Very few appeared to be discontented. The *mayorales*, in addition to directing the work, helped the peons throughout the harvest. The promised alcohol was passed to each *mayoral* after the *mando* was over. Each one received a bottle of alcohol to give to his team. After finishing their bottles the people asked for more alcohol. The *mayorales* refused. The latter appeared to have plans to get drunk by themselves without letting their peons participate. However, the people kept asking and two more bottles were given to each group.

That night most of the peons were drunk. Some stayed in the plaza for several hours after the *mando*, and others went off to places where alcohol was sold where they continued drinking.

The drunkenness of this day was the subject of comment during the following days. What people said was very favorable for the establishment of the custom of having liquor after the weekly labors. They all talked about their deeds and teased each other. Some of them admitted having gotten drunk while others protested that they had not and so it was necessary for them to go where alcohol was sold.

The wives of the drunks, in opposition to their husbands appeared to be quite displeased, and there was not one who did not scold me for giving alcohol to her husband who had lost his poncho (it was recovered). Many of them had spent the money they received at the *mando*, and others had lost the potatoes they had received in the *pelley* [distribution of produce as a gratuity]. (AVP, Mario Vázquez. 26-ii-54.)

Despite much concern and many attempts to improve the situation, absence remained a problem. Thus, Pedro Cruz, although he was an extreme case, was not an exception to some general rule of faithful attendance at Hacienda labors. Moreover, the action taken in his case was not novel, for other settlements of absenteeism had been made which involved property transfer. For examples, two cases from the meetings of the *mayorales* are presented here:

Case 1. Lorenzo Mayhuey has been notified three times about the need for his return to work. He has not done that to date, and so it was agreed to grant Mayhuey's properties to Vicente Evaristo who has petitioned to enter as a peon. This is what was decided: a) Vicente Evaristo, who wants to be a peon, is married to Lorenzo Mayhuey's wife's niece. The parents of the niece live near Mayhuey who agrees that the properties be granted to Evaristo who is a close relative of Mayhuey's wife and the person who has replaced Mayhuey in Hacienda work; b) Vicente Evaristo took advantage of the *mayorales'* meeting to appear and petition that Mayhuey's properties be granted to him.

The *mayorales* made no objection to granting the properties to the petitioner. It was agreed that one of them appear to make the formal transfer of the fields. It was also agreed that Mayhuey and his family could continue to occupy their house and plant in the field around it. On the next day the *mayoral* appointed by the others and I made the formal transfer of Mayhuey's properties to Evaristo. For that purpose we went to the fields and explained to Mayhuey's mother-in-law, the only inhabitant of the house, that the lands had been transferred with Mayhuey's approval.

Case 2. Víctor Cruz, a peon in the Hacienda for two years, stopped coming to Hacienda work. In January of this year, taking advantage of two *mandos*, Cruz was called to come to his usual *tareas*. Since Cruz did not respond to our call, at the *mayorales'* meeting it was agreed to have Cruz appear at the Hacienda along with his brother Alfonso, who according to rumor is working Víctor's fields, Julua Coleto, Víctor's wife who has separated from him and is the mother of his two children, and Simón Cruz, who is also working Víctor's fields. These persons were notified by the authorities [i.e., the *varayoq*] who were also present at the time of the agreement.

When the designated persons, the *mayorales*, the *administrador*, and I met on the appointed day at 7 a.m., this arrangement was made. Víctor Cruz said that he had looked for me three times but had not found me. He admitted his absenteeism because of illness and promised to attend thereafter. Alfonso Cruz denied planting in Víctor's fields and advanced genealogical arguments about the origin of his properties. These affirmations were contradicted as false by two *mayorales*. Julia Coleto, Víctor's ex-wife, said she was planting one section of land in order to maintain his two children. Simón Cruz admitted to planting one of Alfonso's fields because he was accustomed to helping him with agricultural tasks.

In view of the fact that Víctor was ill, lacking in resources for his food supply, and works as a peon for a rich Vicosino, that he is the father of two children who live with his wife, a person without land, it was proposed that all the properties farmed by Víctor now be worked by Julia Coleto as the guardian of the two children, and that the house and adjacent field for maize continue to be occupied by him until he dies. Then these will be passed to Víctor's children.

Our point of view was accepted completely by the *mayorales*, authorities, Julia Coleto, and Víctor Cruz, but not by Alfonso and Simón Cruz. The first argued that the field he was cultivating be excepted, and the second suggested that his uncle should work one *tarea* per week. But since the arrangement we had proposed had been accepted and completed agreed on, Alfonso accepted the verdict that Víctor's goods and lands, with the exception of the field located next to his house, be in Julia's care.

Víctor's name will be erased from the Hacienda's list and replaced by Pablo Cruz Segundo, the name of the oldest son, with Julia. Pablo's older brothers, Julia's other children, will work in the Hacienda for him until he grows up. (AVP, Mario Vázquez, March 1952, 3691.)

The Project did all it could do to make certain that absence from work be made up, and that the Hacienda would receive a worker's labor in return for its allotment of land. However, as I have noted, the land was distributed unevenly and it was impossible to obtain even a measurement of this inequality. There were forty-seven families in Vicos who sent no representative to Hacienda labors, either in return for a land allotment or in alternation with another household with land. In the absence of information, we may only speculate that perhaps some of these had small parcels while others did not, that many of them were part-households, i.e., broken ones, and that they largely consisted of people whom Vicosinos designated "unfortunates" or "orphans," those without the support of relatives. People assess others, also, as "good" or "bad" in terms of whether or not they carry out their obligations. Eduardo Soler recorded the following in one of his interviews:

Juan Coleto: I have equal regard for all my relatives, but I give preference to my children and my brother. My brother lives next door to my house. We always visit and help each other in our work. For example, if we get hold of something special to eat we share it with each other. Still, my cousin, Andrés Evaristo, and I help each other more often. He has several brothers and we all help each other. I weave cloth for them. Because my brother is close by we see each other every day at work, or we visit each other. I also see Andrés every day. We don't separate. I don't help Andrés in work in the fields because he had children who can help him, but I do other things for him like weaving.

My father-in-law and I help each other. Other friends we help in *minka* are Rufino Reyes's sons. My best friend is Herminio Colonia. We've known each other since we were children. If one of us has a fiesta, he invites the other.

Here we say that a good father of a family is a man who carries out his duties toward his family, that is, one who doesn't quarrel with them or make them go without food.. I'm a good father of a family because I carry out all my duties at home. I'm also polite to my neighbors and everybody. Bad fathers are those who forget about their relatives, ones to whom they are not important. They suffer from the lack of food and clothing. Such men quarrel constantly with their wives and others. Among the bad fathers who are well known here in Vicos are Pedro Cruz [the missing worker this chapter is about], Fermín Lázaro, and Pablo Narcizo. They go out to different places to work, so that their relatives suffer at home. . . .

Sometimes it's better to live a little apart from relatives so as not to have trouble with them. But, sure, it's good to live harmoniously with all of them. If there's a lot of trust among siblings or cousins it's good always to be together with them, to look in on them, to help each other because among us we always need that. (MP, August 21.)

There is a difference between working outside Vicos as a susbistence supplement and as a means of avoiding obligations. The latter case is not only an absence from Hacienda *tareas*, which runs the risk of *embargo* and, thus, obliges a family to provide substitutes, but it is disruptive of the network of reciprocities in which Vicosinos are tied to each other, that is, the complex of ritual exchanges of resources ranging from mutual aid to labor festivals. Wage labor is necessary but it is not the desirable mode of working, and it seems likely that the same considerations apply in Vicos that appear elsewhere in the Andes. For example, Enrique Mayer (1974:115-116) writes of reciprocity versus wage labor (*"jornales"*) in Tangor, a community in the Chaupiwaranga Valley southeast of Ancash:

> Although the two forms of work contract are equivalent to each other from a purely formal view . . . in reality this is not the case, since the crucial element is missing: the personalized affective reciprocal relationship between equals. To work for someone without a return in work is perceived as demeaning to oneself. The known *jornaleros* in Tangor considered people with less intrinsic worth than farmers. They are described as lazy people unable to farm and bad managers of their own resources which forces them to look for work in the village. Peons who regularly hire themselves out for work are also the poorest in the village.

In Vicos, one type of man works his tareas in the Hacienda, farms his own fields, and then if there is time left in the week goes to Marcará or Carhuaz to work for a *patrón* there. In return for this work he receives produce, or cash with which he can purchase victuals, cloth, tools, or other household necessities. Such a man is a worker, a good caretaker, one who is viewed with approbation. Another type of man, the *"vago"*, instead of providing for his family, threatens their well-being by going away for extended periods of time. Such "no-goods" find *patrones* to support them in town, or engage in morally marginal or actually criminal activity. Some have the habit of drinking up their earnings, and while drunk acting out violent scenes in fights in the *chicherías*, small bars which serve *chicha* and *aguardiente* [*huashco*, alcohol diluted with water], or at home by beating their women and children when they return.

Norman Pava cites the case of a man known both for his poverty and sloth who managed to live in Vicos without land or the provision of any service to the Hacienda:

> José Tadeo, about 60 years old, has no *chacras*, plants no crops, and is not a peon of the Hacienda. His household, consisting of two round, straw-

thatched huts, stands on a little plot of ground. He has no claim to any of the land around his houses. To earn his livelihood he generally works in Marcará where his employer feeds him. His wife spins wool for other people and receives her pay for this in raw food. He and she supplement their incomes by begging, stealing, and gifts from others who pity them. Delfín Coleto attributes José Tadeo's poverty to the following: He is lazy and doesn't want to work for the Hacienda, and so the Hacienda will not let him plant a *chacra*. His wife has been sick and so he has nobody to care for him. He has two women. He spends all his spare time working in his *compañera's chacra*–as opposed to the other woman who is his wife. The *compañera* gives him food occasionally. He has a son by her. His two sons by his first wife are dead. Today, for breakfast, he and his wife ate about half a medium-sized *mate* [dish] of *shakwi de tzotzoqa*, milled hominy soup, with a bit of salt, about a tablespoon of lard, and a medium-sized *mate* of ocas. For dinner they had *shakwi* made of half a *mate* of *habas*, and a *mate* of *ocas*. This is a very small amount of food for two people to eat, compared with other people.

The food José and his wife ate was obtained as follows: the milled hominy was given to his wife in exchange for her spinning half a ball of yarn. The *ocas* were obtained in trade for some *ají* which José bought in Marcará. The *habas* were a gift from an *ahijada* [goddaughter].

Delfín says that José is "a bad man." He is bad because a man ought to have only one woman, and he ought to work for the Hacienda and have a *chacra* on which to raise food. In contrast, Félix Lázaro is "a good man" because he is a hard worker and a good provider, so that his family eats well. He is also helping to care for his old mother-in-law, María Sánchez. (AVP, April 7, 1952.)

In Vicos there is a close connection between the idea of laziness and the practice of leaving the community to work elsewhere:

Emilio Lázaro: Once I went to Paramonga [a sugar plantation on the coast] just to visit my brothers. I was there for only three days. They told me that there was a lot of work to be had there, but I wasn't interested in staying because I had so much work waiting for me back here. (MP, Soler, July 3.)

Jorge Reyes: (What do you think of the Vicosinos? Is everybody the same or are some worth more than others?) We're not all the same in Vicos. Some are more powerful and others are less so according to their land and other property. Besides that, some are lazier than others and make the land go bad for not planting it, while others are very good workers. Some like to travel around to other places because they don't like to work their fields. Others genuinely like the land because they know how to respect what the land produces in order to satisfy their hunger. (MP, Soler, August 4.)

Ciriaco Evaristo: (What do you think of other Vicosinos?) All of us are the same. None of us becomes very refined. It's just that the rich ones think they are superior to the rest of us. Other times those people who've gone away to work and who've come back with store clothing and speaking Spanish think they are superior. However, they are criticized by everybody. People say that they really go around to other places because they're lazy, because they don't want to work in the fields like the rest of us. Sometimes, with talk like that, they get into fights at fiestas. . . . Those of us who always stay in Vicos are in better condition. That's because the ones who go out to work and get money end up spending all their money in stores. They come back well dressed but their money is gone. It isn't enough for them to keep on living, so they end up by going back to work again. Those of us who stay here at home have enough for the whole family to live well almost all year long. (MP, Soler, August 5 and 10.)

Pedro Meza: Lazy people like to live in the street, but I'm a worker. I'd rather work. (MP, Flores, with Pablo Herrera, July 4.)

Alfonso Cruz: Walto Sánchez was a man who earned lots of money. He planted his fields well. His son went out, and when he came home he said that they made good money there. So the father also went and came back with money. He fed his wife well. But now he's completely lost. He was a working man and he has turned into a vagabond without any hope. That's why I don't want my son to get an *enganche* and go to the coast. I advised him that even if a person can do two *tareas* a day it's better just to work here. Going out of here to those places won't get you anything good. (MP, Flores, with Celso León, August 20.)

Juan Coleto: I like to work, whether it's for the Hacienda or on my own. I like it because I've been used to it since I was a child. If I get sick and stop work for a few days, I miss working. When a person doesn't work his body changes. It makes no difference to me if it's in my own fields, the Hacienda's land, or work in *la república*, I work the same. I believe a man should work the same, no matter where. I've always given my whole attention to work, no matter for whom. However, here in Vicos there are lazy men just as there are good workers. Those lazy ones are those who have little or no interest in working in the fields. It's their destiny to manage to earn a living by working in other places, forsaking their land. Well, it's all right to go away to work for a few weeks, but those lazy people can't be comfortable here any more. I don't care for people like that. Men should always work with interest and in good faith. (MP, Soler, August 8.)

Ambrosio Evaristo: What we like to do is work in the fields, in agriculture. We wouldn't want more than that. When we do that, it isn't easy to go away to the coast. Only lazy men do that, ones who don't like to work in the fields. The rest of us can't do that because we have work to do here. The ones who go away return even lazier. Then they don't want to work in the fields here any more. (MP, Flores, with Ricardo Estremadoyro, July 12.)

Pedro Cruz was well known in Vicos as a lazy man, a "ne'er-do-well" by local standards. He was also reported to be a brawler.[39] He was one of those who spent the money he earned outside the Hacienda drinking *chicha* and *aguardiente* at shops along the road from Marcará to Vicos. This is the background against which we are to understand Vicosinos' reaction to the confiscation of Pedro Cruz's land. It is also evident that this step taken by the Hacienda was influenced by that opinion, for the administration correctly predicted that Cruz could not hope for aid from the community. The Project could, thus, escape from a self-contradiction, because, if you will recall, it had announced when it took over the Hacienda: "The Project will no longer take from the Vicosinos their moveable, semi-moveable, or non-moveable properties." The confiscation was announced at the *mando* of August 19, 1953:

> Having exhausted various measures for obliging the peons to make up their *faltas*, and considering that the inattendance of some is causing disturbances in administrative activity, it was decided to put into practice the threat that was made on taking possession of the Hacienda. The threat was this: if the peons did not come to work they would not have *embargos* taken from them, nor would they be fined or molested, but they would lose the right to the possession of their lands, which would be given over to new peons or planted by the Hacienda.
>
> This threat was put into practice with the goods of Telésforo Reyes and Pedro Cruz, both chronic absentees despite having been given multiple opportunities to make up their *tareas*, like: the acceptance of their children as replacements for these heads of family, even their wives. The fields of both men will be planted with potatoes by the Hacienda. The peons looked at each other without saying a word.
>
> On the next day Telésforo Reyes's son appeared, claiming that he had no *faltas*, and the few that he did have he would make up. However, his mother was summoned. With a tragic attitude and sobbing, she appeared the next day. She pointed out that they did not have many *faltas*, and the ones that existed were her husband's responsibility. He was hardly interested in his small children, while she would promise to have them made up. In view of the woman's firm attitude, she was asked to talk with the *mayoral* from the high part, who would serve as guarantor to the Hacienda and would oblige Telésforo to make up his *faltas*, as the wife indicated. The *mayoral* accepted the proposed solution, and in the

following weeks Telésforo Reyes's sons attended Hacienda labors until they had made up the *faltas*.

Three days after the *mando*, Pedro Cruz's wife appeared at the Hacienda to beg that the Hacienda not plant her land and that their 9 months of *faltas* would be made up. Their *faltas* were her husband's and their son's fault because they did not want to work in the Hacienda. She cited various causes: illness, lack of animals, and lack of victuals. She was asked for a guarantee in order to cancel the Hacienda's decision, but neither she nor her son could find anyone to guarantee that their *faltas* would be made up.

The land was cultivated and potatoes were planted, but one section of potato land and another of maize were reserved to be cropped by Pedro's wife who has small children and also owns a few cattle and sheep. (AVP, Mario Vázquez, 1953.)

The eviction is described in William Blanchard's field notes of August 25, 1953:

At the *mando* last Wednesday it was announced that the Hacienda would begin to cultivate the field belonging to a man who had many, many *faltas*. The matter was reviewed and the man had promised to make them up, but then had left Vicos to go to work in Marcará. The wife had then promised to work but had failed. The son, likewise, had failed to keep his promises. Now it was decided to act decisively. I gathered that the opportunity of bringing this up at a *mando* was a threat aimed at people who aren't showing up, especially since so much trouble has been experienced lately in getting *yuntas*. The man's name is Pedro Cruz.

Yesterday morning I went up to the field with Enrique. They were getting it ready to plant potatoes with several men and a couple of *yuntas*. I asked Enrique if the people had any objection to working on it. He said "why?" in a sort of uncomprehending way.

As we rode on from there we talked more about the case. I asked if it could have been given to a man who had no land, instead of being used for the Hacienda's advantage. He said that would just create bad feeling between the ones who were evicted and the ones who took it over. However, he said, that was done in a case last year and there were no quarrels. In the present case, Pedro Cruz has been left a bit of land and is allowed to keep his house, which would not be torn down.

While we were still within sight of the homestead I looked up at the house and saw no signs of life whatever. I asked Enrique where the man was. He said, with a sort of "oh, hell" gesture, "He's in Marcará working."

When we got up to the Hacienda's field, we found 36 *yuntas* at work. Enrique thought that there was a direct connection between the talk at the *mando* and the eviction, and the number of people who had shown up for work.

Early yesterday morning, before the work day began, a couple of women came to the *casa hacienda* to talk about the matter. Little attention was paid to them. Then, late in the afternoon, a young fellow came out to the warehouse. It turned out to be *Modesto Cruz, the son. He was obviously drunk and his mouth was unusually caked with coca. I had the impression that in addition to being drunk he was also not quite "right in the head." He talked and talked in Quechua. The ones who understood seemed somewhat amused by him, and the mestizos paid not too much attention to him. He seemed to look at no one at all while he talked. Sometimes he aroused much laughter by things he said, especially when he announced that his mother had whipped him. He seemed to pay no attention to being laughed at. The carpenter translated some for me. The fellow said that his mother was feeling terrible about the loss of the land. He said that she had hit him. Then he talked about "a mother's malediction." He said he was going to work the land anyway, that he was going back into the field. My feeling in watching him was strange. There was obviously a deeply felt grievance which brought him there. Whether or not it was just was irrelevant. Yet he aroused only mirth. While he was drunk he showed no signs of aggressiveness. I had the feeling that he represented people so frustrated in their situation that they show no hostility, even when drunk, toward the agents of their grievances.

Enrique mentioned to me earlier that by not giving the land to anyone else, it still left the situation open for the family to make up their *faltas* and resume cultivation of the land. Mario said yesterday evening that there are several cases with large numbers of *faltas*, and that one or two of them are related to such influential people that there is little the Hacienda can do. Mario also said that the eviction is widely known and discussed here in Vicos. (AVP.)

It seems that this Field Director, the representative in Vicos of the principal investigator, Allan Holmberg, is nearly paralyzed by his inability to understand what is going on. He depends on clues from two mestizos to orient himself. While this is going on, these mestizos are running the Hacienda in collaboration with Vicosino power-holders, and convince the Field Director of the rightness of their actions. Later, Blanchard again noted increased attendance in the Hacienda:

On Monday I went to Chullán [a sector where Hacienda land is located] with Enrique. The land had been turned over before planting potatoes. In the highest part, 21 *yuntas* were plowing under a *mayoral*'s supervision. We watched the work. Enrique took down the names of the workers and we left. In the lowest part another *mayoral* was directing the work of 15 *yuntas*. Enrique attributed the presence of such a large number to the impression that Pedro Cruz's eviction had caused. (AVP, August 27, 1953.)

On August 31 Blanchard reported further on the case when he made another visit to the Cruz field:

> Last Thursday I went up again to Pedro Cruz's field with Enrique. We arrived at about 9 o'clock to find most of the men chewing coca. There were about 25 individuals. Enrique said the field is about one hectare in extent. It is irregular in outline and slopes in several directions. In the upper part a *yunta* went to work with two men in addition to the *gañán*, the plowman. Two more teams like that were working the middle and lowest parts of the field. Eight men with hoes worked over the furrows which had been plowed. Enrique said that the field had been in preparation during the first three days of the week and that they were now going to sow it.
>
> I asked Enrique who the men were that were working on a Thursday. He told me that most of them had *faltas*. One man said "no." Enrique told me that he had asked the man to come because he lived nearby. All the rest, he said, had been told to come because they had *falta*. . . .
>
> The Cruz house is just above the very highest part of the field which stretches down in every direction from the house. The upper part slopes gently but lower down the slope increases. The upper part is relatively free of stones, but the lower part is very stony indeed. Enrique says it is pure laziness which has prevented Pedro Cruz from clearing out the stones. . . .
>
> Pedro Cruz has another field that has not been taken away from him. It is higher up and farther away. He owes the Hacienda one day's work a week on that. If he ever expects to get this field back he must make up over 70 days. Enrique said he had been given chances to recover in the past but always broke faith.
>
> At the work break Enrique and I went up to the house. I had seen little sign of life there except for a child and a dog. When we were close to the house, a woman came out and began to speak to Enrique. He told me she was Pedro's wife, the mother of the drunk who was down at the *casa hacienda* late Monday afternoon. She talked to Enrique for several minutes while he sometimes answered or sometimes seemed to pay little or no attention to her. I occasionally asked him what she was saying. She was obviously giving him some kind of sad story. She seemed very upset, and after a bit she began to cry which she kept up for the rest of the time we were near her. Enrique was speaking to her rather briskly, as though offering easy advice, and I could understand enough words to gather that he was referring to her son, husband, and others. At my request he asked her where the son was. She said he was working in Marcará. The husband was working somewhere around Carhuaz. He was not around much. Enrique says that both men are useless and given to vices, presumably drink and coca. He implied that both of them have been known to steal. The son aroused antagonism when he made his attempt to

work in the Hacienda some time ago: he stole the lunches of the other men had gone to the field.

After we left the woman, still weeping and complaining, Enrique said that if Pedro or any of his family can make up the *faltas* they can have the field back for planting next season. He did not seem to think there was much likelihood of the father or son doing anything about it, however. Enrique told me that Pedro has to keep current for the field he has been allowed to retain, as well as to make up his *faltas*. Since Pedro is in Carhuaz and Modesto is in Marcará, the task of making up the *faltas* will apparently fall on the women. (AVP.)

Sarah Levy, of the Methodology Project in Vicos at the time, was quick to understand the significance of the case of Pedro Cruz. She gave her data gatherers special "Instructions" (see Appendix 2) and sent them to find informants. Here is what some Vicosinos had to say about Cruz, his family, and the critical turn of events:

Alejandro Colonia: Pedro Cruz's house is located in Puncucorral [a Vicos neighborhood]. He lives there with his wife and son. Vicos people make fun of Modesto, the son, whom they call *"ishmushqalla"* [shitty] because he is very careless with his clothing. He wears them completely torn and dirty. Besides that he is lazy. That's why he goes around all dirty and defaults in Hacienda work. His father went away to work. He's been doing that for a long time because he's a lazy man too. He ignores his wife and son, and so he stays in other places just looking for his own food. He's always made those trips. When he comes back, he's barely here for a few weeks and everything he's earned is gone. Then he goes off on another *enganche* and uses up the money he gets from it by getting drunk. . . .

Pedro's wife is lazy too. She's an *"usha tziki"* [sheep's ass]. That's what they call lazy women when they don't know how to take care of their husbands and they don't know how to work. They call Pedro a *"purikoq,"* that is, a person who travels around through laziness so as not to work in his fields. He's the Hacienda's person, but since he doesn't pay attention to anything the *mayorales* have been saying that they'd take his fields away from him so the Hacienda could plant them. Because of that, his son has begun to work on the Hacienda. Today he's working on the school. I don't know whether or not they've already taken the fields away. Telésforo Reyes is another lazy man who'd rather work in neighboring towns and forgets about working in the Hacienda. [There seems to be a confusion here between the two men who had been mentioned in the *mando* on August 19.] (MP, Soler, August 25.)

Manuel Reyes: I know Pedro Cruz because we both live here in Vicos, but he's not a friend and I don't know him well. We live in different neighborhoods. I live in the heights and he lives down below in Punkucorral. He has a wife and children but I don't know them at all. When this Pedro was a young man he used to work hard. I mean that he worked the same as other men. After he got married he began to go out to other places to look for work. Like that, little by little, he got into that habit because his relatives always took his place in Hacienda work. Then it happened that they didn't come any more. His wife didn't come either, and so they took their fields away. I don't know why she didn't try to make up her husband's *faltas*. (MP, Soler, August 27.)

Ciriaco Vega: I know Pedro Cruz. That man worked hard in the beginning but gradually he lost interest in work. After he got married, he kept on working in the Hacienda but he really worked less than other men and he was often absent from work. He likes to go out to other places to work, to Marcará or to the plantations on the coast. When he goes far away he stays there working for weeks or months. Sometimes we have to work outside Vicos so as to get victuals for living through the year because we only have a bit of land. Even so, I think he was profiting unduly.

Speaking in general, I think that the Hacienda system of making us work three days every week is not useful or right. It's not possible that they make us work three days for the little land we have, that often doesn't give us a crop when we plant it. If they make us go without the indispensable products for living all year, we are forced to go out and earn a little money to buy them. Even more, for those of us who have no livestock to sell, there's no remedy but to work in other places. (MP, Soler, August 28.)

Francisco Mendoza: I know Pedro Cruz, his wife, and his son. Pedro always goes away to work in other places. He forgets about completing his *tareas* in the Hacienda. He also forgets about his family. I've heard people say that the Hacienda has taken his fields away because of his many *faltas*. . . .

I'm familiar with wage labor. I've worked in Marcará and they've paid me S/. 3.00 plus 50 *centavos* for coca and 50 more as *temple*. We don't pay wages here but sometimes we work in a *minka*, by turns, but with the indispensable attentions for the workers who help out. I'd rather stay at home and work my own land, rather than go out to earn money in other places and pay my helpers with a part of my earnings. That system wouldn't turn out well because money always gets spent fast, and if we haven't seen to having our fields worked well then there is no food to eat. Also, here we think of all the ones that go out to other places as lazy. We say that they go away so as not to work their fields and not to carry out their obligations to the Hacienda, like Pedro Cruz. (MP, Soler, August 28.)

Manuel Reyes: (Have you heard talk about the Pedro Cruz case?) Today at the *mando* they named the ones who have to go tomorrow to work for the Hacienda on Cruz's land. Pedro Cruz stopped working much in the Hacienda. He went to work in Recuay and Marcará. His son should have come to work, but he's also been working outside. Nobody came to Pedro Cruz's defense because he's the only one to blame for leaving the Hacienda's work. (Did the *mayorales* defend him?) Well, how? How is he going to be defended? Pedro Cruz was like a trader, going from place to place. (What do people say about the case?) They're not talking. Nobody says anything about the fields being taken away. They'll take them away from us if we miss work. Everything's quiet. (What do you think of Pedro Cruz?) What should I think of Pedro Cruz for not working in the Hacienda when the work customs are known? Is the Hacienda going to let him do it? Are they going to give him a gift and make up his *faltas*? He's gotten used to things in other places. When he works he has money and he satisfies his desires easily. That's why he can't get used to working in the Hacienda now. That's what must have happened. (And Cruz's wife, what is she like?) I don't know what's going to become of her. They talked to that woman in the Hacienda and they told her that she was accepted for the next day. She must have thought, "I've worked in the Hacienda. How is it that nobody's working my land?" How is a person not going to work if she has land from the Hacienda? (Could Cruz's wife be lazy?) Who knows? The son, too, will follow this road, looking at his father. The son went to the Hacienda to ask that they leave him some land, if only the piece that's near his house. If they go away, it's good that they do it, but they don't work in the Hacienda. It's like it was their own land. They're going out to work elsewhere. The Hacienda is right to get angry. (MP, Flores, with Celso León, August 26.)

Llicu Tadeo: (What do you know about Pedro Cruz's case?) I don't know anything, just that he was a poor man and that he went to work outside in Marcará. I've heard it said that they've taken away his fields. (What kind of person is he?) I don't have any thoughts about him because I live far from his neighborhood. He has babies. There's a family on the land. They ought not to take away the fields they have for planting crops. Now, God knows if those fields are going to yield a harvest what with the curse of those poor children! If the Hacienda had found the fields abandoned, wouldn't it be different? They can take back fields when the people who live there aren't to be found. Otherwise, they can't. (What do you think if Cruz's wife?) Why didn't she work if her husband was away? Only they know why. Now in the Hacienda they're even taking babies to work. Why wouldn't they have gone to work? (Is it good that they take women and children as peons?) It's all right if the father is sick. The son or the daughter can work so there won't be a *falta*, and then nobody gets angry. (Why didn't the son go and take his father's place?) He's lazy. Young people these days give up through laziness. Who knows why? He should have done the work for his father, but because the boy wasn't inclined he didn't work. (MP, Flores, with Celso León, August 29.)

Alfonso Cruz: (Have you heard about Pedro Cruz's case?) I knew that he wasn't present at the Hacienda, and that he'd gone off. So then Cruz's son asked them here at the Hacienda why they were giving land to other people. He said that was why he wasn't inclined to come to work. I don't know if he'll come or not. I've heard it said that they'd take his field, but I don't know if that's happened. (They threw them out yesterday. The Hacienda took their land.) Now maybe that's why I saw Cruz's son asking for Enrique. It still isn't known why it was that they wanted to take the land away, if it was because he didn't complete his *tareas* for the Hacienda, or if it was the wickedness of the Hacienda by giving the land to somebody else while they were working for the Hacienda. (MP, Flores, with Celso León, August 29.)

Emilio Colonia: Pedro Cruz is weak. He doesn't work. It's all right if they take that field away. Why would they take it away from somebody who worked? Why would they take it away from me when I work for the Hacienda every week? If somebody took it from me, I'd hit him even if he was a *patrón*. If he's also the renter, he hasn't bought the land. If they'd pay me double for my work, I'd go to Paramonga even.

In the old days they took land away from other Vicosinos, but I don't remember more than that. It's that people have told me about it and I don't know what happened after that. (MP, Soto, with Ricardo Estremadoyro, August 25.)

Andrés Copitán: I know Pedro Cruz. He lives just over the hill. We're neighbors. I don't know anything about what happened in the Hacienda, but I've heard that the Hacienda took his fields away. That's very well done because this man is very untrustworthy and he leads a very untidy life. That's why he left the Hacienda. (MP, Soto, with Ricardo Estremadoyro, August 29.)

While almost all the Vicosinos interviewed saw a certain justice in the land confiscation, many had doubts as to whether or not it was appropriate. Since the Hacienda had abolished the sanction of taking an *embargo* on moveable property–and seems to have desired to do so with non-moveable property, which led to its ambivalence–confiscation was the only "remedy," as some of the Methodology Project's informants expressed it, in order to maintain work discipline. But "remedy," in the language of Vicos as we will explore it in the next chapter, means not only something curative but something which is quite the opposite, something that can make one sicker or kill. What did some of these Vicosinos have to say about Hacienda punishments? You will note in the interviews the Vicos acceptance of the hacienda system. At the same time, you may well ask why, if so many Hacienda workers conceived of a fair balance between their *tareas* and the lands granted them, the Hacienda was finding it difficult to motivate the workers to appear at work when they were needed.

Alejandro Colonia: It's good that the Hacienda has taken land from Pedro Cruz, or from any person who wasn't fulfilling his obligations. If the Hacienda took land away from a person who did his duty, it would be unjust. If I were a *patrón* I'd do the same. I'd take his land from him. In the old days they took *embargos*, even if people missed just a few days of work. The *embargos* were stored until the owners redeemed them by paying a fine. That's why people didn't worry about it because they thought that their things would stay in storage until they could get them out. Now they make a certain allowance if the *faltas* are justified. They only take land away if people have many *faltas*. It's good that they take land away from people who don't work for the Hacienda. Everybody ought to be able to work on equal terms. It seems to me it's much better to take their land away from then than to take *embargos* of their goods or livestock, because often they don't even plant on their own land. (MP, Soler, August 28.)

Manuel Reyes: We all know that when we don't do our *tareas* they can take our land away. Neither Pedro nor his family did their duty. When people knowingly don't do their duty there's no other remedy but to act this way. In the old days they used to take *embargos* when cases like this came up. But recently this system was abolished. But now a person can have his land taken away after they calculate his many *faltas*. It doesn't seem to me that land should be taken away, because when that happens a person is deprived of satisfying what he needs to feed himself. If it's a large family they'd suffer severely because prices have gone up so much. As I say, there's nothing like planting for oneself. I think it would be better to take *embargos*. (MP, Soler, August 27.)

Ciriaco Vega: Cruz forgot about his *tareas* in the Hacienda. That's surely why the Hacienda has taken his land. I think that's good as a punishment, but I don't agree that the punishment should be in that form. In the old days they took *embargos* of livestock and other properties from people who missed work, but now they take land away. I think they ought to continue with *embargos*, because there's the possibility of getting the *embargos* back after a person finishes the *tareas* he's missed. If they take land away from a person, you know, then we'd have no place to plant. It wouldn't matter to the Hacienda, in that case, even if we were starving. (MP, Soler, August 28.)

Francisco Mendoza: I don't agree that they took land from Pedro Cruz, because now that man and his family don't have any place to plant and they'll suffer from hunger. It would have been better to take an *embargo* from him, like they always used to do. (MP, Soler, August 28.)

Manuel Reyes: (Is what the Hacienda did just?) It's just, because if a man is healthy he can't go for so long with *faltas*. Cruz ordered his wife, "Look, girl, go to the Hacienda. If they take you I'm going to work in Huaraz. If they don't take you I'll work in Huaraz a month and then I'll leave there." So it happened that at the Hacienda the *mayorales* didn't take her because she has a baby and that won't allow her to work. The woman showed up to work, but she was just there a week and then she didn't come any more. It was the same with their son who came to work for a month and then didn't come back. (How ought the Hacienda deal with cases like that? Is it good to take land or could they do something better?) Don Enrique has made this proposal: if they pull themselves together and come back to work, next year they'll give the land back, because that way they won't be taking it completely away. It's just a punishment. Meanwhile, the Hacienda will plant it, and they say, "If you don't conform we'll take the land away and give it to someone else." So it's just like an *embargo*. (They say that Pedro Cruz's son went to the Hacienda to beg that they leave him even a bit of land near their house.) If they behave themselves that can be done, but if they don't work in the Hacienda as if they owned the land, and they keep going off to work elsewhere, the Hacienda is right in being angry.

(Is it good or bad what they've done to Pedro Cruz?) Without working, how is one going to live? How can one provide for oneself like that? Still, if one misses a few days, let's say, the Hacienda says that one has been absent out of some need or necessity. But in this case when one has missed so much, year after year, it's something different. So if one misses a few days it would be unjust to take one's land. . . .

(What obligations, duties, and rights are there between the Hacienda's *patrón* and the peon?) A peon's duty is to obey what they order. Similarly, the Hacienda is obliged when there is a *falta* from sickness or some other problem. They ought to wait for the peon to make up his *falta*, without taking an *embargo* or doing what they did with Pedro Cruz. But if a peon doesn't say anything, then the Hacienda can't have any obligation or consideration for him.

Enrique, on his own account, has talked with the authorities and said that he can pardon three work days if a person goes out to look for victuals, but he must tell them. If I miss work I go to Enrique and ask for my *temple*. He tells me, "But you have a *falta*, Manuel." I answer, "But you know how sickly I've been. I'll make up the *falta*." And he gives me my *temple*. Certainly, a person's word is what counts.

(What do you think about the abolition of *embargos* by the Hacienda?) It's good because in the old days they took *embargos* of our animals which we had to support us, and now the animals are free. (Wouldn't it have been better if they'd taken an *embargo* from Pedro Cruz instead of taking the land?) Well, now there isn't that custom of taking *embargos*. But they've taken it because of the ill temper of Cruz's son. Because

Enrique went to Cruz's place and met up with the son. He asked him why he didn't go to work, and the son told him, "Why are you taking the field away, *carajo*. There's the field. Just leave it there." Such language made Enrique angry. Instead of speaking that way, the boy ought to have answered respectfully. Now they've planted the field. They in ten sacks of seed. The field was fertilized with the manure that Meza's wife put in. (Is what Mario did in taking the field away from them good, then?) It's well done, because if a person isn't respectful he isn't worth anything. In Parash [a Vicos neighborhood] they also sent a *yunta* to Manuel Romano's field. He was an irrigator. The people who knew that he'd been working defended him. What happened was that the senior *tápaco* didn't know he was working. Everybody spoke up with one voice for that man, saying that he'd been working. But for Pedro Cruz, nobody came out in favor of him. . . . (MP, Flores, with Celso León, August 26, 29.)

Llicu Tadeo: (Is what the Hacienda did all right?) They shouldn't have done that. The *mayorales* are for the *patrones*. They are like the Hacienda's family. They must have gone to notify Cruz, to see why he wasn't working. He would then have told why he was defaulting. Since I was a child, I've never seen them take anybody's fields away. The *mayorales* make people work. So if a person has *faltas* in the Hacienda, they go and ask him if he's going to work or not. (Is what the Hacienda did good or bad?) I already told you that it's not the custom to take land away. What more can I say? (How should the Hacienda have arranged things with Pedro Cruz instead of taking his field?) It could order its *mayorales* to go and look at their house, see how they're living, if they are in need, if they have victuals, and find out why they're not working. . . . Then they can say if he missed work from need, if he has the things he needs, if he has maize. Then they can tell why he's leaving to work elsewhere. We are people who belong to the State, and the land belongs to the people as if it were their property. Besides, the people were born here and it's an abuse when they take land away from them, because the land doesn't belong to either the Beneficencia or the State. They didn't buy it. . . .
(Wouldn't it have been better if they'd taken an *embargo* from Pedro Cruz instead of taking the field away?) It's because he doesn't have anything to take as an *embargo*. Otherwise, it would have been good if they'd taken a sheep or a pig, and because of that he'd have worked to redeem them. . . . (What do you think of the abolition of *embargos*?) They used to have *embargos* because the custom was different. Now these ones have other customs and they don't have *embargos*. Now they plan to take land away from the people with many *faltas*. That way they'll be more attentive to Hacienda work. In the old days the *embargo* was the same for everybody. They took *embargos* from the richest people. Now the ones who have many defaults get their land taken away, but also they let people alone when they give their word. (And did Pedro Cruz give his

word?) I don't know how it was, if that shit-beast [*bestia de mierda*] was there in his field. If I'm not there in my field, let them take it away from me too. . . . (Was that just?) Once they gave my grandson a field and then they told him they were going to take it away because he was two weeks behind in work. So he asked them to make up the *faltas* and they accepted that. One's capability isn't worth anything. What's worth something is one's word. What more can I tell you? I don't know if they found Pedro Cruz in his field or not. If they found him, then they could arrange something. Like that they could have investigated his situation at home, seen his needs. . . . (So then, is it good that they threw him out?) That was why, of course. He defaulted year after year. Who's not going to get angry? I wouldn't like it if I gave somebody a field and then he didn't work. You even tell a dog who's not obedient, "Get out of here!" It's the same with somebody who doesn't obey. (MP, Flores, with Celso León, August 29.)

Emilio Colonia: The *patrones* aren't crazy to throw somebody out. They do that to lazy people. Didn't they let him know before they did it? If it was like that, it's fine. If he didn't pay any attention, they were right. They had to throw him out. People ought to work. If he had a grown up son, why didn't the son do it? (MP, Soto, with Ricardo Estremadoyro, August 25.

Andrés Copitán: If the Hacienda took Pedro Cruz's land away from him, that's all right. We all ought to work for the Hacienda equally. Cruz didn't come to work for more than three years even though the Hacienda scolded him several times. They told him that if he didn't come to work they were going to take his land away. His wife is the one who is suffering because she's here. What does it matter to the man? He fills his stomach in peace. (The interpreter asks him, "Haven't you heard it said by other Vicosinos that the Hacienda is abusive? That's what they've told us.) Is that a fact? Is that what they're saying? They took it away from him for being lazy. If I don't work for a month they can excuse me, but if I miss work for three or four years, how are they going to excuse me? Some of us are going to have to work together, and others not. I know that his son is grown up and could easily have replaced him in Hacienda work. His father told him not to work and he added that the land would be safe. But they're kicked out like that and nobody has a right to work on their land.

(We asked him if he had seen Cruz what he would have told him about the affair.) I'd advise him to have respect for his *patrones* because the land isn't yours. It belongs to the Hacienda. . . .

Now the Hacienda has taken away half and planted potatoes there. In the past, like now, they took away half and planted maize. From the wife's tears, when she asked for protection, they gave it back to her, and she promised to work in the Hacienda. Now I don't know what happened.

(We asked him if Cruz's wife had livestock.) She had sheep. The cow she had died. (Where did she pasture her sheep?) Surely in her neighbors' fields. (MP, Soto, with Ricardo Estremadoyro, August 29.)

The Vicosinos appear to have told interviewers what they thought the latter wanted to hear, but in terms of the Vicos conception of collective punishment for transgression, explored in the last chapter, we might speculate that they might have an "Andean" solution in the form of a collective pardon. Jefrey Gamarra (2002:34) finds pardon rituals in communities in Ayacucho affected by the violence which erupted in the region during the 80s and early 90s, in which horrible deeds were performed by some community members:

> The concept of *pardon* from the point of view of Andean culture implies *forgetting* of the acts committed. So the Quechua word *pampachay* (to pardon, to forget) literally means to level, to make a non-level surface flat, to make equal. If this process of pardon be understood as gifts and counter-gifts, whose axis is the *forgetting* of "social interest," it has already taken place in many communities. In what way is a forced and manipulated memory, imposed by the State and other private urban organizations, going to affect communal cohesion?
>
> But now, the matter of pardon and forgetting brings us to another problem. Is this produced on the level of individual memories or those of the group? It is here that the process we call *communal reconciliation* makes sense. Memory, collective or individual, has been and still is in a certain way a *blocked* memory, in the sense that both communal authorities and members seek to forget experiences that could threaten communal cohesion. The heads of these communities not only oblige the ex-members of Shining Path to respect the rules, but they also require all members of the commons not to molest the "repentant." Informants repeatedly mention forgetting as an expression of reconciliation: *"burying all the evil, people become new beings, with a single idea, they don't think any more about the violent time."* To *bury guilt and not speak about what happened* is characteristic of blocked memory, what can be called *voluntary forgetting* or that which is imposed by the group

There is much more, surely, to Pedro Cruz's story, but there is not much more in the archives that I could discover. An anonymous census memo, dated "March, 1954", indicates a resolution of the Hacienda's (the Project's) case against him:

> Pedro Cruz, Weekly *tarea*: 3, an entitled peon. For several years Pedro has not worked in a continuous way in Hacienda work. The present administration, after taking a series of conciliatory measures which had no result, chose to plant one of Pedro's properties, which remains in the

power of the Hacienda. One of Pedro's minor children now gives service to the Hacienda, and so the hand will be returned to him after the harvest. (AVP.)

At some point during the next few months, Pedro Cruz died. His widow found another man, apparently choosing someone who resembled Cruz (or perhaps filled some *absence* in herself). Reference is made to the family in the notes of Héctor Martínez Arrellano[40]:

> Today I gave credit of 60 kilos of potatoes to *Pablo Sánchez, despite the worst reports of the Hacienda *administrador* who told me that before he married Pedro Cruz's widow he was a lazy, careless, and even thieving person, and that the *faltas* he has in the peon register are said by his brother to be his own fault as a person who hasn't carried out his duties in Hacienda work. I granted him credit, thinking that this way I could contribute to his regeneration so he could take a more appropriate status in the community. (AVP, 14-v-55.)

Martínez made two more references to the family:

> Miguel Cruz is one of Pedro Cruz's sons. He must be about 22 years old. I found him sunning himself in the field that lies next to the house where he lives with his mother, siblings, and step-father, Pablo Sánchez. He told me that two days ago he arrived from Capillas where he was working in order to get money to pay a fine that the *varayoq* had imposed on him because he had asked his mother, "Why do you have a thief for a lover and why do you forgive him? Your lover is a lazy man and he ought to take you to his house and not come here to live in my father's house." He informed me: "I said that to her because Pablo Sánchez stole a *lampa* from Andrés Cupitán. So he came with the *varayoq* and took the *lampa* that I'd bought with the money I earned. I asked my mother what had become of my *lampa*. She told me that it must have been stolen, but then I met up with Andrés Cupitán who told me that Pablo Sánchez had stolen his *lampa*, and so he'd taken off a *lampa* that he found in my house, and that he'd return that *lampa* to me when Pablo Sánchez returned his *lampa* to him. When I insulted my mother, she complained to the *varayoq*, and they fined me 12 *soles* which I gave to Espíritu Tafur. Then he insulted me for insulting my mother. Instead of insulting her I should have kept quiet, because that was what a son was for. I don't know what use it is to have my mother when it's she who's the one that has fines imposed on us, instead of preventing that they fine a person, and injuring a person like that. And then they don't want me to stay at home because I prevent my step-father from hitting my small siblings. Then he's a thief and maybe he'll teach my siblings to steal. That's why I have to go to Capillas again to bring back my other brother. Then once that the two of us are here

we'll fix it so my mother goes off to her lover's house and leaves us in the house and the lands that were from my father. It's not fair that a lazy, thieving man live in the house that's from my father. If my mother wants to live with her lover, let her to his house! . . .

"Pablo Sánchez is a thief. He has no shame because he's used to robbing people and taking over other people's possessions without asking permission. Last year, for example, he robbed a sack of *jora* [sprouted purple maize for making *chicha*] from José Colonia. He found out about it and came to get his *jora* back. Then, as a punishment, he took away a sheep. When he took it my mother didn't say anything. Rather, she forgave her lover for his thieving ways. He's shameless because when they got married they went to a person in Marcará to whom I'd given 20 *soles* to keep for me and asked him for 10 *soles* to get married. They did it with that. If he's a man he ought to work and not ask like that, stealing other people's money. He's also a thief and shameless because he takes over my things while I'm watching. For example, the other day he took my *puru* [gourd receptacle of lime for chewing coca] without saying anything to me, because he lost his own *puru* at the maize harvest. Then he doesn't have a single tool for working, so he has to take hold of my father's tools that he left when he died. He also maltreats my small siblings and makes them work. Surely that's because he has no children of his own. Because of all that, when my brother arrives we'll throw him out. Let him go to his own field and his house. And my mother, if she wants, can go with her lover. Then we'll stay at home with my younger siblings. Another time he took 10 *soles* that I'd put away in a pot. When I asked my mother what had become of the 10 *soles*, she told me she didn't know. Later I learned that my stepfather had taken it." (AVP, 24-v-55.)

*Francisca Mendoza is Pedro Cruz's widow and currently Pablo Sánchez's wife. We talked when I went to look at her husband's potato field that he'd planted with credit from the Project. She told me that one of the pieces of land her former husband owned when he was alive was being planted by *Antonio Cruz, Pedro's nephew, who received it from his father, and that the latter had begun to plant it because her husband was a vagabond and didn't bother to plant his land. Since her husband wasn't planting that land, his brother, Sebastián, Antonio's father, said to her, "Well, if your husband isn't planting that land, and since he's my brother, I'm going to plant them and in that way I'll get to you a part of the produce from the harvest so that you can feed your children." Francisca says, "When Sebastián died, those lands passed on to Antonio who is now stopping me from planting , even at the edges of the field. When I claimed that land he told me that he improved it, because at the beginning it was a marsh. Now that there are more of us in the family, you people ought to fix it so that those fields that belonged to my husband are returned to me.

"Similarly, *Marcos Lázaro has other fields from my husband. He began to plant them when my husband died. When I claimed them from him, he told me that he would just plant them this year, and that when he harvested his *ocas* he'd leave those fields so we could plant them with my present husband and my son Miguel." (AVP, 26-v-55.)

There are no more file slips relating to Pedro Cruz in the archives, but I have no doubt that this troubled family continued to trouble the Project, and later the Vicos community, with its troubles.

Conclusions

Let us focus on the vicissitudes of the Project as it was carried into the error of substituting everything else for the two actions it could not perform: liberating the Vicosinos from the hacienda system and redistributing the land more equitably–two possibilities which were deferred until after the Project stopped. If the Project had tried the first it would have failed in its contract with the Beneficencia. If it had tried the second it would have lost the cooperation, indeed support, it received from powerful Vicosinos. Here, the strategic question asked by Johannes Fabian (1983:154) is relevant: "[W]hen we accept domination as a fact, are we not actually playing into the hands of those who dominate?" In this, the Project made itself a part of the "development problem" it desired to overcome, but because it needed to appear to be doing the rational and disinterested action it was unable to "diagnose" itself as problematic, or submit to an objective "diagnosis."[41] But I want to make this critique as an ethnographer of the Project and not as someone condemning it morally. James Ferguson (1994:16-17), in his general introduction to a critique of development discourse in Lesotho, has these guiding comments to offer:

> Empirically, "development projects" . . . do not generally bring about any significant reduction in poverty, but neither do they characteristically introduce any new relations of production (capitalist or otherwise), or bring about any significant economic transformations. They do not bring about "development" in either of the two senses identified above, nor are they set up in such a way that they ever could. . . .
> To take on the task of looking at the "development" apparatus anthropologically is to insist on a particular sort of approach to the material. As an anthropologist, one cannot assume, for instance, as many political economists do, that a structure simply and rationally "represents" or "expresses" a set of "objective interests"; one knows that structures are multi-layered, polyvalent, and often contradictory, and that economic functions and "objective interests" are always located within other,

encompassing structures that may be invisible even to those who inhabit them. The interests may be clear, and the intentions as well; but the anthropologist cannot take "planning" at its word. Instead of ascribing events and institutions to the projects of various actors, an anthropological approach must demote the plans and intentions of even the most powerful interests to the status of an interesting problem, one level among many others, for the anthropologist knows well how easily structures can take on lives of their own that soon enough overtake intentional practices. Whatever interests may be at work, and whatever they may think they are doing, they can only operate through a complex set of social and cultural structures so deeply embedded and so ill-perceived that the outcome may be only a baroque and unrecognizable transformation of the original intention.

The object of the Project's research became a fetish, a substitute for any real resolution of the Hacienda's problems. To borrow a phrase from Anthony Appiah (1990:6), we could call it a "cognitive incapacity." In this its personnel seem to have been mistaken human beings, not villains. E. L. McCallum (1999:142) writes:

> The fetish indicates how reality is permeated with the fantastic forces of desire, but also of knowledge–
> the fantasy of knowledge not only being the projection of mastery and control, but also the investment in belief that contradicts evidence or materiality. . . . As subjects come into being they simultaneously shape the context and objects in which they will exist while incorporating and appropriating those same rules and tools to make themselves who they are. They are not stupid about how they do this, but are aware to a certain extent–though not always completely–of how knowledge and desire direct their efforts. To be smarter and stronger subjects they must work the ambivalence and contradictions more attentively.

She adds that fetishing "offers a way to do this." But the Project staff people were not paying attention.

As for Pedro Cruz, here was an anomaly[42] in Vicos, someone "unusual, unexpected" (Canguilhem 1989:133) in a community whose ego-ideal is the "hard worker." However, despite this maneuver to avoid the term "abnormal," the simple expectation or anticipation of certain behaviors is already the setting of a "norm" which is "a polemical concept which negatively qualifies the sector of the given which does not enter into its extension [i.e., what is abnormal] while it depends on its comprehension" (239). Under the gaze of some informants, who used some favorite Vicos expletives, including the scatological, in reference to Cruz, he seems–to employ Canguilhem's (134) anatomical model as a metaphor--like a "monstrosity," an anomaly that is "very serious, making the performance of one or more functions impossible or difficult, or producing in the individuals so affected a defect in structure very different from that ordinarily found in their species." Mary Douglas (1966:38) writes: "There are several ways of treating anomalies. Negatively, we can ignore, just not perceive them, or perceiving we can condemn. Positively we can deliberately confront the anomaly and try to create a new pattern of reality in which it has a place." She adds that people can take different measures to deal with them: "by settling for one or other interpretation, ambiguity is often reduced . . . the existence of anomaly can be physically controlled . . . a rule of avoiding anomalous things affirms and strengthens the definitions to which they do not conform . . . anomalous events may be labeled dangerous . . . [and] ambiguous symbols can be used in ritual for the same ends as they are used in poetry and mythology, to enrich meaning or to call attention to other levels of existence" (39-40).

Enrique Luna othered Cruz and his family to Blanchard with the epithet "*viciosos,*" vicious people, addicts to coca and alcohol—evil, a disposition to which Blanchard offered no resistance. Frederic Jameson (1981:115) offers this description of the othering process:

> Evil . . ., as Nietsche taught us, continues to characterize whatever is radically different from me, whatever by virtue of precisely that difference seems to constitute a real and urgent threat to my own existence. So from the earliest times, the stranger from another time, the 'barbarian' who speaks an incomprehensible language and follows 'outlandish customs,' but also the woman, whose biological difference simulates fantasies of castration and devoration, or in our own time, the avenger of accumulated resentments from some oppressed class or race, or else that alien being, Jew or Communist, behind whose apparently human features a malignant and preternatural intelligence is thought to lurk: these are some of the archetypical figures of the Other, about whom the essential point to be made is not so much that he is feared because he is evil; rather, he is evil *because* he is Other, alien, different, strange, unclean, and unfamiliar.

Pedro Cruz was certainly "atypical", a nonconformist, passive rebel who appears uncannily to have reminded, not only other Vicosinos, but the Project personnel of their own secret desires, and perhaps their ghosts, which they were unable to acknowledge or recognize. Such anomalies have instructional value. Victor Turner (1967:105) suggests that "monsters are manufactured precisely to teach neophytes to distinguish clearly between the different factors of reality, as it is conceived by their culture. . . . Monsters startle neophytes into thinking about objects, persons, and features of their environment they have hitherto taken for granted."

If Pedro Cruz was a mirror image, he was that only to some informants. The terms which other Vicosinos employed only illustrate their displacement of the fear of something, or perhaps a nothing, an *absence*, in themselves, a secret alterity. Only a few of the informants considered the alternative response of compassion. In this second scenario he may well have been seen, since he was not "working," as "crying." One informant suggested an examination of the family in order to discover what was not right.

How are we to think of him, with all our positive and negative transferences? Here I am intrigued by the possibility of applying what George Marcus (1998:165) has to say about wealthy eccentrics to Pedro Cruz, who was poor: "[T]he defining nonconformism of eccentricity might be associated with the worthless 'drunkard and fool' epithet . . . , or it might be associated with various kinds of clinically assessed mental illness, or it might, alternatively, be associated with the gift of originality and genius." But Marcus (166) adds, and most provocatively, that the wealthy eccentrics "are hyperaware that their selves are being constructed elsewhere by other agencies, that they are keenly aware of their selves being multiply authored. . . . They are more likely to engage with and comment upon the production of their selves by other agencies, and this engagement is less likely to be in the form of literal discourse than in the form of the behaviors, performances, and habits that constitute eccentricity itself." We have no interview materials with Cruz, but it is easy to imagine him as a fragmented person, in great part "authored" or "constructed" by the Hacienda and by other Vicosinos, "agencies" he, the self with no center (171), repudiated as best he could with his behavior.

We can also view his passive rebellion as form of what James Scott (1985:29) refers to as "weapons of the weak" or "*everyday* forms of peasant resistance," like "foot dragging, dissimulation, false compliance, pilfering, feigned ignorance, slander, arson, sabotage, and so forth"–all of which could have been a part of Cruz's repertory. I could wish, though, that circumstances had permitted him to be much less passive about his rebellion for possibly, with his comprehension and rejection of Vicos life under the hacienda system, he might have been a creative leader. Or, too, considering "how things worked" (and still do to some extent) in the social order of the Callejón de Huaylas, as a leader he might have ended his existence (or had it ended for him) much earlier than he did. At the same time, I agree with Nancy Fraser's (1989:93-94) critique of the "somewhat cartoonish characterization of the Romantic impulse which lionizes "the figure of the extraordinary individual who does not simply play out but, rather, rewrites the cultural script his sociohistorical milieu has prepared for him":

> Insofar as the Romantic impulse figures such difference making as the work of extraordinary individuals, insofar as it treats them and their work as the source of all significant historical change, insofar as it views history largely as the succession of such geniuses, it becomes aestheticizing, individualist, and elitist. It is, in short, the impulse to father oneself, to be *causa sui*, to separate from one's community. Thus, the masculine pronoun is appropriate.

Judith Butler (1990:138-139), writing as a radical feminist, suggests that "the normal" or "the original" turns out "to be a copy, and an inevitably failed one, an ideal that no one *can* embody. In this sense, laughter emerges in the realization that all along the original was derived." Here it is obvious that the "industrious worker" model of the Hacienda labor force, the model from which Pedro Cruz was alleged to have departed, was a sham, a "groundless ground." With Vicosinos generally not showing up for work it is impossible to measure Pedro Cruz's absence in terms of some preexisting identity. There would be no true or false, real or unreal worker, so that the postulation of a "true" worker identity would be shown to be a "regulatory fiction." Thus the notion of an essential worker is part of a strategy that conceals the performative character of Hacienda work and the possibilities of taking labor beyond the restrictive frame of Hacienda domination and compulsory work.[43]

We should then turn our attention to the startling difference in the treatment of a non-conformist worker that existed between the pre-Project hacienda system and the hacienda system under the Project's guidance. Non-conformity, mainly in the form of the shirking of Hacienda duties and alcoholism rather than open rebellion, had been treated with confiscation of goods and physical abuse such as kicks and whippings. Barnett (1960:50) reports that past *patrones* relied on the state apparatus to have workers "jailed and fined for stealing, threatening the *patrón* or his employees, or other infractions." He believes that public whippings ceased some time in the 1920's but notes: "Several informants commented that occasional beatings (with fists) as well as blows with a riding crop were given in the fields by the father of the present administrator [i.e., Enrique Luna's father]" (51). Only one possible attempt to injure or kill a *patrón* appears in the data. Barnett's (104) principal informant in Marcará, Adolfo García, told him of the abusive *patrón* Lostaunau who may have been a target around 1912: "Those [Vicosinos] who opposed Lostaunau were put in jail. On the old road, going up to Vicos from Marcará, Lostaunau was wounded by a bullet. He said a Vicosino had shot at him, but some also said he did it himself accidentally, with his own pistol."

There were some marginal Vicosinos who performed no Hacienda labors, owned no recorded farm lands on the estate, but were permitted to maintain homesteads with adjoining land in Vicos. Some were useful as *peones* of rich Vicosinos. Others seem to be living contradictions to the Vicos prescriptions of labor, reciprocity, sobriety, and care for family. They offered no challenge to the system but, rather, seem to have been useful to *patrones* as reinforcers of labor discipline in the role of abjects. In Kristeva's (1982:1-2) terms an abject is a "jettisoned object," driven off by a superego, which "lies outside, beyond the set, and does not seem to agree to the latter's rules of the game." Butler (1990:133-134) comments:

> The "abject" designates that which has been expelled from the body, discharged as excrement, literally rendered "Other." This appears as an expulsion of alien elements, for the alien is effectively established through this expulsion. The construction of the "not-me" as the abject establishes the boundaries of the body which are also the first contours of the subject. ... The boundary of the body as well as the distinction between internal and external is established through the ejection of something originally part of identity into a defiling otherness.... The boundary between the inner and the outer is confounded by those excremental passages in which the inner effectively becomes outer, and this excreting function becomes, as it were, the model by which other forms of identity-differentiation are accomplished. In effect, this is the mode by which Others become shit.

This is what seems to have happened to Pedro Cruz.

The Project could not tolerate this man who constituted a threat to its research performance, that is,--and I say this seriously--its potency as social science, its insatiable desire to prove itself and its methods as a mature scientific undertaking--unconsciously, to achieve an erection. Taussig (1993:226) ponders, "How strange and multitudinous a notion 'society' becomes when we thingify it, as if this very act makes it slip away from us," and then asks, "[S]hould we not allow the terminology to express its sacral bent more fully and instead of saying social facts are *things* say that social facts are *reification* . . .?" He suggests, "The most rigorously sociological sociology in the history of Western Man [sic] turns out to be bound, tooth and claw, to fetishism, from which it is itself inseparable and of which it becomes exemplary" (235). Social science, thus, becomes haunted and more mirror than science, for social scientists who look into their data for reflections of themselves which they may easily misrecognize..

The Project's object, as I have outlined it, was not merely to engage successfully in social science but to attract more research funding and, by its fame, to enhance the careers of its staff. But absenteeism, the "upside-down erection,"[44] threatened to bring disaster. How could it use the Hacienda as a "controlled" experiment in development if its workers did not show up at work? How could it demonstrate and disseminate the virtues and advantages of increased productivity under such conditions. It wanted to liberate the Vicosinos not only from the hacienda system at Vicos but from the inequalities and injustices of their social order. But the Project erred, as "high modernists" are wont to err. James Scott (1998:95) writes:

> The temporal emphasis of high modernism is almost exclusively on the future. Although any ideology with a large altar dedicated to progress is bound to privilege the future, high modernism carries this to great lengths. The past is an impediment, a history that must be transcended; the present is the platform for launching plans for a better future. . . . The strategic choice of the future is freighted with consequences. To the degree that the future is known and achievable–a belief that the faith in progress encourages–the less future benefits are discounted for uncertainty. The practical effect is to convince most high modernists that the certainty of a better future justifies the many short-term sacrifices required to get there.

But in order to achieve its goal the Project became the Hacienda (as ghosts can merge with one another, separate, and blend again). The Project swallowed the Hacienda. It took on this identity "secretly," that is without acknowledging it. In so doing it gulped down its love object, social science. Or, rather, to employ Nicolas Abraham and Maria Torok's (1994:126-127) concept, the Project "incorporated" its science:

> Introducing all or part of a love object or a thing into one's own body, possessing, expelling or alternately acquiring, keeping, losing it–here are varieties of fantasy indicating, in the typical forms of possession or feigned disposession, a basic intrapsychic situation: the situation created by the reality of a loss sustained by the psyche. But the fantasy of incorporation merely simulates profound psychic transformation through magic; it does so by implementing literally something that has only figurative meaning. So in order not to have to "swallow" a loss, we fantasize swallowing (or having swallowed) that which has been lost. . . . The magical "cure" by incorporation exempts the subject from the painful process of reorganization. . . . Incorporation is the refusal to reclaim as our own the part of ourselves that we placed in what we lost; incorporation is the refusal to acknowledge the full import of the loss, a loss that, if recognized as such, would effectively transform us.

In exercising control of the Hacienda work force in the way it did, the Project-Hacienda, by manipulating its "dependent variables," gave up all hope of "controlled experimentation." To gain control, it lost control. And the love object was lost. The equivalence of commodity producers became a fetish, but meanwhile the Project was blind to inequality and injustice and offered no challenge to these conditions.[45] None of this has been said to date. It has remained unsaid for nearly a half century. This is because it has gone without saying. But secrets will out themselves.

Pedro Cruz had to be made an example, perhaps a scapegoat. But the strategy appeared to work, at least temporarily–for workers began to appear for their *tareas*–and sufficiently to allow the Project to congratulate itself for doing the "right" thing, displaying rectitude, constructing not a "permanent revolution" but a "permanent erection." However, it was uncertain, it hesitated, it vacillated, and, while it was planting the Cruz field it was looking for ways to undo what it had done, for, to employ Derrida's (1986:121) metaphor, while it could not close the penal colony and castrate castration, it did not wish to appear vengeful. It found itself in Hamlet's famous role:

Hamlet . . . clearly opposes the being "out of joint" of time to its *being-right*, in the right or the straight path of that which walks upright. He even curses the fate that would have caused him to be born to set right a time that walks crooked. He curses the destiny that would precisely have destined him, Hamlet, to do justice, to put things back in order, to put history, the world, the age, the time *upright*, on the right path, so that, in conformity with the rule of its correct functioning, it advances straight ahead–and following the law. . . . He swears against a destiny that leads him to do justice for a fault, a fault of time and of the times, by rectifying an *address*, by making of rectitude and right ("to set it right") a movement of *correction*, reparation, restitution, vengeance, revenge, punishment. He swears against this misfortune, and this misfortune is unending because it is nothing other than himself, Hamlet. Hamlet is "out of joint" because he curses his own mission, the punishment that consists in having to punish, avenge, exercise justice and right in the form of reprisals, and what he curses in his mission is this expiation of expiation itself. (Derrida 1994:20.)

The Hacienda Vicos and the Project are really, or unreally, fetishes which erase the persons of those subjects who exercised power in their names. The "Hacienda" and the "Project" are abstractions, representations of the local staff, as well as the principal investigator, the absent ghostly Allan Holmberg who was alive in Ithaca while the events recorded here were taking place,[46] the contract with the Beneficencia (two more fetishes which represented the symbolic violence of legality and the physical violence of the propertied mestizo elite of the Callejón de Huaylas), in sum, the field of social relations of the Vicosinos with their Others. Thus, it was not that Vicosinos were "Hacienda people," that they "owed" anything to the Hacienda, or that they were subject to what the Hacienda "wanted" from them, but that, as Eric Wolf (1966:3) asserts, "control of the means of production, including the disposition of human labor," has passed from them, "the primary producers into the hands of groups that do not carry on the productive process themselves, but assume instead special executive and administrative functions, backed by the use of force."

In the writing of this book I confess that I have often lost track of the fetished nature of these entities. But here, consciously, I allow the fetish to use me as it will. Michael Taussig (1998:231) asks: "Can the fetish 'pass'? Can it lurk undetected in the everyday? Can this sensate and mobile tissue evoking an obscure innerness be truly the zone of the fetish? And all along we thought that it was just our familiar friend, old face, far from the traders on the West Coast of Africa and Christian fantasies concerning pagan ritual objects. . . . But then the fetish–as we use the term, and as the term uses us–have this remarkable twofold property of being either in-your-face exotic *or* hidden in the everyday." As Lacan (1994:195) writes of the phallus, that the fetish appears and disappears: "One tries to see where it is and where it is not. It is never truly where it is, nor is it at all absent from where it is not."

Bondage and discipline! Here is the hacienda system fetished out of sight! In the nineteenth century the use of stocks, chains, whips, and other forms of restraint and punishment was common in all parts of Perú. But there were no consenting adults. Yet I think what I am trying to approach here is not a horror show but a secret component which may "slip under the table," the more so if we try to hide what is not there or to obscure what is not clear. The issue may be raised: while the Project might have preferred a free and just Vicos, the contract forced it to continue unfreedom and injustice. Just how secret was its maneuvering to abolish confiscation and then to reinstate it? We are now discussing the vicissitudes of being human, more than those of the Project. However, these conclusions are not irrelevant to the designs of *all* those humans who, by means of development or revolutionary strategies, endeavor to make existence safer for themselves.

The Vicos Project was a creature--a fetish–of the 1950's. It modeled in small-scale the great North American enterprise–one which presented an attractive surface while hiding a wound, an emptiness, a castration--of which Laura Mulvey (1996:74-75) writes:

Reference to the 50s invokes the aftermath of the Korean War and the success of the Marshall Plan, American mass consumption, the "society of the spectacle" and, indeed, the Hollywood melodrama. It was a time when, in the context of the cold war, advertising, movies and the actual packaging and seductiveness of commodities all marketed glamour. Glamour proclaimed the desirability of American capitalism to the outside world and, inside, secured Americanness as an aspiration for the newly suburbanized white population as it buried incompatible memories of immigrant origins. . . . The image of "fifties-ness" as a particular emblem of Americanness also masks the fact that it was a decade of social and political repression while profound changes gathered on the horizon, the transition, that is, from Joe McCarthy to James Dean, from Governor Maddox [of Georgia who stubbornly defended the "color line"] to Martin Luther King.

Here is Mulvey's (xiv) comment on fetishing which she calls, "the most semiotic of perversions":

It does not want its forms to be overlooked but to be gloried in. This is, of course, a ruse to distract the eye and the mind from something that needs to be covered up. And this is also its weakness. The more the fetish exhibits itself, the more the presence of a traumatic past event is signified. The "presence" can only be understood through a process of decoding because the "covered" material has necessarily been distorted into the symptom. The fetish is on the cusp of consciousness, acknowledging its own process of concealment and signaling the presence of , if not the ultimate meaning of, a historical event.

The Vicos Project had much to cover up. There is little to recognize (or perhaps much to misrecognize) in it but its misrecognition. It was not that the Project made petty capitalists out of some Vicosinos but that it did so by continuing for several years nothing less than the simulacrum[47] of a feudal social order. Bourdieu's (1996:39) characterization of academic classifiers who separate the last accepted from the first rejected by an unbridgeable gap applies here: "They only do well what they have to do (objectively) because they think they are doing something other than what they are doing, because they are doing something other than what they think they are doing, and because they believe in what they think they are doing. As fools fooled, they are the primary victims of their own actions." The Project staff concealed from themselves the patronizing and patriarchal implications they did not want to confront, the fields that demand authentic growth in human relations if we ever are to be a *sane* and *social* species.

If I had never been a child experiencing the misapplied and

misrecognized power of adults, if I had never inherited a patriarchal *habitus*--like a gene for some bizarre pathology accompanied by ordinary, unbizarre pain--or found myself in the powerful role of parent in relation to powerless and trusting children, and if I had not recognized in myself a repetition of the same confused, hesitating, anxious, and fearful blindness as that of the Project, I would perhaps be willing to see the Project's personnel as villains. It turns out that they were only engaging in the situated discourse of their location in time and space. In studying genetic pathology from the perspective of molecular biology, Georges Canguilhem (1989:175-279) finds that "error" is a more useful concept than "evil," "deficiency," or "excess." "There is," he says, "no difference between the error of life and the error of thought, between the errors of informing and informed information," and "a genetically determined disease is no longer a mischievous curse but a misunderstanding." Consequently: "As living beings, we are the effect of the very laws of the multiplication of life, as sick people we are the effect of a universal mixing, love and chance." Paul Rabinow (1996:87-88) comments on Canguilhem's work, that people make mistakes; they place themselves "in the wrong relationship with the environment, in the wrong place to receive the information needed to survive, to act, to flourish. We must move, err, adapt to survive. This condition, of 'erring or drift,' is not merely accidental or external to life but its fundamental form." At the same time, we should not forget the horrors that result from placing mountains of money, guns, tanks, bombs, and legions of militaries and paramilitaries who "disappear" children they suspect of being "terrorists"–as if one word could encompass all of worldwide hopelessness's imagined communities–, in the hands of strikebreakers, or white-hooded (in Peru they wear ski-masks) lynch mobs, and skin-headed thugs who murder "guest workers," and those sanitation engineers who call themselves "ethnic cleansers," all of these at the disposal of "erring" persons in positions of command.

I have given much attention here to the Project's errors, and their effect on its scientific pursuits. What effect did it all have on Vicos? Actually, not very much. As Zimmerer (1996:70) says of Peru's land reform of 1969, it simply supplemented "a series of powerful changes rather than dictating them." In his exegesis of Jean-Jacques Rousseau's remarks on sexual supplements, Derrida (1976:150-151) picks up on the theme of danger.[48] While the effects of the agrarian reform on Peru's future are still to be reckoned with, I do not believe that we can say the same for the Project in Vicos where it chose, for the most part, not to exercise power but to be undecided.

Appendix 1

The following interview was conducted by Juan Elías Flores, with Celso León as interpreter, on August 25, 1953, with Alfonso Cruz:

(You were a *mayoral?*) Yes, when Atenio was the renter, and Maxi Flores was his *administrador*. In those days they began to have *enganches* for the coast, to go to San Bartolo. I got the people together to send them with *enganches* to San Bartolo on the Hacienda's account. 30 men went. The renter of San Bartolo was the same one from here in the Hacienda. When somebody asked who was in charge. They said it was I, that I encouraged them by telling them they should go to the coast and make money. Because I got those people together for the *enganche* the *patrones* appointed me *mayoral*. I'd just been a field hand.

(What did you do as a *mayoral?*) When they gave the order that I was to be *mayoral*, they gave me the job of *semanero*. I directed the *tápacos* and the cooks. For that they fired a man called Dolores Tafur. I was directly under the *patrón*. In those days the *semanero* had to order other men to bring firewood to Chancos. When the *patrón* wanted to leave early, I'd tell the *mulero* to saddle the horse. I arranged for the horse's fodder. I directed the shelling of maize and the selection of seed potatoes. Some women didn't do their work well at those jobs and I fixed it so they worked well. I also had a plant called *firito* gathered so as to send it to Lima where they made disinfectants for bugs out of it. The *semanero* was also a field *mayoral*. In those days all the *mayorales* took turns at being *semanero*. Now they've abolished that custom.

In the old days they had *mitaq* who were single girls who came by turns to cook for the Hacienda. The *fiscal* had the job of directing them. Now that the new chiefs have come, they saw that it was a great abuse for the Vicosinos. So now there is no *tápaco* or *mitaq*.

The *tápaco* used to cut fodder for the animals, the guineapigs and rabbits. The Hacienda's *empleados* went out to the fields to supervise the workers, and the *tápaco* was the one who brought lunch out to them.

When I ended my time as *semanero*, I had a week off, and then the next week I went out with the people as *mayoral* to direct the potato harvest in Chullán [a sector of Hacienda land].

(What else did you do as *mayoral* beside work in the fields?) I also had them cut eucalyptus and bake tiles. (What other duties does the *mayoral* have?) To look at the crops to see in what condition they're in for cultivation. Then when the Hacienda was planting flax, we had to work with that.

(Has the duty of the *mayorales* now changed?) It's the same as before. The only thing that's changed is the chief. Before, the *mayorales* had all the people at their disposal. They appointed someone to the position of *cobrador* at the pass. They chose four to ten people by turn, first from one district, one part like Wikuspachán, then from Paltash, Huamantzaca, Cuyhuash, Ukushpampa, and then Wiyash, and from there to Ucaparte [all Vicos neighborhoods and administrative sectors]. The *mayorales* were in charge of all that. It was the custom for the *mayoral* to direct all the work. The *apuntador* named the *mayorales*. Now it's not like that. The *mayorales* don't choose people. Now Enrique and Mario do it. In the old days, the people who were chosen worked on the school, building houses, and all the different jobs. The choice was for the Hacienda, and that way people learned all the Hacienda jobs. Now the choice is made for one job. Now they take people from all the sections, and those people don't work at all the different jobs but at a single job like the ones who are working on the school. Then the rest of the people can't get skilled at those jobs and they're useless.

(I've seen that sometimes the gringos get the *mayorales* together. What would that be for?) I don't know that they talk with the gringos. People don't know about the agreements the *mayorales* make with the *patrones*. They just find out about orders for doing jobs at the *mando*. Only now the *mayorales* give out the list of jobs more clearly so that the people can hear them.

(Is the job of the *mayoral* to defend the *hacendados'* interests or are they on the side of the Indians?) It's half way. The *mayorales* aren't for one or the other. They don't make people work like slaves or drive them harshly. They have to arrange rest times for chewing coca, but when people sit for a long time the *mayorales* have to see that they get up, so that they only rest at the designated time. They tell them when it's time for work

(And when there are troubles between a *patrón* and the Vicosinos, what does a *mayoral* do?) That doesn't happen. When the Hacienda is harsh with the workers who work there, they say, "You're working us like burros!" Also, some saucy workers answer the *mayorales* back. When the *mayoral* gives orders, there are rude people who don't want to obey. Sometimes they say that it's because their tools are broken.

(I thought that the *mayorales* were like older brothers who helped and defended the Indians.) It's not like that. They appoint a *mayoral* to be equal with the Hacienda and with the people. Not to let the people get lazy and not to make them work too hard. It's not like you think, because the *mayorales* also work as if they were workers when they are directing the people. At the maize and potato harvests the workers are used to carrying off a kilo or a kilo and a half to eat. Some are like that, and others don't take anything. The *mayorales* watch out that they don't take any more than that. They scold them, saying "Why are you taking the Hacienda's crops when you have your own fields and you're paid."

(Wouldn't it be good if the Hacienda had representatives who would defend and stand up for the peons?) If there were some support for the people, that would be good. There was an Indians' representative when Maxi Flores was here. They had him called from Carhuaz where he lived. Such representatives should be appointed for the Indians so that they're not made mercilessly to work hard, and also they'd have the duty of disciplining the workers who didn't obey the Hacienda's *empleados*. Those delegates would take care of discipline and they'd defend the Indians from outrages. The *patrones* used to have the custom, and it's written in a document in Carhuaz, to give out coca every day. The order was that if they gave too little coca and outraged the people, Carhuaz would be notified. Those delegates were also *mayorales*. That is, they had two duties: to have the Hacienda worked at the order of the renters, and to be defenders of the Indians, to see that they got all their coca and that there weren't outrages. But now they just go on with the duty of delegates because they haven't appointed any others. These days they keep quiet when the coca is taken away, and if there are abuses they don't do anything. Well, what are they doing? Surely the present *patrones* are corrupting them, and that's why they don't say anything. They keep quiet. They don't report abuses outside. Isn't that so?

(What should a peon do when he has some complaint against the Hacienda? If they take a field away from him? If they don't excuse one day of work? If they've committed some abuse?) A worker like that would come here to the Hacienda to beg that they not take the field. They'd do this only because they're ignorant. They don't know where to go to register a complaint so as to defend their rights. If he knew what to do, he'd get his field back, or his *embargo*. It would be like Pancho Sánchez [one of the delegates who petitioned President Leguía in the mid 1920's] in the time when it was customary to work four days [per week] for the Hacienda. We all worked that way with all the abuses and harshness. But two intelligent and brave man came forward. They were Pancho Sánchez and Ignacio Colonia, and they were Vicosinos. Pancho Sánchez's *yunta* got into the Hacienda's pasture. They took away his *yunta* as an *embargo* for the Hacienda. Pancho Sánchez was a brave man and God helped him. He went silently to Lima with Ignacio Colonia, without asking for any help. He didn't say anything to anyone. He didn't complain to the Hacienda. Mauro Mendoza in Recuayhuanca has a photograph of the two of them in the Government Palace. It seems like they were brave men to go there dressed like Vicosinos with their hats in their hands, and be together with the President. They only found out about it here when [President] Bustamante's order arrived for the renter to get out of the Hacienda. When a new renter came, Pancho Sánchez and Ignacio Colonia asked that it be three days of work. The Government accepted that. They went off not knowing how to read or write, or speak Spanish. And they went into the Government Palace. What strong men they were to go on foot to Lima! When they came back, the ones in the Hacienda were impressed. Those men had the idea that they themselves should pay the rent, but they didn't know how to read. So there were wicked people who understood those papers and they made themselves *patrones*. Then Pancho Sánchez turned bad when they bewitched him out of envy. After that, Teófilo Luna and Domingo León came in as renters. [Cruz appears to be combining two protest movements, one in the mid-twenties when a delegation visited President Leguía, and one, ca. 1946, when another visited President Bustamante.]

(Would you like it if the Indians had some good delegates, good representatives?) It would be better if it were somebody from outside, a soldier because he'd be more upright in his decisions. A civilian is more dishonest. He wouldn't have the character to have laws or customs respected. (Wouldn't you want a Vicosino?) How about that! It wouldn't be good. That's because now people are like "the priest who says mass over his own body." Now the young men who are coming up are less lost, but they don't know about the past, about old customs. The *mayorales* who are old men are doing what they can. So I think it would be better to have somebody from outside, a soldier . . . . Now these *patrones* are good and they're getting crops like never before. They're educated men who know about the world. They're good with the people. They're making advances. People say it's because they know how to work, but it's also because they behave well, and God's blessing is helping them

Appendix 2

The following instructions, reproduced verbatim, for a "Special Task" were given to the Methodology Project's (n.d.:22) field workers, Eduardo Soler, Juan Elías Flores, and Froilán Soto Flores, on August 25, 1953:

Pedro Cruz was a peon of the Hacienda. He always was lacking in work for the Hacienda (that is, he was absent more than he came). When the Project arrived in Vicos, it called all the absent peons and told them that they were going to work because the Project had no interest in enriching itself but in working for the benefit of the Vicosinos. The Project abolished all the abuses of the old *patrón* with the peons who did not come to work: *embargos* were not made and sick people were excused, etc.

One of those who never came to work was Pedro Cruz. Therefore, the case of Pedro Cruz came about. Mario Vázquez spoke with him, telling him and explaining to him the necessity of his work on the Hacienda, because if he did not come to work on the Hacienda, the Hacienda would give his lands to another new peon or it would appropriate his lands.

Therefore, Pedro Cruz came to work on the Hacienda for 6 consecutive weeks. Then he stopped attending. Then, again, Mario Vázquez went to Pedro Cruz's house and he interviewed Pedro Cruz's wife. She said that her husband did not want to work on the Hacienda, and her son did not either, and because she was the owner of some cattle, she herself took over the responsibility of working on the Hacienda.

The wife came to the Hacienda for 4 consecutive weeks. Then she left too, after finishing her work. Again, Mario Vázquez went to her house to talk to her. She gave evidence that she had left working on the Hacienda because she had been sick (she had a baby) and she would send her son to work.

The son came for 5 or 6 days, but then disappeared. In the month of June the peons were notified that the fields of Pedro Cruz were available for anyone who wanted to be a peon, and if there were no one then the Hacienda would plant those lands. Nobody wanted those lands, for fear of having conflict with the original owner.

Cruz's wife, informed about this decision, came to the Hacienda and offered to give a sheep as payment for all the absences from work. It was not accepted. Mario Vázquez told her that her husband and her son had to come to finish what they lacked, because if they did not, the Hacienda would do it: the Hacienda would take their land to cultivate.

She did not return. Last Wednesday, it was announced to the people what the Hacienda had lately decided: to take over the lands. And work was ordered with this end. On Monday (yesterday), the work began for the planting which the Hacienda was doing. On this day, when the Hacienda began with the work, the parcel (a section of their *chacra*) was pointed out that would be cultivated by the Cruz family.

You already have the facts of this business. It seems to us that this is a good opportunity to get the reactions of the Vicosinos with respect to this concrete business, with plan #4, section B-1--attitudes toward work, and perhaps with section A-3--opinions about the hacienda system--and 4--opinions about the personnel of the Hacienda. We are going to use this business as a point of departure to probe these attitudes and opinions.

1. Discover if your informant has heard tell of this business.

2. How do the Vicosinos interpret this business, and how does your informant himself interpret it? Let the informant speak frankly and freely. Be sure to get all the facts and attitudes that he has, before probing or suggesting something. Say: "Do you remember something more that you can tell me about this affair?"–"Can you explain a little more to me?"–etc., in order to obtain all possible information–all that he can tell you on his part, voluntarily.

3. Did the Hacienda act well or not in this affair? With justice or injustice? How should the Hacienda have solved this problem?

4. What does the informant think of Pedro Cruz? Of his wife and son? Probe.

5. What does he think about the abolition of embargos which were applied before in Vicos? Might it have been better if Pedro Cruz had been embargoed? Why?

6. How did Mario Vázquez act in this affair? With justice or with injustice or prejudice? What should he have done? What about Enrique Luna? What about the gringo [i.e., William C. Blanchard]?

7. What are the mutual obligations between the Hacienda and a peon like Pedro Cruz?

These detailed instructions did not mean much to the interviewers, who were experiencing demoralization at the time (see Chapter 2) or to Vicosinos who did not think like social scientists. It is obvious in the interview materials which are presented in the text of this chapter that the interviewers did not follow the outline closely and that the Vicosinos did not respond as the designers of the Methodology Project expected. The latter ultimately discarded the data as quantitatively unanalyzable, useless for their purposes. I think they were correct in making their assessment, but I do not believe that the data are useless. You are the judge of that.

Notes

1. An earlier version of this chapter was published as "El peón que se negaba," *Allpanchis Phuturinqa* 6:79-142, 1974. A later English version, somewhat expanded, appeared as "The peón who wouldn't: a study of the hacienda system

at Vicos," *Papers in Anthropology* 16(2):78-135, 1975. The present context, intent, and text are significantly altered from those of either of these earlier interpretations.

2. Pedro Cruz and the members of his family are the only Vicosinos whose identity I wish to disguise in this chapter. I do this in order to offer them some privacy.

3. Freud (1959:233-234) writes: "The loss of consciousness, the '*absence*', in a hysterical attack is derived from the fleeting but unmistakable lapse of consciousness which is observable at the climax of every intense sexual satisfaction, including auto-erotic ones. This course of development can be traced with most certainty where hysterical *absences* arise from the onset of pollutions in young people of the female sex. The so-called 'hypnoid states'–*absences* during day-dreaming–, which are so common in hysterical subjects, show the same origin. The mechanism of these *absences* is comparatively simple. All the subject's attention is concentrated to begin with on the course of the process of satisfaction; with the occurrence of the satisfaction, the whole of this cathexis of attention is suddenly removed, so that there ensues of momentary void in her consciousness. This gap in consciousness, which might be termed a *physiological one*, is then widened in the service of repression, till it can swallow up everything that the repressing agency rejects." Hysteria is not gendered, so if we can overlook Freud's focus in what he wrote (in order to avoid revealing himself?) in 1908 we can appreciate its possible application to an event in Vicos in 1953 which was overdetermined, and filled with ambivalence for the staff of the Project.

4. Emily Apter (1991:xiii) calls attention to this theoretical need.

5. Freud (1957:87-88) writes: "The first auto-erotic sexual satisfactions are experienced in connection with vital functions which serve the purpose of self-preservation. The sexual instincts [i.e., drives] are at the outset attached to the satisfaction of the ego-instincts; only later do they become independent of these, and even then we have an indication of that original attachment in the fact that the persons who are concerned with a child's feeding, care, and protection become his earliest sexual objects: that is to say, in the first instance his mother or a substitute for her. Side by side, however, with this type and source of object-choice, which may be called the 'anaclitic' or 'attachment' type, psycho-analytic research has revealed a second type, which we were not prepared for finding. We have discovered, especially clearly in people whose libidinal development has suffered some disturbance, . . . that in their later choice of love-objects they have taken as a model not their mother but their own selves. They are plainly seeking *themselves* as a love-object, and are exhibiting a type of object-choice which must be termed 'narcissistic".

6. Laplanche and Pontalis (1973:339) distinguish "two modes of the psychical

apparatus as specified by Freud." One, "the primary process is characteristic of the unconscious system." The other, "the secondary process typifies the preconscious-conscious system.... [I]n the case of the primary process, psychical energy flows freely, passing unhindered, by means of the mechanisms of condensation and displacement, from one idea to another and which are at the root of unconscious wishes (primitive hallucination); in the case of the secondary process, the energy is bound at first and then it flows in a controlled manner: ideas are cathected in a more stable fashion while satisfaction is postponed, so allowing for mental experiments which test out the various possible paths leading to satisfaction."

7. The original passage, written in the language of 1970 is: "The man who deliberates on his culture is already cultivated and the questions of the man who thinks he is questioning the principles of his upbringing still have their roots in his upbringing."

8. Pietz (1993:125) warns: "Derridean post-Marxists would locate the fetish in semantic indeterminacy and the ambivalent oscillation (hence no dialectical resolution) between contrary determinations, a 'space' where codes and their logics break down in a materiality that is conceived in terms of pure difference, contingency, and chance." It is understood that dialectics and *différance* do not speak to each other. Nicolas Abraham (in Abraham and Torok 1994:81) notes that "psychoanalytic concepts, however awkward or incoherent or even scandalous they may appear, possess a sort of power, and they cannot be included in alien systems of reference without deadening their nerves." The same would apply to other kinds of deconstruction.

9. Kobena Mercer (1994:259-260) writes: "[T]oday the word 'revolution' sounds vaguely embarrassing when it comes out of the mouths of people on the Left: it only sounds as if it means what it says when uttered in the mouths of the radicalized Right."

10. *Comunidad Indígena* from 1962 until 1969, and *Comunidad Campesina* after that date, to correspond with the "revolutionary" government's effort to erase a concept, the "native," from Peruvian minds, one which has stubbornly refused to submit to e-race-ure.

11. For an historical outline of the circumstances of the development of haciendas in Peru, see Vázquez 1961:10-17.

12. See Quijano (1968) for a greater discussion of these points.

13. Not so for the coastal plantation owners whose power increased with the impetus given to cotton and sugar production with the North American Civil War and the liberation struggles in Cuba. See my summary of the history of Peruvian

rural labor in Stein (1991c) which contains a more recent bibliography on these matters.

14. Daniel Heyduk (1971:77ff.) calls attention to this shift in his study of "Huayrapampa" in Bolivia. In this regard, Peruvian history follows an Andean pattern.

15. The sources for this table are: Vázquez (1952:36), Mangin (1954:II, 5-6), Barnett (1960:9), and Alers (1965:426). The tabulations of the 1940 Census Have been corrected by Mangin.

16. See also my discussion of the hacienda system of the Callejón de Huaylas in Stein (1974a). For general accounts see also Davies (1974:9-13), Handelman (1975:25-28), and Tullis (1970:90-93) in English; and Bourricaud (1967:128-155), Favre (1964), Montoya Rojas (1970:34-43, and Vázquez (1961) in Spanish. For comparative materials in hacienda systems in Latin America, see Feder (1971:120-167), Mörner (1973), Tannenbaum (1962), and Wolf and Mintz (1957).

17. See also Stein (1991c, 1997b).

18. The following description of the organization of the Hacienda Vicos has been taken from Vázquez (1952:36-41, 1955a:9-11), Mangin (1954:II, 12-24), Stevens (1959:25-31), Barnett (1960:27-37) and Garrido-Lecca (1965:, 18, 25). These sources on Vicos are supplemented by my personal observations in the Province of Carhuaz.

19. Norman Pava was a North American student who worked in Vicos from 1951 to 1953 (Dobyns and Vázquez 1964:6-7). His field notes are identified as AVP, "Archives of the Vicos Project," as will all others from this source.

20. That minifundism existed and exists in Vicos is not to be questioned. However, Andean ecology mandates that a farmer have many plots in the variety of microclimates that usually exist in relatively small areas. In his seminal work on "Andean rationality," Golte (1980:24) comments on "the great diversity of ecological conditions in very small areas and, with it, the multiplicity of crops and forms of agricultural exploitation adapted to variations in nature. At the same time, this wealth and multiplicity of the Andean world are found to be confined to quite limited conditions: there exists a small amount of level land, generally poor soils, fields liable to erosion; on the western slopes a lack of water and, in general the harsh climate of tropical mountains, with a significant number of days characterized by night frosts and marked differences in temperature between day and night and sun and shadow, which increase with altitude." Golte (29) points out, "A household which needs to cover great distances to carry out rather limited labors, in small fields, must associate itself with others so that advantage does not

become again disadvantage from the work time lost on the way. The need exists to find forms of cooperation among several households, which permits one, or a limited number of persons, to carry out farm labor in its fields." Unfortunately, the Project was insensitive to such subtle ecological issues. While it paved the way toward the community's decision to convert the former Hacienda lands into a producers' cooperative, its great emphasis was on making individuals more productive. By so doing it discouraged festive labor groups and made it less feasible to expand the agricultural frontier. Thus, Vicos has become a less habitable microregion than it was before the interventions.

21. Vázquez (1955b:200) reports that, according to the Project's census of 1952, 28 families of the 363 in Vicos were identified as "rich" or "very rich," by local standards. His figures are: 6 very rich, 22 rich, 146 average, 123 poor, 63 very poor, and 3 unknown.

22. One of Juan Elías Flores's informants had been a *mayoral*. I include here, as Appendix 1, the relevant interview materials. They shed additional light on the hacienda system in Vicos, the point of view of an ex- *mayoral*, and the attempt by a group of Vicosinos to rent the Hacienda themselves in the mid-1920s, a topic which is covered in detail in Barnett's (1960) unpublished dissertation.

23. In 1885 the *varayoq* of the Callejón de Huaylas led a rebellion that has been termed "anti-fiscal" by some scholars, since the collection of the *contribución personal* was one of the precipitating factors. The matter is still debatable and the final interpretation has yet to be made. See Stein (1988, 1998) and Thurner (1996, 1997, 2000).

24. The following details on special tasks and services are largely taken from AVP, Mario Vázquez, May 6, 1949, November 16, 1949, and January 2, 1950. See also Vázquez (1952:37-39, 1963a:26).

25. Barnett (1960:32) reports that the schedule changed in 1954 "not without much discontent", in order to eliminate two rest periods and to reduce the mid-day rest by a half hour. Work began and ended a half hour earlier thereafter.

26. The abolition of the *embargo* was one of the Project's reforms. It is worth noting that it reappeared, after Vicos became a *comunidad*, as a means of obliging the *comuneros*, members of the commons, to attend communal labors on the ex-Hacienda lands (Garrido-Lecca 1965:53).

27. The same fact is mentioned in Holmberg (1967:7).

28. Such wage labor is still characteristic of Vicos and other communities in the region, since land reform has not generated a better distribution of land.

29. Descriptions of the *"enganche"* system are to be found in Chaplin (1967:63), Davies (1974:54), and Klarén (1973:26 ff.). With agrarian reform and the population explosion, it is now a thing of the past.

30. Vázquez (1963b:97) reports that approximately one hundred Vicosinos had been living in the lower Santa, Casma, Nepeña, and Pativilca Valleys, the city of Lima, and also on other haciendas in the Callejón de Huaylas. When the hacienda system in Vicos was abolished, 30 heads of family returned and others expected to do so in the near future.

31. This event is reported in Doughty (1966), Dobyns, Doughty, and Holmberg (n.d.:182-188), and Patch (1964). I am indebted to William P. Mangin (personal communication) for calling my attention to the similarities between the Peace Corps disturbance of 1964 and past occurrences of collective unrest. Paul L. Doughty reports on the meeting which he and Mangin, as representatives of the Peace Corps, had at the time with Vicosinos: "The act of 'throwing us out' is in the line of Vicos tradition as Barnett's thesis demonstrates. Both Bill [Mangin] and I came away from the assembly . . . commenting on the obvious glee with which the Vicosinos exercised their power. . . . It is therefore difficult to attribute this expression of community will to the development of community organization and decision-making as sponsored by Cornell [University], or to attribute it to traditional Vicos behavior. I suspect that it involves something of both, but perhaps more of the latter in that . . . the Vicos leaders were ineffectual during the assembly and it was the mass that led. (AVP: March 24, 1964, 4.)

32. The Methodology Project notes will be abbreviated as "MP." See Chapters 2 and 3 for information on the interviewers.

33. I insist here on the term *patza*, earth, as it is in the variety of Ancash Quechua spoken in the Callejón de Huaylas. The term, elsewhere in Peru, is "Pachamama." But "Mama Pacha" in Vicos and elsewhere in the region would mean "Mother Stomach." So much for Quechuista purism!

34. Patch (1966:4-5) states an alternative point of view based on his experiences in the Andes: "It is argued by some that manual labor is rejected as socially demeaning by Spanish-speakers while it is accepted and may be valued as the measure of the man [sic] by peasants. It is my observation that manual labor is basically considered demeaning by mestizos and peasants alike. However, the role of performing it is accepted by the peasant who has no other role open to him within the confines of the world as he conceives it. It may be that within these conceptual bounds he desires to excel in the restricted role, but this does not mean that he is ignorant of larger horizons or of the opprobrium attached to labor with the hands." There can be no questioning of the fact that the commercial orientation has grown in Vicos over the last half century. It also existed in pre-Project Vicos when Vázquez (1952:102) observed: "There are many persons who

display great activity in work which is not oriented [by incentives of wealth, the celebration of fiestas, and the ideal of individual virtue], but by other perspectives in life. Thus, they concern themselves with the greater productivity of their lands, not with the object of having abundant food but with the desire of obtaining a surplus for commercial ends and by commerce improving their domestic economy. Others go with *enganches* to coastal plantations or dedicate themselves to the transport of metal ore, not with the single object of acquiring new clothing, or food, but in order to accumulate small capital and invest it in the purchase of livestock or to the sale of liquor, coca, sugar, and the like."

35. Dr. Blanchard was Field Director in Vicos from 1953 to 1956 (Dobyns and Vázqez 1964:28).

36. Enrique Luna worked with the Project until the Hacienda was abolished in 1956 (Dobyns and Vázquez 1964:30-31).

37. The late Dr. Vázquez later became Project Field Director (Dobyns and Vázquez 1964:4-5). He eventually aligned himself with the Velasco agrarian reform of 1969 and provided input to this sweeping effort from the top to liberate the Peruvian countryside until 1975, when the "second phase of the revolution" dismissed him..

38. This summary is taken from Mario Vázquez's field notes of four *mandos* and one meeting of the *mayorales*. (AVP, Mario Vázquez, 28-xi-51, 27-xii-51, 29-xii-51, 12-i-52, 16-i-52.)

39. Mario Vázquez reported: "The Vicosinos who got drunk in the carpenter's shop at the sawmill in Chancos had a fist fight. People say it was between Pedro Cruz's relatives and people from Wiyash [a Vicos neighborhood], because Cruz had insulted someone from there" (AVP, 12-vi-49).

40. For information about Dr. Martínez, who worked in Vicos as a data gatherer during 1954-1956, see Dobyns and Vázquez (1964:15).

41. The model for this statement is Timothy Mitchell's (1995:150) critique of USAID's (the Agency for International Development, a branch of the U.S. State Department) development discourse in Egypt: "The major goal of USAID programs in Egypt is to develop what is termed the 'private sector.' The actual effect of these programs, however, is to strengthen the power of the state. This is not simply some fault in the design or execution of the programs. USAID itself is a state agency, a part of the 'public sector,' and therefore works in liaison with the public sector in Egypt. By its very presence within the Egyptian public sector it strengthens the wealth and patronage resources of the state. USAID is thus part of the problem it wishes to eradicate. Yet because the discourse of development must present itself as rational, disinterested intelligence existing outside its object,

USAID cannot diagnose itself as an integral aspect of the problem."

42. Canguilhem (1989:132) notes that "in a strictly semantic sense 'anomaly' points to a fact, and is a descriptive term, while 'abnormal' implies reference to a value and is an evaluative, normative term."

43. I owe many thanks here to Judith Butler's (1990:141) discussion of the "natural" and the "normal" in gender identity. Indeed, much of the preceding paragraph is a paraphrase of her text.

44. Derrida (1986:81) writes of Hegel's philosophy: "The possibility of standing upside down, of the upside-down erection, is inscribed in the cycle of the family standing up. The son is son only in his ability to become father, his ability to supply or relieve the father, in his occupying his place by becoming the father of the father, that is, of the son's son. A father is always his grandfather and a son his own grandson. . . . The movement of the upside-down erection describes the structure of the concept's nonconceptual conception." The Project engaged in contortions with a different content, but the contortions themselves seem similar to me.

45. Horkheimer and Adorno (1982:17) say: "Before, the fetishes were subject to the law of equivalence. Now equivalence itself has become a fetish. The blindfold over Justitia's eyes does not only mean that there should be no assault upon justice, but that justice does not originate in freedom."

46. I am intrigued by the resemblances–indeed, to be more direct, the metaphors– which connect my biography with the events described here which have to do with the Vicos Project. The missing principal investigator in Vicos reminds me of the fact that I grew up missing a father. It is said that every biography conceals an autobiography (see Stein 1997a), but I am also convinced that every ethnography conceals an autobiography. And this book constitutes an ethnography of the Vicos Project.

47. A simulacrum is a copy of a copy which has no original. See Baudrillard (1983).

48. Derrida (1976:150-151) writes of Rousseau's texts on the subject: "The experience of auto-eroticism is lived in anguish. Masturbation reassures . . . only through that culpability traditionally attached to the practice, obliging children to assume the fault and to interiorize the threat of castration that always accompanies it. Pleasure is thus lived as the irremediable loss of the vital substance, as exposure to madness and death. . . . The dangerous supplement, which Rousseau calls a 'fatal advantage,' is properly *seductive*; it leads desire away from the good path, makes it err far from natural ways, guides it toward its loss or fall and therefore it is a sort of lapse or scandal. . . . It thus destroys Nature." It does not

exceed the bounds of imagination to think of the 1969 agrarian reform as either dangerous, castrative, or guilty.

Chapter 5

Making a Différance: Medical Intervention at Vicos[1]

The verb "to differ" [*différer*] seems to differ from itself. On the one hand, it indicates difference as distinction, inequality, or discernibility; on the other, it expresses the interposition of delay, the interval of a *spacing* and *temporalizing* that puts off until "later" what is presently denied, the possible that is presently impossible. . . . In the one case "to differ" signifies nonidentity; in the other case it signifies the order of the *same*. . . . We provisionally give the name *differance* [*différance*] to this *sameness* which is not *identical*. . . .

As the condition for signification, [the} principle of difference affects the *whole sign*, that is, both the signified and the signifying aspects. . . . [T]he signified concept is never present in itself, in an adequate presence that would refer only to itself. Every concept is necessarily and essentially inscribed in a chain or a system, within which it refers to another and to other concepts, by the systematic play of differences. Such a play, then–differance–is no longer simply a concept, but the possibility of conceptuality, of the conceptual system and process in general. . . .

Differance is what makes the movement of signification possible only if each element that is said to be "present," appearing on the stage of presence, is related to something other than itself but retains the mark of a past element and already lets itself be hollowed out by the mark of its relation to a future element. (Jacques Derrida 1972:129, 139-140, 142.)

"Making a *différance*, or "a differance," is undecidable. *Maybe* it means change, and *maybe* it means postponing change. It probably means both, and we are well advised not to privilege one meaning over the other. Jean-Luc Nancy (1992:39) writes: *"Différance* is nothing other than the infinite repetition of meaning, which does not consist in its duplication or in a way of always distancing itself to infinity, but which is rather the grounding of meaning, which is to say the absence of a ground, which destines it to be that which it *is*: its own *différance*. If meaning had a ground, if it did not (have to) call and name itself, it would have no more meaning than the immanence of water in water or stone in stone or the closed book in the book never opened. *Différance* is bidding, appeal, request, seduction, imploring, supplication.l *Différance* is passion." Derrida (1982b:21-22) emphasizes the permanent subversion of all authority by *différance*, including its own:

> [*D*]*ifférance* is not. It is not a present being, however excellent, unique, principal, or transcendent. It governs nothing, reigns over nothing, and nowhere exercises any authority. It is not announced by any capital letter. Not only is there no kingdom of *différance*, but *différance* instigates the subversion of every kingdom. Which makes it obviously threatening and infallibly dreaded by everything within us that desires a kingdom, the past or future presence of a kingdom. And it is always in the name of a kingdom that one may reproach *différance* with wishing to reign, believing that one sees it aggrandize itself with a capital letter.

Let us begin our study of differance in medical discourses in Vicos with a Quechua word, *ampi*. *Ampi* is impossible to translate into either Spanish or English because it has oscillating signifieds. It can mean either "medicine" or "anti-medicine," "remedy" or "poison."[2] It is like Greek *pharmakon* which, Derrida (1981:70) notes, was used by Plato in the sense of "both remedy and poison [and which] already introduces itself into the body of the discourse with all its ambivalence.[3] This charm, this spellbinding virtue, this power of fascination, can be–alternately or simultaneously–beneficent or maleficent."—

> The *pharmakon* would be a *substance*–with all that word can connote in terms of matter with occult virtues, cryptic depths refusing to submit their ambivalence to analysis, already paving the way for alchemy–if we didn't have eventually to come to recognize it as antisubstance itself.

Derrida (97) points out that the usual translation of the word as "remedy" is accurate but that this "nonetheless erases, in going outside the Greek language, the other pole reserved in the word. . . . It cancels out the resources of ambiguity and makes more difficult, if not impossible, an understanding of the context . . . thus excluding from the text any leaning toward the magic virtues of a force whose effects are hard to master, a dynamic that constantly surprises the one who tries to manipulate it as master and as subject." It is a translation of what is said, not of what is intended (98). The translation "can thus be neither accepted nor simply rejected" and also there can be "no such thing as a harmless remedy" (99).

Derrida (125-126) adds: "The 'essence' of the *pharmakon* lies in the way in which, having no stable essence, no 'proper' characteristics, it is not, in any sense (metaphysical, physical, chemical, alchemical) of the word, a *substance*." Moreover, the semantic difficulty is that while "two objects cannot coexist in the same place," yet "without changing places, a same object can become 'other'" (160). *Ampi* is like that. Something quite marvelous, something powerful, something magical.

Roland Barthes (1972a:270-271) writes that "the force of a sign (or rather of a system of signs) does not depend on its complete character (fulfilled presence of a signifier and of a signified) but much more on the relations the sign sustains with its (real or virtual) neighbors; in other words, it is the attention paid to the organization of the signifiers which establishes a true 'criticism of signification,' much more than the discovery of the signified and of the relation which unites it to its signifier." Thus, it is the aim of this chapter to place *ampi* in its context.

Vicente Rafael (1993:111, 211) presents a parallel case for Tagalog, in the Philippines, where "the presence of Latin and Castillian terms . . . opened up for the natives the possibility of finding in their language something that resisted translation." He concludes: "The fact that translation lends itself to either affirmation or evasion of social order is what gives it its political dimension. It draws boundaries between what can and cannot be admitted into social discourse even as it misdirects the construction of its conventions." From the point of view of monolingual speakers of Spanish–as well as bilinguals who wish to "sanitize" their first language–, the native languages are, similarly, out-of-frame[4] and subversive of social order. Thus the colonial linkage, which Irene Silverblatt (1987:195) establishes, among "witchcraft, maintenance of ancient traditions, and conscious political resistance" seems to persist into the present. And we can easily understand how satisfying it is for Peruvian military and paramilitary personnel to slaughter unarmed Quechua-speaking farmers who are in their eyes dangerously out-of-frame and perceived as threatening.[5] Militaristic discourse is indeed strange for, as Angela Gilliam (1997:184) points out, the transformation of "the powerless into the more powerful even when the opposite is true, the attack on the unarmed is possible, presumably in self-defense."

Unarmed people are harmless victims in the sights of automatic weapons, but it seems paradoxical that subversion permeates Andean culture as Bruce Mannheim (1998:411-412) so impressively demonstrates in his study of a sixteenth century Quechua hymn, a contemporary song, and a textile in which contestation is both stated and disguised in such a way that it resists translation but allows interpretation. But how are contemporary–any more than colonial–thugs to understand the difference between symbolic resistance and an armed uprising?

While Quechua monolingualism places its speakers in direct contact with brute force, it removes them from the Peruvian field of symbolic power. Pierre Bourdieu (1990:170) writes:

> Symbolic power–as a power of constituting the given through utterances, of making people see and believe, of confirming or transforming the vision of the world and, thereby, action on the world and thus the world itself, an almost magical power which enables one to obtain the equivalent of what is obtained through force (whether physical or economic), by virtue of the specific effect of mobilization–is a power that can be exercised only if it is *recognized*, that is, misrecognized as arbitrary. This means that symbolic power does not reside in "symbolic systems" in the form of an "illocutionary force" but that it is defined in and through a given relation between those who exercise power and those who submit to it, i.e., in the very structure of the field in which *belief* is produced and reproduced. What creates the power of words and slogans, a power capable of maintaining or subverting the social order, is the belief in the legitimacy of words and of those who utter them. And words alone cannot create this belief.

In the case of *ampi* we confront a Quechua medical discourse of ill-being and well-being, of healing and un-healing, of remedy and anti-remedy, and, in no manner incidentally, of medical practice and malpractice. Mestizos, bilinguals, understand this overdetermined significance of *ampi*, as well as that of *ampeq*, one who practices *ampi*, but they tend to view the other pole of meaning as "false belief" subject to "correction." Colonizers, missionaries, government officials, and dominant elite sectors have been doing this for centuries in their unceasing efforts to erase "social memory," a term used by Thomas Abercrombie (1998:21) "to convey the embodied ways by which people constitute themselves and their social formations in communicative actions and interactions, making themselves and their social formations in communicative actions and interactions, making themselves by making rather than inheriting their pasts." Bilinguals translate *ampi* as Spanish *"remedio,"* cure, and *ampeq* as *"curandero,"* curer. Persons "in transition" from Quechua monolingualism to modernity are likely to translate the latter as *"curioso,"* curious or strange person–which actually is closer to the ambivalence in the word.   As Regina Harrison (1989) suggests: "The semantic imprecision" of such terms "would argue that the language of the victor avoids the problem of accuracy." Persons who know only Spanish, or are bilingual in Spanish and English, are removed even farther, and are in no condition to anticipate how the oscillating signifieds bounce, tumble, change places, erase each other and reappear, like unquiet ghosts–ghosts in Avery Gordon's (1997:17) sense of what is excluded and invisible.[6] But translation takes place in a field of symbolic power, as Alton Becker (1995:232-233) reminds us:

> Glossing is clearly a political process. How often do two languages meet as equals, with equal and reciprocal authority? How often, for instance, are the root metaphors of the "exotic" language considered equal in analytic power to those of the language of analysis? Many find the deepest metaphors of another language poetic and defamiliarizing, but few find them to be as useful in analysis as one's own, that is, as pictures of the world "as it is." It takes considerable effort even to see one's own root metaphors as metaphors.
>   The second step in analysis by which dissimilarities are put into the background is abstraction, or, as linguists call it, parsing–putting the glossed language into a grammatical framework, the terms of which are terms in the language of the glossing. This language about language, or metalanguage, is also rarely if ever seen as equal in power in the two languages, and so there is an interesting politics here, too, which is only beginning to be unfolded: the politics of claiming universal explanations from within a particular language.

Translations which suppress the other pole of *ampi* repress signifieds, oppress the living language. Spanish attempts to neutralize Quechua are nothing less than linguistic intimidation, linguistic terrorism, where the Quechua speaker comes to doubt, fear, and hate his/her own language. Such "symbolic violence," as Bourdieu (1991:51) points out, "is not aware of what it is (to the extent that it implies no *act of intimidation*)"; it can only be exerted on a person predisposed (in his [or her] habitus) to feel it." For example, Plaza Martínez (1994:7) says that in Bolivia, tragically, "one no longer has the right to be what one is," and adds: "The imposition of Spanish is justified in different ways: the need for communication, the development of a modern vocabulary, literature, education in Spanish, etc. In contrast, other languages are poor, lacking in writing and literature, and there can be no higher education in them. Common people even continue to believe that they are not even languages but only dialects, hybrid forms, lacking in grammars and dictionaries." His statement is equally applñicable in Peru. Barthes (1983:31-32) writes:

My teacher's speech is, so to speak, never neutral; at the very moment when he seems simply to be telling me that red signals an interdiction, he is telling me other things as well: his mood, his character, the "role" he wishes to assume in my eyes, our relations as student and teacher; these new signifieds are not entrusted to the words of the code being taught, but to other forms of discourse ("values," turns of phrase, information, everything that makes up the instructor's rhetoric and phraseology). In other words, another semantic system almost inevitably builds itself on the instructor's speech, i.e., the system of connotation. . . . I no doubt receive an objective message: *Red is the sign of interdiction* (the proof of this lies in the conformity of my behavior), but what I actually experience is the speech of my teacher, his phraseology; if, for example, this phraseology is intimidating, the meaning of red will inevitably include a certain terror; in the rapid process (as experienced) of the message, I cannot put the signifier of the terminological system to one side, and the signified of the rhetorical system to the other, dissociating red from terror.

If we substitute for "teacher" and "pupil" in Barthes's text to "developer" and "Vicosino" in Vicos, we begin to see (and perhaps for the first time) how linguistic intimidation works. Therefore, we should exercise extreme caution in reading the field notes in the Project's archives but we should not give up the challenge of interpretation.

The Quechua language has other marvels, among which there is one we should understand as an aid to our interpretation of the medical interventions in Vicos. This is Quechua's inflection for evidentiality, of which Wallace Chafe (1986:262) observes that "everything dealt with under this broad interpretation . . . involves attitudes toward knowledge." Gary Parker (1976:150-151) defines three basic modes of discourse in Ancash Quechua: one which "marks speech when the speaker gives information that comes from his/her personal experience," another which "marks speech when the speaker gives information which does not come from his/her own experience," and the third which "marks speech when the speaker is making conjectures." The first, the terminal suffix -*m*, -*mi*, indicating personal knowledge, is either untranslated by interpreters or translated as Spanish "*es (son)*," is (are); while the second, the suffix -*sh*, -*shi*, indicating hearsay may be translated as "*dice (-n)*," "*dice (-n) que*," or often as "*dice (-n) diciendo*," he/she says (they say), he/she says (they say) that, he/she says (they say) saying; and the third, the suffix -*ch*, -*chi*, indicating conjecture may be translated as "*quizás*" or "*posiblemente*," maybe/perhaps or possibly. Quechua orators are judged by the skill with which they employ these modes in conveying delicate shades of meaning which, at best, are difficult to translate and, at worst, are impossible. David Weber (1986:138) points out with regard to Quechua evidentials in

Huánuco which are the same as those of Ancash:

1. [O]nly one's own experience is reliable.
2. Avoid unnecessary risk, as by assuming responsibility for information of which one is not absolutely certain.
3. Don't be gullible. (Witness the many Quechua folktales in which the villain is foiled because of his gullibility.)
4. Assume responsibility only if it is safe to do so. (The successful assumption of responsibility builds stature in the community.)

The utility of *-mi/-shi/-chi* lies in allowing the Quechua speaker to handily assume or defer responsibility for the information he [or she] conveys, thus minimizing his risks while building his stature in the community.

Weber (142) provides this cautionary (for us) narrative:

[A] speaker [of a dialect in northern Junín] wrote a pamphlet on cultivating pastures. His source of information was an agricultural engineer with whom he had talked at length; consequently the author used *-shi* throughout his pamphlet. Readers apparently interpreted this as the author's lack of commitment to the idea: no one was moved by it to plant a pasture.

We need to hold this information in mind as we examine materials on the Project's interventions in Vicos life, and most emphatically in the case of its interventions having to do with medical matters, that is, <u>curing</u>, <u>treatment</u>, and <u>medicine</u>, all of which will be underlined so that we can remind ourselves of the double meanings they carry. Other Vicos concepts like *achachay*, or *calor* and *cálido*, "*hot*", *templado*, warm, and *alalay* or *frío*, "*cold*," will be italicized in both Spanish and English to remind us that we confront a different code. I think this will help us to realize Johannes Fabian's (1993:86) suggestion that we *can* treat old texts dialogically: "To be carried out successfully, making and translating ethnographic texts in the absence of interlocutors still calls for (the substitute of) an inner dialog in which the anthropologist who writes ethnography must *listen* and match recorded sounds and graphic symbols with communicative competences, memories, and imagination." It is in this way that we can begin to understand "resistance to modern medicine" as resistance to translation, resistance to an alien medical language.

Resistance.[7] A polysemic word that defies analysis. Derrida (1998:2) says:

Ever since I can remember, I have always loved this word. Why? How can one cultivate the word "resistance"? And want to save it at any price?

Against analysis, to be sure, but *without* "analysis" and *from* analysis? And from translation? . . . This word, which resonated in my desire and my imagination as the most beautiful word in the politics and history of [France], this word loaded with all the pathos of my nostalgia, as if, at any cost, I would like not to have missed blowing up trains, tanks, and headquarters between 1940 and 1945–why and how did it come to attract, like a magnet, so many other meanings, virtues, semantic or disseminal chances?

In psychoanalysis resistance is the "hidden meaning [that] exceeds the analysis" (4). There the object is to transform "the patient, the resister, into a 'collaborator' (that is Freud's word) to whom one supplies explanations and in whom one arouses an investigator's objective interest in himself," that is, to break down the resistance. "At stake, then, are sense and truth" (17-18). But when something exceeds, rather than resists, analysis? Derrida (30-31) leads us back to "Plato's Pharmacy" and the *pharmakon*, where, "in the back room of the pharmacy," the pharmacist (analyst) "would still like to separate, like chemical elements, the good remedy from the bad poison." Similarly, *ampi* exceeds analysis, exceeds the Project's medical intervention, exceeds modern medical discourse. Resistance? We see it as a ghost, a ghost which invades and pervades modern medical efforts to demonstrate the power of physicians. But neither the Project's staff nor the physicians can see it. However, the Vicosinos can and do.

One of the major stated goals of the Project was to improve well-being in the Vicos population. This was partially accomplished, only partially: as far as matters of health and hygiene were concerned the Project was relatively ineffective. At the outset, Allan Holmberg (1955:23-26) stated his conception of Vicos as a laboratory:

> In many respects the Vicos situation is like a laboratory, and by this I mean more than a natural laboratory. We are trying to manipulate and control large and complex blocks of reality (environment, society, and culture) in their natural setting. At the same time, we are trying to conduct our experiments and our interventions by dealing with subsistence that has real meaning to the Vicosinos (like potatoes, cattle, land, or health). And we are trying to deal with this substance within the total context of culture. This, of course, is not experimentation in the laboratory sense of the measurement of the precise effect of a single variable, but rather the development of a strategy for the manipulation and control of systems or sets of variables in the direction of meaningful and purposeful ends.

But, again, how much "control of systems or sets of variables"? As we have seen in the sphere of potato production, not the slightest resemblance to laboratory control–though the strategy was successful in a supplementary manner for a while for the sector of entrepreneurial Vicosinos. In the sphere of health, the problematic was far different from that of commerce. Holmberg (1965:6) writes frankly:

> In the area of well-being it was much more difficult to devise a strategy of intervention that would show immediate and dramatic pay-off. This is a value area, to be sure, in which great deprivation was felt at Vicos, but it is also one in which the cooperation of all participants in the community was necessary in order to make any appreciable impact on it. The major well-being problems at Vicos, even today, stem from public health conditions. All individuals are deeply concerned about their personal well-being but are unwilling to forego other value indulgences to make this a reality for the community as a whole. Nor were the resources available to do so at the time the project began.
>
> A variety of attempts was made to tackle the most urgent health problems. In collaboration with the Peruvian Ministry of Health and Social Welfare, a mobile clinic was started at Vicos, which made at least one visit to the community each week. Support for this effort came from the community itself in the form of the construction of a small sanitary post at which the sick could be treated. It was hoped to staff this clinic through Public Health services of Peru, but all attempts to do so were frustrated by the lack of budget and responsibly trained personnel. In Peru, such services seldom extend into rural areas because the preferred values of the medical profession are, as almost everywhere, associated with city life. Consequently, no major public health effort was launched and the community's state of well-being has shown little net gain.

The "failure" of the Project's program really represents the failure of modern scientific medicine to respond to the needs of Vicosinos, not to ignore those of other poor people in Peru and elsewhere in the world. But what exactly Holmberg means by "All individuals are deeply concerned about their personal well-being but are unwilling to forego other value indulgences to make this a reality for the community as a whole" is opaque to me. Most Vicosinos had and have limited choice in matters of health and hygiene since they are either uninformed themselves or live in close proximity to others who are uninformed (and so are subject to reinfection), have little access to expensive medical and pharmaceutical supplies, equipment, and services, and are unable to afford expensive medical and pharmaceutical commodities in the first place. Where is the "indulgence," then, in reliance on home remedies, folk medical practitioners, and magic? Or would Vicosinos' persistent use of *ampi* constitute a "perversion" under the gaze of a developer? Maybe Holmberg means simply that rural householders, with hungry household animals, urinate and defecate near the sides of their houses. But is this another case of absence, that absence which seems to haunt the Project and its production? Is Holmberg's view being edited, embellished, transformed, like the painted face of a corpse in a coffin?

The term "modern scientific medicine" is itself misleading. Charles Leslie (1976:6-8) points out:

> The term "modern medicine," used in contrast to traditional medicine, encourages the user to confuse inferences from the modernity-traditionalism dichotomy with reality. For example, the dichotomy opposes the changing and creative nature of modernity to an assumed stagnant and unchanging traditionalism, but acquaintance with historical documents and with the contemporary medical institutions labeled "traditional" reveals that considerable change has occurred in the last century, and that medicine like everything else has been changing throughout the past. . . . The term "scientific medicine" is also misleading. It encourages the assumption that all aspects of cosmopolitan medicine are somehow derived from or conducive to science, but by any ordinary criteria many elements in this system are not scientific–for example, the politics of research funding or of professional associations, various routines of hospital administration, or the etiquette of doctor-patient relationships. A second and equally stultifying assumption is that all medicine other than cosmopolitan medicine is unscientific. . . . Finally, the term "Western medicine" is misleading for obvious reasons. The scientific aspects of Western medicine are transcultural. Ethnic interpretations of modern science are the aberrations of nationalistic and totalitarian ideologies or, in this case, a reflex of colonial and neo-colonial thought.

Peru is not a healthy place. Thomas Hall (1969:194) characterizes the Peruvian population as "suffering primarily from communicable disease, poor nutrition, and the effects of inadequate sanitation." A generation ago it was difficult for Hall to find morbidity and mortality statistics he could rely on. Such problems persist thirty years later, but I also think that Peru's "oversupply" of physicians, as we will note later, for a social majority they do not attend is a tragic paradox. Hall (15) says:

> Tabulations by cause of death are available only in those districts where there are enough physicians to ensure reasonably complete professional death certification. By 1964 the Division of Health Statistics of the Ministry of Health was able to obtain professional certification in 177 of Peru's more than 1,600 districts, covering approximately 43 per cent of the national population. Such districts with professional certification are primarily urban in nature, the population has relatively too good access to

medical care and cannot be considered representative of the country as a whole. . . .
Morbidity statistics are notoriously incomplete in most countries and Peru is no exception. There is compulsory reporting of certain communicable diseases, but published rates are grossly underestimated. With about half the population not utilizing medical services, the failure of physicians to report all notifiable conditions treated represents only a comparatively minor source of error.

Luis Carlos Gómez (1988:30) offers a sobering commentary on these old guesses and brings them up to date: "Accidents and violence are important causes of morbidity and mortality in Peruvians of all ages up to 64 years. They are the primary cause of death in those between 15 and 44 years, and the primary cause of hospitalization in the 5-14 age group"
But let us leave larger Peruvian problems aside for a while and look again at Vicos. In 1952, when the Project began, Holmberg (1952b:6) noted in his first progress report:

In January and March we cooperated with Parke-Davis and Company and the Peruvian Ministry of Public Health in a parasitological study in Vicos. It was the first time that such a study had been made in an Indian community in Peru. The results were little less than surprising. It was found that 99% of the Vicosinos had one or more types of pathological parasites with an average of four of them per person.

Alers (1971:125) reports that sixteen kinds of parasitic intestinal infections were much more frequent in Vicos than in a sample of mestizo communities, and half of the Vicosinos were "hosting at least one and possibly all five" of the most frequent ones. Such infections raised the need for the intake of food, increased the number of cases of gastrointestinal ulcers, and even contributed to respiratory problems. Parasitic intestinal infections constituted the most frequent medical diagnosis. Respiratory disorders were next, and then diseases of the skin and eyes which "are also related to the very intense ultraviolet radiation" at high altitude "and to the dryness of the atmosphere, combined with a very low fat diet." Epidemics of measles, flu, and whooping cough periodically swept the community of its youngest members. Alers (1965b:431-434) tells of five major epidemics suffered by the Vicosinos which his informants remembered: typhoid at the beginning of this century, influenza in 1951, measles in 1956, and whooping cough and measles in 1959 and again in 1964. He concludes that "their effects on the falling rate of population growth have undoubtedly been considerable." Holmberg (1971b:43) notes: "The goal of the traditional Vicosino was simply to survive as long as he possibly could, knowing full well that he

[sic] might be a victim of fate at any moment."

Much of what Aída Milla de Vázquez (1972:126-127) says about Vicos treatment of illness in children holds true for persons of all ages:

> Vicosinos think of their children's illness in terms of the external symptoms they manifest. Any complication is totally ignored by them, and all they can do is to explain them by some meteorological phenomenon or supernatural cause. Many are convinced that the ones who are responsible for double sickness are the *"curios"* who made a mistake or the clinic doctor who did not feel them over correctly. What happens is that people say that their children with dysentery or diarrhea became ill in the stomach from *"empacho"* [dirty stomach], or when they have a cough sometimes with bodily pains that it is from *"calentura"* [heating]. If they get flu or scurvy or measles, it is from *calor* [heat] or *frío* [cold], and they treat them with elements of opposite thermal states. If a child has *"calentura,"* they bathe or rub the patient's body with alcohol, and if the *frío* is intense the patient is rubbed with grease and wrapped up. If a child cries frequently, and there is no way to explain the pain, the parents call in a *"curios"* who tries to localize the disorder with *"shoqma de cuy"* [rubbing with a guineapig[8]] and to cure it with herbs applied to the affected part.
>
> When illness is produced by strange causes, like *"mal de ojo"* [evil eye], they tie colored threads on the fingers or around the neck. If it is from *"turmanyay"* [the rainbow] they carry a child, with rue and garlic in its pockets, to the place where it contracted the illness. When the *"curios"* makes the diagnosis that there is no cure for the illness, and if there is no doctor at the post, the parents expect that they can only wait for the moment of death. If there is a doctor at the Community post, they turn to him or her as a last resort. Then the doctor finds a complicated case: for example, pneumonia instead of simply flu or measles.

As for "mental health,"

> The psychological set of fearful contact with the natural and social worlds, manifested in Vicosino preoccupation with death, appeared in other forms also. In the realm of sensation, the same pattern of personal withdrawal was apparent in the self-images of men reared under manorial conditions. To half these men, a human touch was painful or interpreted as aggressive or bringing injury or death; Hence pleasure was regarded as immoral and a luxury. . . . It should also be noted that . . . there has been an increase in the level of anxiety in the community. Questionnaire surveys [in 1953 and 1963] indicate a substantial increase in the reported incidence of trembling hands, palpitations of the heart, nightmares, headaches, loss of appetite and difficulty in falling asleep. (Alers 1971:128-129.)

Richard Schaedel (1988:769) describes the work in Vicos of "a team of

Sullivanian psychologists invited by Allan Holmberg . . . to carry out an experimental study using clinical interviews and projective tests in the late '50s" [sic]:

> [Ralph] Klein's (1963) dissertation, the only documentation of this group study, concentrated on self- image. His conclusion that the Andean peasants interviewed had a remarkably "low" self-image was hardly surprising and could probably have been extended to most contemporary peasants living under hacienda-serf conditions similar to those of Vicos. The limitations of projective testing . . . were apparent in Klein's work, but his interview data might yet be used to substantiate some of the cognitive constructs of later times.

Klein visited Vicos in 1960 in a team of four psychoanalytically trained clinical psychologists. He produced a series of sketches of the self-images of Vicos men which provide an outside view of the images workers project, in a community which has only recently emerged from the hacienda system–despite the problems and difficulties of researchers who had to cope with double translation via interpreters from Quechua to Spanish, and then from Spanish to English. The sketches may provide a view, as well, of what the researchers were looking for, along with their success or failure in finding it. David Gow (1976:28-29) charges the group with having "little respect" for peasant culture. He points out that their "descriptions conform faithfully to mestizo stereotypes of peasant behavior." Despite such reservations on the part of these "observers of observers," a few extracts from Klein's (1963:53, 73-74, 86-87, 91, 106) sessions with Vicosinos he calls "Antonio," "Dario," "Gregorio,", "Hernán," and "Jorge" illustrate a part of Vicos life under the hacienda system that nobody else has probed:

> [Antonio] experiences his body as very vulnerable and is very much preoccupied with worrying about his health and with the remedies needed in case of sickness. He has often been sick, and every sickness brings to mind the possibility of sudden death. Every bad dream is an ill omen. In spite of all remedies he feels that the only thing one can really do about this is to do nothing and stay under cover. "You will die if it is the day for you to die." Any period of being healthy is an interlude before the next sickness.

> Dario's picture of the world would appear to be organized centrally around the proposition that to be noticed at all is a condition of the gravest danger. In line with this proposition, he is convinced that invisibility would be of the greatest value to him. Any behavior motivated by or even suggesting the presence of initiative will invite total disaster.

He seems to perceive existence as having some elements of safety in it for others but not for him. His image of his body is that it is not quite adequate for survival, that he is somewhat lacking in the minimal adaptive machinery required by his murderous environment.

As [Gregorio] sees it, everything depends on his health, and his health is under the control of higher powers and may be taken away capriciously at any moment. He feels his well-being is out of his hands. Death can catch him anywhere quite suddenly, like lightning. . . . To see anything is dangerous for he might see something that would arouse the ire of the powerful ones under whose surveillance he is. He must simply be a worker and see nothing in order to survive. . . . As he sees it, he lives in a world in which one does not dare to desire.

[Hernán] feels he is as defenseless, as vulnerable, and as inactive as he was when a baby in his mother's presence. He experiences himself as a baby wrapped in its umbilicus–oppressed, starved, and immobilized. He feels that the moment one is born, one is spt to be devoured by hungry beasts. He feels hungry all the time and satisfaction for him does not seem to exist. He sees himself as depending for his survival on being nourished by others.

[Jorge] is so preoccupied with survival that the only feeling he knows is fear, in connection with death. . . . He feels that all the power in the world is in the hands of others. He feels that it is necessary for him to hide behind the anonymity of being just like everyone else. Independent action he sees as very dangerous. . . . He feels that one has to follow in the footsteps of others, particularly one's father. Trying to assert himself and do something radically different is suicidal. The only way to stay alive is to be paralyzed.

These extracts from Klein's sketches can, despite all the difficulties of the research, be interpreted as modes of survival and successful adaptation to an abusive and oppressive existence in the Hacienda Vicos.

Illness and Curing in Vicos

I am going to present some cases of illness and its treatment from the Project Archives (AVP) which contain the unpublished field notes of most of the researchers who passed through Vicos. These archives, which I have discussed earlier, constitute an "upside-down monument" to the Project, another reverse erection, or maybe a limp one, because although these files are packed with thousands of file slips, they have been little used, have had little impact on Andeanist or anthropological thought, and have not contributed to an ethnography of Vicos. It is a loss for everyone because, despite the needs for editing, reevaluation, and reinterpretation, much of the data is of excellent quality. For a view of Vicos folk medicine and the Project's medical interventions, we are especially fortunate in having available the observations and interviews of Abner Montalvo Vidal,[9] a Quechua-speaking anthropologist originally from Huánuco. His field notes constitute a unique record of illness in Vicos, reaction to it, and modes of coping with it. William C. Blanchard, as well as other researchers, also provided records which are useful for our purposes.

The field notes of the Project staff give us a view of Vicos that is more than folkloric. An extract from the raw data is, to employ Clifford Geertz's (1973:9) metaphor, like "a note in a bottle," a message that has floated through time and space to us, and one which is "foreign, faded, full of ellipses, incoherencies, suspicious emendations, and tendentious commentaries." It is, then, up to us to reconstruct and reconstruct these observers' "constructions of other people's constructions of what they and their compatriots [were] up to." These texts are "illness narratives," as Arthur Kleinman (1988:48-49) has suggested:

> The chronically ill become interpreters of good and bad omens. They are archivists researching a disorganized file of past experiences. They are diarists recording the minute ingredients of current difficulties and triumphs. They are cartographers mapping old and new territories. And they are critics of the artifacts of disease (color of sputum, softness of stool, intensity of knee pain, size and form of skin lesions). There is in this persistent reexamination the opportunity for considerable self-knowledge. . . . The point I am making is that the meanings of chronic illness are created by the sick person and his or her circle to make over a wild, disordered *natural* occurrence into a more or less domesticated, mythologize, ritually controlled, therefore *cultural* experience. . . . Thus, patients order their experience of illness– what it means to them and to significant others–as personal narratives. The illness narrative is a story the patient tells, and significant others retell, to give coherence to the distinctive events and long-term course of suffering. The plot lines, core metaphors, and rhetorical devices that structure the illness narrative are drawn from cultural and personal models for arranging experiences in meaningful ways and for effectively communicating those meanings.

Let us examine the cases.

Juana Cilio

This sad story of a woman with an intestinal infection was recorded by Montalvo in November, 1954, but details a series of events that had taken place two months earlier. At the time a mobile clinic from Huaraz was coming to Vicos twice a week, and many Vicosinos were taking advantage of its services. This case is one of a hospital referral by a clinic physician that failed. It is an account of pain which nobody could alleviate, miscues, misunderstandings, and crossed purposes fed by a potent mixture of Vicosino fear of *patrones*–fear of displeasing, of saying "no"–and the overeagerness of Project personnel to justify the existence of the Project by obtaining a "demonstration effect." More than a matter of opposed wills, or willful opposition, it is an example of what Lyotard (1988:8-9) calls a *differend* where: "It is in the nature of a victim not to be able to prove that one has been done a wrong. A plaintiff is someone who has incurred damages and who disposes of the means to prove it. One becomes a victim if one loses these means. One loses them, for example, if the author of the damages turns out directly or indirectly to be one's judge. . . . The plaintiff lodges his or her complaint before the tribunal, the accused argues in such a way as to show the inanity of the accusation, [and] litigation takes place. . . . The plaintiff is divested of the means to argue and becomes for that reason a victim. If the addressor, the addressee, and the sense of the testimony are neutralized, everything takes place as if there were no damages. A case of differend between two parties takes place when the 'regulation' of the conflict that opposes them is done in the idiom of one of the parties while the wrong suffered by the other is not signified in that idiom." By the Project's rational standards, Juana Cilio and her family are completely in the wrong. But then, it is in the "nature" of Vicosinos to be "wrong," since they are judged in an idiom foreign to them.

> September 14: Manuel Alejandro Cruz arrived [at the clinic] and asked the doctor to look at his wife who was very sick. He asked him to go to their house because the patient could not even stand up. The doctor asked him to bring her, and the Indian agreed to do it right away. But then the doctor told him that it was already late and that it would be better to bring her on Tuesday. So it was agreed, even though the man insisted that she would die meanwhile. (APV, Montalvo, 14-ix-54.)

> September 16: On my rounds through Punkucorral neighborhood I visited Juana Cilio and found her very ill. Her body was swollen all over and she complained of dysentery and pain in her eyes. She could not walk. I offered to bring her to the doctor so he could examine her and she asked me to do that. (APV, Montalvo, 16-ix-54.)

> September 17: I told the doctor that Juana Cilio's illness was serious. In view of the impossibility of her coming to the examining room it seemed like a visit was in order, but he disagreed saying that his

obligation was only to give service here [at the mobile clinic]. He said that this matter of going to her house would allow the Indians to get used to asking for treatment at home. Furthermore, if the other doctors did not give similar service, it was not up to him to do it. Finally, he suggested to the nurse that just she might go on a visit, to which she responded saying that this was not permitted if a doctor was there, and that it was only allowed if he was not.

After a bit of embarrassed discussion and indecision, in the end they agreed to make the visit for which purpose the *administrator* [Enrique Luna] provided the mounts. The visit was made by the doctor, the nurse, an assistant, the photographer [John Collier[10]] and me. We walked for 20 minutes to the patient's house.

The doctor examined her thoroughly and saw the urgency of hospitalizing her. The nurse's attention had a great influence on the relatives' spirit, and even that of the patient herself. They gave her injections and left pills. The doctor suggested Huaraz or Carhuaz for hospitalization, but I thought Huaraz would be better because there would be a better opportunity for the people from UNICEF to take care of her, so that when she got well she could serve as a diffusion agent. (APV, Montalvo, 17-ix-54.)

September 18: During yesterday's visit the hospitalization was agreed on by the medical service and the patient's relatives, and even the patient herself–also, that it would take place today. With that in mind I talked with her husband about bringing her to Marcará and then sending her in a truck to Huaraz. The husband would be obliged to carry her, but he said he had not been able to find a *minka* [used here in the sense of "helpers"]. He had tried to get help from his wife's brothers who refused, in particular Natividad Cilio who stated that he had to work in the Hacienda and it would be to his disadvantage. Manuel Alejandro [the husband] says, however, that they did not agree to it because they all bear him ill will, and then when they got together with her it turned out that taking her was against their wishes, and furthermore that they were not even on good terms with their sister.

Today the *administrador* and I got up before dawn, at 4 a.m., to wait for that woman and send her to the hospital. However, she did not appear. So I went to visit them again. I found the husband seated at the door of his house. He greeted me with many complaints of having problems with his vision (he has an infected eye), and said he was suffering sharp pains because he had gone to the Hacienda to work like a strong man because the *administrador* had been urging him to complete his back *tareas*, that is, that he make up his absences. Now he felt he had no strength to carry his wife. After his brothers-in-law refused, nobody else among the rest of his circle agreed to help as a *minka*. For the time being it was better that the patient just remain at home to be cured, if that could be, and to die if not. In any event, what was he to do?

I listened to everything, but my visit was for two reasons: his wife's health and to make arrangements for the damage Manuel's pigs had done in Marcelino Cupitán's potato field, which had been planted on shares with the Hacienda. First I took care of health matters. I gave the woman an injection and I left her the pills prescribed by the medical service. The patient and her relatives accepted and asked for medical assistance. The matter of hospitalization remained, and that was essential for her cure. The members of the family understood and they agreed to take her to Marcará, but just at that moment they rejected hospitalization completely. To justify this lack of compliance, the resistance to going to the hospital, the husband said that she was very sick to the point of final calamity, and that she had revived. Her brother and daughter tried to justify this line of reasoning. When I spoke with them about the seriousness of the case, the impossibility of the doctor's treating her at home, the manner of treating her and caring for her all the time that would be possible only in the hospital, and the approximate time she would be interned, which for those poor people would not cost anything, either for the hospitalization or for medications, they all together, especially the patient, began to cry. They asked how their children would be, what they would eat, and who would look after the livestock. They drew an altogether sentimental picture around these arguments. After they calmed down I told them that all that was painful but it would be much more so if she died, and the children would be without a mother. At that they all agreed because they recognized that it was the truth. So then they were willing again to take her to the hospital. But now they thought about the *minka*. To solve that problem for them I offered to have it done by the Hacienda after I spoke with the *administrator*. With this the husband felt more cheerful, but he continually complained about how sick and impotent he was and how impossible it was to carry his wife. He kept saying, "Ayayay, my eye!" At such an expression of pain I told him that if he were that sick I'd have the doctor look at him. He agreed and said, "I too want to be in the hospital so they can cure my eye which has swollen up like a bladder."

In all that I said I tried to interact with them in the same mood they were in, and to use their phrases at the time, allowing them to express themselves freely. At last a climate of decision was reached, one which would take the patient to the hospital. But then he said that they had nothing to feed her or for her children to eat. I offered to give them some money for food, and they decided to buy barley and *habas* to feed those who would remain. They talked a lot about this matter. The man spoke as though he were sunken in the worse of misfortunes. He even felt unable to go and get the grain supplies they were going to buy from the Hacienda, so he told his daughter, who is about 15 years old, "Now you go and bring the barley and maize. Why are you just looking at me like that when you see that I'm sick?" And then, "It's better if I go. Get a sack, or borrow one. Add up the cost of the barley and the wheat." The girl borrowed a robe from her aunt, while the conversation developed an exaggerated plaintive tone, especially on the part of the man who kept saying, "Ayayay, my eye!"

We were about to leave when the man, seeing that he was going to go alone to bring the supplies, complained to his daughter, "Leave the baby," which she had been carrying on her back, "with your aunt so that she can look after it. I'm a sick man. Don't just look to me to do everything. Help me!" So the daughter unloaded the baby and gave it to her aunt. At that moment everything was resolved in regard to the patient and the family problem. I thought it was opportune to take up the other problem regarding the damage to the potatoes. I told him, "Marcelino Cupitán's mother tells me that your pigs have damaged the potatoes he planted with the Hacienda. Let's see about that so we can agree. He answered, "Yes, of course, *papacito, niño* [little father, child: a respectful way to address a mestizo], my little children couldn't keep the pigs from getting into the field and my oldest daughter was out looking for herbs to <u>cure</u> her mother. It wasn't because they let them do harm but because they couldn't keep them from it." And so on. I told him that it surely was like that, but we should look at the damages with him to see how much they amounted to and to make arrangements. We went to the field which is some 10 meters below his house. Cupitán's mother showed me the marks on the plants. We counted 40 units slightly damaged, and I told Manuel, "It's customary for there to be restitution for such damages. You'll harvest these damaged ridges and the Hacienda and Marcelino will harvest their equivalent from the healthy plants in your field." He answered, "Very good, *papacito*, that's the way it will be." I also told him that so there wouldn't be any more damage in the future, he should fence those three meters from his door that are open and through which the animals came, and also that he should take care of the damaged potatoes because it was to his interest. He accepted everything and we went back to the house.

It was at that moment that the patient's problem was lost again because the man, letting show or hinting at his discontent at the arrangement of the potato matter, said to me, "*Papacito*, my wife won't be able to go now to the hospital in Huaraz. We'll just <u>cure</u> her here if the doctor doesn't come. Let's do what God commands. So then she will die, *papacito*, from all these things that are happening to me, my children, my animals, the damage. Everything then, *papacito*, makes it impossible for me. What are we to do then, *papacito*, if God wants it like that.!" The sister said the same, but I know the motivation of such a change and without giving the matter much importance I said, "Don't worry about the damages. I'm going to pardon you with the condition that you just make the 3-meter fence with spiny branches. With regard to your wife, we've already spoken seriously about the need to hospitalize her." I told him that I was interested only through friendship and not because I was his *patrón*. "Yes, *papacito*, it will be like that then. Tonight I will bring her with the *minka* and right now we'll go to the Hacienda to buy food supplies for my little ones." So it was arranged for the third time to have the patient hospitalized.

At the Hacienda I warned the *administrator* not to ask him for explanations about why he did not bring his wife to Marcará, and why, since he had not brought her, he did not come to work in the Hacienda. I put it rather strongly, as usual, so as to allow him [Cruz] to act spontaneously in order to observe him better, and I asked the *administrator* to help him with the *peón* [i.e., the *minka*] he needed to carry his wife. Enrique Luna told me, "This lazy *pendejo* has observed how the patients with tuberculosis have obtained leave for several months with *temple* paid to them while they're not working. That's why he's making himself sick. It's to justify not bringing his wife and not working in the Hacienda. He surely wants to take a leave and earn *temple* without working. (AVP, Montalvo, 18-ix-54.)

September 19: This morning we got up at 4 a.m. for the second time, because it is the only time when there are trucks for Huaraz. Our object was to send this patient to the hospital because we had agreed that he would bring her at dawn. But he did not bring her. So then I made a visit to Juana Cilio to ask her why they had not brought her. She answered that the *minka* did not come and that her husband could not carry her by himself. She has not taken her pills because they make her nauseous.

Dióscora Venancio, whom I met on the way back from Juana Cilio's, told me that she was a bad woman and was jealous of her own brothers and sisters. They always left her house either angry or weeping. They don't come to see her any more, nor do her neighbors. Since she got sick this last time, she [Dióscora] has not seen anyone other than her sister-in-law, that is, her husband's brother's wife, who has come to visit. (AVP, Montalvo, 19-ix-54.)

September 22: In Marcará I met Juana Cilio's husband and daughter. They indicated that she herself did not want to go to the doctor because her whole body pained her and she was certain that in the hospital she would die. (AVP, Montalvo, 22-ix-54.)

There are no more file slips in the archives on Juana Cilio's case, and Montalvo had other cases to work on. It appears that he, and possibly other Project people, had sought to make a "star group" of this family, whose members were major actors in a "social drama," of which Victor Turner (1982:69) writes:

Social dramas occur within groups bounded by shared values and interests of persons for whom the group which constitutes the field of dramatic action has a high value priority. Most of us have what I like to call our "star" group or groups to which we owe our deepest loyalty and whose fate is for us of the greatest concern. ... In every culture one is *obliged* to belong to certain groups, usually institutionalized ones . . . . But such groups are not necessarily one's beloved chosen star groups. It is in one's star group that one looks most for love, recognition, prestige, office, and other tangible and intangible benefits and rewards. In it one achieves self-respect and a sense of belonging with others for whom one has respect. Now every objective group has members some of whom see it as their star group, while others may regard it with indifference, even dislike. Relations among the "star-groupers," as the first category may be called, are often highly ambivalent, resembling those among members of an elementary family for which, perhaps, the star group is an adult substitute.

While Montalvo is counting on Juana Cilio's family to perform as "stars," these people have other ideas and act out some other drama or dramas. And how can a *"pendejo"* appear in a starring role? Montalvo has given up. Perhaps, from the Project's view of things, to have accepted this family's perspective on its own pain and suffering would have been too painful and, thus, insufferable. As I re-read these field notes I have a feeling about the players like those of Greg Sarris (1993:260), a Native North American who writes, after reading texts from his own group produced by anthropologists, that: "The story was about them in a way that was not them."

Manuel Cruz Cilio

Montalvo recorded another case history on October 18 of the same year. The data show that the informant was tubercular and that he had received treatment, or was receiving it. Circumstances are happier here than in the previous case, but this informant's speculations on *calor* and *frío*[11] indicate the confusion and consternation that accompany illness, and the acting out of wishes to get well. Simply because the patient was receiving modern medical treatment did not prevent him from seeking and receiving home treatment and the services of curers who employed magic in their therapies (or anti-therapies, as the case may be.). Here I wish to let the texts of Vicos medical discourse speak for themselves, leaving fetish discourse to the Project. As William Pietz (1985:14) points out regarding the latter, it "has always been a critical discourse about the false objective values of a culture from which the speaker is personally distanced." I am not seeking such distance from Vicos.[12] I do not intend to write about what Vicosinos "believe," but, rather, only about their discourse. (Note to all ethnographers: If I were writing in Quechua I would inflect for hearsay rather than personal knowledge.)

The art of *shoqma con cuy*, rubbing with a cuy, has been discussed earlier. It is mentioned in this case and will appear in other cases. It is a diagnostic-therapeutic technique in which the cuy both reflects the patient's illness and draws it out. *Shoqma* may also be performed with flowers, especially those used in religious processions, or dirt from magical places. It is a magical intervention by a person skilled in interpreting the signs of illness, transferring the illness from the patient to the material object or objects, and prescribing remedial measures. It takes place in the absence of modern scientific medicine, and is far better than doing nothing, since among those who employ the discourse the magic often works. And when it does not, this is also the nature of *ampi*.

I have characterized *shoqma* as an art. It is a work of art, of which Victor Turner (1982:15) writes: "Works of art are vastly unlike many expressions of political experience, which lie under the power of selfish or partisan interests, and hence suppress, distort, or counterfeit the products of authentic experience. Artists have no motive for deceit or concealment, but strive to find the perfect expressive form for their experience." We might contest the essentialism of this statement but it leads us to a hermeneutic conception of clinical practice which is as true of Vicos medicine as it is of modern scientific medicine. As Good and Good (1981:175) put it:

> The development of a clinical approach that makes social and cultural aspects of a patient's life relevant to the clinician must, it seems to us, be based on a two-fold recognition that *human illness is fundamentally semantic or meaningful* and that *all clinical practice is inherently interpretive or "hermeneutic"*. First, while all disease has biological or psychological correlates or causes, sickness becomes a human experience only as it is apprehended, interpreted, evaluated and communicated–that is, as it enters the world of human meaning and discourse.

Here is Montalvo's case:

> Speculating on the origins or causes of his illness, [Manuel Cruz Cilio] began by telling me that once he played the violin and as such he was a member of all the musical groups at all the fiestas. With this style of life in which he had to bear all the inclemencies of the *frío* to which he was exposed in one way or another, something bad happened to his health. He had to stay seated on the floor in the patio, without even a roof to shelter him, without using fleece wraps, and even on floors that were wet or out in the rain. He had to play because that was what the people who were dancing wanted from him. He had to keep awake until late at night. To all of this it was necessary that he add that he was a weaver and as such had to keep his back close to a cold wall.
>
> However, it was at Calixtura of the present year in which, having played the violin all night and the next day, so that the people could dance, he felt a fever and he began to be bothered by a lot of coughing. The cough was strong and made him bring up a lot of blood. His head ached and he had

to stay in bed. Then a *curandera* who lives in this same neighborhood examined him and then prescribed a *pucha* [a plaster] with herbs, but dry ones, that is, only heating them up in a pan. But his sister, while they were being prepared, added water and so the *pucha* turned out semi-liquid. The preparation consisted in grinding the herbs (he does not remember which herbs they were), adding warm water to them, and applying them as a plaster all over his body.

As a result of this therapy he became sicker. He coughed with greater intensity and he spit out more blood. When he became worse like that, he went to Fernando, a *qarash* [diagnostician/healer] who lived in Recuayhuanca [a community across the river from Vicos]. That one gave him *shoqma* with a cuy and diagnosed the illness as *costado* (pneumonia). He gave him medicine in a bottle (he does not remember what this medicine was) and he rubbed another preparation on his back, covering him with a very clean and new cloak. He paid 20 *soles* for all this.

After I suggested to him that he theorize about his illness, hr explained it, its nature and the way the medicines worked and are working. He says that the time when he came down with the cough, fever, and spitting blood, they gave him the *pucha* and the *curiosa* told him that his illness came from *calor* and so a medicine that was *fresco* was indicated. That medicine was the herb *pucha*. But because his sister added water, the preparation turned out to be much more *fresco*, and so its application turned out to be harmful. This was because the illness was not only due to the *calor* but also to the *alalay*, or the *frío*. He affirms that since he is a worker in the fields where he had to be continually exposed to the *calor* and the *frío*, he had to have both of them.

He makes these ideas function in this way: He then had an illness that was from *calor* and *frío*. If the *pucha* had not contained water it would have relieved what was from *calor* and it would not have aggravated his illness from *frío*, but since the *pucha* had water it became very *fresco*. These reasons are reinforced by the fact that he worked in the *calor* and so he had to have an illness that came from it. So he says that what is the right thing to do is to take medicines that are *cálidas*, but measured in proportion to the *puchas* that are *fresco*. That is to help his illness that comes from *frío*, that is, *costado*. Bronchopneumonia is an illness of this type, and he had to be like that because he went around in the *frío* and he worked on a loom where there was a lot of *frío*. Finally, he says that his illness that came from *calor* has been cured, and that his current illness just comes from *frío*, so that he is *pasmado*, that is, that the *frío* has diffused throughout his body until it went to his bones. That is why the doctor's medicines that are *cálidas* are doing him a lot of good.

He says that the Vicos doctor examined him and said that he was sick. The new *patrones* have been tolerant with him. They have been good because they thought to have him cured, and even though he was an *hacienda nuna*, they have not obliged him to work. When he wanted to send his youngest son to replace him, they did not want to use him. They said he was young and should be in school. So instead they gave him leave for two months. He says that he does not know how to thank them for the good they have done for him, and that in the old days they never would have excused him from work but they would have preferred that he die in the fields rather than concern themselves with his health. (AVP, Montalvo, 18-x-54.)

Dionicia Sánchez

This case, recorded by Montalvo in November, 1954, contains a detailed description of the art of *shoqma*. This common technique of diagnosis and curing was mentioned in the preceding case. Another description is provided in the next case, and I include as an appendix an unpublished account by a North American Student, Cheryl Chadbourn, who underwent the treatment in Vicos in 1962.

Julia Sánchez began to tell me about her sister, Dionicia. First she said, "Well, you, you're like a father and mother the way you look after us. You pay attention to us. You help us. You're having my husband cured too, and like that you must do it for my sister." She was full of expressions like that now and then, and she told me that yesterday the sister came crawling to Julia's house. When she arrived she passed out, and that is the way they found her. So they prepared *gloriado* [hot punch] for her, made with hot water and a little cane alcohol. They had her drink it. Next they prepared other medicines but she did not react well. She reacted slightly. These preparations were infusions based on *casha gaña, casha alonso, marti dolor, violeta, yerba luisa* [a popular tea], *colespa motqon,* and *shura* [sprouted purple maize], all kinds of herbs.

Dionicia had a very swollen stomach. It looked like she was going to explode, but with the medicines she took she came to and they managed to make her more comfortable, but they thought she was going to die. Then they ordered to have *shoqma* with a cuy done on her. The practitioner was Robenza Francisca, a neighbor who lives in this part of Vicos. With that *shoqma* she got better and felt relieved. She could then tell them how she got sick.

She told them that the night before last she had dreamed about her husband, now dead, who asked her why she had slept with a man who lives down below this place (she does not want to identify him), even though he had told her not to do it. She answered that this was untrue, that she hadn't slept with anyone. Then he asked her to keep him company on a visit to the upper part of Vicos, Cullwash, and they went there. There were other men who went with them and after they walked around they returned to the house. Then the husband grabbed the poncho which he wove to wear at the fiesta of San Andrés, the same year he died, and he tore it up. She was very hurt because he had destroyed this keepsake. When she work up she was very sad and she began to get sick around 10 a.m. She had dizzy spells and fell down, losing consciousness.

When she came to, she came down to her sister's house by crawling. When she got there she passed out again. (She says that she died.) While she was in that state she saw her mother, now dead too, come in surrounded by many women. The latter laughed a lot while her mother very seriously beckoned her with one hand while she shook her skirt with the other.

Julia says that these two dreams are signs that somebody has to die. She might have died if her husband had not, in the dream, taken her back to her house and if her mother had followed her after she made that signal.

The *tutu* [youngest] son, named Agustín Cruz, who was listening to the account that his mother was making, interrupted and told me happily that his aunt was not going to die because he had seen it in the cuys with which they had made the *shoqma*. This news spread confidence as much to Julia as to the patient. The latter said weakly, "If I had to die, I would have died already. Her sister said the same and added that the last spells she had were so strong that had put her in such a state that they really had left her dead.

After she revived she still had a swollen belly. So they made *chacchar* [i.e., they had a coca-chewing done] with Daniel Gereda. They say, "*Chaqchatziquiwarqa*" [something like "the backside of the coca bolus has bumps"], which is the act by which a person chewing coca carries out a search for what is going to happen. It is a consultation of the coca, and those who know how to interpret the different positions which the leaves take can learn what it is they want to know. Consulting like that they found out which of the things suggested by the neighbors would be best to give her. Gereda said not to do any of it. While they were in such confusion, her oldest sister sent word that she had consulted with Delfín Silva, a *curioso* in Recuayhuanca. He told her that the patient should be given the infusion of white onion in a liquid of potatoes and herbs. The onion should be ground up.

The patient did not speak because of the state she was in, but she asked me to have her seen by the doctor so he might help her because she was a poor woman. (AVP, Montalvo, 13-xi-54.)

[Two days later, Montalvo and the Project's photographer, John Collier, arrive at Julia Sánchez's house to record a *shoqma* treatment.] They thought about a cuy and told the daughter, a girl of about 12 years, to get a cuy from the kitchen, which she did. It was a black one and John said it wasn't right for photography. Julia said, too, that it was very young. So they sent the girl to an uncle's house to get another cuy. Meanwhile we talked about the course of the illness, and Julia told me that last night the patient had not slept for even a while. When I asked her to explain this lack of sleep, she said to Dionicia, "the *mal traidor* [evil bringer?] has got you." She says that with the *tabardillo* [typhoid? sunstroke?] the *mal traidor*, her blood is turning black from the *calor*.

She has had this illness for a long time, and that is why her husband always told her to take *fresco* things. She has taken many of these medicines and thanks to them she is better. Next, when I asked her about her dreams before she got sick, and at the time she was unconscious she told me the same things that Julia had related the day before yesterday. While we were conversing the girl arrived carrying a cuy of a dark orange color. Then Dionicia stretched out on the floor where they had put down a cloth mantle. They piled up some old petticoats at the head and she placed her head on them. Meanwhile Julia took the cuy in her right hand, holding her thumb around it with her other fingers on the neck, so that her palm remained at the back. Julia sat down next to the patient. We had as spectators Dionicia's two little children and me, while John waited with his camera.

The patient undressed to the waist and shook her petticoats. Julia began to rub her with the cuy in such a way that the animal's back was the part that had contact with the patient's skin. She began by applying it to the head, and to restrain the cuy from scratching the skin with the movement of its feet she held the hind limbs with her left hand. Next she passed to the face with circular movements, then to the back with longitudinal movements from top to bottom, and the same with the arms. Then the patient turned around on her back, for Julia to rub her from breast to waist. She rubbed the stomach, taking care not to uncover it by placing the animal underneath the clothing. Finally she finished with the feet. Then she sat down again and returned to rubbing the head and face with the cuy, especially the head. She said that the head was the part that hurt her more.

To find out the state of the cuy, Julia dropped it on the floor. Seeing that it did not run away even though it was frightened, she said that it was dizzy. She explained, too, that sometimes the cuy runs away and that means that more *shoqma* still has to be done with it. On the other hand, others die before the operation is over, because their blood thickens and they die because they have absorbed all the *calor* from the patient. When she saw the half-alive state of the cuy she said that surely the illness was from *calor* and *frío*. She took up the cuy again and rubbed the head, face, and body of the patient, and as a final movement placed the animal in front of the patient, fixing it so the mouths of both faced each other at a distance of about 3 cm. She told the patient to breathe at the cuy. She did so and then the treatment ended.

While the operation was going on, both the operator and the patient talked about the procedure. I was able to join in with comments. In this conversation Julia announced that some neighbor also was sick and commented on how the aunt could have sold her the cuy knowing that she was poor and sick, and that she should have given it as a gift. They talked about how Dionicia had been a good spinner since she was a girl, and how when she was out of wool she would argue with their father, that Dionicia got married very young when she was only a little bigger than her daughter who is about 12, that the husband was a good man and he got married young too, and in these circumstances it could almost be said that they raised each other, and that he died dynamiting a rock in the field of a neighbor who offered to pay him in wool. Dionicia told the story of how in spite of her opposition he was always handling that material, and that day the neighbor showed up to ask him to dynamite the rock. The husband, arguing that there was no wool for their cloth, went off. From far off they saw that after lighting the fuse he took shelter, but when it did not explode he came back, and it looked like a log brushed by him when it went off. But after the accident they only found a few small pieces of his body. He ended like that, after getting ready so hard to give a good fiesta for San Juan's day because he was a *mayordomo* [in this case a steward of the saint]. Because of the circumstances, everything he had got together for the fiesta was used up in the funeral.

After the rubbing was over Julia sent the girl to fetch water in a *mate* [gourd dish]. She brought the water from the irrigation channel that runs next to the house, from which they take their water. The patient got dressed and then Julia called her to come out. The placed the *mate* of water in the patio and the girl fetched a knife. Julia placed herself next to the *mate* and began by cutting the animal's neck below the jaw, for which the held the cuy below the chin and turning it on its back with her left hand.

After cutting far enough to sever the main blood vessels in the neck, with her right hand she rear limbs holding it very high so that blood flowed from the cut onto the water. The distance between the cut and the surface of the water was about 25 cm. The blood mixed with the water until it had a uniform pink color, but in the trajectory from the cut to the water it could be seen that the blood was dark, for which reason she said it was *calor*. Possibly the blood contained much carbonic anhydride for every time the operator's finger or fingers pressed the respiratory tracts it surely produced an asphyxiation. Because of this action some cuys will die during the operation. Also at the end, that is, when all the blood was out, dark clots of blood were found at the bottom, which provided the reason for a new confirmation of the *calor*.

Next she left the cuy on the floor and carried the water to the channel where she spilled it out and returned with clean water. Then she began to skin it, for which purpose she began by loosening the skin around the mouth and, little by little, turning it over she uncovered the whole body. Holding the animal with her left hand, for which she put it on her palm in an extended dorsal position, she began to examine it. Seeing some white ligaments on the stomach and chest, she said that it was *viento* [wind], and then bathing it with water, for which she used her right hand, she that the ligaments were shrunken and slightly distended. She said that it was because the illness had been produced by *frío*. Then, turning it over to place it extended ventrally, she examined a part between the vertebrae where there was a bit of fat. When she looked at whitish ligaments with bloody stains she said that the white was from the *frío* and the stains were from the *calor*. Then she began to uncover the insides, breaking the tissues only with her fingernails and forcing the ribs to show. When everything was uncovered she noted, sprinkling water continually, first the *kawey willkan*, which is a part of the large intestine which has a projection like a lobe. She said that if it is swollen while water is being thrown on it that this is because it is drinking water, and it means that the patient is dying. In this case sometimes it was swollen and other times not, which means that maybe she will live or die. Second, *aka rosario aqesh*, which is the rosary of the cuy's intestines. This is the section of the small intestine where excrement is already forming in definite pellets for evacuation. The criterion they established is that if on being bathed with water it remains swollen, the patient is going to get up very quickly. If not, it means that the patient is going to continue prostrate.

At the beginning it was swollen and Julia said that the patient would recuperate very quickly, but after many other tests she tried to obtain better evidence with no success. She even tried to help things indirectly with her fingers without positive results. So she said, "Maybe she'll keep on being sick like that." (AVP, Montalvo, 15-xi-54.)

Juandi Sánchez

A brief account of Juandi Sánchez's illness appears in Montalvo's (1967:70-72) where he reports that Sánchez had been consulting *curiosas* for his "cough, headaches, loss of appetite, and weakness" for two years. He had seen eleven of these specialists and finally came to the attention of the doctor who attended the Vicos clinic. This doctor diagnosed Sánchez's condition as tuberculosis and started him on a routine of weekly injections. Juandi Sánchez was one of my oral history informants in 1971, so his case had a favorable outcome and he appeared to be in good health fifteen years after Montalvo's interviews. The materials illustrate the care with which a good ethnographer recorded data, as well as the distance he placed between the informant and himself.

Juandi Sánchez tells me that earlier his house was located in a higher place than where he now lives. Just recently he built the one in which he currently resides. That was, he says, when he got married. He built it on top of the ruins of the *ushnu*, that is the remains of primitive Inca or pre-Inca constructions. Everybody told him that it was the *ushnu*'s place and that they would hurt him. But he paid no attention to all that and he built the house. Now he thinks in a way that his wife died when she was eaten by the *ushnu*, and that it is an *aktzay* place, that is, a bad one. He says that he does not know how they can eat a person, but he affirms that it consumes a person. Now, he tells me, the *ushnu* are eating or consuming him. That is why he is sick and not getting well. He says that everybody believes it is like that, and it ought to be true, but he has not thought about leaving for another place because he does not have the strength to build another house. (AVP, Montalvo, 18-i-56.)

According to the doctor in the Vicos clinic, the one who attended his cure, the illness he has is ganglionar tuberculosis. However, according to the thinking of the patient himself, the causes of his illness are: He believes that from the different accidents he has had he is suffering from *susto* [fright sickness], that the earth, or *patza*, has grabbed him.[13] It also comes from a break in his ribs on the left side which he thinks he has now, the same thing that has produced inflammation in the ganglions in his neck. He also had *susto* from this accident. *Frío* got into him, for he has gone about exposing himself to it in different places. He adds that a *curiosa* in Marcará told him that the *yuraq turmanyay*, the "white rainbow," had got into him. He does not know what that is. Surely, too, the *viento* has touched him, that is, he is *viento toqash*. It is evident that it is like that because he has on many occasions been exposed to this agent which has got into him. Many people tell him that he is *mal brash*, that is, "bewitched." He says that he has been undergoing cures for a long time, but up to now he has not gotten well. It can not be from the *calor*, he says, because when he eats things that are *cálido* his body does not accept them. Further, he can not be exposed to the sun for much time before he feels that his body is burning, his head gets dizzy, and when he is working he feels much fatigue from the *calor*. This fear he has of *calor* makes him certain that it is not from this agent.

Many years ago, when he was going over the Huamantzaca bridge [over one of the tributary streams flowing into the Marcará River in Vicos], the burro he was riding threw him into the river. Both of them fell in. On that occasion he got *susto*. (He says, "*Mantzakarqaa*" [I was frightened]. Besides that, while he was working on a house he also fell and got *susto* again.

Also, years ago, when Jorge Bardales [a mestizo in Marcará] bought a wild bull, Juandi went with a friend to capture it. They were on its trail in a place called Oqoru. They spent almost the whole day chasing it with the intention of taking it down to the *pampa*. It was already very late in the day when they managed to get it out of a thicket and onto the *pampa*, and so as not to let it go back he got the idea of following it on the same trail. The bull was mature, with big horns, and everyone was afraid of it. When he least thought so, the animal was in front of him, charged him, and thrust him against the stones of an abandoned house in that place. But since it had very large horns, they hit the wall and left him in the middle, so he got out quickly below and tried to jump over the wall. But the bull hit him again, striking him with its snout on his buttocks, and one of its horns hit lightly on an old scar that he had on the left side of his chest. He fell into the interior which was very deep. From what the bull had done and from the fall, he was very *asustado* [frightened], and surely he lost his *anima* [soul] there. From then on he felt very ill, until one of the old aunts he had gave him a *shoqma* with flowers from different plants. He felt better for a while, but then everything got worse again. It was more so when he came to live here in his new house constructed on top of the ruins of the ancient inhabitants. Everybody tells him that this place is

eating him, or rather consuming him.
    When he got worse, he had to employ another *curiosa* to cure him. She
told him that she would cure him if he would give her two hundred twenty
soles. Juandi had only one ox that had been a *shunay*, that is a gift of a
newly born calf, and he had to sell it to get the money to pay the
curandera who later became his *comadre* [co-mother, baptismal sponsor]
at the baptism of his son with Sofia Vega. For the treatment she put a
blanket on the floor and had him sit beside her. She had a handful of
papers with little figures in the form of hats on them (possibly playing
cards), and after having him breathe on them she threw the papers at him
on the blanket. Then she told him he had been bewitched. Next she got
together *rayán* [a tree] twigs and other herbs, milled them, and diluted
them with water. She added *pepita* [a fruit] soap and had him drink it.
Then she got some *yerbasanta* [an herb] which she crushed, dissolved in
water, and bathed him. The drink was a purge to get all the witchcraft out.
(AVP, Montalvo, 18-i-56.)

Since Juandi Sánchez was surely being treated with antibiotics there was
nothing more for Montalvo to record.   That there is much more to
Sánchez's story is certain, but neither Montalvo nor I recorded it.   In the
field and later in archives, I took my own field notes about him and those
of Project staff for granted, as documents that could "speak for
themselves." This has proved to be not so. As Paul Rabinow (1977:124)
so eloquently states it: "What seemed to my own naive consciousness, to
'speak for itself' proved to be the most in need of interpretation."

Delfin Coleto

    Delfin Coleto's case is about an intestinal infection and back pains. The
long course of his illness was described by Montalvo and other members
of the Project who followed it from October, 1954, to the end in August,
1955. We confront here a rather more complex collection of reports by
several different observers who sought, unsuccessfully, to obtain a
"demonstration effect" which would convince other Vicosinos of the
efficacy of modern scientific medicine and influence them to utilize it.
Undoubtedly, the Project's interest in the case also had much to do with
Coleto's relation to the Project/Hacienda, for he was a *mayoral*. This
position in the structure of the Project/Hacienda is a strategic factor in the
interaction between him and Project personnel.   If we compare this
solicitude with the Project's view of Manuel Alejandro Cruz, Juana Cilio's
husband in the first case presented here, where a "demonstration effect"
was also sought, we see the differential effects of cultural capital, symbolic
power, and the symbolic violence which dismisses Cruz as a "*pendejo*."
Included in this case is another description of *shoqma*. The story begins

with Montalvo's field notes:

> Thursday, October 28: Delfin says that his illness comes from many years ago but that it became worse at least six years ago. At that time, he says, he went to the mountains to round up his cattle. There was one very wild animal that kept getting away and he had to go looking for it. He was with his brother and they spent a very miserable day in the rain which soaked through all their clothing. On top of that there was hail. At the time they were trying to bring the animal out of a canyon into which it had gone and did not want to leave. They were soaked through and got out of there only to have to go to bed hungry on some straw on which snow fell, covering them over. It was from that, surely, that the *frío* got into his back. From that time on he has been suffering more intensely.
>
> It can also be from *achachay*, or *calor*, because he has always gone about in the sun, in the *calor*, and then in the *frío*. When the *frío* enters people, that is when their backs and their bones ache. Surely the *frío* has gone into his bones because he is feeling intense pains there.
>
> After he was given *shoqma* with cuy, the *entendida* [a woman who "knows," i.e., a *curiosa*] told him that his stomach had *ladeado* [tilted]. He says maybe it's so and maybe not. He asked me if I believed in that, because he does not. I told him that surely in some cases it must be like that and he agreed that was the way it was, and certainly because his stomach hurt and he had diarrhea. At that time they got him up and he was all right, but later he got sick again. (AVP, Montalvo, 28-x-54.)

On the following day Montalvo went to Coleto's house accompanied by John Collier, the photographer, to be witnesses to the *shoqma* treatment administered by Coleto's wife, Corposa Cruz:

> Friday, October 29: The brought out two chairs so that we could sit next to the patient who was fully clothed and reclined on some fleeces placed in the *corredor*[14] of the house. He was covered with some blankets. He sat up while his wife went to the cuy pen and picked a young animal. She says it is two months old. She brought it without any other explanation. She took the animal in her right hand, holding it by the throat so that the palm of her hand was at the back and her thumb, index, and middle fingers were pressed on the throat. While she was coming from the kitchen, and John was taking photographs of the animal, Delfin began to take off his pants and underclothing, being careful all the time not to show any part of his naked body from the waist down, for which he was covered all the time with the blankets. Next he placed his poncho to support his position better and then he fixed the bedding which had become disarranged.
>
> Corposa placed herself to the right of the patient and near his head, because really there was only room on that side because there was a wall on the left. Holding the cuy with her right hand, she began to pass the

cuy's head on the patient's forehead, holding the back of his head with her left hand. After three rubbings which were not very strong but rather light, she moved to his face, the rest of his head, his throat, shoulders, and so on. For these operations, according to the convenience in manipulating the cuy, she changed from one hand to the other. She made the rubbings slowly and softly, stopping a few seconds on each part. On the back, which was the affected zone, the rubbings were more continued and the stoppings more prolonged. From the back she went on to the chest, then to the arms, the waist, and then she repeated the operation on the whole of his upper body starting with the head. When she had finished the upper half of his body, she began rubbings on his feet and went up, little by little, to his waist. She rubbed carefully on his stomach which was another part that also was hurting. When the rubbings were finished the patient could get dressed. Then, for the last time, she returned to rub his head
and, finally, she placed the animal in front of the patient, almost mouth-to-mouth but separated by about 5 cm., at which time the patient several times–about five–breathed directly into the mouth of the animal.

During the whole operation, the patient as well as the *shoqmadora* [one who performs the operation], and the rest of those present like María [the patient's daughter] and ourselves, could converse about matters relating to the cure, as well as other themes which allowed us to laugh at times. Nevertheless, as the treatment went on the commentaries ceased and we concentrated on the illness.

When the so-called *qaqey* [the treatment] was over, Corposa told María to bring water, which she quickly did, bringing a cup-shaped *mate* from the kitchen. The water was taken from the irrigation channel, because there was none in the water jar in the kitchen, and placed on the floor a meter from the patient's head in a place where the light came in more fully. Taking a knife, she cut the throat across and only part way. For this, she held the animal from the back in her left hand in such a way that it was drawn from behind and easy to cut. When the blood began to flow, she took the hind legs with her right hand and raised them while the head was lowered close to the container of water. Thus she let the blood flow into the water and they began the diagnosis. She says that when the illness is from *frío* the cuy does not die during the *qaqey* as in the present case where it was semi-conscious, but when the illness is from *calor* in general they are unconscious, "like dead," or sometimes they really die.

The blood that had spilled into the water partly mixed with it, giving it almost a uniform color, but at the end one part dropped to the bottom of the water giving it a dark coloring from the clot. José Baltazar [María's husband and Coleto's son-in-law], María, and Corposa concluded that the patient had an illness from "*frío* and *calor*," that is, that the weak coloring represented an illness from *frío* and the clot one from *calor*. They said that if it were only from *frío* it would not have coagulated. Otherwise, it would all have had to be clots.

Next Corposa began to skin it from the lips as though she were making sausage, and like that from there to the rump she skinned it without breaking the skin and without detaching the body totally. Then the examination began again.

They noticed a piece of tissue which appeared fatty between two vertebrae on the spinal column and they said it was the "lung." Judging from its pale color and the granulations it showed, they diagnosed that it was from *frío*–its pale color–and from *viento*–the granulations. To obtain some reflex movement, Corposa sprinkled water on this part but said nothing.

Then she turned the animal over with its ventral side up and noted the way the stomach was covered. The swelling there was the reason why the stomach was *ladeado*, but for such a thing there was no evidence because both sides were uniform. They also noticed on the stomach some pieces of white epithelial tissue with bubbles inside which they interpreted as *viento*.

Then they went on to examine the limbs, for which Corposa raised the forelimbs on both sides of the cuy and now and then she bathed them with water without noticing anything strange, but when she examined the hindlimbs she noticed that they were both like sticks which she interpreted as *frío*. The presence of a bloody stain on the cuy's right leg gave them the sign for diagnosing *calor*. At this moment they changed the water, throwing what was in the cup out of the patio, that is, the liquid with the blood. With the new water Corposa kept bathing the animal but they did not notice anything new.

Next, just using her fingernails, she loosened the tissue which covers the stomach below the sternum and forcing them with her fingers she broke the connections between the ribs. She separated the two sides on the midline of the breast, leaving the internal organs exposed. They looked first at the lungs and saw a general paleness inside which was interpreted as *frío*, and there were some red stains from the coagulation of blood which they said was *calor*. They went on to look at the stomach and found it very full and with a whitish coloring on the outside, and some bubbles, which they interpreted as *viento*, *frío*, and *empacho*.

To finish the examination of the stomach, still using her fingernails, she tore it open and found a lot of grass which confirmed the diagnosis of *empacho*. Next she emptied the excrement on her hand and began to rinse it with water. She noted that it was all uniform, which gave rise to no commentary.

In the same way they examined the intestines, first observing in which position they were, and when they noted that there was a large bend they said that certainly it was *ladeado*. They also opened some sections and got out the excrement, which they washed but they made no diagnosis. Judging the paleness of the tissues they said it was from *frío*.

They did not examine the rest of the insides and bony parts but went on to examine the head, first externally. They looked at the paleness and said it was *frío* and from the pinkness at the occiput they said *calor*. Next Corposa took a large needle and separated the parietals, inserting the needle at the point of intersection of these two bones with the occipital. First they looked at the color and found it slightly pink. They diagnosed *achachay*, that is, *calor*, and finally they took note of the brain mass. They observed that it was swollen and said that Delfín was still going to live a long time, surely long enough for him to bury his children.

Ending the action with a series of commentaries, they placed the body again in its skin and said that they were going to hang it on a black *penca* [maguey] plant or on the beams of the house. They made the examination of the cuy for diagnosis. Corposa was the operator. Also there was José Baltazar who, they say, knows more than the other people in the house. Delfín's daughter, María Coleto, participated in the diagnosis in a very secondary way. José made most of the diagnosis and the others followed him, confirming or suggesting that such and such a thing ought to be so. The diagnosis was made in a loud voice and in the presence of the patient who was lying about a meter away, which allowed him also to intervene with questions or providing reasons of the accidents in his life that may have caused such and such an illness that they were discovering.

What is interesting is that at the moment of making the diagnosis of each one of the things they discovered in the cuy, they related it to the situations in which the patient had been during his routine activities. The *frío*, in general, they ascribed to his having walked around late in the night, in the rain, hail, and snow, and so on, and they could reconstruct for the patient that on such and such a day, or season, he had been on the *puna* and it snowed, at a time when he could not conveniently take shelter or cover himself. And the *calor* got into him because he had been in the sun in his activities for the Hacienda.

Since they concluded that his illness comes as much from *frío* as from *calor*, they say that he ought not to take only <u>medicines</u> that are *cálidos* to combat it but also ones that are *frescos*. Then Delfín himself said that as something *cálido* he should be rubbed with *sinapismo* [mustard plaster, or materials for its preparation], and as *fresco* with *saturno* vinegar, which he asked me to buy for him. (AVP, Montalvo, 29-x-54.)

We may note how in Vicos <u>medical practice/malpractice</u>, <u>diagnosis</u>, and <u>treatment</u> are group matters in which a circle of relatives is involved, along with the patient, and all are free to express opinions and make recommendations. In contrast, the code of modern scientific <u>medical practice</u> places a medical authority in a one-on-one situation in which the passive patient listens and obeys, responding only to the physician's initiative (and often, these days, a roomful of physicians interrogate, poke and jab, terrorize, and invade the body of a patient). While physicians know full well that their <u>treatments</u> may not always be effective, modern patients tend to fetish medications and medical equipment. In Vicos people hope to get well but recognize the differences among experience, hearsay, and possibility. *Ampi* does not always work. Indeed, it may work as anti-treatment.

Delfín Coleto and his illness became a focus for the attention of other members of the Project. We also have observations of him and his family recorded by William C. Blanchard, Héctor Martínez Arellano, and Buenaventura Armas Montero.[15] Armas also recorded several visits by him at the Vicos clinic during November and December, some of which are omitted here. Coleto's story continues a few days after Montalvo's observations with these field notes by Blanchard and Armas:

Wednesday, November 3: This afternoon Héctor Martínez and I went on horseback to see Delfín. Martínez had the medicines which Montalvo had got in Marcará. I understood that the *shoqma* with a cuy that took place last week by José Baltazar, Corposa, and María had produced an agreement among these principals that vinegar with *sinapismo* would be hot and cold to counteract the struggle with those two things attacking Delfín.

We found Delfín lying in the *corredor* hunched up on his side. He seemed weaker than he was last week and did not sit up after I told him to lie down again. Martínez told him and Corposa what we had brought. They did not seem to recognize it. They asked about it, they wondered who had suggested it, and they did not seem to know what one did with it. Martínez indicated that it was for external rubbing, so Delfín stirred about as if eager to try something. He took off his poncho, then his wool shirt (he was wearing neither coat nor vest), and let Corposa rub some of the vinegar on his back. (This vinegar was from the pharmacy in Marcará and did not smell unpleasant to me as does cider vinegar.[16]) She put a little in the cup of her hand and then moved the back of that hand, with the liquid not leaving it, over the part of his back she was going to rub. Then she turned her hand over and rubbed it on gently. Meanwhile, they made the observation that it might be good for him to drink some, but we told them no, just to use it for outside application. While we were there they did not use the other two items, both packets of powder or loose material. One was the *sinapismo*.

Delfín said that he was feeling worse. He said that he had been eating little, and hardly anything this day, since everything he ate turned into watery diarrhea anyway. I said that he needed to eat and suggested mutton broth. They did not have a sheep, so I said why not trade a pig for a sheep? But they said they had no pig either.

I told them that I would try to see if I could get the doctor to come up on Friday, but I could not promise. Delfín said he wanted to have the doctor take him to the hospital. As I understood Martínez's translation, it seemed that Delfín had thought he was going to die but then did not, so he wants to go to the hospital. We wondered how he could be gotten down to the Hacienda. They said on a horse if we would lend them one. My own feeling was that he was far too weak for that. There was more talk about food for him. I said that rice would be good and asked if they had any. They said no and asked for *fideos* [noodles] which I was dubious about. I told him not to eat *ají*. He said he had been eating it until a day or two before. I also told him no fat at all. As Martínez and I were leaving I looked at the chickens and we went back to suggest that they kill one an give the broth to Delfín. They asked when, and I told them the sooner the better, since he had eaten practically nothing the whole day. Before that, while Martínez and they were speaking Quechua, the suggestion of an egg came up. Corposa went to the corridor, picked up a fresh one, knocked of the end, and handed it to Delfín. He ate it all, raw.

Delfín had a *minka* [here a work party] working in the field just above the house. He said that he could keep them that day. I gathered that these workers were all the resources he had. He asked if I would let some *peones*, or even one, come to help finish the hilling that was going on. I said I would talk it over with Enrique Luna, and later did so. We decided to send him some help. When the matter of the chicken came up, Delfín wanted to know if the *minka* might have some. We said no, that he should use it all for himself. We left, I again cautioning him to eat, to avoid *ají* and fat, and to keep good and warm. We said we would try to see him on Friday.

While we were there, Corposa said that Delfín had wanted to be taken to the hospital earlier but that she had not been able to take the responsibility of permitting this without talking first with his relatives and *casta* [patrilineal kin group]. (AVP, Blanchard, 3-xi-54.)

Monday, November 8: On Friday morning the clinic came, for the first time in some weeks under Dr. Ponce's direction. I told him soon after he arrived about the case of Delfín, the *mayoral*. He suggested that we go up to Delfín's house, saying that the nurse could take care of the cases at the Hacienda. We left on horseback, getting up to Delfín's in an hour. We went into the patio and found Corposa and some other women there. Delfín was not in the *corredor* and we found, when Corposa opened the small wooden door to the storeroom, that Delfín was lying on the floor in the dark. We were Enrique, Ponce, Max [Mrs. Blanchard], and myself. Enrique acted as interpreter, though Ponce and Delfín could make each other understand a great many things. Delfín, as I noticed on the earlier visit, tends to use Spanish very little, perhaps an effect of his being so ill.

Dr. Ponce asked him a number of questions, eliciting that he had diarrhea or dysentery, showed no evidence of blood, and had taken alcohol the day before but little else. Ponce took his pulse, trying both wrists, and saying it was weak. Delfín said he had a cough, but not a bad one. Ponce said to me that he could not be sure what Delfín had. It might be typhoid. I said that I had, in my visits, not seen him evidencing great fever at all.

Ponce decided, after trying in vain to see in the darkness and even though Corposa had lighted a candle, to get him out. He moved out, Corpora spreading some hides for him. I was surprised to see that he could walk as well as he did. However, he seemed very glad to lie down again. Ponce got out a number of things he had brought up in a saddle bag, an ampule of dextrose and something else, prepared a syringe, and injected the large quantity intravenously, asking via Enrique, how Delfín felt. It seemed that the rate of the injection depended on keeping posted on the reaction of the patient. This was for building up his strength. He told Delfín it was a tonic. Then he gave him an injection of assorted new drugs to kill the bacteria in his hip. During the first injection Delfín had done much groaning, perhaps from the effort of sitting up. He did not seem very happy about all of this, but he submitted with no objections. Ponce talked to him about what he should eat. He told him no *ají*, no alcohol, no solid meat for a while. He recommended broth and a few other things. He told Delfín that he was going to feel better right away, and that he (Ponce) would be back to see him again on Tuesday. Delfín was also urged to take much more liquid.

While the injecting was going on, Corposa was with Delfín, helping him remove his *wachuku* [sash] in order to let the doctor examine him better. (AVP, Blanchrd, 8-ix-54.)

Wednesday, November 10: Yesterday morning, the clinic arrived late. It consisted of Dr. Ponce, the social worker, two nurses, and an assistant. As usual, Armas was also helping them. Ponce and I talked for a bit, and then he, Max, and I went up to Delfín Coleto's on horseback. When we arrived we found that John Collier, who had gone on foot, was ready to take photographs of the treatment by the doctor, to compare with those of the *shoqma* with cuy of two weeks ago.

Corposa was there, and she also complained of feeling bad, having something wrong in the stomach. Ponce said he would look at her later. Delfin was inside the room but sitting with his back against the wall. I did not go in because I could not see well, but John took photos there. Delfín was feeling much better, he said, had eaten something, and seemed to have little or no diarrhea. He talked about how far behind his farming was and said that when he got better he would work hard to make it up, and also his work for the Hacienda.

Ponce got him to come out of the room. He walked out, doing rather well compared with the terrible debility he showed the last time. He had on his shirt and vest, *wara* [pants], and *wachuku*. Corposa, hovering about, threw down three *pellejos* [fleeces] and fixed up a sort of bed for him. Ponce, who communicated partly in Spanish and partly in Quechua with Delfín, got him to lie down and prepared the apparatus for giving him another injection of dextrose. First he checked his pulse, then listened to his heart and breathing. Corposa was very close to Delfín during the injection, holding his arm for the doctor. John got pictures of this. Ponce gave him pills in place of another injection. He left two kinds for Delfín to take, explaining the times to take them in Spanish and Cuzco Quechua. When he told Delfin to take the pills, Corposa ran and got a cup (looking like one of the Project's enamel cups) and Delfín swallowed them down, almost eagerly, as if completely willing to cooperate with the doctor.

Hanging on the wall was a chicken leg that Delfín said he was going to have.   Ponce talked to him about eating more, and about getting some orange juice which would be most difficult for him to get because the oranges that grow here are not fit to eat. (AVP, Blanchard, 10-ix-54.)

Tuesday, November 16:   Max and I left around 9:30 and went up to Delfín's. We found him sitting in the *corredor*, fully dressed, but not with a bed or anything to recline on. Corposa was with him as usual. I asked him how he was. He said he felt better but that he did not want to eat too much because he felt bloated. I suggested that he take something a bit more often than the few means a day they have, five, perhaps, with an egg at one, some milk at another. He said that he cannot take milk, that it does him harm. Then he told me that his little grandchild, María's son, has had diarrhea for a week. I told him that the doctor was here today, that it was a good time to send the child down. María brought the child but said that she had to make chicha, or watch it, for her husband's *minka*. I said that Corposa might be able to watch the chicha, so then María said that she had to take her husband's lunch to him in the Quebrada. I talked a bit about how it would be better to take the child down today, that a week was a long time to have had the diarrhea, and surely he would not start to get better until the doctor gave him something, as had happened in Delfín's case. They seemed to think this over. María let it be known that she would go down today. She had thought it would be soon enough on Friday.

Delfín said he would come down on Friday, walking slowly. Corposa was worried about the sun, and his getting *hot*, but I told him to come early and slowly. I went out with Max and Delfín followed us, walking a bit unsteadily. Then María decided not to go after all but to wait until Friday. However, after I had gotten back and been around for a while, she showed up. The doctor said the child had functional diarrhea, and had had it for some time off and on. María took some powdered preparation up to Delfín with instructions as to how he should take it. (AVP, Blanchard, 16-xi-54.)

Friday, November 19: Delfín Coleto said that he felt a little better. The doctor told him that he needed to be taken care of and prescribed vitamin B for him. His pulse was still weak and he could engage in any effort because of his age. He has great confidence in the doctor, and the same in the medicines. Dr. Ponce examined him like that and recommended rest for him. (AVP, Armas, 19-xi-54.)

Sunday, December 26: This morning Max and I were driving up from Marcará. We picked up César Sánchez and his wife, and then Corposa Cruz. I asked her how Delfín was. César Sánchez acted as interpreter in the conversation. She said he was sick, that he had "the urines," which César agreed was diarrhea. He had had what César called a "*curiosidad*" ["curiosity," surely a *curiosa*] and she [the *curiosa*] had diagnosed his case and told him that what he needed was a change of blood, and that she would change it for him. I asked how she was going to do that. César said to me, with as much amazement as I felt at the idea, "I don't know. How can that be done?" Corposa indicated that Delfín was very much pleased at the diagnosis and the suggested treatment.

I asked if Delfín had been drinking boiled water, and she said no. I told her, via César, that he should drink boiled water. That is, all the water he drank should be boiled. César told her this.

Dr. Ponce came today with his family. I told him that Delfín was ill again. He said that he had some medicine for Delfín but would give him the children's form in pills. I wondered if Ponce had talked with Montalvo, who might have recommended spoonfuls [of liquid medicine] as against pills, because people did not like the pills which some have thought were *hot*. (AVP, Blanchard, 26-xii-54.)

Monday, December 27: Max and I rode up this morning to see Delfín Coleto. I wanted to see how he was, Corposa having said yesterday that he was bad again. We got up there and were met by Corposa who helped tie up the horses. She then led us back to their place where we found Delfín sitting against the post in the shed [i.e., *corredor*] with his back toward the entrance. He greeted us and Corposa brought me a chair from the storeroom.

Delfín said that he was bad. He had only had two days' relief from the diarrhea. I asked him if he had taken all the medicine the doctor had given him, and he said yes. He said he had taken half-doses for a few days. I asked if he were eating, and he said that he had just finished a sixth chicken but that he really had no appetite. For example, he ate only about three little potatoes. Then, without my asking, he volunteered that a *curiosa* had given him a going over with a cuy again. I asked when. He said, Friday, then Tuesday or Wednesday. Not even Corposa could remember when.

Delfín said that the *curiosa* had told him, "No tienes *sangre*" [you don't have any blood]. He went on, "Todo agua adentro, como ovejera, apesta" [all water inside, like a shepherdess, it stinks]–which was supposedly why it came out, as he says, "*orina*" [urine] and very offensive in odor. I inquired what the *curiosa* intended to do about this situation. He said that nothing can be done about it. She had told him, "No se puede curar, capaz tú puedes morir" [it can't be cured, maybe you'll die]. He went on, relating her reactions to his case: "Barriga está a un lado. Así está arreglando barriga no más" [stomach is on its side, like that the stomach is just being arranged.]. He said that he does not want to eat much, telling us that again. He said, "Dos, tres platos, y allá mismo está cagando" [two or three dishes, and there and then it's shit right out]. I asked what things he had been eating. He said *shakwi de trigo* [milled wheat soup], *caldo de gallina* [chicken broth], *habas*, a few potatoes, just 2 or 3, no *ají*, and very little fat in anything –because, he said, they could not afford cooking oil. I asked him if he touched alcohol. He said no, but that he would love to have some chicha. Max and I both told him no chicha. He said that he gets very thirsty, and I told him to drink all the water he wanted to but to make sure it had been boiled. Corposa brought him some water while we were there, putting her finger in it to test how hot it was. He assured me that it had been boiled.

He pulled back the poncho over him to indicate something about his legs. Then he said that he had been massaged, probably by Corposa, with chicken fat on the legs up to the thighs. I asked why and he told me that it was because of the pain. He implied that the treatment had helped. Corposa went into the storeroom and brought out a bottle of something that I smelled and which I tentatively identified as a sweet wine, possibly with something else in it. They said it was called *sikullá*. She brought out another bottle with something that smelled like banana oil. This is called *piña y presku*. Max told me she thought Corposa had brought these things back with her yesterday, having gotten them from Enrique's mother in Marcará. I do not know whether they had been requested by Corposa or suggested by Doña María. They asked if Delfín could take them. I said it would be better to wait until they hear from the doctor tomorrow.

I thought he showed signs of being tired. Corposa was saying something that sounded like that Max and I were like *compadres* to him, but who would help her? She began to cry. I asked why she was sad. He said it was because he was sick. He said he had been thinking he might die, so I told him that he would get better if he would do what the doctor told him. I had told him earlier that the doctor had some new medicine for him, and that Corposa should come and get it at the clinic, since Delfín had said he did not think he could get down. Max and I left around 11:30. (AVP, Blanchard, 27-xii-54.)

Monday, January 10: This morning Delfín came back to work for the first time in months. He worked at the *depósito* [storage facility] where women were sorting *chochos* [*tawri*, or lupine beans], and did not have to do anything strenuous. He did not look any too well but, compared with the way he looked a few weeks ago, he has apparently made quite a recovery. He told me that he liked the medicine that the doctor gave him (Palmitato de Chloromycetin) to take by the spoonful, and that he had finished it all up. It would have lasted at best three or four days. He said that he had the label which shows the name of it, in case he could get some more. It did him so much good that he wants to continue taking it. I asked if he had diarrhea and he said no. I told him that the medicine was to cure that, and that was why the doctor had given it to him. (AVP, Blanchard, 10-i-55.)

Tuesday, January 11: Delfín Coleto said that he had felt a little improvement with the medicine that Dr. Ponce de León had given him, but when the medicine was finished the pains in the stomach had come back and he had no appetite but, rather, a weakness all over his body. Dr. Ramírez examined him and ordered that they give him an ampule of "*emitana*" and <u>pills</u> to take three times a day, and that when he was thirsty he should take *cold boiled* water, eat meat, soft-boiled eggs, and milk. He said that Coleto needed much <u>care</u>. (AVP, Armas, 11-i-55.)

All these instructions to boil water for drinking from doctors and several members of the Project are made without the additional caution that all vessels in which food is prepared and served, as well as all eating implements, be cleaned in boiled water too. Furthermore, in the language of Vicos, the concept of "*cold boiled*" water is an oxymoron! Coleto's case was far from over: it seems as though he was continually being reinfected from some source in or about his house. Montalvo observed him at the same time, but whether or not Coleto was "responding to two independent medical systems" or whether he was"passing one to the other," is more problematic than Montalvo's wishes in that regard.

Sunday, January 9: *Assimilation of scientific medicine*: When I visit Delfín, each time he must tell me that he is not only undergoing the <u>therapy</u> that the doctor has indicated but also home <u>therapy</u>. It is curious that Delfín, who accepts scientific <u>medicine</u> without protest, is not entirely confident in it. Currently, his <u>medication</u> is a response to two independent systems, scientific and folk. Now for example, he tells me that he went again to consult with a *curiosa* to be <u>cured,</u> and that he is taking <u>medicines</u> prescribed by her. In this sense, he is then passing from one system to another without rejecting either one. (AVP, Montalvo, 9-i-55.)

Tuesday, January 18: A week ago last Friday Delfín came to the nurse to have her give him an <u>injection</u> and give him some spoonfuls of <u>medicine</u>. Delfín reports that the injections were given him, and that the spoonfuls of oral <u>medicine</u> did him great harm because they gave him a stomachache. Therefore he did not take any more of them. On that same day, he says, he had a <u>drink</u> prepared for him that they told him was very good for diarrhea. This <u>home remedy</u> is what has done him good, because it calmed the diarrhea he had by Wednesday.
Delfín had been willing to enter the hospital, and he should have gone on Friday in the same vehicle as the doctor, but he did not show up. We supposed that he would do it today but, suspecting that he would not, I went to visit him to see what things he would tell me. I found him seated and his wife, with whom I spoke first, confirmed it. He told me that they had told him to enter the hospital but that he was not willing to go because his daughter was opposed to it. She said that he would die there, and she asked, when he died, who was going to bury him in strange ground, far from his family? Corposa joined in, saying that she could not get him to go to the hospital because Delfín's daughter and her children blamed her. They told her, "You, it'll be your fault if he dies in the hospital!" So, for those reasons, they should decide how to do those things.

Delfín said that he had not talked at all with his daughter about entering the hospital, and that, besides that, he himself was doubtful whether or not he would get well or he would get caught by it. They asked me to tell them about how it was to be in the hospital and if one had to pay for it. I told them that there was no charge in the case of poor people, and that there was a better chance there that any patient could be cured because the doctor is there every day and not like the present case in Vicos where he comes only twice a week.

Then Corposa said to me, "They say that you told Jorge Reyes to go to a *curiosa* in Carhuaz. It wouldn't be a bad thing if you also told us about that woman so we could go there. They say that Jorge Reyes also says that you sent him to the *curiosa* there." I told him that what Jorge Reyes had been saying about me was false. Instead, one day I went to visit him and he told me that he had gone to see that woman, that he had paid her one hundred *soles* for the consultation, and that she was curing him. So she said to me that it surely was a lie, and turning to her husband she said, "For your health it doesn't matter if you pay, even one hundred *soles*." He remained thoughtful.

From what Delfín has told us about his possible hospitalization the following can be deduced: 1. Fear that he will die far away from his locality. 2. Fear of his spouse of her husband's family, in case of a serious outcome, if she exerts influence for his hospitalization. 3. The need for family consent to make his entrance possible. 4. Ignorance about admission procedure and conditions for the stay and the cure. That is, they believe they must pay for it. 5. The belief that hospital medicine, and medicine in general, is only one of the possibilities for a cure. (AVP, Montalvo, 18-i-55.)

Wednesday, January 19: Delfín Coleto Durán, age 65, residing in Wiyash [a division of Vicos], has been sick for a long time and attended by the physician, Dr. Julio Ramírez Jácome. When the latter came to the clinic yesterday, he asked me how Delfín was feeling. I told him that I could not tell him anything because I had not gone to see him.

Today I came to Delfín Coleto's house at 10:30 in the morning. I found him sitting on a bench when I went inside his house. I surprised him with coca in his mouth, and I asked him why he was chewing coca. I told him that it would do him great harm, and because he was taking medications it was even worse. After listening to me, he went out to his patio and spit out all the coca. He rinsed his mouth, and a little while later Corposa, his third wife, came in. He told her, "The Sergeant [see note 11] has come to visit me and he got angry when he saw me with coca in my mouth." Corposa said to me that it bothered her more because Delfín was not paying any attention to her. Delfín told her that he would chew no more coca. He had had a little wrapped in a cloth and that was why he began to chew it so as to find out if I were going to come today or not, but now he was not going to do things like that. The medicine that the doctor gave him on Friday, the 14th of this month, he had begun to take at noon and he kept taking it every two hours until the bottle was finished. He did not feel an improvement. The diarrhea was the same. Also the stomach pain was not relieved. Yesterday he did not send Corposa to the doctor's but had told her, "I see that it isn't doing me any good, so don't go down there and don't bother the doctor."

Corposa had fixed a medicine of forage plants like thistle, *amor seco* [?], sage, and milled avocado seed. She boiled all those herbs and gave the mixture to him as a tea. The first cup he took was at 11 in the morning, and he had another in the afternoon. According to what Delfín reported he felt better, and it had stopped the diarrhea, the stomach pain, and he had more appetite. This morning he had eaten three dishes of soup and he had also eaten some fox meat. He told me that he was going to find somebody to hunt fox for him. I asked him that if the doctor told him to go to the Carhuaz hospital, would he be ready to go? He told me that he was ready to go to the hospital, but on Sunday or Tuesday because he could not do it before then because he had to turn over the keys to the cemetery and take an inventory of things, leaving in his place some other person to take over the duties of *Tesorero* [a member of the *varayoq* organization who "is in charge of the control and conservation of the cemetery" (Vázquez 1964:47)]. (AVP, Armas, 19-i-55.)

We should take note of how Armas, a mestizo from Carhuaz, employs a negative discourse on coca-chewing to intimidate and shame Coleto. (Armas belongs to a social sector which makes a good living selling coca and alcohol to farmers.) It is rhetoric that conveys disdain, superiority of the mestizo and inferiority of the rural person, suggesting that Coleto practices a "dirty" habit, a secret "vice," and is somehow "bad." How this Project employee believes he can "help" Coleto get well while insulting him is something only a mestizo can know, and one with development discourse on his mind as well!

Tuesday, January 25: This morning I was going to see Delfín Coleto to find out if he had lost interest in going to the hospital to get cured. I met him on the way, for he was already on his way to the clinic to tell the doctor that he could not go to the hospital this time because he still had not taken an inventory of the church's goods according to his duty as *Tesorero* which he had just taken on this year. Also he says that the home remedies have made him better and he is walking now. Otherwise, he thinks that he is not going to get well in the hospital. That is what he believes. (AVP, Montalvo, 25-i-55.)

Monday, January 31: Delfín Coleto tells me that he has no desire to eat anything and that the only thing he has been able to eat in several days has been a little *shakwi*, a soup of pea flour. (AVP, Montalvo, 31-i-55.)

Tuesday, February 8: Delfín came to the clinic today saying that because his illness was better he was there so that the doctor might give him more medicines and examine him thoroughly. I asked him why he had not come on Friday, the 4th of this month, and he answered saying that on that day he was still in bed, and that was why he could not come to the clinic. He told me that the medicine the doctor had given him had done him good. Now he did not have diarrhea or the stomach pains. I asked him if he had taken some medicine at home, and he told me no but that his wife had given him massages with chicken fat on the parts that hurt him and that it had done him good.

When his turn came, the young lady who was assisting called him to go into the examination room where the doctor was. He greeted the latter and told him that now he was feeling better with the pills that the latter had prescribed for him. When the examination was over, the doctor ordered that he be given an injection from an ampule. The doctor asked him if he were ready to go into the Carhuaz hospital. Delfin answered negatively, saying that I had told his wife that the doctor would wait for him on the 11th in order to take him in the vehicle. (AVP, Armas, 8-ii.55.)

Friday, February 11: Delfin tells me today that the doctor told him he would take him to the Carhuaz hospital, and that he was willing to stay in that medical facility to get cured once and for all, because he was not improving with anything and his health was continually in danger. Since the patient was willing, I went in to see the doctor and asked him if he had decided to admit him. He said yes. I asked him if he did not consider some possibility of failure which would be viewed negatively in Vicos and would produce resistance in other more favorable cases which could end with favorable outcomes from the medical and social point of view. He responded with a little ill humor that in medicine both failure and success were common, and that it would be very foolish to expect successes. Moreover, he believed that he could get cured in the hospital with hospital routine alone, the better availability of medicines, and daily care.

So admission is recommended without prior study of the consequences it will have later, whether the outcome is positive or negative. (AVP, Montalvo, 11-ii-55.)

Montalvo appears to be having second thoughts about the matter of hospitalization. We do not know how this changed outlook came about. As succeeding references to the event indicate, Coleto was indeed hospitalized in Carhuaz. Nevertheless, despite an intensive search in the archives I could find no file slips reporting on his experience. It was apparently a disaster, and it would be useful to know more details of how this happened. I am left with the questions: could field notes have been removed, or was it that Project personnel were so embarrassed not simply by their failure to obtain a positive "demonstration effect" but as well by the negative consequences of the event that nobody saw fit to write about it? After Coleto returned to Vicos there were still attempts, unsuccessful ones, made to get him to the hospital in Huaraz which, as the departmental capital, had more and better medical resources than the small provincial hospital in Carhuaz.

Tuesday, March 1: The clinic arrived soon after eight this morning and worked until almost eleven, at which time Max, Montalvo, and Dr. Ramírez went up to see Delfín. I had been surprised at Dr. Ramírez's interest in seeing Delfín. When he got back he told me that Delfín was a bit better and that he would like to provide him with some more of the same medicine sent by Dr. Ponce, and that he is taking now. (AVP, Blanchard, 1-iii-55.)

Friday, March 4: Dr Ponce had said in Huaraz yesterday that he was coming to Vicos today. In the afternoon, about 3:30, the chauffeur came to say that the doctor could not come because he had to give a talk in Marcará but had sent him up to get Delfín to take to the hospital. However, Montalvo had already found out that Delfín would not come. Dr. Ramírez knew that. Is there no communication between the two doctors? Or had Dr. Ponce not even waited to ask Dr. Ramírez in Marcará, where he presumably was holding a clinic. I sent a note to Ponce. (AVP, Blanchard, 4-iii-55.)

Sunday, March 5: Corposa Cruz came down this morning. Aliro [the Project handyman] acted as interpreter, although he did not bother to translate much of what she said. It seems that she came to say that Delfín is not going to the hospital on Tuesday. Dr. Ponce had wanted to take him in on Friday but he could not go without consulting his family, he said, so he thought he might go on Tuesday. Corposa said that Delfín would rather die at home.
She did not seem consistent in what she had to say. As Aliro explained it to me, she or Delfín, or both of them, were undecided and wanted me to make the decision. I said that it was up to them, that I was not sick but Delfín was. I said that the doctor had said that in Huaraz it would be different from what it had been in Carhuaz, in that the doctor of the UNICEF would still have control, not lose it as happened before. She said that they charge for food in the hospital in Huaraz. We told her that was not so. I said that the doctor had suggested it so that he could take better care of his patient in the sense of knowing what he had to eat, and so forth.
Then she began to say more about Delfín. He did not want to go because he did not trust her, or any of the others at the place, with his grain which was stored there. He was most unhappy about this. Then she said that José Baltazar, the son-in-law, wanted Delfín to go. Finally, she said that she would go back and they would talk it over again, and she would tell us whether he would go or not. (AVP, Blanchard, 5-iii-55.)

Tuesday, March 15: Today Dr. Ramírez indicated that he wanted to make house visits in at least two neighborhoods. This intention of his is to be explained by the fact that he had come to Vicos with a newspaper reporter. So the three of us went–the doctor, the reporter, and I. We rode horseback. Delfín was, like always, lying on some fleeces in his *corredor*. He welcomed us, shaking hands. The doctor asked him about his condition and he said that he had diarrhea again. He had only eaten a soup of *habas* and wheat and now his "companion" [penis] hurt. When he was asked what he had been taking after the pills were gone, he said *harún oregano*. Delfín's wife says it is a wild plant that is made into an infusion, and is taken with a little sugar.

Then, when the doctor asked him, he said that he was not willing to go to the hospital because, "I left the Carhuaz hospital almost dead, and when I think about that I'm not interested. Besides, if a person doesn't have any money he suffers from hunger to eat things like bread." The doctor said to him that this time not just any doctor would take care of him but he would himself. Listening to that, Delfín's wife said, "Please find out if he's going to live or die. Take his pulse well and see how it's going, see if it's for the good or the bad," and then she began to cry. She said that she was there to take care of him, even though his daughter and her husband don't recognize her, even though they intend to kick her out after he dies, and that she had come to this house maybe only because they asked for her and begged her so much to come and live with Delfín, and that because of all that she was also going to be forsaken, and so on. The doctor told her not to cry, that what was important was curing Delfín, and that having used up so much medicine it was not worth it to leave him in that condition. Then Delfín said that he had been thinking that if he died in the hospital, God knows who would get his body, and that this was what his family was afraid of. He says that surely he ought to die in his own house and in Vicos so that they can keep him company.

Nevertheless, later he was again interested and he said he would go next Tuesday, because currently they have been spreading manure on a field and he could not go until they finished that. He did not explain why. He also said that when he went he would go with his wife so she could attend him.

We said goodbye and left. As usual, he asked me to give him some cigarettes.

This time the doctor examined his stomach lightly, took his pulse, and listened to his heart, but he did not look at the sexual "companion" even though he had been told about it. The reporter took no notes of any kind but looked absent-mindedly at the doctor's examination. He did not ask about anything, either. (AVP, Montalvo, 14-iii-55.)

Thursday, April 14: Today, after a long while, I went to visit Delfín. When I came into his house I found him in the part that is occupied by his son-in-law, José Baltazar. They were both installing the loom in a new location because, he says, before it took up too much of their space. Delfín appeared healthy. After many visits during which I have not seen him with coca in his mouth, this time it was there. His color is darker and he is not as pale as he has been at other times. His first words were that he was now feeling better and eating well, that his stools have been dry, and that all the improvement was due to a plant that they found in the garden of the Carhuaz hospital.

One of his relatives, who had taken the plant with orange peel, *allqo shoqlla*, rosemary, and *molancuyá*, told him about it. But then a person from Recuayhuanca came and told him that he should take it without mixing it. They brought him this plant, then, and every morning he has kept on taking it without sugar. He began this therapy a week after the chloromycetin was used up. He says that those pills did not get rid of his diarrhea because a week after they were gone he was sick again, but when he took that plant he improved.

On the other hand, now his abdomen, stomach, and back hurt, and he will go to see the doctor to be cured of those things. Corposa joined in the conversation saying that Delfín wasn't going to get better because now he was well for one or two days, and then he went to bed with the same sickness as ever. Now it hit him like malaria and his whole body shook, and so even he thinks he is dying. The plant has cured his diarrhea completely, but now he has something else. She does not believe he will get better, and surely tomorrow he will wake up sick. About the hospital, she said that his family was not willing because, in the first place, he is much improved. In the second place, his family says that he will certainly die there, and who knows where they might throw his body. Fears like these are also making Delfín himself lose interest, although he was willing at the beginning. (AVP, Montalvo, 14-iv-55.)

Monday, May 16: While I was walking in Parash I stopped to see Delfín Coleto because I knew that he had been sick for a long time. I found him lying on a bed of fleeces. He told me that for several days he had been worse than usual, and that yesterday he had eaten a little *shakwi* but today he had not tasted a thing because his stomach was hurting unbearably, like his back and abdomen.

He told me, "For several days I've been taking sweet watercress which is *fresco* and was calming my stomach pains, but now it's not doing me any good. Instead, when I take it my stomach hurts more. Nobody recommended that I take it, but we know that it's good because we used to take it when there wasn't any medicine.

"I haven't gone back to visit the doctor because the medicines he gave me haven't done me any good. On the contrary, the pills I took gave me stomach pain. Besides that, I can't go now because I can't walk, because my legs are weak. A few days ago Señora María (Mary Collier) gave my wife Corposa 4 pills which did me a lot of good. They calmed the pain in my stomach, back, and ribs. My wife went to ask for more yesterday, but they told her they were all gone."

Corposa tells me that when Delfín was coming back from the Carhuaz hospital they met a woman known as "Rogopa," who is from Huaraz and knows about <u>curing</u>. When she saw the state Delfín was in she told him that he was surely sick in the kidneys, for which every morning he ought to take lemon juice and this would do him a lot of good. She said to me, "But I don't know how to give it to him, and that's why I want to take Delfín to that woman's to have her <u>cure</u> him. Since he can't walk I can't carry him, so would you people in the Hacienda please lend me a horse or make the car available for taking him to Marcará where this woman is living and running a shop. Before, when José Baltazar's daughter was sick with stomach pains, "La Rogopa" examined her and gave her a bottle containing <u>some kind of a liquid</u> which made my niece throw up the worms she had, and then the stomach pains were <u>cured</u>. She's a woman who <u>knows</u>." (AVP, Martínez, 16-v-55.)

Further complications ensued–as if this case had not already been tangled in a web of medical failures to prevent Coleto's continual reinfections, errors in his one hospitalization, the passivity of Project personnel who took seriously their role as participant observer-interveners but yet could not intervene in any helpful way, and mismanagement in general–when his marriage to Corposa Cruz ended. This marriage appears to have been encouraged by romantic notions in the minds of Project people. Norman Pava, the North American anthropology student who lived in Coleto's house, and who left Vicos long before the latter's illness, was the marriage *padrino* [wedding godfather], and Ana de Almandoz, Aliro's wife, was the *madrina* [wedding godmother]. Such matchmaking, a fetishing of romance, may be ascribed to misplaced intervention by persons who gazed at a widower and a widow and wished to see their own narratives of a "happy ending" reflected.

Middle-class North Americans and Peruvians seem unconsciously to have projected their own notions of romantic love and "family values" into Vicosinos. To employ the metaphor of the oscillating *pharmakon* here, this one-sided and static tendency–nothing less than heterosexism–to conceive marital union as <u>remedial</u>, a <u>remedy</u> which will make up for life's deficits, <u>medicine</u> to heal injuries to the souls of the persons involved which have made them heretofore unlovable, a <u>cure</u> for loneliness, and <u>treatment</u> for an anomalous single state, is a reading which ignores the realities of marital misery, family violence, and divorce statistics. We say that loving spouses are "taking care" of each other, but we also employ the phrase "take care!" in the sense of "watch out!" Why do we not say "giving care" and "give care!"? Possibly because "caregiving" has been medicalized. It would seem that most Vicosinos look at marriage in terms of reciprocity rather than romance: this seems to be in Coleto's wife's mind when she demands a share of a maize crop in return for her work in preparing food and drink for the *minka* that cultivated the maize field. We read in the field notes of Project people–all of them male– the image of Corposa Cruz as a dutiful wife who is attending her husband in the best way she can: conducting a *shoqma* session, preparing his food, running errands, seeking alternative medications, with no hint of difficulties between her and Delfín Coleto. Yet, when we come to his words, if we are willing to take them at their face value, it seems he has been enduring a distasteful and downright painful relationship, one that has aroused his anger rather than his love. I would also like to suggest–which in no way precludes other suggestions, readings, and interpretations–that Coleto may also be unconsciously seeking his own body image in his wife, the image of a body that has been failing him, giving him much pain, and one from which he would like to rid himself. And Corposa Cruz, resenting his miserly gaze–actually more like surveillance by a higher power– which counts how much she eats and the time she spends conversing with neighbors, seems also to have had enough of their relationship. Perhaps their dead baby has something to do with their troubles. And we might also include in the production of their separation some tension between Coleto's daughter and her husband with Corposa Cruz.

The instability of "peaceful union" is suddenly revealed. Drucilla Cornell (1991:1309, 1314, cited in Davies 2001:227) states: "When there is not peace, we should not pretend there is. Certainly the patriarchal order does not provide a 'peaceful' world for women." Margaret Davies's comments follow: "The arguments that gender is a violent hierarchy, or that heterosexuality is compulsory, do not amount to an approval of force but rather a revelation of the fact of violence in the very concept (and therefore the practice) of sexual relationship as traditionally understood." Coleto, too, broke his silence:

Wednesday, June 1: I found Delfín Coleto, as usual for some time, lying in bed. He told me that his wife, Corposa Cruz, left his house Sunday afternoon, taking with her a ring, a blanket, a *wishlla* [wooden spoon], and half an *arroba* of *habas*. He told me, "She went because I told her to get out. I've been married for two years and in all that time she's kept on making me angry because she's gone out on the footpath to talk with people without doing anything in the house since I've been sick. Then, about eight months ago, she became more bothersome. She made me angry all the time. Then, when I couldn't bear any more of it, I told her to get out. So that's why she left. This morning she came with my marriage *madrina*, Ana de Almandoz, and Sergeant Buenaventura Armas. My *madrina* told me that Corposa should remain at home but I refused that because I know she'll keep on making me angry, and I can't bear that. The day she left she took with her some cloth, a ring, a shirt, a few potatoes, and a pot. Now that Corposa's gone, my daughter, José

Baltazar's wife, will be the one who looks after me. When I die my grandson, Pedro, will be the one who replaces me in my obligations to the Hacienda.

"I'm surely going to die, like Jorge Reyes, at the end of a year's illness. If it's like that, I only lack four months. But I'd like to go to the coast. Maybe I could get better there. Over the last few days I've gotten a little better, and now I can sleep a little more peacefully at night. My bones don't hurt me as much now. Before, my bones hurt me unbearably, and I couldn't sleep at night. Now I'm not being cured with any home remedy. They don't have any effect on me. The food I'm taking is *shakwi* with *chochoca* [cornmeal], and sometimes a few potatoes. (AVP, Martínez, 1-vi-55.)

Thursday, June 2: At 7:30 in the morning there appeared Corposa Cruz, Delfín Coleto's wife, both of them residents of Cachipachán. She arrived at the *casa hacienda* and the first thing she did was to go to Señora Ana de Almandoz, wife of the construction boss. Corposa spoke with her about her husband, Delfín Coleto, who had thrown her out of his house. It was the third time that Delfín had thrown her out.

After she talked with Señora Ana, Corposa gave an account to me, telling me that she was coming to ask for help and to offer a complaint about the troubles she had had with her husband Delfín. I asked her why it was that she had appealed first to Señora Ana, and Corposa answered, telling me that she had gone to her because she was her wedding *madrina*, while the *padrino* had been the anthropologist, Norman Pava. She said that since the *madrina* was available she had to appeal to her, and that she is the one who is called on to do justice. Corposa told me that it was the third time that Delfín had thrown her out of the house. He had always been looking for some excuse to tell Corposa to get out of his house. She told me that today she had come to advise her *madrina* that Delfín has thrown her out for good. He had told her to leave the house immediately, and that Corposa's presence bothered him a great deal, and that he didn't need her company because he would rather die alone than in Corposa's presence. That was the way Corposa expressed herself about her husband.

She told me that she had asked her *madrina* to go to Delfín's house so that Corposa could get her things out in the *madrina*'s presence. She also asked me to accompany her for that purpose. I agreed and, since the *madrina* agreed, I had to go there with Señora Ana.

We arrived at 8 a.m. in the morning, finding Delfín lying in bed. He greeted us and shook hands. Señora Ana asked him how he was feeling. Delfín answered, saying that he felt the same, that he wasn't getting better. After having spoken with him about his health, the *madrina* began to ask him what had happened with Corposa and why he had thrown her out of his house. Delfín responded, saying that she had left the house without saying anything to him. After having denied it like that, and having said that Corposa had left for no reason, he began to tell the truth. The *madrina* interrogated him, asking him why he had behaved like that with his wife, instead of spending his life being harmonious and being without angry feelings. Besides that, she told him, "When you were going to get married, *ahijado* [Godson], I asked both of you, my *ahijada* and you, to search your minds carefully. At that time you both answered me, saying that you agreed with each other and that you both loved each other like husband and wife. That's why I was willing to serve as your *madrina.*" That is how the *madrina* expressed herself. Delfin answered, saying that it had really been like that, but now it was his wife's behavior that did not please him. He said that when they were married, Delfin had bought her a skirt and had told her to wear it, but Corposa, in defiance of him and not obeying him, had not worn it. According to what Delfin said, she had taken that skirt to her daughter's in Wiyash, and when some time had gone by Corposa had brought the skirt back to Delfin's house but it was then worn out. That was the first time that there was a reason for them to be fighting, and it was when he began to hate his wife. He said that the second time was when Delfin had given a chicken to Corposa, telling her to raise it and buy something with the sale of the eggs. Corposa had taken it from him and thanked him but, he says, after a month went by the chicken disappeared. Delfin then said to her, saying that surely Corposa had taken it to her daughter's. Corposa had assured him that the truth was that the chicken had disappeared from Delfin's house because a hawk had eaten it, and that it was a lie when Delfin had blamed her. After Delfin stopped talking and telling about the reasons why they had had arguments, and that he did not want Corposa's presence, he said that Corposa should leave his house the same way she had entered it, and that he no longer even wanted to see her.

At 8:10 in the morning Corposa showed up at Delfin's house. She went inside where Delfin was lying but she did not greet him. The *madrina* told him to make up with her because Delfin was now an old man and needed a person to be together with him and take care of [*cuidar*] him, even to bring him a glass of water, and that was why he had a wife and they had got married so they could take care of each other [*cuidarse*], and that they should get along with each other because it was the duty of husband and wife. Then Delfin answered, saying that he did not want to get along with his wife because it was a worse torment to have his wife present at his side, and that was why he preferred to be alone and die without his wife looking at him. He also asked that she do him the favor of taking her things out immediately and stop walking around in his house, because when he saw his wife at his side it gave him more pains. He said that it could be that she was the cause of his death, and it was urgent that Corposa take her things away.

Having listened to all those words from Delfin, Corposa entered the room and began to take her things out into the patio. She said that she too was not agreeable to making up with her husband because he was so ridiculous and very bad tempered, and always noticed little things, and that she had entered Delfin's house just to fetch her things. Corposa began to take her things, beginning first with a little wheat in a middle-sized pot, an ounce of spun thread, two skirts already worn, two rings, and a little aluminum pot that had been a gift from Norman, her *padrino*. She also took out three empty pisco bottles, and when he noticed that one of the bottles had a cork in it, Delfín told her not to take the cork because it was his. Corposa answered, saying that the cork was a present from her *madrina* and she had to take it with her. Corposa also insisted that he give her as much as a sack of maize because she was the one who had put in more work feeding the *minkas* and that was why she claimed it. Delfín told her that he was going to give it to her after the harvest. That was the way that Corposa got her things out and they separated for good. After having witnessed that, we took our leave. At the door we met up with Delfín's son-in-law, José Baltazar, who told us that he had not interfered in any way and that later it could be that Corposa might say something. He had not gotten involved in order to avoid the consequences. We said goodbye. (AVP, Armas, 2-vi-55.)

Monday, June 13: Ana de Almandoz says she is the wedding *madrina* to Delfín and Corposa. She came to be that in company with the North American, Norman Pava. She says that it is the custom in the region of the Santa Valley [i.e., the Callejón de Huaylas] that the *padrino* is the one who should intervene through the course of his *ahijados'* marriage. Here in Vicos it is the same. When the *ahijados* quarrel the *padrinos* are called in. They look for reasons and decide which of the spouses is guilty. Based on the findings of their investigation, they impose their authority first by scolding the bad behavior of the guilty party. The *padrino* can come to his *ahijados'* house early in the morning to whip them with a rope even while they are still asleep. She tells me that she sponsored the marriage of Delfín and Corposa along with Norman Pava, that she knew that Delfín was marrying this time for the third time, that there were many times when he quarreled with his wife, and that they had already separated twice and this was the final one. Since Corposa, Delfín's wife, had already gone, Ana had first come to her to ask, as *madrina*, that they make up, but she discovered that Delfín had already thrown her out of his house for the third time. She had also complained to Enrique, not as a *padrino* but as the *patron* who has authority over the *mayorales* and everyone in Vicos. . . .

Ana says that in Delfín's case she has intervened only because the *padrino* is absent. It is better, she says, if the *padrino* goes to settle things. However, she went and everything came out in her presence. She was consulted and then taken by Corposa who, at her suggestion at the beginning accepted reconciliation, but when Delfín took it into his head not to want to welcome her, she also said that she did not want to remain. In this way the first problem which was to find reconciliation changed into the manner of arranging the division of produce and other small things.

With regard to the produce, Delfín said that he was going to give her a sack of maize, and that he could not give her more because it was needed for his funeral and so that the one who replaced him in the Hacienda would have something to eat. He could not give her anything yet from the wheat, the seed for which belonged to Corposa, because it was growing. He would give it to her when it was ripe, and that if she wanted to have her wheat that much she should transplant it to her fields so as to be more at peace. Corposa also took, with Delfín's consent, a new ring which was put on at the wedding and which Norman, she says, bought for her. She also took a sack of potatoes which, Corposa says, was what they owed her for what she had spun. . . .

Ana tells me that one day while she was washing clothes by the river, Corposa came. When she got near she sat down, at which time Ana saw she was pregnant. So she asked her when she was going to give birth, and Corposa answered that she did not know.

When Delfín entered the Carhuaz hospital Corposa he visited Ana's house. At that time she asked him again if they were getting clothes ready for when the baby was born. He answered that they were going to buy them.

Finally, Corposa came again to Ana's, and she noticed that she was no longer pregnant and she asked, "Well, have you given birth?" She answered yes, that it had been a girl but born dead.

The day that Ana went to Delfín's, she asked him what had become of the child that his wife had been pregnant with. He told her that he did not know about such a thing, that maybe she was, but that if it was so he did not know anything about it, that it might be from someone else. Ana reminded him that he himself had affirmed that it was his child. Ana says that then he told he that he never had said that. Ana thinks that the child could have been from Delfín but that, because he was angry, he did not want to recognize it in the end. (AVP, Montalvo, 13-vi-55.)

Tuesday, June 14: In the case of Delfín Coleto and Corposa Cruz, Enrique says that the cause of the break-up of this marriage more than anything is because of Delfín's stinginess. He says that Corposa has been telling him that Delfín was measuring even the food she prepared at home. He scolded her for wearing out clothing that he had given her, even though she should be the one to be angry because she let his daughter wear it. Then she had to bear it that she had to share the food she had prepared with Delfín's daughter. (AVP, Montalvo, 14-vi-55.)

Wednesday, June 22: Corposa Cruz informs me that she left her husband, Delfín Coleto, because his attitude was so stingy, both for the food she ate and for the work she did, about which he appeared to be very unhappy. His unhappiness was fed by his daughter, José Baltazar's wife, who told her father that her step-mother did not take good care of her and that all she did was to talk with people or take food to her children's places. That is a lie because she never has taken food to her daughters' homes, and she wasn't just talking with the neighbors. On the contrary, she says, "I'd even go out to find kindling so as to cook food for my husband when he was sick, and also I've taken care of him as well as I could since he got sick, and that was many months ago.

"After I left his house I came back a few days later in the company of my *madrina*, young Anita de Armandoz, but then I didn't want to stay because I knew that he'd be bothering me every day by saying, 'Well, you've gone to your *madrina* so she'd make me let you stay in my house.' To avoid that I've had to return to the house that I left three years ago when that miserable man got me out by fooling me and then later causing me to suffer from want. If I left there it was because my mother-in-law [of a former marriage], Vicetana Reyes, told me to go and live with him because she thought he was a good man. I also went to live with him because the one who was going to be my *padrino* [Pava] later told me I should go and live with him. He told me that Delfín was a good man and had nobody to help him.

"From the first moment I was in his house I helped him because he didn't have anything. It wasn't like I believed, that a mature man like Delfín would have things to eat and clothes to wear. After I lived with him for a while he started to watch me carefully, even the food I was eating, and he wasn't satisfied with the way I did things. When he got sick I took care of him all the time. Even in the Carhuaz hospital I cleaned up his messes, so that now he can tell me, 'Get out, you lazy woman, you're only good for eating food.' I know that in all of that he was helped by his son-in-law and his daughter. Now that I've returned to this house, I'll stay with my mother-in-law, if I have to eat dirt and water, but I won't have anyone telling me, 'You're lazy, you're good for nothing, and get out of my house!' But I still want him to give me a share of the maize harvest in payment for all that I've helped him with all these three years. If he doesn't share it with me I'll go to Don Enrique to make him do it. If Don Enrique can't, I'll go to the Police Post and have them make him pay for my services for the three years I've helped him. My *madrina* told Delfín to give me a share of the harvest, but up to now he hasn't done it even though I know he's been harvesting that maize that I had cultivated because he's been sick all that time."

Vicetana Reyes tells me that Corposa married Delfín because she believed he was a good man and could provide for her. She also said, "I was afraid that the gringo who was living with Delfín, Norman Pava, would be angry and blame me for being the one who didn't want Corposa to go and live with Delfín, and also because my grandson, José Baltazar, would be angry and say that I was getting in the way of Corposa's going to live with his father-in-law. When his *padrino*, Norman, was living in his house, Delfín was very good to Corposa, but when he left Delfín began to bother her a lot, watching what she was doing and what she was eating. Soon after Delfín came to get Corposa she told me that people talked about Delfín, saying that he was a very stingy and suspicious person, but I didn't believe it until recently."

Now Corposa wants to go off and work on the coast, or to some other place. Just yesterday, Abner Montalvo said to her, "Let's go to Lima and there you can be with my wife." But she does not want to leave even for a short time because, she says, there she will miss her two daughters who live here." (AVP, Martínez, 22-vi-55.)

Tuesday, July 5: Delfín is newly very ill and he tells me about his relatives that have been visiting him. One of them is his sister Ursula who lives in Cullwash. She has come to see him several times, especially when he had just separated from his wife Corposa, but currently she has not come to see him for many days. He assumes that she must be very busy with things. We cannot guess to what degree she has hard feelings toward Delfín, although when he speaks of her he feels a little like crying.

I made a visit to Ursula Coleto. We talked about her brother Delfín's illness, and her words were of a complete resignation to the demise which was going to take place. That is, she now feels certain that he is going to die and that now there is no remedy to hold back the event. She also told me that she had visited him at different times, but that she had not done so for several days. She gave for a reason that she had been very busy with her livestock. Nevertheless, from the time I arrived I could see that it was not the animals that were the compelling reason, because she was just spinning and she told me that her daughter had gone out to pasture the animals. One must think that surely on some occasions she has to go out herding, but she has a daughter who is of the right age and can go and take care of such duties. (AVP, Montalvo, 5-vii-55.)

Monday, August 1: While going through Wiyash, the army veteran who was with me told me about the death of the ex-*mayoral* Delfín Coleto, saying that he had passed away yesterday, on Sunday. After I heard all of that I asked him to go to the deceased's house, and we went there. José Baltazar, who is the deceased's son-in-law, came out to greet me and shake hands. I asked him if it was true that his father-in-law had died. José told me that the *ruku* [the deceased] had died on Sunday, July 31, around 5 in the afternoon, and that they hadn't been able to cure him with anything in the last moments.

After giving me that news, José Baltazar invited me into the room where what was left of Delfín Coleto reposed. I saw that they had him laid out on a blanket. We left and he took me to another room where they were weaving a cloth for the *ruku*'s shroud. He told me that the funeral would be with a mass if the priest was willing. The mass was going to be celebrated in the Hacienda's church, but it was changed to Marcará. He said the funeral was going to be on Thursday, the 4th of this month.

After he finished telling be all this about his father-in-law's death, he began to speak about the deceased's ex-wife, telling me that the deceased had left a sack of maize for her, that is Señora Corposa Cruz. She had not wanted to receive it, or take it away. He had offered it to her and the deceased had made good on his promise to give it to her.

When José Baltazar said all that to me, I told him that the best thing to do would be to have the deceased's ex-wife sent for. So then he told me that he was going to send her a message, and about a half hour later

Corposa Cruz appeared. She greeted me and the others, but she did not even say so much as, "I'm going to look at my husband." On the contrary she wanted to quarrel with her step-daughter about some wheat. I told her that the deceased, as he had offered, was giving her that sack of maize and that she should take it with her or she would lose it. But Corposa told me that the amount of maize was too small, because the *ruku* had had a big harvest. Then she said that she had the right to receive some wheat from them because she had provided the seed. María, the deceased's daughter, told me that the wheat was going to be used up in a meal for the people who were coming there today and tomorrow, and so because of that she could not give any to Corposa. Corposa only had the right to take her maize.

After Corposa had argued with her step-daughter, I said to her that, instead of giving condolences or having pain at the death of her husband, she had come to make trouble, and that this was not right. I immediately made her take the sack of maize that the deceased had left for her.

Corposa's step-daughter was seated in the patio rolling a skein of black thread which was so that they could make a ribbon for the deceased. Corposa recognized that the thread had been spun by her, and she approached her step-daughter to tell her that the thread belonged to herself. The step-daughter answered, saying that the thread was needed, that they were going to use it for a ribbon for the deceased. Corposa grabbed one of the skeins and went into the kitchen saying that she had forgotten to take her wooden spoon. She also brought out a pot that belonged to her. That is the way Corposa behaved in the deceased's house, raising such a stir and quarreling with her step-daughter. Then she sought out one of the people she knew among those who were going by on the footpath and called him to help her take out the sack of maize. After that, Corposa left the deceased's house. José Baltazar's wife came crying to me, saying that her step-mother was not grieving for her father's death but that, on the contrary, she was very happy, and that was why she was making such a disturbance in the house. After that I left the deceased's house. (AVP, Armas, 1-viii-55.)

Tuesday, August 2: Delfín Coleto, former *mayoral* of the Hacienda Vicos, died on Sunday, July 31, at 4 in the afternoon. He will be burried on Thursday. Last night Enrique Luna, Aliro Armandoz, Buenaventura Armas, Federico Kauffman, and I, went to the wake. His family was there, including his son-in-law, José Baltazar, his daughter, José Baltazar's wife, his grandson, Andrés Sánchez with his wife, and Marcos Cruz, Pedro Meza, Domingo Tafur with his wife and small son, Modesto Colonia with his wife and son, Delfín's cousin Hipólito Lázaro, Justina Tadeo who is Andrés Cruz's daughter-in-law, Victoria Meza, and the *cantor* [chanter] Nicanor Sánchez.

Delfín was on a table covered with blankets and a poncho, his head covered with a white cloth, and on top of this a hat. At Delfín's head was a crucifix, and near it a very thin candle which was slowly burning.

The room where Delfín was laid out was small, so that some people were outside in the *corredor*. In the room the men were separated from the woman, each on opposite sides of the table. Under the latter was a woman and her small son. There were also some children wrapped in blankets who were sleeping.

Near to the *cantor* were some men. Nicanor had a small book with funeral chants in Quechua and Spanish. Each chant had two verses which they were repeating in a slow manner with very hoarse voices, possibly from the coca and alcohol. The men who surrounded the *cantor* repeated the verses after he had finished them. When Nicanor finished his two verses was quiet while the others finished their response in a chorus. Nicanor Sánchez knows how to read but he does it with difficulty. His little black book is now old and there are some lines which can not be read clearly any more. Domingo Tafur held another candle to give them light.

All the men had their ordinary hats on, except Domingo Tafur who was wearing a black hat. Similarly, the women wore hats of that color.

When Enrique Luna noticed that the *mayoral* Delfín's whip was at his side, he said, "They've given him his *mayoral*'s whip!" Domingo Tafur replied, saying, "Let's see the one he's punishing now." Enrique answered that there was only punishment in this life, to which Domingo said, "That's true, thanks sir." Then Enrique said, "Delfín was already old and he had to die, but the relatives who have come are few. Poor Delfín!"

Aliro and Enrique brought two bottles of alcohol, one of which was given to José Baltazar and the other to Delfín's daughter, but neither one of them offered us any even though they were drinking. Later they brought us out a *mate* of sweetened chicha. Maybe they prepared it for us because they were just drinking unsweetened chicha.

The men chewed coca. They drank alcohol along with the women.

A little while after we came, the *mayorales* Herminio Colonia and Fortunato Reyes showed up. The hosts offered them chicha and alcohol. They had brought nothing. When Herminio Colonia came in, Domingo Tafur made this comment: "The bully has come!" He said it in a very low voice which could barely be heard.

José Baltazar said that the Marcará priest would come to Delfín's funeral. He will pay just 110 *soles*, because Delfín always employed him and his name shows up in the priest's register. Otherwise, he would have charged him 200 *soles*.

Corposa Cruz did not come to the wake.

When we left the chants with their sad responses were going on, the same as when we came in. (AVP, Martínez, 2-viii-55.)

It seems in these field materials as if everything has turned around, that an uncanny spirit has taken possession of a romantic narrative and twisted it into something unrecognizable where nothing is as it was at the beginning, not even the ethnographers' scientific detachment and distance. From a simple matter of exploring <u>patient care</u> in folk and scientific medical systems the series of "messages in bottles" seems to have become not only tragic but ugly and mean as well. The "stars" of this social drama, a "folkloric" and "demonstration" one staged by the Project, performed another drama or series of dramas completely opposed to Project expectations. It or they resist interpretation; indeed, they defy it. An interpretation depends upon a kind of cultural synonymy, but where synonymy is missing the interpretation is not necessarily invalid.[17] Or is synonymy missing?

In fact, there are several narratives constructed in these field notes: not merely the stories of Delfín Coleto and Corposa Cruz but those of the writers and of you and me, the readers. For us—you and me–because those narratives of the writers of the observations are forever fixed–we have good reason to suspend judgment and disappointment as we did with Sarah Levy's story. Especially with Cruz whose life went on. What I read in the notes is an unwarranted reaction to her, a kind of "loss of Eden," a blaming of "all the world's discomfort on the female" (Millett 2000:53), on the part of the mestizo ethnographers who appear to have interpreted her actions, negatively, as a shameful display of greed and uncaring. But these are narratives seen through an optic of Peruvian patriarchy which is not identical with that of North America, for all patriarchies are not one. Theirs were not Vicos narratives but mestizo ones. They "expected more" from her, more care, more love, more abjectivity, more passivity, and, clearly, more silence, than she was willing to provide. That was *their* narrative. From her point of view, that of a Vicosina and not that of a mestizo male, she was entitled to compensation for the labor she had contributed. That was *her* narrative. Millett (39-40) writes of the modernity to which the fieldworkers aspired: "[W]omen have certain economic rights, yet the 'women's work' in which some two thirds of the female population in most developed countries are engaged is work that is not paid for. In a money economy where autonomy and prestige depend upon currency, this is a fact of great importance. In general, the position of women in patriarchy is a continuous function of their economic dependence." Cruz's behavior seems to have offended some masculine sensibilities, and it may yet offend more, for her anything-but-passive actions. She was only being her own woman. Since Vicos patriarchy was incomplete from the point of view of either North American or Peruvian machismo, the opposite of "disappointment" in Cruz is called for. Her independence can be celebrated! But that is *my* narrative. You are free to construct something close to *your own*.

If I had never felt love and hatred simultaneously, fear and rage, pleasure and unpleasure, sadness and elation, and if I had never felt completely cut off from others, unable to articulate pain or joy, I might then be in some kind of non-site that would permit me to pass judgment on Corposa Cruz and Delfín Coleto. But their performance in all the narratives– really an "overperformance," as overdetermined, as a palimpsest–is not alien to me, and I do not think it will be alien to you. Their separateness and loss are familiar. The uncanniness of the drama dissolves and we suddenly become close to the players. The tragedy relocates itself into the heart of the Project, where the players were abandoned.

There remains one issue to pursue: Andeanists' neglect of the abuse of women in the Andes. This is to be observed in the Project's work on this case. Orin Starn (1999:175-176) points out:

> Until quite recently, many anthropologists had ignored or downplayed the question of power and inequality between the sexes in Andean society.... The enthusiasm for things Andean carried over into a benign view of gender in the region as a matter of complementarity and cooperation. Too many studies glossed over the frequency of wife beating, the reluctance of parents to educate girls, the exclusion of women from village leadership, and other obvious indications of inequity. Although the emphasis on the richness of village ritual, religion, and ecology was a valuable antidote to stereotypes of Andean inferiority, the desire to see the best in the Andes meant anthropologists simply failed to grapple fully with the serious discrimination and violence against women.

Perhaps the case of Corposa Cruz and Delfín Coleto can help us see what we have overlooked.

Ill-Being in Vicos and Peru

We are now outside the folkloric. Dirks, Eley, and Ortner (1994:6) point to "a growing tendency to move culture out of the realm of the exotic custom, the festival, the ritual, and the like and into the center of the historical problematic, or, rather, to recognize that the rituals and festivals are sites in which larger and more dynamic fields of discourse, larger and more powerful hegemonies, are being constituted, contested, and transformed." At this point I think we may be ready to raise the question: what, really, do the concepts of *calor* and *frío*, indeed the whole "rigamarole" of the folklore of sickness and curing in Vicos, represent? Our response must be that they are metaphors for the feelings of pain, suffering, and unpleasure that flow through people in an oppressed and exploited community in which misery is abundant and there are not enough good things to go around. They are religious concepts and, as such are not subject to testing for "truth" or "falsity" but should be examined in order to ascertain their meaning.[18] "As a religious problem," Geertz (1973:104-105) says, "the problem of suffering is, paradoxically, not how to avoid suffering but how to suffer, how to make of physical pain, personal loss, worldly defeat, or the helpless contemplation of others' agony something bearable, supportable–something, as we say, sufferable." The Vicos concepts cope with suffering "by placing it in a meaningful context, providing a mode of action through which it can be expressed, being expressed understood, and being understood, endured." The Project did its best to keep its distance by focusing on development, "potato power," and "demonstration effect," because there was simply no way for it to alleviate or even address these elemental issues of unhappiness, dis-ease, and ill-being in Vicos–the alterity of Vicos, the difference that was deferred.

Sherry Ortner (1999:11) writes in her introduction to the recent celebration of the work of Clifford Geertz: "'Culture,' if it is to continue to be understood as a vital part of the social process, must be located and examined in very different ways: as the clash of meanings in borderlands; as public culture that has its own textual coherence but is always locally interpreted; in fragile webs of story and meaning woven by vulnerable actors in nightmarish situations; as the grounds of agency and intentionality in ongoing social practice." We see all of these processes in the Vicos culture of pain. Further, we see in the cases presented that the Project's efforts to bring the advantages of "modern scientific medicine" to Vicos succeeded only partially, more often by chance than by plan. The mobile clinic and the dispensary brought medications to Vicos which would not otherwise have reached many people, and we may not deny the good that they did.

Scientific physicians examine their patients' physical signs and listen to their reported symptoms. They do not debate the nature of pathology with their patients, nor do they decide on therapeutic measures in joint discussion with them. If we compare this with the give and take of a Vicos diagnostic-therapeutic session, in which the medical practitioner is likely to be a relative or a skilled neighbor, where other persons are present and participating in the diagnosis, where both the illness and the therapy are subject to debate by everyone, and where patients and their families are free to repeat the session with as many healers as they can find or to try a variety of remedial alternatives. Moreover, in modern scientific medical practice, as Albrecht and Levy (1984:48) note: "What is good for the doctor, hospital, medical supply company or pharmaceutical firm may not be good for the patient. We possess a medical care system appears to have many ineffective parts and which may actually cause a great deal of harm." And Lois Pratt (1976:201) presents a stinging indictment of modern medicine in the United States:

> One consumer problem which is clearly rooted in the structure of medical care is the impotence of the patient and family in medical care transactions–their lack of control over the care received and the arrangements for obtaining care. As a result, consumers may not get the care they want or need, and they cannot protect themselves against hazardous medical practices.
> The professionals' dominance is sustained by laws and other formal arrangements which protect the profession from monitoring by consumers; for example, physicians control the state medical boards and accrediting agencies, individual physicians are assured a high degree of autonomy by licensing laws that make renewal of a license a routine matter and by weak peer review mechanisms. Physicians have maintained control over medical information by establishing their right to own medical records and test materials, by the custom of carefully screening information given to patients about medical procedures and findings, and by the formal channels of authority within hospitals which protect the physician's exclusive right to communicate with patients about diagnosis and therapy.

In general, the idiom of the physicians did not erase Vicos medical discourse as much as it was erased by it. This was less the Project's failure and more the failure of modern scientific medical practice. Yet the Project, giving preference to its study of "beliefs," made little or no attempt to interpret Vicos medical language. The providers of illness narratives were treated as sources of data and evaluated in terms of their "demonstration potential." Is this not the fate of all monological and unreflexive modernity projects that wish to extend their forms of enlightened opacity to their Others? While we cannot ask the Project to leap ahead of its time, we cannot excuse it either. Its principal error was its blindness to the elitist nature of scientific medicine. It also failed to grasp the commodified nature of modern scientific medicine, where the high cost of medical education combined with the high cost of outfitting new physicians with the instruments they need to practice medicine as they know it, effectively erases poor people from the benefits of their intervention. If this is an aporia in wealthy North America, a place which tolerates hoards of street people, what are we to expect in a poor country like Peru, and for the poorest strata in Vicos? Thus, modern scientific medical discourse is erased by poverty.

Although a sector exists that is served by modern medicine in Peru, medical facilities are distributed most unequally. A quarter of a century ago, on the national level there existed one physician for 2,070 persons and 435 persons for each hospital bed (Guerra, et al. 1973:v). Yet, according to Hall (1969:100-101), while there was one physician for every

700 persons in the Department of Lima, there was only one physician for every 26,500 in the Department of Huancavelica, one of the least modernized departments in the country. Hall adds, "In five departments the ratio was worse than one per 15,000 and in only three was it better than the national average of one per 2,200." In 1964, while 5.6% of the hospital beds per thousand population were in the Lima metropolitan area, only 0.6% of them were located in population groupings of less than 10,000 people (53).

In the decade of the 1970s, Doughty (1976:101) notes that the Department of Lima had only 25.7% of the country's population while it had 45% of the hospital beds and was served by 57% of the physicians. In 1986, according to Lip. Lazo, and Brito (1990:69) "38% of the hospitals and 55 per cent of the beds" were in the Lima-Callao area which contained 31% of Peru's population. These researchers comment that "30 years later . . . centralism has become more pronounced" (184). Moreover, with budget cuts hospitals have begun to come apart structurally. Carrillo (1988:110) reports: "Deterioration was particularly evident in building walls and in surgery areas; in contrast, administrative offices were in the best repair."

Zschock (1988:4) notes that "Peru uses three-fourths of its health sector resources to support expensive urban hospitals, and only one-fourth for lower-cost health centers and health posts providing primary health care to its urban and rural poor. As a result, six million Peruvians–almost a third of the Peruvian population–have no access to modern health services." In relation to the largest urban area, Paul Doughty (1976:100 comments:

> The clustering of medical personnel and facilities within Lima and Callao leaves no doubt that these are the places to go when one requires serious medical care, bypassing the provincial clinics and hospitals where understaffing is a chronic trait, and the lack of equipment bewilders medical doctors accustomed to urban facilities. Since there are frequently operating rooms without lights or perhaps scissors, laboratories without modern hypodermic needles, and wards with no nurses, peasants surmise–often correctly–that one only goes to the provincial hospital when he [sic] is about to die. A review of hospital statistics supports this observation, only 3 percent of patients succumb in Lima hospitals, which handled 44.5 percent of all the nation's patients in 1965, whereas 4.4 percent of those in other hospitals died. In Lima, medical care can be truly excellent; in rural areas, it may be altogether absent.

The skewed nature of the distribution of health care is accented by Mesa-Lago (1988:236-237) who reports on the treatment of a tiny minority of patients under the care of Peru's social security systems: "The most extravagant medical care program expenditures for contracted services have probably been payments for medical care abroad. From 1978 to 1982, 326 beneficiaries were treated in the US, Canada, the UK, and Spain at a total cost of US $7.25 million. In 1982 alone, 131 insured benefitted from this service at a cost of US $5 million–a figure equivalent to 1.6 percent of total [social security] medical care expenditures for that year. The average cost of this benefit was US $38,168 per beneficiary."

With regard to the supply of physicians, Hall (1969:108) observes: "It is clear that Peru could benefit from many more doctors. The question is whether they can be paid for and effectively put to work." Hall (69) notes that "a reasonable supply of health personnel" could be provided "in accord with the country's ability to support this personnel and the principal health problems encountered." However, he finds evidence that suggests that conditions of "unmet demand . . . do not exist in Peru and indeed for some professions the reverse situation prevails." A large supply of health personnel exists exactly where unresolved health problems are the most severe. He describes the development of the medical career:

> The paths a young medical graduate may follow in developing his [sic] professional career are varied, though several patterns predominate. After internship, almost half of the graduates seek employment in the provinces, where competition is less than in the capital and the chances of a steady income during the first few years are better. Almost 10 per cent leave the country for advanced study abroad, primarily in the United States, and according to recent information, a substantial number decide not to return to Peru.
>
> The majority of those who prefer to remain in Lima or other large cities seek government positions in order to obtain a measure of economic security during the period when they are developing their private practice. The positions are limited, however, and many cannot find employment. As a result, a large number end up working without pay in a charity hospital hoping to attract a few paying patients or eventually be named to one of the salaried jobs. (98.)

Lip, Lazo, and Brito (1990:52-53) rely on older statistics from 1964– presumably because there have been no updates and there is little evidence that the situation has changed. They report that of 5,235 physicians in Peru, 28.6% had to rely on salaried work while only 3.7% were self-employed. The rest combined self-employment with teaching or with work in a variety of public and private occupations. The same authors note, with regard to a current sample they took of 367 physicians, that only 67.03% were adequately employed while 25.4% were underemployed and 1.63% were unemployed. 6% were not available for employment in medicine because they were retired, ill, or had left the profession: "In the cases of their condition of having abandoned professional practice, they had been fully employed before entering their current occupational status. The cause of their abandonment of medicine was the decision to devote themselves fully to non-medical occupations with greater incomes." 10.6% of the sample "indicated that they had taken up commercial and service activities out of the medical field, and to a lesser degree in industry, agriculture, and construction" (136-137).

The Vicos situation illustrates well the conditions prevailing in Peruvian rural communities relative to health. If a dispensary-clinic–now officially designated as a "health-post"–was finally built there, it was probably due in great part to the road which connects Vicos with Marcará, one which was built in Hacienda times, in the early 1940s, for the purpose of transporting produce to the market. This road made possible the free access of health teams from Huaraz in the 1950s. It was the Project's existence that created interest among high-level officials in the Peruvian Ministry of Public Health, and whose objective was a preventive health plan rather than a curative one. Nevertheless, the plan's strategy was to introduce a curative program with a view to "attract and familiarize the people with health workers and their duties" (Montalvo 1967:94-96).

The 1954-55 annual report of the Project, contains a few details of the arrangement between the Ministry and the Project, a description of Abner Montalvo's activities, and an account of the new clinic:

> Since the end of June a health team has been coming to Vicos twice a week. It consists of five people: a physician, a nurse, two assistants, and a social worker. It is here to extend to the Indians the services of a modern clinic. The initial reaction of the Vicosinos was curiosity, but more and more patients are attending it, both children and adults, for the Program takes care of anyone in Vicos, not just parents and children as in other places. At the end of 1954 some 150 families, that is, almost half of the total number of Vicos families had members registered in the clinic. . .
> . Provisionally, the locale of the clinic consists of a *corredor* and some rustic rooms in the Hacienda, there being no other place big enough for it. The army reservists of Vicos have voluntarily offered their services for the construction of a modern and convenient locale for the clinic to function. The Program's Sanitary Engineer has been supervising the work which has already started with materials provided by the Project. (Blanchard 1955:1.)

At the end of the second year of the clinic's existence it had come to have a daily attendance of around 40 or 50 people, both children and adults (Blanchard 1956:1), and 63% of the total of 396 families were registered there (Montalvo 1967:19). Attendance at the clinic fluctuated in relation to the services available and the cost of medications (110). In

1957 a resident physician was assigned to service in the Vicos school by the Ministry of Education, and only later took charge of the clinic. Over the next years there came and went sanitary inspectors, laboratory technicians, radiologists, and also Peace Corps volunteers. In 1966 a Vicosino who had been trained in practical nursing in a Huaraz hospital was sent to the Vicos clinic (98-99). When I visited Vicos in 1971 the health-post was functioning and the same Vicosino was still there, offering first aid and operating a drug dispensary selling products at cost. He conducted examinations of patients between the now occasional visits from health teams stationed in Huaraz, who came to Vicos in specially equipped vehicles. However, the Vicos health-post exists at the end of a long bureaucratic chain, described by Enge and Harrison (1986:214-215):

> The Health Post is the smallest fixed-facility providing only out-patient and preventive services to semi-rural and rural populations in towns of 500 to 2,000 inhabitants. The post is simply equipped and staffed by an auxiliary nurse or a health technician with about one year of medical training who performs basic curative procedures, attends emergencies, and provides health and family planning education.
>
> At all levels in the health system, and certainly at the lowest levels, health workers constantly complain about low salaries, a chronic lack of medicines and supplies, and that the higher level officials have no interest or concern for their plight. . . . Financial and material deficiencies appear to have two causes: First, the administrative and management systems do not deliver resources where and when they are needed. Second, a chronic lack of financial resources limits the Ministry of Health's ability to support existing health infrastructure with resulting low productivity and cost-effectiveness. . . . The ministry's budget has increased drastically since 1980, but the purchasing power of the Peruvian Sol has decreased even more rapidly. The result is a net decrease in resources while the target population has increased by more than 10 percent. . . . To further complicate the picture, the ministry has since 1980 shifted financial resources away from supplies and services toward the payment of salaries. . . . Of the entire health budget, about 80 percent is spent at the central level, and then the remaining 20 percent is allocated to the regions.

In a sample made by Montalvo (1967:4) in Vicos in 1956, of 70 heads of family only 8% indicated that they had occasionally seen a physician before the establishment of the Vicos clinic, and these cases were apparently due to the fact that they had been in military service. Montalvo (19) writes:

> The physicians, socially assimilated as mestizos, were accepted by some persons as acceptable for curing mestizos but not Indians, who were

considered by the mestizos themselves as possessing a human condition which was different from that of the mestizos. Many people also wondered if the doctors really knew the way to diagnose their own illnesses. Diagnostic techniques: questioning patients, listening to the heart beat, taking samples of blood and feces, and the use of cold instruments like x-ray machines– were not considered as good as those of local *curanderos* who touched the pulse at the wrist. Such people compared *curanderos* favorably with the physicians, saying that the *curanderos* knew the illness simply by taking the patient's pulse while the physicians had to ask patients what was happening to them.

Finally, people began to question whether or not the medicine administered by physicians was desirable for the curing of illnesses caused by *frío, calor, viento*, and other magical agents.

Montalvo (24) cites an unpublished study by Héctor Martínez, carried out in 1955, on the reasons why people decide to consult a physician:

Failure of folkloric therapy	38%
Failure of therapy conducted by a *curiosa* (or *curandera*)	26%
Failure of medicine from a pharmacy	16%
Family pressure	6%
Curiosity	6%
Suggestion by a *curiosa*	4%
Suggestion by a *bruja* (witch)	2%
Not specified	2%
Total	100%

Montalvo's (111-112) study compares the responses given by Vicosinos over the decade from 1956 to 1966. It shows an increase of confidence by people in physicians, if not in the concepts of modern medicine. Between those years the number of people who believed that doctors were capable of curing illnesses caused by *calor, frío*, and *viento* increased from 3% to 47%. Those who thought physicians could cure *patza* increased from 1% to 18%, and those who believed that they could cure *susto* increased from 0% to 29%, *cólera* (anger) from 5% to 5'%, and witchcraft sickness from 0% to 5%. Of the sample, 9%, most of whom were army veterans, knew that tuberculosis was caused by germs and 16% understood that the cause of typhus was lice.

The development efforts carried out in Vicos also gave the people greater access to medical facilities outside the community. Despite an initial resistance to hospitalization, in 1966, 24 patients from Vicos who were seriously ill were taken to the Huaraz hospital (107). This hospital lacked funds and personnel, and Lancaster (1965:4) characterizes the scarcity of equipment: "The hospital's laboratory is nonexistent in that it lacks microscopes, tubes, blood-typing serums, centrifuges. . . . The truth is that it takes more paper to list its 'lacks' than its 'has.' Occasionally a microscope is borrowed from the UNICEF clinic which is located a few blocks away. Because no blood types are determined, no whole blood transfusions are made although saline and serum transfusions are possible. . . . The pharmacy, deficient in supplies, is stocked with samples from the United States and Canada. The patients sometimes fill their prescriptions here but more often go to a public pharmacy." In this capital city of the Department of Ancash, the sixth largest political division of Peru, the class structure of regional society is firmly installed. This is clearly to be noted in the treatment people receive in the hospital. Lancaster (13) observes:

> The patients are treated equally by the Nuns except whites and upper class Peruvians are given preferential treatment, because they expect and demand it. . . . The two classes could be determined by observing the reactions and methods employed by the aides. Two aides in particular resented administering to the Indian patients. One man with severe leg laceration . . . was ordered out of bed and was forced to lean against the wall while his bed was deloused. . . . Another Indian man was about 70 years old, moaned constantly which irritated one of the aides. She yelled at him and turned him roughly while straightening his bed, although he cried out in pain whenever she turned him. The old man was dead by morning not necessarily due to her handling, but his pain was genuine and she was inconsiderate.

We can hardly wonder, then, why many Vicosinos preferred home treatment, viewed modern medicine as an alternative if and when it was available, and remained victims of both infectious diseases *and* folk medical practice/malpractice. The extension of medical facilities to Vicos seemed to be a ministerial game dependent on whims, budgets, and which party was in power at any particular time. Furthermore, Peru cannot afford to put more than minimal resources into its health and welfare systems because it needs public funds to pay off foreign indebtedness. Daniel Miller (1997:41) notes: "If Communism was castigated by the West as the power of extreme left-wing ideologies to reconstitute societies in their image of the future ideal society, it seems just as reasonable to suggest that the IMF and the World Bank are agencies that have allowed extreme right-wing ideologies to activate their transformation of the world into their pure market ideal by starting with the weakest countries of the world. Just as with Communism, the ultimate justification is constantly reiterated as being the elimination of world poverty." Meanwhile, many Vicosinos have remained as needy and pained as ever. Well-being hovers around the borders of Vicos, tapped only by those who are able to penetrate them advantageously, while those who are unable to do so remain as they have been. For them, well-being continues to be erased by poverty, the power/knowledge of others, and both national and international politics.

Appendix

We are fortunate to have a description of a *shoqma* treatment by a North American student, Cheryl Chadbourn (1962:22-26) who received it from a *curandera* as a part of her research project. She describes her experience in her essay on Vicos medicine:

With the help of Enrique Luna I was able not only to interview [two] *curanderas* on the use and interpretation of *shoqma*, but also to arrange to see a *shoqma* performed by one of them [on a patient] and to have the other do a *shoqma* on me. . . . The *shoqma* which was performed on me by Nicolasa Castillo was done in Enrique Luna's home in Marcará. Nicolasa grasped the cuy firmly around the neck and began rubbing it over my body. . . . I was surprised at the amount of pressure applied; the animal gasped constantly and uttered a few squeaks, but remained passive.

The cuy is a fairly delicate animal and is often smothered or internally damaged in the process. I found it amusing that the liver, being a large and easily damaged organ, is often diagnosed as the cause of illness by the *curandera*. This seems to correspond rather well with the incidence of liver ailments in Vicos! After splitting the throat, Nicolasa held the cuy upside down over a basin of water and allowed the blood to drip in several circles. Although I was not able to find out how she reached the diagnosis, Nicolasa said that my blood was sad and "in pain." I must be suffering from sorrow. Upon opening the body wall, Nicolasa discovered that there were ridges along the stomach and said that I had frequent stomach aches. I also had chills, for when water was sprinkled on the organs they trembled. Tissues of a recently killed animal will respond in some way; they do not remain inert.

An informant said that one *curandera* sprinkled water to make her prognosis. In this case, if the lungs open and close around the heart, the patient is to have a long life and easy recovery. If they only open, recovery will be difficult or impossible. If the colon rises and falls, the patient will die; if it only rises, he or she will have a long life. . . . The *curandera* became very concerned over the fact that the stomach was not in the middle of the body but only on one side. This was explained to be the main cause of my stomach cramps and diarrhea. (I think it well to note here that I did not give Nicolasa any symptoms. She told me that I was sorrowing and had intestinal troubles, rather than the reverse.) Next she palpated the heart which she announced to be *calor*. She then washed the remaining organs separately, but they were uninterestingly normal, save the uterus which was slightly inflamed and another cause of my stomach aches. She said that she could not tell if this were caused by *calor* or *fresco*.

Nicolasa then proceeded to treat me. The major problem was to get my stomach back into its proper position, and she decided that mechanical means was the only way to accomplish the move. Placing me in a supine position, she first grasped me under the axilla and pulled, twisting and shaking me to the left. Then she grasped me around the waist and, finally, the hips, doing the same. She pressed my stomach to the middle of the abdomen and then repeated the complete procedure on the other side. For the inflammation I was advised to take two herbs, *acorma* and *huamllasin*, mashing them and drinking them with hot water. She said that sorrow was the cause of both the hot heart and the sad blood. She advised me to put some blossoms of either an orange or lemon tree in hot water and drink the mixture.

The *curandera* is believed to be able to diagnose any illness by the use of *shoqma* with cuy. I asked both [informants] how they were able to tell what is wrong, and the following is a resumé of their replies: "The heart of the cuy is enlarged and white if the person has *susto*; it is colored in a well person. I may also see that the person does not have *susto*. If there is something wrong with the heart, the animal's heart in water acts like a sponge. It seems to want to drink water. When I cut into the heart there is blood in it. There is no blood in the heart in the case of a well person. . . . The kidneys look broken or abnormal if they are not well. . . . When the lungs are bad there is a little white cap on them. Or sometimes, when you squeeze them, blood comes out. There is also much of the thing you see when you spit out or cough. . . . When a person has colic the intestine is twisted around. It and the stomach look abnormal."

Notes

1. Parts of this chapter originally appeared in "Modernización y retroceso del mito: diagnosis por medio de la magia y curación en el pueblo de Vicos, Perú." *América Indígena* 37:671-747, 1977. Other parts of that essay were included in Stein (1991d) and are omitted from this version. I have chosen to retain much of the data from the original but have rewritten a piece that is over two decades old since, within that span of time I have changed my mind. Some of the new material also appears in Stein (n.d.a).

2. I do not wish to detract from Gary Parker's excellent work on Ancash Quechua. However, in the Parker and Chávez (1976) dictionary, based on the dialect spoken in the southern part of the Callejón de Huaylas which retains an initial /h/ that is missing in the Province of Carhuaz and other northern provinces, *hampeq*, *hampi*, *hampikuy*, and *hampiy* are defined respectively as "curandero [healer] . . . remedio, curación, medicina [remedy, cure, medicine] . . . curarse [to get well] . . . medicinar [to treat or cure] . . . .", not incorrect translations but incomplete ones.

3. Derrida's (1981:61-171) essay, "Plato's pharmacy," focuses on a discussion of writing as *pharmakon* in the *Phaedrus*, a text by Plato. Derrida emphasizes writing, rather than healing, and so his intention may differ/be deferred in relation to mine in this chapter. Christopher Norris (1991:63) says: "The *Phaedrus* is . . .

a crucial text for Derrida's reading of Greek philosophy. It contains Plato's most vigorous attack on writing, couched in the same familiar terms–'presence' versus 'absence', living speech versus the dead letter. . . . To commit one's thoughts to writing is to yield them up to the public domain, to risk being misconstrued by all the promiscuous wiles of interpretation. Writing is the 'death' that lies in wait for living thought, the subtle agent of corruption whose workings infect the very sources of truth." Tom Cohen (2001:20, note 14) observes: "'Plato's Pharmacy' analyzes the pharmacological role of (the deaths of) Socrates and writing under the fictive if powerful logics of the parricide, the putting out of Being or father Parmenides (or 'Plato'), the theatrical drama of the overthrow in part. The rhetoric of this presentation keeps the index of generational replacement, overthrows, dawns, and historical effects in position for the reader, on display repeatedly." What I am extracting from Derrida's exciting commentary is his demonstration of the extremes to which thought can be carried by the privileging of speech over writing. In the Vicos cases I examine here it is the privileging of medicine over poison. This would apply to all binary oppositions. What should be emphasized, in this examination of the Project's work in Vicos, is its inability to leave *ampi* undecidable. In other words, the staff persisted in assigning a specific meaning to the term in the context of its training in Western metaphysical thinking: "obviously," *medicine* was *good*, while *poison* would "clearly" have been *bad*.

4. Erving Goffman (1986:201) writes: "Given a spate of activity that is framed in a particular way and that provides an official main focus of attention for ratified participants, it seems inevitable that other modes and lines of activity occur in the same locale, segregated from what officially dominates, and will be treated, when treated at all, as something apart. In other words, participants pursue a line of activity–a story line–across a range of events that are treated as out of frame, subordinated in this particular way to what has come to be defined as the main action."

5. Goffman (1986:202) adds to his discussion of out-of-frame action (see Note 4): "A significant feature of any strip of activity is the capacity of the participants to 'disattend' competing events–both in fact and in appearance–here using 'disattend' to refer to the withdrawal of all attention and awareness. This capacity of participants, this channel in the situation, covers a range of potentially distracting events, some a threat to appropriate involvement because they are immediately present, others a threat in spite of having their prime location elsewhere."

6. Gordon (1997:17) says: "To write stories concerning exclusions and invisibilities is to write ghost stories. To write ghost stories implies that ghosts are real, that is to say, that they produce material effects. To impute a kind of objectivity to ghosts implies that, from certain standpoints, the dialectics of visibility and invisibility involve a constant negotiation between what can be seen

and what is in the shadows."

7. Gupta and Ferguson (1997b:28, note 14) caution that we need a political perspective which "is neither a naïve celebration of resistance for its own sake (a temptation to which anthropologists in particular have too often succumbed) nor a cold analytic detachment from the compromised ground of real-world political struggles (the curse of American academia in general) but a combination of real political engagement with a skeptical strategic analysis."

8. The diagnostic/treatment technique of *shoqma* will be treated in some detail later in this chapter. We should think of it as both diagnostic and therapeutic since the cuy or guineapig is believed not only to reflect the disorder, which is why it is sometimes referred to as an "Andean x-ray," but it also absorbs the disorder from the patient. A post-mortem examination of the cuy is believed to reveal details of the illness. See also Ghersi (1960, II:94) and the Appendix to this chapter.

9. Dobyns and Vázquez (1964:16-17) identify Dr. Montalvo as an investigator of "medical and sanitary aspects of Vicos culture during field investigations conducted in 1954-56. . . . The information he collected in Vicos provided him with his bachelor's degree thesis." He received the doctorate from Cornell University in 1967. See Montalvo Vidal (1967).

10. John Collier is identified by Dobyns and Vázquez (1964:30-31) as a member of the "Vicos experiment staff" who "made a photographic study of Vicos ethnology . . . during 1954-1955."

11. *Calor* and *frío*, or *hot* and *cold*, seem only to have a slight relationship to thermal state, but, rather, refer to magical non-substances which can invade the human body. For more discussion and references, see Stein (1991d:112; 132, note 7).

12. Pietz (1985:14) writes: "Fetish discourse always posits this double consciousness of absorbed credulity and degraded or distanced incredulity. The site of this latter disillusioned judgment by its very nature seems to represent a power of the ultimate degradation and, by implication, of the radical creation of value."

13. Several cases of *susto*, Spanish for "fright," *patza* [earth sickness] in Quechua, also known as "magical fright," are discussed in Stein (1991d) in which additional references are cited. This illness, people say, is the result of a fright, being startled by something unexpected, and consequent soul-loss in which the soul is "grabbed" by the earth. See Rubel, O'Nell, and Collado-Ardón (1984, 1985) who, while they focus on *susto* in Mexico, have some general statements to make about the syndrome. Arthur Kleinman (1980:76) writes: "Hispanic-American patients who apply the illness category *susto* to depressive or anxiety

symptoms do not merely construe these symptoms differently than do members of other groups in American society but actually construct distinctive illness experiences that resemble their expectations of how patients with this culture-specific disorder are supposed to feel and behave." The same might be said of patients with *susto* or *patza* in Peru. Rubel, O'Nell and Collado Ardón (1984:112) ask these significant questions: "In communities in which the culture links onset of a folk illness to a frightening event, what distinguishes those who fall victim from those who do not? . . . For those who fall ill, what consequences do they suffer? . . . Among the victims, why are some more seriously affected than others?"

14. What is called the *corredor* is a roofed extension of a house, facing the patio, generally with a floor that is raised from the level of the patio, where much of the daily activity of the members of a household takes place when they are at home. Fleeces and blankets are spread out on the floor of the *corredor* in the evening, and that is where the family sleeps. At the back of it a door or doors lead into a room or rooms which are used for storage. When someone is sick, a bed for him or her may be laid out inside a room.

15. See Dobyns and Vázquez (1964:15, 31) for references to these individuals. The reference to Armas, a mestizo from Carhuaz who worked for the Project, identifies him as "Sargento" because he had been a *sargento* [sergeant] in the Peruvian army and had led the weekly drill of the district's *movilizables*, army veterans.

16. The late Maruja Martínez, translator of the Spanish edition of this book (Stein 2000), kindly provided this note: "This refers to *Vinagre Bully*, a preparation widely used in Peru to lower fever and relieve headaches."

17. I take my model for this statement from William Frawley's (1982:160-161) discussion of "translation as recodification," in which he asserts that "a theory of translation must indeed say something about the possibility of synonymy across codes, but if it turns out that there is *no* synonymy, the act of translation is in no way discredited or disproved. In other words, translation theory assumes that remodification occurs (and is valid) no matter what the status of identity across codes. To reduce translation thus to the question of identity is likewise to construe the act too narrowly since the falsification of identity would consequently eliminate translation, and it is patently obvious that code-crossing is occurring at present while the question of identity remains unsolved."

18. Here Geertz's (1973:123) advice is applicable: "One of the main methodological problems in writing about religion scientifically is to put aside at once the tone of the village atheist and that of the village preacher, as well as their more sophisticated equivalents, so that the social and psychological implications of particular religious beliefs can emerge in a clear and neutral light. And when

that is done, overall questions about whether religion is 'good' or 'bad,' 'functional' or 'dysfunctional,' 'ego strengthening' or 'anxiety producing,' disappear like the chimeras they are, and one is left with particular evaluations, assessments, and diagnoses in particular cases. There remain, of course, the hardly unimportant questions of whether this or that religious assertion is true, this or that religious experience genuine, or whether true religious assertions and genuine religious experiences are possible at all. But such questions cannot even be asked, much less answered, within the self-imposed limitations of the scientific perspective."

We will probably go on asking people what their "religion" is, but it's relevant to point out that Derrida (2002d:66-67) emphasizes the Latin origin (*"religio"*) of the word: "Religion circulates in the world, one might say, like an *English word*. . . that has been to Rome and taken a detour to the United States. Well beyond its strictly capitalist or politico-military figures, a hyper-imperialist appropriation has been underway now for centuries. It imposes itself in a particularly palpable manner within the conceptual apparatus of international law and of global political threats. Wherever this apparatus dominates, it articulates itself through a discourse on religion. From here on, the word 'religion' is calmly (and violently) applied to things which have always been and remain foreign to what this word names and arrests in its history. . . . *Globalatinization* (essentially Christian, to be sure), this word names a unique event to which a meta-language seems incapable of acceding, although such a language remains, all the same, of the greatest necessity here."

Chapter 6

Deconstruction and the Vicos Project[1]

A title is always a promise. Here the title does not constitute a "sentence."
It therefore has no "meaning." It acts out a "promise" in a statement
which "properly speaking" has no "meaning." ... But this literary fiction,
if it really is one, nonetheless would seek (and up to a certain point
successfully) to produce political effects and change conventions, to
legitimize or de-legitimize, to constitute, through its very irony, a new
right. In any case, this fiction cannot be *totally* grounded in existing
conventions in order to define sentences in which a word has "meaning."
This is because everything depends upon contexts which are always open,
non-saturable, because a single word (for example, a word in a title)
begins to bear the meaning of all the political phrases in which it is to be
inscribed (and therefore begins to promise, to violently ground its own
right and other conventions, since it does not yet *totally* have the right to
promise) and because, inversely, no phrase has an absolutely determinable
"meaning": it is always in the situation of a word or title in relation to the
always open context which always promises it more meaning. (Jacques
Derrida 1989b:115-116)

This goes for "deconstruction," Derrida adds, among other words in a
title. And we could apply it to the "Vicos Project," or recalling this book's
title, "the modernity project at Vicos." A project that set out to do
modernization in Vicos, and which can be deconstructed. One can make a
promise in a title, of course, knowing that one doesn't intend to fulfill it.

Derrida (2001d:66) points out: "One does not lie simply by saying what is false, as long as one believes in good faith in the truth of what one believes or assents to in one's opinions." So a title wouldn't lie if circumstances beyond one's control kept one from fulfilling a title's promise, if undecidability intervened as it always already does. I wouldn't have been lying when I said in the Preface that I was going to "apply" deconstruction to Project texts, although I might not have been in possession of sufficient information, or formation, or competence to carry it out. Derrida (67) leaves us with questions: "[I]s it possible to lie to oneself, and does every kind of self-deception, every ruse with oneself deserve to be called a lie?" I believe that all these possibilities are undecidable: I don't have the information that would let me decide rationally, but I decide just the same. Beyond all that, I have no reason to believe that I've "deconstructed" anything. I've written about the Project and I've let it deconstruct itself, during which time I've let my self deconstruct its self. A self is impossible any way, or anyway, for that matter, because "it" contains otherness, the voices of alien others, what Freud was saying in what he said when he invented the binary "conscious/ unconscious." I inherited "my self"; I did not invent it.

Here's where deconstruction begins. Derrida (2001e:102) tells us: "[W]hat does it mean to 'inherit' a tradition, when one thinks from its perspective, in its name, certainly, but precisely *against it in its name*, against the very thing it will have felt obligated to save in order to survive while vanishing? Again the possibility of the impossible: the heritage wouldn't be possible except where it becomes im-possible. This is one of the possible definitions of deconstruction– precisely as an inheritance." And then: "If deconstruction were a destruction, nothing would be possible any longer. The least desire, the least language would be impossible. Thus, within deconstruction, if one can speak here of an inside, there is this negotiation.... One could also say that deconstruction 'involves the structures' or the constructa, the things that make life or existence possible. Deconstruction makes the constructed character appear as such, which is not artificial in opposition to the natural (precisely this opposition needs to be deconstructed) but constructed or structured in view of making possible–of making possible ... what? Not only consciousness, the person, the ego, the unconscious" (Derrida 2002b:16). Deconstruction has been misunderstood as a "technique," as "interpretation," as "apolitical" (by some) and "political" (by others), as "nihilistic,"and as an irresponsible "anything goes." Derrida (1992d:22-23) maintains:

If, then, it lays claim to any consequence, what is hastily called deconstruction *as such* is never a technical set of discursive procedures, still less a new hermeneutic method operating on archives or utterances in the shelter of a given and stable institution; it is also, and at the least, the taking of a position, in work itself, toward the politico-institutional structures that constitute and regulate our practice, our competences, and our performances. Precisely because deconstruction has never been concerned with the contents alone of meaning, it must not be separable from this politico-institutional problematic, and has to require a new questioning about responsibility, an inquiry that should no longer necessarily rely on codes inherited from politics or ethics. Which is why, though too political in the eyes of some, deconstruction can seem demobilizing in the eyes of those who recognize the political only with the help of prewar road signs. Deconstruction is limited neither to a methodological reform that would reassure the given orgainzation, nor inversely, to a parade of irresponsible or irresponsibilizing destruction, whose surest effect would be to leave everything as is . . . .

This said, I now apply deconstruction (or deconstruction applies me) to the questions of whether or not the Vicos Project did (or wanted to do) good in or for Vicos, was a change agent, what is remembered of it, and whether or not it did (or wanted to do) harm. Derrida (2001e:104) says: "Answer and delay, then: an answer, at least according to good sense, is always second and secondary. It lags behind the question or the request, behind the expectation in any case. And yet everything starts with an answer." If that is so, then everything ends with a question.

Did the Vicos Project Do Good?

People can *intend* to do good, but they can also *intend* to do harm. Derrida (1978:27) points out that there is a tension in in-tention-ality. ("In-tension-ality" would sound just the same and would be written phonemically the same.) One of the best authorities on the alternating signifieds of *intention* is Jacques Lacan (1988b:234, 237) who points to a binary structure in his vision of desire to do good and its tearing:

We will now define the ego ideal of the subject as representing the power to do good, which then opens up within itself the beyond that concerns us today. How is it that as soon as everything is organized around the power to do good, something enigmatic appears and returns to us again and again from our own action–like the ever-growing threat within us of a powerful demand whose consequences are unknown? As for the ideal ego, which is the imaginary other who faces us at the same level, it represents by itself the one who deprives us.

The desire of the man [sic] of good will is to do good, to do the right thing, and he who comes to seek you out, does so in order to feel good, to be in agreement with himself, to identify with or be in conformity with some norm. Now you all know what we nevertheless find in the margin, but also perhaps at the limit of that which occurs on the level of the dialectic and progress of the knowledge of the unconscious. In the irreducible margin as well as at the limit of his own good, the subject reveals himself to the never entirely resolved mystery of the nature of his desire.

It is to be understood that desire, in Lacan's discourse, is symbolic and impressed into human subjects at an early age. Lacan (1988a:166) says: "Man's [sic] ideal unity, which is never attained as such and escapes him at every moment, is evoked at every moment in this perception. The object is never for him definitively the final object, except in exceptional circumstances. But it thus appears in the guise of an object from which man is irremediably separated and which shows him the very figure of his dehiscence within the world–object which by essence destroys him, anxiety, which he cannot recapture, in which he will never truly be able to find reconciliation, his adhesion to the world, his perfect complementarity on the level of desire. It is in the nature of desire to be radically torn. The very image of man brings in here a mediation which is always imaginary, always problematic, and which is therefore never completely fulfilled. It is maintained by a succession of momentary experiences, and this experience either alienates man from himself, or else ends in a destruction, a negation of the object." Desire to do good is torn apart at the moment it comes into existence.

It seemed clear (which suggests that it might have been unclear) to me, in retrospect, when I began this book five years ago that the Vicos Project desired to do good. Now that all seems undecidable. The Project not only kept secrets from the Vicosinos; It kept secrets from itself. After all is said and done, Derrida (1992e24) suggests: "One can stop and examine . . . a secret, make it say things, make out that . . . there is something there when there is not. One can lie, cheat, seduce by making use of it. One can play with the secret as with a simulacrum, with a lure or yet another strategy. One can cite it as an impregnable resource. One can try in this way to secure oneself a phantasmatic power over others. That happens every day. But this very simulacrum still bears witness to a possibility which exceeds it." Despite Holmberg's stated goal of "working himself out of a job," in his absence the Project's secret was its desire for power.

It also seems now that *desire-its-self* contains otherness. Lacan expresses this with the notion of "radical tearing": desire is wanting (in its many senses), doing without, wishing for, needing, a rip, a tear, a ring around a hole .... Otherness is embedded in the texts. No cause for alarm. It happens.

Derrida (1976:162) tells us: "We must begin *wherever we are* and the thought of the trace, which cannot take the scent into account, has already taught us that it was impossible to justify a point of departure absolutely. *Wherever we are*: in a text where we already believe ourselves to be." In a later work Derrida (1996c:86) adds: "If we analyzed the concepts of decision and responsibility in a cool manner, we would find that undecidability is irreducible within them. If one does not take rigorous account of undecidability, it will not only be the case that one cannot act, decide or assume responsibility, but one will not even be able to *think* the concepts of decision and responsibility." This frees us to view "undecidables, that is, unities of simulacrum, 'false' verbal properties (nominal or semantic) that can no longer be included within philosophical (binary) opposition, but which, however, inhabit philosophical opposition, resisting and disorganizing it, *without ever* constituting a third term, without ever leaving room for a solution in the form of speculative dialectics. ... Neither/nor, that is, *simultaneously* either/or" (Derrida 1982a:43).

We can now return to the Vicos Project's intention to do good, bearing in mind that development/underdevelopment, remedy/antiremedy, practice/malpractice are undecidables rather than binaries. The goal of its research was to find ways of allowing Vicos to develop, to take remedial measures, to practice applied anthropology. Immediate land reform, i.e., the erasure of the hacienda system, would have placed Vicos in the situation of thousands of other Peruvian rural communities, in which case the Project and other observers would not have needed to intervene but could merely have observed Peruvian change processes taking place over the next half century in Vicos. Unfortunately, in its brief moment of only five years, the one intervention the Project could not bring about–the *sine qua non*, the indispensable, the strategic, the key–was that one. At that initial point the Project made its decision to accept the terms of its contract and continue the hacienda regimen. At that point, too, it began what James Fairhead and Melissa Leach (1997:54-55) call "the continual production of supportive knowledge" within a "methodologically supported certainty that alternative methods and data sets [were] disqualified as inadequate, naive, unscientific or simply improbable." The knowledge it produced excluded all evidence to the contrary. We can call this, with Pierre Bourdieu (1977:19) "*learned ignorance* . . . a mode of practical knowledge not comprising knowledge of its own principles."

This does not mean that the Project was *wrong*. P. H. Gulliver (1985:53) asks, "should anthropologists work in the applied field if and where that involves work in a regime that is colonialist, neo-colonialist, oppressive or otherwise abhorrent?" This is not easy to answer,

> if only because moral and ideological views differ as much among anthropologists as among any other people. The probable fact that in many regimes there is not an environment benevolent to the anthropological enterprise should debar applied anthropology there. The work would be a failure, a cover-up, and quite possibly to the disadvantage of the people studied. On the other hand, where some policy is in prospect–say, the building of a large dam or the definition and registration of land titles–and where there is reasonable opportunity for the anthropologist to work and genuinely to be heeded, his [sic] involvement in the applied field can be advantageous. I think it is easy to exaggerate the probable contribution of anthropology under almost any regime; nevertheless, it is no less easy to exaggerate its uselessness and to abandon anthropological skills and perceptions in the face of the real difficulties of making them in any way effective.

Except for its assistance in the final expropriation in favor of the Vicosinos in 1962, in which Vicos was overcharged for the land, the Project probably did some good. As Gulliver has so well stated the case, "it is easy to exaggerate the probable contribution of anthropology under almost any regime." Despite the posturing, fetishing, and self-promotion of Project personnel, there was an element of permissiveness that reached Vicos from Ithaca, where Holmberg was most of the time. But Holmberg stated his desire "to work himself out of a job." Tragically, he did so prematurely and to the detriment of the Project.

The other major impediment to doing good, for the Project, consisted in its failure to acquire language skills. Not one of the North American staff was able, or took the trouble, or deemed it important to learn Quechua. Would this have been good?   No, indispensable!   Of all the "methodological" skills, the years of training in anthropology and related disciplines, shelves of books read, and progress reports written, there was nothing that could substitute for it. The lack of language skills effectively placed a screen between the Vicosinos and the "gringos," a screen of mestizo and Vicosino intermediaries and interpreters of varying degrees of interestedness and disinterestedness.[2]

It was not inappropriate to hope for the development of Vicos. "Development" is an overdetermined sign. Alan Rew (1997:81) says:

> "Development" is as much a set of currently existing institutions and practices with an international remit and compass as it is sets of concepts containing powerful ideological visions with normative tools of reform on

behalf of economic growth and poverty alleviation. Development is therefore at the same time rhetoric, official practice and political theory, while also serving as a framework for descriptions, on a global scale, of human misery and hope.

So too are "modernity" and "rationality" overdetermined. One face of modernity is not a happy one. Whether or not we agree with what he says about our favorite fetishes, Stephen Tyler (1991:81) writes a compelling indictment of patriarchal, phallic, exploitative, utopian, insensitive modernity:

Modernist works are global and transcendent discourses and solutions. The fairy tales of those grim brothers of the nineteenth century, Darwin, Marx, Freud, and Einstein are paragons of the type. Nothing less than the whole here–of organisms, of history, of the mind, of the universe. These master narratives command sub mission and signify the author's and man's victory over the mystery, recalcitrance, and chance of nature. Heavy, heroic characters contest here. Man and nature are joined in a combat that will ultimately end in man's complete control over the dark powers of the mother. Man, the hero, wars with nature, the mother, the source, and his persistence in the face of vicissitude and trickery leads to the inevitable victory that transforms nature from source to resource, something to be exploited. Direct confrontation and force overwhelm the resistant negativity of nature unrevealed, and the wily feminine forces of darkness are dispersed by the light of reason. Such are the meta-narratives of emancipation, liberation, and enlightenment that tell of the overcoming of arbitrary authority by technology, by rational work. Reason, that technology of thought, liberates the mind from ignorance, superstition, and illusion. Industry, the technology of work, emancipates the laborer from nature just as evolution, the great technology of nature, liberates man from animal and frees energy from inert mass. One monological tale tells this story again and again. Modernist discourse is always utopian, and its message is the meaning of the "final solution." (Emphases omitted.)

Yet we should not freeze modernity at one pole. It is undecidable. Néstor García Canclini (1995:268) writes:

[M]odernity is not only a space or a state one enters into or from which one emigrates. It is a condition that involves us, in the cities and in the countryside, in the metropolises and in the underdeveloped countries. With all the contradictions that exist between modernism and modernization–and precisely because of them–it is a situation of unending transit in which the uncertainty of what it means to be modern is never eliminated. To radicalize the project of modernity is to sharpen and renew this uncertainty, to create new possibilities for modernity always to be able to be something different and something more.

In this sense, the modernizing movement–among whose contradictions is having contributed to engendering new fundamentalisms, strengthening them, and making them more threatening–is the adversary of all fundamentalism. It is the (uncertain) certainty that there is no dogma, no absolute foundation, that proscribes doubt and innovation.

As James Carrier (1995a:204) says of "the notion of autonomous and calculating market actors" in "capitalist markets": the connection of rationality "with real markets and market actors needs to be demonstrated rather than assumed." I think that it is precisely because capitalism is irrational that it does so much harm in the world. The Vicos Project did no rational calculation. On the contrary, it was rooted irrationally in a desire–and a rather insatiable one–to see its version of "development" occur in Vicos, to foment it, control it, and point to it with pride. Indeed, observing the gringos in Vicos reminds me of the state that Emma Crewe (1997:75) characterizes as "deliciously reassuring, because it shatter[s] the stereotypes of whites being essentially efficient, punctual and sharp-witted."

Carrier (1995a:205) concludes that the "allure of absolute difference, of the distinctiveness of the modern West from all the rest, makes it hard to see similarities among different types of society, just as it makes it hard to see differences within a single type." In other words, by yielding to a "demand for difference" and framing the Vicosinos as "Others," Project staff failed to grasp Vicos rationalities as well as their own irrationalities.[3] In this process, it is evident to me that the Project "orientalized" the Vicosinos and "occidentalized" themselves: it reduced the complexity of Vicos to a mirror-image of its own irrationality and it reduced its own complexity to a mirror-image of what it saw in Vicos (cf. Carrier 201). Thus, it engaged in the monologue of "the West talking to itself about itself and its dominance in the world" (202). This said, it should surprise no one to learn that "critical anti-market strands in modern thought," as well as "the Market triumphalism of Adam Smith and his successors . . . stand in an interior rather than exterior relationship to one another," and "firmly within, rather than outside, modernity" (Kahn 1997:76). We are confronting nothing less than Bourdieu's (1977:79) "intentionless invention of regulated improvisation," and I concur with his statement that "because subjects do not, strictly speaking, know what they are doing . . . what they do has more meaning than they know."

Was the Vicos Project an Agent of Change?

Michel Foucault (1977:137-138) raises some questions which have bearing on the notion of the subject as agent:

> Is it not possible to reexamine . . . the privileges of the subject? Clearly, in undertaking an internal and architectonic analysis of a work (whether it be a literary text, a philosophical system, or a scientific work) and in delimiting psychological and biographical references, suspicions arise concerning the absolute nature and creative role of the subject. But the subject should not be entirely abandoned. It should be reconsidered, not to restore the theme of an originating subject, but to seize its functions, its intervention in discourse, and its system of dependencies. We should suspend the typical questions: how does a free subject penetrate the density of things and endow them with meaning; how does it accomplish its design by animating the rules of discourse from within? Rather, we should ask: under what conditions and through what forms can an entity like the subject appear in the order of discourse; what position does it occupy; what functions does it exhibit; and what rules does it follow in each type of discourse. In short, the subject (and its substitutes) must be stripped of its creative role and analyzed as a complex and variable function of discourse.

Foucault does not ask us to dispense with the subject. Rather, what he urges us to do is deconstruct it.

A new generation of scholars is appearing, one which is bypassing a certain "structuralist solicitude and solicitation" (Derrida 1978:6) in the fierce but sterile debate on the "essential" question of whether or not human beings can be agents in resisting oppression and determining the conditions of their own existence. This is doubtlessly a consequence of the decline of what Samuel Weber (2001:55) calls "the ego psychology of the autonomous subject so dear to American liberal culture." In *The Interpretation of Dreams*, Freud (`1965b:563) states: "The question whether it is possible to interpret *every* dream must be answered in the negative. It must not be forgotten that in interpreting a dream we are opposed by the psychical forces which were responsible for its distortion. It is thus a question of relative strength whether our intellectual interest, our capacity for self-discipline, our psychological knowledge and our practice in interpreting dreams enable us to master our internal resistances." Weber (2001:57-58) responds:

> Interpretation, for Freud, does not reconstruct and resuscitate so that we may register and apprehend—it partakes of, and in a process of conflict

that no totalization can ever comprehend. . . . [In Freud's text], the ambivalence can be retraced to the exigency of *Selbstüberwindung*—a term that means practically the opposite of its translation in the Standard Edition [of Freud's work], which reads "self-discipline," since what is both required, and stated, is the overcoming-of-self, i.e., of the ego. Such overcoming, however, the "mastering of internal resistances," still inevitably entails mastery, control, discipline, and hence, as such, appeals to the very ego that it seeks to "overcome."

Sherry Ortner (1995:186) points out: "Agency is not an entity that exists apart from cultural construction (nor is it a quality one has only when one is whole, or even when one is an individual). Every culture, every subculture, every historical moment, constructs its own forms of agency, its own modes of enacting the process of reflecting on the self and the world and of acting simultaneously within and upon what one finds there." Johannes Fabian (1998:20-21) observes: "If freedom is conceived not just as free will plus the absence of domination and constraint, but as the potential to transform one's thoughts, emotions, and experiences into creations that can be communicated and shared, and if 'potential,' unless it is just another abstract condition like absence of constraint, is recognized by its realizations, then it follows that there can never be freedom as a state of grace, permanent and continuous. As a quality of the process of human self-realization, freedom cannot be anything but contestatory and discontinuous or precarious. Freedom, in dialectical parlance, comes in moments." How then can we question the indisputable fact that people are creative and adaptable? Agency needs deconstruction, for people are not equal: some are women and others are men, children and adults, motivated and unmotivated, more and less competent, and presented with different opportunities. (See Amartya Sen 1992, particularly his chapter on "agency achievement" [56-72] and his statement on "freedom to achieve" vs. "actual achievements" [148].)   Gayatri Spivak (1996:294) points out that agency can mean anything: "When one posits an agency from the miraculating ground of identity, the question that should come up is, 'What kind of agency?' Agency is a blank word."   Then, too, agency is further complicated by theatricality, as Catherine Liu (2000:113) points out:

Linguistic performance is always susceptible to theatricalization. ., . . [T]he problem is that any speaker at any time can be simply *acting*. What acting might in fact be is, of course, highly problematic in all cases, but when we are dealing with actors we are perhaps adding to the confusion of agency: an actor follows a script and a nonactor supposedly does not. But it is certainly possible to imagine that a certain amount of acting takes place far from, the stages of the world.

Florencia Mallon (1994:1511) says:

> The question of complicity, hierarchy, and surveillance within subaltern communities and subaltern cultures is a thorny one indeed, one that cries out for nuanced and sympathetic treatment. On one side, raising this question makes clear that no subaltern identity can be pure and transparent; most subalterns are both dominated and dominating subjects, depending on circumstances or location in which we encounter them. A leader of a movement can become a collaborator or go home and beat up a wife or children; a collaborator can use power to protect a subaltern community or individual; or, as happened repeatedly in anticolonial rebellions, individuals who had profited personally from the power structure reneged on their earlier complicity and led major upheavals. On the other side, complicity or hierarchy does not make impossible, in any larger sense, the occasional, partial, contingent achievement of a measure of unity, collaboration, even solidarity. These ever-shifting lines of alliance or confrontation, then, are not deduced from specific, already existing subaltern identities or subject positions. They are constructed historically and politically, in struggle and in discourse.

Agency is problematic. Freud has shown us that human beings are not only motivated by their conscious wishes but by their unconscious desires and fears. In a parallel manner, Marx observed that we do not fashion historical events according to our will but, rather, we are haunted by ghosts from the past.[4] Just as Jameson (1981:61-68) calls attention to the "political unconscious" of psychoanalytic theory (e.g., "childhood traumas, primal scene fantasies, Oedipal conflicts, 'period' illnesses such as hysteria" in relation to "the historical institution of the nuclear family" and "the historicity of the sexual phenomenon"), we can likewise call attention to the primary process (i.e., the psychoanalytic unconscious) in historical writing on agency. Barthes (1968:10-11) writes: "[U]nder the name of style a self-sufficient language is evolved which has its roots only in the depths of the author's personal and secret mythology, that subnature of expression where the first coition of words and things takes place, where once and for all the great verbal themes of his [or her] existence come to be installed. Whatever its sophistication, style has always something crude about it: it is a form with no clear destination, the product of a thrust, not an intention, and, as it were, a vertical and lonely dimension of thought. Its frame of reference is biological or biographical, not historical: it is the writer's 'thing,' his glory and his prison, it is his solitude." There can be little doubt that the matter of agency touches the emotional issues that drive historians and anthropologists, indeed, all of us, to fight bitter battles over the contested bodies of who, we or the others or both, are "victims" and who are "agents." Or we can declare war on ourselves, hoping to replace "id" with "ego," the favored one, the one we'd like to be ruled by. Derrida (1978:198) deconstructs:

> *Différance*, the pre-opening of the ontic-ontological difference . . . , and of all the differences which furrow Freudian conceptuality, such that they may be organized, and this is only an example, around the difference between 'pleasure' and 'reality,' or may be derived from this difference. The difference between the pleasure principle and the reality principle, for example, is not uniquely, not primarily, a distinction, an exteriority, but rather the original possibility, within life, of the detour, of deferral . . . and the original possibility of the economy of death.

If we question the Project's agency "as change agent," then we should also question the Project's changes–and not only the changes it introduced in Vicos but in the context of changes which have been taking place in Perú as a whole. First, as in the rest of the country, a population explosion: the number of Vicosinos more than doubled in the three decades from the 1950s to the 1980s. In 1982 there were 4,820 people in the community (Doughty 1987:146), too many for too little land despite increasing productivity. Vicos had become an exporter of people, and there were enough Vicosinos in Lima and Huaral to form "regional associations" (147). Doughty (2002:238) reports the current population as 5,500: a decade and a half ago, the community decided to distribute its commons lands, resulting "in the formation of an instant 'minifundia' [microholding] system of property ownership, with the average family plot being about one hectare."

We have seen how some Vicosinos entered modern markets by becoming producers of commodities. During the times of intensified potato production in Vicos, however, I see no evidence that Vicosinos fetished potatoes. Arjun Appadurai (1986:54) links "the fetishism of commodities" to "sharp discontinuities in the distribution of knowledge concerning their trajectories of circulation." And Igor Kopytoff (1986:83) follows this briefer statement by pointing out that

> even things that unambiguously carry an exchange value–formally speaking, therefore, commodities–do absorb the other kind of worth, one that is non-monetary and goes beyond exchange worth. We may take this to be the missing non-economic side of what Marx called commodity fetishism. For Marx, the worth of commodities is determined by the social relations of their production; but the existence of the exchange

system makes the production process remote and misperceived, and it "masks" the commodity's true worth (as, say, in the case of diamonds). This allows the commodity to be socially endowed with a fetishlike "power" that is unrelated to its true worth.

Kopytoff (66-67) introduces the notion of "a kind of biography of things in terms of ownership," in association with the people who make them, endow them with meaning, use them, circulate them, change their meaning and use, and terminate them." This in no way gives "life" to things. If Dobyns (see Chapter 3), therefore, endowed potatoes with "power," this was his problem. The Vicosinos, in contrast, learned more about the market. I should write "markets," since *The Market* is an abstract model and does not take account of the irrationalities of real life (Carrier 1997). At the same time, *The Market* is a discourse, as Carrier (48) notes:

> To see the Market model as being like a language suggests that the empirical adequacy of the model is not the point, at least for explaining why it is so common. While a language may have a vocabulary that is rich in certain areas and impoverished in others, we would not normally assess it in terms of whether it is right or wrong, internally consistent or inconsistent. Rather, a language provides the tools by which its speakers communicate with each other about the world.

Here the point is that Vicosinos have learned this language, and that this enabled them to function in the several kinds of marketing situations that are found in the region and the nation. The acquisition of greater power over production also constitutes the learning of a new language and leaving behind an older one. This is not just a Vicos process, or a Peruvian process, but a world process. David Ludden (1992:270-272) observes with regard to India, but globally as well:

> Capitalism wrote a new kind of agricultural text. In the old text, authors gleaned knowledge from peasants; farm practice was expertise. But capitalist Europe disseminated progressive techniques authorized by science, which invented a new agricultural semantics. Peasant wisdom became folklore. Experts spoke the language of laboratory, model farm, efficiency, and statistics. . . .
>   Agriculture thus became an object for development by being abstracted from society and culture, broken into input-output data, translated out of the vernaculars into the English of scientific semantics, and projected back onto farmers by institutions that imagined localities only as identically empirical units, passive under their gaze, objects of observation and responsibility. Thus became necessary to talk about the "average village" or "typical peasant" in statistical terms. Developing

agriculture in the farm world of capitalism transformed agricultural knowledge in India by changing its mode of production, shifting its creative focus to the metropolis, and obliterating local experience as an active agent in the formation of expertise.

However, the process of market participation is not something new for Vicos or any other Andean community. Joel Kahn (1997:90) points out that the

> notion that there are non-modern terrains in the remoter regions of South America, and that their occupants have an external perspective on modernity, is highly problematic. Such occupants prove remarkably difficult to locate in a region of the world that has been effectively re-made by European conquest, the forced movement of peoples, the extraction of wealth, the rise of "modern" nation-states, the activities of multinational corporations over a period of almost 500 years, to say nothing of processes of cultural imperialism and cultural globalization that began with the Iberian missionaries.

Penelope Harvey (1994:68) comments that "this implicit division of local practices into the authentically indigenous and the imported western or mestizo has equally detrimental effects both rendering most contemporary Andean social practice inauthentic, and essentializing a notion of authentic indigenous culture in opposition to, and separate from, recognizably western practices. For the past five hundred years Andean peoples have engaged with outsiders– Europeans, North Americans, each other! There is no justification for limiting Andean cultural authenticity to the pre-Hispanic." Steve Stern (1995:77) writes, "Andean peoples, as individuals and as corporate groups," have "intervened in all kinds of product, land, and labor markets . . . throughout the colonial period," a process which "cast them in diverse roles–as collaborative allies, as junior and senior partners, and as competitive rivals" with non-Andean actors; moreover, "Andean initiatives played a major role in determining the specific character and workings of the colonial market economy." Tristan Platt (1995:262-263) notes for Bolivia what is also true for Perú, that "liberal policies in the second half of the nineteenth century marginalized many" rural communities "that, at the beginning of the Republic, had enjoyed greater commercial opportunities," a history which challenges the misconception that Andean "approaches to the market only began to intensify during recent decades of 'development' in a unidirectional advance toward 'progress.'" And Olivia Harris (1995:351-352) observes that while the definition of "Indianness" at the present time "is a function of . . . limited market participation," we see "that the commonplace idea that Andean peasants were and are resistant to participation in commercial circuits cannot be sustained." Small farmers and farm workers have not resisted "markets as such," but rather "to certain forms of coercion by which they have been forced to hand over their surplus, to offer their labor and produce at disadvantageous or unjust rates, or to sell or give up land vital for the reproduction of their agriculture." The Vicos Project in no way brought Vicosinos into the market because they were already there..

Vicosinos have learned not only Spanish but the content of Peruvian primary and secondary education, for a *colegio* has been established in Vicos.[5] This, combined with the new language of agricultural inputs and outputs, and the language of modern commerce, situated them in regional and national markets as Peruvians, not as Vicosinos. Here, most appropriately, we may pose James Clifford's (1988:175) question: "How does one grasp, translate a language that is blatantly making itself up?" To paraphrase Clifford's self response: we are called on to confront the limits of our language or of any single language; we are called on to construct a reading "from a debris of historical and future possibilities," a construction which is "hybrid and heteroglot."

The school, one of the Project's monuments, can also be viewed as one of the Vicos undecidables. This is so in the national context as well. Bourdieu (1974:32) points out:

> It is probably cultural inertia which still makes us see education in terms of the ideology of the school as a liberating force . . . and as a means of increasing social mobility, even when the indications tend to be that it is in fact one of the most effective means of perpetuating the existing social pattern, as it both provides an apparent justification for social inequalities and gives recognition to the cultural heritage, that is to a *social* gift treated as a *natural* one.

In the school, Bourdieu (35) continues, "the handicaps are *cumulative*, as children from the lower and middle classes who overall achieve a lower success rate must be more successful for their family and their teachers to consider encouraging further study." Thus:

> By giving individuals educational aspirations strictly tailored to their position in the social hierarchy, and by operating a selection procedure which, although apparently formally equitable, endorses real inequalities, schools help both to perpetuate and legitimize inequalities. By awarding allegedly impartial qualifications (which are also largely accepted as such) for socially conditioned aptitudes which it treats as unequal "gifts" it transforms *de facto* inequalities into *de jure* ones and *economic and social* differences into *distinctions of quality*, and legitimates the transmission of

the cultural heritage. In doing so, it is performing a confidence trick (42).

Timothy Mitchell (1991:73) describes the 1844 Egyptian School in Paris, which is not unlike what I have observed of the school in twentieth century Peru: "Like the army, the school offers unprecidented techniques by which students can be 'fixed' in their place and their lives meticulously regulated. Every hour of the day has been marked out, divided into separate activities whose boundaries are given not in the unfolding of the activity but in the abstract dimensions of hours and minutes."

Bourdieu (in Bourdieu and Wacquant 1992:166-167) has noted how "France has eliminated a large chunk of its peasantry in the space of three decades without any state violence" through differential out-migration of women and the resulting increase in bachelorhood. This is a case of "symbolic violence," that is a "violence which is exercised upon a social agent with his or her complicity." Education, similarly, is but another way to "disappear" small farmers and farm workers.

One can, then, feel a certain degree of sympathy for Claude Lévi-Strauss who writes:

> The only phenomenon with which writing has always been concomitant is the creation of cities and empires, that is the integration of large numbers of individuals into a political system, and their grading into castes or classes. Such, at any rate, is the typical pattern of development to be observed from Egypt to China, at the time when writing first emerged: it seems to have favored the exploitation of human beings rather than their enlightenment. This exploitation, which made it possible to assemble thousands of workers and force them to carry out exhausting tasks, is a much more likely explanation of the birth of architecture than the direct link referred to above. My hypothesis, if correct, would oblige us to recognize the fact that the primary function of written communication is to facilitate slavery. The use of writing for disinterested purposes, and as a source of intellectual and aesthetic pleasure, is a secondary result, and more often than not it may even be turned into a means of strengthening, justifying or concealing the other.

But is it fair to express contempt for writing, when one has disseminated via writing–and most seminally–one's theories to so many, and with such hegemonic results for a time? David Olson (1985:15) observes:

> [T]he effects of literacy on intellectual and social change are not straightforward. As we noted at the outset, it is misleading to think of literacy in terms of consequences. What matters is what people do with literacy, not what literacy does to people. Literacy does not cause a new

mode of thought, but having a written record may permit people to do something they could not do before–such as look back, study, interpret, and so on.   Similarly, literacy does not cause social change, modernization, or industrialization. But being able to read and write may be vital to playing certain roles in an industrial society and completely irrelevant to other roles in a traditional society. Literacy is important for what it permits people to do–to achieve their goals or to bring new goals into play.

Derrrida (1976:109-110) calls the "scorn for writing" an "ethnocentric oneirism," a dream, and concludes that writing is undecidable, "beyond good and evil" (314).[6] Would we wish, because the pedagogic system is so bad and social opportunities for literate people so limited, to withhold literacy from Vicosinos? Since it is undecidable, we can also examine its empowering side. Bourdieu and Passeron (1990:127) offer us a possibility of a change in the field:

> Maximizing the productivity of pedagogic work would ultimately imply not only recognition of the gap between the linguistic competences of transmitter and receiver but also knowledge of the social conditions of the production and reproduction of that gap, that is, knowledge both of the modes of acquisition of the different class languages and of the scholastic mechanisms which consecrate and so help to perpetuate inter-class linguistic differences. It is immediately clear that, short of relying on the accidents or miracles of individual conversions, such practice can be expected only from teachers objectively constrained to satisfy a specifically and exclusively pedagogic demand; to put it another way, it would require a pedagogic action directed towards the inculcation of a different relation to language and culture, i.e. subordinated to the objective interests of a quite different public, and teachers recruited and trained to satisfy the requirements of posts that were differentiated technically–and not merely hierarchically–and thus capable of preventing the play of circular alibis that is authorized by the traditional cumulation of the tasks of teaching, research and even management. In short, only a school system serving another system of external functions and, correlatively, another state of the balance of power between the classes, could make such pedagogic action possible.

Ulf Hannerz (1992:87) points out that there is "no sharp break between contemporary literate cultures and what one might facetiously call an idiocy of oral life," but instead "a long series of small and large steps by which humankind has gradually realized the potential of writing." We could just as easily see an idiocy of literate life, perhaps not so facetiously, in Hannerz's depiction of "a literacy of street signs and birthday cards, of cereal packages and newspaper obituaries, of shopping lists and car license plates," a literacy he calls "petty literacy, not the high-power critical literacy of the bookish." With reference to the work of Shirley Brice Heath, Hannerz admits that there are more kinds of literacy than these two extremes: "And we can safely assume that literacies such as these differ not merely in frequency and intensity of use but also in the cultivation of levels of skill, with regard to reading as well as writing." In her stimulating study of two poor "communities," black and white, and the "community" of the unpoor black and white, all in the Piedmont region of the Carolinas, Heath (1996) outlines radically different cultural profiles of reading and writing that originate in different lifestyles. Of the unpoor, both black and white, she says:

> As the children . . . learn the distinctiveness between contextualized first-hand experiences and decontextualized representations of experience, they come to act like literates before they can read. They acquire habits of talk, associated with written materials, and they use appropriate behaviors for either cooperative negotiation of meaning in book-reading episodes or story-creation before they are themselves readers. . . . At home, children see adults and older siblings reading for various purposes and in different ways. . . . There are similar rules for using writing and for recognizing the functions it serves family members. (256-257.)

Heath (355) notes that poor children in school "had to learn to 'code-switch' between systems." In other words, the task for Vicos children—monolingual in Quechua and inexperienced with literacy in their homes—had, and still have, rather formidable obstacles to overcome in achieving literacy of any degree and quality. That some of them have achieved it is testimony for the human will to know.

The relative isolation of the Callejón de Huaylas that prevailed for several decades into the twentieth century, combined with the relative weakness of the central government in Lima, limited the presence of the state. Eric Wolf (1982:81) described such a situation in which "strategic elements of production as well as means of coercion are in the hands of local surplus takers":

> Under such conditions local figures can intercept the flow of tribute to the center, strengthen their grip over land and the population working it, and enter into local or regional alliances on their own. Such local alliances, however, are frequently directed against the center but also against members of their own class, with the result that factional struggles will ramify throughout the countryside, thus weakening their class position. Factional struggles, in turn, may allow the elite at the center to survive by

strategems of divide-and-rule. Paradoxically, internecine faction fights also weaken the position of the primary producers, since in the absence of strong central control they must seek protectors against unrest and predation.

The extension of the state into Perú's hinterland, so well described by Nugent (1994, 1996, 1997, 1998) has severely limited what is left of *gamonalismo*. There is much more democracy than there was a half century ago, but the state is another undecidable, for state power can also commit horrors. Nevertheless, the restrictions of the hacienda system are gone from Vicos and other rural communities, along with the *hacendados*. In the Callejón de Huaylas, as in other regions, new elites in formation are too busy trading commodities in markets to concern themselves with the phantom of "peasant revolt," a fear which characterizes agrarian societies around the world (cf. Chatterjee 1993:171). The term "peasant" is already outmoded, and it's disappearing–but, to paraphrase a well known quip by Mariátegui, it's not disappearing fast enough! We should speak, rather, of "farmers" and "farm laborers." In Vicos, as in the community studied by Linda Seligmann (1995:180-181) in southern Perú, a "new stratum of intermediaries," people who worked with campesinos as "teachers, bureaucrats, extension agents, and entrepreneurs" brought new ideas about "the meaning of national integration, the exercise of legitimate authority, and the kinds of objectives that communities could strive to meet through their local political organizations." New culturally hybridized identities have been formed. I use "hybridity" here in the sense of an acknowledgment "that identity is constructed through a negotiation of difference, and that the presence of fissures, gaps and contradictions is not necessarily a sign of failure" (Papastergiadis 1997:258).[7] With a changed relation to the land, voting rights, commodification, and social mobility, both horizontal and vertical, Vicosinos employ a new set of discourses in combination with old ones. It is a part of the crisis which Perú has experienced over the last half century with the transition from a predominantly rural to a predominantly urban country. This has been taking place everywhere in the Andes, with the construction of roads, the extension of education, judicial reform, the decline of agriculture in the GNP, agrarian reform, and the dissemination of constitutional rights along with knowledge of legal procedures for demanding them. As a consequence of the state's reach, bringing modernity, more democracy (however incomplete), and the displacement of *gamonalismo* (see Nugent 1997),[8] postmodern changes are now becoming apparent. The new languages have resituated Vicos, along with thousands of other rural communities by making it possible for people to question what Bourdieu

(1977:168-169) calls "doxa, the sum total of the theses tacitly posited on the hither side of all inquiry." This constitutes a popular "critique which brings the undiscussed into discussion, the unformulated into formulation." He adds: "Crisis is a necessary condition for a questioning of doxa but is not in itself a sufficient condition for the production of a critical discourse. . . . It is only when the dominated have the material and symbolic means of rejecting the definition of the real that is imposed on them through logical structures reproducing the social structures (i.e., the state of the power relations) and to lift the (institutionalized or internalized) censorships which it implies . . . that the arbitrary principles of the prevailing classification can appear as such." And, thus, "the boundary between the universe of (orthodox or heterodox) discourse and the universe of doxa, in the twofold sense of what goes without saying and what cannot be said for lack of an available discourse, represents the dividing-line between the most radical form of misrecognition and the awakening of political consciousness" (170).[9]

Part of the rural "resituation" involves what Marisol de la Cadena (1990:90-91) refers to as ethnic "volatilidad". She goes on to comment:

> In Andean populations neither *mistis* [mestizos in the Quechua of southern Peru] nor Indians are essentially or exclusively one or the other. The daily dynamic is charged with the force of *ceasing to be Indians*, because being such today means embodying the *impotence* of servility. Far from being submission, it is resistance. Resistance to the oppression of the colonial inheritance. . . . One of the central aspects of this is ceasing to be poor, which is equivalent to ceasing to be Indians.

As Homi Bhabha (1994:114-115) points out, hybridity intervenes in the cultural to change values and rules of recognition so that the identity of authority is altered. Cultural items are retained, but they no longer represent an essence: "The partializing process of hybridity is best described as a metonymy of presence. . . . It is the power of this strange metonymy . . . to so disturb the systematic (and systemic) construction of discriminatory knowledges that the cultural, once recognized as the medium of authority, becomes virtually unrecognizable." When I visited Vicos in 1971 the style of clothing which identified persons as Vicosinos was rapidly disappearing, faster among men than among women (cf. de la Cadena 1991), but more people of both genders had the purchasing power to obtain the clothing they wanted and which they used not only to dress themselves but to assert their changing identity. Carola Lentz (1995) reports, similarly, for Shamanga, Ecuador: "Male migrant workers respond to the discrimination they experience on the coast with attempts to hide their ethnic affiliation by adopting mestizo dress. Wearing 'modern' clothing upon returning to the highland, however, is also a way for them to display their access to cash and to rebel against the mestizos who attempt to stigmatize them as members of an inferior, race. Many men use this adoption of mestizo dress as a way of emphasizing their raised consciousness. Women, on the other hand, held and hold on to their 'traditional' dress–which is very distinct from that of the mestizos–though they supplement this dress with new fabrics and colors." In this, Shamanga is much like Vicos. Elsewhere in Ecuador dress and identity are variable, as Mary Weismantel (1998:76) shows in her study of ethnic identity in Zumbagua, Ecuador:

> Ethnicity in the parish is primarily marked by clothing or by language. "Indians" speak Quichua, "whites" speak Spanish. "Indian" clothing is unconstructed; it consists of lengths of cloth that can be wrapped or folded about the body to form ponchos, shirts, shawls, sashes, and carrying cloths. . . . The more tightly fitting and tailored a person's clothing, the "whiter" he or she is. Also, "Indian" clothing, whether handwoven or purchased, is heavy and thick and worn in many layers as protection against the cold. "Whites" wear thin polyester clothing, though they may don heavy "Indian" ponchos at night. This thin clothing represents the fact that "whites" typically spend their days indoors in shops or buses, while "Indians" work out-of-doors, unprotected from the elements. . . . Dressing styles also correlate youth, masculinity, whiteness, and wealth. Young people's clothing is more "white" than that of their elders, while Indian male dress becomes part of the lexicon of "white" female dress. "White" women and cholas wear trousers, and when a "white" woman is cold, she dons not an Indian shawl but rather the masculine poncho.

Barthes (1990:26) employs what he calls "a *vestimentary code* in written clothing, in which a class of signifiers (the garment) will *stand for* a class of signifieds (the world of Fashion) even more than the sign itself." Surely we could construct "vestimentary codes" in spoken clothing and worn clothing as well, thus, languages of clothing:[10] in the latter case, "what I wear" tells you "who I am" and "how I expect you to relate to me, and what I expect you to expect that I expect".[11] De la Cadena (1991:18) writes of Chitapampa, a rural community near Cusco:

> The city, which accommodated Indians at the beginning of the century, is changing ideologically and its influence is becoming a "deindigenizing" one. The features which had served as "markers" of interethnic differences–*chullos* [wool caps with ear flaps], *ojotas* [sandals], and

bayeta [homespun cloth]–are disappearing, and are being replaced by others, effective in regional culture to indicate the differences between "Indians" and *mistis*, but less visible and much more quantifiable. . . . Only one very small part of the population of Chitapampa has a definite ethnic identity, as Indian or mestizo. When any Chitapampino [resident of Chitapampa] is asked for the ethnic status of another inhabitant of the community, the most common response is that "he or she is in process," which emphasizes the nebulous quality of peasant ethnic identity.

Such oscillation between one set of codes and another seems to be nothing new in the Andes: Regina Harrison (1989:58) employs the same concept in her analysis of an early seventeenth century document. Similarly, in de la Cadena's Chitapampa case, people are neither "peasants," nor intermediaries, nor elites, that is, not "Indians," not mestizos, and not whites. Oscillating between one "essence" and another is about as de-essentialized[12] as one can get. Elsewhere, de la Cadena (1996:40) discusses race-switching in Cusco historically: "[The] relational or context-sensitive aspect of racial interactions allowed a person who was 'Indian' in a given relationship to become mestizo in another, depending on who was inferior and who was superior in the relationship. In certain circumstances, identifying oneself as Indian could even be a personal choice subject to change."

In her most recent work, appropriately entitled *Indigenous Mestizos*, de la Cadena (2000:316-317) writes abut market women and then generalizes to both genders:

The notion of indigenous mestizaje [the process of becoming mestizo] is . . . evident in everyday subordinate discourses and is concretely embodied in the figure of mestiza market women. They fuse the dominant rural-urban divide, and the elite would not hesitate to call them "uppity" Indians. Their gendered identity, which slipped through the grasp of class rhetoric . . . connotes a notion of mestizaje that runs counter to its dominant definition. I see mestizas as Andean indigenous individuals, mostly non-Indian, yet occasionally and relatively Indians, whose identities combine the endless motion between contestation and acquiescence. . . . By calling themselves mestizas/os and silencing Indianness, urban indigenous Cusqueños [inhabitants of Cusco] rebuke stigmas of all sorts and proceed to de-Indianization, which consists of (among other things) producing, celebrating, and staging a very "impure" indigenous culture, which is empowering because it has been stripped of such elements of Indianness as illiteracy, poverty, exclusive rurality, and urban defeat.

Despite great regional differences in Peru, Vicosinos are also "in process." People are learning new codes and idioms. Thomas Turino (1992:451) quotes one of the Lima migrants from Conima, in the Department of Puno:

> In Conima people depend on nature for their subsistence. Here we work for wages, for money, and so we don't need those beliefs any more. Since they [the people in Conima] depend on nature, if it doesn't rain one year, they bring water from the *montaña* [eastern slopes of the Andes] and it always rains; or if there's a downpour they have a ceremony to stop the rain. *T'inka* and *ch'alla* are like prayers. But we work for wages and we don't need these things.

Turino comments: "This is not a declaration of skepticism with regard to these highland beliefs and practices, it is simply a pragmatic affirmation which maintains that such things are not relevant in the current situation of the residents. Conimeños in Lima explain that they do not speak Aymara any more for similar reasons." Nevertheless, it is not that easy to switch grammars. Deborah Tannen (1996) shows that while modern Greek is disappearing among third generation Greek-Americans, and will be gone in the fourth generation, "those very third generation Greek-Americans who have lost the Greek language may not have lost, or not lost entirely, Greek communicative strategies." I think a similar process is going on in Peru. Old languages can be replaced by new ones, but the old grammars have ways of influencing the new ones, and similarly old, dead ones revived are influenced by new contexts; and languages can turn against their speakers.[13]

We could speak of "linguistic hybridization," much like what has happened to Peruvian music. The Lima-born children of Turino's Conimeños who learn to play *zampoñas* (panpipes) in Lima, play music which, because of differences in "musical values and practices", sounds different (Turino 1992:440).[14] Copies of folkloric performances of Andean music and dancing in Lima also have a different context and a different intention from the original.

Zoila Mendoza (1998:170) notes with regard to the performance of folk music and dance in Cusco: "During the first decades of this century *indigenistas* [indigenists] faced a paradox. The cultural elements that they promoted as 'authentic' and vulnerable belonged to a subordinated majority that, through the political struggle, was questioning the legitimacy of the existing power structure. In the light of this paradox, the *indigenista* founders of the *instituciones culturales* [cultural institutions] used the concept of 'folklore'. This concept was readily applicable to the conflictual arena of the public expressive forms and offered the possibility to reinterpret and curb the potential threat posed by those cultural elements." Mendoza (179) concludes:

> Although public and private *instituciones culturales* have attempted to establish boundaries around the forms and meanings of highland music and dance by classifying them as 'folkloric', 'indigenous', or 'mestizo', and modeling them after 'invented traditions', these expressive forms have constantly surpassed these boundaries even in the context of contests and other staged presentations. Outside this context the performers who consider their music and dance 'folkloric' have used this concept to validate their creative efforts and to gain new spaces and recognition for their performances. Thanks to this acknowledgment within the regional and national arena, the performers of Andean music and dance have been able to give new meanings to these performances. Even though the concept of 'folklore' has pejoratively marked the performances of Andean music and dance at the national level (mostly because these forms are supposed to represent the highlanders), and many gender and ethnic/racial stereotypes have been fostered through folkloric events, this concept has helped legitimate a field where in Cusco people rework their ethnic/racial, gender, and social-class identities.[15]

Interest in folklore has grown in recent years and there is a purpose in preserving, revising, and inventing codes. Paerregaard (1997b:223) observes:

> Formerly regarded as the by-product of an unappreciated rural life style, Andean folk culture is today viewed with fascination and admiration. Although cultural prejudices against Andean people still prevail in Perú, many urban migrants now regard their cultural background as a potential source of income as well as a strategic vehicle to change social status and redefine ethnic identity.

Zygmunt Bauman (1997:57) finds in the postmodern a "true emancipatory chance" which "does not lie in the celebration of born-again ethnicity and in genuine or invented tribal tradition, but in bringing to its conclusion the 'disembedding' work of modernity: through revealing conditions of individual freedom which transcend both national and ethnic/tribal limitations; through focusing on the right to choose as the sole human universality, on the ultimate, inalienable individual responsibility for that choice, and on the complex State- or tribe-managed mechanisms aimed at depriving the individual of that freedom of choice and that responsibility." This chance is not easily attainable, however. As Laclau (1996:49-50) points out, "Whether . . . new groups will manage to transform [existing] institutions, or whether the logic of the institutions will manage to dilute–via co-optation–the identity of those groups is something which, of course, cannot be decided beforehand and depends on a hegemonic struggle. But what is certain is that there is no major historical change in which the identity of *all* intervening forces is not transformed." Perú has changed profoundly and is changing. For the twenty-first century we must alter Mariátegui's maxim to read: without the hybrid no Peruvianness is possible! In this way, to paraphrase optimistically the choice offered by Jorge Basadre, Perú is a possibility rather than a problem.

Face-to-face with such "process," we can no longer support an "essential" conception of Vicos, that is, the assumption "that certain mental phenomena or ways of thought are essential attributes" of a society or culture–in this case Vicos–"and that, because of this, they are explanantions of choice for the actions of people who, by criteria of birth, upbringing, citizenship, and/or residence, might be regarded as belonging to" it (Vayda 1994:326). In other words, we should try to avoid any "emphasis on cultural uniformity, structure, and stasis at the expense of diversity, mobility, and change" (324). This not only applies to Vicos but to Perú, and even to ourselves, for that matter. However, "de-essentializing," in the same way that deconstruction is also reconstruction, carries with it a "re-essentializing" component (see Note 11). James Carrier (1995b:28) points out with regard to Western anthropologists who have studied Melanesian societies:

> The people and societies they confronted really were different from urban America, Britain, and Australia, home to most of those researchers. It should be neither a surprise nor a cause for censure that those anthropologists sought to explain that difference or that they sought to do so by developing and invoking a set of principles that accounted for what they saw, or even that those principles defined some of what they saw as more important and worthy of attention, and some as less. It is difficult to imagine how people could conduct research, much less live their daily lives, in any other way. And, to continue the example, if such selective perception is unexceptionable for Western anthropologists studying closely the societies of Melanesia that they confront in their field-work, it is even more unexceptionable for their understanding of the taken-for-granted Western societies from which they came.
>
> In other words, the sheer existence of essentialist rendering and selective perception is likely to be routine. Pointing out that existence is not very revealing. Even pointing out that it causes errors and misperceptions, though worthwhile, is not very exciting, for these are inevitable. Instead, it is necessary . . . to begin to show how that essentialist and selective

vision arises, how it reflects people's social and political situations, and how it affects their lives and works.

It would, then, be an error to essentialize participants in the Peruvian marketplace as "commodified." Moreover, as David Nugent (1996:263) shows, historically in twentieth century Peru, "commerce and accumulation" have been seen "as liberating and empowering at one time, but as evil and dangerous at another." As I suggested at the beginning of this chapter, there is no purpose in invoking only the negative poles in concepts like "commodity," "modernity," "integration," "development," or even "essence," although such demonizing has a strong "resonance" (Kahn 1997:69-71) in many scholars. Rather, as Diana Fuss (1989:20) suggests, whether they are used in defense of subaltern people or in assertion of some metaphysical authority depends on *who* uses them, *how* they are deployed, and *where* their effects are felt:

> There is an important distinction to be made ... between "deploying" or "activating" essentialism and "falling into" or "lapsing into" essentialism. "Falling into" or "lapsing into" implies that essentialism is inherently reactionary—inevitably and inescapably a problem or a mistake. "Deploying" or "activating," on the other hand, implies that essentialism may have some strategic or interventionary value. What I am suggesting is that the political investments of the sign "essence" are predicated on the subject's complex positioning in a particular social field, and that the appraisal of this investment depends not on any interior values intrinsic to the sign itself but rather on the shifting and determanitive discursive relations which produced it. . . . [T]he radicality or conservatism of essentialism depends to a significant degree, on *who* is utilizing it, *how* it is deployed, and *where* its effects are concentrated.

"Essence" is undecidable. James Clifford (1997:331) has made a significant contribution to the understanding of global socio-economic process by suggesting what is essentially (and I choose the word deliberately) a "de-essentializing" of capitalism[16]:

> Commodities and markets release forces that tear down borders and unsettle empires; they also consolidate dominant polities. Because economic globalization works both with and against national attachments, it is premature to decree either the end or the consolidation of nation-states. And although the centers of capitalist power are still largely in the European and North American "West," this is changing. Asian economic power [recent economic disasters to the contrary notwithstanding!] is an inescapable reality, whether centered in Japan, Korea, Indonesia, or—most powerfully perhaps—in diasporic and mainland China. Can we still say

that global economics, because it is capitalist, is inherently "Western"? As Marx understood, capitalism is revolutionary, destructive *and* productive. And it does not usher in a unified, "bourgeois", or "Western" sociocultural order as it spreads. It has proved to be flexible, working through as well as against regional differences, partially accommodating to local cultures and political regimes, grafting its symbols and practices onto whatever non-Western forms transculturate its logic. It does business with monarchies, dictatorships, oligarchic bureaucracies, and democracies, with neo-Confucians, Hindus, Orthodox Jews, a range of Islamic societies.

Arrighi, Hopkins, and Wallerstein (1989:40-45) point out that what they call "antisystemic movements," that is, movements against capitalism, all the "failed" or "co-opted" movements that have called themselves "revolutions," have actually been successful in altering "social relations of accumulation" and ending the existence of "stateless" peoples, or "the deepening of stateness," "growth in the density of the interstate system," and the opening of international borders. All of which strongly suggests the possibility–and not the problem–that the Vicosinos along with millions like them, neither "Andean", nor "mestizo", nor "criollo", nor any other designation which opposes some Peruvians to other Peruvians, might someday not only manage the Peruvian economy but might direct the future of Perú. As Deborah Poole (1992:219) states: "If there were a common conclusion to anthropology and history during the 80s, it would be that the essence of pan-Andean culture does not reside in inherited traditions or in ecological adaptations, but rather in the common repertory of strategic responses with which Andean peoples have confronted both Spanish colonialism and capitalism."

Memories of the Vicos Project

Let us also de-essentialize the Project. It, too, has changed just as Perú has changed around its memory. And memory is situated in the present, as Adrienne Rich (1986:15) reminds us (in case we have forgotten): "Every journey into the past is complicated by delusions, false memories, false naming of real events." Memory changes as we grow. So the memory of the Project has changed and has, as well, changed the remembered Project. We now have new languages for remembering it. And writing, or rewriting, the Project changes it more; Arthur Jacobson (1992:113) comments on what Yahweh made Moses write:

Writing changes *what* we remember, and the *way* we remember it. We write in order to remember what we wish or fear to forget. Writing to remember is writing to forget–to forget in order to be reminded by the writing. To remember through the written record of an event is to forget the immediate experience of it.

The Project is only remembered in a language which exists at this turn of a new century. Our memory, then is memory in the year 2000. This is what we know. Donna Haraway (1991:196, 198) writes: "The only way to find a larger vision is to be somewhere in particular." She adds: "Situated knowledges require that the object of knowledge be pictured as an actor and agent, not a screen or a ground or a resource, never finally as a slave to the master that closes off the dialectic in his unique agency and authorship of 'objective' knowledge." Knowledge, then, is contingent (Clifford 1986:109). Not only does the ethnographic object change but I change as I write about it.

"Agrarian reform" looks different now from its appearance in the early 1950s. It is apparent now that Vicos would only have needed to wait seven years, from 1962 to 1969, to be liberated finally from the Beneficencia and handed over to the agrarian reform. Instead, in 1956, it was delivered into the hands of the Programa Ancash, the first of a series of governmental agencies which all turned out to be as corrupt and inefficient as the Beneficencia, but in different ways. Changes have assisted what and who is "in process", however, and many Vicosinos are enjoying improved living standards, indeed, prosperity. Vicosinos, as the electoral majority in the District of Marcará have emerged from powerlessness to empowerment. In 1986 A Vicosino was elected *alcalde* (mayor) of the District (Doughty 1987:147). But since these kinds of changes are reported for many other rural communities in Perú, we can hardly call them achievements of the Project. They mark the coming of modernity to the Andes. This is what the Project wished for, but not precisely what it wished for because it was not completely conscious of its wishes (i.e., desires). This is what it looked for, but again not precisely, because it feared to look at the obliteration of what was not present, to gaze at the absence of what was missing in itself.

In focusing on modernity, and the vicissitudes of modern development discourse in Perú, in this examination of the Vicos Project I have inevitably drawn on materials that say much about Vicos and the Vicosinos. But, as I have pointed out in the Preface, I have endeavored to keep Laura Nader's (1972) advice to the anthropologist: to "study up." Essentially, this means to study dominance, power and wealth, and the misuse of these human resources in the interests of the few. I have also, I think, tried to follow a model constructed by Roland Barthes (1972b:135) for the subversion of myth, in my treatment of development discourse:

> It . . . appears that it is extremely difficult to vanquish myth from the inside: for the very effort one makes in order to escape its stranglehold becomes in its turn the prey of myth: myth can always, as a last resort, signify the resistance which is brought to bear against it. Truth to tell, the best weapon against myth is perhaps to mythify it in its turn, and to produce an *artificial myth*: and this reconstituted myth will in fact be a mythology. Since myth robs language of something, why not rob myth?

I have, thus, tried to employ the fetish, the phallus, castration, mirrors, and blindness in a discourse of counter-mythification. In his discussion of Russian formalism, Frederic Jameson (1972:50-51, 55, 57) refers to the model of *ostranenie*, the "making strange of objects, a renewal of perceptions," viewing things "in a new and utterly unforseen light, as though for the first time," and what "we have come to take for granted as something natural and eternal, and which therefore cries out for defamiliarization." Such a model is "based on the opposition between habituation and perception, between mechanical and thoughtless performance, and a sudden awareness of the very textures and surfaces of the world and of language." Mark Schneider (1993:19) observes: "[E]nchanted phenomena that today *do* pose pragmatic difficulties for us are often encountered simply as unusual but at the same time rather unremarkable features of our world. Appreciating their true strangeness would require that we shed some of the conventions that make the world seem normal to us in the first place. To *really* sense the peculiarity of our own circumstances, in other words, we would first have to defamiliarize them–a trick not easy to accomplish." Thus, a gringo calls on himself to other not the Other but himself and *his* kind, to see strangers who came to the Callejón de Huaylas in the early 1950s as stranger themselves than their own perceptions of strangeness. And their misrecognition of where strangeness was. Todorov (1975:158-159) defends the use of the fantastic in literature: "[T]he fantastic permits us to cross certain frontiers that are inaccessible so long as we have no recourse to it. . . . Apart from institutionalized censorship, there is another kind, more subtle and more general: the censorship which functions in the psyche of the authors themselves. The penalization of certain acts society provokes a penalization invoked in and by the individual himself [sic], forbidding him to approach certain taboo themes. More than a simple pretext, the fantastic is a means of combat against this kind of censorship as well as the other."

In portraying blindness–for that is the condition of the dominant–I find myself in a rather similar frame of mind to that of Derrida (1993:2-3) who, in his somewhat autobiographical analysis of drawings of the blind, points out that, first, "the drawing is blind, if not the draftsman or draftswoman," and that, second, "a drawing of the *blind* is a drawing *of* the blind":

> Double genitive. There is no tautology here, only a destiny of the self-portrait. Every time a draftsman lets himself be fascinated by the blind, every time he makes the blind a *theme* of his drawing, he projects, dreams, or hallucinates a figure of a draftsman, or sometimes, more precisely, some draftswoman. Or more precisely still, he begins to *represent* a drawing potency at work, the very act of drawing. He invents drawing. The *trait* is not then paralyzed in a tautology that folds the same onto the same. On the contrary, it becomes prey to *allegory*, to this strange self-portrait of drawing given over to the speech and gaze of the other. The subtitle of all these scenes of the blind is thus: *the origin of drawing*. Or, if you prefer, *the thought of drawing*, a certain pensive pose, a *memory of the trait* that speculates, as in a dream, about its own possibility. Its potency always develops on the brink of blindness. Blindness pierces through right at that point and thereby gains *in potential*, *in potency*: the angle of a sight that is threatened *or* promised, lost *or* restored, given. There is in this gift a sort of *re-drawing*, a *with-drawing*, or *retreat*, at once the interposition of a mirror, an impossible reappropriation or mourning, the intervention of a paradoxical Narcissus, sometimes lost *en abyme*, in short a specular *folding* or *falling back*–and a supplementary *trait*.

Like Derrida, accidentally, "and sometimes on the brink of an accident, I find myself writing without seeing." When I began the project of writing this book about the Project, I did not see how close to me it was (nor did I really see *it*), nor how my portrayal of the Project's blindness was at the same time a portrayal *of* blindness, blindness in me. If Derrida and I share this trait, why not other writers, all writers? However, I am not writing on grammatology but on the Vicos Project. So I turn to the "Introduction" written by Dobyns, Doughty y Lasswell (1971b) to their monument erected to the memory of this Project. They define it as "a project to improve the standard of living of a few thousand rural Peruvian highland Indians," whose "anthropologists provided their skills as data collectors to find out what the Indians themselves wanted" (10). With this "knowledge" (and I am presuming that this is the authors' intent), it was possible "to implement, on a national scale, many of the measures tested and proved during the Vicos experiment toward developing a prototype for improving peasant life by increasing the peasant share of power.... In a word [actually, several words!], the research and development program at Vicos, officially or not, has played a significant part in the changing national policy of Perú's traditional land tenancy systems. At times Vicos stood at the forefront of reform, a lonely and isolated show-piece," but when "national sentiment solidified in favor of . . . agrarian reform, Vicos . . . became only one project among many agrarian reform programs" looking for ways not only to liberate *colonos* from hacienda systems, to convert the latter into commodity-producing farmers, and to "create truly national loyalties among hitherto physically and socially isolated rural populations so as to avoid more serious guerrilla-style peasant armed movements" (14). Dobyns and Doughty (1971:18-19) characterize Project researchers at Vicos as "highly motivated anthropologists" acting from "strong feeling[s] of responsibility for carrying the findings of social science into the world of practical affairs." They represent "the really revolutionary anthropologist . . . who employs his best disciplinary skills as both data collector and theorist, working directly both with decision-makers and the people in seeking to broaden in fundamental ways the distribution of power within a national society," as opposed to the kind of anthropologist "who most frequently publishes papers pleading for economic and social reforms, or seeks to find occasions for physical confrontation with officialdom to shout provocative slogans." And Dobyns (1974:209-210) affirms: "Unlike the vast majority of social scientists, who must attempt to identify causation *ex post facto*, Cornell-Perú Project researchers knew with certainty what caused numerous changes among Vicosinos. As participant interveners, the researchers themselves carried out or instituted actions, whose consequences they first predicted and then observed. Anthropological intervention in Vicos provided, in other words, the nearest approach to truly experimental research design that social scientists seem likely to achieve for some time to come." Erectile and unreal! A fetish! A large and unsatisfying phallacy![17]

Already, two decades ago, after a detailed study of the so-called "agrarian reform," José Matos Mar and José Manuel Mejía (1980:161) pointed out its consequences in Perú: while "there has occurred a redistribution of landed property without precedent in Peru," and "it has been accompanied by the institution of an associative type of organization in the agricultural regions with the greatest economic importance, . . . it has not had great impact in the traditional sector and has left the greater part of the rural population marginalized." One of their major conclusions is: "Because it did not benefit the major part of the rural population of the country, and because it also did not represent a valid alternative formula for the population involved, it can be affirmed as the conclusion of the analysis carried out so far that the reform has not resolved the land problem of Peruvian history." It was an agrarian "reform" which built the foundation for the terrors of the 1980s and 1990s. A "reform" that Michael Woost (1997:249) likens to "riding in a top-down vehicle of development whose wheels are greased with a vocabulary of bottom-up discourse," in which "the vocabulary of participation has become one of subordination," under the terms of which "to participate is to bend one's purpose, goals and strategies to fit the official mold."[18]

It would be ludicrous to suggest that the agrarian reform which was coming, and independently of the Project's will, would not have arrived without the Project's interventions.[19] And it would be absurd to assume that the agrarian reform would have been more or less inefficient, inadequate, self-defeating, or corrupt with or without any alleged input from the Project. Without the Project, would the Peruvian state have extended less into Vicos and would the voting rights of the 1979 Constitution not have made Vicosinos the majority in their political district? And if becoming political agents "depeasantizes" rural people, would Vicosinos in 2002 be any more or less depeasantized?

As for "guerrilla-style peasant armed movements," entire farming communities in large areas of the country have been dispersed in the "dirty war" between the state apparatus and the Senderista (Shining Path) guerrillas. Nelson Manrique (2002:21) reports that between a million and a million-and-a-half people have been affected by this violence, including 30,000 killed, 600,000 displaced, 40,000 orphaned, 20,000 widowed, 4,000 disappeared, 500,000 children with post-traumatic stress, and 435 communities razed. The Senderistas were far from "peasants," despite their rural roots.[20] They illustrate the tragedy of overeducation transformed into mis-education; and what is good for these modern-day extirpators of idolatry appears to be catastrophic for almost everyone else. Manrique (2002:102-103) characterizes their outlook as a "colonial" anachronism, the granting of patronage to rural clients (much in the spirit of the class from which they come):

> [Their] measures . . . had unanimous acceptance, and even though *comuneros* [members of rural commons] were conscious that their margins of individual liberty were being continually restricted, they considered that paying that price was acceptable in exchange for the security that Sendero offered them. A *comunero* explained, "That's the way it has to be because we Peruvians are carried away by evil." The expression means that they could not obtain the same results "through good." Vertical and violently authoritarian paternalism has legitimacy because it is deemed inevitable: old reflexes of fatalism and passivity appear, interiorized long ago in colonial times. Freedom exchanged for security: the exchange can appear hard to bear, but in contemporary Peru the freedom a person can enjoy is not very great, especially if one is an

Indian and poor.

We could call this a "dominator-subaltern *habitus*." The Senderistas (as well as the military and para-military authorities) replaced the *patrones* who disappeared with agrarian reform. Yet Sendero contradicted itself. Gonzalo Portocarrero (1998:60-61) points out that "Sendero's ideology is distinctively modern. It involves a cult of movement, an unlimited fascination for the ability to act. It rejects calmness. The alternative to movement cannot be tranquility but rather pessimism and depression."

> What is most interesting is that this romantic modernism is strongly linked to a resistance to the individuation which would modify it, transforming its meaning. In effect, the celebration of change, which is an aspect of modernity, together with the cult of will and ethics, characteristics of romanticism, are accompanied by a renunciation of freedom, by reliance on submission. That is, there is no question of seeking individual development. What is desired is giving oneself unconditionally to the party collective. It is a traditional and authoritarian discourse. . . .
> What kinds of people are seduced by these ideas? What can there be behind the red figure? Probably a young person, filled with impulses and anxieties, who wishes to be good and thoughtful but who, without a definite direction, decides to give up his or her privacy and autonomy in exchange for peace, location, and meaning. So I think that the rejection of individualism expressed in the militant's engagement is based on two motives. The first represents a moral mandate and has to do with Catholic tradition and its exaltation of solidarity, and its distrust of pleasure and personal matters. From this perspective individualism is selfish and sinful. The second motive has to do with the limitation of the individualist option in the surroundings through which the candidate moves to militancy. In an environment dominated by poverty and the lack of opportunities, the stake of personal development can have no meaning since frustration is most likely.

This suggests that there has been an "interesting"[21] change in the code "from the religious to the militant" (cf. Spivak 1988:197). Could it be that the Senderistas have not merely substituted the worship of one set of icons for another but have hybridized what many of us have taken for distinct and contradictory codes? Thus, the ghost of patriarchy lurked in the pores of a revolutionary movement.[22] As de la Cadena (1998:54-55) concludes, "The perversity of history in the case of the Shining Path was that it was precisely the survival of Peruvian social hierarchies within their party that permitted the grand leaders to situate themselves above hierarchy. When all was said and done, 'the party' was a part of Peruvian society." Despite the great difference between Sendero and the *Khmer Rouge*, Iván Hinojosa

(1992:93) makes this comparison of the two movements:

> There exist . . . many similarities between both groups, like the character of the small cadres, closed, paranoiac, and authoritarian, the emphasis on surrounding the cities from the countryside, the dogmatism of misinterpreting reality, the xenophobia of defining foreign domination, and the voluntarism of completing planned projects on time. In the same way, despite great differences between Peru and Cambodia, the expansion of public education in both cases did not fulfill its original commitment to strengthen the State, but rather it undermined it ideologically because of the severe crises in these societies.

But let us remember that "development" is a sign with multiple signifiers and signifieds. It also pertains to human development, growth, growing up, which can sometimes be a very painful process. We may very well ask, rhetorically, if the Vicos "developers," oddly enough resembling senderistas, may not be portraying, blindly, an ideal kind of growth, an everything-is-as-it-should-be assertion that agony and trauma are to be hidden in the process of turning out "model citizens?" As in obligatory "family values." Were they simply repeating their traumas silently in saying that what was done, was done in the best interests of their Others (and their others in themselves)? Why did they deal with rebellion and revolution in such an oblique, stereotyped, and, yes, even fearful way? Could they, possibly, have been repressing rebellious impulses and otherness in themselves, veiled wishes to challenge paternal, patriarchal, authority, and fears of castration? So much for the repressive, suppressive, and oppressive "sanctity" of the authoritarian patriarchal family and its "values." But let us try to replace re-pression with a post-structural "post-pression"! From that vantage point we may probe at the heart of "family values" in order to reveal their fundamental insanity.

Did the Project Do Harm in Vicos?

In connection with "failed projects" of literature, Deborah Esch (1989:77) says: "We commemorate (and fail to commemorate) them not by erecting monuments . . . but by reading and rereading. We 'mourn' them otherwise, by remembering and remarking, however prosaically, the difference between a funeral march and a triumph of reading." But failure is not injury. As I've noted, after the first year of the Project, Allan Holmberg was able to spend only a few weeks every summer in Vicos. This was not a "major error," as much as it was a key failure–though there may not be a great difference between them. We could call it "misrecognition." The absence of the Principal Investigator also signifies blindness, Holmberg's blindness to what was happening in Vicos and the Project's blindness in having to function with his absence, an absence a system of "field directors" and "field coordinators" was employed to cover. Holmberg's spirit is absent from all the reports prepared by his epigones after his death, and they even serve as ventriloquists to a mock-up of his ghost when they have the latter report on conditions in Vicos in 1967 (Holmberg 1971b:53), a year after his death. Holmberg is absent, as well, from the ethnographic part of the Archives: no field notes of his are included in the wealth of ethnographic and developmental reports to be found there. We can only wonder at his presence in publications (like those cited in the foregoing) in view of so much absence.

The Archives offer a rather different view of relations between the Vicosinos and the Project than the epigones' proclamations: these field notes reveal a classic struggle between "liberators and their liberated" (cf. Mehlman 1977:53), which is, in the case of Vicos, between "developers and their developed." Is the nature of "development" necessarily that of controlling authorities and resisting subjects? The data from Vicos confirm Brooke Larson's (1998:324) view of Andean history as "a fundamentally contested historical process" for the hacienda system, both in general and specifically in Vicos, and for the brief moment of the Project in Vicos. Indeed, the Project's problem was that it could not conform to its ideal experimental model because its experimental objects were not passive. The Vicosinos were not "dependent variables," but rather "independent" ones. We see these relations between authorities and subalterns as contested, negotiated, and shaped as much by the latter as by the former. Another example of what Steve Stern (1987:11) calls "resistant adaptation."

As it turned out, developmentalist authority was neither as comfortable in its patriarchal self-assertion or in its ability to perform miracles in Vicos, as in its' model's more recent attempts to control the world as a dominant and "peace-loving" power. The Project's development discourse turns out to be yet another form of "white mythology", an idiom which reflects a single culture's aberration, one that is quite limited in time and space (Derrida 1982b:213). The blind Project exposed itself through its apprehensiveness about space (Derrida 1993:5), that is, the space of its science, whether it might trip and fall (as do the blind [21]) into insignificance or oblivion–where nobody would recognize or value its work, nobody admire its accomplishments–a condition that would not leave it a social scientific leg to stand on. It needed to be upright. It needed demonstration to the point where it could not see pretense, injustice and untruth. The Project, in losing control by taking control, was beset by "the fear of seeing *and* of not seeing what one must not see, hence the very thing one must see" (48), that is, its infirmity in its firmness. "Blindness does not prohibit tears" (127), either. It is hard to find evidence of regret in the many (yet hasty, insufficient, and incomplete) Project documentations, except in Allan Holmberg's statement (1958:12– see Chapter 1) that if he could do it again, he was not certain that he would repeat it.

No one in the year 2002 would even consider the possibility of designing such a project. Nevertheless, we have inherited it, whether we like it or not. It is a root, and José Carlos Mariátegui's (1970;74) vision of 1925 in which he conceives of a revolutionary indigenismo which "thinks of the past as a root, but not as a program" is as relevant for us today as it was in his time. Frank Salomon (1982:97) writes of a "Vicos legacy" in "an older meliorist tradition of community development through social scientific intervention" which "continued to produce programmatic statements" in the 1970s, and opposed it to "an internationalist movement for the defense of cultural minority rights, rooted in part in the critique of modernization theory" which "questioned the viability of local reform apart from recognition of deep-rooted conflict between national institutions and ethnic minorities." Such solicitude for "ethnic minorities" would be effective if we knew what they were. It favors one pole of a binary opposition which is in need of deconstruction.

If I have helped in this book to explode the idea that the Vicos Project is some kind of angry ghost which threatens anthropologists, I will be satisfied. I like Manrique's (1999:76-77) approach to texts that were written decades ago: "We ought not to lose sight of the fact that history is always written in the present, from a historically determined situation. If . . . it is necessary to avoid committing the anachronism of attributing our own rationality to authors of other times, it is at the same time indispensable to incorporate in the analysis the retrospective knowledge which the intervening decades have offered us. Otherwise we would be condemned to enclose ourselves in the illusions–ideological ones–of the protagonists of those times."

Never a horrible monster, the Vicos Project was much more helpful than harmful. We can view it in the spirit of Clifford Geertz (1984:263) who begins his "Distinguished lecture: Anti anti-relativism," and which is distinguished in its text as well as its title, with the words: "A scholar can hardly be better employed than in destroying a fear"–and ends: "Looking into dragons,[23] not domesticating or abominating them, not drowning them in vats of theory, is what anthropology has been all about. . . . We have, with no little success, sought to keep the world off balance: pulling out rugs, upsetting tea tables, setting off firecrackers. It has been the office of others to reassure; ours to unsettle. Australopithecines, Tricksters, Clicks, Megaliths–we hawk the anomalous, peddle the strange. Merchants of astonishment." Well, why not!

Peruvians might find it useful to understand better this very hesitant dragon which is a piece of their history–one that is still mentioned in Peruvian publications but whose significance is little grasped–a little better through any light I might shed on what happened in Vicos. Jaime Urrutia (1992:8-9), for example, mentions the Vicos Project, does not seem willing to take more than a superficial glance at it, and engages with no publication about it after 1970. It is regrettable that so limited a bibliography was available to this author, but this is no fault of the author but, rather, the fault of North Americans who have written more recent accounts of events in Vicos and failed to circulate them in Peru. More recently, in an encyclopedic volume on Peruvian anthropology, a book which was published almost simultaneously with the Lima edition of this study of Vicos, Carlos Iván Degregori (2000a), the editor appears to have based his brief remarks on the Vicos Project on Holmberg's (1966) collection of essays.[24] In his introductory chapter, Degregori (2000b:41-42) comments on Holmberg's desire to "modernize" and "Westernize" Vicos:

> These affirmations have to do with a conception in which tradition and modernity are two opposed and mutually exclusive poles. But more than their functional relation to power or their own multiplying effect, what calls for attention in the Project is not in Vicos itself. I refer to the massive mobilizations which appeared throughout the Andes toward the end of the 1950s and the first half of the 1960s, when thousands of organized *campesinos* who had never so much as heard of the Vicos Project "reoccupied" hundreds of thousands of hectares of lands which, according to them, had been illegally taken from them. It was like the upside down image of that "orientalist," if not racist, movie scene in which an Arab plants himself in front of Indiana Jones and begins to make threatening gestures with his scimitar, attempting to frighten the Western and Christian hero, who looks back impassively and then takes out his pistol. With just one shot he ends the circus. Only here the roles are reversed and it is the Indian *campesinos* who, without much theory or many resources, wound to the death the precapitalist landlord in a series of quite bloodless movements, given their magnitude, and the lamentable sequel which followed, that is the land problem.

While I would seriously question the existence of "precapitalist landlords" in Peru in the middle of the twentieth century, and I herewith raise the issue of the revindicators' "misrecognition" of their problem in that the land seizures did not resolve farm workers' difficulties. Degregori is quite correct in indicating that rural workers in the late 1950s needed no "therapeutic" policy narratives to recover lands that really had been stolen from their ancestors. That such an assertion of agency in the 1850s would have been impossible needs no explanation. Another contributor to the same collection of essays writes in regard to the Vicos Project:

> Initiated in 1952, this Project formed part of the "Program of Culture and Applied Social Science" that Cornell University implemented at the conclusion of World War II in five communities in different parts of the world. . . . The goal of the program was to carry out an experimental program of research and development, oriented fundamentally to the carrying out of studies of induced change and the improvement of the quality of life of their inhabitants, and their "integration" into the modern sector of their societies. In Peru, the program was assigned to Allan Holmberg. It took place in Vicos, an hacienda located in the Callejón de Huaylas, which was chosen because of the advantages its availability offered–it could be rented because it belonged to the Beneficencia Pública de Huaraz–and its small number of inhabitants (around two thousand). Vicosinos constituted the most backward group, with the lowest level of income in Ancash.. . . .
>
> Vicos became a real laboratory of research in applied anthropology, and more than one generation of Peruvian and foreign anthropologists participated in it. While, when the Project came to an end, it was shown that reality did not always correspond with good intentions, for the "miracle" of the modernization of Vicos could not be sustained with the same intensity when the injection of outside resources was eliminated, the Project alone could not be considered a failure since it achieved some of the proposed objectives in great measure. In 1952, when the Project began, Vicos was one of the most backward haciendas in the Callejón de Huaylas, with *colonos* subject to precapitalist relations of servitude and domination. They had to give 159 days of labor per year to the *hacendado* as compensation for the usufruct of lands and pastures. In 1962, when the transfer took place, Vicos was already a cooperative, and conditions of life had improved enormously in comparison with those of a decade earlier. . . .
>
> Nevertheless, the great paradox of the Project was that in those same years, without the great quantity of experts, funds, and time invested in the "Vicos laboratory," the hacienda system was dismantled not just in one or two neighboring haciendas, as a product of "demonstration effect," but in a good part of the Andes by the action of *campesinos* themselves, without having so much as heard of the Project. (Avila Molero 200:418-422,)

In this case, the author cites Vázquez (1951), Holmberg (1966), and an article by Héctor Martínez (1989).

North American anthropologists have less understanding of the Project. It is still discussed but it has been treated as a fetish in many of the primary accounts, and poorly portrayed in all the secondary accounts that I have seen. In what appears to be an introductory text in *Applied Anthropology*, John van Willigen (1986:79-91) devotes a chapter of thirteen pages, entitled "Research and development anthropology," to the Vicos Project. It is largely a summary of Dobyns, Doughty and Lasswell (1971a), and no source later than 1971 is cited. This author concludes a bibliographic note at the end of the chapter with this statement: "Unfortunately, there is no single comprehensive description of the Project, but this volume [i.e., Dobyns, Doughty and Lasswell, cited above] is an excellent substitute." My comment is: when pigs fly!

Robert Borofsky (1994:415-416), in a concise paragraph in which four very diverse comments on the Project contend with one another, demonstrates that discussion has not closed. He concludes: "In the final analysis [presumably when we have disappeared?], one's assessment of the Vicos Project depends on what one deems is possible within a political-economic setting where an entrenched elite enforces its dominance over a rural peasantry, sometimes brutally, with tacit governmental support." And John Bennett (1996), in what appears to be a review article on applied anthropology but is in reality a tribute to the North American anthropologist Sol Tax, devotes only a few lines to the Vicos Project. That is to be expected in portrayals of the blind, or even of the sighted in their self-portraits with the use of mirrors.

In response to those Andeanists who still view the Vicos Project as an "abomination," and those who other me as an "abomination's" offspring,[25]–I would like to quote Mary Douglas (1966:165) in reference to our Andeanist sub-culture:

> In a given culture it seems that some kinds of behavior or natural phenomena are recognized as utterly wrong by all the principles which govern the universe. There are different kinds of impossibilities, anomalies, bad mixings and abominations. Most of the items receive varying degrees of condemnation and avoidance. Then suddenly we find that one of the most abominable or impossible is singled out and put into a very special kind of ritual frame that marks it off from other experience. The frame ensures that the categories which the normal avoidances sustain are not threatened or affected in any way. Within the ritual frame the abomination is then handled as a source of tremendous power.

Hardly an "abomination," despite all its weaknesses, false starts, misrecognitions, lapses of judgment, and Cold War intentions, and most certainly not a nest of *pishtacos* (see Chapter 3), the Project is characterized by some, particularly those who were part of the structuralist ferment (or were fermented by structuralism) of the 1970s, as consisting of less-than-humans sucking the culture out of Andean people and "integrating" them into national society as low-class zombies. This is an unfair, demeaning, careless, and perhaps even racist image, *not* of the Project's image but that of Peruvians who would so easily allow their identity to be sucked out![26]–although, as Manrique (1999:78) suggests, the question of who is going to integrate whom in Peru is by no means settled.

Perhaps the Project has been nothing more than a *pishtacos' pishtaco*, that is, a meta-*pishtaco*, or metavampire. In her study of vampire literature which focuses on Bram Stoker's novel *Dracula*, Carol Senf (1997:82-83) points out: "Almost every detail in *Dracula* underlines that a sophisticated group of human beings is waging war on a primitive, even animalistic being. The triumph of human beings at the conclusion might even be said to reinforce the idea of progress that was so common in the nineteenth century, an idea commonly associated with biological evolutionism. . . . The conclusion . . . suggests that the past has been entirely annihilated. If one were to read *Dracula* in the context of contemporary social and political ideology, one might say that it exudes confidence in progressionist notions, in the triumph of the present over the past." This suggests to me that, more than ageism, some Andeanists are unconsciously repeating the "developmentalism" they consciously detest.

Then, too do we not, all of us students of *"lo andino"* (the Andean) suck at the Andes so that we may write dissertations, obtain academic positions and promotions, and write articles and books (including this one!). We accumulate symbolic and cultural capital like capitalists who, Ken Gelder (1994:20) points out in his discussion of Marx's use of the vampire metaphor, suck at farmers and workers and get rich. Vampires are queer, culturally marginal (141-142). And they do not see themselves in mirrors–which is why, I suspect, such a fuss is made about the Vicos Project. But I think that the point is: if I were not something of a vampire myself I would not so easily see the trait in others.

This train of thought is problematic because it leaves something out. Roland Barthes (1972b:142-143) shows how myth is a depoliticization: it performs a "conjuring trick" by turning reality "inside out" and "removed from things their human meaning." It "does not deny things, on the contrary its function is to talk about them" by purifying them: "it makes them innocent, it gives them a natural and eternal justification." In abolishing "the complexity of human acts, it gives them the simplicity of essences." The *pishtaco* myth applied to ourselves must include our struggles in fields of symbolic power. The practice of anthropology is at the same time a malpractice, a "remedy" and a "poison," clarification and obfuscation. I doubt that we shall ever "purify" it. Roy Wagner (1981:158) offers us a commentary:

> The future of anthropology lies in its ability to exorcise "difference" and make it conscious and explicit, both with regard to its subject matter and to itself. Especially in America, we have an "anthropology of fact and fiction," focusing explicitly on factual consistency, knowledge, and professional brotherhood, but full of implicit and furtive differences, rivalries, jealousies, and quite unprofessional ambitions that are the more destructive (and politically vicious) for being unspoken. It is a fact-producing "industry" that *suffers* the dialectic as history, polemic, and factional squabble, living a cultic succession of jargons, bandwagons, and "needs" of the department or the discipline, "setting up" its own surreptitious revolutions and cataclysms by projecting optimistic and unrealistic "programs" for concerted action.

In other words, there is something of the *pishtaco* in all of us.

Near the beginning of her interpretive commentary on Freud's *The Uncanny* (1955b). Hélène Cixous (1976:526) asks the critical question: "Doesn't the analysis which brings up the whole question of repressions imprint them at once upon the one who undertakes the analysis?" The *pishtaco* myth, after all, is a fiction and so some of Cixous's (547) conclusions are relevant: "As a Reserve of the Repressed, fiction is finally that which resists analysis and, thus, it attracts it the most. Only the writer 'knows' and has the *freedom* to evoke or inhibit the [uncanny]. In other words, only the writer has the freedom to raise or repress the Repression. But this 'freedom' defies all analysis; as another form of the [uncanny] it is like that which should have 'remained . . . hidden." At the same time there is love of the familiar:

> "Love is a yearning for a country, according to popular wisdom. . . . [A] yearning for a country is a formulation which is always interrupted by the interpretation which reads: regret and the desire for 'yearning.' Which country? The one from which we come, 'the place where everyone dwelt once upon a time and in the beginning.' The country from which we come is always the one to which we are returning. You are on the return road which passes through the country of children in the maternal body. You have already passed through here: You recognize the landscape. You have always been on the return road. Why is it that the maternal landscape . . . and the familiar become so disquieting? The answer is less buried than we might suspect. The obliteration of any separation, the realization of the desire which in itself obliterates a limit; all that which,

in effecting the movement of life in reality, allows us to come closer to a goal, the short cuts, the crossing accomplished especially at the end of our lives;   all that which overcomes, shortens, economizes, and assures satisfaction appears to affirm the life forces. All of that has another face turned toward death which *is* the *detour* of life. The abbreviating effect which affirms life asserts death. (544-545.)

Eros and Thanatos. All of this suggests that we are simply humans oscillating between our love at one pole and our fear at the Other. I read in Andeanist literature not simply a desire for career maintenance but a great love for a foster country. The same must be said of the Project's people.

I think we all ought to try harder to read with *intellectual love*. I find this sometimes difficult to live up to–it resolves itself into the aching question, "how to be good in a bad society?" (Barthes 1972a:75). Pierre Bourdieu (1999:614) concludes the large work in which he and his associates present a series of interviews on *The Weight of the World* with a rather inspiring statement which actually applies to all reading and writing:

> [A]t the risk of shocking both the rigorous methodologist and the inspired hermeneutic scholar, I would say that the interview can be considered a sort of *spiritual exercise* that, through *forgetfulness of self,* aims at a true *conversion of the way we look at* other people in the ordinary circumstances of life. The welcoming disposition, which leads one to make the respondent's problems one's own, the capacity to take that person and understand them just as they are in their distinctive necessity, is a sort of *intellectual love*: a gaze that consents to necessity in the manner of the "intellectual love of God," that is, of the natural order, which Spinoza held to be the supreme form of knowledge.

What effect, then, did the Project have on Vicos? Over the course of a half century, I think not much. It did no lasting harm, and in its time I think it did some good by investing the community's profits at home in the form of a school, teachers' quarters, a health post, the acquisition of Chancos, the lower part of Vicos, which had been separated for some time, and other improvements. It prolonged the lives of some Vicosinos, and possibly improved the quality of those lives at least a little. I imagine Vicos very much like the fishing villages on the shores of Lake Titicaca which Ben Orlove (2002:231-232, 234) describes:

> [T]he villagers do not speak of development. They hear the word *desarrollo*, the Spanish term for this concept, in radio news programs and in speeches by political officials and candidates, but they do not use it

when they speak Quechua. Nor have they adapted any Quechua term meaning "growth" or "unfolding" to use in its place, as speakers of indigenous languages in other parts of the world have done. . . . The absence of any term for *development* in Quechua stems, in part, from the concrete recognition of the failures of local projects carried out in the name of *desarrollo* . . . . It also reflects a general skepticism toward the government. Though villagers seek recognition from the government and welcome certain projects such as schools and clinics, they often doubt its blandishments. . . .

Rather than discussing the economic factors alone, the villagers often speak of the end of the *abusos*, injustices, that prevented them from building schoolhouses or opening markets in rural areas, and that led them to be subject to the arbitrary whim of police and judges. However, the changes are not all positive. Villagers note also that the fields do not produce crops as abundantly as they once did, that thieves are more numerous and more brazen than they once were, and that people do not live as long as they used to.

The Vicos Project has had lasting effects in Andean studies, both in the Andean countries and North America for it is still discussed. Introductory anthropology texts offer it as a model of applied anthropology and, as we've already read, professional scholars still write about it. At Cornell University Allan Holmberg's more "biodegradable" (to borrow a term from Derrida [1989e][27]) developmental and working-oneself-out-of-a job Andeanism was replaced by John Murra's more monumental vertical control which sought permanence and hegemony in Andean studies. Holmberg was loved, while Murra was followed; and it seemed as though the new order set about deliberately to extirpate any loving memory of the Project. It was as if the deceased were condemned to death, as Derrida (861) puts it in his commentary on reaction in the late 1980s to Paul de Man's wartime journalism of 1942:

Yes, to condemn the dead man to death: they would like him *not to be dead* yet so they could put him to death (preferably along with a few of the most intolerable among the living). To put him to death this time without remainder. Since that is difficult, they would want him to be *already dead without remainder*, so that they can put him to death without remainder. Well, the fact is he is dead (they will no longer be able to do anything in order to kill him), and there are remains, something surviving that bears his name. Difficult to decipher, translate, assimilate. Not only can they do nothing against that which survives, but they cannot keep themselves from taking the noisiest part in that survival. Plus there are other survivors, aren't there, who are interested in survival, who talk, respond, discuss, *analyze* endlessly. We'll never have done with it. It's as if something nonbiodegradable had been submerged at the bottom of the sea. It irradiates.

There were Project members who forgot themselves long enough to love Vicos, Paul Doughty for example. Otherwise, Vicos has grown and changed in the context of national events. Although I have not visited there in recent years, my impression from those who have is that the community is much like thousands of other rural communities in Peru: net exporters of people to urban centers and struggling to survive in a poor country which bears the burden of a large external debt and lacks the resources to provide basic services to its people equitably. One might say that Peru specializes in poverty. Enrique Mayer (2002:320), basing his list on the work of Peruvians who study poverty (almost obsessively), notes: "[T]here are now many categories of poor–the extremely poor, the merely poor, the chronically poor, the indigent, the temporary poor, the structurally poor, and so on." It should be no surprise that small farmers and farm laborers are the poorest, Vicosinos included.

Asking a Question

Derrida (1978b:79) raises the question: Since we're all dying, is there a future? He can't answer an impossible question, but he provides a comment on the following page regarding the foundation of

> A community of the question, therefore, within the fragile moment when the question is not yet determined enough for the hypocrisy of an answer to have already initiated itself beneath the mask of the question, and not yet determined enough for its voice to have been already and fraudulently articulated within the very syntax of the question. A community of decision of initiative, of absolute initiality, but also a threatened community, in which the question has not yet found the language it has decided to seek, is not yet sure of its own possibility within the community. A community of the question about the possibility of the question. . . . The question has already begun–we know it has–and this strange certainty about an *other* absolute origin, an other absolute decision that has secured the past of the question, liberates an incomparable instruction: the discipline of the question. (80.)

As for me, while I'm "biodegradable," I'm still alive (even if I'm not when you read this, I am while I'm writing it) and looking forward to a future, the future, my future,–only a trace at this point–when I can ask the question in different ways. So the end of this book is simply . . . .

Notes

1. Parts of this chapter also appear in Stein (n.d.a).

2. This criticism applies to my own work in Hualcán, where in 1951 and 1952 I was only a little better off than the North Americans in Vicos. There was nothing more important for me to learn about Hualcán than its language, and I have no excuse for not doing so. I had learned enough to check on my interpreter by the end of my stay there, but I could not dispense with him because I was unable to speak the language.

3. Natalia Majluf (1997) has written a fascinating account of the representation of Peru at the Universal Exhibition of 1855 in Paris by Peruvian artists, and by the faulty French interpretation of works displayed. It reminds me of ways in which Vicosinos and other Peruvians have been viewed by North Americans in search of difference. She writes: "The demand for difference was not simply a victory for romantic notions of cultural relativism, for the manner in which it was deployed to redefine France's relationship to the rest of the world served to establish a new international hierarchy. The Mexican and Peruvian painters had exhibited their works as representatives of their nations, but they had also aspired to equal participation in a contemporary exhibition, as cosmopolitans, as members of a world culture. However, within the context of an exhibition that set down the borders of the nation, their works were forcibly tied only to the national and the particular. The exhibition interpellated them for the difference they could produce, framed them as others, and in so doing broke the spell of their identity as cosmopolitans. Subjected to this critical strategy, they found they had no place in the new hierarchy except as the transparent vehicles for exoticism or as simple appendages of an expanding French culture" (875).

4. In this well known opening to his text, *The Eighteenth Brumaire*, Marx (1963:15) was writing in a discursive mode that could be described as the "philosophy of history". This was a half-century earlier than psychoanalytic discourse appeared and so, despite what may have been exclusively his historiographic intention, what he wrote can now be interpreted in a way that he could not anticipate. For us, his written words take on an autobiographical significance. (See the discussion of Marx's conception of "commodity fetishism" in Chapter 3.)

5. Doughty (1987:146) reports a 1982 enrollment of 500 in Vicos primary schools, and 78 in a secondary school. Thus, only a minority of pupils is exposed to secondary content, but these figures represent a narrowing of the gap I observed in 1971 when there were some 300 primary pupils in Vicos and only a dozen or so Vicosinos in the Carhuaz colegio and other post-primary institutions.

6. Dennis Tedlock (1983), in a work that has also been widely disseminated, and seminally as well, gives the same kind of priority to the "spoken word." Much of his urging for a "dialogical anthropology," in written form, is intellectually exciting, but I cannot accept his privileging of the written word.

7. Papastergiadis (1997:259) adds: "Hybridity evokes narratives of origin and encounter. Whenever the process of identity formation is premised on an exclusive boundary between 'us' and 'them', the hybrid, born out of the transgression of this boundary, figures as a form of danger, loss and degeneration. If, however, the boundary is marked positively–to solicit exchange and inclusion– then the hybrid may yield strength and vitality."

In the same collection of articles, Friedman (1997:82-83) warns: "Hybridity is founded on the metaphor of purity." This sense of the term can hardly apply to Perú, so I would conceive of this on-going process as a "hybridization of hybrids."

8. David Nugent (1994:338) writes of a significant expansion of the circulation of commodities the effect of which is an "annihilation of regional space" that "has helped to create new material dependencies among the populace of Peru and has linked individuals to a growing national (as opposed to regional) economy via the creation of a national market." Then, "by expanding and integrating its control over communication and education, the central government has extended the ideological and cultural bases on which individuals may imagine the nation as a single community and themselves as its citizens." And, finally, "the progressive annihilation of regional boundaries has made it possible for the central government to apply armed force and impose bureaucratic control with greater ease throughout more of its territory."

9. The transformation of rural Perú is overdetermined and so, far more complicated than a matter of national agrarian movements breaking the hegemony of the landed elite, as one noted (but unidentified) Andeanist has recently stated. Without the "tectonic" change in the receptivity for agrarian reform in an urban population, in a country where agriculture had become of minor importance, no questioning of that hegemony would have been admitted, for "what goes without saying . . . comes without saying" and "tradition is silent, not least about itself as a tradition" (Bourdieu 1977:167)!

10. One can experience difficulties in "reading" clothing, however, and so what one thinks one has "read" is not necessarily shared with more discriminating (i.e., persons more familiar with the culture) "readers-" Weismantel and Eisenman (1998:132) offer the example of drag: while "some drag performances undermine gender stereotypes, drag can also reinscribe patriarchy when male performers use an exaggerated womanliness to show women how to be truly feminine."

11. Cf. Larson (1998:363): "Even the most casual traveler to Bolivia today cannot help but notice the distinctive dress of urban market women (often mislabeled by

tourists as "Indians"). They stand out amid the mass of haggling humanity, thanks to their elaborate (regionally varied) clothing code: white top hats . . ., *polleras* (layered cotton or velvet skirts), aprons, striped *aguayos* [colorful, stripped, square pieces of cloth that women wrap around their shoulders and often carry loads in– Personal communication, Brooke Larson, November 30, 1998], earrings, and money purses dangling from their layered petticoats. Clothing (and other implicit ethnic markers) serve a crucial function in assigning legitimate membership in marketplace culture and in the collective representation of cholitas (not all of whom are market vendors)."

12.   "De-essentializing," in the way that deconstruction is also reconstruction, carries with it a "re-essentializing face. J. Hillis Miller (1979:250-251) deconstructs "deconstruction":

The word, like other words in "de," "decrepitude," for example, or "denotation," describes a paradoxical action which is negative and positive at once. In this it is like all words with a double antithetical prefix, words in "ana," like "analysis," or words in "para," like "parasite." These words tend to come in pairs which are not opposites, positive against negative. They are related in a systematic differentiation which requires a different analysis or untying in each case, but which in each case leads in a different way each time, to the tying up of a double bind. This tying up is at the same time a loosening. It is paralysis of thought in the face of what cannot be thought rationally: analysis, paralysis; solution, dissolution; composition, decomposition;   construction, deconstruction; mantling, dismantling; canny, uncanny; competence, incompetence; apocalyptic, anacalyptic; constituting, deconstituting. Deconstructive criticism moves back and forth between the poles of these pairs, proving in its own activity, for example, that there is no deconstruction which is not at the same time constructive, affirmative. The word says this in juxtaposing "de" and "con."

13.   See Derrida's (2002e:195) discussion of Gershom Scholem's mystical application, in 1926, of the term "catastrophe" to the Zionist revival of the sacred language, Hebrew, for contemporary secular usage. Such "linguistic sin" will surely "turn . . . against those who have desecrated it. Then terrible things will not fail to happen." Derrida (209-210) comments that the revivalists (or fetishers) are like "sorcerers' apprentices gifted with an unconscious courage that pushes them to manipulate forces which surpass them. . . . Here is a dead language, which in truth was not dead, but *surviving*, living over and above what one calls a living language, a language that one pretends to resuscitate . . . ; here is a language that turns against those who speak it but who, in truth, only believe that they are speaking it . . . "

14.   Turino (1993:155) says of the middle-class Puneño musicians in Lima, the

Asociación Juvenil Puno: "Since the members of AJP Base Puno were primarily reared in urban Peruvian society, where the Western tuning system predominated, and they learned to perform panpipes largely while living in the city, it is understandable that . . . they did not yet tune, or *hear*, their tropas precisely as rural Andeans do. AJP's attitudes about rehearsing music . . . were also logically different from those of musicians in the ayllus; AJP members had different goals for performance, and a different social style and philosophy that aided them in approaching their goals."

15. For more discussion of folklore as accommodating rural music and dance to urban tastes, see de la Cadena (2000, Chapter 6).

16. This also suggests to me, and especially in the light of world events in the waning twentieth century, that it would be a good idea to "de-essentialize" socialism, a project which Marx and Engels began a long time ago.

17. I am impressed here with the similarity of these developers' discourse to Emma Crewe's (1997:75) comment on "development tales told by expatriate experts about their success with the 'locals.' Such ravings "affirm the authors' place in the wider social order of the development industry. Their body of superior knowledge does not exist in any objective sense, but relies on constant reiteration and renewal of development language, methods and rules. This process is silent so that the experts appear neutral in theory, while in practice they reinvent their powerful position."

18. However, to view the 1968 "Peruvian Revolution" almost as a conspiracy "to construct a mestizo hegemony," and one which failed because it "could not 'domesticate' Indianness," as Florencia Mallon (1992:47, 50) views it, is something of an oversimplification, a case of "di-vision," and perhaps even unkind to most of the Peruvian population consisting of people who would, if asked, define themselves as "mestizo."

19. Frank Salomon (1982:98) notes that "[r]etrospective treatments of the Vicos project . . . suggest that the Vicos experience may have contributed to defining the terms of discussion as the Velasco government sought to create successor institutions replacing latifundios." He does not state whether or not he believes such "treatments." However, since one of the members of the Project, the late Mario Vázquez, occupied an influential agrarian reform office in Velasco's government, it is possible that he *believed* he was applying what he *believed* he had learned in Vicos. Sadly, we cannot ask him.

20. Deborah Poole (1994:4) notes that "Sendero . . . has recruited both its leadership and militants from a provincial elite and a generation of rural youth whose identities and aspirations often straddle the idealized cultural and ethnic divide which the literature would have us believe separates indigenous peasants

from *mestizo* elites." An elite that has suffered from agrarian reform and perhaps is "in process" in reverse; and rural youth whose "process" is blocked.

21. I employ/deploy the word "interesting" in Lyotard's (1997:50) sense: the word "is very convenient. It suspends both engagement and disengagement. It fends off at a slight distance. Always followed by elipses. A nuance in one's voice urges it toward the yes, another toward the no. But it always says 'maybe.'"

22. Isabel Coral Cordero (1998:349-350) provides a chilling commentary on Sendero's misogyny: "Shining Path established an instrumentalist relationship with women, whereby patriarchal relations were reproduced to benefit the party... . Shining Path's ideology and actions on gender were contradictory. On the one hand they conceived of politics and particularly war as the work of *machos* and attacked their opponents as "fags" (*maricones*), "cowards," and "little women" (*mujercitas*). On the other hand they made significant efforts to recruit women... . But the acceptance of these woman did not imply changes in gender relations." A woman's committee responsible for "providing security for the top leader of the 'mass front,'" turned out to be "no more than ladies-in-waiting who, in disciplined shifts, were responsible not only for minor political tasks but for attending to his domestic and personal needs. . . . But what most surprises about Shining Path is the manner in which senderista men and women confronted their adversaries by denigrating women." What fascinates me is this senderista image of its women as *both* caretakers *and* slaughterers: true phallic mothers!

23. On a tour of China with a group of anthropological colleagues in October, 1999, our national guide informed us why dragons were popular in his country: You wouldn't want to try to make a pet of one, he said, but dragons are very useful because they have good vision and they warn you when trouble is approaching. This is not irrelevant to the topic at hand.

24. Degregori (personal communication, June 13, 2001) has informed me that a new edition of the book is in preparation, with addenda and corrections.

25. I am othered, anyway! In his generous review of my book on Mariátegui (Stein 1997), Peter Klarén (1999:166) notes "the difficulties that Stein himself confronted as an 'othered' young Jewish boy in the America" of the 1930s." But that was only the beginning! Since I am not a religious Jew, do not believe that people should be circumcised without their permission, do not look to Israel as a "homeland," do believe that Zionism is and has been a tragic mistake (though it is much to late to reverse history), believe that Palestinians should have their own nation-state if they want it, and believe that Palestinians in Israel should be accorded the status of first-class citizens and that all confiscated land should be returned to them. In consequence, other Jews have othered me as well. If the only discourses available to me had been those of Jews ("chosen people") and Gentiles (anti-Semitism), I would have been discourseless. I find myself in the absurd

situation which Derrida (1978:75) describes as a "noncoincidence of the self and the self," that is, "both more and less Jewish than the Jew."

26. What kind of scholarship is this which, armed to the teeth, only defends the agency of rural workers and denies it to its non-vision of "decultured" ex-rural workers!

[27] . Derrida (1989:813) uses the term "biodegradability" in these ways: *"On the one hand,* this thing is not a thing, not—as one ordinarily believes things to be—a *natural* thing: in fact 'biodegradable,' on the contrary, is generally said of an artificial product, most often an industrial product, whenever it lets itself be decomposed by microorganisms. *On the other hand,* the 'biodegradable' is hardly a thing since it remains a thing that does not remain, an essentially decomposable thing, destined to pass away, to lose its identity as a thing and to become again a non-thing. . . . Can one say, figuratively, that a 'publication' is biodegradable and distinguish here the degrees of degradation, the rhythms, the laws, the aleatory factors, the detours and the disguises, the transmutations, the cycles of recycling?"

References Cited

ABERCROMBIE, THOMAS A.
1998 *Pathways of Memory and Power, Ethnography and History among an Andean People.* Madison: The University of Wisconsin Press.

ABRAHAM, NICOLAS, AND MARIA TOROK
1986 *The Wolf Man's Magic Word: A Cryptonomy.* Translated by Nicholas Rand. Minneapolis: University of Minnesota Press.
1994 *The Shell and the Kernel, Renewals of Psychoanalysis, Volume I.* Edited, translated, and with an Introduction by Nicholas T. Rand. Chicago and London: The University of Chicago Press.

ADAMS, RICHARD N., AND CHARLES C. CUMBERLAND
1960 *United States University Cooperation in Latin America.* East Lansing: Michigan State University Institute of Research on Overseas Programs.

ADORNO, THEODOR
1978 *Minima Moralia, Reflections from Damaged Life.* Translated from the German by E. F. N Jephcott. London: Verso.

ALBRECHT, GARY L., and JUDITH A. LEVY
1984 A sociological perspective of physical disability. In *Advances in Medical Social Science, Volume 2*, Julio Ruffini, ed. New York: Gordon and Breach Science Publishers.

ALERS, J. OSCAR
1965 Population and development in a Peruvian community. *Journal of Inter-American Studies* 7:422-448.
1965b The quest for well-being. *The American Behavioral Scientist* 8(7):18-22.
1966 *Population, Attitudes, and Development: The Case of Vicos.* Ph.D. Thesis, Cornell University. Ann Arbor, MI: University Microfilms International.

1971 Well-being. In Dobyns, Doughty and Lasswell 1971a.
APPADURAI, ARJUN
1986 Introduction: commodities and the politics of value. In *The Social Life of Things, Commodities in Cultural Perspective*, Arjun Appadurai, ed. Cambridge, UK: Cambridge University Press.
1996   *Modernity at Large, Cultural Dimensions of Globalization.* Minneapolis and London: University of Minnesota Press.
APPIAH, KWAME ANTHONY
1990   Racisms. In *Anatomy of Racism*, David Theo Goldberg, ed. Minneapolis and London: University of Minnesota Press.
APTER, EMILY
1991 *Feminizing the Fetish, Psychoanalysis and Narrative Obsession in Turn-of-the-Century France.* Ithaca, NY, and London: Cornell University Press.
ARAMBURÚ, CARLOS EDUARDO
1978 Aspectos del desarrollo de la antropología en el Perú. In *Estado de las ciencias sociales en el Perú*, Bruno Podestá, ed. Lima: Centro de Investigación de la Universidad del Pacífico.
ARRIGHI, GIOVANNI, TERENCE K. HOPKINS, and IMMANUEL WALLERSTEIN
1989 *Antisystemic Movements.* London and New York: Verso.
AUGÉ, MARC
1998 *La guerra de los sueños, Ejercicios de etno-ficción.* Translated by Alberto Luis Bixio. Barcelona: Editorial Gedisa.
ÁVILA MOLERO, JAVIER
2000 Los dilemas del desarrollo: Antropología y promoción en el Perú. In *No hay país más diverso, Compendio de antropología peruana*, Carlos Iván Degregori, ed. Lima: Red para el Desarrollo de las Ciencias Sociales en el Perú.
BABB, FLORENCE E.
1980 *Women and Men in Vicos, Peru: A Case of Unequal Development.* Michigan Occasional Papers in Women's Studies, No. XI. University of Michigan. Ann Arbor.
BAKER, PAUL T., and MICHAEL A. LITTLE, eds.
1976 *Man in the Andes, a Multidisciplinary Study of High-Altitude Quechua.* Stroudsburg, PA: Dowden, Hutchinson & Ross.
BARNETT, CLIFFORD R.
1960 *An Analysis of Social Movements on a Peruvian Highland Hacienda.* Ph.D. Thesis, Cornell University. Ann Arbor, MI: University Microfilms International.
BARTHES, ROLAND
1968 *Writing Degree Zero.* Translated from the French by Annette Lavers and Colin Smith. New York: Hill and Wang.
1972a *Critical Essays.* Translated from the French by Richard Howard. Evanston, IL: Northwestern University Press.
1972b *Mythologies.* Selected and translated from the French by Annette Lavers. New York: Hill and Wang.

1990   *The Fashion System.* Translated by Matthew Ward and Richard Howard. Berkeley: University of California Press.

BATAILLE, GEORGES
1973   *Literature and Evil.* Translated by Alastair Hamilton. New York: Urizen Books.

BAUDRILLARD, JEAN
1975   *The Mirror of Production.* Translated by Mark Poster. St. Louis: Telos Press.
1981   *For a Critique of the Political Economy of the Sign.* Translated by Charles Levin. St. Louis: Telos Press.
1994   *The Illusion of the End.* Translated by Chris Turner. Stanford, CA: Stanford University Press.

BAUMAN, ZYGMUNT
1989   *Modernity and the Holocaust.* Ithaca, NY: Cornell University Press.
1991   *Modernity and Ambivalence.* Ithaca, NY: Cornell University Press.
1997   The making and unmaking of strangers. In *Debating Cultural Hybridity, Multi/Cultural Identities and the Politics of Anti/Racism,* Pnina Werbner and Tariq Modood, eds. London and Atlantic Highlands, NJ: Zed Books.

BECKER, ALTON L.
1995   *Beyond Translation, Essays toward a Modern Philology.* Ann Arbor, MI: University of Michigan Press.

BENNETT, JOHN W.
1996   Applied and action anthropology, Ideological and conceptual aspects. *Current Anthropology* 36(Supplement):S23-S53.

BHABHA, HOMI K.
1994   *The Location of Culture.* London and New York: Routledge.

BLANCHARD, WILLIAM C.
1955   *Proyecto Perú-Cornell, Cuarto Informe.* Mimeographed. Lima: Instituto Indigenista Peruano.
1956   *Proyecto Perú-Cornell, Quinto Informe.* Mimeographed. Lima: Instituto Indigenista Peruano.

BLOCH, MAURICE
1989   The symbolism of money in Imerina. In *Money and the Morality of Exchange,* Jonathan Parry and Maurice Bloch, eds. Cambridge, UK, and New York: Cambridge University Press.

BOON, JAMES A.
1982   *Other Tribes, Other Scribes, Symbolic Anthropology in the Comparative Study of Cultures, Histories, Religions, and Texts.* Cambridge, UK: Cambridge University Press.

BOROFSKY, ROBERT
1994   Applying anthropological perspectives. In *Assessing Cultural Anthropoloogy,* Robert Borofsky, ed. New York: McGraw-Hill.

BOURDIEU, PIERRE
1974   The school as a conservative force: scholastic and cultural inequalities. Translated by J. C. Whitehouse. In *Contemporary Research in the Sociology*

of Education, John Eggleston, ed. London: Methuen.

1977a The economics of linguistic exchanges. *Social Science Information* 16:645-668.

1977b *Outline of a Theory of Practice*. Translated by Richard Nice. Cambridge, UK: Cambridge University Press.

1984 *Distinction, A Social Critique of the Judgement of Taste*. Translated by Richard Nice. Cambridge, MA: Harvard University Press.

1989 Social space and symbolic power. *Sociological Theory* 7(1):14-25.

1990a. *The Logic of Practice*. Translated by Richard Nice. Stanford, CA: Stanford University Press.

1990b *In Other Words, Essays Towards a Reflexive Sociology*. Translated by Matthew Adamson. Stanford, CA: Stanford University Press.

1991 *Language and Symbolic Power*. Translated by Gino Raymond and Matthew Adamson. Cambridge, MA: Harvard University Press.

1993 *Sociology in Question*. Translated by Richard Nice. London: Sage Publications.

1996 *The State Nobility, Elite Schools in the Field of Power*. With the collaboration of Monique de Saint Martin. Translated by Lauretta C. Clough. Stanford, CA: Stanford University Press.

1998 *Practical Reason, On the Theory of Action*. Stanford, CA: Stanford University Press.

1999 Understanding. In *The Weight of the World, Social Suffering in Contemporary Society*, Pierre Bourdieu, et al., eds. Translated by Priscilla Parkhurst Ferguson, Susan Emanuel, Joe Johnson and Shoggy T. Waryn. Stanford, CA: Stanford University Press.

2000a *Pascalian Meditations*. Translated by Richard Nice. Stanford, CA: Stanford University Press.

2000b *La dominación masculina*. Translated by Joaquín Jordá. Barcelona: Editorial Anagrama.

BOURDIEU, PIERRE, and JEAN-CLAUDE PASSERON

1990 *Reproduction in Education, Society and Culture*. Translated from the French by Richard Nice. Second edition. London: Sage Publications.

BOURDIEU, PIERRE, and LOÏC J. D. WACQUANT

1990 The purpose of reflexive sociology (the Chicago Workshop). In *An Invitation to Reflexive Sociology*, Pierre Bourdieu and Loïc J. D. Wacquant. Chicago: University of Chicago Press.

BOURRICAUD, FRANÇOIS

1967 *Cambios en Puno, Estudios de Sociología Andina*. México: Instituto Indigenista Interamericano.

BOYARIN, DANIEL

1998 What does a Jew want?; Or, The political meaning of the phallus. In *The Psychoanalysis of Race*, Christopher Lane, ed. New York: Columbia University Press.

BRAIDOTTI, ROSI

1989 Envy: Or With Your Brains and My Looks. In *Men in Feminism*, Alice Jardine & Paul Smith, eds. New York and London: Routledge.

BRITZOLAKIS, CHRISTINA

1999 Phantasmagoria: Walter Benjamin and the poetics of urban modernism. In *Ghosts, Deconstruction, Psychoanalysis, History*, Peter Buse and Andrew Stott, eds. London and New York: Macmillan Press/St. Martin's Press.

BRUNER, EDWARD M.
1993 Introduction: The ethnographic self and the personal self. In *Anthropology and Literature*, Paul Benson, ed. Urbana and Chicago: University of Illinois Press.

BRUSH, STEPHEN B.
1999 Bioprospecting the Public Domain. *Cultural Anthropology* 14:535-555.

BÜRGER, PETER
1992 *The Decline of Modernism*. Translated by Nicholas Walker. University Park, PA: The Pennsylvania State University Press.

BURTON, W. G.
1985 The industrial uses of the potato. In *The History and Social Influence of the Potato*, Radcliffe Salaman. Revised impression. Cambridge, UK: Cambridge University Press.

BUTLER, JUDITH
1990 *Gender Trouble, Feminism and the Subversion of Identity*. New York and London: Routledge.
1993 *Bodies That Matter, On the Discursive Limits of "Sex"*. New York and London: Routledge.

CANGUILHEM, GEORGES
1989 *The Normal and the Pathological*. Translated by Carolyn R. Fawcett in collaboration with Robert S. Cohen. New York: Zone Books.

CAPUTO, JOHN D.
1997a A commentary: Deconstruction in a nutshell. In *Deconstruction in a Nutshell, A Conversation with Jacques Derrida*, John D. Caputo,ed. New York: Fordham University Press.
1997b Dreaming of the innumerable, Derrida, Drucilla Cornell, and the dance of gender. In *Derrida and Feminism, Recasting the Question of Woman*, Ellen K. Feder, Mary C. Rawlinson, and Emily Zakin, eds. New York and London: Routledge.
1997c *The Prayers and Tears of Jacques Derrida, Religion without Religion*. Bloomington and Indianapolis: Indiana University Press.

CARRIER, JAMES G.
1995a *Gifts and Commodities, Exchange and Western Capitalism since 1700*. London and New York: Routledge.
1995b Introduction. In *Occidentalism, Images of the West*. Oxford, UK: Clarendon Press.
1997 Introduction. In *Meanings of the Market, The Free Market in Western Culture*, James G. Carrier, ed. Oxford, UK, and New York: Berg.

CARTER, MICHAEL R., and ELENA ALVAREZ
1989 Changing paths: the decollectivization of agrarian reform agriculture in coastal Peru. In *Searching for Agrarian Reform in Latin America*, William

C. Thiesenhusen, ed. Boston and London: Unwin Hyman.

CARRILLO, ETHEL R.
1988   Distribution of health Care facilities. In *Health Care in Peru: Resources and Policy*, Dieter K. Zschock, ed. Boulder, CO, and London: Westview Press.

CERTEAU, MICHEL DE
1997   *The Capture of Speech and Other Political Writings*. Translated by Tom Conley. Minneapolis and London: University of Minnesota Press.

CHADBOURN, CHERYL
1962   *Concepts of Disease in a Peruvian Indian Community*. Columbia, Cornell, Harvard, Illinois Summer Field Studies Program. Mimeographed. Ithaca, New York: Department of Anthropology, Cornell University.

CHAFE, WALLACE
1986   Evidentiality in English conversation and academic writing. In *Evidentiality: The Linguistic Coding of Epistemology*, Wallace Chafe and Johanna Nichols, eds. Norwood, NJ: Ablex Publishing Company.

CHAPLIN, DAVID
1967   *The Peruvian Industrial Labor Force*. Princeton, NJ: Princeton University Press.

CHARI, HEMA
2001   Colonial fantasies and postcolonial identities, Elaboration of postcolonial masculinity and homoerotic desire. In *Postcolonial, Queer, Theoretical intersections*, John C. Hawley, ed. Albany: State University of New York Press.

CHATTERJEE, PARTHA
1993   *The Nation and Its Fragments, Colonial and Postcolonial Histories*. Princeton, NJ: Princeton University Press.

CHENG HURTADO, ALBERTO
1958   La minka en Vicos. *Anales de la Universidad Nacional Mayor de San Marcos*, Segunda época, Nos. 19-20:16-22.

CIXOUS, HÉLÈNE
1976   Fiction and its phantoms: A reading of Freud's *Das Unheimliche* (The 'uncanny'). Translated by Robert Dennomé. *New Literary History* 7:525-548.

_____. 1994 *The Hélène Cixous Reader*. Edited by Susan Sellers. London and New York: Routledge.

CLIFFORD, JAMES
1986   On ethnographic allegory. In *Writing Culture, The Poetics and Politics of Ethnography*, James Clifford and George E. Marcus, eds. Berkeley, Los Angeles, and London: University of California Press.
1988   *The Predicament of Culture, Twentieth-Century Ethnography, Literature, and Art*. Cambridge, MA, and London: Harvard University Press.
1997   *Routes, Travel and Translation in the Late Twentieth Century*. Cambridge, MA, and London: Harvard University Press.

COCHRANE, GLYNN
1971   *Development Anthropology*. New York: Oxford University Press.

COHEN, TOM

2001 Introduction: Derrida and the future of . . . In *Jacques Derrida and the Humanities, A Critical Reader*, Tom Cohen, ed. Cambridge, UK: Cambridge University Press.

CONSUMER REPORTS
1998 Test, inform, protect. 63(9):6-7.

CORAL CORDERO, ISABEL
1998 Women in war: impact and responses. In *Shining and Other Paths, War and Society in Peru, 1980-1995*, Steve J. Stern, ed. Durham, NC, and London: Duke University Press.

CORNELL, DRUCILLA
1991 Civil disobedience and deconstruction. *Cardozo Law Review* 13:1309, 1314.

COUTU, ARTHUR J., and RICHARD A. KING
1969 *The Agricultural Development of Peru*. New York: Frederick A. Praeger.

CREWE, EMMA
1997 The silent traditions of developing cooks. In *Discourses of Development, Anthropological Perspectives*, R. D. Grillo and R. L. Stirrat, eds. Oxford, UK, and New York: Berg.

DAVIES, MARGARET
2001 Derrida and law: Legitimate fictions. In *Jacques Derrida and the Humanities, A Critical Reader*, Tom Cohen, ed. Cambridge, UK: Cambridge University Press.

DAVIES, THOMAS M., JR.
1974 *Indian Integration in Peru, A Half Century of Experience, 1900-1948*. Lincoln: University of Nebraska Press.

DEGREGORI, CARLOS IVÁN, ed.
2000a *No hay país más diverso, Compendio de antropolgía peruana*. Lima: Red para el desarrollo de las ciencias sociales.

DEGREGORI, CARLOS IVÁN
2000b Panorama de la antropología en el Perú: Del estudio del Otro a la construcción de un Nosotros diverso. In *No hay país más diverso, Compendio de antropología peruana*, Carlos Iván Degregori, ed. Lima: Red para el Desarrollo de las Ciencias Sociales.

DE LA CADENA, MARISOL
1990 De utopías y contrahegemonías: el proceso de la cultura popular. *Revista Andina* 15:65-76.
1991 "Las mujeres son más indias": Etnicidad y género en una comunidad del Cusco. *Revista Andina* 17:7-47.
1996 *Race, Ethnicity, and the Struggle for Indigenous Self-Representation: De-Indianization in Cuzco, Peru (1919-1992)*. Ph.D. Dissertation, University of Wisconsin-Madison. Ann Arbor, MI: University Microfilms International.
1998 From race to class: insurgent intellectuals *de provincia* in Peru, 1910-1970. In *Shining and Other Paths, War and Society in Peru, 1980-1995*, Steve J. Stern, ed. Durham, NC, and London: Duke University Press.
2000 *Indigenous Mestizos, The Politics of Race and Gender in Cuzco, Peru,*

1919-1991. Durham, NC, and London: Duke University Press.

DE LAURENTIS, TERESA
1984 *Alice Doesn't, Feminism, Semiotics, Cinema.* Bloomington: Indiana University Press.
DE MAN, PAUL
1979 *Allegories of Reading, Figural Language in Rousseau, Nietzsche, Rilke, and Proust.* New Haven, CT, and London: Yale University Press.
1983 *Blindness and Insight, Essays in the Rhetoric of Contemporary Criticism.* Second edition, revised. Minneapolis: University of Minnesota Press.
1984 *Th Rhetoric of Romanticism.* New York: Columbia University Press.
DERRIDA, JACQUES
1972 *Speech and Phenomena, And Other Essays on Husserl's Theory of Signs.* Translated by David B. Allison. Evanston, IL: Northwestern University Press.
1976 *Of Grammatology.* Translated by Gayatri Chakravorty Spivak. Baltimore and London: The Johns Hopkins University Press.
1978a *Spurs, Nietzsche's Styles.* English translation by Barbara Harlow. Chicago and London: University of Chicago Press.
1978b *Writing and Difference.* Translated by Alan Bass. Chicago: The University of Chicago Press.
1981 *Dissemination.* Translated with an Introduction and Additional Notes by Barbara Johnson. Chicago: The University of Chicago Press.
1982a *Positions.* Translated by Alan Bass. Paperback edition. Chicago: The University of Chicago Press.
1982b *Margins of Philosophy.* Translated by Alan Bass. Chicago: The University of Chicago Press.
1986 *Glas.* English translation by John P. Leavey, Jr., and Richard Rand. Lincoln and London: University of Nebraska Press.
1988a *Limited Inc.* Evanston, IL: Northwestern University Press.
1988b *The Ear of the Other, Otobiography, Transference, Translation.* English edition edited by Christie McDonald. A translation by Peggy Kamuf of the French edition edited by Claude Levesque and Christie McDonald. Lincoln and London: University of Nebraska Press.
1989a Psyche: Inventions of the other. Translated by Catherine Porter. In *Reading de Man Reading,* Lindsay Waters and Wlad Godzich, eds. Minneapolis: University of Minnesota Press.
1989b *Edmund Husserl's Origin of Geometry: An Introduction.* Translated by John P. Leavey, Jr. Lincoln and London: University of Nebraska Press.
1989c *Of Spirit, Heidegger and the Question.* Translated by Geoffrey Bennington and Rachel Bowlby. Chicago and London: The University of Chicago Press.
1989d Acts, The Meaning of a given word. Translated by Eduardo Cadava. In *Memoires for Paul de Man.* New York: Columbia University Press.
1989e Biodegradables, Seven diary fragments. Translated by Peggy Kamuf. *Critical Inquiry* 15:812-873.

1992a *Given Time: I. Counterfeit Money*. Translated by Peggy Kamuf. Chicago and London: The University of Chicago Press.

1992b Before the law. Translated by Avital Ronell, with additional material translated by Christine Roulston. In *Acts of Literature*, Derek Attridge, ed. New York and London: Routledge.

1992c How to avoid speaking: Denials. Translated by Ken Frieden. In *Derrida and Negative Theology*, Harold Coward and Toby Foshay, eds. Albany: State University of New York Press.

1992d Mochlos; or, The conflict of the faculties. Translated by Richard Rand and Amy Wygant. In *Logomachia, The Conflict of the Faculties*, Richard Rand, ed. Lincoln: University of Nebraska Press.

1992e Passions: "An oblique offering." In *Derrida: A Critical Reader*, David Wood, ed. Oxford, UK, and Cambridge, MA: Blackwell.

1993 *Memoirs of the Blind, The Self-Portrait and Other Ruins*. Translated by Pascale-Anne Brault and Michael Naas. Chicago and London: The University of Chicago Press.

1994 *Specters of Marx, The State of the Debt, the Work of Mourning, and the New International*. Translated by Peggy Kamuf. New York and London: Routledge.

1995 The time is out of joint. In *Deconstruction is/in America, A New Sense of the Political*, Anselm Haverkamp, ed. New York and London: New York University Press.

1996a As *if* I were dead: An interview with Jacques Derrida. In *Applying: To Derrida*, John Brannigan, Ruth Robbins, and Julian Wolfreys, eds. Houndmills, UK, and New York: Macmillan Press/St. Martin's Press.

1996b *Archive Fever, A Freudian Impression*. Translated by Eric Prenowitz. Chicago and London: The University of Chicago Press.

1996c Remarks on deconstruction and pragmatism. In *Deconstruction and Pragmatism*, Chantal Mouffe, ed. London and New York: Routledge.

1997 *Politics of Friendship*. Translated by George Collins. London and New York: Verso.

1998 *Resistances of Psychoanalysis*. Translated by Peggy Kamuf, Pascale-Anne Brault, and Michael Naas. Stanford, CA: Stanford University Press.

1999a *Adieu to Emmanuel Levinas*. Translated by Pascale-Anne Brault and Michael Naas. Stanford, CA: Stanford University Press.

1999b Marx & sons. In *Ghostly Demarcations, A Symposium on Jacques Derrida's* Specters of Marx, Michael Sprinker, ed. London and New York: Verso.

2001a The future of the profession or the university without condition (thanks to the "Humanities," what could take place tomorrow). In *Jacques Derrida and the Humanities, A Critical Reader*, Tom Cohen, ed. Cambridge, UK: Cambridge University Press.

2001b "The deconstruction of actuality: An interview with Jacques Derrida." In *Deconstruction, A Reader*, Martin McQuillan, ed. New York: Routledge. [1994.]

2001c "I have a taste for the secret. In *A Taste for the Secret*, Jacues Derrida and Maurizio Ferrarís. Translated by Giacomo Donis. Cambridge, UK: Polity.

2001d History of the lie, Prolegomena. In *Futures, Of Jacques Derrida*, Richard Rand, ed. Stanford, CA: Stanford University Press.

2001e As if it were Possible, "within such limits" . . . In *Questioning Derrida, With his replies on philosophy*, Michel Meyer, ed. Aldershot, UK: Ashgate.

2002a *Who's Afraid of Philosophy?, Right to Philosophy I*. Translated by Jan Plug. Stanford, CA: Stanford University Press.

2002b *Negotiations, Interventions and Interviews, 1971-2001*. Translated by Elizabeth Rottenberg. Stanford, CA: Stanford University Press.

2002c *Without Alibi*. Translated by Peggy Kamuf. Stanford, CA: Stanford University Press.

2002d Faith and knowledge, The two sources of "religion" at the limits of reason alone. Translated by Samuel Weber. In *Acts of Religion*. New York and London: Routledge.

2002e The Eyes of language, The Abyss and the volcano. Translated by Gil Anidjar. In *Acts of Religion*. New York and London: Routledge.

DES CHENE, MARY

1997 Locating the past. In *Anthropological Locations, Boundaries and Grounds of a Field Science*, Akhil Gupta and James Ferguson, eds. Berkeley, Los Angeles, and London: University of California Press.

DIRKS, NICHOLAS B., GEOFF ELEY, and SHERRY B. ORTNER

1994 Introduction. In *Culture/Power/History, A Reader in Contemporary Social Theory*, Nicholas B. Dirks, Geoff Eley, and Sherry B. Ortner, eds. Princeton, NJ: Princeton University Press.

DOBYNS, HENRY F.

1971 Enlightenment and skill foundations of power. In Dobyns, Doughty, and Lasswell 1971a.

1974 The Cornell-Peru Project: experimental intervention in Vicos. In *Contemporary Cultures and Societies of Latin America*, Dwight B. Heath, ed. New York: Random House.

DOBYNS, HENRY F., and PAUL L. DOUGHTY

1971 A note to anthropologists. In Dobyns, Doughty and Lasswell 1971a.

DOBYNS, HENRY F., PAUL L. DOUGHTY, and HAROLD D. LASSWELL, eds.

1971a *Peasants, Power, and Applied Social Change, Vicos As a Model*. Beverly Hills, California: Sage Publications.

1971b Introduction. In Dobyns, Doughty and Lasswell 1971a.

DOBYNS, HENRY F., PAUL L. DOUGHTY, and ALLAN R. HOLMBERG

n.d. *Peace Corps Program Impact in the Peruvian Andes, Final Report*. Cornell Peru Project, Department of Anthropology, Cornell University. Mimeographed. Ithaca, New York.

DOBYNS, HENRY F., and MARIO C. VÁZQUEZ

1964 *The Cornell-Perú Project Bibliography and Personnel*. Ithaca, New York: Cornell-Perú Project, Department of Anthropology, Cornell University.

DORNER, PETER

1992 *Latin American Land Reforms in Theory and Practice, A Retrospective Analysis.* Madison, WI, and London: The University of Wisconsin Press.
DOUGHTY, PAUL L.
1966 Pitfalls and progress in the Peruvian sierra. In *Cultural Frontiers of the Peace Corps,* Robert B. Textor, ed. Cambridge, MA: The M.I.T. Press.
1971 Human relations: affection, rectitude, and respect. In Dobyns, Doughty, and Lasswell 1971a.
1976 Social policy and urban problems in Lima. In *Peruvian Nationalism, a Corporatist Revolution,* David Chaplin, ed. New Brunswick, NJ: Transaction Books.
1982 What has become of Vicos? The aftermath of a classic program. Presented at the Annual Meeting of the Society for Applied Anthropology. Typescript. Gainesville, Florida.
1986 Directed change and the hope for peace: Peruvian experiences. In *Peace and War, Cross-Cultural Perspectives,* Mary LeCron Foster and Robert A. Rubenstein, eds. New Brunswick, NJ, and Oxford, UK: Transaction Books.
1987a Vicos: success, rejection, and rediscovery of a classic program. In *Applied Anthropology in America,* Elizabeth M. Eddy y William L. Partridge, eds. Second edition. New York: Columbia University Press.
1987b Against the odds: collaboration and development at Vicos. In *Collaborative Research and Social Change, Applied Anthropology in Action.* Boulder, CO, and London: Westview Press.
2002 Ending serfdom in Peru, The struggle for land and freedom in Vicos. In *Contemporary Cultures and Societies of Latin America, A Reader in the Social Anthropology of Middle and South America.* Third edition. Prospect Heights, IL: Waveland Press.
DOUGLAS, MARY
1966 *Purity and Danger, An Analysis of Concepts of Pollution and Taboo.* New York and Washington: Frederick A. Praeger, Publishers.
DUBERMAN, MARTIN
1994 *Stonewall.* New York: Plume.
DYER, RICHARD
1997 *White.* London and New York: Routledge.
ENGE, KJELL, and POLY HARRISON
1986 The locals fight back when times are tough: The ethnography of health care in Peru. In *Practicing Development Anthropology,* Edward C. Green, ed. Boulder, CO, Westview Press.
EPSTEIN, T. S.
1962 *Economic Development and Social Change in South India.* Manchester, UK: The University Press.
ERIKSEN, THOMAS HYLLAND
1997 The nation as a human being–a metaphor in a mid-life crisis? Notes on the imminent collapse of Norwegian national identity. In *Siting Culture, The Shifting Anthropological Object,* Karen Fog Olwig and Kirsten Hastrup, eds. London and New York: Routledge.

ESCH, DEBORAH
    1989   A defense of rhetoric/The triumph of reading. In *Reading de Man Reading*, Lindsay Waters and Wlad Godzich, eds. Minneapolis: University of Minnesota Press.
ESCOBAR, ARTURO
    1995   *Encountering Development, the Making and Unmaking of the Third World*. Princeton, NJ: Princeton University Press.
FABIAN, JOHANNES
    1983   *Time and the Other, How Anthropology Makes Its Object*. New York: Columbia University Press.
    1993   Keep listening: ethnography and reading. In *The Ethnography of Reading*, Jonathan Boyarin, ed. Berkeley, Los Angeles, and London: University of California Press.
    1998   *Moments of Freedom: Anthropology and Popular Culture*. Charlottesville and London: University Press of Virginia.
FAIRHEAD, JAMES, and MELISSA LEACH
    1997   Webs of power and the construction of environmental policy problems: forest loss in Guinea. In *Discourses of Development, Anthropological Perspectives*, R. D. Grillo and R. L. Stirrat, eds. Oxford, UK, and New York: Berg.
FANON, FRANTZ
    1963   *The Wretched of the Earth*. Translated by Constance Farrington. New York: Grove Press.
FAVRE, HENRI
    1964   Evolución y situación de las haciendas en la región de Huancavelica, Perú. *Revista del Museo Nacional* (Lima) 28:237-257.
FEDER, ERNEST
    1971   *The Rape of the Peasantry: Latin America's Landholding System*. Garden City: Doubleday Anchor Books.
FELMAN, SHOSHANA
    1985   *Writing and Madness (Literature/Philosophy/Psychoanalysis)*. Translated by Martha Noel Evans and the author with the assistance of Brian Massumi. Ithaca, NY: Cornell University Press.
    1993   *What Does a Woman Want? Reading and Sexual Difference*. Baltimore and London: The Johns Hopkins University Press.
FERGUSON, JAMES
    1994   *The Anti-Politics Machine, "Development," Depoliticization, and Bureaucratic Power in Lesotho*. Minneapolis and London: University of Minnesota Press.
FLORES GALINDO ALBERTO
    1989   Lo andino en la encrucijada (conversatorio). In *Encuentros*, Carlos Arroyo. Lima: Ediciones Memoriangosta.
FORD, THOMAS R.
    1955   *Man and Land in Peru*. Gainesville: University of Florida Press.
FORTY, ADRIAN
    1986   *Objects of Desire, Design and Society since 1750*. London: Thames and Hudson.

FOSTER, GEORGE M.
1969 *Applied Anthropology.* Boston: Little, Brown and Company.
FOUCAULT, MICHEL
1972 *The Archaeology of Knowledge and the Discourse on Language.* Translated from the French by A. M. Sheridan Smith. New York: Pantheon Books.
1977a *Discipline and Punish, the Birth of the Prison.* Translated from the French by Alan Sheridan. New York: Pantheon Books.
1977b *Language, Counter-Memory, Practice, Selected Essays and Interviews.* Translated from the French by Donald F. Bouchard and Sherry Simon. Ithaca, NY: Cornell University Press.
1980a *Power/Knowledge, Selected Interviews and Other Writings, 1972-1977.* Edited by Colin Gordon. *Translated by Colin Gordon, Leo Marshall, John Mepham, and Kate Soper.* New York: Pantheon Books.
1980b *The History of Sexuality, Volume I: An Introduction.* Translated from the French by Robert Hurley. New York: Vintage Books.
1994 *The Order of Things, an Archaeology of the Human Sciences.* New York: Vintage Books.
1997 Polemics, politics, and problematizations: An interview with Michel Foucault. In *The Essential Works of Michel Foucault, Volume One, Ethics, Subjectivity and Truth,* Paul Rabinow, ed. New York: The New Press.
FRASER, NANCY
1989 *Unruly Practices: Power, Discourse, and Gender in Contemporary Society.* Minneapolis: University of Minnesota Press.
FRAWLEY, WILLIAM
1984 Prolegomenon to a theory of Translation. In *Translation, Literary, Linguistic, and Philosophical Perspectives,* William Frawley, ed. Newark, /London and Toronto: University of Delaware Press/Associated University Presses.
FREUD, SIGMUND
1955a The psychotherapy of hysteria. In Studies on Hysteria by Joseph Breuer and Sigmund Freud. In *The Standard Edition of the Complete Psychological Works of Sigmund Freud.* Volume 2. London: The Hogarth Press and the Institute of Psycho-Analysis.
1955b The "uncanny." In *The Standard Edition of the Complete Psychological Works of Sigmund Freud.* Volume 17. London: The Hogarth Press and the Institute of Psycho-Analysis.
1957 On narcissism: an introduction. In *The Standard Edition of the Complete Psychological Works of Sigmund Freud.* Volume 14. London: The Hogarth Press and the Institute of Psycho-Analysis.
1961 Fetishism. In *The Standard Edition of the Complete Psychological Works of Sigmund Freud.* Volume 21. London: The Hogarth Press and the Institute of Psycho-Analysis.
1965a *New Introductory Lectures on Psychoanalysis.* Translated and edited by James Strachey. New York and London: W. W. Norton & Company.
1965b *The Interpretation of Dreams.* Translated from the German and edited

by James Strachey. New York: Avon Books.
1988   Freud and fetishism: Previously unpublished minutes of the Vienna Psychoanalytic Society. Edited and translated by Louis Rose. *Psychoanalytic Quarterly* 57:147-165.

FRIEDMAN, JONATHAN
1997   Global crises, the struggle for cultural identity and intellectual porkbarreling: cosmopolitans versus locals, ethnics and nationals in an era of de/hegemonization. In *Debating Cultural Hybridity, Multi-Cultural Identities and the Politics of Anti/Racism*, Pnina Werbner and Tariq Modood, eds. London and Atlantic Highlands, NJ: Zed Books.

FROMM-REICHMANN, FRIEDA
1959   *Psychoanalysis and Psychotherapy, Selected Papers*, Dexter M. Bullard, ed. Chicago: The University of Chicago Press.

FURNHAM, ADRIAN, and STEPHEN BOCHNER
1986   *Culture Shock, Psychological Reactions to Unfamiliar Environments*. London and New York: Methuen.

FUSS, DIANA
1989   *Essentially Speaking, Feminism, Nature & Difference*. New York and London: Routledge.
1995   *Identification Papers*. New York and London: Routledge.

GAMARRA C., JEFREY
2002   Las dificultades de la memoria, el poder y la reconciliación. IPAZ. Oficina de Investigación, Universidad Nacional de San Cristóbal de Huamanga. Ayacucho, Peru.

GAMMAN, LORRAINE, and MERJA MAKINEN
1995   *Female Fetishism*. New York: New York University Press.

GARCÍA CANCLINI, NÉSTOR
1995   *Hybrid Cultures, Strategies for Entering and Leaving Modernity*. Translated by Christopher L. Chiappari and Silvia L. López. Minneapolis and London: University of Minnesota Press.

GARRIDO-LECCA, GUILLERMO
1965   *The Measurement of Production Efficiency in Peruvian Traditional Agriculture, The Case of Vicos*. M.S. Thesis, Cornell University. Ithaca, New York.

GEERTZ, CLIFFORD
1973   *The Interpretation of Culture, Selected Essays*. New York: Basic Books.
1984   Distinguished lecture: Anti anti-relativism. *American Anthropologist* 86:263-278.
1995   *After the Fact, Two Countries, Four Decades, One Anthropologist*. Cambridge, MA: Harvard University Press.

GELDER, KEN
1994   *Reading the Vampire*. London and New York: Routledge.

GELL, ALFRED
1992   Inter-tribal commodity barter and reproductive gift-exchange in old Melanesia. In *Barter, Exchange and Value, An Anthropological Approach*, Caroline Humphrey and Stephen Hugh-Jones, eds. Cambridge, UK:

Cambridge University Press.

GELLES, PAUL H.
1994   Channels of power, fields of contention: the politics of irrigation and land recovery in an Andean peasant community. In *Irrigation at High Altitudes: The Social Organization of Water Control Systems in the Andes*, William P. Mitchell and David Guillet, eds. Washington: American Anthropological Association.

GHERSI B., HUMBERTO
1959-1961   El indígena y el mestizo en la comunidad de Marcará. *Revista del Museo Nacional* (Lima) 28:117-187, 29:47-127, 30:95-176.

GILLIAM, ANGELA
1997   Militarism and accumulation as cargo cult. In *Decolonizing Anthropology, Moving Further toward an Anthropology for Liberation*, Faye. V. Harrison, ed. Arlington, VA: Association of Black Anthropologists/American Anthropological Association.

GILMAN, SANDER L.
1986   *Jewish Self-Hatred, Anti-Semitism and the Hidden Language of the Jews*. Baltimore and London: The Johns Hopkins University Press.

GILROY, PAUL
1990   One nation under a groove: the cultural politics of "race" and racism in modern Britain. In *Anatomy of Racism*, David Theo Goldberg, ed. Minneapolis: University of Minnesota Press.

GODELIER, MAURICE
1999   *The Enigma of the Gift*. Chicago: The University of Chicago Press.

GODOY, RICARDO A.
1990   *Mining and Agriculture in Highland Bolivia, Ecology, History, and Commerce Among the Jukumanis*. Tucson, AZ: The University of Arizona Press.

GOFFMAN, ERVING
1986   *Frame Analysis, An Essay on the Organization of Experience*. Boston: Northeastern University Press.

GOLTE, JÜRGEN
1980   *La racionalidad de la organización andina*. Lima: Instituto de Estudios Peruanos.

GÓMEZ, LUIS CARLOS
1988   Health status of the Peruvian population. In *Health Care in Peru: Resources and Policy*, Dieter K. Zschock, ed. Boulder, CO, and London: Westview Press.

GOOD, BYRON J., and MARY-JO DELVECCHIO GOOD
1981   The meaning of symptoms: A cultural hermeneutic model for clinical practice. In *The Relevance of Social Science for Medicine*, Leon Eisenberg and Arthur Kleinman, eds. Dordrecht, Holland, Boston and London: D. Reidel Publishing Company.

GORDON, AVERY F.
1997   *Ghostly Matters, Haunting and the Sociological Imagination*. Minneapolis and London: University of Minnesota Press.

GOSE, PETER

1986 Sacrifice and the commodity form in the Andes. *Man* 20(2):296-310.

1991 House rethatching in an Andean annual cycle: practice, meaning, and contradiction. *American Ethnologist* 18:39-66.

1994a Embodied violence: racial identity and the semiotics of property in Huaquirca, Antabamba (Apurímac). In *Unruly Order, Violence, Power, and Cultural Identity in the High Provinces of Southern Peru*, Deborah Poole, ed. Boulder, CO: Westview Press.

1994b *Deathly Waters and Hungry Mountains, Agrarian Ritual and Class Formation in an Andean Town.* Toronto: University of Toronto Press.

GOW, DAVID D.

1976 *The Gods and Social Change in the High Andes.* Ph.D. Thesis, University of Wisconsin-Madison. Ann Arbor, MI: University Microfilms International.

GREENE, SHANE

n.d. Gringos do the damndest things: Rumor as political strategy in the Peruvian Amazon. Presented at the 101st Annual Meeting, American Anthropological Association, New Orleans, November 21, 2002.

GROSZ, ELIZABETH

1993 Lesbian fetishism? In *Fetishism as Cultural Discourse*, Emily Apter and William Pietz, eds. Ithaca, NY, and London: Cornell University Press.

1997 Ontology and equivocation, Derrida's politics of sexual difference. In *Feminist Interpretations of Jacques Derrida*, Nancy J. Holland, ed. University Park: The Pennsylvania State University Press.

GUERRA, JOSÉ A., et al.

1973 *Current Economic Position and Prospects of Peru.* Washington International Bank for Reconstruction and Development.

GUHA, RANAJIT

1988a The prose of counter-insurgency. In *Selected Subaltern Studies*, Ranajit Guha and Gayatri Chakravorty Spivak, eds. New York and Oxford, UK: Oxford University Press.

1988b Preface. In *Selected Subaltern Studies*, Ranajit Guha and Gayatri Chakravorty Spivak, eds. New York and Oxford, UK: Oxford University Press.

GULLIVER, P. H.

1985 An applied anthropologist in East Africa during the colonial era. In *Social Anthropology and Development Policy*, Ralph Grillo and Alan Rew, eds. London and New York: Tavistock Publications.

GUPTA, AKHIL, and JAMES FERGUSON

1997a Discipline and practice: "The Field" as site, method, and location in anthropology. In *Anthropological Locations, Boundaries and Grounds of a Field Science*, Akhil Gupta and James Ferguson, eds. Berkeley, Los Angeles, and London: University of California Press.

_____. 1997b Culture, power, place: Ethnography and the end of an era. In *Culture, Power, Place, Explorations in Critical Anthropology*, Akhil Gupta and James Ferguson, eds. Durham, NC, and London: Duke University Press.

GUSFIELD, JOSEPH R.

1996   Contested Meanings, The Construction of Alcohol Problems. Madison: The University of Wisconsin Press.

HABERMAS, JÜRGEN
1987   The Philosophical Discourse of Modernity, Twelve Lectures. Translated by Frederick Lawrence. Cambridge, MA: The MIT Press.

HALL, THOMAS L.
1969   Health Manpower in Peru, a Case Study in Planning. Baltimore: The Johns Hopkins Press.

HANDELMAN, HOWARD
1975   Struggle in the Andes: Peasant Political Mobilization in Perú. Austin and London: University of Texas Press.

HANNERZ, ULF
1992   Cultural Complexity, Studies in the Social Organization of Meaning. New York: Columbia University Press.

HARAWAY, DONNA
1989   Primate Visions, Gender, Race, and Nature in the World of Modern Science. New York and London: Routledge.
1991   Simians, Cyborgs, and Women, The Reinvention of Nature. New York: Routledge.
1997   Modest_Witness@Second__millenium.Female.Man$^\theta$__Meets__OncoMouse, Feminism and Technoscience. New York and London: Routledge.

HARRIS, OLIVIA
1989   The earth and the state: the sources and meanings of money in Northern Potosí, Bolivia. In Money and the Morality of Exchange, Jonathan Parry and Maurice Bloch, eds. Cambridge, UK: Cambridge University Press.
1994   Comment. In Starn 1994.
1995   Ethnic identity and market relations: Indians and mestizos in the Andes. In Ethnicity, Markets, and Migration in the Andes, at the Crossroads of History and Anthropology, Brooke Larson, Olivia Harris, and Enrique Tandeter, eds. Durham, NC, and London: Duke University Press.

HARRISON, REGINA
1989   Signs, Songs, and Memory in the Andes, Translating Quechua Language and Culture. Austin: University of Texas Press.

HARVEY, PENELOPE
1994   Domestic violence in the Peruvian Andes. In Sex and Violence, Issues in Representation and Experience, Penelope Harvey and Peter Gow, eds. London and New York: Routledge.

HEATH, SHIRLEY BRICE
1996   Ways with Words, Language, Life, and Work in Communities and Classrooms. Second edition. Cambridge, UK: Cambridge University Press.

HEATH, STEPHEN
1989   Male feminism. In Men in Feminism, Alice Jardine & Paul Smith, eds. New Yoirk: Routledge.

HELLER, AGNES
1990   Can Modernity Survive? Berkeley and Los Angeles: University of

California Press.

HEYDUK, DANIEL

1971   *Huayrapampa: Bolivian Highland Peasants and the New Social Order.* Ithaca, NY: Cornell University Latin American Studies Program, Dissertation Series, Number 27.

HIMES, JAMES R.

1972   *The Utilization of Research for Development: Two Case Studies in Rural Modernization and Agriculture in Peru.* Ph.D. Dissertation, Princeton University. Ann Arbor, MI: University Microfilms International.

1981   The impact in Peru of the Vicos Project. In *Research in Economic Anthropology*, George Dalton, ed. Volume 4. Greenwich, CT, and London: JAI Press.

HINOJOSA, IVÁN

1992   Entre el poder y la ilusión: Pol Pot, Sendero y las utopías campesinas. *Debate Agrario* 15:69-93.

HOLMBERG, ALLAN R.

1952   *Progress Report, Cornell Peru Project.* Mimeographed. Department of Sociology and Anthropology, Cornell University. Ithaca, New York.

1952b *Proyecto Perú-Cornell, Primer Informe.* Mimeographed. Lima: Instituto Indigenista Peruano.

1955   Participant intervention in the field. *Human Organization* 14(1):23-26.

1958   The research and development approach to the study of change. *Human Organization* 17(1):12-16.

1959   Land tenure and planned social change: a case from Vicos, Peru. *Human Organization* 18(1):7-10.

1960   Changing community attitudes and values in Peru: a case study in guided change. In *Social Change in Latin America Today, Its Implications for United States Policy*, Richard N. Adams, et al. New York: Harper and Brothers.

1965   The changing values and institutions of Vicos in the context of national development. *The American Behavioral Scientist* 8(7):3-8.

1966   *Vicos, método y práctica de antropología aplicada.* Lima: Editorial Estudios Andinos.

1967   Algunas relaciones entre la privación psicobiológica y el cambio cultural en los Andes. *América Indígena* 27:3-24.

1971a Experimental intervention in the field. In Dobyns, Doughty and Lasswell 1971a.

1971b The role of power in changing values and institutions of Vicos. In Dobyns, Doughty and Lasswell 1971a.

HOLMBERG, ALLAN R., and HENRY F. DOBYNS

1965   *Case Studies of Subsistence and Transition, Vicos, Peru.* Comparative Studies of Cultural Change, Department of Anthropology, Cornell University. Mimeographed. Ithaca, New York.

1969   The Cornell Program in Vicos, Perú. In *Subsistence, Agriculture and Economic Development*, Clifton R. Wharton, Jr., ed. Chicago: Aldine Publishing Company.

HORKHEIMER, MAX, and THEODOR W. ADORNO

1982   *Dialectic of Enlightenment.* Translated by John Cumming. New York: Continuum.

HORNBERGER, NANCY H.
1995   Five vowels or three? Linguistics and politics in Quechua language planning in Peru. In *Power and Inequality in Language Education,* James W. Tollefson, ed. Cambridge, UK: Cambridge University Press.

HORNE, DONALD
1984   *The Great Museum, The Re-Presentation of History.* London and Sydney: Pluto Press.

HORTON, DOUGLAS
1981   Potato. *Ceres,* January-February:28-32.
_____. 1983   Potato Farming in the Andes: Some Lessons from On-Farm Research in Peru's Mantaro Valley. *Agricultural Systems* 12:171-184.

HURTADO SUÁREZ, WILFREDO
1997   La música y los jóvenes de hoy: Los hijos de la chicha. In *Lima, Aspiraciones, reconocimiento y ciudadanía en los noventa,* Carmen Rosa Balbi, ed. Lima: Fondo Editorial de la Pontificia Universidad Católica del Perú.

IAN, MARCIA
1993   *Remembering the Phallic Mother, Psychoanalysis, Modernism, and the Fetish.* Ithaca, NY, and London: Cornell University Press.

IRIGARAY, LUCE
1985   *This Sex Which Not One.* Translated by Catherine Porter with Carolyn Burke. Ithaca, NY: Cornell University Press.

ISBELL, BILLIE JEAN
1998   Violence in Peru: Performances and dialogues. *American Anthropologist* 100:282-292.

JACOBSON, ARTHUR J.
1992   The idolatry of rules: Writing law according to Moses, with reference to other jurisprudences. In *Deconstruction and the Possibility of Justice,* Drucilla Cornell, Michel Rosenfeld, and David Gray Carlson, eds. New York and London: Routledge.

JAMESON, FREDERIC
1972   *The Prison-House of Language, A Critical Account of Structuralism and Russian Formalism.* Princeton, NJ: Princeton University Press.
1981   *The Political Unconscious, Narrative as a Socially Symbolic Act.* Ithaca, NY: Cornell University Press.
1991   *Postmodernism, or, The Cultural Logic of Late Capitalism.* Durham, NC: Duke University Press.

JOHNSON, ALLAN G.
1997   *The Gender Knot, Unraveling Our Patriarchal Legacy.* Philadelphia: Temple University Press.

JOHNSON, CHRISTOPHER
2001   Derrida and science. In *Questioning Derrida, With His Replies on Philosophy,* Michel Meyer, ed. Aldershot, UK, and Burlington, VT: Ashgate.

JONES, DELMOS J.

1997 Epilogue. In *Decolonizing Anthropology, Moving Further toward an Anthropology for Liberation*, Faye V. Harrison, ed. Arlington, VA: Association of Black Anthropologists/American Anthropological Association.

JORDAN, JUNE
1981 *Civil Wars*. Boston: Beacon Press.

KAHN, JOEL S.
1997 Demons, commodities and the history of Anthropology. In *Meanings of the Market. The Free Market in Western Culture*, James G. Carrier, ed. Oxford, UK, and New York: Berg.

KEARNEY, MICHAEL
1996 *Reconceptualizing the Peasantry, Anthropology in Global Perspective*. Boulder, CO: Westview Press.

KEENAN, THOMAS
1997 *Fables or Responsibility, Aberrations and Predicaments in Ethics and Politics*. Stanford, CA: Stanford University Press.

KLARÉN, PETER F.
1973 *Modernization, Dislocation, and Aprismo: Origins of the Peruvian Aprista Party, 1870-1932*. Austin and London: University of Texas Press.
1999 Review of *Dance in the Cemetery: José Carlos Mariátegui and the Lima Scandal of 1917*, William W. Stein (Lanham, Maryland: University Press of America, 1997). *Hispanic American Historical Review* 79:165-166.

KLEIN, MELANIE
1975 *Envy and Gratitude, and Other Works, 1946-1963*. London: The Hogarth Press and the Institute of Psycho-Analysis.

KLEIN, RALPH
1963 *The Self-Image of Adult Males in an Andean Culture, a Clinical Exploration of a Dynamic Personality Construct*. Ph.D. Dissertation, New York University. Ann Arbor, MI: University Microfilms International.

KLEINMAN, ARTHUR
1980 *Patients and Healers in the Context of Culture, An Exploration of the Borderland between Anthropology, Medicine, and Psychiatry*. Berkeley, Los Angeles, and London: University of California Press.
1988 *The Illness Narratives, Suffering, Healing, and the Human Condition*. New York: Basic Books.

KOESTENBAUM, WAYNE
1989 *Double Talk, The Erotics of Male Literary Collaboration*. New York and London: Routledge.

KÖHLER, ULRICH
1981 Integrated community development: Vicos in Peru. In *Research in Economic Anthropology*, George Dalton, ed. Volume 4. Greenwich, CT, and London: JAI Press.

KOPYTOFF, IGOR
1986 The cultural biography of things: commoditization as process. In *The Social Life of Things, Commodities in Cultural Perspective*, Arjun Appadurai, ed. Cambridge, UK: Cambridge University Press..

KOROVKIN, TANYA
1990 *Politics of Agricultural Co-Operativism: Peru, 1969-1983*.

Vancouver: University of British Columbia Press.

KRISTEVA, JULIA

1981 Interview. Translated by Claire Pajaczkowska. *m/f* 5/6. [1974.]

1982 *Powers of Horror, an Essay on Abjection.* Translated by Leon S. Roudiez. New York: Columbia University Press.

1989 *Black Sun, Depression and Melancholia.* Translated by Leon S. Roudiez. New York: Columbia University Press.

KULICK, DON

n.d. Discussant's presentation, Invited Session: Homophobias: Lust and Loathing, Past, Present and Future. 101st Annual Meeting, American Anthropological Association, November 22, 2002.

LACAN, JACQUES

1977 *Ecrits, A Selection.* Translated from the French by Alan Sheridan. New York and London: W. W. Norton & Company.

1978 *The Four Fundamental Concepts of Psycho-Analysis.* Edited by Jacques-Alain Miller. Translated from the French by Allan Sheridan. First American edition. New York and London: W. W. Norton & Company.

1985 *Feminine Sexuality.* Edited by Juliet Mitchell and Jacqueline Rose. Translated by Jacqueline Rose. New York and London: W. W. Norton & Company/Pantheon Books.

1988a *The Seminar of Jacques Lacan, Book II. The Ego in Freud's Theory and in the Technique of Psychoanalysis, 1954-1955.* Edited by Jacques-Alain Miller. Translated by Sylvana Tomaselli. New York and London: W. W. Norton & Company.

1988b *The Seminar of Jacques Lacan, Book VII, The Ethics of Psychoanalysis, 1959-1960.* Edited by Jacques Alain Miller. Translated by Dennis Porter. New York and London: W. W. Norton & Company.

1994 *La relación de objeto.* El Seminario de Jacques Lacan, Libro 4. Edited by Jacues-Alain Miller. Translated by Enric Berenguer. Barcelona: Ediciones Paidós.

LACLAU, ERNESTO

1996 *Emancipation(s).* London and New York: Verso.

LAGOS, MARIA L.

1994 *Autonomy and Power, The Dynamics of Class and Culture in Rural Bolivia.* Philadelphia: University of Pennsylvania Press.

LANCASTER, NADJA BEE

1965 *Hospital de Belén in Huaraz, Perú.* Columbia, Cornell, Harvard, University of Illinois Summer Field Studies Program, 1963. Mimeographed. Ithaca, New York: Comparative Studies of Cultural Change, Department of Anthropology, Cornell University.

LAPLANCHE, J., and J.-B. PONTALIS

1973 *The Language of Psycho-Analysis.* Translated by Donald Nicholson-Smith. New York and London: W. W. Norton & Company.

LARSON, BROOKE

1998 *Cochabamba, 1550-1900, Colonialism and Agrarian Transformation in Bolivia.* Expanded edition. Durham, NC, and London: Duke University

Press.

LATOUR, BRUNO
1993   *We Have Never Been Modern.* Translated by Catherine Porter. Cambridge, MA: Harvard University Press.

LAUER, MIRKO
1991   La modernidad, un fin incómodo. In *Modernidad en los Andes*, Henrique Urbano, comp. Cusco: Centro de Estudios Regionales Andinos "Bartolomé de Las Casas."

LASSWELL, HAROLD D.
1971   The transferability of Vicos strategy. In Dobyns, Doughty and Lasswell 1971a..

LASTARRIA-CORNHIEL, SUSANA
1989   Agrarian reforms of the 1960s and 1970s in Peru. In *Searching for Agrarian Reform in Latin America*, William C. Thiesenhusen, ed. Boston and London: Unwin Hyman.

LEACOCK, ELEANOR, and RICHARD LEE, eds.
1982   *Politics and History in Band Societies.* Cambridge, UK: Cambridge University Press.

LEAVEY, JOHN. P., JR.
1999   French kissing, Whose tongue is it anyway? In *The French Connections of Jacques Derrida*, Julian Wolfreys, John Brannigan, and Ruth Robbins, eds. Albany: State University of New York Press.

LENTZ, CAROLA
1995   Ethnic conflict and changing dress codes: a case study of an Indian migrant village in highland Ecuador. Translated from the German by Allison Brown. In *Dress and Ethnicity, Change Across Space and Time*, Joanne B. Eicher, ed. Oxford, UK, and Washington: Berg.

LESLIE, CHARLES
1976   Introduction. In *Asian Medical Systems: A Comparative Study*, Charles Leslie, ed.. Berkeley: University of California Press.

LÉVI-STRAUSS, CLAUDE
1963   *Structural Anthropology.* Translated from the French by Claire Jacobson and Brooke Grundfest Schoepf. New York: Basic Books.
_____. 1992 *Tristes Tropiques.* Translated from the French by John and Doreen Weightman. New York and London: Penguin Books.

LEYS, COLIN
1996   *The Rise & Fall of Development Theory.* Nairobi, Bloomington, IN, and London: East African Educational Publishers, Indiana University Press, and James Curry.

LINGIS, ALPHONSO
1993   Schizoanalysis of race. In *The Psychoanalysis of Race*, Christopher Jones, ed. New York: Columbia University Press.

LIP, CÉSAR, OSWALDO LAZO and PEDRO BRITO
1990   *El trabajo médico en el Perú.* Lima: Organización Panamericana de la Salud y la Universidad Peruana Cayetano Heredia.

LIU, CATHERINE
2000   *Copying Machines, Taking Notes for the Automaton.* Minneapolis and

London: University of Minnesota Press.

LUCKHURST, ROGER

1999 "Something tremendous, something elemental": On the ghostly origins of psychoanalysis. In *Ghosts, Deconstruction, Psychoanalysis, History*, Peter Buse and Andrew Stott, eds. London and New York: Macmillan Press/St. Martin's Press.

LUDDEN, DAVID

1992 India's Development Regime. In *Colonialism and Culture*, Nicholas B. Dirks, ed. Ann Arbor, MI: The University of Michigan Press.

LYNCH, BARBARA D.

1982 *The Vicos Experiment, a Study of the Impacts of the Cornell-Peru Project in a Highland Community.* Washington: U. S. Agency for International Development.

LYOTARD, JEAN-FRANÇOIS

1988 *The Differend, Phrases in Dispute.* Translation by Georges Van Den Abeele. Minneapolis: University of Minnesota Press.

1993 *Toward the Postmodern.* Edited by Robert Harvey and Mark S. Roberts. Atlantic Highlands, NJ: Humanities Press.

1997 *Postmodern Fables.* Translated by Georges Van Den Abbeele. Minneapolis and London: University of Minnesota Press.

MACCANNELL, DEAN

1976 *The Tourist, A New Theory of the Leisure Class.* New York: Schocken Books.

MACDONALD, LAURA

1995 NGOs and the problematic discourse of participation: cases from Costa Rica. In *Debating Development Discourse, Institutional and Popular Perspectives*, David B. Moore and Gerald J. Schmitz, eds. Houndmills, UK, and New York: Macmillan Press/St. Martin's Press.

MANGANARO, MARC

1990 Textual play, power, and cultural critique: an orientation to modernist anthropology. In *Modernist Anthropology, from Fieldwork to Text*, Marc Manganaro, ed. Princeton, NJ: Princeton University Press.

MAJLUF, NATALIA

1997 "Ce n'est pas le Pérou," or, the failure of authenticity: marginal cosmopolitans at the Paris Universal Exhibition of 1855. *Critical Inquiry* 23:868-893.

MALLON, FLORENCIA

1992 Indian communities, political cultures, and the state in Latin America, 1780-1990. *Journal of Latin American Studies* 24 (Quincentenary Supplement):35-53.

1994 The promise and dilemma of subaltern studies: perspectives from Latin American history. *American Historical Review* 99:1491-1515.

MANGIN, WILLIAM P.

1954 *The Cultural Significance of the Fiesta Complex in an Indian Hacienda in Perú.* Ph.D. Dissertation, Yale University. Ann Arbor, MI: University Microfilms International.

1955   Estratificación social en el Callejón de Huaylas. *Revista del Museo Nacional* (Lima) 24:174-189.

1979   Thoughts on twenty-four years' work in Peru: the Vicos Project and me. In *Long-Term Field Research in Social Anthropology*, George M. Foster, et al., eds. New York: Academic Press.

MANNHEIM, BRUCE1
1991   *The Language of the Inka since the European Invasion.* Austin: University of Texas Press.
1998   A nation surrounded. In *Native Traditions in the Postconquest World*, Elizabeth Hill Boone and Tom Cummins, eds. Washington: Dumbarton Oaks Library and Collections.

MANNHEIM, BRUCE, and KRISTA VAN VLEET
1998   The dialogics of Southern Quechua narrative. *American Anthropologist* 100:326-346.

MANRIQUE, NELSON
1999   *La piel y la pluma, Escritos sobre literature, etnicidad y racism.* Lima: SUR, Casa de Estudios del Socialismo/Centro de informe y Desarrollo Integral de Autogestión.
2002   *El tiempo de miedo, La violencia política en el Perú, 1980-1996.* Lima: Fondo Editorial del Congreso del Perú.

MARCUS, GEORGE E.
1998   *Ethnography through Thick and Thin.* Princeton, NJ: Princeton University Press.

MARCUS, GEORGE E., and MICHAEL M. J. FISCHER
1986   *Anthropology as Cultural Critique, an Experimental Moment in the Human Sciences.* Chicago and London: The University of Chicago Press.

MARIÁTEGUI, JOSÉ CARLOS
1959   *Siete ensayos de interpretación de la realidad peruana.* Sétima edición. Lima: Biblioteca Amauta.
1970   *Peruanicemos al Perú.* Lima: Biblioteca Amauta.

MARTÍNEZ, HÉCTOR
1989   Vicos: Comunidad y cambio. *Socialismo y Participación* (Lima) 44.
n.d.   *Vicos: continuidad y cambio.* Manuscript. Lima.

MARTÍNEZ, HÉCTOR, and CARLOS SAMANIEGO
1978   La política indigenista. In *Campesinado e indigenismo en América Latina*, Enrique Valencia, et al. Lima: Ediciones CELATS, Centro Latinoamericano de Trabajo Social.

MARX, KARL
1963   *The Eighteenth Brumaire of Louis Bonaparte.* New York: International Publishers.
1976   *Capital, A Critique of Political Economy. Volume One.* Translated by Ben Fowkes. London: Penguin Books.

MATOS MAR, JOSÉ, and JOSÉ MANUEL MEJÍA
1980   *La reforma agraria en el Perú.* Lima: Instituto de Estudios Peruanos.

MAYER, ENRIQUE
1974   *Reciprocity, Self-Sufficiency and Market Relations in a Contemporary Community in the Central Andes of Perú.* Ithaca, New York: Cornell

University Latin American Studies Program Dissertation Series, Number 72.
1979 *Land-Use in the Andes: Ecology and Agriculture in the Mantaro Valley of Peru with Special Reference to Potatoes.* Lima: Centro Internacional de la Papa.
1991 Peru in deep trouble: Mario Vargas Llosa's "Inquest in the Andes" reexamined. *Cultural Anthropology* 6:466-504.
2002 *The Articulated Peasant, Household Economies in the Andes.* Boulder, CO, and London: Westview.

MCCALLUM, E. L.
1999 *Object Lessons, How to Do Things with Fetishism.* Albany, NY: State University of New York Press.

MCCLINTOCK, ANNE
1995 *Imperial Leather, Race, Gender and Sexuality in the Colonial Contest.* New York and London: Routledge.

MEHLMAN, JEFFREY
1977 *Revolution and Repetition, Marx/Hugo/Balzac.* Berkeley: University of California Press.

MÉNDEZ G., CECILIA
1992 República sin indios: la comunidad imaginada del Perú. In *Tradición y Modernidad en los Andes*, Henrique Urbano, comp. Cusco: Centro de Estudios Regionales Andinos "Bartolomé de Las Casas."

MENDOZA, ZOILA S.
1998 Defining folklore: Mestizo and indigenous identities on the move. (In Special Issue, *Race and Ethnicity in the Andes*, Mary Weismantel, ed.) *Bulletin of Latin American Research* 17:165-183.

MERCER, KOBENA
1994 *Welcome to the Jungle, New Positions in Black Cultural Studies.* New York and London: Routledge.

MESA-LAGO, CARMELO
1988 Medical care under social security: Coverage, costs, and financing. In *Health Care in Peru: Resources and Policy*, Dieter K. Zschock, ed. Boulder, CO, and London: Westview Press.

METHODOLOGY PROJECT
1954 *Instructions given to fieldworkers, Peuvian study.* Cross Cultural Methodology Project. Dittoed. Department of Sociology and Anthropology, Cornell University. Ithaca, New York.
1955 *Progress report, Project for the Development of Social Science Research Methods in Cross Cultural Research.* Dittoed. Department of Sociology and Anthropology, Cornell University. Ithaca, New York.
1956 *Report, Cornell Methodology Project for the Development and Testing of Improved Methods for Studying Underdeveloped Areas.* Dittoed. Department of Sociology and Anthropology, Cornell University. Ithaca, New York.

MILLA DE VÁZQUEZ, AÍDA
1972 *Estudio de la socialización en la Comunidad Indígena de Vicos (Ancash).* Tesis para optar el grado de Bachiller en Antropología. Lima:

Programa Académico de Ciencias Sociales, Universidad Nacional Mayor de San Marcos.

MILLER, DANIEL
1997   *Capitalism, an Ethnographic Approach.* Oxford, UK, and New York: Berg.

MILLER, J. HILLIS
1979   The critic as host. In *Deconstruction and Criticism*, Harold Bloom, et al. New York: Continuum.

MILLETT, KATE
2000   *Sexual Politics.* Urbana and Chicago: University of Illinois Press.

MITCHELL, TIMOTHY
1991   *Colonising Egypt.* Berkeley, Los Angeles, and London: University of California Press.
1995   The object of development, America's Egypt. In *Power of Development*, Jonathan Crush, ed. London and New York: Routledge.

MONTALVO, ABNER SELIM
1967   *Sociocultural Change and Differentiation in a Rural Peruvian Community, an Analysis in Health Culture.* Ithaca, NY: Cornell University Latin American Studies Program Dissertation Series, Number 5.

MONTOYA ROJAS, RODRIGO
1970   *A propósito del carácter predominantemente capitalista de la economía peruana actual.* Lima: Ediciones Teoría y Realidad.

MORALES, EDMUNDO
1995   *The Guinea Pig, Healing, Food, and Ritual in the Andes.* Tucson: The University of Arizona Press.

MÖRNER, MAGNUS
1973   The Spanish American hacienda: a survey of recent research and debate. *Hispanic American Historical Review* 53:183.216.

MOSHER, ARTHUR T.
1957   *Technical Co-operation in Latin American Agriculture.* Chicago: The University of Chicago Press.

MULVEY, LAURA
1996   *Fetishism and Curiosity.* London and Bloomington: Indiana University Press.

MURRA, JOHN
1966   New data on retainer and servile populations in Tawantinsuyu. *XXXVI congreso internacional de Americanistas, España, 1964, Actas y Memorias, Vol. 2.* Sevilla.
_____. 2000   *Nispa ninchis/decimos diciendo, Conversaciones con John Murra.* Edited by Victoria Castro, Carlos Aldunate, and Jorge Hidalgo. Lima/New York: Instituto de Estudios Peruanos/Institute of Andean Research.

MURRA, JOHN V., and MERCEDES LÓPEZ-BARALT, eds.
1996   *Las cartas de Arguedas.* Lima: Pontificia Universidad Católica del Perú.

NADER, LAURA
1972   Up the anthropologist–perspectives gained from studying up. In

Reinventing Anthropology, Dell Hymes, ed. New York: Pantheon Books.
NANCY, JEAN-LUC
    1992 Elliptical sense. In *Derrida: A Critical Reader*, David Wood, ed. Oxford, UK, and Cambridge, MA: Blackwell.
NELSON, CARY
    1989 Men, feminism: the materiality of discourse. In *Men in Feminism*, Alice Jardine & Paul Smith, eds. New York and London: Routledge.
NEIRA, ELOY, and PATRICIA RUIZ BRAVO
    2000 Enfrentados al patrón: Una aproximación al estudio de las masculinidades en el medio rural peruano. In *Estudios culturales: Discursos, poderes, pulsiones*, Santiago López Maguiña, Gonzalo Portocarrero, Rocío Silva Santisteban, and Víctor Vich, eds. Lima: Red para el Desarrollo de las Ciencias Sociales en el Perú.
NORRIS, CHRISTOPHER
    1987 *Derrida*. Cambridge, MA: Harvard University Press.
    1991 *Deconstruction, Theory and Practice*. Revised edition. London and New York: Routledge.
NUGENT, DAVID
    1994 Building the state, making the nation: the bases and limits of state centralization in "modern" Peru. *American Anthropologist* 96:333-369.
    1996 From devil pacts to drug deals: commerce, unnatural accumulation, and moral community in "modern" Peru. *American Ethnologist* 23:259-290.
    1997 *Modernity at the Edge of Empire, State, Individual, and Nation in the Northern Peruvian Andes, 1885-1935*. Stanford, California: Stanford University Press.
    1998 The morality of modernity and the travails of tradition, nationhood and the subaltern in northern Peru. *Critique of Anthropology* 18:7-33.
OBERG, KALERVO
    1960 Cultural shock: adjustment to new cultural environments. *Practical Anthropology* 7:177-182.
OLSON, DAVID R.
    1985 Introduction. In *Literacy, Language, and Learning, The Nature and Consequences of Reading and Writing*, David R. Olson, Nancy Torrance, and Angela Hildyard, eds. Cambridge, UK: Cambridge University Press.
OMI, MICHAEL, and HOWARD WINANT
    1994 *Racial Formation in the United States, from the 1960s to the 1990s*. Second edition. New York and London: Routledge.
ORTA, ANDREW
    n.d. *Seductive Strangers and Saturated Symbols: Fat Stealing, Catechists and the Porous Production of Andean Locality*. Department of Anthropology, University of Illinois at Urbana-Champaign. Urbana, Illinois.
ORTNER, SHERRY B.
    1995 Resistance and the problem of ethnographic refusal. *Comparative Studies in Society and History* 37:173-193.
    1999a Thick resistance: Death and the cultural construction of agency in Himalayan mountaineering. In *The Fate of "Culture", Geertz and Beyond*,

Sherry B. Ortner, ed. Berkeley, Los Angeles, and London: University of California Press.

1999b Introduction. In *The Fate of "Culture", Geertz and Beyond*, Sherry B. Ortner, ed. Berkeley, Los Angeles, and London: University of California Press.

OSTERLING, JORGE P.
1983 *Reply to* Notes for a history of Peruvian social anthropology, 1940-1980. *Current Anthropology* 24:355-357.

OSTERLING, JORGE P.,and HÉCTOR MARTÍNEZ
1983 Notes for a history of Peruvian social anthropology. *Current Anthropology* 24:343-360.

PAERREGAARD, KARSTEN
1997a Imagining a place in the Andes, In the borderland of lived, invented, and analyzed culture. In *Siting Culture, The Shifting Anthropological Object*, Karen Fog Olwig and Kirsten Hastrup, eds. London and New York: Routledge.

1997b *Linking Separate Worlds, Urban Migrants and Rural Lives in Peru*. Oxford, UK, and New York: Berg.

PAIGE, JEFFREY M
1975 *Agrarian Revolution, Social Movements and Export Agriculture in the Underdeveloped World*. New York: The Free Press.

PAPASTERGIADIS, NIKOS
1997 Tracing hybridity in theory. In *Debating Cultural Hybridity, Multi/Cultural Identities and the Politics of Anti/Racism*, Pnina Werbner and Tariq Modood, eds. London and Atlantic Highlands, NJ: Zed Books.

_____. 1998 *Dialogues in the Diasporas, Essays and Conversations on Cultural Identity*. London and New York: Rivers Oram Press.

PARKER, ANDREW
1993 Unthinking sex: Marx, Engels, and the scene of writing. In *Fear of a Queer Planet, Queer Politics and Social Theory*, Michael Warner, ed. Minneapolis and London: University of Minnesota Press.

PARKER, GARY J.
1976 *Gramática quechua: Ancash-Huaylas*. Lima: Ministerio de Educación y Instituto de Estudios Peruanos.

PARKER, GARY J., and AMANCIO CHAVEZ
1976 *Diccionario quechua: Ancash-Huaylas*. Lima: Ministerio de Educación y Instituto de Estudios Peruanos.

PARRY, JONATHAN
1989 On the moral perils of exchange. In *Money and the Morality of Exchange*, Jonathan Parry and Maurice Bloch, eds. Cambridge, UK: Cambridge University Press.

PATCH, RICHARD W.
1964 Vicos and the Peace Corps, a failure in intercultural communication. *American Universities Field Staff Reports Service, West Coast of South America Series* 11(2).

PELS, PETER
1998 The spirit of matter: on fetish, rarity, fact, and fancy. In *Border*

Fetishisms: Material Objects in Unstable Spaces, Patricia Spyer, ed. New York and London: Routledge.

PIETZ, WILLIAM

    1985   The problem of the fetish. *Res* 9:5-17.

    1987   The problem of the fetish, II, the origin of the fetish. *Res* 13:23-45.

    1988   The problem of the fetish, IIIa, Bosman's *Guinea* and the enlightenment theory of fetishism. *Res* 16:105-123.

    1993   Fetishism and materialism: the limits of theory in Marx. In *Fetishism as Cultural Discourse*, Emily Apter and William Pietz, eds. Ithaca, NY, and London: Cornell University Press.

PLATT, TRISTAN

    1995   Ethnic calendars and market interventions among the *ayllus* of Lipes during the nineteenth century. In *Ethnicity, Markets, and Migration in the Andes, at the Crossroads of History and Anthropology*, Brooke Larson, Olivia Harris, and Enrique Tandeter, eds. Durham, NC, and London: Duke University Press.

PLAZA MARTÍNEZ, PEDRO

    1994   Tendencias sociolingüisticas en Bolivia. In *Language in the Andes*, Peter Cole, Gabriela Hermon, and Mario Daniel Martín, eds. Newark: Latin American Studies Program, University of Delaware.

PLOEG, JAN DOUWE VAN DER

    1993   Potatoes and knowledge. In *An Anthropological Critique of Development, The Growth of Ignorance*, Mark Hobart, ed. London and New York: Routledge.

POATS, SUSAN V.

    1982a Beyond the farmer: potato consumption in the tropics. In *Research for the Potato in the Year 2000*, W. J. Hooker, ed. Proceedings of the International Congress, CIP Tenth Anniversary. Lima: Centro Internacional de la Papa.

    1982b *Potato Preferences: A Preliminary Examination*. Lima: Centro Internacional de la Papa.

POOLE, DEBORAH

    1988   Landscapes of power in a cattle-rustling culture of southern Andean Peru. *Dialectical Anthropology* 12:367-398.

    1992   Antropología e historia andinas en los EE.UU.: Buscando un reencuentro. *Revista Andina* 19:209-245.

    1994   Introduction: anthropological perspectives on violence and culture–a view from the Peruvian high provinces. In *Unruly Order, Violence, Power, and Cultural Identity in the High Provinces of Southern Peru*, Deborah Poole, ed. Boulder, CO: Westview Press.

    1997   *Vision, Race, and Modernity, a Visual Economy of the Andean Image World*. Princeton, NJ: Princeton University Press.

PORTOCARRERO MAISCH, GONZALO

    1993   *Racismo y mestizaje*. Lima: Casa SUR.

    1998   *Razones de sangre, aproximaciones a la violencia política*. Lima: Pontificia Universidad Católica del Perú, Fondo Editorial.

PRATT, LOIS V.
1976   Reshaping the consumer's posture in health care.   In *The Doctor-Patient Relationship in the Changing Health Scene*, Eugene B. Gallagher, ed. DHEW Publication No. (NIH) 78-183. Washington: U. S. Department of Health, Education, and Welfare.

PRATT, MARY LOUISE
1992. *Imperial Eyes, Travel Writing and Transculturation*. London and New York: Routledge.

PRICE, RICHARD
1961   *Watanaki: Courtship and Marriage Institutions in Vicos, Perú*. Cambridge, Massachusetts: Harvard University, Columbia-Cornell-Harvard Universities Summer Field Studies Program in Perú. Mimeographed.

QUIJANO OBREGÓN, ANÍBAL
1968   Tendencies in Peruvian development and in the class structure.   In *Latin America, Reform or Revolution?*, James Petras and Maurice Zeitlin, eds. Greenwich, CT: Fawcett Publications.

RABINOW, PAUL
1977   *Reflections on Fieldwork in Morocco*. Berkeley, Los Angeles, and London: University of California Press.
1986   Representations are social facts: Modernity and Post-Modernity in Anthropology. In *Writing Culture, The Poetics and Politics of Ethnography*, James Clifford and George E. Marcus, eds. Berkeley, Los Angeles, and London: University of California Press.

RAFAEL, VICENTE L.
1993   Contracting Colonialism, Translation and Christian Conversion in Tagalog Society under Early Spanish Rule. Durham, NC, and London: Duke University Press.

RATTANSI, ALI
1994   "Western" racisms, ethnicities and identities in a "postmodern" frame. In *Racism, Modernity and Identity, on the Western Front*, Ali Rattansi y Sallie Westwood, eds. Cambridge, UK: Polity Press.

READINGS, BILL
1989   The deconstruction of politics. In *Reading de Man Reading*, Lindsay Waters and Wlad Godzich, eds. Minneapolis: University of Minnesota Press.

REW, ALAN
1997   The donors' discourse: official social development knowledge in the 1980s. In *Discourses of Development, Anthropological Perspectives*, R. D. Grillo and R. L. Stirrat, eds. Oxford, UK, and New York: Berg.

RICH, ADRIENNE
1979   *On Lies, Secrets, and Silence, Selected Prose, 1966-1978*. New York and London: W. W. Norton & Company.
1986   *Of Woman Born, Motherhood as Experience and Institution*. New York and London: W. W. Norton & Company.

ROSALDO, RENATO
1986   From the door of his tent: The fieldworker and the inquisitor. In *Writing Culture, The Poetics and Politics of Ethnography*, James Clifford and George E. Marcus, eds. Berkeley, Los Angeles, and London: University of

California Press.

ROSS, ANDREW

1989   No question of silence. In *Men in Feminism*, Alice Jardine & Paul Smith, eds. New York and London: Routledge.

RUBEL, ARTHUR J., CARL W. O'NELL and ROLANDO COLLADO-ARDÓN.

1984   *Susto, a Folk Illness*. Berkeley, Los Angeles, and London: University of California Press.

1985   The folk illness called *susto*. In *The Culture-Bound Syndromes, Folk Illnesses of Psychiatric and Anthropological Interest*, Ronald C. Simmons and Charles C. Hughes, eds. Dordrecht, Holland, Boston, Lancaster, UK, and Tokyo: D. Reidel Publishing Company.

SAID, EDWARD W.

1978   *Orientalism*. New York: Pantheon Books.

1988   *Beginnings, Intention and Method*. New York: Columbia University Press.

SALAMAN, REDCLIFFE

1985   *The History and Social Influence of the Potato*. Revised impression edited by J. G. Hawkes. Cambridge, UK: Cambridge University Press.

SALOMON, FRANK

1982   Andean ethnology in the 1970s: A retrospective. *Latin American Research Review* 16(2):75-128.

SARRIS, GREG

1993   Keeping Slug Woman alive: The challenge of reading in a reservation classroom. In *The Ethnography of Reading*, Jonathan Boyarin, ed. Berkeley, Los Angeles, and Oxford, UK: University of California Press.

SCHAEDEL, RICHARD P.

1988   Andean world view: hierarchy or reciprocity, regulation or control? *Current Anthropology* 29:768-775.

SCHNEIDER, MARK A.

1993   *Culture and Enchantment*. Chicago and London: University of Chicago Press.

SCHOR, NAOMI

1985   Female fetishism: The case of George Sand. *Poetics Today* 6:301-310.

1994   This essentialism which is not one: coming to grips with Irigaray. In *The Essential Difference*, Naomi Schor and Elizabeth Weed, eds. Bloomington and Indianapolis: Indiana University Press.

SCOTT, JAMES C.

1985   *Weapons of the Weak, Everyday Forms of Peasant Resistance*. New Haven, CT, and London: Yale University Press.

1998   *Seeing Like a State, How Certain Schemes to Improve the Human Condition Have Failed*. New Haven, CT, and London: Yale University Press.

SEDGWICK, EVE KOSOFSKY

1985   *Between Men, English Literature and Male Homosocial Desire*. New York: Columbia University Press.

SELIGMANN, LINDA J.
1995   *Between Reform & Revolution, Political Struggles in the Peruvian Andes, 1969-1991.* Stanford, CA: Stanford University Press.
SELIGMANN, LINDA J., and STEPHEN G. BUNKER
1994   An Andean Irrigation system: ecological visions and social organization. In*Irrigation at High Altitudes: The Social Organization of Water Control Systems in the Andes,* William P. Mitchell and David Guillet, eds.   Washington: American Anthropological Association.
SEN, AMARTYA
1995   *Inequality Reexamined.* New York/Cambridge, MA: Russell Sage Foundation/Harvard University Press.
SENF, CAROL A.
1997 *Dracula, The Jewl of Seven Stars,* and Stoker's "burden of the past. In *Bram Stoker's Dracula, Sucking Through the Century, 1897-1997,* Carol Margaret Davison, ed.   With the participation of Paul Simpson-Housley. Toronto and Oxford, UK: Dundurn Press.
SHERBONDY, JEANETTE E.
1992 Water ideology in Inca ethnogenesis. In*Andean Cosmologies through Time, Persistence and Emergence,* Robert V. H. Dover, Katharine E. Seibold, and John H. McDowell, eds.   Bloomington and Indianapolis: Indiana University Press.
SILVERBLATT, IRENE
1987   *Moon, Sun, and Witches, Gender Ideologies and Class in Inca and Colonial Peru.* Princeton, New Jersey: Princeton University Press.
SLOTERDIJK, PETER
1987   *Critique of Cynical Reason.*   Translation by Michael Eldred. Minneapolis and London: University of Minnesota Press.
SMITH, PAUL
1989   Men in feminism: men and feminist theory. In *Men in Feminism,* Alice Jardine & Paul Smith, eds. New York and London: Routledge.
SNYDER, JOAN
1960   *Group Relations and Social Change in an Andean Village.* Ph.D. Thesis, Cornell University.   Ann Arbor, MI: University Microfilms International.
SOLER, COLETTE
1996 The symbolic order (II). In *Reading Seminars I and II, Lacan's Return to Freud,* Richard Feldstein, Bruce Fink, and Maire Jaanus, eds. Albany, NY: State University of New York Press.
SPIVAK, GAYATRI CHAKRAVORTY
1976   Translator's Preface. In *Of Grammatology,* Jacques Derrida. Translated by Gayatri Chakravorty Spivak. Baltimore and London: The Johns Hopkins University Press.
1988   Subaltern studies: deconstructing historiography.   In *Selected Subaltern Studies,* Ranajit Guha and Gayatri Chakravorty Spivak, eds. New York and Oxford, UK: Oxford University Press.
1990 *The Post-Colonial Critic, Interviews, Strategies, Dialogues.* New York and London: Routledge.

1996   Subaltern talk, Interview with the Editors. In *The Spivak Reader, Selected Works of Gayatri Chakravorty Spivak*, Donna Landry and Gerald MacLean, eds. New York and London: Routledge.

2000   Deconstruction and Cultural Studies: Arguments for a deconstructive Cultural Studies. In *Deconstruction, A User's Guide*, Nicholas Royle, ed. Houndmills, UK, and New York: Palgrave.

STAKMAN, E. C., RICHARD BRADFIELD, and PAUL C. MANGELSDORF
1967   *Campaigns Against Hunger.* Cambridge, MA: Harvard University Press.

STARN, ORIN
1994   Rethinking the politics of anthropology, The case of the Andes. *Current Anthropology* 35:13-38.

1999   *Nightwatch, The Politics of Protest in the Andes.* Durham, NC, and London: Duke University Press.

STEIN, WILLIAM W.
1988   *El levantamiento de Atusparia, el movimiento popular ancashino de 1885: un estudio de documentos.* Lima: Mosca Azul Editores.

1991a   El "Problema indígena" puesto a prueba mediante el uso de un documento personal. In *El caso de los becerros hambrientos, y otros ensayos de antropología económica peruana.* Lima: Mosca Azul Editores.

1991b   La lucha por la mano de obra campesina en el Perú rural. In *El caso de los becerros hambrientos, y otros ensayos de antropología económica peruana.* Lima: Mosca Azul Editores.

1991c   La situación de la clase trabajadora rural en el Perú. In *El caso de los becerros hambrientos, y otros ensayos de antropología económica peruana.* Lima: Mosca Azul Editores.

1991d   El mal folk, ¿entidad o ficción?, un ensayo sobre la ideología de la enfermedad en Vicos. In *El caso de los becerros hambrientos y otros ensayos de antropología económica peruana.* Lima: Mosca Azul Editores.

1996   Patronage. In *Encyclopedia of Cultural Anthropology*, David Levinson y Melvin Ember, eds. New York: Henry Holt and Company.

1997a   *Dance in the Cemetery, José Carlos Mariátegui and the Lima Scandal of 1917.* Lanham, MD: University Press of America.

1997b   El destino de "El process del gamonalismo": Algunas vicissitudes acerca del Otro. *Anuario Mariageguiano* 9:59-70. Lima: Empresa Editora Amauta.

1998   Next to nothing: more on Pedro Pablo Atusparia. *Hispanic American Historical Review* 78:307-315.

2000a   *Vicisitudes del discurso del desarrollo en el Perú, Una etnografía de la modernidad del Proyecto de Vicos.* Lima: Casa SUR.

2000b   Food and Fetish in Peru: "Potato Power and the Vicos Project. *Irish Journal of Anthropology* 5(1):63-87.

2001   Lo post-étnico y la persistencia de la diferencia. In *Estudios culturales: discursos, poderes, pulsiones*, Santiago López Maguiña, Gonzalo Portocarrero, Rocío Silva Santisteban, asnd Víctor Vich, eds. Lima: Red para el Desarrollo de las Ciencias Sociales en el Perú.

n.d.a Los letreros de las calles del Centro de Lima: Memoria e identidad en el Perú. In *Batallas por la Memoria: Antagonismos de la promesa peruana*, Jorge Bracamonte, et al., eds. Lima: Red para el desarrollo de las Ciencias Sociales en el Perú, in press.

n.d.b   *Rethinking Andeanist Discourse, De-Essentializing the Andean: Toward a Reflexive Ethnology.* Revision of a paper presented at the American Ethnological Society Meetings, Portland, Oregon, March 25-28, 1999.

n.d.c   *The Post-Ethnic: Race-ing, Race Formation, and Racism In and Out of Peru.* Presentation to the Latin American and Iberian Studies Committee, Texas Tech University, Lubbock, September 22, 2000.

STERN, STEVE J.

1987   *Resistance, Rebellion, and Consciousness in the Andean Peasant World, 18th to 20th Centuries.* Madison, WI: University of Wisconsin Press.

1995   The variety and ambiguity of native Andean Intervention in European Colonial Markets. In *Ethnicity, Markets, and Migration in the Andes, at the Crossroads of History and Anthropology*, Brooke Larson, Olivia Harris, and Enrique Tandeter, eds. Durham, NC, and London: Duke University Press.

STEVENS, ROBERT D.

1959   *Agricultural Production on Hacienda Vicos: Description and Analysis of a Hacienda Agricultural Society in the Andes of Peru.* Cornell-Peru Project, Department of Sociology and Anthropology, Cornell University. Mimeographed. Ithaca, New York.

STEWART, SUSAN

1980   *Nonsense, Aspects of Intertextuality in Folklore and Literature.* Baltimore and London: The Johns Hopkins University Press.

STOKES, SUSAN C.

1995   *Cultures in Conflict, Social Movements and the State in Peru.* Berkeley, Los Angeles, and London: University of California Press.

TANNEN, DEBORAH

1996   *Gender and Discourse.* New York and Oxford, UK: Oxford University Press.

TANNENBAUM, FRANK

1962   *Ten Keys to Latin America.* New York: Alfred A. Knopf.

TAUSSIG, MICHAEL

1980   *The Devil and Commodity Fetishism in South America.* Chapel Hill: The University of North Carolina Press.

1992   *The Nervous System.* New York and London: Routledge.

1993   *Maleficium:* state fetishism. In *Fetishism as Cultural Discourse*, Emily Apter and William Pietz, eds. Ithaca, NY, and London: Cornell University Press.

1997   *Mimesis and Alterity, A Particular History of the Senses.* New York and London: Routledge.

1998   Crossing the face. In *Border Fetishisms: Material Objects in Unstable Spaces*, Patricia Spyer, ed. New York and London: Routledge.

TAYLOR, MARK C.

1993   *Nots.* Chicago and London: The University of Chicago Press.

TEDLOCK, DENNIS

1983   *The Spoken Word and the Work of Interpretation.* Philadelphia: University of Pennsylvania Press.

THURNER, MARK
1990   Reseña de *El levantamiento de Atusparia*, William W. Stein (Lima: Mosca Azul, 1988). *Revista Andina* 15:300-303.
1997   *From Two Republics to One Divided, Contradictions of Postcolonial Nationmaking in Andean Perú.* Durham, NC, and London: Duke University Press.
2000   Less on Atusparia. *Hispanic American Historical Review* 80:137-140.

TODOROV, TZVETAN
1975   *The Fantastic, A Structural Approach to a Literary Genre.* Translated from the French by Richard Howard. Ithaca, NY: Cornell University Press.
1984   *The Conquest of America, the Question of the Other.* Translated from the French by Richard Howard. New York: Harper & Row, Publishers.

TRINH T. MINH-HA
1998   Difference: "a special Third World women's issue." In *The Feminist Critique of Language: A Reader.* Second edition. London and New York: Routledge.

TROUILLOT, MICHEL-ROLPH
1991   Anthropology and the savage slot, The poetics and politics of otherness. In *Recapturing Anthropology, Working in the Present*, Richard G. Fox, ed. Santa Fe, New Mexico: School of American Research Press.

TULLIS, F. LAMOND
1970   *Lord and Peasant in Peru: A Paradigm of Political and Social Change.* Cambridge, Massachusetts: Harvard University Press.

TURINO, THOMAS
1992   Del esencialismo a lo esencial: Pragmática y significado de la interpretación de los sikuri puneños en Lima. *Revista Andina* 20:441-456.
_____. 1993   *Moving Away from Silence, Music of the Peruvian Altiplano and the Experience of Urban Migration.* Chicago and London: The University of Chicago Press.

TURNER, VICTOR
1967   *The Forest of Symbols, Aspects of Ndembu Ritual.* Ithaca, NY, and London: Cornell University Press.
_____. 1982   *From Ritual to Theatre, The Human Seriousness of Play.* New York: Performing Arts Journal Publications.

TYLER, STEPHEN A.
1986   Post-modern ethnography: from document of the occult to occult document. In *Writing Culture, the Poetics and Politics of Ethnography*, James Clifford and George E. Marcus, eds. Berkeley, Los Angeles, and London: University of California Press.
1987   *The Unspeakable, Discourse, Dialogue, and Rhetoric in the Postmodern World.* Madison: The University of Wisconsin Press.
1991   A post-modern in-stance. In *Constructing Knowledge, Authority and Critique in Social Science*, Lorraine Nencel y Peter Pels, eds. London: Sage Publications.

TYLER, STEPHEN A., and GEORGE E. MARCUS
    1990 Comment. In *Modernist Anthropology, from Fieldwork to Text*, Marc Manganaro, ed. Princeton, NJ: Princeton University Press.
URRUTIA, JAIME
    1992 Comunidades campesinas y antropología: historia de un amor (casi) eterno. *Debate Agrario* 14:1-16.
VAN WILLIGEN, JOHN
    1986 *Applied Anthropology, An Introduction*. South Hadley, MA: Bergin & Garvey Publishers.
    1996 Comment. *In* Bennett 1996.
VAYDA, ANDREW P.
    1994 Actions, variations, and change: the emerging anti-essentialist view in anthropology. In *Assessing Cultural Anthropology*, Robert Borofsky, ed. New York: McGraw-Hill.
VÁZQUEZ, MARIO C.
    1952 La antropología cultural y nuestro Problema del indio. *Perú Indígena* 2(5/6):7-157.
    _____. 1955 *A Study of Technological Change in Vicos, Peru: Cornell-Peru Project*. M.A. Thesis, Cornell University. Ithaca, New York.
    _____. 1961 *Hacienda, peonaje y servidumbre en los Andes peruanos.* Lima: Editorial Estudios Andinos.
    _____. 1963a Autoridades de una hacienda andina peruana. *Perú Indígena* 10(24/25):24-36.
    _____. 1963b Proceso de migración en la comunidad de Vicos--Ancash. In *Migración e integración en el Perú*, Henry F. Dobyns and Mario C. Vázquez, eds. Lima: Editorial Estudios Andinos.
    _____. 1964 *The Varayoq System in Vicos*. Comparative Studies of Cultural Change, Department of Anthropology, Cornell University. Ithaca, New York.
    _____. 1967 Un caso de discriminación en las elecciones municipales de 1966. *Wamani* (Ayacucho) 2(1):30-44.
VITEBSKY, PIERS
    1992 Landscape and self-determination among the Eveny: The political environment of Siberian reindeer herders today. In *Bush Base: Forest Farm, Culture, Environment and Development*, Elisabeth Croll and David Parkin, eds. London and New York: Routledge.
VON GLEICH, UTTA, and WOLFGANG WÖLCK
    1994 Changes in language use and attitudes of Quechua-Spanish bilinguals in Peru. In *Language in the Andes*, Peter Cole, Gabriela Hermon, and Mario Daniel Martín, eds. Newark, DE: Latin American Studies, University of Delaware.
WAGNER, ROY
    1981 *The Invention of Culture*. Revised and expanded edition. Chicago and London: The University of Chicago Press.
WALLERSTEIN, IMMANUEL
    1991 Class conflict in the capitalist world-economy. In *Race, Nation, Class, Ambiguous Identities*, Etienne Balibar and Immanuel Wallerstein. London

and New York: Verso.

WEBER, DAVID J.
1986   Information perspective, profile, and patterns in Quechua. In *Evidentiality: The Linguistic Coding of Epistemology*, Wallace Chafe and Johanna Nichols, eds. Norwood, NJ: Ablex Publishing Company.

WEBER, SAMUEL
2001   *Institution and Interpretation.* Expanded edition. Stanford, CA: Stanford University Press.

WEINER, ANNETTE B.
1992   *Inalienable Possessions, The Paradox of Keeping-While-Giving.* Berkeley, Los Angeles, and Oxford, UK: University of California Press.

WEISMANTEL, MARY
1997a White cannibals: fantasies of racial violence in the Andes. *Identities* 4(1):9-43.
Race Rape: The Andean Pishtaco as White Rapist. Paper prepared for the 1997 American Anthropology Meetings in Washington, D.C. Manuscript. Department of Anthropology, Northwestern University. Evanston, Illinois.
1998   *Food, Gender, and Poverty in the Ecuadorian Andes.* Prospect Heights, IL: Waveland Press.
2001   *Cholas and Pishtacos, Stories of Race and Sex in the Andes.* Chicago and London: The University of Chicago Press.

WEISMANTEL, MARY, and STEPHEN F. EISENMAN
1998   Race in the Andes: Global movements and popular ontologies. (In Special issue, *Race and Ethnicity in the Andes*, Mary Weismantel, ed.) *Bulletin of Latin American Research* 17:121-142.

WEISS, PETER
1976-81 *Die Ästhetik des Widerstrands.* 3 volumes. Frankfurt-am-Main: Suhrkamp.

WERBNER, PNINA
1997   Essentializing essentialism, essentializing silence: ambivalence and multiplicity in the constructions of racism and ethnicity. In *Debating Cultural Hybridity, Multi-Cultural Identities and the Politics of Anti-Racism*, Pnina Werbner and Tariq Modood, eds. London and New York: Zed Books.

WHITE, HAYDEN
1978   *Tropics of Discourse, Essays in Cultural Criticism.* Baltimore and London: The Johns Hopkins University Press.

WHYTE, WILLIAM FOOTE
1965 High-level manpower for Peru. In *Manpower and Education: Country Studies in Economic Development*, Frederick Harbison and Charles A. Myers, eds. New York: McGraw-Hill Book Company.

WOLF, ERIC R.
1966   *Peasants.* Englewood Cliffs, New Jersey: Prentice-Hall.
1982   *Europe and the People Without History.* Berkeley: University of California Press.

WOLF, ERIC R., and SIDNEY W. MINTZ
Haciendas and plantations in Middle America and the Antilles. *Social and*

Economic Studies 6:380-412.

WOOST, MICHAEL D.
    1997   Alternative vocabularies of development?   "Community" and "participation" in development discourse in Sri Lanka.   In *Discourses of Development, Anthropological Perspectives*, R. D. Grillo and R. L. Stirrat, eds. Oxford, UK, and New York: Berg.

YOUNG, ROBERT J. C.
    1995   *Colonial Desire, Hybridity in Theory, Culture and Race*. London and New York: Routledge.

ZACK, NAOMI
    1993   *Race and Mixed Race*. Philadelphia: Temple University Press.

ZIAREK, EWA PLONOWSKA
    1997   From euthnasia to the Other of reason, Performativity and the deconstruction of sexual difference.   In *Derrida and Feminism, Recasting the Question of Woman*, Ellen K Feder, Mary C. Rawlinson, and Emily Zakin, eds. New York and London: Routledge.

ZSCHOCK, DIETER K.
    1988.   Introduction.   In *Health Care in Peru: Resources and Policy*, Dieter K. Zschock, ed. Boulder, Colorado, and London: Westview Press.

ZULAWSKI, ANN
    1995   *They Eat from Their Labor, Work and Social Change in Colonial Bolivia*. Pittsburgh and London: University of Pittsburgh Press.

Index

Note: Some entries that appear throughout this book, such as Vicos, Vicosinos, and Vicos Project, are not listed in the Index; nor are personnel of the Methodology Project who are given fictitious names in Chapter 2 but are identified in Chapters 3 and 4. Vicos informants are listed here.